Today's Teen

Fourth Edition

Joan Kelly-Plate, Ed.D.
Former Associate Professor
Department of Home Economics Education
Texas Tech University

Eddye Eubanks, Ph.D.
Education Specialist
Formerly of the Texas Education Agency

Today's Teen

Fourth Edition

GLENCOE

Macmillan/McGraw-Hill

New York, New York   Columbus, Ohio   Mission Hills, California   Peoria, Illinois

Send all inquiries to:
GLENCOE DIVISION
Macmillan/McGraw-Hill
3008 W. Willow Knolls Drive
Peoria, Illinois 61614

ISBN 0-02-675428-2 (Student Edition)
ISBN 0-02-675429-0 (Teacher's Wraparound Edition)

Printed in the United States of America

2 3 4 5 6 7 8 9 RRW 99 98 97 96 95 94

Contributors

Linda Glosson, Ph.D.
Consumer Homemaking Instructor
Wylie High School
Wylie, Texas

Mark Bregman

Christine Venzon

Reviewers

Catherine Gay
Home Economics Instructor
Pinellas County Schools
St. Petersburg, Florida

Linda Glosson, Ph.D.
Consumer Homemaking Instructor
Wylie High School
Wylie, Texas

Chris Moore
Home Economics Instructor
Salt Lake City, Utah

Joanne Reid
Supervisor of Special Vocational Populations
and Occupational Home Economics
Evansville-Vanderburgh School Corporation
Evansville, Indiana

Contents

Unit 1 — Self-Discovery 16

Unit 2 — Relationships 98

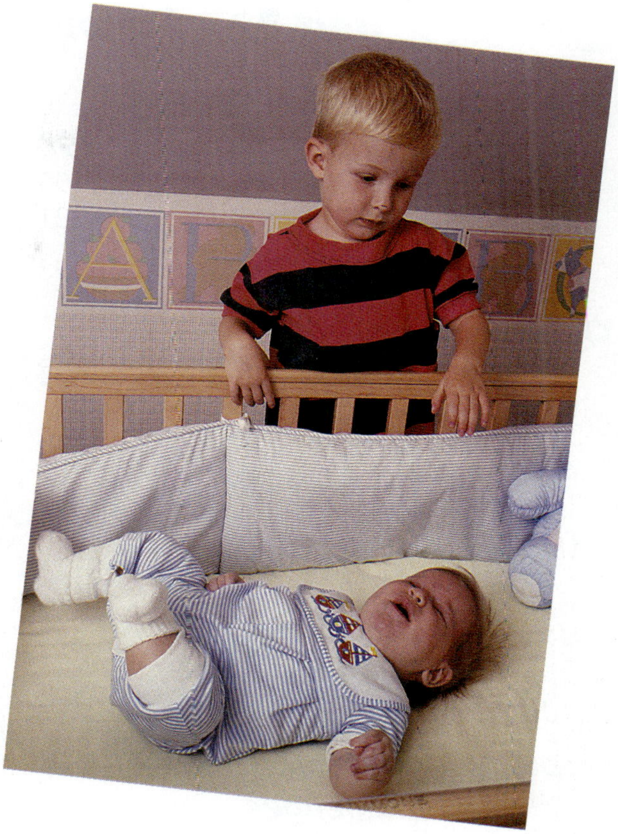

Unit 3 — Resources to Manage 192

Unit 4 — Housing 248

Unit 5 — Clothing 298

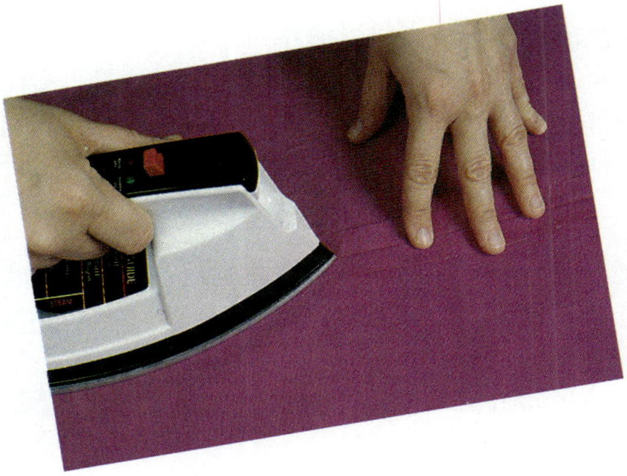

Unit 6 — Foods 426

UNIT 1

Self-Discovery

CHAPTERS

CHAPTER 1

Making the Most of Yourself

OBJECTIVES

- *Define self-concept and identify ways to boost self-esteem.*
- *Discuss how heredity and environment influence personality.*
- *Identify strategies for reaching your potential and using your resources.*

TERMS TO LEARN

- ***self-concept***
- ***self-esteem***
- ***personality***
- ***heredity***
- ***environment***
- ***potential***
- ***resource***
- ***human resources***
- ***material resources***
- ***resourceful***

"I did it!" Sean thought to himself with satisfaction. What a good feeling it was. To anyone else it might not have seemed like much, but, to him, this success in track meant a great deal. Now he felt confident. Now he felt good about himself. All of a sudden, it occurred to him that there was so much else he could do if he worked at it. He was ready and eager to try.

Getting Ready for Success

Did you ever wonder why some people succeed and others don't? The answer is not a simple one.

For one thing, success means different things to different people. Mr. Salazar felt successful when the business he built from the ground up brought him a good income. Maribeth O'Sullivan, a Peace Corps volunteer in Nepal, felt successful when she showed a group of women how to prepare healthy meals for their families. Sam Yoo knew success when he won the spelling bee at his school. For Andrea, passing her biology test was an achievement. What does success mean to you?

All of these people were successful in different ways. Something had to be working for them, however, in order to find their own successes. What worked for them can work for you too. You're in charge — if you decide to be.

Taking a Look at You

"They are able because they think they are able." In this quote, the Roman poet Virgil is stating that it is very important to believe in yourself. Nate had trouble with this. Because of a few mistakes, he no longer wanted to try anything. He branded himself as a failure. The image that Nate had of himself was affected by his past experiences.

Your Self-Concept

The picture you have of yourself and the way you believe others see you is your **self-concept**. Your self-concept is shaped by the experiences you have throughout your lifetime. Your self-concept can change, depending upon experiences you have along life's path. The way people are treated by family and friends from the time they are babies until they are senior citizens contributes to the images they have of themselves.

Can you put your own self-concept into words? Try it. Think about the kind of person you are. Don't label as "good" or "bad"; just describe.

Your Self-Esteem

Your **self-esteem** is the way you feel about yourself — the confidence and happiness you have in yourself. Self-esteem can range anywhere from low to high. If you like who you are and believe in yourself and your abilities, you have high self-esteem. If you do not like who you are very much and do not believe in yourself, you have low self-esteem. When your self-esteem is on the high side, you are self-confident. Your confidence makes you willing to try more, to take risks. You are more likely to accomplish things and be successful. Keep in mind, however, that everyone will have a low day now and then — a day when self-esteem may not be as high as usual. This is normal. Keeping a positive attitude through the low days and getting support from family and friends will help you maintain high self-esteem.

Amy never tries to do well in school or be part of a group. Often, she feels that other people do not like her. Sometimes she shows a dislike for herself by the way she treats others. When she is angry with herself, she often directs this anger at a friend. How would you describe Amy's self-esteem?

In contrast, Gabriela takes pride in her accomplishments and is not afraid to try new things. She is not afraid to make mistakes. Gabriela is happy and pleasant to be around. She smiles, has a good sense of humor, and isn't too hard on herself when she makes a mistake. She gets pleasure from making other people feel good about themselves. Even on her low days, Gabriela tries to keep her spirits up and brighten someone else's day. How do Amy and Gabriela differ in self-esteem?

AROUND THE WORLD

Getting involved in worthy causes is a great way to improve self-esteem. Many programs allow young people to offer their skills and services to people in other countries. Through *Amigos de las Americas*, for example, volunteers travel to South America and the Caribbean to help with health programs. In the *Earthwatch Research Corps*, volunteers help others study and protect natural resources. How does helping others benefit the volunteers as well as those they serve?

Your Personality

Your self-esteem and self-concept are often apparent to others. They show in your personality. Your **personality** is the combination of feelings, character traits, attitudes, and habits that you display to others. This combination of characteristics makes you unique, or one-of-a-kind.

The stage was first set for your personality before you were born. You are probably already aware that you received genes from each of your parents that determined your physical traits, such as your eye and hair color and your height. This passing along of traits and characteristics from parents to children is called **heredity** (huh-RED-uh-tee). Heredity also influences your personal characteristics, such as your intelligence, abilities, and your emotional responses.

Although your personality began with your heredity, it has been shaped much further by your environment. Your **environment** (in-VY-run-munt) is everything around you, including people, places, and events. The family is usually the most important environmental influence on a person.

How might the development of self-esteem be encouraged in this family?

Within the family, the seeds of self-concept and self-esteem are sown. For example, children who live in an environment filled with love and encouragement are much more likely to feel good about themselves. This, in turn, contributes to a pleasing personality.

Building Self-Esteem

Felipe's life has not been easy. His father left the family several years ago. His mother has struggled to raise four children in the best way she can. Felipe remembers little of his father except the harsh words he always had for Felipe. Now Felipe believes he is not as smart or as strong as his older brothers. Felipe fears he will never be good enough to succeed at anything, so he acts as though he doesn't care about his future.

Felipe feels defeated. Can he turn his life around? What do you think? Felipe needs a big boost in his self-esteem to help him become successful. Examine your own self-esteem. If it needs a boost, here are some ideas to explore:

- ***Accept yourself.*** Differences make people interesting. Learn to value the qualities that make you a unique person. Remember that your true worth comes from inside, not outside.
- ***Dare to dream.*** Set your sights high. Plan to take little steps in order to get there. Working toward a dream can be helpful in itself. If the dream is too lofty, you will still profit from what you learn along the way. Who knows? You might even achieve the dream.

- ***Be realistic.*** Some things can be changed; others cannot. Time and energy wasted on unrealistic wishes is self-defeating and interferes with accomplishing other more realistic goals. Lora Lee spends much of her time worrying about her appearance. She wishes she had a smaller nose, straighter hair, and more height. Everyone thinks Lora Lee looks fine — everyone, that is, except Lora Lee.
- ***Don't settle for what is.*** In other words, know that some things can be changed. Just because Ray is shy doesn't mean he can't take some steps to turn that around a bit. You, too, can make changes in yourself and in your life, if you need and want to.
- ***Focus on your strengths.*** Everyone has strengths and weaknesses. Strengths, or the things you do well, help you work effectively toward your goals. Avoid worrying about your weaknesses. However, if a weakness is interfering with your goals, think about ways that you can overcome or compensate for that weakness. You may discover some new strengths.
- ***Turn to others for help.*** Ideas and assistance from others may help you affirm your strengths and find new ways to deal with your weaknesses.
- ***Get involved.*** Becoming involved in worthwhile activities, such as volunteer work or belonging to an interesting club, can really boost your self-esteem. Looking for ways to help or work with others can enable you to see new strengths and understand ways that you can assist others with their needs.
- ***Be proud of your accomplishments.*** Even small accomplishments are worthy. Often they are the stepping stones to bigger and better things.
- ***Believe in yourself.*** Remove statements like these from your thinking: "How could I be so stupid?" "What's the matter with me anyway?" "I can't do anything right." Instead, learn to forgive yourself for your mistakes and try again. People seldom succeed without some failure along the way. Only by trying can you become what you want to be.

What steps can you take to work toward your dreams?

Overcoming Barriers

Someone once said, "The control center of your life is attitude." Every person can point to reasons why he or she cannot succeed. One says, "I am female." Another says, "It's my race." Another explains, "I have no opportunity." Still another says, "I have lost my sight." Should these factors

How to . . .
Feel Good about Yourself

Sometimes this is easier said than done. You may have a bad day. You think you don't look right or act right. You want to feel good, but it just isn't happening. How can you turn things around? Read what these teens have to say.

- ***Brittany***. "Talking always saves me. Whenever I need to feel better, I find someone to whom I can talk. My stepfather is super. He listens and just seems to know what to say to make me have confidence in myself again."
- ***Dominick.*** "Some people I know like to put others down. They've done it to me. I took it all seriously for a long time. Finally, it hit me. They were just saying those things to make themselves look better. Now I either avoid them or don't listen. That has made a big difference in how I feel about myself."
- ***Heidi.*** "Boredom is my worst enemy. When I don't have anything to do, I start feeling sorry for myself. I think of more things that are wrong with me. Now that I realize this, I try to get involved in activities that are interesting. Joining a club at school has helped. We have projects to work on and leaders with plenty of ideas."

Determination and the right attitude help people succeed regardless of their limitations.

hold people back? In an imperfect world, any of these factors can get in the way.

The truth is people are not limited by their heredity, their environment, or even physical disabilities — if they have determination and the right attitude. Think about it. A pitcher makes it into the big leagues, even though he has only one arm. A young woman who cannot see learns to travel by herself. A young man graduates from college with honors after growing up in poverty. All of these are true examples of people who have succeeded because they have determination and postive attitudes. They believed in themselves. They did not let the attitudes of others hinder them. Their own positive attitudes helped them take charge and overcome the barriers to their successes.

The hurdles you have to jump may not be as high as those just described, or they may be higher. Whatever the case, you can move toward success. As society tries to solve the problems that hold people back, you have a choice to make. Do you wait for the solutions, hoping that someone else will make it easier for you, or do you take charge of your own life? Most people would agree that you can't sit back and wait. You must take charge, because no one else is aware of the skills and talents that you have to share.

Taking Risks

One of the scariest parts of taking charge is facing risk. It often feels safer to do nothing. A couple of Victor's friends scorned him when he worked to improve his grades. People in Noreen's community laughed when she decided to try out for the school's soccer team, since it had always been an all-male team. These individuals could have given up and chosen comfort and safety over risk. They could have also sacrificed the possibility for success.

How is the teen in this photo taking a risk by helping this young mother? What benefits are there in taking a risk like this?

Reaching Your Potential

All people have **potential** (puh-TEN-chul), or the possibility of becoming more than they are right now. Reaching your potential means becoming all that you can be. Because Kwang has good math and science skills, he has the potential to be an engineer if he wants to and if he works at it. Monica has the potential to be a competitive gymnast if she spends more time and effort in training.

Your potential is within your reach. Here are some suggestions for identifying and reaching it:

- ***Examine your interests and abilities.*** Make a list of each, asking others for input. Match interests and abilities. For example, Cassie loves children and gets along well with others. Because of this combined interest and ability, she plans to coach a beginning level girls' softball team in the summer. This will allow her to develop a skill, explore an interest, and decide what steps she might take next.
- ***Keep your efforts focused.*** Many people do not reach their potential because they allow themselves to get distracted along the way. When you decide to accomplish something, stay focused. Remember what is best for you and your future and stay on that path.

This Will Make You Feel Better

If you sometimes get discouraged, consider this fellow: He dropped out of grade school. Ran a country store. Went broke. Took 15 years to pay off his bills. Took a wife. Unhappy marriage. Ran for House. Lost twice. Ran for Senate. Lost twice. Delivered speech that became a classic. Audience indifferent. Attacked daily by the press and despised by half the country. Despite all this, imagine how many people all over the world have been inspired by this awkward, rumpled, brooding man who signed his name simply, A. Lincoln.

Learning to use the resources available to you can lead to future successes.

- ***Take care of yourself.*** You are more likely to develop your potential if you are healthy and full of energy. Eat foods that promote good health. (You will learn about healthful foods and eating habits in Unit 6.) Get enough sleep. Exercise and stay fit. Reject what is harmful to you, such as tobacco and drugs, including alcohol.
- ***Use your potential in positive ways.*** Luis is a talker. He is charming, convincing, and has a way of making others feel good about themselves. Some people might use such a skill in negative ways, persuading people to do what is harmful. Luis is not like this, however. He wants to find a way to use his skills, such as working with the homeless or elderly, to help himself and others.

Using Your Resources

Michael's older brother, Travis, wanted to go to college, but he did not have the money. Michael thought he might like to go too in a few years, so he watched closely as Travis made his plans. First, Travis kept his grades high. He talked to his counselor and a few teachers at school. The counselor gave him pamphlets and flyers about many scholarships for which he could apply. Travis applied for all of these. He found books about colleges, scholarships, and financial aid at the library. His father brought home an application for a scholarship that was offered through his place of employment. By the time Travis was ready, he had several offers for financial assistance. College became a reality for him. Travis knew how to use his resources.

Identifying Resources

Anything you use to help you accomplish something is a **resource**. Resources can be either human or material. Resources that have to do with people are called **human resources**. All other resources are material resources. **Material resources** are often objects. They include money, property, supplies, and tools. Material resources also include community resources, such as libraries, schools, churches, hospitals, clinics, and parks.

Like Travis, you might use family members and teachers as resources. Friends, neighbors, employers, and community contacts are other possibilities. For counseling, you might go to educators or religious leaders. For enrichment, you might go to a local artist, writer, or musician. Physicians, police officers, firefighters, and emergency service personnel are also resources. What might cause you to turn to these people as resources? A fee may be attached to using some of these resources, but many are available at little or no cost to you.

Personal qualities are also human resources. These include health, interests, skills, knowledge, abilities, and attitudes. Even your personality may be counted as a resource.

Making the Most of Resources

Once you identify your resources, you need to make them work for you. This can be done in several ways.

First, strive to increase your resources. People you meet may be able to help you, now or later. Read newspapers, bulletin boards, and pamphlets that are displayed in public places to learn what is going on. Discover what you can learn and with whom you can make useful contact. Develop your own knowledge and abilities. These resources are yours to keep. Sharpening them may increase other resources. For example, education and training can result in a higher salary when you have a career. Money can be an important resource.

Second, conserve your resources. Spending all your money on arcade games brings pleasure at the moment. Putting some money in a savings account brings more money later. Taking care of your possessions means they last longer. You won't have to spend time and money replacing them as often. Can you think of other ways to conserve resources?

In what ways might your teachers serve as resources for you?

Third, learn to substitute resources. For example, substitute the resource of personal energy for the resource of money by making a birthday gift. Instead of buying books and tapes, use the library. Instead of keeping the temperature high during the winter, put on warmer clothes.

Finally, share resources. Work together in a study group for a difficult class or assignment. Repair something for a friend who in return will teach you a new skill. Trade books, tapes, CDs, or clothes as long as both parties agree to take good care of the items. Sharing can be useful.

Resources are all around you. They are shared among people, communities, states, and countries. You only have to find them and learn how to use them to help you accomplish your goals and the goals of groups you are involved with. When you do this, you can be described as **resourceful**. Resourceful people can solve problems, an important skill for anyone who wants to succeed.

Using a library broadens the number of resources available to you.

How might helping others succeed benefit you as well?

Helping Others Succeed

"I know you can do it."

"I'd like to help you."

"I'm glad you're my friend."

How often do you say things like these to family and friends? Sometimes people become so caught up in their own concerns that they forget about others. Your life is closely intertwined with many people. *What you are depends on them, and what they are depends on you.* As you become older, remember that the positive way you treat others returns to you. In what ways may an attitude like this help make society stronger?

Ramona takes time to listen to her friends. She wants them to know that she enjoys being with them. She doesn't put them down or gossip about them to others. She is genuinely warm and gives trust whenever she can. All of this helps build self-esteem in Ramona's friends. They are better equipped to reach their own potential. In turn, they feel good about Ramona and support her, too. The same thing can happen to you. This, in itself, is a success like no other.

TAKING ACTION

Jerry has a strong self-concept and a generally positive attitude. He also has a talent for making others feel good about themselves. Recently, Mr. Cutler asked Jerry if he would be interested in helping form a counseling program for students in his age group at school.

According to Mr. Cutler's plan, student counselors would be available to talk confidentially with any student who wanted to share personal problems, such as family conflicts or difficulties with schoolwork. In the case of family conflict, the counselors would provide information about community resources that could provide help. The counselors might recommend student tutors for those in need of academic help. The counselors would be carefully trained by Mr. Cutler. Jerry asks you if you would consider being a student counselor.

Using Your Resourcefulness

- After considering Jerry's request, would you be interested in becoming a student counselor? Why or why not?
- Do you think someone who has experienced deep personal conflicts could help others successfully? Why or why not?
- Does your school have a student counseling program? What do you think about Mr. Cutler's plan? How would you design a student program for your school?
- What resources can help you learn more about student programs?

Chapter 1 Review

Summary

In this chapter, you have read about:

- Factors that affect self-concept and self-esteem.
- How to move toward success by raising your self-esteem.
- Taking charge of your life and sometimes dealing with risks when you take charge.
- How to identify and reach your potential.
- Identifying, using, and conserving your resources.

Facts to Recall

1. Explain the relationship between self-esteem, confidence, and success.
2. How does a person's self-esteem affect his or her behavior?
3. What are two important factors that help shape your personality?
4. List five things you can do to boost your self-esteem.
5. How can getting involved help raise self-esteem?
6. Explain why it can be difficult to take charge of your own life.
7. What is potential? What are four ways of identifying and reaching it?
8. Define resource. Give five examples of human resources and five examples of material resources.
9. Identify four ways to make the most of your resources.
10. How can helping others build self-esteem also help you succeed?

Ideas to Explore

1. Identify specific factors that affect your own self-esteem.
2. Discuss specific ways in which your heredity and your environment have influenced your personality — your likes and dislikes, your interests, your attitudes.
3. Use the list of suggestions for boosting self-esteem found in this chapter and explain one way that you can apply each point to your life.

Activities to Try

1. As a class, develop a list of as many things as you can think of that you can do every day to raise other people's self-esteem.
2. On a sheet of paper, list all your resources — human and material. On a separate sheet of paper, list your goals and interests. Exchange your list of goals and interests with a group of two or three other classmates. List ways in which each of you can use your resources to help the others in the group succeed.

LINK TO *Communication*

IDENTIFYING QUALITIES FOR SUCCESS

Read a magazine article or book about a successful person whom you admire. Write a two-page summary about the factors that contributed to this person's success. In your summary, answer the following questions:

- How did this person get ready for success?
- What helped to develop this person's self-concept and self-esteem?
- How did others influence this person's success?
- How were barriers to his or her success eliminated?
- How did this person work to reach his or her potential?
- How did this person use resources to achieve success?
- In what ways has this person helped others succeed?

CHAPTER 2

Your Values and Goals

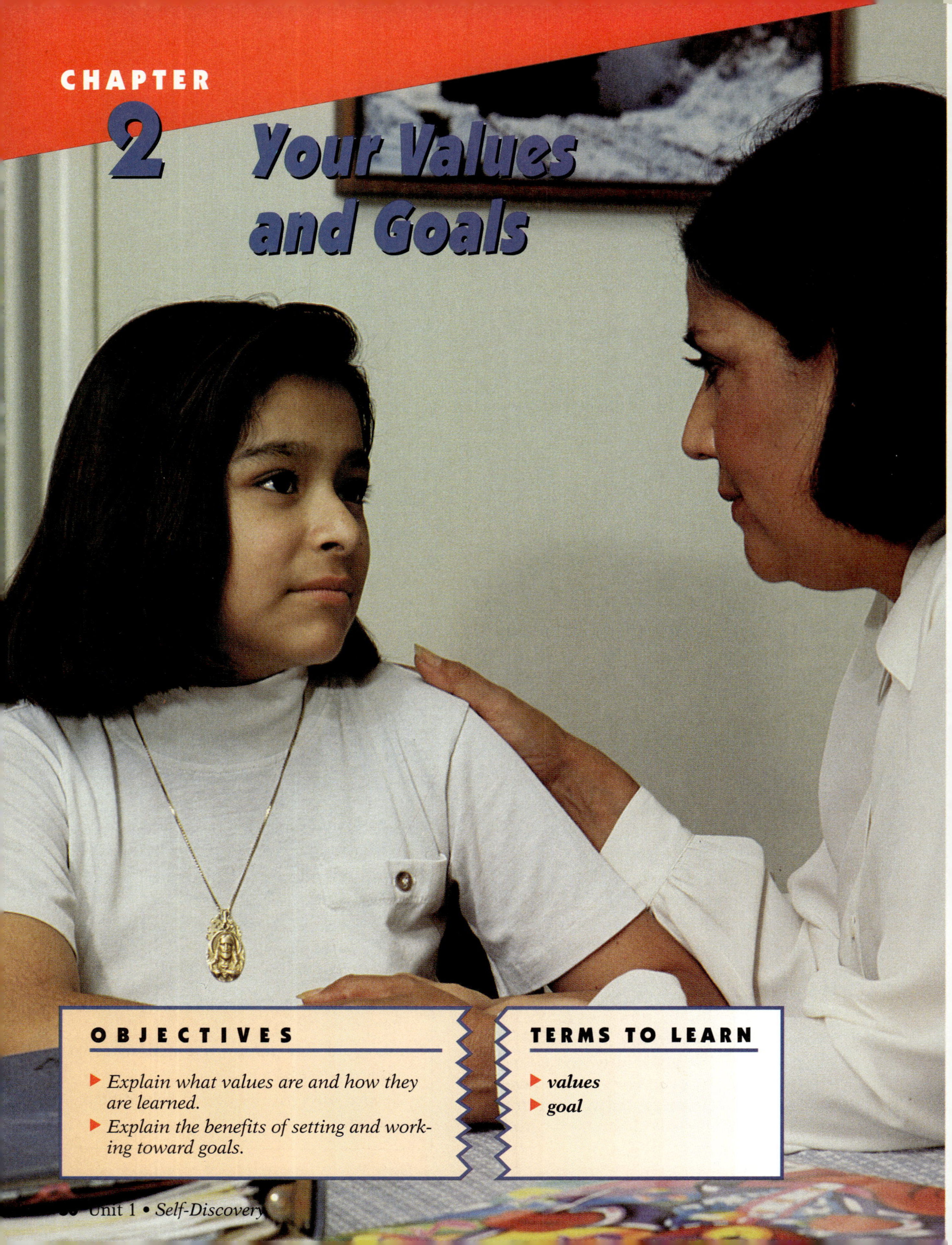

OBJECTIVES

- *Explain what values are and how they are learned.*
- *Explain the benefits of setting and working toward goals.*

TERMS TO LEARN

- ***values***
- ***goal***

If he made the team, basketball shoes would be expensive. Andre knew that. He also knew that his mother didn't have the money, nor did he. As he thought about tryouts, Andre wondered what to do. If he said something to his mother, he knew she would struggle to find a way to get the shoes. She might even make sacrifices to buy them. She would be very sad if there was no way that she could provide the shoes. For several long minutes, Andre stared at the sign-up sheet for tryouts. Then he turned and walked slowly away.

What's Important to You?

Making decisions is not always easy. What will you choose? Which way will you go? More importantly, what will influence your decision?

Values

Every day you use values to help you make decisions. Your **values** are the beliefs, ideas, and feelings about what is important to you. Deciding to have healthy lunches every day rather than having a soft drink and a candy bar shows that you value good health. Deciding to read a story to a younger brother shows that you value family relationships. Your values serve as guidelines by which to make decisions. Without values to guide you, these decisions might not be easily made.

Your values are always showing. For example, they are reflected in how you act. A person who values honesty believes it is wrong to cheat on tests. This value will guide this person's actions, even when exams are tough. Values also show in what you say. A person who cares about the feelings of others will speak kindly to them. In addition, values can be seen in how you spend your resources. Giving to a charity instead of buying new clothes shows you value the health or well-being of others over material things. Finally, values show in what you are willing to stand up for. A person who risks the opinions of others — and sometimes even his or her own personal safety — to stand up for a principle gives a clear message about values.

The directions people take in life are influenced by the values they hold as important. You may never have thought about the values that are important to you. By thinking about your values now, you can learn more about yourself. You may even discover something you'd like to change.

By returning a missing billfold, this teen is showing he values honesty.

Basic values are generally acquired at home. However, values may also be acquired through friends, religious teachings, books, and magazines. Think about the ways you have acquired your values.

How Are Values Acquired?

Most people acquire basic values in the home. Family members pass on their beliefs and feelings to younger members through examples and teaching. Many of the values acquired at home last a lifetime. They provide a constant means for guiding action. They can become a source of strength. As you can see, teaching values is an important responsibility. When children learn values that can help them in life, they are more likely to be successful and happy.

Values are also acquired in other places. Religion teaches values. Some values are acquired in school. Still others come from friends, television, books, and magazines. What values might a person acquire from each of these sources? Could a person learn to value something that is harmful?

Types of Values

Some people value things that can hurt themselves as well as others. These are called negative values. Think about the people who value only their own needs, comforts, and desires and have no regard for the needs, feelings, rights, or property of others. They may not take care of what they borrow. They may destroy property, causing financial troubles and pain for people. They may even steal, never giving a thought to the anguish they cause.

Not all negative values are as obvious. What do you think about the following situations? Earl doesn't speak to the new student in school because he doesn't like the way Corbin looks. Because Marla spends all her time with her friends, she often forgets to feed her dog. Her pet goes hungry on some days. How do these examples show negative values?

AROUND THE WORLD

Identifying values and goals is difficult for all young people. For young Native Americans who live on a reservation but go away to school, it is even harder. At home, they learn values that are traditional to their culture. They learn ways to express these values through such experiences as prayers, dancing, and other ceremonies. The lifestyles of young Native Americans at boarding school, however, are usually much different.

Some Native American parents feel their children are being pushed into giving up the values and traditions they have been taught at home and forced to accept the attitudes and culture of the rest of society. This confuses the young people, who feel caught between two different, and sometimes opposing, sets of values.

Negative values need to be changed. However, first you must identify the fact that they are negative. How can this be done? When you want to test a value, ask yourself: "Will my actions hurt me or anyone else, either now or later? Could this cause others to lose respect for me?" A "yes" answer to either question means that you are acting on a negative value. Rethink your behavior and look for a more positive approach.

Positive values are just the opposite of negative ones. They do not cause harm — to you or to anyone or anything else. Often they make your life and the lives of others better. What are some ways you've chosen to use positive values in your life?

Look around and you'll see that people's values often vary. Some values, such as truth and honesty, are valued worldwide, by all people of all cultures. However, in many cases, what's important to one person or culture may not be equally important to another. This does not mean that some values are right and others are wrong. Sarah prizes independence. Paul feels a need for security. When Sarah looked for a job, she moved away from the town where she had been raised. Paul looked for and found a job close to home. Values entered into the decision that each made. They each made the decision that was right for them.

These teens are sharing their positive values by painting over some graffiti on a wall in their community. What are some ways that you can share your positive values?

Setting short-term and long-term goals helps you gain a sense of accomplishment when you achieve them. What short-term and long-term goals are you setting for yourself?

What Are Goals?

Your values have a strong impact on the goals you set for yourself. A **goal** is something you plan to be, do, or have and for which you are willing to work. Any time you set a goal, you are placing value on the objective. The goals you choose and the actions you take to reach them show what is important to you — your values.

Types of Goals

Some goals are as simple as getting a homework assignment done. This is a *short-term* goal. It can be achieved in the near future. Other goals are more broad. A plan to earn enough money to visit the country where your ancestors grew up is a *long-term* goal. It takes time to achieve goals of this type.

Both short- and long-term goals are important. Short-term goals, such as reading a book, cleaning your room, writing a letter, are easier to reach than long-term goals. By setting short-term goals, you gain a sense of accomplishment when you reach them.

Long-term goals may be more easily met if short-term goals are set first. Cicely wanted to go to a summer computer camp recommended by her teacher. She thought she could pay for it by babysitting. She set a goal of earning a specific amount of money each week. The smaller amounts were easier to deal with than the total cost of the camp.

▼ Group Goals ▼

People often share goals, with all members of a group working for the same goal. For example, families have common goals. The Chungs planned a family reunion last year — a goal they set together. As a group, they decided where to hold the reunion, what food to serve, who would prepare it, and what entertainment and games to provide. Working together to achieve their goal was rewarding, as was the end result. At times, working for group goals means that some individual goals will not be met. What examples can you think of?

You probably belong to a number of groups besides your family. These other groups also have goals that you share. Bart's youth group at church wanted to buy gifts for residents at a nursing home. They met this goal by holding a car wash to raise money. When Sonia's volleyball team won their conference championship, they felt they had a chance to go to state. Going to the state tournament became their goal, and they worked hard to move toward it. When people work together on common goals, much can be accomplished.

Many people prefer to work for goals that they help set. If you feel this way, keep that fact in mind when you join other groups. In some groups you will be able to help set goals, and in others the goals will already be in place. You will be expected to help work for the goals of any group you join.

Aim So High You'll Never Be Bored

The greatest waste of our natural resources is the number of people who never achieve their potential. Get out of that slow lane. Shift into that fast lane. If you think you can't, you won't. If you think you can, there's a good chance you will. Even making the effort will make you feel like a new person. Reputations are made by searching for things that can't be done and doing them. Aim low: boring. Aim high: soaring.

© United Technologies Corporation

How are these teens working together toward a common goal? How will they benefit from working together cooperatively?

Why Set Goals?

Think for a moment about what you accomplished yesterday. Can you list specific achievements? Do the same thing for the last month. When people look back in time, they often discover that they did not accomplish nearly what they had wanted to accomplish. The missed opportunities may cause regrets. Goals can give you direction. They force you to think about what you want and to take the necessary steps to meet your goals. By setting goals and working to achieve them, you are more likely to find success and satisfaction in life.

Choosing Goals

When choosing goals, you must reflect on your own values — to determine what is important to you. Parents, friends, and relatives may influence your goals. However, you must be sure that the goals you set reflect what *you* want, not what others want for you. To achieve any goal, you must be committed to it so you will work hard to achieve it.

Dreams vs. Reality

Deciding what goals to set is not always easy. You may need to draw the line between dreams and reality.

The chances of becoming a professional basketball player are very limited, yet millions of teens share this same dream. Lofty dreams are considered impractical by many people, yet often they are the motivators for success. The highest hopes will never be reached if you don't strive for them. Moreover, much can be gained along the way to a lofty dream.

Playing in the NBA was Victor's dream. The thought sparked him to work hard at basketball. He learned much, including teamwork, dedication, and discipline. He made good friends and stayed out of trouble. Eventually Victor realized that the NBA was far out of his reach, but he set a new goal for himself — playing junior college basketball.

The risk with dreaming is the possibility of disappointment. It can't hurt to try for something grand if you understand that it might not work out. Still, you may need to examine the goal carefully. Aiming to cut a record in Nashville is probably not a good idea if you sing off key. A goal that is totally unrealistic may not be worth spending time on, especially if you may be hurt by the outcome.

When setting goals, you may have to choose between your dreams and reality. Do you have the skills and resources necessary to achieve your goals? Is your goal realistic and worthy of spending time on?

Achieving Goals

Once you have set meaningful, realistic goals, use the following guidelines as you work to achieve them:

- ***Keep goals in mind.*** Have you ever made a New Year's resolution and later forgotten it? The same thing can happen with any goal you set if you are not careful. Maintain a mental picture of your goal. Also, write it down on paper. Whatever your goal, read it aloud every morning and every night.
- ***Actively pursue goals.*** Just wanting to participate in a 5-kilometer (about 3 miles) run isn't enough. Even though it is a fine goal, it won't get you anywhere without action. To meet his running goal, Kevin made a commitment to follow a safe training program in which he gradually increased how far he ran. He set goals for the distance he wanted to achieve by the end of each week. With each new distance that he achieved, Kevin gave himself a positive reward — an incentive to reach his final goal.
- ***Be determined.*** Even though you have a goal and the will to succeed, stumbling blocks may come along. Like roads, most goals have a few bumps, detours, or other obstacles that can get in the way. Tackle these with confidence and enthusiasm. You often benefit as much from working toward a goal as you do from eventually meeting it.

If you are not careful, it is very easy to forget your goals — much like this teen girl has forgotten about her New Year's resolution to cut back on sweets.

TAKING ACTION

Your home economics teacher has asked you to perform a valuable service for the entire class. She explains that volunteer work — work without pay — is one very rewarding way to develop self-esteem and help learn how to get along and work with others. It lets others know you're a responsible worker and can provide experience that may help you get a paying job in the future. It's also a great way to find out about yourself. You can learn what kind of work you like and don't like, and whether you prefer working indoors or outdoors.

Your teacher asks you to find volunteer work that best suits each classmate's personality. You'll have to take into account each person's abilities and qualities (as you know them). You'll also have to research a variety of volunteer services in your community.

Using Your Resourcefulness

- What resources would you use to find out about volunteer programs in your area?
- Evaluate each classmate and offer volunteer work that would suit each person's abilities and qualities.
- What volunteer job would suit your own personality? Would you be willing to do volunteer work? Why or why not?

Chapter 2 Review

Summary

In this chapter, you have read about:

- How values affect your decisions.
- The ways in which you show your values.
- How and where values are learned.
- Positive and negative values.
- Different types of goals and why it is important to set them.
- The need to set meaningful goals and to balance your goals with reality.
- How to achieve goals.

Facts to Recall

1. What are values? How do they help you make decisions?
2. List four ways in which your values show.
3. Why is teaching children values an important responsibility?
4. What is a negative value? How can you discover whether you are acting on a negative value?
5. What is a goal?
6. Explain how reaching short-term goals can help you achieve a long-term goal.
7. Why is setting goals important?
8. Identify two benefits of striving for dreams.
9. List four guidelines that will help you achieve your goals.

Ideas to Explore

1. Do you think it is possible to live without any values or goals? Explain.
2. Give a specific example of how your values have affected a decision you have made or an action you have taken.

Activities to Try

1. On a sheet of paper, write down a long-term goal. Then list five short-term goals that could be helpful in achieving it.
2. Write down a long-term goal on a sheet of paper. Exchange your paper with a classmate. Read your classmate's goal. Then write down below it an obstacle that would make achieving the goal more difficult. Return the paper. Read the obstacle your classmate has written on your paper. Write a paragraph explaining how you would overcome this obstacle. How might you change your goal to make it reachable in light of this obstacle?
3. Select two of your favorite songs. Examine the lyrics (words of the song) carefully to determine what values are expressed. Write several sentences about the underlying values in the lyrics of each song. Do the lyrics reflect positive or negative values? Discuss your findings with the class.

LINK TO *Social Studies*

EVALUATING THE EFFECTS OF VALUES

Values show the importance of people and things in your life. They affect your life in many ways including what you say and do, how you use money, and how you treat others. Think about the values you hold and then write your response to the following:

- Choose one value that you feel has had a great impact on your life.
- How does this value affect the way that you treat others?

(**Note:** Your answers are private and for your personal use only. Share them only if you want to.)

CHAPTER 3

Making Decisions and Managing Your Life

OBJECTIVES

- *Explain how values and goals influence decisions.*
- *Describe the decision-making process and how decisions may affect others.*
- *Describe the management process.*

TERMS TO LEARN

- ***decision making***
- ***needs***
- ***wants***
- ***alternatives***
- ***management***

It was a decision that Christa didn't think she could make. How could she choose? It would be like taking sides, and she didn't want to hurt anyone.

"Who do you want to live with," her grandfather had asked, "your mother or your father?"

Now that the divorce was certain, Christa wondered if her parents would ask her the same thing. She thought about what she would say if the question arose.

Making Decisions

Every day you make decisions. Some are easy; others are not. **Decision making** is the act of making a choice. It might involve something as simple as deciding what to eat or as complicated as picking a college.

Simple decisions are usually made almost without your noticing. When a decision has little effect on your life, it can be made this way. The route you take to school, for example, may not be important. If taking the long route will make you late, however, some thought should go into the decision. Which of the following decisions do you think could be made without much consideration?

- Which socks to put on in the morning.
- What classes to take next year.
- Which movie to see on Friday night.
- Who will be your closest friend.

Making some decisions may not be easy. You may need to do a lot of thinking before making a choice.

What Influences Decisions?

The decisions you make are influenced by many factors. Some are external and some are internal. That is, some come from people and things around you, and others come from the knowledge and attitudes within you.

Family

"I'm not going to tell you what to do, but . . ." Has anyone ever said this to you? Comments like this one are typical in families. As a small child, you could make few decisions on your own. During the teen years, however, more and more decisions become your responsibility. You need to learn decision-making skills in order to be able to do a good job of taking care of yourself both today and in the future.

Family members are usually willing and eager to help teens learn to make good decisions. To do this, they may offer advice and information to help the young person make

Decisions, Decisions

Sometimes the decision to do nothing is wise. But you can't make a career of doing nothing. Freddie Fulcrum weighed everything too carefully. He would say, "On the one hand. . . but then, on the other," and his arguments weighed out so evenly he never did anything. When Freddie died, they carved a big zero on his tombstone. If you decide to fish — fine. Or, if you decide to cut bait — fine. But if you decide to do nothing, you're not going to have fish for dinner.

Talking through serious decisions with a trusted adult can help you make responsible choices.

his or her own decision. Sometimes they may make the decision for the teen. When might this be necessary? The adults in a family do not want to see teens make serious mistakes. They may even feel that the teen is not ready or able to make the decision alone. Although they know that young people learn by some mistakes, adults have a responsibility to protect and teach.

Families have a very strong influence on decisions. Even when family members are not providing direct input into a decision, the effect of the family is there. Everything you have experienced and learned within the family will come to bear upon the decisions you make and your ability to make them.

Friends

As you grow older, do you find yourself turning more often to friends for help with decisions? This is often the case. Friends have a strong influence on each other. Remember a couple points, however. Your friends often have no more experience or knowledge than you do. Some may even want to influence you for their own reasons. Be smart about seeking their help. You can always listen and learn, but, in the end, you must make your own decisions.

Resources

Decisions are often affected by resources including time, knowledge, money, and skills. Money, for example, is a common influence. While his stepfather was on strike for several months, Brett made some decisions related to the situation.

He decided to look for a part-time job. He also decided to wear his track shoes for another season. In addition, he decided to stay home more on weekends in order to save gas. All of these decisions were directly linked to his family's reduced income during the strike.

Values

Should you get a job or play a team sport at school? Should you study or watch television? Should you buy a new sweater or save the money? The decisions you make are nearly always based on what you feel is important. As you read in the last chapter, these are your values. The decisions you make are a showcase for your values.

Sometimes problems arise when people base decisions on a negative value. If you don't have your values in order, you may pay the price of living with the consequences of a bad decision. Some people make decisions that go against their values because they give in to other outside influences. Believing in honesty and then letting someone talk you into doing something dishonest can cause real feelings of conflict, not to mention other problems.

Good decisions are much more likely to result when your values are clearly and carefully defined and carefully followed.

Decisions involve choosing one thing over another. Clearly defined values help you make good decisions.

Needs and Wants

As you make decisions, your needs and wants will be a strong influence. All human beings have certain needs. **Needs** are things that are essential for your health and well-being. You have physical, emotional, mental, and social needs.

You have three basic physical needs: food, clothing, and shelter. Your basic emotional needs include affection, security and safety, independence, belonging or acceptance, and achievement. Your desire to learn and experience the world around you is an intellectual need. Socially, you need to establish positive relationships with other people, including family, friends, and acquaintances.

Wants are those things you desire even though they are not essential for your health and well-being. Sometimes wants are viewed as needs even though they really aren't. Sometimes the line between the two is hard to see. Does Leila *want* a new dress for the prom or does she *need* one? What do you think?

The decision-making process can be used for all types of decisions, but is especially critical for major decisions. How is the teen in this drawing using the decision-making process?

▼ Steps in Decision Making ▼

One of the tricks to making good decisions is in knowing when to make them quickly and when to think them through. Read Emil's description of Wes:

"Wes never seems afraid to make a decision. You can see him thinking, and then he just says it. When no one else can decide what to do or how to handle something, Wes is willing to take a stand. It makes him look confident, and everybody admires that. Of course, I've seen him hold back, too. He might say something like, 'Well, I'll have to think about that.' When this happens, you know it's more complicated. Wes can stop and take a close look when he needs to, and I like that."

The process that Wes uses to make decisions is basically a simple one. It can be used for all types of decisions, although it becomes more critical for major decisions. If you are making a major decision, you may find it helpful to write down your ideas for each step as you work through the process. This will help you keep your attention focused on the decision to be made. Follow these steps in making decisions:

- ***Step 1: Identify the Decision to Be Made.*** Clearly defining the situation or problem that requires a decision helps you know exactly what must be decided upon. Thinking about your goal or desired outcome can help you make a more effective decision. For example, your goal might be to buy a new camera for a family trip. You need to decide what type of camera and features — 35mm or automatic focus, built-in flash or flash attachment — will meet your needs and budget.

- ***Step 2: Analyze Your Resources.*** What do you need and what do you have that will help you resolve the situation, reach the goal, or solve the problem? Are time and energy all you need? If money is needed, how much can you spend? Do you have skills that would help? Where can you get more information?
- ***Step 3: List the Alternatives.*** Several ways of dealing with a situation are usually possible. Think about the different **alternatives** (ahl-TUR-nuh-tivs), or choices you have, and make a list. The more alternatives you think of, the more likely you are to find one that works.
- ***Step 4: Examine the Alternatives.*** Think through the decision in your mind. Consider the possible results of each alternative — listing the advantages and disadvantages of each. You may need to learn more about each alternative to do this. Here's where some of the resources you identified in step 2 can be helpful. You may find more information from family members and teachers. Books, magazines, and newspapers can also be helpful. An informed decision is more likely to be a good decision. Some people skip this step and make a quick decision at the wrong time. Such decisions may not lead to the results they want or expect.
- ***Step 5: Choose the Best Alternative.*** Think about your values, goals, wants, and/or needs. Make a choice that best fits them.
- ***Step 6: Act on Your Decision.*** Carry it out to the best of your ability. You may need to make a plan of action for carrying it through. Sometimes people willingly go through the process of reaching a decision, but they stop short of taking action. Have enough confidence in your decision to see it through.
- ***Step 7: Evaluate Your Decision.*** When you evaluate a decision, you judge its quality or how well it worked for you. If the outcome of a decision is not what you expected or hoped for, you may have to make a new decision. By analyzing your decision and determining what went wrong, you can avoid making the same error another time.

Listing and examining the alternatives are important to making an informed decision.

Learning from Your Decisions

A good decision is something to be proud of — you may even discover things that will work for you in the future. However, not all decisions will work out right for you. When your decisions don't work out, keep your chin up. No one makes the right decision all the time. Sometimes you have to live with the consequences of a wrong decision. You have to say, "Okay, this was my decision, and it didn't turn out the way I had hoped. I'll just accept my error and try to do better the next time. Since everyone makes mistakes, I won't let this stop me from making decisions with confidence in the future."

The Impact of Decisions

In one afternoon, Jon changed the direction of his life. At sixteen he decided to quit school. The decisions he would make from that point on would be quite different. This is the way it is with many decisions. It's like a chain reaction. You make one decision that sets you on a certain course. If the decision is a big one, everything else from that point on may be different. Do you see why making the right decision can be very important?

How Others Are Affected

Sometimes the decisions you make affect only you. Many, however, affect others as well. The effects can range from minor to very serious. Think about the decisions made in the following situations. Who, in addition to the decision maker, was affected?

- One of Marla's friends invited her to spend the night at her house. Marla accepted but changed her mind at the last minute when something came up that she wanted to do more.
- Roland, age fifteen, invited friends to his apartment for a party while his parents were gone. The party got out of hand with loud music, too many people, and a mess in the apartment. The police responded to complaint calls from other people in the building.

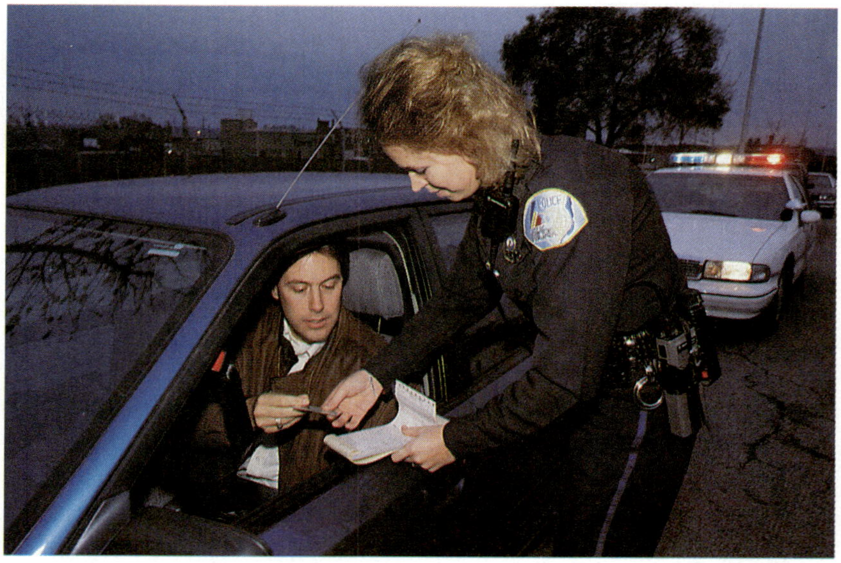

Think through the possible consequences of each decision. Who will your decision affect? This young man made the decision to disobey a traffic law. How might his decision affect others negatively?

AROUND THE WORLD

In 1987, some school children in Sweden set themselves a giant goal — saving the world's rain forests. They began small, with a bake sale that raised enough money to protect ten acres of rain forest. Soon, children and adults across Sweden were involved in raising funds and educating people about the importance of rain forests. The effort has spread among young people in over a dozen countries, including Great Britain, Australia, Costa Rica, and the United States. Over 20,000 acres of rain forest have been purchased and protected. How have the decisions and actions of a small group of students affected — and continue to affect — the lives of many other people?

It's far too easy to make decisions without regard for the consequences to yourself and others. Choosing an alternative that protects another person's feelings and well-being, but does not produce the result you really wanted is more difficult. It may not be what is the most pleasing to you at the time. However, the self-centered alternative — one with no regard to its effects on others — can backfire on you. Think about all the consequences as you enter into the decision-making process. It can save many regrets.

Making decisions in a group is similar to making individual decisions. One big difference, however, is that the majority or all group members must agree upon the decision. What difficulties might there be in making group decisions? Read more about group decision making and improving relationship skills in Chapter 9.

Solving Problems

Sometimes the situations you face are more involved and require more than just making a single decision. For example, when Aleesha moved to a new city, she felt lonely. It didn't seem like home to her. Aleesha had a problem. It could not be solved by making a single decision. What she needed to do was break the problem down into parts that she could better handle. Several decisions might need to be made.

When Aleesha tackled her problem from several angles, she was able to solve it. Some of the decisions she made concerned how to find new friends, how to get to know her neighborhood and community, and in what types of activities she could get involved. Her problem was not as overwhelming when she took this approach.

TIPS: *Problem Solving*

Here are some helpful tips for solving problems:

- **Prepare yourself.** Gather the information you need to solve the problem.
- **Give yourself some "think" time.** Allow enough time to sort through the information you gathered. Spend time reflecting on all ideas and alternatives.
- **Take time to test the solution.** Apply the solution to the problem. Ask yourself, "Does the solution give me the results that I want?"

Some situations require more than making a single decision. They may involve reaching out to others.

Learning to Manage

Camille never seemed to get much done. Even though she was able to do enough to get by, she had many things she wanted to accomplish. "What am I doing wrong?" she wondered.

The Management Process

A lesson in management could help Camille. **Management** means wisely using resources to achieve goals. In other words, management involves using what you have to get what you need or want. A good manager will use decision-making, problem-solving, organizing, and planning skills. What other skills do you think might be helpful for a good manager?

Management may occur in many situations — from simple to complex. For example, using resources to manage a study schedule may be more easily accomplished than managing a small business.

When Camille learned a few basic steps in the management process, she found that she had much better control over her life. You, too, may find the following management process helpful.

- ***Step 1: Set a Goal.*** Nothing will be accomplished until you decide what you want or need to do. Write your goal down in specific terms. Include a time frame. Instead of saying, "I want to do better in school," say "I plan to raise my English grade to a B by the end of the semester." This way you can see exactly what the expected result is and how long you have to achieve your goal. A time frame helps you pace yourself in working toward your goal.

Write your goals in specific terms.

Luisa's Attempt to Manage

4:00 p.m. — Luisa rushes into the house. She should have been home an hour ago.

4:15 p.m. — Luisa gets out all the ingredients to make hamburgers, french fries, and tossed salad. She also sets out the salad dressing and milk.

4:20 p.m. — Luisa peels and slices the potatoes.

4:35 p.m. — She finds that the hamburger patties are still frozen, so she begins to cook them anyway at a low temperature so they can defrost.

4:40 p.m. — Luisa's best friend, Esther, calls and they talk for 10 minutes.

4:50 p.m. — Luisa's mother comes home from work. Luisa had promised that dinner would be ready at 5 p.m. because her mother has plans for the evening.

4:55 p.m. — Luisa begins heating up the oil to fry the potatoes.

5:00 p.m. — She begins tearing up the lettuce but finds that it has gotten warm from sitting by the range. She puts it into the freezer to cool quickly. Luisa finally puts the potatoes into the hot oil.

5:10 p.m. — Luisa cuts up the tomatoes. She calls to her little brother, asking him to set the table.

5:15 p.m. — The hamburgers are sticking to the pan from cooking too long on one side. Luisa flips them over.

5:20 p.m. — Mother helps Luisa finish the salad, although Luisa promised to do everything by herself. Most of the lettuce has frozen and cannot be used.

5:25 p.m. — The hamburgers are done — well done. The french fries still have 10 more minutes to go. They must be eaten last. The salad dressing and the milk are too warm. Luisa blames everything on her friend's telephone call. She decides to serve peanut butter sandwiches the next time.

What specific problems can you identify in Luisa's management plan? What could she have changed to bring about better results?

- ***Step 2: Make a Plan.*** Now use your decision-making and problem-solving skills to determine what must be done to reach your goal. What steps must be taken? When, where, and how will you proceed? What resources can provide help? Put your plan in writing. It may take the form of a checklist, a schedule, a calendar, or reminder notes to yourself. Whatever you use, keep it handy for regular reference.

- **Step 3: Act on the Plan.** Putting the plan into action is an easy step for some people but a hard one for others. Remember that a plan without action won't get you anywhere.
- **Step 4: Control the Plan.** This helps you keep the plan working. It involves checking the progress of your plan and making decisions about any needed changes along the way. For instance, you might say something like, "Because I didn't pass my English test, I will add half an hour per day to my study schedule."
- **Step 5: Evaluate the Results.** Was the goal reached? If so, remember what worked well for you. If not, determine what went wrong and think about revising your plan. You may need to set a different goal. Becoming a goal-oriented person can put an "A" for accomplishment in your life.

Good management skills take practice. Developing your decision-making and problem-solving skills is part of learning to manage effectively. Management skills may be used in any number of situations throughout life. As you read through other chapters in this book, you will learn more ways to use your management skills.

TAKING ACTION

"Help me figure out what to do!" Trish nearly cries when she calls you on the phone. She had planned to work after school tomorrow at her part-time job at Henderson's athletic-goods store. Trish had also promised her mother, who works full-time, that she'd shop for food on the way home tomorrow since Aunt Sue is coming for dinner and Trish's mom plans to cook a special meal. After tomorrow's dinner, Trish had intended to study for a big test the next day.

Now Trish's friend Libby has called with a last-minute surprise. On a call-in radio program, Libby had won two tickets for the concert event of the year — tomorrow night. Trish has wanted to go for ages, but the concert was sold out before she could buy tickets. Now Libby has asked her to go, and Trish is torn over what to do. She needs your advice, especially since you sometimes fill in for her at her part-time job.

Using Your Resourcefulness

- After considering the choices and decisions that Trish needs to make, explain what course of action you would suggest.
- Could Trish manage her time in such a way as to fulfill all responsibilities and still attend the concert? If so, draw up a schedule for Trish.
- Suppose you have the same test as Trish. Would you be willing to fill in for her at work? Why or why not?

Chapter 3 Review

Summary

In this chapter, you have read about:

- Things that influence the decisions you make.
- The seven steps of the decision-making process.
- How the decisions you make can affect others.
- The five steps of the management process.

Facts to Recall

1. What is decision making? Identify six things that may influence your decisions.
2. Why is it sometimes necessary for an adult in a family to make a decision for a teen?
3. What are two problems with turning to friends for help with decisions?
4. What happens if you make a decision that goes against your values?
5. Identify the four types of needs and give an example of each.
6. List the seven steps in the decision-making process.
7. Briefly explain how you choose the best alternative when making a decision.
8. How can decision making have a "chain reaction" effect?
9. List the five steps of the management process.
10. How is it helpful to give yourself a time frame in which to accomplish a goal?

Ideas to Explore

1. Who do you think has more influence on a teen's decision making, family or friends? Explain.
2. Discuss how it can be difficult to tell the difference between needs and wants.
3. There is often conflict between teens and adults in a family as teens begin to want to make their own decisions. How might this conflict be avoided?

Activities to Try

1. Make a list of ten decisions you have made in the last week. For each one, write down what things influenced your decision and what effects your decision had on you and others.
2. Write a short essay explaining how you would use the seven-step decision-making process to help make one of the following decisions: where to go to college; what type of summer job you should look for; how to best use your allowance.

LINK TO *Communication*

MAKING AN EFFECTIVE DECISION

Create a skit in which someone needs to make a major decision. Write two versions of the skit. The question or course of action that needs to be decided upon will be the same for both versions; how the decision is made will be different. The first version should show the person taking a shortcut in decision making. The second version should show the same person using the seven-step decision-making process. Share the skit with the class. Discuss the following:

- How did the results of each method of decision making compare?
- Which method of decision making was the most effective?
- What are the benefits of using the decision-making process for major decisions?

CHAPTER

4 Coping with Change and Stress

OBJECTIVES

- *Discuss the types of changes typical during adolescence and ways to cope with them.*
- *Identify signs of stress and ways to manage stress positively.*

TERMS TO LEARN

- ***adolescence***
- ***puberty***
- ***growth spurt***
- ***hormones***
- ***character***
- ***ethics***
- ***stress***

Looking at old family photo albums was always fun. It had been a few years since anyone had dug them out at Ben and Joy's house. One rainy Sunday afternoon, they decided to browse through them. Seeing Uncle Bill and Grandma Lacey as teens was always cause for a chuckle. Not only had styles changed, but they both looked so different. Everyone had changed, from childhood through the teen years to adulthood, including Ben and Joy. They wondered what changes were yet ahead for them. Someday the family album would tell.

Understanding Change

Adolescence (ad-uh-LESS-unts), or the stage of growth between childhood and adulthood, is a time of many changes. During these years, teens change faster than they ever will again. Like Ben and Joy, you have changed since you were younger, and the process is continuing.

During adolescence, teens often experience a rapid growth spurt.

Physical Changes

Right now your body is probably changing rapidly. These rapid changes affect the way you feel, behave, and think about yourself.

It is helpful to know some facts about adolescence. The beginning of adolescence is marked by puberty. **Puberty** (PYOO-burt-ee) is the time when boys and girls start to develop the physical characteristics of adult women and men. For girls, the beginning of **menstruation** — a monthly discharge of blood from the uterus — is an early sign that puberty has begun. For boys, the reproductive system begins producing sperm. Both girls and boys usually experience a rapid increase in height, a **growth spurt**. Girls may notice their body shape changes. Boys often notice facial hair growth and their voices deepening. Both boys and girls may notice strong surges of physical energy.

During puberty, your **hormones**, or chemical substances in your body, are at a very high level. They help stimulate body changes and the development of the male and female reproductive systems.

Puberty lasts an average of three years, but it can start at different ages. Boys usually begin puberty around age thirteen, but it can come as early as eleven or as late as fifteen, or even older. Girls usually begin puberty around age eleven, but it is normal for it to start any time between nine and thirteen. Some begin even later. For example, one fifteen-year-old girl may have completed her development. Another may be just beginning puberty at the same age.

Teens sometimes feel awkward with rapid changes in height and build. Eventually, the awkward feelings disappear, as teens adjust to the new growth and development.

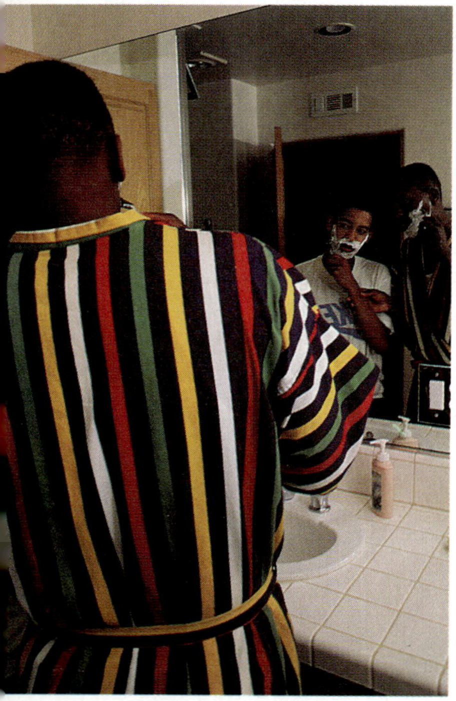

Teens go through rapid changes during puberty as they grow to adulthood. What are some changes that you've experienced?

It is common to worry that you are changing too slowly or too quickly. Teresa is thirteen but looks like seventeen. She feels out of place among her friends. Rob is seventeen and doesn't need to shave. His younger brother Drake, however, is already shaving. Teens develop at different rates. If you are not growing and changing as quickly as your friends, don't worry. Every healthy human being grows up. Whether you start early or late has no effect upon the end product — the adult you.

▼ Emotional Changes ▼

Do you sometimes feel on top of the world one day and down in the dumps the next? Along with spurts of physical growth and energy come surges of strong emotions. Emotions and feelings can change rapidly during puberty. They can make you feel restless and irritable or happy and full of life.

These surges of emotion are also affected by the changing hormones in your body. They can cause emotions to be very intense and swing rapidly — part of the "growing pains" of adolescence.

Knowledge is a special ally during this stage of your life. When you know what is happening to your body and causing your emotional ups and downs, you can understand some things better. Some teens tend to think that if they feel down about something, that feeling will never go away. This is not true. You need to know that the strong emotions you sometimes feel will probably last just a short time. The emotional swings you experience in adolescence eventually settle down as you enter adulthood.

There are many positive ways to deal with strong emotions and use the extra energy of the teen years. Get involved in physical activities, such as intramural sports, pep squad, or an exercise program that you enjoy. Try helping other people. You will feel better and worry less about yourself.

▼ Social and Intellectual Changes ▼

Although physical and emotional development are most apparent, you are also developing socially and intellectually. All of these areas of development are related.

As physical and emotional changes occur, teens are growing socially and intellectually, too. Developing good social skills as a teen will serve you well in relationships with others throughout your life.

You have many opportunities for learning how to get along with others — family, friends, and acquaintances. This is social development. Your relationships change throughout your life. As you change and grow, your interests may change, leading to new friendships. Developing good social skills will serve you well throughout life.

At the same time that you are growing socially, you are gaining both knowledge and experience. This is your intellectual development. The education you receive, and the school and community activities in which you participate, give you new insights and ways of looking at things.

Moral Development

At times you will face decisions that deal with issues of right and wrong. In a complex situation, these decisions can be difficult. Although you want to do what's right, sometimes it's not clear which course of action is right and which is wrong. Your choices may also be more difficult if you feel pressure from others.

The challenge is to learn to base important decisions on a set of **ethics** or moral principles — generally accepted guidelines for right and wrong behavior. For example, telling the truth and treating people fairly are commonly accepted as standards of right behavior. Strong ethics, based on positive

The Snake That Poisons Everybody

It topples governments, wrecks marriages, ruins careers, busts reputations, causes heartaches, nightmares, indigestion, spawns suspicion, generates grief, and dispatches innocent people to cry in their pillows. Even its name hisses. It's called gossip. Office gossip. Shop gossip. Party gossip. It makes headlines and headaches. Before you repeat a story, ask yourself: Is it true? Is it fair? Is it necessary? If not, shut up.

values, can guide you through difficult times. When making difficult choices, it is also helpful to seek guidance from parents, teachers, religious leaders, or counselors. When you act according to a set of high ethical principles, you are said to be a person of good **character**. People of good character gain respect and trust from others.

Managing Stress

While change goes on within you, it goes on around you as well. All of these changes can cause pressures, fears, self-doubt, feelings of self-consciousness, and emotional highs and lows. Sometimes the combination can be challenging to handle and lead to a great deal of stress.

What Is Stress?

Stress is the physical or emotional strain or tension that is caused by pressures, fears, worries, and changes in your life. During adolescence, you may find that you have increased responsibilities and others expect more of you. This may add even more pressure and stress.

Everyone has stress. Anyone who moves to a new city, job, or school experiences stress. Divorce or remarriage can cause stress for everyone involved — children, parents, grandparents, and close friends. Trying to meet a deadline for school or work can also cause stress. You can never be completely free of it. You can, however, learn how to manage it.

TIPS: ***Character Development***

Here are some tips that may indicate your progress in developing a positive character:

- Your willingness to act without rewards or acknowledgement.
- Your ability to control strong emotions and find ways to express them constructively.
- Developing patience in delaying personal pleasure or reward when needed.
- Showing your dependability by keeping promises.
- Showing your ability to admit mistakes rather than making excuses for yourself.
- Developing your ability to look at problems and situations from all angles.

Everyone experiences stress. Some learn to manage that stress better than others. What are some healthful ways to manage your stress?

▼ What Can You Do? ▼

How you react to the stress you face every day is important. Some stress is helpful because it keeps you on your toes. It pushes you to do better and work harder. Too much stress, however, can cause emotional strain and may even lead to physical problems. Think of stress as the tension, or tightness, of a violin string. You need enough to make music, but not so much that the string snaps. In the section that follows, you will learn ways to identify and manage stress — to keep yourself well tuned, just like that violin.

Identify Signs of Stress

How do you know if you are suffering from stress? Your body will give you physical signs of stress. It will also give you emotional signs. For example, a pounding heart when you are scared and sweating hands when you are nervous are physical signs of stress. You may find it hard to go to sleep when you are worrying about something. These are some ways in which your body reacts to stress. Other physical signs of stress include:

- Headaches and backaches
- Upset stomach or other digestive problems
- Tight muscles or pain in the shoulders or neck
- Dizziness
- Eating too much or too little
- Feeling tired much of the time

Symptoms of stress may be physical or emotional and are common to people of all ages.

These physical symptoms could be caused by problems other than stress. There might be some other reason for a headache or sleeplessness. Stress, however, is a very common problem among people of all ages. When you suffer physical symptoms such as those just listed, stress may be the cause.

Emotional signs of stress are often more difficult to detect than physical signs. Matt has learned that when he starts getting too critical of himself and his friends, it is a sign that he has too much stress. Midori becomes depressed when she is stressed. Other emotional signs of stress include:

- Restlessness
- Boredom with school or work
- Irritability and difficulty in getting along with others
- Anger at self and others
- Carelessness about mistakes

Signs of stress are like warning lights. They could be warning you of serious problems. Stress can sometimes

AROUND THE WORLD

Education is very important in Japan. Young people are expected to study hard to get into good schools and find high-paying jobs after graduating. Students must pass entrance exams to get into high school and universities — the best schools have the toughest exams. Therefore, many students, some as young as age seven, take extra classes to improve their studying and test-taking skills. Like American youths, Japanese young people deal with stress through sports such as baseball and judo, or by joining youth clubs or listening to music.

cause illnesses, such as high blood pressure and heart disease. Ulcers can also be caused by stress. These diseases often afflict young people as well as adults. To protect your health, you need to be alert for signs of stress. When you see signs of stress in yourself, you need to find healthful ways to reduce stress in your life. Consider the tips that follow.

Look at Your Attitude

Much of the time, it's your attitude about an event, not the event itself, that results in stress. For example, if you have to stand in a long line, your attitude about waiting will determine how stressful the situation will be. You can become frustrated and angry about the delay. On the other hand, you can choose not to be upset. Instead, you can use the time to plan your day's activities or just relax and watch the people around you. Which attitude would create stress? Here are some tips for reducing or avoiding stress by having the right attitude:

- ***Think about the positive side of a situation.*** If you are moving to another city, think about the opportunities and the new friendships the move will bring.
- ***Be choosy about the problems you decide to meet head on.*** Don't let small irritations become large problems. If something is important to you, by all means stand up for your beliefs. However, learn to keep your reaction in proportion to the situation. Adding frustration — your own and everyone else's — only increases the stress.
- ***Give yourself time to examine your attitude.*** Sometimes you can change your attitude by backing off and leaving the room, taking a walk, jogging, or watching a favorite television show. Taking a little break gives you time to get control of your emotions and will help you see the situation more clearly.

Giving yourself time to examine your attitude is a helpful way to manage your stress. Backing off from a situation and taking time to play a family game or go for a walk can help you control your emotions and lessen the stress in your life.

- ***Learn to be more accepting.*** Some things just can't be changed. You will be much happier if you say something like, "Well, since I can't change this situation, I may as well make the best of it."
- ***Be open to other points of view.*** Looking at stressful situations from the viewpoint of others, and not just your own, can help you understand all angles of the situation. This can help you change your attitude.

Relax

Learn how to relax. When you relax, you loosen up. You become less tense and are more at ease. When you feel tension building up, try to get away from the cause of your stress for a while.

Sometimes it helps to occasionally sit in a chair and daydream. Keep your thoughts positive, or think about a beautiful beach you saw in a magazine. Try reading a good book to take your mind off your troubles.

Exercise

Physical exercise can help too. If you are upset, work off your stress with physical activity. Get a hard workout by playing something you enjoy, such as basketball or tennis.

Participating in a physical activity that you enjoy can help you work off your stress and leave little time for worrying.

Try running or jogging. The energy it takes won't leave you much energy for worrying. Let off steam by doing household tasks, such as cleaning out a closet or doing yard work. This will help you do two things at once — get some work done and work off your stress.

Set Realistic Goals

Setting goals may help you reduce or manage stress. If you have a goal to work toward, extra tasks and responsibilities will be more meaningful. A goal will also help you measure your work. You'll be able to see how much you have accomplished and how much more there is to do.

Remember to be realistic about your goals. You can challenge yourself and dare to dream, but setting too many goals that are beyond your reach may add stress to your life. You must be realistic about the number of goals you set for yourself, too. Don't expect to be able to do everything at once; take one thing at a time. If you set unrealistic goals, you'll end up working too long and worrying too much about failure.

Plan Your Days

Many people find it helpful to do their planning on paper by making lists. Try making daily and weekly activity lists and crossing off items as you finish them. This will let you see what you've accomplished. At the end of each day, and at the end of each week, you can check your progress. You will learn more about managing your time in Chapter 18.

Develop Healthy Habits

Eat a balanced diet, including a variety of healthful foods. Get plenty of sleep, rest, and exercise. Lack of sleep reduces your ability to manage stress. It can also make you tired and irritable.

Do not use alcohol and other drugs. These present legal as well as health problems. The ability to manage stress comes from within you. Pills, alcohol, and other drugs reduce your ability to manage stress and add new problems. If you try to cope this way, you will never learn how to manage stress. Instead, you will have more stress.

Help Others

Sometimes when you feel stressed, you may be thinking too much about yourself. You might be all wrapped up in your own problems and too close to the situation to see a positive solution.

When managing stress, it often helps to get your mind off yourself. By doing something for others, you forget your own stress for awhile. Doing something extra around the house, helping a younger brother or sister with school work, running an errand for an elderly neighbor, and visiting someone in the hospital are just a few examples of ways you can help others and deal with stress at the same time.

Developing healthy habits shows you care about yourself and can help you manage stress.

Talking with a youth worker or a trusted friend can help you find constructive ways to cope with change and stress.

Sources of Help

Don't hesitate to ask for help when you feel stressed. For example, your family — including grandparents, aunts, and uncles — may be able to help you understand and deal with a problem. Adults at school, such as a counselor or trusted teacher, can also help. Choose someone you are comfortable talking with.

Your family doctor or the school nurse may be especially helpful in dealing with stress. Like family members and school personnel, they can put you in touch with social agencies and professionals who can provide additional help when needed.

Community organizations, such as the YMCA, YWCA, recreation centers, or the Red Cross, may have a youth worker. This person's job is to work with young people as individuals and in groups. A youth worker can help you find ways to cope with change and stress.

Sometimes talking over difficult problems with a trusted friend or religious leader is just the help you need. You may find that just talking about a problem out loud helps your outlook toward the problem.

Never be hesitant to ask for help. Think about it. If someone came to you with a problem, how would you feel? Chances are, you would feel good about giving help. The same is true in reverse. People are willing to be there for you too.

TAKING ACTION

"Living with a single parent can be trying," Garrett says. "My mom depends on me to do most chores and watch over my sister and two brothers. One brother doesn't do his share at all. We argue all the time, and it's stressful."

Garrett doesn't have much time to see friends except on weekends. Lately as he heads out the door on a Friday or Saturday night, his mother will ask him to stay home and spend "quality" time with her. Garrett enjoys spending time with his mother but wants to see more of his friends too. Between school, the track team, homework, and chores at home, he sometimes feels "burned out."

Using Your Resourcefulness

- What options does Garrett have to deal with and relieve stress?
- How should he communicate his needs to his mother, brother, and friends so that they help him out?
- How do you deal with personal and family stress?
- What resources are available to you for coping with stress?

Chapter 4 Review

Summary

In this chapter, you have read about:

- How you change physically, emotionally, intellectually, socially, and morally during adolescence.
- How change in your life can cause stress.
- How stress can cause physical and emotional problems.
- What you can do to cope with stress.
- Where you can turn for help in dealing with stress.

Facts to Recall

1. What is adolescence? In what five ways do you change during this period?
2. List three changes in physical development that occur during adolescence.
3. What are hormones? How can they cause difficulties during adolescence?
4. Explain how adolescence can be an opportunity for social and intellectual growth.
5. Name two qualities that identify a person of strong character.
6. What is stress? What changes during adolescence can cause stress?
7. List five physical signs and three emotional signs of stress.
8. Explain how your attitude can make a situation less stressful.
9. How can setting reasonable goals and planning your day reduce stress?
10. Identify four sources of help in dealing with stress.

Ideas to Explore

1. Do you think teens today face more stress than their parents did as young people? What pressures or concerns might they have faced that you do not?
2. Discuss the relationship between feeling in control of a situation and stress. What can you do to feel more in control of a situation when stressful change occurs?

Activities to Try

1. With one or two classmates, write and perform two skits. In the first, show a teen reacting to a specific change in life with a negative attitude. In the second, show the person dealing with the situation positively.
2. Using newspapers and magazines, find articles about different resources available to help people cope with change and stress. Write down the name, address, and/or phone number of each resource. Share these with the class.

LINK TO *Health*

Identifying Stress in Your Life

In itself, stress is neither good nor bad, harmful nor beneficial. Too little stress may be just as bad as too much stress. Because people react differently to the same events, the best amount of stress for you is very personal. The sources of your stress may be yourself, your family, school, or work. Sometimes stress in one area of your life causes stress in another area. For example, your work schedule allows you less time for family and school work. On a sheet of paper:

1. Identify the things in your life which are stressful to you.
2. Indicate whether each stress is positive or negative.
3. Identify the source(s) of each stress.
4. Describe ways to manage the stress in your life.

(**Note:** Your answers are private and for your personal use only. Share them only if you want to.)

CHAPTER

5 Moving Toward Maturity

OBJECTIVES

- *Describe the signs of maturity and give examples of mature actions.*
- *Explain how role models can help you.*

TERMS TO LEARN

- ***maturity***
- ***independence***
- ***role model***
- ***modeling***
- ***roles***

"Sometimes it's hard to figure. I'm too young to vote, too young to drive, too young to stay out late, and too young to go camping alone with my friends. On the other hand, I'm old enough to take care of my brothers, work on the farm, and help with my aunt's campaign for a seat on the county board.

"It's frustrating to have people expect things from you one minute and hold you back the next. My sister says she remembers feeling the same way a few years ago. She says to be patient and enjoy my 'carefree' years. Well, I'm trying."

Seeking Maturity

Can you identify in some way with the speaker in the previous paragraphs? Most teens can. The desire to become an adult is normal and necessary. This is what gives teens the incentive to learn what they need to know and to test their wings as they move toward adulthood.

Simply becoming an adult is not the real goal, however. Becoming mature is. There is a difference. **Maturity** (muh-TUR-uht-ee) means reaching full development. People mature in all the areas of development — physical, emotional, social, intellectual, and moral. That is, they gradually move toward full development in each area. However, not everyone matures at the same rate. In addition, some people mature rapidly in one area, but lag behind in other areas. As a matter of fact, some people never reach maturity in some areas of development. What characteristics do you think go along with the development of maturity?

Age is used as a legal measure of maturity, as in determining when you can drive or vote.

Age is a commonly used indicator of maturity. This is the basis for laws that require you to be a certain age before you can get a work permit, a driver's license, or a marriage license. The right to vote also depends on your age. Different states may set different ages for these rights, but age is a legal measure of maturity almost everywhere. It is not a complete one, however.

At age twenty-one, Justin is legally an adult. His temper and his lack of ability to manage his money, however, show some immaturity. As you can see, age alone does not determine maturity.

MEETING SPECIAL NEEDS

Through Understanding

Think about someone you know who has a disability. How do you view this person? Often, the first reaction is to focus on a person's disability. However, people with disabilities are people first. They have the same feelings, problems, and the need for friends that you have.

Devon, a teen with a learning disability, shared what life was like for himself with some of his classmates. "Sometimes people ignore me or make fun of me because they think I'm different. That hurts! Whenever I can, I try to find ways to let people know that I'm no different from other teens — they just need to understand more about me. I like to do the same things that other teens like to do — listen to music, talk, eat pizza, watch movies, and go to football games."

Ask yourself the following questions in thinking about people with disabilities:

- Do you see the person's abilities or disabilities first?
- How might you feel if people only looked at you in terms of a disability?

(Continued on next page)

Signs of Maturity

- "What a mature child she is!"
- "Oh, I would never go out with him. He's too immature."
- "Why don't you just grow up?"

Have you ever heard people make comments like these? They are evaluations of maturity. What makes some people more mature than others? You can probably list some qualities. See how your list compares with the ideas that follow.

Dealing with Emotions

Happy, sad, fearful, glad, jealous, lonely, peaceful, and loved. What do all these terms have in common? If you identified them as emotions, you are absolutely correct. How many other emotions can you name? You may wonder what emotions have to do with maturity — the fact is they have a lot to do with maturity.

Learning to label your emotions and express them in a healthful way is an important part of maturing. Everyone has emotions. However, the way you choose to act on your emotions can be appropriate or inappropriate. How can you tell if you are choosing a healthful, or right, response to your emotions? Try asking yourself the following questions:

- Do I respond to my emotions in a way that is harmful to myself or others?
- Do I respond to my emotions in ways that are appropriate for the time?

The way you choose to act on your emotions can be appropriate or inappropriate. In what ways is this teen acting on his emotions inappropriately?

Mature people learn to be in charge of their emotions, rather than letting their emotions be in charge of them. They show their feelings in constructive ways, and they don't go to pieces whenever something goes wrong. They know that everyone has difficulty dealing with emotions at one time or another.

Lenny was twenty-three years old when he lost his third job. He quit the first one in a moment of anger. On the other two jobs, he was fired after too many arguments with bosses and employees. Unfortunately, Lenny had never learned to control his emotions. Even little things made him lash out in anger.

Most people respond in a positive, healthful way to emotions such as love and hopefulness. However, learning to control emotions such as anger in a positive, healthful way is easier for some than for others. Here are some ways to help control difficult feelings:

- ***Think about the way you feel before reacting.*** If necessary, count to ten or walk away from the situation for a short time.
- ***Avoid letting small irritations upset you.*** You may find your attitude improving if you can let go of the little things.
- ***Talk about the way you feel.*** Naming your emotions as you talk with someone you trust can help you put a positive perspective on your feelings.

Allowing yourself to feel your emotions and deal with them in an appropriate, healthful way shows you are well on your way to emotional maturity.

Acceptance

Another sign of maturity is the ability to be accepting. This comes in two ways.

In the first place, a mature person is accepting of others. Can you imagine your classroom filled with people who all look and act just alike? What if people were all the same everywhere you went? How boring the world would be if this were true! Differences make people interesting; they do not make people wrong or unacceptable. Anyone who judges people or hurts them according to their differences — whether the difference is in appearance, attitude, ability, custom, or any other way — shows a lack of maturity. This doesn't mean that you have to like everyone you meet. It does mean that you should be tolerant and not view their differences as wrong.

Through Understanding (Continued)

- How can you appreciate and affirm the abilities in someone who has a disability?
- How can you encourage others to look beyond the disabilities and focus on the abilities that people have?

Try getting to know someone with a disability a little better. You will gain maturity and build your self-esteem as well as the self-esteem of the disabled person. Who knows — you might just find a good friend.

Working together cooperatively can be fun and rewarding for all those involved.

Don't Be Afraid to Fail

You've failed many times, although you may not remember. You fell down the first time you tried to walk. You almost drowned the first time you tried to swim, didn't you? Did you hit the ball the first time you swung a bat? Heavy hitters, the ones who hit the most home runs, also strike out a lot. R.H. Macy failed seven times before his store in New York caught on. English novelist John Creasey got 753 rejection slips before he published 564 books. Babe Ruth struck out 1,330 times, but he also hit 714 home runs. Don't worry about failure. Worry about the chances you miss when you don't even try.

Another form of acceptance involves circumstances. When things cannot be changed, a person needs to understand and accept that fact. After an auto accident, Beth went through some difficult times. It wasn't until she accepted her resulting disability that she was able to get on with her life.

Remember there is another side to this coin, however. In some situations, acceptance is the wrong approach. This is true when positive change is possible. Kent knew his family could not finance his college education, but did he simply accept this and let go of his dream? No! Instead, Kent looked for ways to get help and worked for what he wanted. In this case, acceptance would have been a mistake.

Willingness to Work Hard

The decorating committee was hard at work getting ready for the homecoming dance. Ellie was up to her usual tricks. She loved to volunteer so she could be in the middle of all the activity. When it came down to work, however, she drew the line. Instead Ellie would flit around, talking to people, joking with them, and not getting anything done. Her immaturity was showing.

Very little is accomplished without work. Good grades come with effort. Winning teams develop with practice. Successful employees are rewarded for giving their all. People admire those who do their part. These are the people you want on your committee, team, or staff.

Around the World

May 5 is celebrated as *Children's Day* in Japan. It expresses the love and respect the Japanese feel for their children. It also sends a message to young people about growing up. On *Children's Day,* large kites shaped like carp are flown from the rooftops. The carp, a fish that swims against the current, symbolizes the difficulties to be overcome in life.

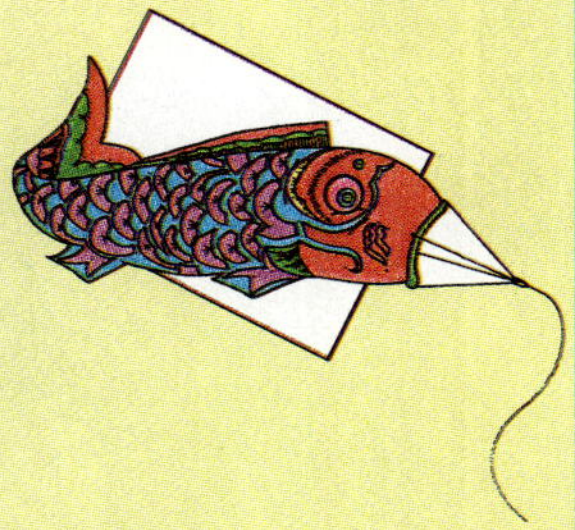

When the "Ellies" of the world are around, what do you do? Some people respond by stating: "Well, if she's not going to do anything, I'm not either." Following Ellie's example is not a good idea. First, the job does not get done. Second, you become just like Ellie. Others will see you in the same light. A more mature attitude is to do your part — and more, if necessary. There is satisfaction — and often eventual reward — in knowing that you put forth your best effort to get a job done.

Good grades come with effort. How do you think this teen feels about her efforts?

Patience

Long lines, heavy traffic, slow service — all of these and more can bring out the impatient nature of some people. What other examples can you think of that cause people to become impatient?

Impatience indicates self-interest. It says, "My wants and needs come first and now." Patience, on the other hand, says, "I can wait to have what I want or need, because the wants and needs of others are important too."

You have no doubt seen children hovering around a teacher, all trying to get attention at once. A few may be willing to wait, realizing that their turn will come. They know that patience is in order and that they must sometimes delay satisfying their own needs. This shows they are developing maturity.

Dependability

One quality most people like to find in their friends is dependability. It's nice to know that you can count on someone. This is one more characteristic of a mature person.

How would you rate the dependability of the following people?

- In over a year on the job, Tina has never been late for work.
- Chelsie takes phone calls for others in her family but doesn't write down or remember to pass along the messages.

- Even though Arlo doesn't get much actual playing time in the basketball games, he never misses a practice.
- Once a week, Joe picks up groceries for his grandmother and delivers them to her.

How is this teen showing maturity and responsibility?

Independence

Independence, or the ability to take care of one's self, is perhaps what every teen is striving for. A mature person learns the skills that make this possible. Just think about what you need to know and be able to do in order to be independent. You must be able to make good decisions. You will need money-making and management abilities. You will also need knowledge about taking care of housing and health needs. Self confidence is a necessary quality for those learning how to be independent.

Without such skills as these, a person remains dependent on others. As a teen, you are steadily gathering the information you need to become an independent person. This comes through your family, friends, and education.

Good Judgment

Why is it that some people get themselves in trouble all the time and others don't? It may be a matter of judgment.

Some people have developed the ability to see all sides of an issue. They have what might be called a broader vision. They are able to look at a situation and see the positive and negative effects — on themselves or on others. This helps them make decisions about what is good, right, or practical.

You can see real-life examples of this all around you. Think about people you know who get themselves into tough situations. Is bad judgment a factor? Chances are, it is. Developing good judgment takes time, effort, and learning from your past experiences and the experiences of others. Once acquired, it can make your life move along much more smoothly.

Responsibility

Few qualities of mature people are more valued than responsibility. Responsibility involves knowing what is expected of you and following through with the appropriate behavior. It involves knowing that you are accountable for your actions. Admitting your mistakes, rather than blaming someone else, shows you can be trusted. This is one quality that families often look for in their growing children. A teen who shows a sense of responsibility earns trust and, therefore, the privileges that go along with that trust. Too often, teens want to be trusted before they have proven their ability to be responsible.

Callie was seldom home on time. She often missed dinners and arrived home after curfew. Because she didn't call, her family worried about what might have happened to her. When Callie was invited to go with a group of friends on a weekend trip to an amusement park, her parents said no. Callie was upset and couldn't understand why they were doing this. Do you?

Mature people often take responsibility for more than themselves — for family, friends, and community. They are willing to help others and even put the needs of others before their own needs at times. For example, if Callie had acted responsibly, she would have had some concern for her parents' feelings as well as her own. A sense of responsibility toward community shows in such ways as having respect for property and concern for the environment. When a group of teens work together to clean up a vacant lot, they are showing community responsibility.

Being willing to put the needs of others before your own is a true sign of maturity.

Using Role Models

Patterning yourself after role models can help as you seek maturity. **Role models** are people who, through their behavior and attitude, serve as an example for others. Who are some of your role models?

Even when you are not aware of it, you model people. **Modeling**, or watching and imitating the behavior of others, gives you a chance to act like them and see if their behavior works for you. You try out their **roles**, or the parts they play in life. For example, a person may play the part of a football player, president of the student body, or a teacher. Within the family, a person may be a mother, father, sister, brother, or grandparent, to name a few. When you follow the actions of a role model, you may dress like them, talk the way they talk, and do the things they do. People may fulfill several roles at one time. For example, you may be a brother or sister, soccer player, and student all at the same time.

How do role models help you as you grow in maturity?

Sometimes people choose the wrong role models. In trying to be like another person, you may find yourself acting in ways that cause problems. You may go against your own values and goals. This is an example of using poor judgment and shows a lack of maturity.

It is true that you can learn a great deal from someone you admire, but you need to ask yourself if your role model will send you in the right direction. Are there signs of maturity? Are the values shown positive ones? Only if these answers are "yes" will the role model be helpful to you.

Your Level of Maturity

By now you should have a pretty good idea of what it means to be mature. You may even have additional ideas about what maturity is. Now take a look at yourself. Where are you on the maturity scale?

At this stage of your life, the important thing is to be moving in the right direction. You should be able to identify ways you have changed since childhood. You should also see ways in which you can move closer to maturity in the future. Why not make this your goal?

TAKING ACTION

You're going out with a new group of acquaintances, some of whom are older than you are. They are all part of the most popular crowd in school and you feel flattered to be included.

Walt has a car and is driving the group to a movie. On the way, Anthony produces a six-pack of beer his brother bought for him. He offers everyone a can. As Walt drinks and speeds along the highway, he and Anthony keep everybody laughing with their jokes. When they finish their beers, they toss their cans out the window. After Walt parks the car, Anthony starts to scrawl graffiti on the wall of a building. The rest of the group encourage him and have a good time.

Using Your Resourcefulness

- If you were a passenger in the car, how would you honestly react to the situation? What would you say?
- Do you think it's hard to resist negative pressure from friends? Why or why not?
- What is the connection between going against the crowd and maturity? Why do you think some teens act more responsibly and use better judgment than others? How can one change to become more responsible?

Chapter 5 Review

Summary

In this chapter, you have read about:

- The difference between age and maturity.
- Types of mature behavior.
- The function of role models.
- Rating your own development in maturity.

Facts to Recall

1. What is maturity? How can it be a source of confusion and frustration for teens?
2. Is age the same as maturity? Explain.
3. List three ways mature people deal with emotions.
4. In what two situations is acceptance a sign of maturity? When is it the wrong approach?
5. What is a mature response to someone who shows an immature attitude toward hard work?
6. How do people show self-interest by impatience?
7. Identify three skills or characteristics needed for independence.
8. What abilities are involved in good judgment?
9. How do mature people show responsibility toward others?
10. How can role models help you?

Ideas to Explore

1. In what ways or situations are teens encouraged or required to show maturity? When are they not?
2. Can a person be mature in some ways — physically, emotionally, socially — but immature in others? Explain.
3. How can you tell when a situation should be accepted as something you cannot change, and when you should work to try to make it better?
4. Debate the following statement: "Teens are given too much (or not enough) responsibility in our society."

Activities to Try

1. Make a list of five situations in which you have trouble controlling your emotions. Beside each one, write down something you can do to deal with your emotions maturely.
2. Make a maturity timeline. Begin with your birth and mark off each year. Write down major events or significant points on your road to maturity — physical, emotional, social, intellectual, and moral. Project the timeline five years into the future, showing the ways you hope to develop in that time span.
3. Describe an incident or tell a short story in which you made a conscious effort to behave maturely. Explain how this was a step forward in your physical, emotional, social, intellectual, or moral development.

LINK TO *Communication*

Choosing a Mentor

Mentor was the elderly friend and adviser of Odysseus (oh-dis-ee-us), the hero of the *Odyssey* — an ancient Greek play. Today, the word "mentor" means a wise and faithful counselor. Young adults are often advised to find a mentor in their career field to guide and advise them. Identify an adult you might choose as a mentor. Write a one-page paper describing the qualities that would make this person a good choice for your personal mentor. How could this person help you as you move toward maturity?

CHAPTER 6

Citizenship and Leadership

OBJECTIVES

- *Describe the qualities of a good citizen.*
- *Identify ways to show citizenship.*
- *Describe the qualities of a good leader.*
- *Give examples of ways to practice leadership.*

TERMS TO LEARN

- ***citizen***
- ***citizenship***
- ***volunteers***
- ***vandalism***
- ***apathy***
- ***leader***
- ***leadership***
- ***parliamentary procedure***
- ***graffiti***

The doors in the front-hall restroom were a mess. Kimi was tired of looking at them. The scribbled names and senseless messages were everywhere, a lasting reminder of the ignorance of some people. It was then that Kimi decided to do something.

"We need more pride," she thought. "We need to find ways to make people want to take care of school property. I think a school-pride campaign might work. Then we need some volunteers to repaint the restroom doors."

With these thoughts, Kimi began her first organized effort at active citizenship. Along the way she would learn some new leadership skills as well.

What Is Citizenship?

A **citizen** (SIT-uh-zen) is someone who is a member of a community, such as a city or town, state, or country. The fact that you are a citizen doesn't automatically make you a good one. The way that you handle your responsibilities as a citizen is known as **citizenship**. Some people do this well; others do not.

Citizens are entitled to the rights and privileges that come with being a member of a certain community. In return, they have duties and responsibilities that must be returned to the community. This allows the community to survive and function well. A community that thrives has many good citizens. In one that does not, too many people place no value on good citizenship.

In a community that thrives, people take the duties and responsibilities that come with citizenship seriously. What duties and responsibilities do you think come with being a citizen?

You're The Finest

In just 200 years, your country, through freedom and hard work, has changed the world. In agriculture, industry, education, medicine, law, transportation, and on and on. No country can match America's record in religious freedom, civil freedom, human rights, the importance and dignity of the individual. We do have our differences. But when we join together in times of crisis, our strength is awesome. Among all the world's nations, America still stands out front. You're an American. You're the finest ever — and don't you ever, ever forget it.

Becoming a Good Citizen

You first learn and practice citizenship in your home and school. If you can make them better places in which to live and learn, then you can do the same in your community. No matter what the setting is, good citizenship involves using many of the same skills and qualities.

Qualities of Good Citizenship

To be a good citizen, you must meet two basic requirements. First, you must care. Second, you must act on your concerns.

In the home, you show a concern for others when you willingly do your part to help family members. A person who cares enough to do this at home will transfer the same attitude into the community. This is also true with such attitudes as respect, honesty, and courtesy.

The members of Leroy's family have respect for each other's property. When one member borrows something, it is returned in good condition. They also take care of their home. Although it is small, it is clean and neat.

This is the attitude that Leroy carries with him — to school and to other places in the community. When he borrowed some supplies from the art teacher for a committee he was on, Leroy made sure everything was returned in good condition. He cared enough to show respect for the teacher's property. When a group of neighbors decided to repair the fence around the community center, Leroy was there to help. He cared about the children who use the center and wanted to make it a better place for them.

There are many ways that people can practice good citizenship. For example, citizens can work together to improve their surroundings.

Leroy learned about caring at home. Now this attitude is helping him become a good citizen. Just caring is not enough, however. To be a good citizen, you must act on your feelings, just as Leroy did at the community center. There are many ways for people to take an active part in practicing good citizenship.

Volunteering

Every community has needs that often go unmet. Through volunteers, much can be done. **Volunteers,** people who offer their services free of charge, help meet these needs. They put caring into action.

People who volunteer are not motivated by money. They have discovered rewards that mean much more. The good feeling that comes from helping others is the first reward. In addition, it is a good way to make new friends. Getting to know people who have similar interests is often one of the aims of volunteers. For many teens, volunteer work offers an opportunity to learn new job skills and gain valuable work experience. They may even make contacts that may later result in employment.

In almost any community, you can find ways to become involved. Look in the yellow pages of your telephone directory under volunteer services or social service organizations. You may find opportunities there. School counselors may also be able to direct you to organizations that need help in your community. There may even be service clubs in your school that you can join.

Being part of the Future Homemakers of America (FHA) is one way to get started in volunteer work. This organization offers a variety of ways to contribute to your home, school, and community. By becoming a member of FHA, you can also make new friends and get involved in activities that will help you grow as a person.

Stopping Crime

Crime hurts people. It ruins neighborhoods. It creates fear and anger.

Most people learn to live by rules as children. These rules are learned at home and in school. Rules, in the form of laws, also exist in communities. Good citizens follow the laws because they care about the welfare of all people. They want order in the community, and they want to live where people feel safe, secure, and happy.

Unfortunately, some people have never learned to live by rules. They have no respect for them. They care only about themselves, never facing or understanding how their actions affect others.

TIPS: *Volunteer Activities*

- Form a group that will clean up **graffiti** (gruh-FEE-tee), unwanted drawings and writing on walls and other property.
- Tutor students who need help with a particular subject.
- Run for student government. Then you can help set rules and policies to make your school a better place.
- Start a community service program if your school does not already have one.
- Join or start a group that is interested in cleaning up the environment.
- Become a hospital volunteer.
- Participate in a charity walk-a-thon.
- Visit shut-ins and run errands for them.
- Visit nursing home residents.
- Organize games for children in your neighborhood.
- Beautify your neighborhood by planting trees and flowers.
- Participate in a food drive for those in need.
- Collect recyclable materials.

AROUND THE WORLD

In Cuba, volunteerism is strongly encouraged and supported by the government through its state-owned businesses, farms, and factories. Volunteers earn points for every hour of service. Everyone's points are posted in their workplace. At year's end, their fellow workers vote for whom they think is most deserving. A yearly reward may be a large appliance at a low price or a vacation at a beach resort. Over many years, a volunteer may accumulate enough points for a car or an apartment.

Gathering food for hungry people is one way these teens are being good citizens.

Crime affects everyone — the criminal and the victims. Good citizens obey laws.

Crime occurs at many levels. It may begin as **vandalism**, the deliberate destruction of property, and move on to stealing and acts of violence. Every criminal act has consequences that affect the victims of a crime, the criminal, and all citizens. Think about these consequences:

- ***Someone pays for the criminal acts of others.*** Shoplifting, for example, occurs when people steal items from stores. In order to make up for lost goods, stores have to charge higher prices. Everyone must pay these higher costs. Vandalism is expensive, too. Every time property is destroyed, someone has to pay the cost of repairs. When the property is public, everyone pays through tax dollars, leaving less money for other needs. If vandalism gets out of hand in a neighborhood and repairs cannot be made, the consequence may be a ruined community. In the saddest of cases, some people pay the ultimate cost of crime — their lives.
- ***Crime has long-lasting effects on its victims.*** After Mrs. Carrera's purse was yanked from her arm by a youth on a bicycle, she was never the same. She was elderly and lived in fear from that point on in her life. The few dollars she lost were nothing compared to what the incident did to her emotionally.
- ***A criminal record lasts a lifetime.*** It can affect a person's ability to get a job. It definitely affects the attitudes others have toward the person.

These are only a few of the consequences of crime. There are many others. Indeed, the more serious the crime, the greater the consequences to everyone involved.

What can good citizens do to stop crime? The first line of defense is to follow the law yourself. Avoid people who are already mixed up in the wrong kinds of activity. Choose friends who want to make your community a better place,

How to . . .

Be a Good Citizen

You have learned that a good citizen cares about others and acts on his or her concerns. Here are some specific ways to do this, now and in the future:

- Take care of public property, as well as your own.
- Don't litter. Pick up litter when you see it.
- Follow rules and laws.
- Respect the rights of all people. Public places are shared by all. Your conduct should reflect this.
- Stay informed.
- Vote in all elections.
- Find ways to make your community a better place for everyone.

not a worse one. If people scorn you for trying to do what is right, reject their reasoning. They are likely to pay a price for their attitude, a price that you will not want to pay too.

Second, be willing to take action. Report any criminal activity you see. Many communities have *Crime Watch* programs that enable you to do this easily. You might even become involved in setting up a neighborhood program that encourages people to look out for each other.

Over the years, crime has become a more serious problem. As a good citizen, you need to be part of the solution, not part of the problem. If you treat others in a positive way — showing care, respect, and courtesy — you send them a clear message that you expect to be treated in the same manner. If your actions don't show this, then making a change is in order.

Good citizens look out for one another.

Staying Informed

Good citizenship involves staying informed. Your ability to contribute to your community hinges on what you know.

Eventually as a voter, you can help choose leaders. The more you know, the better equipped you will be to make such decisions.

By reading the newspaper and listening to radio and television broadcasts, you can keep up with what is going on within your community and the world. You will have informed opinions that may even enable you to influence others. When you know what is going on in your world, you will know who needs help and when.

Avoiding the Problem of Apathy

The headline reads: "Crowd Watches While Elderly Man Is Assaulted." This sad story smacks of a problem that is seen all too often in society — **apathy**. This is just the opposite of caring and taking action. It is a lack of feeling or interest. People who have apathy see what's going on around them as someone else's problem or responsibility. They don't care enough to get involved.

Apathy occurs for a variety of complex reasons. It's more important to focus on curing apathy than to worry about why people are apathetic. You need to know that you can make a difference in the world. Even though ten people around you are doing nothing, you can step forward and help. You can take on that responsibility. It will bring you respect and admiration plus a good feeling inside. Even when ten people around you are doing a lot, you can make a contribution. There is room for everyone when it comes to caring.

A good leader provides positive guidance to a group.

What Is Leadership?

Anyone can be a citizen, but not everyone is a leader. A **leader** is a person who has influence over and guides a group. **Leadership** is not just holding an office, such as student body president, it is the ability to lead. In fact, a good deal of leadership comes from people with no title at all. It is influencing people in other, more informal, ways too. Leadership can be learned and practiced — just like skating, skiing, or making speeches.

What Makes a Good Leader?

Leaders have two main functions. One, they get the job done. Two, they keep the group together. The "job" is whatever the group is organized to do. It might be a game, a contest, or a committee project.

Good leaders share certain qualities. Think about which of the following qualities you have already and which ones you might work to develop. Good leaders:

- ***Listen to the ideas, problems, and concerns of group members.*** Good leaders listen to the feelings behind what is said as well as to the words. This brings about a positive attitude within the group and encourages commitment to the project.
- ***Build a team from the members of the group.*** Good leaders must build a team, not just expect it to fall into place. A way to do this is to recognize the worth of each member and his or her ideas. The group can then build on those ideas to make them more workable. As a result, members can see that their ideas play a role in the group's decision. They will be more enthusiastic about carrying out the decision.
- ***Think creatively to aid the goals of the group.*** They aren't afraid to try new ways to achieve goals, to look for new solutions to old problems, or to risk failure.
- ***Clearly identify group goals.*** They provide each member with information and direction about the goals. As a result, group members don't lose focus of what they are trying to accomplish.
- ***Organize activities, projects, and tasks of the group.*** Good leaders must have a clear picture of what needs to be done and of the steps necessary to carry out the task. They make sure each member understands his or her specific role in accomplishing group activities, projects, and tasks.
- ***Solve conflicts within the group.*** Conflicts may occur when members try to influence the leader or other members. Personality clashes and unpleasant past experiences can also cause differences that leaders must handle.
- ***Direct group decision making.*** They make sure the group doesn't get sidetracked. Good leaders know and follow rules, known as **parliamentary procedure** (PAR-luh-MENT-uh-ree), established years ago by the English Parliament. These rules, listed in a book called *Robert's Rules of Order*, allow leaders to keep order while group members voice their opinions and reach a majority decision.
- ***Participate with group members.*** They do not consider themselves to be more important than the rest of the group. They are willing to pitch in and do the work, too.
- ***Show appreciation for group members.*** They are aware that a group becomes strong when individual members feel special and wanted.

Good leaders help the team work effectively. What leadership skills do you have?

TIPS: *Working with Leaders*

Responsible group members show the following characteristics:

- Work cooperatively with leaders and other group members toward common goals.
- Show that they are trustworthy.
- Speak positively about leaders and other group members.
- Promote unity among group members.

Setting examples for good behavior and giving encouragement are ways that you can practice leadership with those around you. How is the teen in this photo demonstrating his leadership capabilities?

- ***Manage time, money, and other resources for the group.*** They make sure all members share the workload equally. They schedule what must be done and when it must be done in order to meet the group goal. Also, good leaders are honest and are able to account for money and other resources that belong to the group.

Practicing Leadership

You don't need to be appointed or win an election to be a leader. Opportunities for leadership are all around you. In a group of friends, someone leads the rest in deciding where to go and what to do. In school, some students spark the class discussion and influence others by what they say.

With younger family members, an older brother or sister sets an example for behavior and gives encouragement. Just as you may look up to someone for guidance and behavior worth imitating, young people may do the same with you. This is providing a role model instead of using one. A senior on the track team can show a freshman what it means to win or lose with a positive attitude. A veteran employee at the fast-food restaurant can show the new person how to work well with others.

All of these are examples of leadership. Making the effort to practice leadership today can get you ready for even bigger opportunities in the future.

TAKING ACTION

Marianne, your class president, has asked several students for their help. She hopes to raise money for class projects through activities that highlight different areas of the school.

Marianne asks you to represent the home economics department. She wants you to generate ideas, such as a recycled clothing sale, that create both positive public relations for home economics and help raise money for the class treasury. Marianne expects you to offer several ideas that are fun yet practical. She also wants you to organize specific groups and appoint leaders from your home economics class to carry out the ideas.

Using Your Resourcefulness

- Think of three ideas that would promote home economics and raise money in your school.
- Divide members of your home economics class into three groups who will carry out your ideas. Appoint three group leaders.
- What would influence your choice of leaders? What leadership qualities do they have?

Chapter 6 Review

Summary

In this chapter, you have read about:

- Ways in which good citizens show they care about their community.
- Ideas for volunteering.
- How a good leader helps a group achieve its goals.

Facts to Recall

1. Name three qualities of a good citizen learned in the home.
2. Why is "just caring" about your community not enough to make you a good citizen?
3. Identify three rewards of volunteering.
4. Explain how shoplifting and vandalism hurt the whole community.
5. What are two ways good citizens can help stop crime?
6. How is staying informed important to good citizenship?
7. What is apathy? How can you fight it?
8. List four specific ways you can act as a good citizen.
9. What are two main functions of a good leader?
10. List seven characteristics of good leaders.

Ideas to Explore

1. You have read about a leader's responsibilities to the group. What are the group's responsibilities to its leader?
2. Discuss the conflict that arises when citizens of a group cannot follow certain rules that they believe are wrong. Suggest ways of resolving this problem.
3. What action would you take, individually or within a group, if you felt your leader was a poor one or had made a poor decision for the group?

Activities to Try

1. Make a collage of pictures, photographs, and headlines illustrating good citizenship.
2. As a class, brainstorm a list of things you can do today to make your home, school, and community better places in which to live and work.
3. On a sheet of paper, write the term "citizen," "volunteer," or "leader" down the left-hand margin. Next to each letter, write a word beginning with that letter that relates to the term you've chosen.

LINK TO *Social Studies*

Identifying Leadership Characteristics

Some people believe that leadership ability is inherited. However, many people who are not "born" leaders can and do learn to be good leaders. Many people believe that authority makes a leader. Today, however, authority is a much less effective basis for leadership than in the past. Today's leaders *guide* groups rather than *rule* them. Certain personal qualities are also associated with good leaders. At the same time, the characteristics of great leaders are as varied as the leaders themselves. Using your knowledge of history:

- Identify three great leaders.
- List at least five of each individual's personal qualities that made him or her an outstanding leader.

CHAPTER 7 Exploring Careers

OBJECTIVES

- *Explain how interests, aptitudes, and skills influence career choices.*
- *Identify ways to gain work skills.*
- *Discuss sources for finding jobs.*
- *Give strategies for applying and interviewing for a job.*

TERMS TO LEARN

- ***career***
- ***interests***
- ***aptitudes***
- ***skills***
- ***paraprofessionals***
- ***apprenticeship***
- ***entrepreneur***
- ***interview***

Have you ever wondered where the future will lead you? One of the most important decisions you'll make in the next few years about your future concerns the type of **career**, or chosen occupation, you want. With thousands of jobs to choose from, it's never too early to begin thinking about your future career.

Adrienne, an active teen, has been thinking a lot about her future. After a conversation with the guidance counselor at her school, she discovered that she can expect to work at least 35 years with several job changes along the way. The counselor said that changes in the world will affect the jobs available. "The best advice I can give you," said the counselor, "is to get a good education and some training that will allow you to branch out into other career areas during your work life."

Your Future Career

To find a career that you'll enjoy, you need to look at more than just the type of work involved. How does your career choice relate to your family and way of life? How much stress are you willing to work under? What are your interests, aptitudes, and skills? What kind of education do you want? The answers to these questions will have a big influence on your career decision.

Work and Family

A job that sounds interesting may have other qualities that might not fit your needs or way of living. Many times people forget to consider how personal and family life relates to their careers. For example, a person who values time with his or her family, but chooses a job that requires a lot of overtime, will not be happy. Someone who likes independence and flexible work hours — often to help meet the needs of children in a family — won't like a highly structured nine-to-five job. If a family depends on a steady income, then work that is seasonal — or only available part of the year — might not be the answer. Take time to consider the schedule, the number of hours, and income to achieve happiness in your chosen job.

What type of job might fit your needs now? How might this affect the career you choose in the future?

The amount of stress on the job varies from job to job. How much stress do you think this man faces daily on the job?

Stress on the Job

Stress on the job is another important factor to consider. All jobs have stress — some have more than others. In many jobs, stress is a positive, motivating factor that encourages creativity and accomplishment. In others, stress is a negative factor that keeps employees from meeting goals.

Remember that job stress can carry over to your personal life. The opposite is also true. Personal problems can make people less productive at work. Finding a career that is satisfying is one way to decrease the problems caused by stress. Learning ways to manage stress is another. (See pages 56-62 in Chapter 4 for ways to manage stress.)

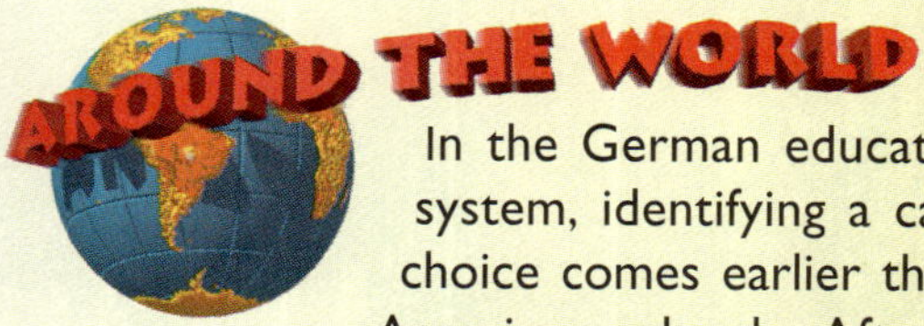

In the German educational system, identifying a career choice comes earlier than in American schools. After the tenth grade, some students begin preparing for university entrance exams. However, about two thirds of all German young people attend vocational/technical schools instead of the university after the tenth grade. They take courses in their chosen profession or trade, such as restaurant management, engineering, or metalworking. In addition, they work for pay at a firm or business in their chosen field to gain hands-on experience. After graduation from vocational/technical school at age 19, many students are fully prepared for work in their chosen career.

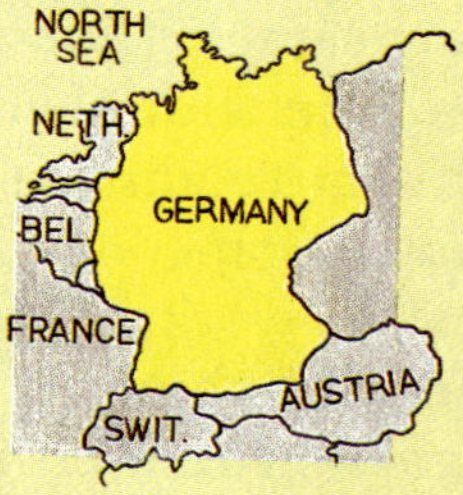

Your Interests

Considering your **interests**, or what you like to do, is one factor to think about when looking at career options. Hobbies and the other ways you spend your free time tell about your interests. You may enjoy working with people or working with your hands. Perhaps you like reading, using words, and writing. On the other hand, numbers and solving problems may hold a special appeal to you. Whatever your interests, consider careers that will make those interests part of your working life.

Your Aptitudes and Skills

Everyone has **aptitudes**, or natural abilities or talents for learning certain skills. A **skill** on the other hand, is the ability to do something that comes from training and practice. A skill that comes to you easily is often something you have an aptitude for. Even when you have an aptitude for a certain skill, it still requires hard work, training, and practice to be developed.

How can you find out what your aptitudes and skills are? One way is to ask yourself these questions:

- In what school subjects do I make the highest grades?
- What do I think I could learn to do well?
- What skills do I have?
- Which of these skills were easiest for me to learn?
- What aptitudes or skills do other people see in me?

Hey, Kids

Just before you go to sleep tonight, check this list: Did you get up on time? Did you make your bed? Did you eat a good breakfast? Did you read something interesting? Did you learn something? Were you polite? Did you help a friend? Did you do some work around the house? Did you try to earn some money to help pay for your clothes? Did you think about your future? Did you read a newspaper or watch a newscast? Did you brush your teeth? Twice? Did you tell your parents how much you appreciate them? Imagine how good you'll feel about yourself if you can say "yes" to these questions, today, and every day.

This teen is developing her aptitude toward art. She might consider a career as a commercial artist or an illustrator of children's books. What are your aptitudes?

Aptitude tests provide another way to find out about your natural abilities and skills. Some tests predict how easy or difficult it would be for you to develop the skills needed for a certain career. Check with your school counselor or the state employment office about aptitude tests that you could take.

Education

Where do you see education fitting into career choices? The less education and training a worker has, the less chance there is for obtaining a steady job. Lack of education and training also make it more difficult to change to other jobs in the future. A high school graduate has a better chance than a dropout does for finding a job that provides interesting work, good wages, and steady employment.

The type and level of training you need varies with the type of job you want. Some jobs require little or no training, while others require four years of college plus an advanced degree. The following outlines the various levels of jobs:

- ***Entry-level jobs.*** Entry-level jobs require little or no training. The training that is needed is usually provided on the job. Types of jobs in this category include a maintenance worker, a counter person at a fast food restaurant, a dishwasher at a hospital or restaurant, a sales clerk, or a nurses' aide.
- ***Paraprofessional jobs.*** **Paraprofessionals** are trained to assist professional people. These jobs require a high school diploma and some additional education at a vocational/technical school or a 2-year college. Some states require a special license for some paraprofessional jobs. Emergency medical technicians (EMTs), child care workers, and dietary assistants are examples of paraprofessionals. Skilled-trade jobs, such as carpentry and plumbing, are also included in the paraprofessional category. Some skilled-trade jobs offer **apprenticeships**, or on-the-job training with pay. An apprentice works under the guidance of a skilled tradesperson to learn a trade.
- **Professional jobs.** Jobs at the professional level require four years of college and often an advanced degree from a graduate school. Teachers, doctors, counselors, architects, and social workers are examples of professional workers.

Paraprofessional jobs require education and training beyond high school.

Your Opportunities Now

There are always jobs to be done. Most of these jobs are for adults who have completed the necessary education or training. However, there are many jobs that you could do right now. Most are part-time and offer paid wages. Others are volunteer jobs that provide pay in the form of skills learned and personal satisfaction.

Volunteer Opportunities

Before you consider getting a part-time job, you may want to try volunteer work. Volunteering gives you an opportunity to develop new interests, test your aptitudes, and develop skills. Volunteer experiences may also offer acceptable workplace references for a person seeking employment without other employment experience. Volunteer opportunities are often available at hospitals, schools, the American Red Cross, and humane societies. See page 77 for more ideas about volunteering.

Volunteer jobs provide a wealth of experience. This teen volunteers at a community center for the elderly. How might this experience help him as he decides on a career?

Part-time Work Opportunities

One of the best ways to learn about a career is by working at a part-time job in a field that interests you. Most part-time jobs offer work during the summer, after school, or on the weekends.

A good part-time job is one that you can do well and that you find interesting. Most importantly, it should give you an opportunity to observe various jobs in the career of your choice.

Working at a variety of part-time jobs over a period of time, gives you a chance to compare the characteristics and duties of different jobs in a variety of areas. In addition, knowing that you can adjust to different work situations and different job demands can help build your confidence and self-esteem.

Opportunities for Entrepreneurs

Are you a goal-oriented, self-disciplined person that has good decision-making skills? Perhaps you have what it takes to be an **entrepreneur** (AHN-truh-pruh-NUR) — a person who starts and manages his or her own business.

Many teens have found creative ways to start a business and make money on their own. For example, Jason started his own lawn-mowing and gardening service when he was 13 years old. He enjoyed the outdoors and found that he had a

As an entrepreneur, you can manage your own business. What skills do you have that might lead to owning and managing your own business?

real aptitude for working with lawns and outdoor plants. Kristin, on the other hand, had developed bicycle repair skills while working beside her father as a child. At age 14, she put these skills to good use by starting her own bicycle repair service.

Special operating permits are required for all businesses. In addition to operating permits, a tax number is assigned to all businesses. Check with your local government offices about the requirements for running your own business.

Getting a Job

Finding a job that you can do well and that you will enjoy takes some careful thought and planning.

Looking for a Job

Have you ever thought about how to get a job? Ann wants a job to earn money for her post-high school education. Her big problem right now is where to start looking for a job. She is aware of her skills and knows she would be a reliable, courteous employee. However, she first has to find a job.

Job hunting takes a lot of hard work. Jobs won't come to you; you have to go to the jobs. When looking for job openings, it helps to have a plan of action to find employers who are looking for a worker with your qualifications.

How do you find these employers? There are a variety of sources you can use, including personal contacts, school counselors, direct contact with employers, newspaper ads, and employment agencies. The more sources you use, the more job openings you're likely to find. You will have a better chance of finding a job you really like instead of taking the first job that comes along.

Talk with Friends and Relatives

Friends and relatives can be one of your best sources of job leads. They may know of employers who need someone with your skills. In addition, they may know people who do the kind of work that interests you.

Although you should not be timid about asking friends and relatives for job leads, do not expect them to find you a job. It is your responsibility to follow up on job leads, set up interviews, and make a good impression with potential employers.

School counselors and job placement offices are often good resources for locating jobs. However, you will want to investigate as many sources as possible.

Check with Your School Counselor

Many schools have a school or vocational counselor to help students find jobs in the community. Other schools may have placement offices where students may register for jobs.

Although your school may be a good source for job information, remember you may be one of many selected to interview for available jobs. Don't depend on your school as your only source of job leads. Investigate and use other sources available to you.

Contact Employers Directly

One of the best ways to find job openings is to contact employers directly. About half of all people who use this method of looking for a job are successful in finding one.

Before talking to employers, do some research to locate employers that need people with your skills. Look through the telephone book and make a list of possible employers. You can also check with the Chamber of Commerce or public library for potential employers.

Once you have a list of employers, contact the person in each company who has hiring authority. This may be the personnel director, the department manager, or the owner. If you do not know the name of this person, call the company and ask the receptionist. When you find out the name of the person to contact, write him or her a letter, make a phone call, visit the company, or use a combination of these methods.

Follow up on job leads as quickly as possible.

Read Newspaper Ads

Newspaper ads are another place to look for a job. Jobs are listed in newspapers under the section called the "Classified Ads" or the "Want Ads." You can learn what types of jobs are most available, what skills are needed for certain jobs, and what salaries are being paid.

Sunday is one of the best days to find job leads in the paper. Circle the ads that match your job interests and skills. Respond to the ads as quickly as possible. The longer you wait to apply, the more likely it is that the jobs will be filled by other applicants.

How to ...
Be a Responsible Employee

It's an exciting moment when you hear the magic words, "The job is yours." However, what's next? The next step is to show that you are a responsible employee. Here are some guidelines for showing that you are responsible:

- Arrive at work on time.
- Avoid long breaks. Take only the amount of time given for breaks.
- Follow safety rules and business procedures.
- Be honest and loyal to your employer.
- Be pleasant, friendly, and cooperative.
- Do your share of the work.
- Be willing to learn new things at work.
- Give two weeks' notice if you decide to leave a job.

Fill out job applications carefully to avoid making any errors.

Check with Employment Agencies

Government and private employment agencies help people find jobs. Government agencies provide free services. You may be asked to fill out a personal information sheet that identifies your skills and interests. A counselor will then tell you about jobs available that match some or all of your skills.

Private employment agencies charge a fee for helping people find jobs. Depending on the situation, either the employer or the person looking for work will pay the agency fee. Private agencies generally require that you sign a contract. Be sure that you understand everything in the contract before you sign it. *Do not sign anything that you do not understand.* You may want to have a knowledgeable person that you trust read through the contract before you sign it.

Applying for a Job

Before applying for a job, there are a few facts that you should know. First, you must have a Social Security card. If you do not have one, you can get one free of charge from the Social Security office in your community. Second, the United States Department of Labor has guidelines for employing young people. Check with your local Labor Department office to find out the minimum age guidelines that affect teens.

When you apply for a job, you'll be competing with others. Be prepared to give an employer complete information. Prepare a list of personal information to carry with you that includes:

- Full name, address, and telephone number.
- Social Security number.
- Work experience including dates when you began and left each job and a description of your job duties.
- Schools you have attended including when you attended them and any certificate, diploma, or degree you received.
- Special training you've received including when and where you received it.
- Skills or aptitudes you may have.
- Personal interests, hobbies, and activities.
- References. List the full names, addresses, and telephone numbers of at least three people. Do not use relatives as references. Be sure to contact your references and ask for permission to give their names to possible employers.
- Telephone numbers of persons to contact in case of emergency.

Some employers request a letter of application for employment. A good letter takes time and thought to write. It will tell the employer about your interest in the job, your skills, your education and training, and your work experience. It will also show your ability to express ideas. Be sure to use correct grammar, spelling, and punctuation. It's a good idea to have someone proofread your letter for any errors.

When applying for a job, fill out job applications carefully. Read through any application before filling it out. Ask questions about anything you do not understand. These forms will ask for the information you have prepared for the personal information list discussed on this page.

Keep the application form neat. Use ink instead of pencil. Print rather than write. Correctly spell each word you use and fill in all blanks on the application. If you have nothing to write, put "does not apply" or "N/A" (not applicable) in the appropriate blank. This way, the employer will know you did not overlook a question.

TIPS: *Interview Know-How*

The following tips may help you make a good impression and come out of an interview with a smile:

- Know where to go for the interview. If you do not know the location of the business, call and ask for directions.
- Arrive five to ten minutes early. Tell the receptionist who you are and with whom you have an appointment.
- Go to the interview alone.
- Wear simple, clean, and neatly pressed clothes. Try to look your very best so you'll make a good impression. Go light on makeup and jewelry. Avoid wearing jeans, T-shirts, and tennis shoes.
- Greet the interviewer with a firm handshake and a friendly smile. Wait to be offered a seat, and then sit up straight. Look alert and interested.
- Avoid distractions such as chewing gum and cracking your knuckles. Try to look relaxed even if you're not.
- Listen carefully to what the interviewer says. Keep good eye contact with the interviewer.

When applying for a job, first impressions are important. Many employers know within the first few minutes of an interview whether they want to hire a person or not.

Interviewing for a Job

A job **interview**, or a meeting between a potential employer and a job-seeker, is part of the process in applying for most jobs. The interviewer will explain the job and ask you questions. An interview also gives you a chance to ask questions about both the job and the company.

When interviewers finish talking, they will ask if you have any questions. Be sure to ask about any points you do not understand. After your questions are answered, the interview is just about over. At this time, thank the interviewer for seeing you. Tell him or her you would like the job.

People rarely are offered a job at the end of the interview. Employers usually interview several people before making a decision. If no mention is made of what is to happen next, ask when a decision to hire will be reached.

After the interview, write a short thank-you note to the employer. Simply state that you enjoyed the meeting and appreciated the chance to interview for the position. Such a note shows that you are interested in the job. It will also show you are a thoughtful person.

If you do not receive any news after several weeks, call and ask if a decision has been made. If you are not hired, you may wish to politely ask why. In this way, you can find out the points you need to work on to be more successful in future interviews.

TAKING ACTION

The students in Mrs. Dawson's home economics class have been thinking about their future careers. Gene is skilled at using his hands and enjoys building models and making household repairs. Many of Sarah's friends talk to her when they have personal problems because she's a good listener and offers helpful advice. Tony has already made a small profit by investing the earnings he has saved from his two newspaper routes. Carlene enjoys taking care of young children and volunteers after school at a local nursery school. Robert has won a school award for a short story in a literary magazine. Bernice is a math whiz and helps her mother balance the household budget.

Using Your Resourcefulness

- For each of Mrs. Dawson's students, offer six possible career choices that would suit their interests and skills.
- Choose one career goal for each student and then research what education, training, and experience is necessary to achieve that goal.
- What resource materials can help you learn more about future career opportunities?
- How can you learn which are the fastest growing and fastest declining jobs of the near future?

Chapter 7 Review

Summary

In this chapter, you have read about:

- Factors to consider when choosing a career.
- Job and volunteer opportunities for teens.
- Sources for locating job possibilities.
- Helpful guidelines for applying for a job.
- Tips on interviewing for a job.

Facts to Recall

1. Name three ways attitude toward family life influence your choice of a career.
2. List three questions you can ask yourself to identify your aptitudes and skills.
3. Explain the importance of education and training in career choices.
4. What are three benefits of volunteer jobs?
5. What is an entrepreneur?
6. Explain how to go about making contact with possible employers.
7. Give five ways of showing that you are a responsible employee.
8. List four guidelines to follow when applying for a job.
9. Give six tips for interviewing for a job.

Ideas to Explore

1. What can businesses do to reduce conflicts between family and work obligations? How does reducing these conflicts benefit both employers and families?
2. What types of jobs are available to most teens? What can you learn from these jobs?
3. Why might an employer ask you about your personal interests during an interview?

Activities to Try

1. Bring job applications from different employers to class. Practice filling them out.
2. Find articles about the job market in magazines and newspapers. How is the job market expected to change in the future? What types of skills will be in demand? Report your findings to the class.
3. Research the history of child labor laws in the United States and elsewhere. Also, research the current child labor laws in your state. Prepare a short report for the class.
4. Find articles about teens involved in volunteer work or unusual jobs in magazines and newspapers. Share them with the class.

LINK TO *Health*

WORK, HEALTH, AND WELL-BEING

Your ability to get and keep a job is directly related to your health. Being healthy means more than not being sick. It means having energy and a feeling of well-being. In other words, health involves both your mind and your body. Without good health, you may be unable to work to support yourself. Think about your health as an employee and complete the following:

- Make a list of ways health can affect your work. What signs of illness should workers watch for?
- Develop a list of guidelines for maintaining good health as an employee. (Refer to Chapter 37 if necessary.)

CAREER Connections

Get Ready for Your Future Through Volunteering

Janell

"I think I always knew I liked helping people, but it wasn't until I began volunteering at Brandis Nursing Home that I realized how much it meant to me.

"The first time I even knew Brandis existed was when Ms. Applegate, the director, spoke to our home economics class. She explained how the home was operated and described how the elderly residents craved special attention. She said that many of the residents' families live far away and aren't able to visit often. They need people to talk to, and Ms. Applegate wondered if any of us would like to help.

"Although I was a little nervous about going, I went anyway. I wasn't sure what I would say to the elderly people. My first few visits were awkward. I guess it was more me than them. It was like any new situation, though; it just takes a little while to feel comfortable.

"Now I have many friends at Brandis. Annie is like a grandmother to me, but many of the other residents are special too. I have learned what they need and how to meet those needs. This may mean reading letters for one, threading a needle for another, pouring a glass of water, or just listening. I feel very useful to my new friends, and I guess the director thinks that I am too. She asked me to become a part-time employee this spring. That means I'll get paid for what I already enjoy doing. I'm not sure what kind of job I want in my future, but I have discovered one thing for certain. I want to work where I can help people."

Katrina

"As a nursing student, I was headed for a career that would allow me to care for people. That was always important to me. After working with the elderly during my training, I decided to become a geriatric nurse. I suppose my close relationship with my grandfather pushed me in this direction.

"Every year our population grows a little older. People are living longer, making the needs of the elderly an increasing concern. I work in a nursing home where my duties cover a wide range of activities. I monitor the condition of patients and keep the physicians who visit our facility up-to-date. I keep track of medications and make sure residents take what they are supposed to in the correct dosages. I have also become very knowledgeable about Alzheimer's disease and how to deal with it. Sometimes I have to work with families to help them understand the needs and problems of their loved ones. Every day I know that I make a difference in people's lives, and that feels good."

"I love working with people, especially the elderly. That's why I decided to become a recreation director in a nursing home. I don't think any group of people anywhere could be more grateful for the small pleasures I create for them. We sing, dance, play games, exercise, and have parties for every special occasion. I plan activities that help them stay in touch—with life and good health.

"My first interest in the recreation field came when I was a volunteer for the Park District in my home town. I worked with youth. Young or old, it doesn't matter. I find a real reward in enriching the lives of others."

MAKING THE CONNECTION

- What qualities do the individuals above have in common?
- Describe how Janell has benefitted from her volunteer work.
- Explain why Janell might be happy in either of the careers described above. What other jobs might she consider?
- Why is working with older people a good job possibility for the future?
- Describe any experiences you have had that involved relating to older adults.

UNIT 2 Relationships

CHAPTERS

PULSE• •TONE OFF• •ON-RINGER
REDIAL
LONESTAR

CHAPTER

8 Communicating Effectively

OBJECTIVES

- *Explain how good communication helps build relationships.*
- *Distinguish between verbal and nonverbal messages.*
- *Explain the listening process.*
- *Identify barriers to communication and describe assertive communication.*

TERMS TO LEARN

- ***relationship***
- ***communication***
- ***verbal communication***
- ***nonverbal communication***
- ***body language***
- ***rapport***
- ***interpreting***
- ***responding***
- ***assertive***

Kaitlin and Tessa are two very different people. Kaitlin gets along well with others. People seem to like her; not just her friends and classmates, but others as well. Tessa, on the other hand, often finds herself in difficult situations. Friendships come and go quickly. There are very few adults she likes, and her family life is stormy. Which of these two girls do you think is more likely to be happy in life?

Relationships Count

Every day you come in touch with all kinds of people. Besides family and friends, your list might include a school bus driver, teachers, store clerks, and your friends' families. Each encounter will indicate how well you get along with others.

When you connect with another person, a relationship of some type forms. A **relationship** is a bond between people. The people may be friends, family members, or people you know but are not close to. The bond may include shared interests, an exchange of information, or shared feelings. Some relationships never grow much beyond a casual conversation whenever you happen to see that person. Others become deep and lasting. Most deep relationships develop over time.

Quality relationships can make a difference in your life. Most people enjoy life more when they have people with whom to share thoughts, feelings, experiences, and interests. In sharing, you are able to get support when you need it and help others when they are in need. When people have good relationships at home, at school, and on the job, they function better in life.

Peers can be good friends that help meet your relationship needs. How do your friends meet your needs?

▼ Making Relationships Work ▼

Tessa knows that she doesn't get along well with others. Figuring out how to improve her relationships is the challenge she faces. Most people find that sharpening communication skills makes relationships work better.

What Is Communication?

Communication (kuh-MYOO-nuh-KAY-shun) is the exchange of information — facts, opinions, and feelings. Exchanging information means sending and receiving messages. You send others these messages through what you say and how you say it. You receive messages when you listen carefully. In any day, most people spend 60 to 80 percent of their time communicating, both as speakers and listeners.

When you speak, you send verbal messages, which are made of spoken words. This is called **verbal communication**. Other messages that you send make up **nonverbal communication**; they are sent without words. Instead you use facial expressions and body movements to communicate. You may give a smile, a frown, a hug, a nod, a wave, or a handshake. Sometimes nonverbal communication is called **body language**.

Communication is usually a mixture of verbal and nonverbal messages. How well you send and receive messages will influence your school, work, and personal life.

Think about the words you use in communicating. How might the way this teen talks to her peers in class be different from the way she talks with them in the hallway or at a party?

▼ Verbal Messages ▼

Although communication is more than just talk, you must use words effectively to communicate a message well. The following tips may help:

- ***Think about your audience.*** Select words that will be clearly understood. For example, the words you use during a class discussion may be different from the ones you use when talking to a three-year-old.
- ***Be clear and specific in what you say.*** Organize your thoughts before you speak. First think about the main point you want to make, and then list the facts that will support your point. Others will not understand your message if it isn't clear in your own mind.
- ***Think before you talk.*** Ask yourself if this is really something you want to say. Choose your words carefully to avoid hurting someone. Words are not easily taken back after you say them.

AROUND THE WORLD

The centuries-old Hawaiian hula dance is a beautiful example of both verbal and nonverbal communication. Dancers, both women and men, chant a story while a drummer beats to the rhythm of their poetry. The dancers, in turn, move their hips and feet in time to the drum beat, while their gestures and facial expressions emphasize the words of their story. The dancers' words, faces, and bodies combine to relate a story in a uniquely expressive way.

- ***Speak clearly.*** Pronounce words correctly and avoid slurring words together. Speak loudly enough to be heard clearly, but not so loud people pull back.

Nonverbal Messages

With tear-filled eyes, eighteen-month-old Ben reached out to his father. Without a word, the child had sent a message — he was tired and needed comforting. The nonverbal message was easily received and understood by Mr. Defabio.

Body language is a powerful communicator. It often says more than your words. Your facial expressions show enthusiasm, thoughtfulness, or sadness. Your hand and arm gestures and your body posture can reflect your true inner feelings.

People send mixed messages when their words don't match their nonverbal messages. What they say is different from what they feel or think. The difference shows in their actions and facial expressions.

Body language can be useful. Try these suggestions to make it work for you:

- ***Smile as you speak.*** You are more likely to get a positive response.
- ***Use direct eye contact.*** Looking away can weaken your message.
- ***Make sure your nonverbal messages are accurate.*** If you are tapping your fingers or tightly folding your arms, you may be saying that you are angry, impatient, or frustrated — whether you want to say this or not.

Make sure that your body language communicates the same message as your verbal language.

Delivering Your Message

Repeat the sentence "I would be glad to do that for you." out loud four times, emphasizing a different word (*I, glad, that,* and *you*) each time. How does the meaning of the sentence change each time?

The way you speak is often as important as what you say. Your tone of voice shows whether you are happy or sad, relieved, or upset. When you keep your emotions in control, it is easier for people to understand your message. Your tone of voice affects how well your message is received.

For good communication, choose a time when the listener is interested in communicating with you. When people are tired, hungry, or busy, they may not be willing to give you their full attention.

Even if you're speaking in a clear, organized manner, successful communication will not take place unless you have rapport with your listener. **Rapport** (rah-POHR) is harmony or understanding between people. It is the feeling of being listened to and accepted.

One way to establish rapport is to put other people at ease. Show interest in them. Make them feel comfortable. Call them by name, and get them involved in the conversation. Ask them questions for their opinions on a topic. Give listeners time to respond to your questions. Also, be yourself. If you are relaxed and comfortable, others will be too.

Developing Listening Skills

In what ways are these teens showing that they are good listeners?

About 60 percent of communication time is spent listening, not talking. In fact, your role as a listener is as important to communication as your role as a speaker.

Have you ever noticed a person in a group trying to say something when others are not paying any attention? How do you think that individual felt? A caring person in the group can "rescue" the speaker by quickly becoming a good listener. Eye contact and a nodding head are appreciated by the speaker. Sometimes listening is more than just looking for messages you want to hear. It involves showing respect for other people.

You can be a good listener if you sharpen your skills in each of these four areas:

- ***Hearing.*** Tune in to what people are saying. Give the speaker your full attention.

- ▶ ***Interpreting.*** Understanding what the speaker actually says and means, is called **interpreting** the message. Be alert for nonverbal messages.
- ▶ ***Evaluating.*** Weigh the information and decide how you will use it. Evaluate the words, not the person speaking. Avoid letting preformed ideas or feelings get in the way of your evaluation.
- ▶ ***Responding.*** Your reaction (in words and actions) to what is being communicated is called **responding**. Your response shows the speaker whether you understand the message. Look at the speaker and nod your head to indicate understanding. If you do not understand the message, ask questions or ask for an example. You may try rephrasing in your own words what you think has been said.

Success at school or on the job often depends on hearing and understanding directions or instructions. Also, misunderstandings are more likely avoided when you take time to hear, interpret, evaluate, and respond correctly.

Barriers to Communication

Some messages discourage rather than encourage communication. Talk that hurts may even destroy relationships. Gossip, lies, insults, threats, and accusations are well-known barriers to communication. They close lines of communication very quickly and show little concern for others.

Nagging and preaching turn listeners off. "You should have called last night" and "You should exercise more" are some examples. How might these same messages be better stated? Messages that focus more on "I" rather than "you" are usually more effective.

A "know-it-all" stops communication because he or she is not open to other people's thoughts, ideas, or opinions. There are usually many ways to look at any situation.

Sometimes people use a tone that shows they mean the opposite of what they are saying. This is called *sarcasm*. For example, one might say, "Julian is really something," but the tone of voice says just the opposite. Sarcasm can be hurtful as well as preventing good communication.

How should you respond to someone who interrupts before you are finished speaking? Because the receiver responds to only part of the message, his or her response may not be right. If someone interrupts you, continue or repeat your message in a patient, yet determined way. In some cases, you may need to say something like, "Excuse me. I didn't get to finish what I wanted to say. Let me try again."

Barriers to communication cause people to be hurt or become defensive. Either way, good communication stops.

Assertive Communication

Assertive people express their opinions in a positive way without hurting others. How are you assertive in your communication?

Many people are afraid to express their own feelings. They feel uncomfortable saying what they think or pressing for what they want. They are passive. *Passive* people do not stand up for themselves. They are afraid to say anything that might make others angry.

Other people are *aggressive* when communicating. They are often thought of as pushy and rude, concerned mostly with their own needs and wants. They want to be in control. They may try to get their way by bullying others.

People who communicate assertively are neither passive nor aggressive. **Assertive** (uh-SURT-iv) people stand up for themselves in a determined or confident manner, but they do not bully others with their words and actions. They not only express their opinions, but they also listen to the opinions of others. When opinions differ, they try to reach an agreement acceptable to all involved.

Your opinion and your wishes are worthwhile. You have the right to express them, even though others may disagree at times. Everyone has to learn to accept give-and-take as part of the communication process. When you strive for confidence and you practice the skills you have learned, you will be well on the way to becoming a good communicator.

TAKING ACTION

"A lot of people think I'm not friendly, but I'm really just shy," Tina Marie says to you. Tina Marie is new at your school and the students don't know her well. You have been asked to show Tina Marie around, so you have gotten to know her a little in the past few days.

One thing you've noticed is that Tina Marie has a habit of not looking people in the eye. If she passes someone in the halls, she looks away nervously. She never speaks first to anyone. Instead, she waits for others to take the first step.

You have learned that Tina Marie has very definite interests. Her music collection is large and varied. She loves to swim. She also enjoys reading, especially about American history. You find her interesting and fun to be with as you get to know her.

Tina Marie wants to make new friends but doesn't know where to start. For one thing, she cannot walk up to people she doesn't know well and start a conversation. It isn't her personal style. As a result, she feels lost and unsure of herself.

Using Your Resourcefulness

- Are Tina Marie's feelings typical ones? Describe any similar feelings you may have had.
- What are some possible reasons for Tina Marie's feelings?
- What action can you take to help Tina Marie in this situation?
- What might Tina Marie do to help herself?

Chapter 8 Review

Summary

In this chapter, you have read about:

- The importance of good communication skills to strong, rewarding relationships.
- Using verbal and nonverbal communication to express yourself clearly.
- Establishing rapport with others to encourage them to listen to your message.
- How to be a good listener.
- Types of messages and behavior that are destructive to communication.
- The role of assertiveness in successful communication.

Facts to Recall

1. Why are good relationships important in life?
2. What is communication? Explain the difference between verbal and nonverbal communication.
3. Identify four ways to improve your verbal communication skills.
4. Give three suggestions for making body language work for you.
5. Give three suggestions for delivering messages successfully.
6. Name and describe the four areas you should work on to become a good listener.
7. List three benefits of being a good listener.
8. Describe five barriers to good communication.
9. What is the difference between being aggressive and being assertive in communication?

Ideas to Explore

1. Evaluate your own communication skills, both as a speaker and a listener. How do you send messages? How are your listening skills? How could you improve?
2. When might it be appropriate to interrupt a speaker? If people interrupt Jay all the time, who is at fault, Jay or the interrupters? Explain your answer.
3. How can body language both help and hurt communication between two persons from different cultures?
4. Explain what you think this quotation by Carlo Goldoni means: "He who talks much cannot talk well."

Activities to Try

1. Use body language to pantomime different emotions. Have the rest of the class try to identify the emotion you are expressing.
2. With a partner, perform two short skits. In one, portray a poor speaker or listener. In the other, show a good speaker and/or listener. Have the rest of the class identify the good or bad habits of each character.

LINK TO *Social Studies*

SOLVING MISCOMMUNICATION

Embarrassing miscommunications are often the result when words are not pronounced or interpreted correctly. Communication errors may also result from a lack of awareness about foreign cultures. Some people believe that a single, international written and spoken language would solve many of our world communication problems. Do you agree or disagree? What might be some advantages and disadvantages of such a language? How might this affect communication problems related to the lack of understanding about cultural differences?

CHAPTER

9 Improving Relationship Skills

OBJECTIVES

- *Describe qualities that strengthen relationships.*
- *Explain why stereotypes and prejudice are harmful.*
- *Identify strategies for resolving conflicts.*
- *Describe ways to control anger.*

TERMS TO LEARN

- ***empathy***
- ***cooperation***
- ***stereotype***
- ***prejudice***
- ***conflict***
- ***compromise***
- ***mediator***

Marcus is someone everybody likes. One day Shana was trying to pinpoint just what it is that makes Marcus so successful with people.

One quality that immediately came to Shana's mind was Marcus's skill in communication. He can speak his mind with confidence and yet still be sensitive to other viewpoints. When he listens to people, he stands silent and thoughtful, giving them his full attention. His responses are directly related to what they have said.

Communication, however, is not the only skill Marcus possesses. He gets along well because of other qualities too. Recognizing this, Shana decided to pay attention to how Marcus deals with people. She wanted to learn something from him.

Qualities That Count

Today, relationships are challenged in many ways. Busy schedules and a changing world can make good relationships difficult to maintain. You can make them work, however, just as Marcus has. By showing you care, empathizing with others, cooperating, being accepting, and keeping your sense of humor you will have the qualities that are key to maintaining good relationships.

Show You Care

First you must learn to care about others. Then you must show it. When people become too focused on themselves, they are viewed as self-centered. What do you think would happen in a society where most people thought only of themselves?

When you reach out to others and show that you care, it gives people a good impression of you. Reaching out to others also gives you a good feeling about yourself.

See if you can add to the following list of ways to show people that you care.

- Point out their special qualities with sincerity.
- Give sincere praise whenever you can.
- Use peoples' names when you talk to them.
- Encourage people to talk about themselves by asking questions and listening. Include subjects that are of interest to others in your conversations.
- Do a favor when possible.

Lending a helping hand to someone is a positive way to show that you care.

AROUND THE WORLD

In Japanese society, one of the most important traits for building strong personal and professional relationships is humility. Everyone, from the youngest student to the most powerful business executive, is expected to show some degree of humility. This means accepting praise graciously, admitting mistakes honestly, and respecting the ideas and needs of others. Humility is based not on feelings of low self-esteem, but on a desire for the social harmony that comes from placing others before one's self.

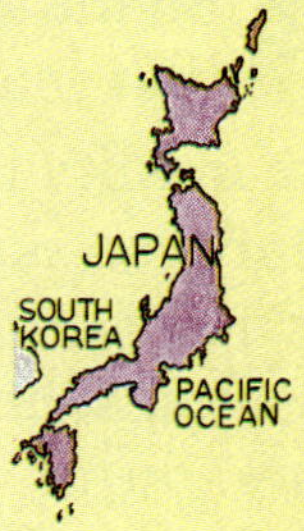

▼ Have Empathy ▼

Empathy (EM-puh-thee) is the ability to understand what someone else is experiencing. You empathize by putting yourself in another's place and trying to see things from their point of view. Empathy has been well described in this well-known Native American prayer: "Great Spirit, grant that I may not criticize my neighbor until I have walked a mile in his mocassins."

Empathy helps form good relationships because it prevents many misunderstandings. When Dorita had very little to say to Frank, he could have easily been offended. Instead he thought about how she was feeling after her parents' divorce and understood her actions. Empathy allowed him to be sensitive to her needs.

▼ Cooperate ▼

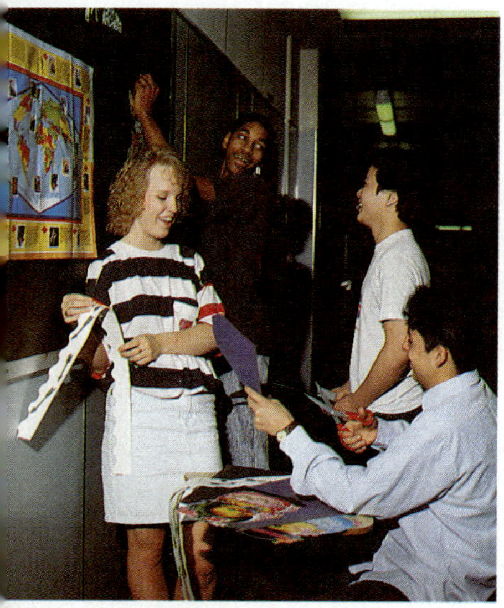

Working together can be fun and accomplish great things, too!

Cooperation is working together with others for the good of all. Another name for cooperation is teamwork. A group of junior high students were asked to make a video that showed a scene from *Tom Sawyer*. Two of the six students forgot props, failed to learn their lines, and constantly distracted the group from the project. As a result, the video was not what the rest had hoped it would be. By not cooperating, the two troublesome students damaged their relationship with the others.

To improve your cooperation skills, try these ideas:

- Do your share. Focus on the goal and participate in reaching it.
- Be agreeable. Some tasks are not fun but they must be done.
- Be willing to use another's ideas or plan. Express your own ideas, but realize that yours won't always be selected.

▼ Be Accepting ▼

No matter where you go in life you will find many people who are different from you. In fact, most people in the world are different from you in one way or another. That does not make them inferior or wrong. As you read in an earlier chapter, differences are refreshing. You can also learn from them. Differences should be a reason for appreciating others, not rejecting them.

Stereotypes

Until recently, Chuck believed that all homeless people were lazy. He felt that they were homeless simply because they refused to get a job. Chuck had stereotyped the homeless. A **stereotype** is a belief that an entire group of people fit a fixed, common pattern — that they are all alike in certain ways. When Chuck stereotyped all homeless people, he didn't see them as individuals; he saw them as a group who all shared the same characteristic of being lazy and not wanting to work.

After joining a volunteer program that provided help for the homeless, Chuck's stereotype of the homeless began to change. He met a homeless family whose small house had burned to the ground. The single mother had a part-time job, but it didn't pay enough for housing. There was no low-income housing in the community that she could afford. As he heard about this family's situation and other similar situations, Chuck began to question his thinking. He was learning to look at people as individuals rather than using stereotypes.

TIPS: *Avoiding Gossip*

Gossip communicates hurtful messages or rumors that are not to be believed. Many friendships and families have often been hurt or destroyed by careless gossip passed from one person to the next.

How can you tell the difference between what is truth and what is gossip? Here are some tips to help you uncover the truth in messages:

- Reject messages that are not based in fact.
- Consider the source of the message. Is this person trustworthy and reliable?
- Talk with the person who is the subject of the message before you believe what is said.
- Use direct questions of those involved to uncover the truth.

Prejudice

Stereotypes often lead to prejudice. When people use differences to dislike or hurt others, they are showing prejudice. **Prejudice** (PREJ-ud-us) is an unfair or biased opinion. Often it is a judgment against a person or a group formed without knowing the facts or by ignoring the facts. For example, prejudice may be directed against people because of their race, religion, or gender (male or female). Age and disabilities are also sometimes used as a basis for prejudice.

The sad thing about prejudice is that it causes people to distrust and hate without just cause. Some people even act on that hate. How do you want to be treated? No doubt, you want others to look beyond what they see and discover who you are inside as an individual person. That is exactly what you must do when you relate to others.

Differences in people are refreshing.

Keep a Sense of Humor

Relationships are more likely to thrive when people find humor around them. Sometimes you may have to make an effort to find it.

When Tamica accidentally dropped Danette's purse through a sidewalk grate, the two spent an hour retrieving it. Instead of feeling angry, Danette laughed about how the purse got there in the first place and about the things they had to do to get it back. Danette had an amusing story to tell others, and her relationship with Tamica stayed as strong as ever.

Look for More

The list of qualities that are useful in building and keeping good relationships goes on. Showing respect and courtesy for others is important. Being patient also helps keep relationships on track. Having a positive attitude can help, too. All of these are tools to use and improve. They can make your life and your relationships happier.

Resolving Conflicts

Conflict can threaten relationships. How might these teens resolve their conflict without destroying their relationship?

One of the greatest threats to relationships is conflict. A **conflict** is a disagreement or struggle between two or more people or groups who have opposing points of view. A conflict may be short and personal, as in a brief argument with a friend; or it may be a long, continuous struggle, as within a family or between countries. Without the ability to settle problems, your relationships with others will suffer.

Conflict can be either positive or negative. It is positive when problems are brought out into the open and settled in a satisfying manner. It is negative when people use destructive tactics in trying to solve the problem.

Most conflicts grow out of disagreements over territory (or space), property, values and beliefs, power and authority, and who gets rewards or privileges. You can't avoid conflicts, but you can work to resolve them. Read "How To Resolve Conflicts" on page 113 for some ideas.

Mediators

Sometimes you may find it impossible to work through a problem, even with cooperation and communication. Deadlocks, in which no one will budge, occur when people can't agree on a solution.

How to ...
Resolve Conflicts

Settling differences is easier if you follow some basic suggestions:

- ***Confront the problem.*** Some people find conflicts so difficult or frightening that they run away from them. They may pretend they don't exist or make excuses for not dealing with them. Avoid conflict only if your safety is at stake or the problem is not worth worrying about.
- ***If possible, choose the right time and location to discuss the issue.*** When people are in the right frame of mind, it is easier to discuss sensitive topics.
- ***Identify the problem.*** Make sure that both sides agree on what it is. Ask questions of each other to find out.
- ***Don't get sidetracked by other issues.*** Save them for another time.
- ***Discuss the issue, not the people involved.*** Hurtful statements directed at people will not be helpful.
- ***Use good communication skills.*** State your position clearly so that it can be fully understood. Listen carefully to the other person's position so that you will understand.
- ***Avoid jumping to conclusions.*** Determine the facts and look for options.
- ***Stay calm and objective.*** Being objective involves sticking to the facts and not being influenced by stereotypes and prejudices. You need to see both sides of the issue clearly.
- ***Cooperate with each other.*** Conflict is not a competitive sport. You will both win when the problem is solved.
- ***Learn to compromise.*** Through **compromise**, each person gives up something in order to reach a satisfactory solution. Compromise is also known as give-and-take.

Sometimes a person not directly involved in a conflict can help people identify the problem and work toward a positive solution.

A **mediator** (MEED-ee-ATE-ur), or someone who is not directly involved in a conflict, can help people look at a problem and work toward a solution. In some schools, mediators are used when students experience conflict with others. School counselors, teachers, social workers, members of the clergy, and mature students may serve as mediators. They are trained to suspend judgment. As careful observers and listeners, they ask questions and respond to both parties. Mediators try to resolve the conflict by determining the problem and suggesting acceptable solutions.

Dealing with Anger

Everyone feels anger. Not everyone knows how to handle it. Evan used to react physically when he was angry. Because fist fights were common for him, many people began to avoid him.

When Evan learned that violence does not solve problems, his life began to change. He learned to let little annoyances go and allowed himself time to cool off before reacting at all. He doesn't keep his feelings locked inside now, but he does control himself. When the feelings are very strong, he does something physically active, such as playing basketball. Now people like to be around Evan. His relationships have improved, just as yours can when you look for better ways to get along.

TAKING ACTION

"I don't understand teamwork," Jared thinks to himself. Maybe it's because he's an only child. Jared isn't used to sharing possessions or playing with a sister or brother. He likes to work on his own rather than in a group. He enjoys spending time by himself drawing. For a home economics project on family conflict, he created a comic book that surprised and impressed everyone.

Jared has a few friends, most of whom are quiet and different from the norm. Sometimes he feels he's missing out on what others call "being part of the crowd," but he isn't sure he wants to change. Mostly, he thinks of himself as content and doesn't feel lonely.

Using Your Resourcefulness

- How would you explain the concept and value of teamwork so Jared might consider it more? Identify resource materials, such as movies, novels, or magazine articles, that illustrate the meaning of teamwork.
- Do you have a friend who seems unusual or different? If so, how do you let that friend know you care?
- Do you think Jared is someone you might want to know? Why or why not? What steps might you take to get to know him?

Chapter 9 Review

Summary

In this chapter, you have read about:

- Personal qualities that help you build good relationships with others.
- How stereotypes and prejudice discourage the development of strong personal relationships.
- Ways of resolving conflict.
- How to deal with anger constructively.

Facts to Recall

1. Name three ways of showing people that you care about them.
2. What is empathy? Why is it important in a relationship?
3. List three suggestions for improving cooperation skills.
4. How do stereotypes and prejudice hurt relationships?
5. How can a sense of humor help with relationships?
6. What is a conflict?
7. How can conflict be positive? When is it negative?
8. List six suggestions for resolving conflicts.
9. What purpose does a mediator serve in resolving conflict?
10. How might a person handle angry feelings in a positive manner?

Ideas to Explore

1. Can people learn personal traits — caring, empathy, respect for others — that enable them to relate successfully to others, or must they feel them instinctively?
2. What conflicts have you experienced? How did you solve them? Were all the parties involved satisfied with the solution? If not, how could the conflict have been resolved more acceptably?
3. Discuss the importance of relationship-building qualities — such as empathy, cooperation, and humor — in resolving conflicts.
4. Is anger always negative? Discuss ways in which it can be turned into a positive reaction.

Activities to Try

1. With two other students, perform a skit in which one student acts as a mediator in solving a conflict between the other two. Have the rest of the class identify the qualities of the mediator that enabled him or her to help reach a resolution.
2. In current newspapers and magazines, find examples of how conflicts between opposing groups were resolved.

LINK TO *Social Studies*

ELIMINATING STEREOTYPES AND PREJUDICE

Everyone has some trait or characteristic that has served as the basis for stereotyping and prejudice. Males, females, teens, redheads, senior citizens, blondes, people who are overweight or underweight, as well as persons of various ethnic origins, races, religions, or regions of the country have all been unfairly judged by others. Choose a group that has been the target of stereotyping and prejudice. Identify some common stereotypes about the group. Then do some research about ways to help correct these false ideas. Perhaps get involved in some volunteer work with this group. Write a one- or two-page report summarizing what you have learned.

CHAPTER 10 Friends and You

OBJECTIVES

- *Describe the benefits of various kinds of friendship.*
- *Discuss how you can make and keep friends.*
- *Explain how to end a friendship when necessary.*

TERMS TO LEARN

- ***acquaintances***
- ***peers***
- ***peer pressure***
- ***clique***

Anna is one of fourteen-year-old Ming's best friends. As far as Ming is concerned, there is no one like Anna. When Ming is troubled, he goes to Anna for advice or just a willing ear. Anna listens to him and gives him support. Sometimes she even confides in Ming, sharing her concerns with him. They enjoy their time together even though it is limited. Anna lives next door to Ming. She is eighty years old.

Regardless of age, friendship is important to nearly everyone. Most people enjoy the companionship that comes with friendship. They like having someone to share with. The benefits of friendship are many. Friends can broaden your life. They provide advice and show understanding. They make you feel accepted and give support when you need it.

All Kinds of Friends

Friendship comes in all degrees. People you know, but who are not personal friends, are **acquaintances** (uh-KWAINT-uhnt-sehs). For example, a cashier at the supermarket or a neighbor down the street might be an acquaintance. A friendship generally goes through stages on the way to becoming a close relationship.

Unfortunately, some people use differences, such as age, race, and nationality, to limit their opportunities for friendship. Even differences in income level may be used to prevent friendship at times. People need to realize that satisfying friendships are based on something other than what you see. True friendship goes much deeper than this.

Peers

Your **peers** are the people you associate with who are about your age. During the teen years, peer friendships are usually the most important kind.

When Shelette thought about friendship, she was often discouraged. She had one close friend and a few others who were not so close. Often she found herself wishing she were like Joy or Amelia, who both had many friends and who always seemed to be included in everything.

Friendships are based on more than what you see. What qualities do you appreciate most in your friends?

It wasn't until Shelette had a heart-to-heart talk with her sister-in-law, Yolanda, that she began to put things in perspective. Yolanda pointed out that Shelette always had a good time with her best friend. Wasn't that of value to her? Yolanda also explained that sometimes "popular" people are not as happy as people think. They may have many friends, but not someone who is very special to them. They may struggle to be popular or even do things they shouldn't in order to be accepted. Yolanda told Shelette that people who like themselves don't always need others around them to boost their self-esteem.

Cliques

In any setting where people gather, they tend to move into groups where they feel comfortable. There is nothing wrong with this common practice. Many teens, as well as adults, form groups to have a sense of belonging.

Cliques often exclude people from the group for superficial reasons. What do you think the teen on the right is feeling about being excluded from the group?

Unfortunately, some groups go too far by excluding people from their circle. A group that does this is called a **clique** (klick). In some way or another, the members of a clique reject those who are on the outside. Only by the group's approval can someone join in. The basis for acceptance is often superficial, based on external qualities such as appearance, clothing, income, or status. When rejection occurs, it hurts.

This is a dilemma for teens. How do you fulfill a need for belonging without rejecting others? First, stand by your principles. Avoid groups that treat others unfairly. Try forming your own circle of friends who do not exclude or judge people. If the clique mentality arises in your group, be courageous enough to challenge it. Strive to include people rather than reject them. It isn't always easy, but peace of mind can come from doing what is right.

Peer Pressure

Because teens look to others for approval, they sometimes give in to pressure from their peers to do something they do not want to do. The pressure or stress you feel to do what others your age are doing is called **peer pressure**. Peer pressure can be good if it encourages you to do something positive, but it's bad if it causes you to go against your own values.

How do you react when people want you to do something wrong? First, think carefully about what they are pressuring you to do. Then ask yourself these questions: Will this hurt anyone? Will it be harmful to me? Are there risks involved? Could there be negative effects, either now or in the future? If any of the answers are "yes," then you must respond with a clear "no." Offer a simple reason for not going along with what they want if you feel you need to. Then change the

AROUND THE WORLD

For many years, apartheid (uh-PAR-tide) was the law of the land in South Africa. This meant that people were limited by their skin color in where they could live and work and with whom they could socialize. Recent legal reforms, however, are allowing people of all racial backgrounds to work, attend schools, and enjoy leisure activities together. Some South Africans, though, still oppose sharing public places with people of different races. Why do you suppose this is? How can this prejudice be changed?

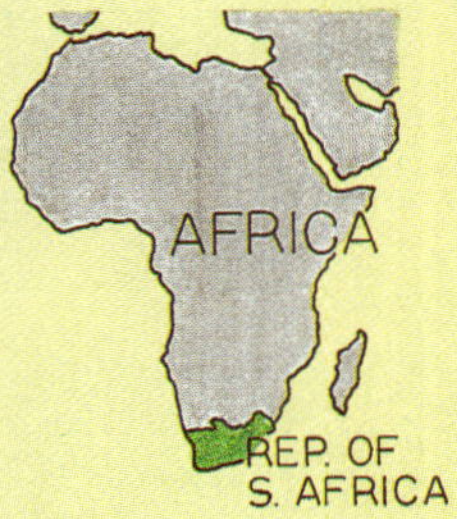

subject or walk away, saying that you have something you need to do. Finally, realize that you don't need friends who don't care about your well-being or their own. Look around you to find someone who does.

Adults

Many adults have authority over teens. This means the adults are in charge. They set the rules to be followed. When a teen is learning and striving for independence, this is not always easy to handle.

Mr. Pratt, a math teacher, cares about his students. Blake is always causing a disturbance in class. Rules mean nothing to him. He doesn't care whether or not classmates learn anything because *he* doesn't want to. Mr. Pratt knows that it is his responsibility to keep order in the classroom. If his students cannot perform on the district proficiency exams, his teaching will be called into question. If students do not learn the math, they will have a harder time in future math classes — and in life. He sees that Blake, in particular, is headed down a destructive path, and he wants to do something to change that. If it means being tough, then that's what must happen.

For adults like Mr. Pratt, setting and enforcing rules is part of their responsibility to young people. Enforcing rules is not fun, nor is it always easy. Rules are made to provide guidance for appropriate behavior — a necessary part of functioning in an orderly, safe world.

Although adults are responsible for guiding young people and enforcing rules, they enjoy friendship with young people, too! What adult friendships do you have?

Most adults, even when they have authority over you, want to be your friend, too. Often they have many concerns, such as taking care of a family. Your responsibility as a maturing teen is to offer respect and friendship to adults. When you do, they will return these to you.

Like you, adults can make mistakes. When you do not understand why an adult does something, you may want to talk about it with that person. The best approach is to use all the relationship skills you read about in the previous chapters.

Friendships with adults can provide you a valuable source of support and fun.

Older Adults

You live in a country that has more and more older citizens. This is because people are living longer today than ever before. Because of this, you may find increasing opportunities to relate to older adults.

As a teen, you are greatly distanced in years from the concerns of older adults. If you are close to aging family members, however, you may have some understanding of their concerns. Elderly people often have health concerns. Reduced ability to move around may contribute to loneliness and make it difficult for them to take care of routine tasks.

Friendship with older adults can provide mutually-rewarding relationships. You can provide them with companionship and lend them a helping hand occasionally. They can give you the benefit of all the wisdom and understanding they have gained from years of living. Older adults can be a valuable source of advice and support.

Children

Although most of your friends are probably other teens, children make good friends, too. Because you're older, your attention is very special to them. You may feel more relaxed and appreciated with children than you do with others.

In today's world, there are children who could use your input. Many children spend time alone while their parents are working. The quality of their lives could improve greatly if you could give them some time. You might teach them a skill you have, go for ice cream, or just sit on the step and talk. What you learn about children can be carried over to your own future, perhaps as a parent someday.

Making Friends

Because most people find pleasure in friendship, they are often looking for ways to begin new ones. Here are some ideas:

- ***Smile.*** A friendly face is the first signal that you are willing to begin a friendship.
- ***Start a conversation.*** Ask a question that doesn't require a simple "yes" or "no" answer. Then respond to the answer. Look for common interests. Great friendships can begin with a simple conversation.
- ***Practice relationship skills.*** Make the relationship skills, including listening and speaking skills, a habit. This will make you a person that others want to be around.
- ***Go where there are people.*** Schools, religious organizations, and communities all offer clubs and programs.
- ***Invite someone to do something.*** Don't wait to be asked. That's what the other person may be doing. If you are turned down, don't worry about it. This happens to everyone. Just try again with someone else.
- ***Give it some time.*** Friendships take time and effort to build. The more time you spend together, the easier the relationship will be to handle.

Keeping Friends

Friendship carries responsibilities with it. If you want a friendship to last, you must give as well as take. How do you think friendship will be affected in the following situations?

- When Lurleen tells Jessica something private, Jessica passes the information along to others.
- Drake listens to all Marty's complaints, but Marty will never take time to listen to him.
- Tonya doesn't want Stacey to have any other friends but her.

Friendships are very valuable. Effort must be made to make them and to *keep* them.

Younger children often need and enjoy the friendship of teens. How can you be a friend to younger children?

Ending a friendship can be difficult, but sensitivity and kindness go a long way in easing the pain of loss. What suggestions do you have for these two teens who are struggling in ending a friendship?

Ending a Friendship

Because people change, not all friendships last forever. New interests, goals, and experiences can cause you to drift away from some people and link with new ones. In some cases, you may discover that the relationship is destructive. If someone causes problems or is unpleasant to be around, the friendship won't be worthwhile. Sometimes outside circumstances interrupt friendships. For example, a friend may move away, causing the relationship to end. A very strong friendship might survive if the two individuals are committed to keeping in touch through the mail and telephone.

If you must deliberately end a friendship, do so with sensitivity. Be direct, but kind. Explain why you need to end the friendship. Focus on how you feel, not on the other person, and be honest about the reasons.

If a friendship ends against your wishes, understand that this just happens sometimes. The good times you had will be remembered. As you move on to other friendships, you can take what you have learned with you.

TAKING ACTION

Rachel can't believe her own eyes. Two weeks ago she and Joelle were practically inseparable, going everywhere together and talking on the phone at night. Now Joelle seems distant at school and appears to look away or lower her head when she passes Rachel in the halls. If Rachel calls Joelle at home, Joelle's sister tells her Joelle is out. And Joelle doesn't call back.

What happened? Rachel wants to know. How can close friends turn into strangers so quickly? What should she do? Should she try to talk to Joelle or let it go and concentrate on other friends? Rachel feels sad and confused.

Using Your Resourcefulness

- What do you think Rachel should do? How should she communicate her feelings? What should or shouldn't she say? Why?
- What does Joelle's body language tell you? What kind of person is Joelle?
- Is ending a friendship difficult for you? Why or why not? What personal resources can help you get over losing a friendship?

Chapter 10 Review

Summary

In this chapter, you have read about:

- How having friends helps your emotional well-being.
- Having friends of all types, including adults and children.
- How to handle peer pressure and cliques.
- The responsibilities of being a friend.
- How friendships can begin and why they sometimes end.

Facts to Recall

1. Name three benefits of friendship.
2. Why may "popular" people be less happy than others think?
3. What are cliques? How can cliques be a problem?
4. Name three ways you can fulfill the need for acceptance without rejecting others.
5. What is peer pressure? How can it be both helpful and hurtful?
6. Give three suggestions for handling negative peer pressure.
7. What do you need to understand about adults in order to get along with them?
8. How can teens benefit from friendships with children and older adults? How do children and older adults benefit from friendships with teens?
9. List four ways to begin a new friendship.
10. List three things to remember when ending a friendship.

Ideas to Explore

1. You have probably heard the expression, "Opposites attract." Can this be true in friendships? How can having friends whose tastes or personalities differ from your own be rewarding?
2. Suppose you saw a good friend doing something that you felt was harmful, even dangerous. How would you persuade your friend to stop without ending the friendship?
3. Sometimes a person can be friends with two people who do not like each other. How can this situation be resolved without ending one of the relationships?
4. Do you think it is easier for small children to make and keep friends than it is for teens? Why or why not?

Activities to Try

1. List the five most important qualities you want in a friend. Compare lists in the class and see if you can agree on a group list.
2. Create a collage entitled, "Friendship is..." Use pictures and words from magazines and newspapers showing the different aspects of friendship.

LINK TO *Geography*

PEN PAL EXCHANGE

One way to learn about other parts of the United States or even another country is from a pen pal. A pen pal is someone you may never meet in person, but, instead, get to know through writing letters. Pen pals share information about their daily lives — interests, activities, and goals. Pen pals often exchange pictures. These long-distance friendships sometimes last for years and may even result in exchange visits. The sharing that takes place through letters can lead to a better understanding of people in another region or country. Ask your teacher or librarian for assistance in finding a pen pal. Write a letter to your new pen pal describing yourself, your home, the area in which you live, and your lifestyle.

CHAPTER

11 Dating

OBJECTIVES

- *Explain how group and single dating differ.*
- *Discuss challenges of dating and how to handle them.*
- *Explain the importance of time and patience in finding real love.*

TERMS TO LEARN

- ***group dating***
- ***crush***

When Carrie looked around the classroom, it occurred to her that they were a very mixed group. Ages ranged probably from thirteen to fifteen, but you couldn't tell by looking. Some of her friends looked very mature. They acted that way too. Others had not matured yet and seemed to have a long ways to go. As far as dating was concerned, some were interested and some weren't. Carrie explored her own readiness for dating often. Time would tell what was ahead for her.

Everyone Is Different

Your class may be very much like Carrie's. Teens mature at different rates. This is especially noticeable during the early teen years. Although some may be ready for dating relationships with others, many are not. This is normal and should not be cause for concern.

Enrico likes girls as friends. He is not interested in dating, however. For him, spending time with his male friends is first priority. If he is anything like his older brother, he might not even start dating until after high school.

Meg is just the opposite. She began dating at an early age. Although she sometimes goes places with the young men in her class at school, she more typically dates those who are a year or two older.

Dora Lee thinks she would like to date, but the opportunities are not there. She expects that it will happen sometime, so she has decided to be patient. She will enjoy her girlfriends and her active life and not worry about the rest.

Friendship groups allow you to get to know a variety of people without the pressures of dating. What do you think about friendship groups or group dating?

Friendship Groups

One of the first steps that many teens take toward dating is getting together in groups that include both males and females. Many teens think of this as a form of **group dating**. They have a chance to go out in a mixed group without having an actual date. Getting together this way helps build understanding the easy way. The feelings, thoughts, and actions of male and female friends can be examined and compared. The pressures that can come in a dating situation are not as likely to be present.

AROUND THE WORLD

Love Park in China's capital city of Beijing is a popular meeting place for single persons interested in marriage. Marriage is highly valued in Chinese society; married people have a better chance at finding jobs, finding housing, and getting an education. What do young Chinese people look for in a possible partner? According to China's marriage law, it should be "character" and "compatibility." According to a Beijing University study, however, it is appearance, education, and social standing. How do you think this compares with American attitudes toward marriage?

When teens gather in groups, they are often looking for something to do. Some communities offer a wide variety of fun places to go and things to do. Other communities offer a very limited choice. In such cases, some creative thinking can help provide ideas. What kinds of group activities can you think of?

Cost and transportation can restrict what many teens are able to do. If this is true for you and your friends, look for inexpensive and simple ways to spend time. Planning activities to do at home may be a good alternative. An afternoon or evening spent watching a video, playing games, listening to music, or having a pizza party can be fun.

When you spend time with others in a group, remember that you have some responsibilities. Often the places where teens go are used by other people as well. Businesses must make money to survive. People who own property want to preserve its value. Teens who gather in community places need to think about how their actions affect others. For example, what might happen to a restaurant if a large group of people routinely take up booth space by ordering only soft drinks? If you were the owner, how would you react?

Although dating may be fun, it is a challenge, too.

Single Dating

Eventually many young people turn to single dating as another stage in their relationships with others. Single dating allows two people to explore how a male-female relationship works. New feelings of attraction and affection are examined. Close friendships can turn to romantic interests. As people date, they begin to discover what they might like in a partner if they decide to marry someday.

Dating can be a challenge for people at any age, but during the early teen years this may be especially true. Without experience as a guide, concerns may arise. Some teens have had questions like these: How do I ask someone out? How do I talk to someone as more than a friend? How do I turn down an invitation? The answers are not always simple.

Gaining Confidence

Few people get through their first dates without some discomfort. Trying to work up the courage to ask someone out, asking someone out, what to do or say on the date itself — any or all of these can be a source of discomfort. Keep a few things in mind if you need to boost your confidence.

Feelings of insecurity are common. Many people have them and overcome them. Chances are, when you feel uncomfortable, so does the other person. Focus on putting the other person at ease instead of thinking about yourself.

Practice and plan what to say. Doing this will help give you confidence conversing. It also helps to plan dates that are activity oriented. Having something to do reduces the need for continual conversation.

Think positively about yourself and about your strengths rather than your weaknesses. A positive attitude makes you more attractive to others, both as a friend and a date.

Choosing a Date

"Your problem, Taylor, is that you only want to go out with the cutest girl in school." Jim's comment to his friend points to an attitude that prevents many good relationships from happening. When you stop to notice, you will see that many of the finest people are not necessarily the best looking. People who focus only on appearances often miss the more important qualities in others. As you look at others with the thought of dating in mind, who would you pick? How often do you let your friends influence your opinions about others? Take a second look around and see if you are eliminating some people for the wrong reasons.

What qualities do you look for in a date? Do you eliminate people for the wrong reasons?

TIPS: *Handling Rejection or Rejecting a Date*

Here are some helpful tips for handling rejection or rejecting a date:

- Don't be afraid of rejection; you can learn from it.
- To deal with disappointment, think positively. There are others to date even if one person turns you down.
- Recognize that you are a good person and remind yourself of that when facing rejection.
- Try again. Asking others for a date may not be easy, but it's worth the effort.
- If you are rejecting a date, do it with kindness in an honest, gentle, supportive way. You might want to say: "It was nice of you to ask me, but I just don't think we have a lot in common. I hope we can still be friends even if we don't date."
- Remember that rejection can hurt if not handled in a positive way. You may want to think about ways that you might gently reject (or accept) a date.

Handling Rejection

Rejection is part of the dating process. It only stands to reason that sometimes two people may not always share the same feelings for each other. Sometimes one person knows this immediately and turns down the invitation for a first date. Sometimes it takes several dates or even a long relationship before the discovery is made. Whatever the case, one party may have to experience rejection.

Responsibility

Along with dating come several responsibilities. The first is to yourself. As you begin to date, you must make decisions about your conduct. Setting your standards of behavior ahead of time can help you if any difficult situations arise.

You also have a responsibility to your date. The person you go out with deserves your respect. Treat your date the same way that you would want to be treated. Think about how you would handle each of the following when on a date: choosing a time to leave and to return; picking up your date; deciding what to do; handling expenses; showing consideration and appreciation; and ending the date.

Still another responsibility is to your family. Young teens need to talk over the rules with responsible family members when they are ready to date. Some families have a particular age in mind to begin dating. Other families look for signs of readiness in the young person. Family rules may involve curfew times, transportation, and where teens may and may not go. A teen who disagrees with the family rules may need to discuss them and show a willingness to listen. This is much more likely to lead to cooperation and perhaps compromise than arguing will.

Showing consideration and appreciation are two of your responsibilities to your date. What are some ways that you can show appreciation to someone you care about?

Once the rules are set, abiding by them is important. Families make rules because they are responsible for your safety and well-being. Breaking rules causes family members to worry and lose trust. Any teen who cares about family members would not want to let this happen.

Thinking about Love

For Kathleen it was her science teacher. For Mike it was a movie star. For Jamal it was the high school girl next door. Each of these teens was experiencing what is known as a crush. A **crush** is a strong attraction to someone. Usually a crush is one-sided. In fact, a crush may be felt for someone you don't even know, such as Mike's crush on a movie star.

Although a crush may be mistaken for love, it really isn't. Crushes seldom last long. Once over, you may even wonder why you felt the way you did.

Crushes are common, especially for teens. The emotions may be powerful. Most teens simply let such feelings run their course. Talking can help, perhaps to friends. If the feelings are difficult to handle, a trusted adult may be able to help.

Sometimes a crush is mistaken for love, but it really isn't. The emotions may be powerful, but crushes seldom last long. Talking with someone you trust can help you cope with the feelings.

Real Love

Becca says she is in love. Her relationship with Ryan is close and special, but is it really love? Defining love is not easy to do. Frank may use the word to talk about his family, a pet, his favorite food, a movie, friends, and a special person in his life. His feelings for a hamburger, however, can hardly be the same as those he has for his beloved dog, Frisky.

Real love is what many people try to identify when they pair up with someone special. Having many experiences with friendships and close relationships can make real love easier to have and to identify. This takes time. It takes most people until at least their late teens or early twenties to be able to identify true love. For others, it may take even longer.

Most people feel that love is a two-way street of give-and-take. It is sharing and trusting and having mutual respect for one another. When you are together, it feels right. Even more important, it is wanting what's best for the other person. Furthermore, it lasts. Whenever there is doubt, a wait-and-see attitude is best.

The road to real love begins within you. Loving and respecting yourself makes you capable of loving and respecting others. It helps prepare you for real love later on.

Later in life, some people choose to marry. As you date different people, think about the qualities that you might want in a mate.

Looking Ahead

When people find real love, marriage is often the next step. The decision to marry cannot be taken lightly. It means looking closely at each other before making a commitment. Dating different people as you mature will help you understand yourself and others better and can help you decide what qualities you value.

As you think about the kind of mate you might want in the future, ask yourself these questions: What kind of person do I want for a mate? What kind of person do I need to be in order to attract the kind of person I want? What changes do I need to make? Am I willing to make those changes?

Marriage, of course, is not for everyone. It's quite common to stay single — or to marry later in life. Many people remain single because they value their independence and the opportunity to pursue their own goals.

Whatever you choose to do with your life, it's too early right now to make such a major decision. Instead, take the time to prepare yourself for the future. Look at how you relate to others and strive for improvement. What you learn during your teen years can help you develop and maintain a long-term relationship in the future.

TAKING ACTION

"It's really common at my school to date in groups," Nona explains. "Four or six friends go to the movies or ice skating together instead of dating separately. The couples are 'loosely' formed but don't really date. We're not old enough to drive," she says.

Nona has known Ken a few months, and likes spending time with him. Sometimes she feels Ken pressures her to be closer emotionally. He would like to start single dating, but Nona doesn't feel ready yet. "I've thought a lot about it. I've made the decision to postpone single dating until I'm a little older. I would like to get to know many different people rather than limiting myself to just one right now," says Nona. Still Ken's pressure makes her anxious on occasion. She wishes she could handle the issue more successfully.

Using Your Resourcefulness

- How should Nona communicate her feelings to Ken? What options does she have to make the relationship work and grow slowly?
- What resources are available to help you better understand dating and developing relationships?
- Would the idea of "group dating" appeal to you? Why or why not?

Chapter 11 Review

Summary

In this chapter, you have read about:

- How individual teens differ from one another in maturity and dating relationships.
- How group dating can pave the way to single dating.
- Challenges that go along with single dating.
- Responsibilities of dating.
- The differences between a crush and real love.

Facts to Recall

1. Explain why some teens begin to date at an earlier age than others.
2. Explain how group dating can help prepare teens for single dating.
3. What responsibilities do teens have when they go places in groups?
4. How can single dating better equip a person for selecting a marriage partner?
5. What are three things to remember if you need to build confidence for dating?
6. How can you reject someone who asks you for a date in a positive way?
7. Describe the responsibilities you have to yourself, your date, and your family when dating.
8. Explain the difference between a crush and real love.
9. Explain why "the road to real love begins within you."
10. What four questions should you ask yourself as you think about selecting a mate for the future?

Ideas to Explore

1. What qualities do you, or would you, look for in a date? Are these the same qualities that you might look for in a marriage partner? Explain.
2. Which do you think would be better, going out with someone you're not really interested in or risking hurt feelings by turning the person down? Explain your answer.
3. Why is it important to know and understand yourself before trying to begin a serious relationship with another person? What might happen if you do not have this self-understanding?

Activities to Try

1. Make a list of activity ideas for teens who are dating, either in groups or on single dates. Think about the resources available in your community. Work in groups or individually and share your lists with the class.
2. Work in pairs to plan a date, focusing on the costs involved. Determine how the costs could be met.
3. Write a paragraph explaining what this quotation from John Donne means to you: "Love built on beauty, soon as beauty, dies."

LINK TO *Geography*

DATING AND MARRIAGE CUSTOMS

Dating and marriage customs vary from one culture to another. In India and many other countries, most marriages are arranged by parents. In some cultures, marriage involves a gift — called a dowry — from the family of the bride or groom to the other family. Research the dating and marriage customs of another culture that you are interested in. How are these customs similar to and different from those in the United States? Share your findings with the class.

CHAPTER

12 A Look at Families

OBJECTIVES

- Identify various family forms.
- Explain the family life cycle and how roles affect families.
- Describe factors that make families unique.

TERMS TO LEARN

- *nuclear families*
- *single-parent family*
- *custody*
- *blended families*
- *extended family*

In thinking about her family, Paula realized just how fortunate she was. Of course the ache of her mother's death was still there. However, she knew that she was probably closer to her dad and younger brother because of it. Their laughter and support could be counted on to help her through the rough spots. She knew they counted on her, too. In what ways do you count on your family for support?

Families Are Important

Most people live their lives as part of a family. Although families today may differ from those in the past, their importance to individual members and to society remains the same.

What Families Provide

Families still serve the basic functions that they have throughout history. The first function of the family is to satisfy the basic physical needs of all members — young and old. These needs include food, clothing, and shelter. Health and safety are other important needs. The safety needs of a young child are quite different from those of a teen.

Families not only provide for physical needs, they also help members grow socially, intellectually, and emotionally. Social growth is promoted when adult family members teach younger ones how to behave in different situations and how to get along with others. Intellectual growth comes through education. Families must see that children learn both at school and at home, so that the children can eventually become independent. Emotional growth develops in a loving, caring environment. Children learn how to express feelings and give, as well as receive, support. They also learn respect and responsibility.

Having fun together is one way that families supply social and emotional support. What other ways can you think of?

Families have a very strong influence on their members. Within the family, you learn values and attitudes that are carried with you throughout life. If you have children someday, many of these will be passed on to them. As you can see, a positive environment is very important.

Types of Families

Even though families serve the same functions that they always have, their forms may not be the same. A look around your neighborhood or school will show you that not all families are alike. What families can you think of that fit the forms described in the following paragraphs?

Nuclear Families

Families in which two parents share a household with their children are called **nuclear families** (NOO-klee-ur). The family may consist of two parents and one child or perhaps a dozen children. The children may be adopted, born into the family, or both.

Spending time together relaxing and enjoying each other is especially important in single-parent families.

Single-Parent Families

A family that has only one parent living in the household is called a **single-parent family**. Most often the parent is the mother, especially after divorce or separation. This is because the court generally awards the care, or **custody** (CUS-tud-ee) of the children to the mother. A growing number of fathers, however, are seeking and receiving custody of their children. Another type of single-parent family is a single adult who has adopted one or more children.

Over 11 million children — more than one out of every five under the age of eighteen — live in a single-parent home today. This is largely the result of an increasing divorce rate. The parent in these families often faces extra challenges. With no other adult to share the responsibilities, it can be difficult. Many children in single-parent homes take on extra responsibilities to help the parent. They often learn independence earlier than they otherwise might.

Blended Families

Families that include a stepparent and stepchildren are called **blended families**. These families are a type of nuclear family in which one or both adults have been married before and one or both may have children from a previous marriage.

Blended families are very common today. When blended families first form, an adjustment period may be needed. The family may feel very different for awhile. Members must learn to share space, manage schedules, and relate in all new

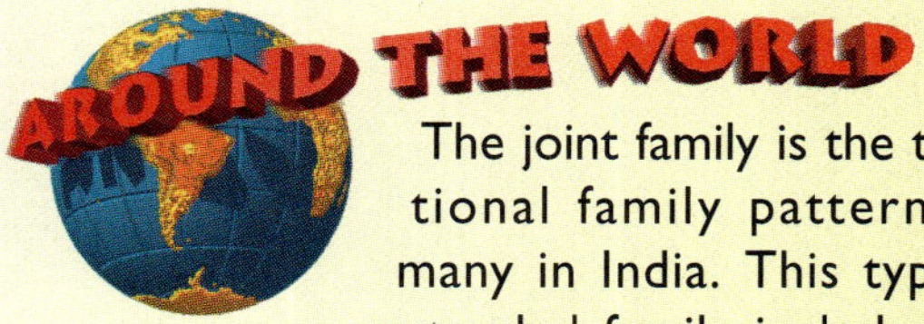

The joint family is the traditional family pattern for many in India. This type of extended family includes the husband and wife; the sons, their wives, and children; and unmarried daughters. There are several advantages to this arrangement. It is convenient for family members who work together in the same business. There are more people to help with household tasks. Young children almost always have others to play with and adults to look after them.

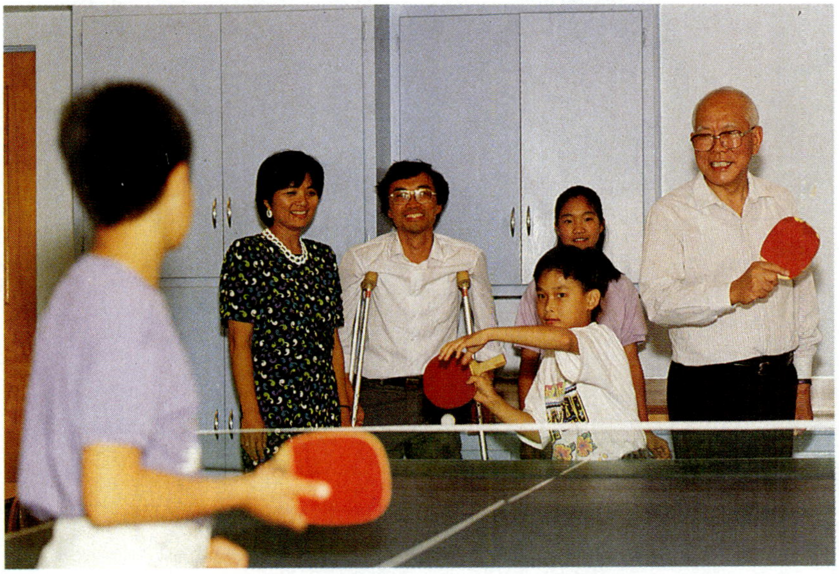

Members of an extended family share good times together as well as household responsibilities.

ways. Feelings of friendship and love may take awhile in coming. With patience, understanding, and a sense of humor, most blended families make the adjustment well.

Extended Families

An **extended family** includes one or more relatives in addition to the basic family unit. Melissa's grandfather, for example, lives with her family. Todd's aunt shares a home with his family. Extended family members — grandparents, aunts, uncles, and cousins — can serve as an extra support system for the family.

Adoptive Families

These families may be nuclear, single-parent, blended, or extended families. The adopted children are not related by birth to one or both parents. Through a legal adoption process, one or more children can become part of a family. The parent or parents are responsible for the care of the children they have adopted as though they were their children by birth.

Foster Families

A foster family can also be a nuclear, single-parent, blended, or extended family. One or more of its children are not the birth or adopted children of the parents. Instead, government agencies or other organizations make arrangements for a particular family to care for children from another family or families. Sometimes the children stay for extended periods of time; in other cases, they stay only for a short time. In some circumstances, the children are adopted later by the foster family.

TIPS: ***Making Blended Families Work***

To help make life go more smoothly in a blended family, try the following tips:

- Keep your sense of humor. Things will not go smoothly all the time. It helps to be able to laugh during the difficult times.
- Set aside some time to spend with each new family member. Taking genuine interest in another person makes him or her feel good and helps you to get to know that person.
- Keep the lines of communication open. Talk about problems openly and work to find positive solutions.
- Look for the little things that can help break down barriers. For example, does your new stepsister or stepbrother like chocolate chip cookies? Try baking a batch together. Working on a simple task together can help break the ice.

Some families include adopted children. There are many reasons why some people adopt children. However, the most important reason is that they want to provide a loving home for children that are already in the world — even if they are of another race.

Other Kinds of Families

Many couples do not have children but are considered to be a family because of the way they fulfill needs. In some situations, people have few or no family members. They may band together to take care of each other. For example, Mrs. Collins, an elderly widow, likes to think of her friends as "family." Mrs. Collins and her friends care about and support each other just as family members do.

The Family Life Cycle

Typically, families go through a series of stages known as the family life cycle. In the typical cycle, a couple marries, adjusts to the new relationship, and eventually has children. Over the next several years, the children are raised and then launched from the family home. The couple must then adjust to the *empty nest* — a home with children no longer present. They go through the middle years and, in time, experience the retirement and aging stage of the cycle.

Not all families follow the standard life cycle. If a couple remains childless, the pattern will not be the same for them. When adult children return home after they have left, the characteristics of the empty nest stage are different. Can you think of other situations that alter the family life cycle?

The concerns that families have at different stages of the cycle vary along the way. As Fred and Alma Perry looked at their photo albums one day, they reminisced about what their lives had been like. They recalled starting out as a young married couple with a low income and few responsibilities. When the children came along, things changed. They had many expenses and less time for each other. Once the children were raised, they had some time and money to spend on themselves. They bought a camper so that they could see more of the country. At retirement, their income decreased. Now they enjoy their grandchildren and travel when they can. They are planning for their aging years. Although health has not been a problem thus far, they know that it is likely to be in the future.

Family Roles

Whatever the stage, living in a family means fulfilling one or more roles. Tom's mother has a number of roles. She's a wife, mother, daughter, and sister. Outside the home she is also an employee. What roles do you have in life?

Problems can come when people do not agree on what a role should be. Who will be the breadwinner in a family? Who will handle household duties? Who will care for the children? What responsibilities do teens have to the family? Reaching agreement on these role-related questions requires effort, understanding, and compromise.

One of the trends seen in recent years has been the change in women's and men's roles. Today many women are employed outside the home. For many, the income is needed. Others choose careers for fulfillment.

Almost one-third of the women who are employed have preschool children. Concern has been raised about how these children fare in child care situations. Some studies have shown that, with quality care, the children can do just fine. Some families still feel that young children thrive best at home with a parent present. Not everyone can choose this option, however.

The family role of men has changed, too. Men are now taking a more active role in parenting and in sharing household responsibilities. Both fathers and children benefit by the closer bond that results.

Family roles and responsibilities change from time to time. What's routine in one family may be a role reversal in another. How do you think roles have changed for this family?

Families Are Unique

Think about the families you have seen on television. Some seem to be perfect. They are attractive people with fashionable clothes, new cars, and beautiful places to live. Others are just the opposite. Most of them can solve almost any problem, large or small, in a half hour. Did you ever wonder if any families like these fictional families exist in the real world? Chances are, they don't. Although the families you know may share some characteristics with those you see on television, most real-life families are not the same at all.

Working together as a family encourages communication and strengthens families.

Families are unique, or unlike other families, in many ways. Some families are different in the way they show feelings. In Webb's house, for example, people express their emotions freely. Hugs are common among family members. Dean's family is the opposite. They love each other just as much as Webb's family, but they are very private people. They find it hard to show their feelings openly with each other.

Families are also unique in their interests and traditions. For instance, the Wongs and the Garcias have very special traditions they have passed on to their children. Their traditions are a unique part of their culture and their family life. Shared family interests may involve music, sports, religious activities, or hobbies. Sharing these interests can help create bonds in a family.

Families are also unique in the ways they use resources to reach their goals. They may use material resources, such as money, housing, equipment, and transportation. They may also use personal resources, such as energy, interests, skills, and knowledge.

A family's uniqueness also depends on how its members work together at home. When all family members commit to making a good life together, it doesn't matter that one family is different from another. Strong families can be happy families regardless of their form, expression of affection, traditions, interests, and resources.

TAKING ACTION

Gavin and his sister Toni were spending part of the summer with their grandparents on Lake Waramug. Toni's best friend, Ruby, and Gavin's best friend, Tom, would soon be coming to visit Gavin, Toni, and their grandparents. Ruby's parents are divorced. Tom lives in a blended family that includes his two sisters and two stepbrothers. This led to a conversation about current changes in family life.

"In my day, two parents usually stayed together for the sake of the children despite any personal problems," their grandmother said.

"Growing up, I never knew anybody who was divorced, but I don't think parents who are unhappy together should stay married for the sake of their children," their grandfather replied.

Using Your Resourcefulness

- How would you respond to the statements made by Gavin's and Toni's grandparents? Do you agree or disagree with the statements? Why?
- What different types of family groups do your friends have? Which families seem positive and supportive? Which seem negative and unsupportive?
- What are some reasons for the change in family groups today? What resources can help you learn more about family life and various family groups?

Chapter 12 Review

Summary

In this chapter, you have read about:

- How families meet the physical, social, mental, and emotional needs of their members.
- The variety of forms a family may take.
- How families experience the family life cycle.
- The roles that people have within families.
- The uniqueness of each family in interests, resources, and lifestyles.

Facts to Recall

1. What is the first function of a family?
2. Describe how families help people grow socially, intellectually, and emotionally.
3. How do nuclear and extended families differ?
4. What extra challenges face both children and parents of single-parent families?
5. What is a blended family?
6. How are adoptive and foster families similar? How do they differ?
7. Briefly describe the standard family life cycle.
8. How do roles affect families?
9. Identify three ways that families can be unique.

Ideas to Explore

1. What is the form of your family? How has its form changed over time?
2. What suggestions can you offer to the members of a recently-formed blended family?
3. What roles do you have in your family? How may the different roles you have now conflict with one another? Explain which of your roles you think is most important.
4. Briefly describe what you believe the roles of a husband and a wife should be in a marriage. What might happen if a couple does not agree on these roles? When should a couple make decisions about role responsibilities?

Activities to Try

1. Write a short television commercial for any product you choose. Include characters, dialogue, and settings that you believe reflect real family life today.
2. Work with a group of class members to list challenges that families face at each stage of the family life cycle. What are some possible solutions for these family challenges?
3. As a class, debate the following statement: "Children who are raised in a family in which one parent stays at home are happier, better cared for, and more emotionally secure than children raised by parents who both work outside the home."

LINK TO *Social Studies*

TRACING FAMILY ROLES

The roles of family members have changed over time. Trace the development of the family from its origins among prehistoric people more than 300,000 years ago to today. Note how the roles played by men, women, and children within the family changed over time. How did the family itself and its roles in society change? Using the information you've gathered, make a time line tracing the history of the family up to the present time. Develop a creative way to present your time line to the class.

CHAPTER

13 Building a Strong Family

OBJECTIVES

- *Explain why it takes effort to build a strong family.*
- *Describe ways to improve relationships with other family members.*

TERMS TO LEARN

- ***siblings***
- ***age span***
- ***sibling rivalry***

Sometimes it takes a near tragedy to wake people up. That's what happened to Alejandro. A heart attack put his father in the hospital and left him near death for several weeks. Alejandro, caught up in his own problems, had been spending as much time as possible away from home. He and his father had not been getting along. When death loomed, however, Alejandro did some soul searching. So much of what had seemed important to him before suddenly seemed unimportant. He began to see that he wanted a second chance with his father. He was willing, even eager, to take the first steps to make things better. That's just what he did.

Your Role in a Strong Family

Strong families don't just happen; it takes time and effort from every family member to keep a family strong. Alejandro realized how important his father is to him and also realized it would take time and effort to build a strong relationship with his father. Family members build stronger bonds when attitudes and actions are constructive rather than destructive. Read "How to Build a Strong Family" on page 142 for more ideas on strengthening families.

Getting Along in a Family

Think of all the ways that family members can be different. Age, gender, and life experiences all set them apart right away. By the time you add interests, obligations, and abilities, you can have a set of very different individuals, all living under the same roof. Effort must be made to bridge the differences. A strong family can be created when attitudes and actions are constructive, not destructive.

If friendships seem easier to maintain than family relationships at times, think about why this may be true. You can choose supportive friends and drop those who are disagreeable. You can base friendship on shared interests and attitudes. Moreover, you can easily decide how much time to spend with friends. You have far less control over family situations. What you do control, however, are your attitude and actions within the family.

Individuals in families can be very different from one another. It takes effort to bridge the differences and get along.

How to . . .
Build a Strong Family

Families can become stronger by:

- ***Spending time together.*** Join each other regularly at certain meals. Play games. Go on an outing. Attend events that concern individual family members such as a music recital, a play, a debate, or a team sport.
- ***Observing traditions***. These may relate to holidays, religion, or routine activities — such as picking apples at an orchard — that the family decides to turn into tradition.
- ***Communicating.*** Share your ideas and thoughts with others and listen to theirs.
- ***Working together to solve problems.*** Discuss problems when they arise. Consider holding family council meetings.
- ***Sharing the work load.*** Set up a schedule and do your part willingly. Be ready to help others when they need it.
- ***Respecting the privacy of others.*** Learn to knock on closed doors and listen only to conversations that concern you.
- ***Showing consideration.*** Think about how you use the phone, treat others' belongings, and use family space.
- ***Putting family needs first.*** Remember that a "me-first" attitude is not constructive. Friends are important, but families are too.
- ***Sharing beliefs.*** These may be religious, political, or community concerns. Act on these beliefs together.
- ***Showing appreciation and love for each other.*** Remember birthdays and anniversaries. Give a hug. Learn to say, "I love you."
- ***Being tolerant.*** Forgive and forget when family members do something you don't like. Most incidents are not worth making an issue of.
- ***Having a positive attitude.*** You'll be pleasant to be around.

When you work out ways to relate well to your parents, brothers and sisters, and other family members, you are doing your share to promote family strength. Sometimes you must be willing to take the first step.

▼ Relating to Parents and Guardians ▼

Learning to get along with people begins at home. The way you act and react will set life-long patterns of behavior.

Understanding

The first step toward a good relationship is understanding. How well do you know your parents? Answers to these questions may help you see more clearly: What has life been like for them over the years? Can you list all the responsibilities they have? What problems must they deal with?

Understanding your parents means trying to walk in their shoes some of the time. You may discover that they have their own reasons for what they do. Recognizing this is very helpful. In addition, allow room for them to be human — parents make mistakes just like everyone else.

Keep in mind that parents' past experiences affect the decisions they make now. For instance, they may try to protect you from problems they had when they were your age. They may also act in ways that reflect how they grew up. Tara's mother was raised in a home where money was scarce. As a child, Mrs. Holmes never had more than the basics. She learned what it was like to scrimp in order to survive. Tara has not had to live like that, so she is often frustrated by her mother's efforts to economize. After a little thought and conversation about her mother's childhood, Tara saw her mother's point of view more clearly.

Discussing your differences and feelings with your parents openly and honestly is a step toward building a strong family. You might try asking your parents what life was like for them as teens.

Understanding is a two-way street. You want your parents to understand you, too. Even though teens want this, many of them hide their thoughts and feelings. This just blocks understanding. Your friends understand you because you talk to them. The same can be true with your parents.

Respect

Respect follows understanding. When you know why people act as they do, it is easier to give them respect. Respect is shown in what you say as well as how you say it. When people talk to you, what words and tones of voice turn you off? Listen to them and then to yourself. Practice the kinds of things you like to hear and then try them out. You may be surprised to discover that you receive more respect when you learn to give it more often.

Appreciation

People who respect others find ways to show appreciation. Sometimes friends do this without even thinking. Showing appreciation is just as important in families, but sometimes is overlooked. Family members have a tendency to take each other for granted. Can you add to the following list of ways to show appreciation for your parents?

- Give a hug or a smile.
- Give a sincere compliment.
- Ask for their help or advice. You may be surprised at how much they have to offer and how willing they are to support you.
- Say "thank you."
- Buy or make a card and include a note of appreciation.
- Offer your help without being asked.
- Show concern. When problems arise, listen and offer to help find a solution.

AROUND THE WORLD

For many Italian-American families, the decision to place an aged family member in a nursing home is especially hard. Italian tradition places high value on family loyalty and respect to elderly family members. Some older Italian-Americans were born in Italy and feel misunderstood in American nursing homes. The respect shown to elderly people is not the same as they feel it should be. One solution to this problem has been the creation of nursing homes run by Italian-Americans for Italian-Americans. These retirement communities provide their residents not only with health care, but with understanding of their history, their culture, and their traditions.

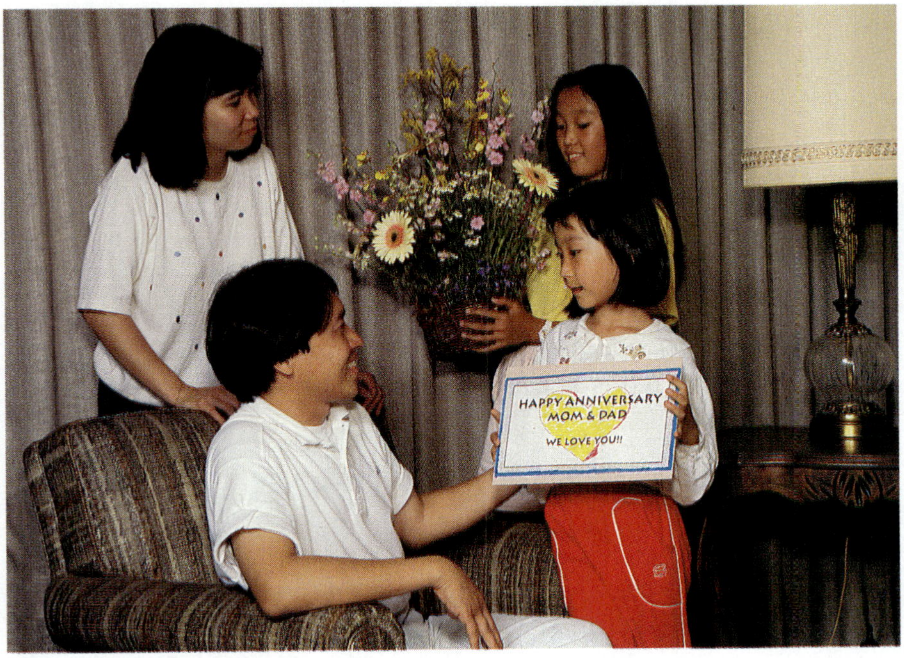

How do you feel when someone shows appreciation to you? How might you strengthen your relationship with your parents by showing your appreciation to them?

Responsibility

Good relationships with parents depend on one more thing — a sense of responsibility. For many years, children rely on parents and guardians to provide for their needs. This is the responsibility of parenthood. Eventually children grow, and it's their turn to begin taking on responsibilities. This is part of growing toward maturity and independence. Teens who are willing to be responsible usually get along better and are often given more privileges. Responsible teens are more likely to be trusted.

What does it mean to be responsible? Here are some examples:

- Justine has certain jobs to do at home. She carries them out without reminders. Sometimes she does extra tasks, especially when she notices that someone in the family is overburdened.
- Carlton is honest with his parents. He admits his mistakes. His parents appreciate this and reward him with trust.
- Shelly lets her parents know where she is going to be when she will be away from home. This is important information for her parents. It gives them peace of mind to know that she is safe. It is important for other reasons, too. When Shelly's older brother had a car accident several months ago, her stepfather needed to reach her quickly. This was easy to do because Shelly had just called home to tell them where she and her friends were going for pizza.

- Tony watches out for his younger brother. Sometimes this is his job. Other times he just sees that Steven needs him, so he helps out.
- Billy Jo works to keep her grades as high as possible. She includes study time in her daily schedule and uses this time wisely. Billy Jo knows that her future depends on what she does now. Her foster parents never have to prod her to get her work done.

All of these teens are showing responsibility. Even though their families don't always say so, they do notice. What's more, these teens get along well in their families. That's the best part.

Relating to Siblings

The same skills that you use in getting along with parents or guardians are useful when relating to **siblings**, or brothers and sisters. Trying to understand them will help you give them respect. Showing that you appreciate them will make them feel good, and they are likely to return the positive feelings to you in some way.

The **age span**, or number of years between children, affects sibling relationships. Sixteen-year-old Tim likes to rebuild car engines, but his ten-year-old brother Michael hangs around and asks endless questions while Tim is working. How would you handle this if you were Tim?

It is easy to think of younger siblings as bothersome. Put yourself in their place, though, and you may think differently. Young children in a family often idolize older siblings. They may want to be like them and do what they do. They are anxious to be older, too. Rejecting them or becoming angry with them just frustrates them and may even turn them into pests. A far better approach is to give them some attention, include them when you can, and distract them some of the time. One day Tim gave Michael some whitewall cleaner and let him work on making the car tires look like new. Michael was happy to be included while Tim went about his work.

Spending time with your siblings, even if it's working at a task together, is a way to build positive feelings. If you have them, what can you do to help strengthen your relationship with your siblings?

What might be some ways to eliminate sibling rivalry in this family?

TIPS: *Getting Along with Siblings*

Here are some tips for getting along with siblings:

- Ask permission before borrowing possessions. Return what you borrow on time and in good condition.
- Don't expect to be included every time an older sibling has friends over for a visit.
- Talk out your disagreements. Be ready to compromise. Then stick to your agreement.
- Be supportive of your siblings.
- Find similar interests you can talk about or do together.
- Teach each other new skills.
- Do household jobs together. They will be easier and more fun to do.
- Compliment your siblings on what they do well.
- Talk to them. Share your feelings, and let them get to know you.

Here's one last thought to remember about siblings. At some point in their lives, most people need the support and friendship of their siblings. Friends can drift apart, but siblings have a bond like no other. If you want them to be there for you when you need them someday, then you must work to keep the relationship in good shape.

Competition

Competition for parents' and other family members' love and attention is a common problem between siblings. This is called **sibling rivalry**. Sibling rivalry can cause people to feel down about themselves. Rebecca feels that her sister gets more privileges than she does. Taylor wishes he could play basketball the way his older brother did in high school. Maria gets tired of listening to people talk about her sister's good grades.

If you ever feel that fairness is a problem in your family, remember this. Parents have a great deal to think about. It is almost impossible for them to keep track of everything said to, bought for, or rewarded to each child. Children have a remarkable ability to tally up all these things — from their own viewpoint. Try not to fall into this trap. Everyone and every situation is different. Some children are more responsible at an earlier age than others. Rewards and discipline that work for one child may not work for another. Making things perfectly even among siblings is practically impossible, and it can even work against you. As one mother put it: "Denise doesn't even see what she would have lost if we had tried to make everything the same for her and her sister. She has gotten to do many things at a younger age than her sister did. She doesn't even think about that when she complains about equal treatment."

When competitive feelings strike, it also helps to remember that you have your own special qualities and abilities. They may not be the same as those of your siblings, but that doesn't matter. Discover what you do well, and develop those skills.

▼ Relating to Other Family Members ▼

Relatives are family members, including those outside the immediate household. They are related by birth, adoption, or marriage. Some families have many relatives who get together for birthdays, graduations, and holidays. Other families have few relatives, or they may live too far away to see them often.

By learning to get along with — and enjoy — your relatives, you will have a fuller life. You can learn about family history from them. Often relatives turn out to be good friends and a tremendous support system in tough situations. These relationships are well worth nurturing through visits and through correspondence when separated by distance.

TAKING ACTION

Family life has been a difficult issue for Adam for a long time. His parents used to argue a lot. Eventually they divorced and he lived with his mother. It took Adam a while to make the adjustment, especially since he'd felt closer to his father. He was extremely distressed when his father relocated to another city, and found himself fighting with his mother too much. Over time, they worked out differences and developed a smoother relationship.

Then, six months ago, Adam's mother remarried. Now he and his stepfather don't get along. To complicate things, Renee, a stepsister one year younger than Adam, is at odds with her own mother and has come to stay with them for a while. She seems to get all the attention and Adam gets the blame when things go wrong. He knows he needs help quickly, but doesn't know what to do.

Using Your Resourcefulness

- What options does Adam have in changing and improving his family conflicts? What would happen if he did nothing to change the situation?
- If he decides to talk to any or all family members, how should he communicate his feelings? What should he say? What shouldn't he say?
- What resources in your community could help Adam and his family? What kind of services do counselors and support groups offer? How does one contact such resources?

Chapter 13 Review

Summary

In this chapter, you have read about:

- Why it sometimes takes a greater effort to get along with family members than with friends.
- How understanding, respect, and appreciation affect relationships with parents and guardians.
- Ways of showing responsibility within the family.
- Things you can do to strengthen your relationships with siblings.
- The contributions of other relatives to your life.

Facts to Recall

1. Explain why it can sometimes be more challenging to get along with family members than with friends.
2. List five ways to help make a family stronger.
3. Why is it easier to respect parents and guardians when you understand them?
4. List five ways to show appreciation for parents.
5. How can responsible behavior lead to greater independence for teens?
6. What is helpful to remember when someone feels that fairness is a problem in the family?
7. List five tips for getting along with siblings.
8. How can relatives outside your immediate household make your life more full?

Ideas to Explore

1. Discuss two ways in which the experiences of your parents or guardians as teens were different from your experiences as a teen. How has that made their attitudes and opinions different from yours?
2. Why do you think some teens have trouble talking with their parents? What suggestions do you have for improving the lines of communication?
3. How can asking a family member for advice show appreciation?

Activities to Try

1. Develop a questionnaire that could be used to help you better understand a parent or guardian.
2. Imagine you are the parent or guardian of a child who is your age. Write a letter explaining your reasons for making a decision or taking an action that the child thinks is unfair.
3. Imagine that you are your own eight-year-old brother or sister. Write a short essay describing your daily activities as your younger sibling might see them.

LINK TO *Geography*

FAMILY LIFE AROUND THE WORLD

Throughout the world, a variety of family patterns exist. People may live in nuclear or extended families. The amount of respect given to women and the elderly depends largely on the culture. The way families trace their ancestry also differs — some trace the mother's family line, others the father's family line. A variety of family customs exist in different parts of the world. Examine family life in another country by completing the following:

- Choose a country.
- Read about families and their ways of life in this country.
- Write a skit describing family life in the country you chose.
- Work with several classmates to present your skit to the class.

CHAPTER

14 Handling Challenges

OBJECTIVES

- *Describe ways families can handle life's challenges.*
- *List resources available to families who need help.*

TERMS TO LEARN

- ***financial***
- ***credit rating***
- ***addicted***
- ***alcoholism***
- ***alcoholics***
- ***spouse***

If there was one thing that Dorita learned through her ordeal, it was that a crisis should not be faced alone. First she had tried to deny that anything was wrong. Even when she accepted the reality of what was happening, she locked so much inside. Everything stayed there until Dorita couldn't handle it anymore. Confiding in her best friend's mother made all the difference in the world. Once it was out, Dorita began to deal with it, looking for other sources of help. She hoped that she would never have to face anything like this again, but if she did, she knew that she would never choose to go it alone.

The Challenges People Face

Life is not without its ups and downs. Many people find themselves somewhere in the middle most of the time, with day-to-day challenges to meet. Sometimes, however, challenges have high impact. When this happens, people must know how to cope. All problems can be handled; the question is *how*.

New Family Members

When new members are added to a family, some adjustments may be needed. Adding members to a family can upset routines. Space and possessions must be shared. Feelings like resentment and insecurity may surface. This is the negative, or down side — if you choose to see it that way.

A healthier approach is to look at the positive side. A baby is entertaining and loving. A new sibling means one more lifelong source of support. A grandmother who moves in may have interesting stories and information to share. A grandparent may be a source of support when a parent is not available or doesn't seem to understand. You can, no doubt, think of other reasons to value the addition of a new family member. Such thoughts make it easier to accept change, and acceptance is essential.

Many times facing personal and family challenges can be difficult. Reaching out to others and finding ways to cope enables you to work through difficult times.

Moving

Have you ever moved to a new community? If so, you know that it can be difficult. Adults and children in a family have many adjustments to make. They will have to adjust to new schools, a new neighborhood, and new people. The feeling of strangeness about a new place is normal, and it goes away after awhile.

Moving can be an adventure and a challenge, too! What are some ways that people can make the transition to a new neighborhood or community easier?

When you begin classes at a new school, sign up for an activity or sport that interests you. This will make it easier for you to meet other students with similar interests. Finding classmates who share your interests is the first step in making new friends. Be friendly and show your interest in others. New friendships come in time.

Unemployment

Unemployment complicated Youseff's life. Both of his parents were laid off for several months. This kind of temporary unemployment is a fact of life for many families. As Youseff found out, it was very stressful for the entire family. In addition to surviving on a reduced income, Youseff found his family members having to cope with feelings of low self-esteem, anger, and frustration.

Youseff tried to keep a positive attitude for his parents' sake. He didn't want to make them feel guilty about what they couldn't provide. Youseff found extra ways to help at home and even got a part-time job to pay for school supplies and other expenses. Youseff's parents were proud of the efforts he made.

Financial Problems

Financial, or money-related, problems can be very stressful. They may be caused by the lack of a job, serious illness, a natural disaster, or even death. Some families routinely struggle with financial problems because their income doesn't stretch far enough.

When bills are overdue, creditors welcome a talk to make new arrangements for payment. This can protect a person's **credit rating** — a record that shows a person's ability and willingness to pay his or her debts. Usually for a fee, consumer credit counseling services offer ideas to people who need to control their spending. They also suggest methods for getting out of debt. These services are listed in the yellow pages of the phone book under "Credit."

Understanding helps when this kind of problem exists. Money for clothes and entertainment may be scarce. Altering clothing (see "How to Alter and Recycle Clothing" in Chapter 36) and finding free sources of entertainment can be helpful. A young person's ability to handle financial difficulties in a positive way can take some of the pressure off parents. Although it may seem difficult at the time, learning to manage with very little often makes people better money managers throughout life. They may also be more appreciative of what they have.

Homelessness

This problem has become more common in recent years. When people lose their homes, financial troubles or job loss is usually the reason. Poor economic conditions in a country can cause this to happen to large numbers of people, often through no fault of their own. Natural disasters such as major flooding, hurricanes, and tornadoes also lead to homelessness, although this is more often temporary. Fires can also lead to homelessness. Most communities try to provide a safety net for those who find themselves with nowhere to go. The Red Cross, Salvation Army, and other agencies are usually able to place people in shelters until they can get on their feet again.

Illness and Disabilities

When illness or disability strikes a family, stress comes to all members. Families who pull together manage best. Learning all you can about the illness or disability is a good idea. Libraries and physicians have information. Others who have gone through similar difficulties have firsthand experience. They can offer valuable information, advice, and support. Attitudes of understanding, compassion, sacrifice, and a willingness to help are useful.

The cost of child care outside the home can cause financial difficulties for many people. This family solved this problem by having one parent work out of the home and provide child care at the same time. What other solutions do you see for this challenge?

Around the World

In recent years, many countries in Africa were affected by severe droughts. Without water, farmers were not able to grow crops to supply food in these countries. Food surpluses were used up quickly and many Africans died from hunger. Many Western countries sent food and millions of dollars of aid to African countries. However, much of the food did not reach needy Africans in time. The challenge that many researchers feel is to find better means of monitoring weather, developing better agricultural methods, and monitoring the health of people (especially children) in high-risk areas to help solve the devastating effects of the hunger problem.

Separation and Divorce

Children of parents who are separated or getting a divorce go through a difficult period of emotional adjustment. When separation or divorce occurs, children sometimes feel they are the cause of the problems. They need reassurance that this is not true and loving support from both parents.

Some parents make mistakes when the separation or divorce process is emotional. They say negative things about each other to the children. They may want the children to take sides. One parent may even try to take the children illegally. This is not good for children, but it does happen. Children have the right to say how this makes them feel.

Coping after a divorce requires special effort. Children may have increased responsibilities in the home and may spend less time with both parents — not just the absent one.

Children sometimes feel torn between their parents during a divorce or separation. It's important for children to spend time with both parents and talk about their feelings.

Ricky lives with his mother and sees his father on certain weekends. Handling the schedule was awkward at first, especially since he missed having his father around. The weekend visits with his father are packed with fun activities, no strong rules, and no limits on watching television or listening to music. This makes it important for Ricky to be careful about how he views each of his parents. It would be easy to see his mother as the tough parent and his father as the fun one.

Even though many of the effects of divorce are unpleasant, most people make adjustments and accept their new way of life. Talking with parents can help a young person understand the parents' decision. A trusted adult — perhaps a teacher, school counselor, or religious leader — may also be able to help.

Substance abuse affects more people than just the abuser. It's important to keep the lines of communication open and get help with coping when you need it.

Substance Abuse

When people use substances that cause them harm, the effects are far-reaching. Substance abuse occurs when medications are misused. It also occurs when other drugs, such as alcohol, inhalants (substances that are breathed in), tobacco, and illegal drugs are used. Often people become **addicted** (uhd-IK-ted) to a drug. That is, they have a physical or psychological dependence on the substance — their body tells them they need it; their brain tells them they need it. They cannot give it up. They will do almost anything to get it. Serious health problems and even death result from substance abuse.

Alcoholism is one type of drug problem. Those who are addicted to alcohol, in the form of beer, wine, or other liquor, have this disease. They are called **alcoholics**.

The Effects

Young or old, people with any drug problem can make life very difficult for their families. Their behavior often becomes troublesome. Out of touch with themselves and reality, they may say what they normally would not. Often they deny that they have a problem. Their actions may be abusive, endangering themselves and others. They often neglect their responsibilities. Financial problems may occur due to the cost of the drug or perhaps the loss of a job. They may even turn to crime to pay for a drug habit.

When teens use alcohol and other drugs, they face serious consequences that can affect them for life. Long-lasting physical, psychological, and emotional effects, can interfere with how well teens do in school or on the job. They frequently fight with their parents and have a "don't care" attitude. Sometimes they even turn to additional drugs. Also, since their use of alcohol and many other drugs is against the law, they may face serious legal troubles.

Loved ones are saddened, frustrated, and angered when a family member has a subtance abuse problem. The result is often hurt and broken families. As you can see, this is a problem for society, too. A society with many troubled families cannot be strong. Obviously, the way to break the cycle is to stop substance abuse at its base — with the individual.

Looking for Solutions

The best solution to the substance abuse problem is prevention. If you don't start — with alcohol or any other kind of drug — you won't have a problem.

Unfortunately for some people, it is too late for prevention. They already have the problem and they need somewhere to turn. If you need help for yourself, a friend, or a family member, look in the yellow pages of area phone books

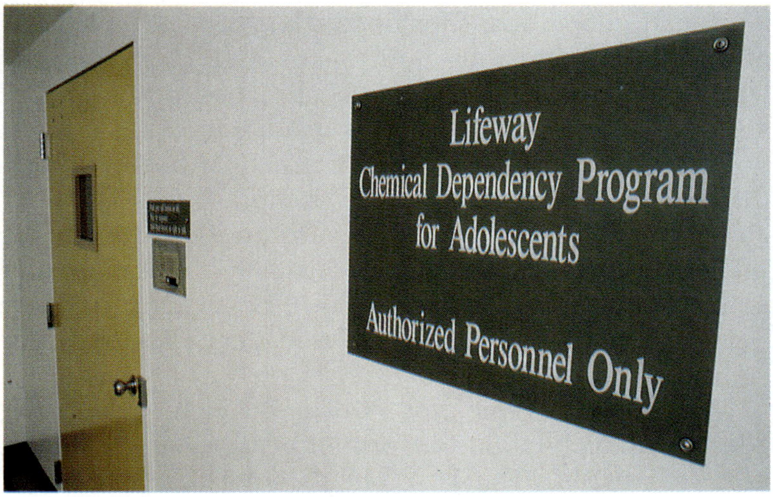

For people that need help with substance abuse, there are many counseling centers and programs that provide the help that is needed.

How to ...

Get Help for Alcoholism

The following organizations provide help for alcoholics and their families. Look for locations for the first three in the telephone directory.

- ***Alcoholics Anonymous (AA)***. All members are recovering alcoholics. The members provide support to others who are trying to remain sober. This is done through regular meetings.
- ***Alateen.*** Children and teens who have an alcoholic parent(s) are helped in Alateen.
- ***Al-Anon.*** This group helps the friends, husbands, wives, and other relatives of alcoholics.
- ***National Council on Alcoholism and Drug Dependence.*** The council provides information and a list of organizations that can help. The address is 12 W. 21st St., 8th Floor, New York, NY, 10010.

under "Drug Abuse" or "Alcoholism." You will find lists of counselors and programs that provide help with every kind of drug problem.

If you are concerned about someone close to you who is an alcoholic, some specific guidelines may be useful.

- Let the person know you are concerned and willing to help.
- Discuss the problem calmly and specifically. Call the problem by its name, alcoholism, and tell the person what is happening to the family and the alcoholic because of the addiction.
- Don't assume responsibilities for the drinker. This just enables the person to continue drinking.
- Never argue with someone who has been drinking. The person is not able to think clearly and may react in a violent way.

Let the alcoholic know that help is available. Talk about the agencies listed in the chart on page 157. Realize, however, that the alcoholic must be ready to seek assistance. You cannot do this for the person. Even when the alcoholic is unwilling to find help, friends and family members can. They can learn how to deal with an alcoholic in order to promote possible recovery. Alateen and Al-Anon, described in the chart, have suggestions. With help, many alcoholics and their families have succeeded in finding the road to recovery.

Violence is destructive to families and is never acceptable. Help is available for individuals and families dealing with domestic violence. Many times, the victims of abuse need to seek help before the abuser gets help.

Violence in the Home

Another kind of abuse occurs when someone harms or threatens another's physical or mental health. Abuse can be aimed at a **spouse** (one's husband or wife), a child, a disabled person, or an older adult.

Abuse comes in several forms. Emil grew up feeling that he was worthless. Constant put-downs from his father caused this *emotional abuse*. Mr. Brown *physically abused* his wife by hitting her when he was angry. *Neglect* was cited when two small children were found in an apartment without food or adult supervision. *Sexual abuse* happened when Tracy was subjected to sexual activity by an adult.

Every one of these types of abuse is wrong. No excuse can make them right for anyone. People who are abused need help. The risk of serious physical and emotional damage cannot be ignored. An abused person must find someone who will listen and provide shelter if needed. Some teens try to run away from abusive situations. The result can be more trouble from strangers who take advantage of them. Many communities have safe places for abused people to go. You can locate them by calling 911 (or the emergency number in your area) or asking for a referral at a hospital emergency room or from a religious organization.

Violence is destructive to families. A person who is abusive in any way needs to learn self-control. This may not happen unless the victims seek help first.

▼ Crime ▼

The fear of becoming a victim of crime can be very stressful. Anyone can become a victim of crime. Those who live alone or are elderly or disabled feel especially at risk. Following safety rules is the best defense. What safety rules do you and your family follow to prevent crime?

Victims of crime can be deeply scarred. Family and friends need to rally around to give support. Crimes, as well as any suspicious activity, should be reported to the police immediately.

When a family member commits a crime, the rest of the family suffers. The best approach is to seek legal help and work to get the person's life back on track.

▼ Death ▼

No family can escape death. When it happens, a grieving process follows. People go through grief in very different ways. Family members need to allow each other to mourn in their own ways.

In handling grief, talking and crying are useful. It is important to release the strong feelings that are inside. Try to think about the good memories you have of the deceased, and give yourself some time to recover.

If you know someone who is grieving, reach out in some way. Simple acts are usually most appreciated — a card, a phone call, or a short visit, for example. Simple words are

SAFETY CHECK ✓

Here are some safety rules to follow to help prevent crime:

- Keep doors and windows locked on the inside.
- Never give your address and telephone number to people you do not know well.
- Keep emergency telephone numbers next to the telephone especially if your area does not have 9-1-1 service.
- Let someone know where you are when you are away from home.
- Carry a whistle when you walk alone or find others to walk with you.
- Always carry identification and telephone numbers of people to contact in case of emergency.

Talking with a trusted adult or qualified counselor can help you cope with many different types of problems. Where could you turn for help if you needed it?

helpful, too. Be a good listener both now and later, when the grieving person may feel that everyone has forgotten about the person who died.

As with any other serious problem that people face, counseling is available. Counseling can be especially useful to people who have been through a particularly difficult loss.

Getting Help

People need not face challenges alone. Relatives, neighbors, and friends can help in times of need. Many willing people stand ready to give emotional and financial support.

Communities have many services for families. Libraries are a good source of information. Police and fire departments provide assistance in emergencies. Medical services and support groups are available in most communities. Support groups are made up of people who have personal experience with specific problems. Welfare assistance is available to families who cannot meet their basic physical needs. Religious and community organizations provide families with many services, such as crisis centers and hot lines. Professionals, including social workers, religious leaders, school counselors and trusted teachers, also give aid. Help is just around the corner if people will only ask.

TAKING ACTION

Your friends have gathered to watch a video together. No one is really focused on the movie. Although Carter would normally never miss a get-together, he is not with you tonight. His father died last month after a long bout with cancer, and Carter is home with his family tonight.

Since the funeral, Carter has seemed distanced from all of you. He hasn't shown up for lunch in the cafeteria since returning to school. You've all seen him in the halls and in classes, but he hasn't really had anything to say. "I don't know what to say to him anyway," Devon points out.

Without saying so, you silently agree with Devon, but you know that avoiding Carter is not the answer. Aaron wants to just leave Carter alone, thinking he'll come around when he wants to. You are not so sure.

Using Your Resourcefulness

- Why do you think Carter is acting in the manner described?
- Evaluate the responses of Carter's friends.
- What suggestions do you have for Carter and the others?

Chapter 14 Review

Summary

In this chapter, you have read about:

- Challenges that families must handle.
- How a positive attitude can help you cope with different situations.
- How you can help others in their hard times.
- Outside resources that can help you cope with challenges.

Facts to Recall

1. How can your attitude hurt or help the situation when a new member is added to the family?
2. How can a teen help parents if one or both become unemployed?
3. Identify three sources of information about illnesses and disabilities.
4. Explain the special difficulties that children face during and after a divorce.
5. Describe how substance abuse affects individuals and families.
6. List six guidelines for confronting an alcoholic about his or her problem.
7. Is abuse always physical? Explain.
8. Why is it important for abused people to seek help?
9. What people are especially at risk of crime?
10. What are some simple but effective ways of reaching out to a grieving person?
11. Name four community resources available to families in times of difficulty.

Ideas to Explore

1. What would you do to support a friend whose family was having problems?
2. Why do you think many people have trouble asking for help in times of crisis?
3. Why do you think some people stay in abusive situations?
4. Why do you think some people have difficulty reaching out to a grieving person?
5. What time do you think is worse for a person who is grieving over the death of a loved one — the time of the funeral or the days that follow? Defend your answer.

Activities to Try

1. Working together as a class, try to rank all the challenges described in the chapter in order of difficulty. Start with the least difficult to handle and end with the most. Why is it hard to agree on the ranking?
2. List ways you could help your family through tough financial times or unemployment.
3. Investigate the resources available in your community for families who need help with different problems.

LINK TO *Communication*

CRISIS ASSISTANCE

Teens may feel overwhelmed, helpless, and alone when confronted by one of the challenges that families may face. Friends may not know how to help. Work with your classmates to develop a student assistance program for your school. Your efforts might include the following:

1. Develop a crisis handbook that provides facts about a variety of crises that families may face. In the handbook, include tips on ways teens can help their families and each other during times of crisis. In addition, create a directory of sources of information and organizations that provide help to families with problems.
2. Work with a faculty sponsor (such as a guidance counselor) to develop a student counseling program for your school.

CHAPTER

15 Understanding How Children Grow

OBJECTIVES

- *Describe the four main stages of development.*
- *Explain how children develop physically, intellectually, emotionally, socially, and morally.*
- *Discuss influences on development.*

TERMS TO LEARN

- ***fetus***
- ***infancy***
- ***toddler***
- ***preschooler***
- ***conscience***

When Valerie took her first steps at eight months of age, her parents were delighted. They placed a chair close to the sofa and encouraged her to let go of one and toddle in the direction of the other. By twelve months, she was walking well. A few years later Valerie's little brother, Dylan, was still scooting along the floor at the age of thirteen months. Mr. Davis began to worry about his son. After all, Valerie had walked so much earlier. Then, one day his mind was put at ease. All of a sudden, Dylan just stood up and walked with very little trouble. Both children, the Davis family realized, were quite normal. They had just developed at different rates.

Stages of Development

Even though children develop at different rates, they still go through four main stages of development, or growth:

- ***Prenatal stage.*** This stage usually lasts about nine months as the **fetus** (FEE-tus), or unborn child, develops inside the mother's body. During this time, a single cell develops into a baby capable of surviving in the outside world.
- ***Infancy.*** The stage called **infancy** begins at birth and lasts about one year. Physical development occurs more quickly during infancy than any other stage of life.
- ***Childhood.*** This period begins at about one year of age. It lasts until the beginning of adolescence — at about eleven or twelve years. During childhood, a number of changes take place as the child grows and develops. To make it easier to understand this age group, many people break it into three smaller groups. A **toddler** is a child one to three years of age. A **preschooler** is three to five years old. Children enter the *school-age* category at age five and leave it when they enter adolescence.
- ***Adolescence.*** Next to infancy, the second fastest period of growth is adolescence. As you read in an earlier chapter, adolescence is the time of life between childhood and adulthood. Adolescence continues until the young person is able to assume adult responsibilities, usually between ages eighteen and twenty-two.

Children grow and develop in four main stages, but may grow at different rates.

Except for infancy, adolescence is the second fastest period of growth. How have you noticed growth changes in yourself?

How Children Grow and Develop

Children grow and develop in several different ways. They grow in size and in muscle strength and coordination. This is called *physical development*. They grow in their ability to learn, think, and judge. This is *intellectual (mental) development*. *Emotional development* means learning to control emotions and to express them in acceptable ways. Through *social development*, children learn to interact with people in various situations. They must also learn to tell right from wrong. This is known as *moral development*.

Children grow in all of these areas at the same time. They don't develop physically one month and intellectually the next. In addition, children may be advanced in one area of development, but lag behind in another. They are learning right from wrong at the same time that they are learning to relate to people.

Physical Development

When Tyler was born, he had wrinkled skin and an oddly-shaped head. Because infants grow quickly, Tyler's parents knew that he would be very different in a short time. Not only would his appearance change, but his abilities would, too.

Gaining control over body muscles is one part of physical development. The skills needed for this control are called *motor skills*. During the first five years of life, children learn to master control of the large muscles needed for activities such as walking and running. They also start gaining better control of smaller muscles. These are needed for such skills as writing, throwing and catching balls, and using tools.

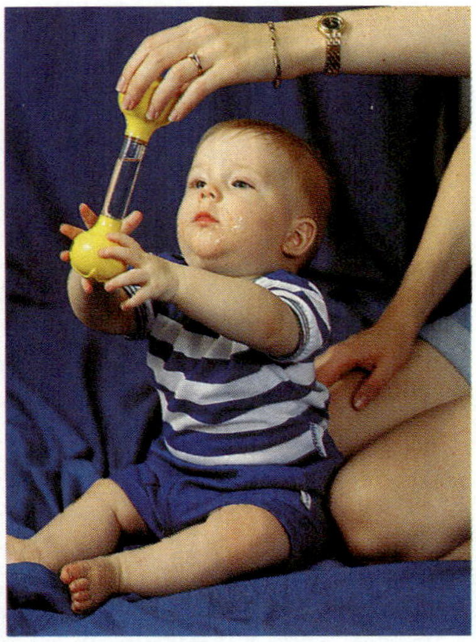

Gaining control over motor skills is an important part of infancy. During this time, infants learn to use their large muscles for walking and running. Control of smaller muscles is used for grasping objects, catching balls, and writing.

Infants learn to control their body movements beginning with their head and gradually working toward other parts of the body. At one month, an infant can briefly lift its chin when lying on its stomach. From three to four months, many infants can hold their heads steady, roll from side to back, and reach for objects such as toys. At five to six months, many infants can usually roll over completely, sit with support, and reach and grasp objects successfully. By seven months, most infants can sit alone and feed themselves some finger foods.

Babies must learn to use their eyes, arms, and hands together. Learning to grasp an object means that the baby knows exactly where the object is and can touch it. This takes time. By the ninth month, most babies can reach for an object and grasp it.

Walking movements begin at birth or perhaps even before. Newborn infants make kicking movements that look like walking. By stretching and kicking, babies strengthen and learn to control muscles of the legs and trunk. With increased strength and muscle control, babies can get up on their knees and crawl. The next step is to stand while holding onto furniture or a person. This helps develop balance, which is necessary before babies can walk alone. Some babies start to walk almost as soon as they can stand. Others take a month or more to try their first step. Many babies will walk with support by one year of age. Others take a little longer.

AROUND THE WORLD

The importance of protecting children against disease is demonstrated by the success of the United Nations World Health Organization's (WHO) vaccination program. When it was begun in 1974, less than 5% of children in developing nations were protected against childhood diseases, and over 3 million children died of diseases such as measles, polio, and whooping cough. Today, WHO workers vaccinate 80% of the world's children against these and other life-threatening diseases. WHO hopes to increase that number to 90% by the year 2000. The organization also hopes to reduce death from measles by 95% and to wipe out polio completely by the turn of the century.

Intellectual Development

As children grow intellectually, they develop the ability to learn, think, and judge. How will you see evidence of this growth? For one thing, children gradually understand more words and ideas. They can also pay attention for a longer time.

Infants learn with their eyes, ears, mouth, and hands. Colorful toys, trips to the store, reading books, and simple songs all provide learning experiences.

The main intellectual skill young children learn is language. Most children begin to talk around the middle of their second year. First, they speak individual words and phrases. By the third year, they speak full sentences. They can connect two thoughts, such as "The stove is hot and can burn me!" or "I'll hurt my brother if I hit him."

By their fourth year, most children seem to ask questions continually. They may ask questions like: "Why does Daddy have hair on his face?" "Why does my hair stay on my head?"

Children need to hear words in order to learn to speak. They must also have someone to talk with. All family members are important in helping children grow intellectually.

Spending time talking with children encourages intellectual development.

Children show their emotions easily. What emotion is this young girl displaying?

Emotional Development

At first, infants can show emotions only by making body movements and facial expressions. They show they're unhappy by crying, kicking, and squirming. Infants respond in a happy way when sucking milk, when being rocked, or when someone speaks soothingly to them.

As children grow older, their emotions become more specific. They show joy, anger, fear, curiosity, jealousy, and affection. Children develop some of their emotional reactions by imitating, or copying, other people.

Children's emotions change rapidly. They may cry one moment and laugh the next. As children grow older, they learn to control their emotions.

Social Development

Social growth involves learning to interact with people in socially acceptable ways. Social development is closely linked to emotional development. Trusting others is the first step in developing socially. Children learn to trust when their caregivers feed them, answer their cries, and give them love and affection.

A second step in social development is to learn independence. Parents can help their children become independent. For instance, children's clothes should be easy to put on so that they can learn to dress themselves.

A third step is to learn acceptable behavior. At age two Michael threw his toys and screamed, "No, no!" when he was told to share them with another child. At age three, he clutched a toy tightly and refused to share it. By the time Michael was five, through consistent interaction with his parents and other children, he had learned to share his toys. He discovered that not only would his toys be returned, but he would also get to play with someone else's toys.

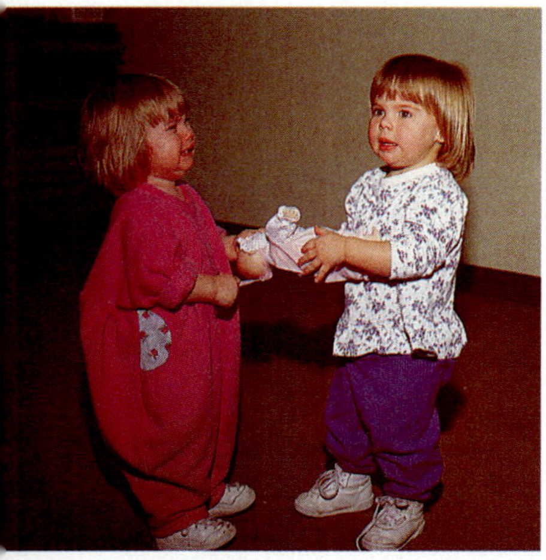

Learning to share is a challenging part of social development for a toddler.

Moral Development

Morals are generally accepted guidelines for right and wrong behavior. Children learn morals mainly in the home, in their place of worship, and in school.

At first, young children really don't understand the difference between right and wrong. They only know that some behavior makes adults upset or angry. Other behavior makes them happy. Gradually, they learn why certain actions are good or bad. With help from parents and caregivers, they develop a **conscience** (KAHN-chunts), an inner sense of right or wrong. This helps children monitor their own behavior.

What Influences Development?

Two factors work together to shape a child into a unique — or special — individual. These are heredity and environment.

Heredity plays a part in who you are and what you look like. What hereditary traits do these young girls have?

Heredity and Environment

In an earlier chapter, you learned that heredity refers to the traits that you inherit from your parents. It includes such characteristics as eye color, hair color and texture, height, and even some abilities. Environment is everything that surrounds you and affects your development and behavior. The way a family treats a child and the opportunities the child has to grow and develop are environmental influences.

Which do you think affects children more, heredity or environment? In truth, both heredity and environment are responsible for how children grow and develop. Children need both the ability to learn (heredity) and the opportunity to learn (environment). What if a child's diet is poor? With poor physical health, children may not have the energy to devote to learning new things. Without a good educational environment at home and at school, children may not develop their intellectual abilities. As you can see, both heredity and environment are important.

Schools

School has high impact on children. Through this environmental influence, children gain knowledge and skills that prepare them for life. Schools teach reading, writing, and mathematics, which are all basic tools in today's world. Schools also teach important ideas about morality and social behavior. In school, children learn to relate to those outside the family. School is a testing ground for finding out what is socially accepted.

At school, children further develop their personality and self-concept. As Karin studies different subjects and meets

The first day of school is often an exciting day for young children. Schools provide an environmental influence in the development of children.

new people, she learns more about her own likes and dislikes and her strengths and weaknesses. As she relates to older children and adults, she begins to think about the future. "What will I be like as an adult? What will I do?" she wonders. The world is opening up to her through education. If she seizes the opportunities, success will surely follow.

Family

Even though schools have a great impact on children, nothing quite compares to the effects that families have. To do well in school and in life, children need to feel good about themselves. Praise, encouragement, and support from family members is important to developing self-esteem. Children who feel good about themselves are better able to work and complete tasks. On the other hand, children who are not encouraged may not be sure about what they can do and may feel their efforts are hopeless.

In addition to encouraging the development of self-esteem, families can help children develop their learning ability in a variety of ways. Family field trips to museums, dance classes, working on projects at home such as building models, and playing games together, are all ways that families encourage learning.

TAKING ACTION

Ronny gets credit toward a home economics class project when he volunteers after school at the Kaiser Day Care Center. His job is to assist an aide caring for a group of two-year-olds.

On his first day, he approaches and picks up a girl who is chewing on a block. She starts to wail loudly. Ronny quickly puts her down and goes over to a boy who is crawling on all fours. Ronny tries to talk to him, but the boy merely points at Ronny's shoes and replies, "Ga-ga." Then the boy sits on Ronny's foot and tries to untie his shoelaces. "Don't do that!" Ronny orders. A third child walks over holding a toybox. She proceeds to drop the box and spill toys all over the floor. Ronny tries to get her to pick them up, but she doesn't understand what he's saying.

Using Your Resourcefulness

- Evaluate Ronny's behavior with each child. What other options of behavior does he have?
- Is each child's behavior appropriate for the physical and mental development of a two-year-old? Why or why not? What resource materials can teach you more about child development?
- Are there volunteer services that work with small children in your area? How would one find them?

Chapter 15 Review

Summary

In this chapter you have read about:
- The stages of a child's development.
- How children develop physically, intellectually, emotionally, socially, and morally.
- How heredity and environment work together to affect a child's development.
- What children learn about themselves and their world in school.

Facts to Recall

1. Name and briefly describe the four main stages of child development.
2. During which two stages is growth the greatest?
3. What are motor skills? Put the following motor skills in order as they are learned by infants: reaching for an object and grasping it; turning the body from side to back; walking; sitting alone.
4. What is the main intellectual skill young children learn?
5. What is the first step in a child's social development? How can caregivers help children learn this?
6. How can parents help children become independent?
7. A five-year-old who shares her toys with her brother is displaying what type of growth?
8. How do heredity and environment work together to affect learning?
9. Besides skills like reading and mathematics, what do children learn in school?

Ideas to Explore

1. What do you think is the most important thing you can teach children to help them become happy, successful adults?
2. Discuss the conflict between teaching a child obedience, yet also encouraging independence. How can this problem be resolved?
3. After reading about the high impact of education on children, what qualities do you think a good teacher should have, besides knowledge of the subject taught?

Activities to Try

1. Choose one talent that you have. In a short paragraph, explain how it was developed through both heredity and environment.
2. List ten ways in which you can help a young child grow intellectually.
3. Discuss ten ways of helping children feel good about themselves when starting school.

LINK TO *Health*

GROWTH AND DEVELOPMENT CHART

A child's development progresses through different stages. The events of normal development do not always occur at the same age for all children. However, they usually occur in the same order. Develop a chart showing the events of normal development during infancy, the toddler stage, the preschool years, the early school years, and the adolescent years. You may need to check the library for additional resources. In the chart include physical, intellectual, emotional, social, and moral development at each stage.

CHAPTER

16 Taking Care of Children

OBJECTIVES

- Describe appropriate care for children of various ages.
- Identify special safety guidelines for children.
- Describe what to do in an emergency.

TERMS TO LEARN

- *poison control centers*
- *first aid course*

Jason didn't know much about taking care of children until his sister and her son and daughter moved back home. Jason had to help out, and that meant doing everything from changing diapers to singing nursery rhymes. For the year that they were there, Jason learned so much. Sometimes it wasn't easy, but by the time they left, he knew more about children than he ever had before. He figured it all might come in handy someday.

Caring for Children

Children enter most people's lives at some point or another. Even if you never have any of your own, you may have to care for the children of friends and relatives sometime. Knowing what to expect will help you do a better job.

Playtime

Children need to play in order to grow and learn. In fact, play is sometimes called children's work.

Playing with Infants

Until he began looking after his eight-month-old niece Lara, Jason thought that babies must have a boring life. Like other infants around six to twelve months of age, Lara constantly tried to touch, taste, smell, and feel everything within reach. She was learning about the world through her senses.

Lara loved the games that Jason played with her. When he handed her a soft ball, she dropped it on the floor and watched him pick it up — again and again. Games like "pat-a-cake" and "peek-a-boo" delighted her. Lara's favorite toys were brightly colored ones. She had a variety of toys, including small blocks, big wooden beads, and rubber and plastic rings and balls. Jason even entertained her with plastic measuring cups and puppets he made from an old pair of socks. He talked to her as they played, which helped her with language skills.

Playing with Toddlers

A toddler's play is more active than an infant's. Toddlers can also concentrate on an activity longer. They like to play with simple toys that can be taken apart and put together again. Blocks and boxes of different sizes make ideal toys. Toddlers ages two to three also enjoy simple puzzles, storybooks, coloring books, large crayons, and paper.

Laticia's caregiver, Mrs. Odell, makes sure Laticia has room for walking and running during playtime. When two-year-old Laticia gets bored or frustrated, Mrs. Odell helps her

TIPS:
Babysitting Basics

Some teens earn money by taking care of children. Here are some tips that can help:

- Write down the name, address, and telephone number of the people you work for. Have this available for your family while you are gone.
- Find out about the job before you go: time and date (write this down); names and ages of children; transportation.
- Agree on your fee and duties.
- Be prompt.
- Ask the parents where they can be reached.
- Be sure that emergency phone numbers — doctor, police, fire department, ambulance, poison control center — are available. Keep these and the phone number of a nearby neighbor by the phone. Also write down the address of the home you are in and put this by the phone. It must be accurate for emergency personnel to find you quickly.
- Ask parents for any special instructions about medication for children, meals or snacks, bathing and bedtime routines and times, and television viewing.

(Continued on next page)

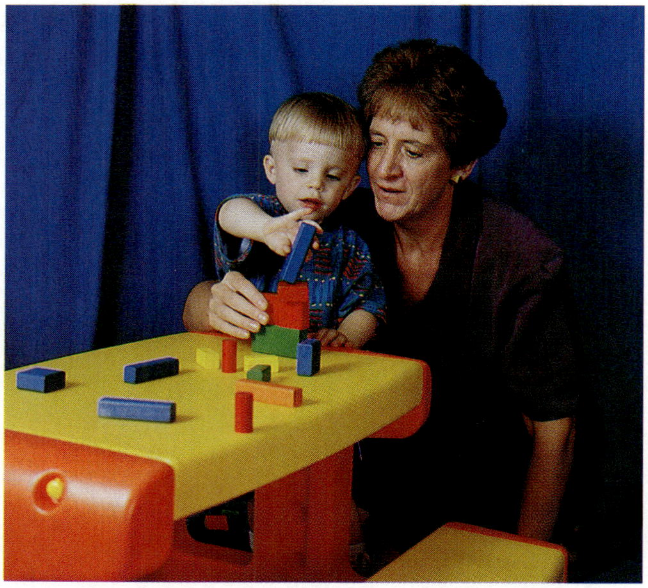

Playing with toddlers can require a lot of patience. When you care for toddlers, be sure to plan a variety of active and quiet play experiences.

find a different activity. She often alternates active play, such as running or throwing a ball, with quiet play. Mrs. Odell talks to Laticia often, describing what she is doing and what she sees.

Playing with Preschoolers

As a preschooler, Charlie is very proud of his new abilities. Often he says something like, "Watch me!" or "I'm the best!" He also has many questions. He is very curious, trying to understand so many new things. Charlie's parents and older sister try to answer his questions as patiently and clearly as they can.

Preschoolers like both active and quiet play. Many can ride a tricycle with ease. They may like to throw and catch balls. For quiet play, they enjoy books, finger paints, clay, crayons, and coloring books. They can also learn to cut with blunt scissors. When you care for preschoolers, take time to read them stories, making sure they see books as fun. Ask them to tell you stories of their own.

Preschoolers love exploration. For example, try turning over a rock to see what you find. On a tour through the neighborhood, a park, or a store, talk about what you see. Even the simplest occasions are opportunities for discovery.

Preschoolers love to pretend. Dressing up and acting like other people is fun. A box of old clothes and accessories can be a treasure to a child of this age.

Learning to play with others is important to preschoolers. Encourage them to join with others and share their toys.

Playing with School-Age Children

Older children are better at playing on their own but will still want your attention. School-age children like to take part in running games, such as tag and hide-and-seek. When they are with others, you can be sure there will be plenty of activity and noise.

Mealtime

As a caregiver, you are responsible for a child's meals. This includes not only preparing healthy meals and snacks, but also serving them safely and making mealtime relaxing and refreshing. Here are some tips for feeding children:

- ***Infants.*** When you care for an infant, you may need to give a bottle. Many caregivers will warm the milk by setting the bottle in a bowl of warm tap water for a couple of minutes. Check the temperature by shaking the bottle upside down over your wrist. The milk should feel warm, not hot. Do you know why the bottle should not be heated in the microwave? The liquid heats unevenly and may be too hot in places.

  If feeding the infant baby food that is to be served warm, make sure the food is no warmer than body temperature. It is not necessary to warm baby food. Give small spoonfuls. Be prepared for messiness. For a baby, eating is a new skill to learn as well as an opportunity for fun by sputtering and playing with the food.

Feeding infants can provide a real challenge to the caregiver. Be sure to ask the parents for specific instructions about what to feed infants and when to feed them.

Babysitting Basics (Continued)

- Ask parents for instructions about answering the phone and the door. Do not give information about where you are or about parents being gone to anyone on the phone. The safest approach to a knock at the door is to not answer it.
- Before the parents leave, locate the children's rooms and bathroom, first aid supplies, fire extinguishers, fire exits, and flashlights.
- Distract children with a game or toy if they are unhappy when parents leave.
- Be attentive to children at all times. Stay awake and keep the television volume low while children are sleeping so that you can hear any cries.
- Don't talk on the phone to your friends. It distracts you from caring for the children. The phone should be free for a call from the parents.
- Respect the family's property. This means cleaning up after yourself, eating only what you have permission to, and leaving closets, drawers, and mail alone.

MEETING SPECIAL NEEDS

Caring for Children with Disabilities

In many ways, children with physical and mental disabilities are like all others. They need love, attention, friendship, and family. Caregivers may need to provide special education, special exercises, and equipment. Patience and encouragement are important qualities for a caregiver.

Shawn first met Damon when Shawn's family living class put on a puppet show for severely disabled children. At first, Shawn was uncomfortable and afraid he would accidentally hurt Damon. Mrs. Davis, Damon's primary teacher, assured Shawn that Damon just needed love and attention like other children.

After several visits, Shawn was an expert at feeding Damon, playing with him, and entertaining Damon with books and stories. Although he could not speak, Damon's affection for Shawn sparkled in his eyes when his friend Shawn entered the room.

When the challenges are met, children with special needs can develop to their fullest potential. Many communities have support groups and services that help special needs children and their families succeed.

Following a regular bedtime routine helps make bedtime a comfortable and enjoyable experience for children and parents or caregivers.

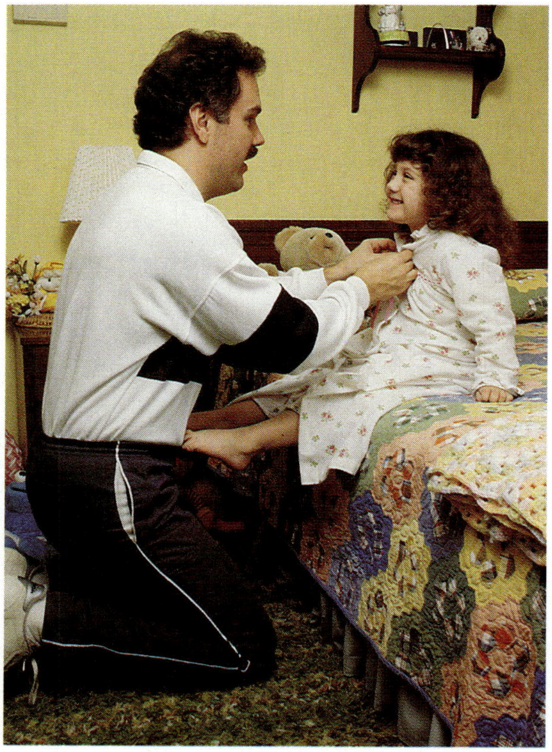

- ***Toddlers.*** A toddler's first solid food is usually simple finger foods. Cut foods into bite-sized pieces to prevent choking. If a high chair is used, place it in a safe, easy-to-clean location. A bib can help protect the child's clothes.
- ***Preschoolers.*** Simple foods, such as milk, cheese, crackers, peanut butter, fresh and dried fruit, and vegetable sticks are popular as well as healthful foods for preschoolers. Even though they may lack neatness and good manners, they are somewhat skillful at eating. Keep mealtimes pleasant, without too many directions. Avoid giving foods that are high in fat and sugar. Never give small children hard candy, nuts, popcorn, or any other food that might cause them to choke.

Bedtime

Shawna leads her son in a quiet activity like coloring before bedtime to help settle him down. She lets Corey know about fifteen minutes early that bedtime is coming. Her attitude is kind but firm.

By following a bedtime routine every evening, Corey knows what to expect and is usually cooperative. A story and his special stuffed bear make bedtime comfortable and enjoyable for him. These techniques are helpful for most young children at bedtime.

How to . . .
Change a Diaper

When changing a baby's diaper, try to make the experience a pleasant one. Talk or sing to the baby while you are diapering. Make up a game, such as patting the feet rhythmically, to associate with the process. The task will be easier if the child is willing. Here are the steps to follow:

1. Place everything you need within easy reach.
2. Place the child face up on a clean, flat surface. You might use a changing table, the crib, or a towel on the floor.
3. Remove the old diaper with the soiled part folded in. Keep one hand on the baby at all times.
4. Clean the baby with disposable wipes or a clean, damp, warm washcloth. It is important to wipe from front to back on female babies.
5. Lift the baby's legs with one hand, and slip a clean diaper underneath.
6. Secure disposable diapers with the tapes attached. Pin a cloth diaper with diaper pins. Always put your finger inside the diaper to protect the baby from being stuck as you pin.
7. Place the baby in the crib while you dispose of the old diaper. If it is disposable, put it in the garbage. If it is a cloth diaper, hold it firmly in a flushing toilet to rinse. Then place it in a diaper pail. Be sure to wash your hands thoroughly after diapering a baby.

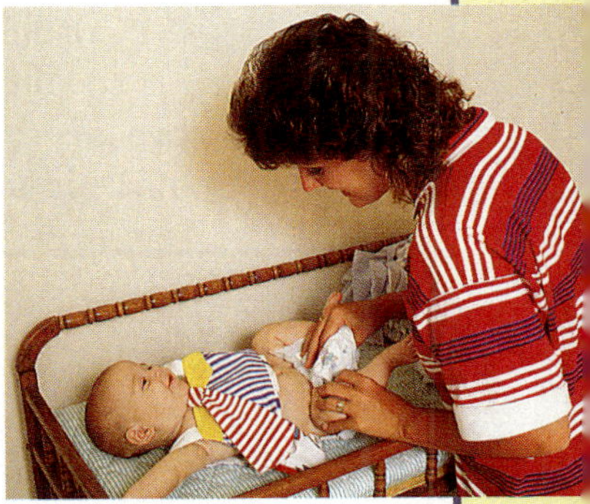

Steps 1, 2, and 3

Step 4

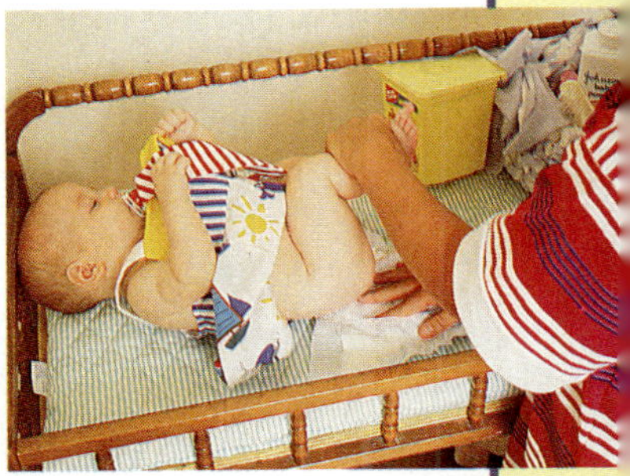

Step 5

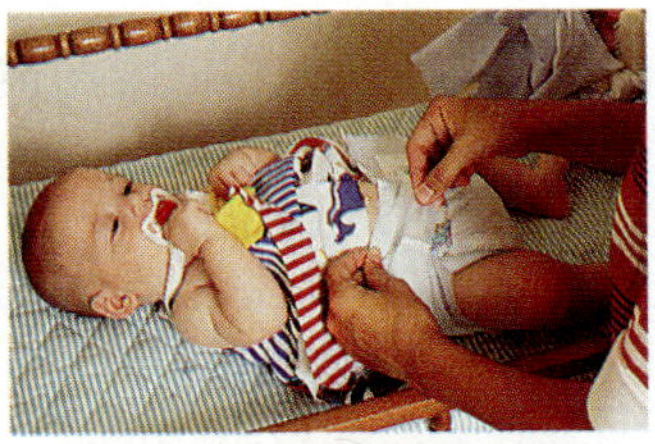

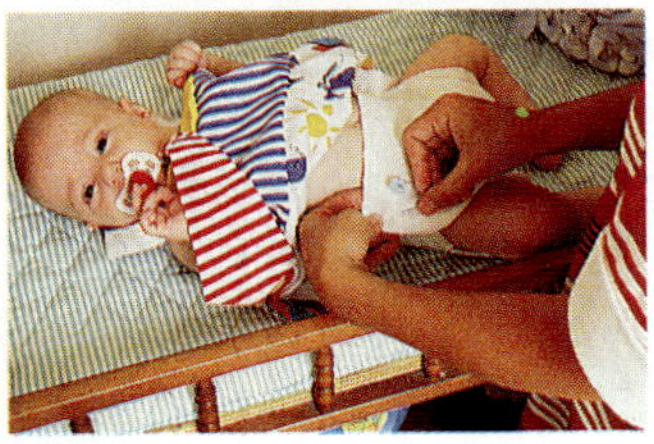

Step 6

Step 7

Around the World

The preschools of the Italian city of Reggio Emilia (REJ-joe ay-MEE-lee-ah) are designed to encourage creativity and love of learning and exploration. Children paint pictures on the classroom windows. They send letters to one another through the classroom "communication center." Classrooms even have dressing rooms with costumes for children who wish to "disguise" themselves for the day.

Keeping Children Safe

Part of being a good caregiver involves watching both the children and their surroundings. Your job is to make sure those under your care are safe, both inside and outside the home.

Indoors

When you're caring for small children, think about how *they* see things. Try getting down on the floor to check for anything that could hurt a crawling baby. Look for any small items a young child might put in his or her mouth. (Young children explore *everything* with their mouths.) Electrical outlets are less tempting to a child if they are covered. If this hasn't been done, put a chair or another large object in front of the outlet to keep the child away. Avoid placing items on the edge of a table where a crawling infant or toddler might pull them off.

The most important step you can take to keep children safe is to stay with them all the time. Until children are about five, don't let them stay in the bathroom alone. They may lock themselves in the room or get into the medicine cabinet where dangerous items like medicines and razor blades are stored.

Safety is very important when you bathe a child. Make sure you never leave young children alone in a bathtub. Even a minute away to answer the phone or get clean clothes can be tragic.

Stairways can be dangerous to children of all ages. Infants and younger toddlers can fall down stairs very easily. You may want to install and fasten gates at the top and bottom of stairs. Older toddlers and preschoolers need to be taught to hold onto the handrail to prevent falls.

Never leave a young child alone in the bathtub. If you must answer the telephone, take the child with you.

MEETING SPECIAL NEEDS

Encouraging Gifted Children

Children who have an especially high level of ability in one or more areas, such as reading, math, music, or art, are known as gifted children. They often learn to read before starting school and enjoy adult company. Gifted children may constantly ask questions that show surprisingly advanced thought.

Gifted children need to be challenged without making them feel superior to, or different from, other children. Many schools and communities have programs that provide stimulating activities for gifted children.

Doors and Windows

Make sure that all windows and outside doors are locked when small children are around. This will keep intruders out and the child safely inside. Falls from windows are more common than you might think. Safety is especially important in high-rise apartment buildings where windows can be many stories above the ground.

Poisons, Matches, and Lighters

Many ordinary products can be dangerous for children. Some are poisonous if swallowed. Others cause damage if breathed into the lungs or if they touch the skin or eyes. Common household poisons include insecticides, cleaning fluids and powders, furniture polish, and drugs, such as baby aspirin and vitamin pills. Even many houseplants are poisonous. Store poisonous products in a locked place.

How can you tell if a child has been poisoned? Here are some symptoms that can give you a clue:

- Choking, coughing, nausea, or dizziness.
- Unconsciousness or difficulty breathing.
- Vomiting from swallowing poisons or chemicals (may cause some burns around the mouth).
- Skin rashes or burns.

If you suspect that a child has been poisoned, immediately call the poison control center. **Poison control centers** have a special staff of people who advise and treat poison

SAFETY CHECK✓

Lead poisoning can cause anemia and permanent brain damage. Sources of lead include painted surfaces (often found in older homes), magazines, some pottery, lead water pipes, and some insecticides. Here are some ways to prevent lead poisoning:

- Keep children busy and away from possible sources of lead poisoning.
- Do not let children eat anything but food.
- Keep children from chewing on paint, plaster, or wood surfaces such as window sills.
- Cover walls with paneling or vinyl wallpaper to cover up possible sources of lead if you own a home.
- If you rent a home, have your landlord fix the walls and ceilings — it's the law in most states.

When choosing toys for children, be sure that they are unbreakable, too large to swallow, and free of sharp edges and small parts. Be sure to keep toys clean, too!

victims. They are often located in hospitals. People at the center will tell you exactly what to do. If your community doesn't have a poison control center, call a hospital emergency room or a doctor right away.

Matches and lighters can be deadly in little hands, so keep them out of reach. Also, keep children away from ranges, wood-burning stoves, heaters, hot water faucets, and hot drinks.

Toys

Some toys can be highly dangerous to infants and small children. When you give a toy to a baby, sooner or later it will go into the baby's mouth. Be sure that each toy you give a baby is unbreakable, too large to swallow, free of sharp edges that can cut, and free of small parts that can come off and be swallowed. Also, be sure the toy is clean, since it may eventually go into the baby's mouth.

Beware of noise-making guns and other toys that make very loud sounds. Some can damage hearing. Toys with long strings or cords may also be dangerous. The cords can become wrapped around an infant's neck and cause choking. Never hang toys with long strings, cords, loops, or ribbons in cribs or playpens where children can get tangled in them.

You need to consider the safety of toys for older children, too. Be certain toys are in good working condition. Don't let children play with broken toys or use them as they were not intended. Five-year-old Kelvin wanted to give his two-year-old sister a ride in his plastic wheelbarrow. His father explained that the wheelbarrow can only carry plastic tools and toys. It is not strong enough to hold Alicia — and neither is Kelvin.

Outdoors

The world gets bigger for children as they begin to play outdoors. Caregivers must supervise young children at all times wherever they go.

- ***Streets and Roads.*** Never let children play in the street or road, and teach them not to chase balls that roll into the street. Fasten gates if the yard is fenced in. When children are old enough, show them the proper way to cross streets and help them cross safely. Most children are active and want to be independent. If you're not careful, they can dart away from you and into the street without thinking. Point out rules for bicycle safety for older children.
- ***Wading and Swimming Pools.*** Another place to keep a sharp eye on children is a wading pool or swimming pool. Never leave children alone in a pool of any kind.
- ***Playgrounds.*** Most neighborhood playgrounds can provide wonderful entertainment for the children in your care. Check the condition of the play equipment to see if it looks safe. Don't let children play on broken or damaged equipment.

Children need supervision as they play outside. Sometimes children are so caught up in their play that they don't realize when situations are dangerous. Keep a close watch on children at all times.

Handling Emergencies

Suppose you were walking through the park where children were playing on the equipment. Would you know what to do if a child fell? When Ruben saw this happen, he remained calm. His quiet, soothing approach was reassuring to the injured child.

While evaluating the situation, Ruben decided that there might be serious injury. The angle of the little boy's arm just didn't look right. Ruben would not let anyone move the boy because that might worsen the injury. He kept the child warm by covering him with his own jacket. He then told the boy's friend to go to the nearest house to get help.

It was this incident that prompted Ruben to take a first aid course. He wanted to know more about handling emergencies in the future. **First aid courses** are available in schools and through the Red Cross and other community agencies. They provide instruction in basic emergency care for injuries of all types.

TAKING ACTION

Gwen is considered an entrepreneur by everyone who knows her. (As you learned in Chapter 7, an entrepreneur is someone who owns and manages his or her own business.) Among other projects, she plans to organize an informal babysitting pool in your neighborhood. Gwen has checked around and discovered many families in need of babysitters. She plans to maintain contact with each family, coordinate their needs and schedules, provide them with responsible babysitters, and collect a portion of each babysitting fee in order to run her service and earn a profit.

She needs to recruit six teenagers who will make excellent babysitters. The ages of the children to be cared for range from one to five. She asks you if you're interested and to suggest friends who would be right for the job.

Using Your Resourcefulness

- Name and evaluate six personal qualities or skills that make someone a good babysitter.
- Would you be interested in such a job? Why or why not? Do you have friends who would be right for the job? Who? Why?
- What qualities and skills does Gwen need to be a successful entrepreneur?

Chapter 16 Review

Summary

In this chapter, you have read about:

- Helping children learn about their world through play.
- Making children's mealtime safe and enjoyable.
- Keeping children safe in the home.
- Identifying unsafe toys.
- Supervising children outdoors.
- Babysitting for children.

Facts to Recall

1. Explain how adults can play with infants.
2. How is a toddler's play different from an infant's? What kinds of toys do they like?
3. List four "quiet play" activities that preschoolers enjoy.
4. Why shouldn't you heat an infant's bottle in a microwave? How should you heat the bottle?
5. How is following a routine helpful to young children at bedtime?
6. What is the most important step you can take to keep children safe?
7. Name four common household poisons. What should you do if you suspect a child has been poisoned?
8. List four characteristics of a toy that is safe for a baby.
9. Identify six characteristics of a good babysitter.

Ideas to Explore

1. Of the four stages of childhood discussed here — infancy, toddler, preschooler, and school-age — which do you think is the most exciting for the child? Explain your answer.
2. How are the needs of children with physical and mental disabilities and the needs of gifted children similar? What challenges do both face?

Activities to Try

1. Imagine yourself as an infant, a toddler, or a preschooler. Write a short story about an everyday event, such as a meal or a trip to a grocery store, as you experience it.
2. Plan a day's schedule for an infant, toddler, or preschooler. Include such things as: what toys you will give the child to play with; what activities you will do with him or her; what you will feed the child, and if and when the child will nap.
3. Get down on a child's eye level and find anything that might be a safety hazard for a child. Identify ways of eliminating the potential hazards.

LINK TO *Art*

ART MATERIALS AND EQUIPMENT

Children use all of their senses in learning. One way to encourage learning and creative expression in children is through art. Put together a variety of materials and equipment — such as tempera paint, finger paint, paper, crayons, clay, paste, felt and scraps of lace and trims, and safety scissors — you think would be helpful to have in a "babysitter's bag." Remember to keep safety in mind as you gather materials. Avoid small items that could cause choking and poisonous materials.

CHAPTER

17 A Look at Parenting

OBJECTIVES

- *Discuss important considerations in the decision to become a parent.*
- *Describe the problems that result when teens become parents.*
- *Identify and explain the responsibilities of parenthood.*
- *Identify resources available to parents.*

TERMS TO LEARN

- ***parenting***
- ***nurturing***
- ***discipline***
- ***time out***

"Let's have a show of hands. How many of you plan to get a degree in parenting someday?"

Virgil thought Mr. Antoine's question was an attempt at humor. In fact, the whole class reacted the same way — until they gave it some thought. As Mr. Antoine pointed out, hardly a job in society is tackled without some kind of training, yet every day people become parents without any formal preparation. There is no aptitude test. There is no supervisor. There are no evaluations. When mistakes are made, however, a price is paid — by parents and children.

The Parenting Question

People have children for different reasons. Not all reasons are good ones. They may feel pressure from family or friends. They may want to pass on the family name and heredity. They may simply have children because it is the thing to do. The decision to have children should be taken more seriously than this.

Deciding to Be a Parent

A decision about becoming a parent should be made carefully with a great deal of thought. People must first ask themselves, "Do we want to have children?" For many people, having children because they want them is the right decision. Having children just because "everyone does" or because of pressure from others, may not be the best reason for having children. Remaining childless may be the right decision for some.

People who are committed to loving and caring for children may deal with a second question — when to have children. They are ready to ask:

- "Do we have enough money to support ourselves and the baby on our own?"
- "Have we finished our schooling?"
- "How will a baby affect our relationship at this time? What about our social life?"
- "Can we make the personal sacrifices needed to care for another person?"
- "What do we know about babies, children, and the responsibilities of parenthood?"

Making the decision to become a parent requires a great deal of communication and thought.

AROUND THE WORLD

Social and economic conditions in Germany make it more difficult for people to decide to become parents. The cost of living in Germany is very high, often requiring that both a husband and a wife work. However, day care is hard to find, so if a couple decides to have children, one parent must stay home to care for them. About half of all German couples have no children. The government is trying to help. It offers child support payments to couples who otherwise could not afford to have children. It also uses advertisements to promote parenthood.

The answers to these questions can help a couple decide when to have children. Waiting can give them a better start in life and make it easier and more enjoyable to raise children later.

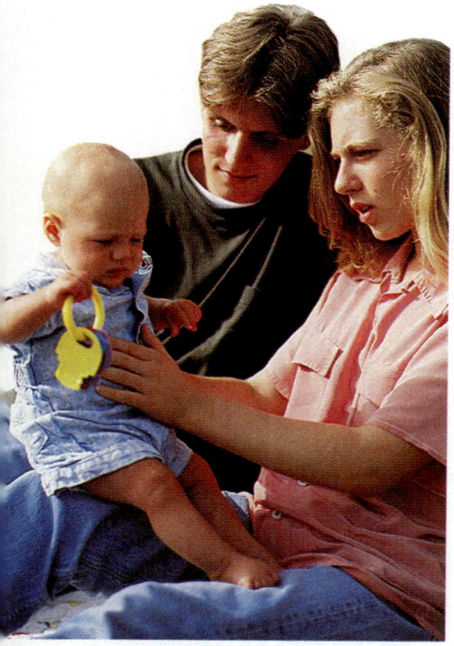
Teen parents face many difficult challenges.

Teens as Parents

Parenthood too soon is tough in many ways. That's why there is so much concern about the increase in the number of teen parents. Parenthood disrupts the lives of teens and pushes them down a difficult road they are not ready to handle. It can hurt the children, too. Many are raised by parents without the resources, knowledge, and readiness needed to be *good* parents.

Often the responsibility for the child falls mainly on the mother. Some teen fathers take an active role in parenting. Many, however, don't live up to their legal and moral responsibilities to their child. If either teen parent drops out of school, the lack of a diploma becomes a lifelong barrier to a good job.

Do you think most teens are emotionally, socially, and financially ready for parenthood? Are they ready to make the personal sacrifices needed to provide total care for another person? What can you personally do to help solve this problem?

The Responsibilities of Parenthood

Have you ever watched or played a team sport at school? Imagine what it would be like for a team to go out on the field or court with very little idea of what they were supposed to do. They would probably lose the game.

You can lose at anything in life, or at least have a tough time, when you don't know what you are doing. Parenting is no exception. **Parenting** is the process of caring for children and helping them grow and develop. Many parenting skills are learned by trial and error. There are better ways. Reading, talking, and thinking about these skills early can help.

Remember that parenting skills are useful to many people. Parents are not the only ones who care for children. Relatives, friends, and professional child care workers all do, too. These people need these skills as much as parents do. Knowing what the responsibilities of parenting are and how to carry them out can make for success when caring for children in any situation.

Meeting Physical Needs

Try making a list of the physical needs that children have. The first things that come to mind are probably food, clothing, and shelter. Did you think to include health needs? The foods children eat must be healthy and contain everything they need to grow and develop properly. They need adequate rest and exercise too. Medical care and protection against common childhood diseases, such as diptheria, polio, and measles, must also be provided. A knowledgeable parent is better able to take care of all this.

Teaching Children

Can you imagine knowing nothing? That's the way an infant begins life. Immediately, caregivers begin the infant's learning process. Parents must provide the tools and opportunities for intellectual development of their children.

Reading to children and looking at pictures is a special time for families. It not only encourages intellectual development, but also provides some time to enjoy each other as a family.

As a parent or other caregiver, what can you do? Talk, read, and listen to children from the time they are born. Avoid baby talk so that children learn correct language skills. Provide opportunities for children to play and learn. Most communities have a number of resources, such as library story hours, that can help satisfy children's intellectual needs.

Nurturing Children

Children need a great deal of **nurturing** (NUR-chur-ing). This means giving love, affection, attention, and encouragement. Without nurturing, they may not develop right physically, intellectually, socially, or emotionally. Nurturing makes children feel secure and accepted as they are. It gives them a sense of worth and adequacy. It also helps them relate well to others. Children who are comfortable with themselves and secure in the family can reach out to others more easily.

Guiding Children

Through guidance, parents and caregivers encourage appropriate behaviors in children. How is this dad providing guidance?

Through effective guidance or **discipline**, parents and other caregivers provide the training that helps children become responsible and cooperative. Many people think of guidance and discipline only in terms of punishment, however, it is much more. Effective discipline helps children learn to get along with others and deal with their own feelings in acceptable ways. Gradually, children begin to see why certain actions are right or wrong. They learn to control their own behavior and take responsibility for their actions.

One way that parents provide guidance is by example. Children imitate what adults say and do. Setting a good example often works better than telling children what to do.

Another way of providing guidance is to explain what behavior is inappropriate and why it is inappropriate. Children need to know what they're doing wrong, why it's wrong, and what should be done instead. When Craig grabbed a book from another child in the doctor's waiting room, his mother said to him, "She chose that book first, Craig. Which one of these would you like to read?"

Messages must be suited to a child's age and level of understanding. At first, you do not need to explain the reasons behind what is expected. Saying, "Pat the kitty," along with a demonstration of gentle handling, is sufficient. Later, simple reasoning may be added: "It hurts the cat when you pull her tail. If you want to play with her, you will have to be gentle."

Praise is an important part of guiding children. Children feel good about themselves when given praise. They are also more likely to continue the desired behavior.

Setting simple and clear limits of behavior is another way to guide children. Children both want and need limits. They don't have the maturity to make good judgments in all areas of their life. Limits help them know what is acceptable, appropriate, and safe for them to do.

A mistake or accident is not misbehavior.

Handling Misbehavior

When children break limits, discipline takes on another role. Parents need to respond to misbehavior in some way. The aim is to help children learn appropriate behavior.

Knowing when to discipline can be tricky. A mistake is not misbehavior. Andrew dropped a glass of milk because he lacked coordination. He needed encouragement and help in cleaning up the spill, not angry words. When three-year-old Sheri pulled up the tulips by the roots, she was only trying to find out what makes them grow. She needed some explanation, not discipline.

Deliberate misbehavior, on the other hand, needs a stronger response and should be appropriate to the child's level of understanding. Discipline can be handled in several ways. Taking away privileges is one method used. For misbehaving, Mattie was not allowed to go outdoors to play with a friend for the afternoon. Enforcing this was hard for Mattie's grandmother, since she had to keep Mattie inside and deal with her mood for the afternoon. It was worth the effort, though, because Mattie learned something that would affect her future behavior.

"Time out" is often helpful in handling misbehavior.

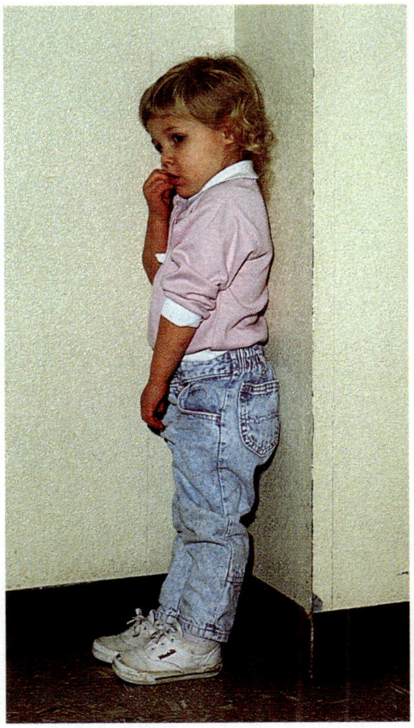

Ignoring misbehavior is another discipline technique. Devon always whined when he wanted his father to buy him something at the store. When Mr. Talbott gave in, Devon learned that whining worked. Finally Mr. Talbott decided to ignore Devon's whining after giving him a simple "no." Before long Devon gave up whining because it no longer produced results.

Removing a child from the activity for a short period of time can also be helpful. This is called **time out**. A parent might say, "I know you're angry, but you still can't hit people. When you can play without hitting, you may go back with the others." This helps reinforce the idea that the child must learn to control behavior.

Handling discipline correctly takes thought, practice, and dedication. Here are some tips to keep in mind:

- Be consistent in your actions and words. If you laugh at Raoul's action one day and discipline him for the same thing the next, you will confuse him.
- Let children know you mean what you say. If you tell Tanisha that it is bedtime and then allow her to stay up longer, she learns that you didn't really mean it.

- Discipline should not be an outlet for the caregiver's anger or frustration. Instead it should be carried out with thought and control.
- Make sure children understand that you still love them even when you disapprove of their behavior.

Resources for Parents

As any parent can tell you, caring for children can be demanding. Physical and emotional fatigue are common. Anyone who cares for children needs some time to get away on a regular basis. Even two or three hours a week is refreshing. Many couples share child care so that all the burden is not on one parent.

Parents need some time to themselves, too. If a paid babysitter is not possible, family members and friends may offer to help out. Taking turns giving each other some time off works well for many people.

Occasionally, a parent may feel at risk of hurting a child. Actions that injure a child either emotionally or physically cannot be allowed to happen. Parents must seek help if they cannot handle their own emotions. Many telephone directories have information on service agencies and hot lines where support can be sought.

TAKING ACTION

Van and Meegan, both 18, are planning their futures. They've been dating for two years, and they want to get married soon and have a child. They think of themselves as caring and responsible teenagers, but Meegan's family is extremely upset by her plans. They want her to go to college and wait several years to marry Van.

The young couple hope to live with Van's parents until they can afford to rent an apartment of their own. So far, the only jobs Van has been able to find pay minimum wage, so Meegan is looking for work, too. They know they're going to face a lot of stress and pressure, but they believe their relationship is strong enough to last. They want to know your opinion about their plans.

Using Your Resourcefulness

- What do you think of Meegan and Van's plans? Are they ready to become parents? Why or why not?
- What resource materials can help them determine the costs of raising a baby? How much will it cost them to raise a child for the first three years?
- In your opinion, what are the three most important personal qualities or skills that make a successful parent?

Chapter 17 Review

Summary

In this chapter, you have read about:

- How people decide if and when to have children.
- The problems facing teen parents.
- Parents' responsibilities for meeting children's physical, intellectual, and emotional needs.
- How parents and other caregivers provide guidance and discipline for children.
- When and how to take action when children misbehave.
- The resources that are available to parents.

Facts to Recall

1. What are three questions that people should ask themselves in deciding when to have children?
2. How can becoming a parent too soon hurt the parents, their children, and society?
3. What is parenting?
4. Besides food, clothing, and shelter, what physical needs do children have?
5. What is nurturing? How does it benefit children?
6. Identify three ways in which parents provide positive discipline and guidance.
7. Name three ways that parents can deal with misbehavior.
8. Identify two ways in which parents can prevent physical and emotional fatigue, that might result in their hurting their children.

Ideas to Explore

1. Do you think most teens have a realistic view of parenting? If not, in what ways is it unrealistic?
2. In your own words, define discipline and punishment. Are they the same thing? If not, how do they differ?
3. Do you think schools should offer teens more classes on parenting? Where else might people of all ages learn about parenting before having or caring for children?

Activities to Try

1. With a classmate, act out a situation showing a child's misbehavior and the parent's response. Have the rest of the class evaluate the effectiveness of the discipline technique used.
2. As a class, brainstorm ideas and images associated with the word "baby." Evaluate the list. Which ideas or images are positive? Which are negative? Which reflect the responsibilities of raising a child?

LINK TO *Health*

COPING WITH CHILDHOOD PROBLEMS

During childhood, children may experience physical or emotional problems that require special attention. Some children develop unrealistic fears as a result of a frightening experience. Some exhibit aggressive behavior (a tendency to start frequent fights and quarrels) or have temper tantrums. Other special problems of childhood may include hyperactivity (inability to control one's activity or concentrate for a normal length of time), poor performance in school, extreme shyness, or bedwetting.

- Read more about one of these problems and make a brief report to the class.
- Identify the symptoms of the problem, possible causes, and actions parents and caregivers should take to help the child.

CAREER Connections

Get Ready for Your Future Through Volunteering

"A friend and I recently volunteered to become summer interns at Camp Hawthorne — a camp for physically disabled teens. We worked for Ramon Aldonza, our supervisor. Ramon trained us to make sure newcomers are comfortable and help them adjust to their surroundings. For some teens who come here for the first time, the experience is stressful. We act like 'buddies' and end up making all kinds of friends.

"I've also volunteered at the Beverly Child Center in my town. There I played with small children. Some days I taught a new song or game, or helped the children fingerpaint. I felt good about myself because I think it's important to take care of another human being.

"My goal is to be a licensed child care teacher. The child care field is growing due to the number of families with both parents working. These families need proper day care for their children. That means there should be many job opportunities no matter where I want to live. I believe volunteer work paves the road for the future and offers a world of experience right now."

"I've always enjoyed being around kids. During high school, I worked at Camp Hawthorne for physically disabled teens. In college, I majored in physical education. I planned to coach sports at a middle school. However, while counseling at a summer camp for teenagers, I became friends with the camp director. He asked me to assist him full-time and after graduation I agreed. I learned how to run a camp and supervise the staff. Two years later when the director left the job, I replaced him.

"I enjoy introducing teens to nature and all kinds of outdoor activities and sports. However, that's only part of what I like about the job. I don't have to commute to work; I live right on the grounds. I like working with my hands. Off-season my biggest responsibility is maintaining the facilities. I fix roofs, deal with plumbing and electrical problems, and paint cabins.

"Still another part of the job is scheduling the campers and informal fundraising. I meet with and talk to interested organizations about the camp and its needs. I hire all summer camp counselors, cooks, maintenance crew members, and lifeguards. The staff works and plays together, and becomes just like a family over time. I certainly don't expect to make a lot of money at this job, but do I love the work and living in a beautiful countryside."

"Teacher, public-relations expert, business person — like Ramon, I'm all these things. I received a bachelor's degree in early childhood education and taught for several years. Now I am the director of the Beverly Children's Center. Companies in the area set up the center for their employees and the community. Every day I'm responsible for the education and care of up to one hundred infants and young children.

"I spend part of the morning in eight classrooms where I oversee teachers, change diapers, or just play with kids. However, most of the time I make sure the nonprofit center operates smoothly. This includes hiring a staff of 15 to 20 teachers and aides, paying bills, and interacting with parents.

"At weekly staff meetings we discuss curriculum development and the problems and progress of each child. If it sounds like a juggling act — it is. I'm also the mother of two children that need care and attention at home, too. This job requires a love of small children, infinite patience, and a strong sense of humor. I can't imagine doing anything else."

MAKING THE CONNECTION

- Do you think working with young children or teenagers might interest you as a career? Why or why not?
- What related career options do Yvonne, Ramon, and Cindy have with their training? What resource materials can help you learn more about child care careers?
- How might you go about learning business and public relations skills?

UNIT 3

Resources to Manage

CHAPTERS

American M.A.D.E.
MAKING. A. DIFFERENCE. ENVIRONMENTALLY.

CHAPTER

18 Managing Time and Energy

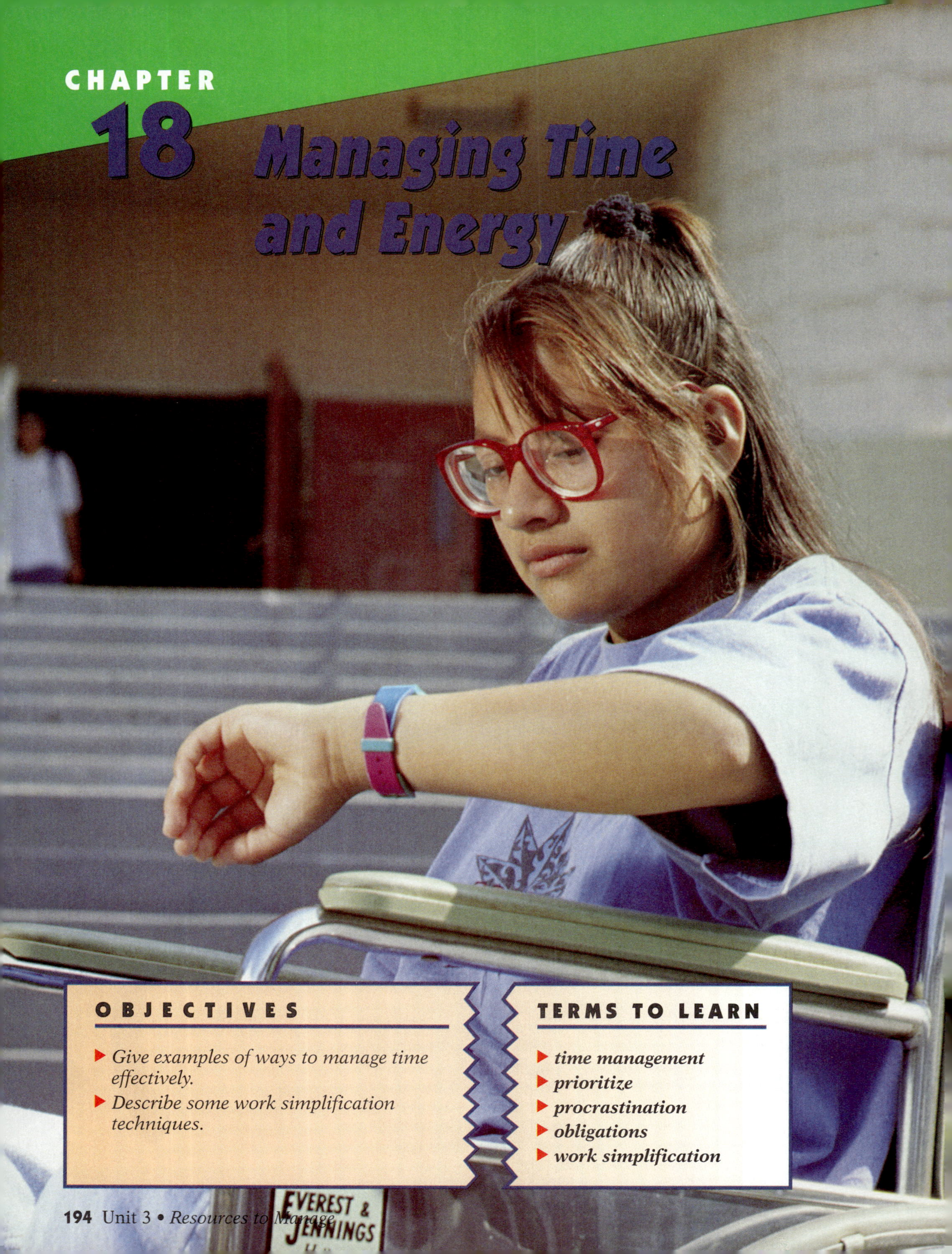

OBJECTIVES

- *Give examples of ways to manage time effectively.*
- *Describe some work simplification techniques.*

TERMS TO LEARN

- ***time management***
- ***prioritize***
- ***procrastination***
- ***obligations***
- ***work simplification***

Mona is an active, full-time student who has a part-time job after school. In addition to classes, homework, and her job, she develops photographs for her school's yearbook. Mona enjoys photography. In fact, she plans on a career as a newspaper photographer. She wishes she had more time to give to photography now, but somehow she always feels rushed. There's just so much to do!

Mona would like to have more time to spend with family and friends and more energy to use for all her activities. "Everyone has the same amount of time each day," she protests. "How do some people accomplish so much and still have time to relax, while my days are a race with the clock — a race that leaves me exhausted?"

Does Mona's complaint sound familiar to you? Do you often find yourself short of time and energy? You can stretch your time and energy resources by learning to manage them more efficiently.

Managing Your Time

Everything that you do requires a certain amount of time. Do you ever say "yes" to a number of activities and then wonder how you will find the time to do them all? When you agree to participate in an activity, you are agreeing to spend some time on it. You can be sure you will have enough time to go around if you take charge of your time and manage it.

Building some extra time into your plan gives you some flexibility when projects take longer than expected.

Around the World

A recent survey of how people in Japan and the United States spend their time produced some interesting results. Adults in both countries spend about the same amount of time working, eating, and sleeping, and on leisure activities. However, Japanese children spend a vastly different amount of time on school work than American children. Japanese school children spend about 55% more hours in class than American children and about five times as many hours on homework. What factors might be responsible for this great difference?

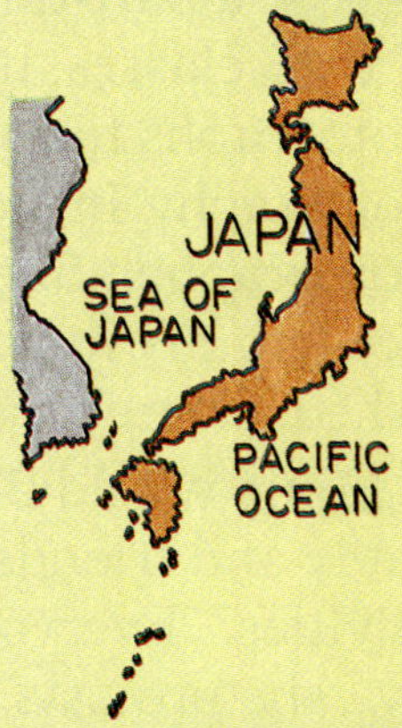

Time management involves planning your use of time so that you can get the most out of the time you have. Taking charge of your time allows you to do what needs to be done and still have time left for doing those things that you like best.

Becoming an Effective Time Manager

To begin managing your time, look at how you use your time now. Keep a record of your activities in a small notebook for a single day. Include such categories as sleeping, eating, bathing, going to school, studying, working, helping out at home, visiting with friends, participating in sports, etc. As you complete each activity, write down the amount of time you spent on that activity. Then, at the end of the day, total up the time that you have spent on each category. Your record will give you a good idea of where your time goes. You may also be able to see if you are wasting time.

Once you have a picture of your current time use, you can start to improve your time management skills. The following techniques will help you take charge of your time and use it more to your advantage.

- ***Set goals for yourself.*** Decide what you want to accomplish in a certain time period. You might set goals for a day. You could also set goals for a week, a month, or even a year. When you know your goals, write down what tasks you must do in order to achieve them. Then estimate how long it will take you to complete each task. Allow enough time to do the job right without feeling rushed. Establishing goals is a key to successful time management. Goal setting helps you focus on what you need and want to do. It also gets you started on planning your use of time.

- ▶ ***Make a daily "To Do" list.*** Planning ahead saves time. You can follow your daily plan instead of always stopping to think what you should do next. Cross off each task on the list as you complete it. This will allow you to see how much you have succeeded in doing that day. See "How to Make a 'To Do' List" on page 198.

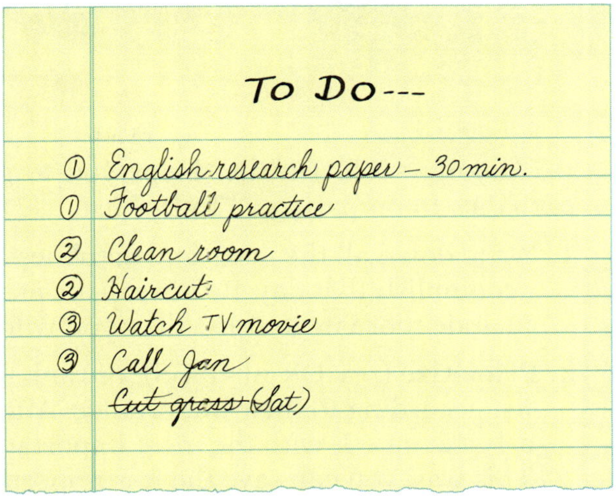

Making a list of things you need to accomplish helps keep you organized and allows you to make the best use of your time.

- ▶ ***Use a monthly calendar to help schedule your time.*** Record important events, meetings, and due dates for the month on your calendar as soon as you know when they will be. Estimate the time that each activity or event will take. This way, you will know how much time is accounted for, and you will be able to prevent scheduling conflicts. Look at your monthly calendar before you say "yes" to anything that will require your time. Use your calendar as a reference when you prepare your daily "To Do" list.
- ▶ ***Group together activities that can successfully be done at once.*** For example, you might be able to make your lunch while you are helping prepare your family's breakfast. You could put your clothes in the washing machine then do your homework while your clothes are washing. You could sew a button on your shirt or blouse while you are talking on the telephone. Be careful, however. Not all activities lend themselves well to doing two things at once. Studying, for instance, requires your full attention. Don't plan to combine studying with watching television.
- ▶ ***Make use of all the time you have, even the short segments.*** You would probably be surprised how much you could accomplish in fifteen minutes or a half hour, if you decided to do so. Instead of wasting short periods because you don't think they are long enough, see how you can make them work effectively for you. Find the right tasks for those times. You might start something and finish it later. Remember that several short periods add up to a lot of time.
- ▶ ***Prevent interruptions whenever possible.*** When people and telephones break into your train of thought, it takes a while to get back on track. You lose time in this process. As a time manager, it is up to you to see that your own schedule gets carried out. Sticking to your schedule often means choosing to stay away from places where you know you will be interrupted.

How to . . .
Make a "To Do" List

Making a "To Do" list helps you to get the most out of each day. In preparing a "To Do" list, use the following steps:

1. Write down all the tasks and activities that you intend to accomplish that day. Be as realistic as possible. Don't include more in your list than you will be able to do.
2. **Prioritize** (pry-OR-uh-TIES), or rank the items on your list according to their importance. After each item, place a 1, a 2, or a 3, with the most important items rating a 1. This way, you can save the less important items for another day if you run out of time.
3. Keep your list handy so that you can cross off items as you complete them.

Putting projects off to the last minute generally results in unnecessary feelings of stress and pressure.

- ***Avoid procrastination.*** Putting off, or postponing, what you have to do is called **procrastination** (proh-KRAS-tuh-NAY-shun). The only result from procrastination is feeling pressured for time when you get around to doing what you have put off until later. Take a positive attitude toward your work. Schedule it, and do it promptly. You will feel good about yourself when your work is complete and you can spend some time having fun.
- ***Build a reward system into your time management approach.*** Rewarding yourself for successes will encourage you to keep taking charge of your time. For example, you could treat yourself to a little free time after you complete your first-priority tasks for the day. You might take a few minutes to talk to a family member or friend. You could also use your time off to just relax. After your reward for a job well done, you will find that you proceed to your next group of tasks refreshed.

Periodically, evaluate how your time management skills are serving you. If you find your "To Do" lists include too much, make the next ones shorter. If you forget to check your monthly calendar, put it in a place where you will remember it. The object is to learn what works and what doesn't so that you can become a better time manager.

Balancing Schoolwork, Family Life, and Activities

Keeping up with your homework and paying attention in class help you get the most out of your class time.

Having enough time for schoolwork, your family, and your friends isn't easy. It means keeping your goals and values in mind as you schedule your use of time. You most likely have **obligations**, or things that you must do or have promised to do. After you finish those, you can spend what time you have left on other activities.

Making Time for Learning

Half of your waking hours are spent at school or doing schoolwork. Thus it is important that you learn to manage your school-related hours well.

You can get more out of class time if you have done your homework and know what the day's subject is about. Then, by listening closely and paying attention, you can better understand what your teacher is talking about. You will also learn the subject matter better and more easily. Take notes on the important points that are presented and discussed in class. Good notes will help jog your memory when you study after class. Also write down assignments, instructions for doing them, and the dates when they are due.

As soon after class as possible, find a few minutes to review your notes. Going over your notes while they are fresh in your mind allows you to clarify the information. You may also find it helpful to rewrite your class notes in a more organized way.

Developing Good Study Skills

Before you sit down to study, gather everything that you will need for your work. This may include pencils, pens, paper, calculator, ruler, eraser, textbooks, and reference books, such as a dictionary.

Take your study materials to a well-lighted place where you will be able to concentrate. Stay away from loud noise and interruptions so that you won't lose study time. Sit at a desk or table rather than on a sofa or bed, where you could easily fall asleep. Avoid stuffy rooms that might make you drowsy. Fresh air will keep you awake and alert for your homework.

Set several goals for your study time. Knowing what you need and want to accomplish will help you make the most of

Studying at a table or desk in a well-lighted place will help you get the most out of your study time. Interruptions like the television and the telephone interfere with what you want or need to accomplish. Getting your studying done early gives you more time to spend with friends and family.

TIPS:
Taking Notes

To take effective notes, try these tips:

- Take notes in outline form, focusing on main ideas.
- Use a few words to write down the main ideas and supporting details. It's impossible to write down every word your teacher says.
- Abbreviate words when you can. For example, use "3" instead of "three."
- Double or triple space your notes. You can fill in more details later if needed.
- Review your notes frequently.
- Use different colored highlighter markers to emphasize main ideas and supporting details.

your time. Study your most difficult subjects first. Then go on to the less difficult ones. Reward yourself with a five- or ten-minute break after you have accomplished a certain amount. Use your break to stand up and stretch, walk around, drink a glass of water, or eat a piece of fruit. By keeping you refreshed, short breaks may save you time in the long run.

Making Time for Family, Friends, and Activities

When you aren't involved in school activities, there are still many things that you may want or need to do. It takes time to be a good family member and to be a good friend. In addition, you need time for yourself to pursue your interests or relax. Careful time management is required to have plenty of time for everything.

One way to avoid time shortages in your out-of-school life is planning. Decide ahead of time what you will do, and set aside the time for it. Make plans with your parents or your brothers and sisters. Record those plans on your monthly calendar as discussed earlier in the chapter. Plan to share a favorite activity with a friend or friends. Find out when everyone is free, and commit to that time.

Planning ahead keeps you from wasting time. You won't suddenly find yourself with nothing to do. It also helps you to focus on what is important to you. People tend to spend more time on the things that they value. If you value time with your brother, you might plan to talk with him, play catch, or go fishing. If you and your friend share an interest in art, you might skip watching television to go to the museum. To manage your time well, you need to make choices — often based on the things that you value — about how to get the most out of it. This might mean limiting telephone time in order to exercise. It could also mean giving some of your time to help others.

Managing Your Energy

Do you operate in high gear in the morning and slow down in the afternoon? Perhaps, instead, you get off to a slow start but become so energetic at night that it's hard to go to sleep. Whether you are a morning person or a night person, you — like all people — have a regular energy cycle. It helps to remember this and schedule jobs that require alertness and energy when you are at your peak.

You can increase your energy level in general by improving your health habits. Eat healthful foods. Get adequate rest. Exercise regularly and avoid harmful substances. Chapter 37 will give you more specifics about health habits and good health.

Another important aspect of energy management is saving energy through **work simplification**. This means finding the easiest and quickest way to do each job well. Here are some ideas that will help you conserve your energy as you work:

Day people rise early, do their best work in the morning, slow down in the afternoon, and fade in the evening. Night people are slow starters in the morning, pick up in the afternoon, and are at their best during the evening.

- ***Analyze each job, thinking about what it involves.*** Can any steps in the process be omitted or combined? For example, when you wash dishes by hand, you may also be drying them. If you skip this step and let the dishes air dry, you can do something else with the time you would have spent drying dishes.
- ***Always use the best tool or utensil for the job.*** If you choose the wrong tool just because it is easily found, you will waste time and possibly energy, too.
- ***Conserve your energy by conserving motion.*** For example, you might use a tray, basket, or cart to carry several items at once so you only have to make one trip instead of several trips.
- ***Organize your storage areas.*** Store articles where they are used most often. Place the items that you use frequently where you can easily see and reach them. Make use of free or inexpensive containers to separate articles in drawers and on shelves. That way, you won't waste your energy hunting for things when you need them.

You can probably think of many other ways to save yourself time and energy. Give your own ideas a try, along with the suggestions in this chapter. Do whatever works best for you in managing your time and energy. The important thing is for you to take charge of your time and energy resources.

TAKING ACTION

Nicole clears tables and washes dishes at Dino's restaurant four times a week. Her work shift starts at 5 p.m. Sometimes she doesn't get home until after midnight.

Trying to juggle schoolwork, swim team practice, her job, and a social life puts Nicole under strain. If she has a test, she ends up studying after work and misses out on a good night's sleep. Nicole gets sick more often since she started her job. Her grades have also suffered. She breaks dates on weekends simply because she's too tired to go out. However, Nicole insists that she needs her job for extra spending money and to help save for college. She comes to you for some help with her schedule.

Using Your Resourcefulness

- What options does Nicole have to manage her time and energy more effectively?
- How would you suggest that she change or eliminate activities to reduce her stress?
- List two or three activities that you would like to add to your life. How would you manage your time and energy to get the most out of these?
- Make a monthly schedule of your own. Indicate how you will use your time each day.

Chapter 18 Review

Summary

In this chapter, you have read about:

- Tips on getting the most out of your time to accomplish what you want.
- Tactics for using study time more efficiently.
- Finding time for out-of-school interests through planning and making choices.
- Managing your energy through work simplification.

Facts to Recall

1. What is time management?
2. How can recording your activities for one day help you begin to manage your time?
3. What does setting goals involve? How does goal setting help you manage your time?
4. Explain how making a daily "To Do" list and using a monthly calendar can help you use your time well.
5. What time management problems are caused by interruptions? By procrastination?
6. Explain how being prepared for class and taking good notes can help you get the most out of class time.
7. How do the things you value affect the way you plan your time?
8. Explain how to organize storage areas to save your energy.

Ideas to Explore

1. What do you find is the biggest obstacle to managing your time? How can it be overcome?
2. Describe an incident in which your values helped you solve a time or energy management problem when one or both were limited.
3. Theresa and Anton have promised to fix a pasta dinner for their family. They must warm the tomato sauce, cook the noodles, prepare a tossed salad, set the table, and clean up the kitchen before serving dinner. Give an example of two tasks that they can do at the same time to save time.
4. Why do you think people procrastinate? How can this habit be corrected?

Activities to Try

1. Make a "To Do" list for one day. Prioritize your tasks. See how many you have accomplished when your class meets again.
2. Write a short paragraph identifying three times during the past week when your schedule has been interrupted. Suggest ways of avoiding those situations in the future.

LINK TO *Science*

IMPROVING EFFICIENCY

The study of *human engineering*, or *ergonomics*, applies scientific knowledge about the human body and behavior to designing and building better tools and equipment. Today, this knowledge is applied to office equipment, farm and industrial machines, and other mechanical devices. The object is to reduce fatigue and health-related problems and to increase speed and accuracy. Human engineering also takes into account the lighting, spacing, ventilation (circulation of fresh air), noise level, and location of equipment. Try to think of ways that a work area or piece of equipment you use at home could be improved to make it easier to use. Draw a sketch of your improved version. Write down the details that support the changes you have made in your improved version.

CHAPTER 19 Managing Money

OBJECTIVES

- *Use records of your income and expenses to make a budget.*
- *Give guidelines for using checking and savings accounts and credit.*

TERMS TO LEARN

- ***income***
- ***expenses***
- ***budget***
- ***endorse***
- ***deposit slip***
- ***check register***
- ***balance***
- ***interest***
- ***credit***

Managing your money effectively is a skill you will need throughout life. Whether you have little money or a great deal, money management skills are still important. People who manage their money well will achieve a balance between money going out and money coming in. They get what they need and want without wasting money on things they don't really need or want. Good money managers are careful not to spend more than they can actually afford. They also plan ahead for future spending. This allows them to meet the costs of their future goals.

Looking at Your Current Financial Picture

Before you can begin managing money better, it helps to know how you're managing money now. You may not even think about where your money goes or about how much money you have for spending and saving. One way to clarify your current financial (money-related) picture is to keep simple financial records. You might keep a weekly record for several weeks and then study and compare these records to learn from them.

To start a weekly record, first write down your **income**. That's the amount of money that you have coming in. It may be the pay you receive from babysitting or from a part-time job. Your income might also come from an allowance that your parents give you. Figure out the total of your weekly income by adding together all money received from various sources. Getting a clear idea of your income will allow you to see how much money you have available for use.

Next, keep track of your **expenses**. These are the things on which you spend money. Common teen expenses include snacks and meals, clothing, and entertainment such as movies.

Learning to manage your money as a teen will be a benefit in adulthood.

Transportation to school is a fixed expense for many teens. What are some of your fixed expenses?

Some expenses come about regularly. They are the same, or about the same, all the time. These are called *fixed expenses*. Many fixed expenses are costs for items and services that you need. Your fixed expenses might include such things as lunch, transportation, savings, and school activity fees. Divide your fixed expenses into categories. Then record how much you spend in each category.

After your fixed expenses, record the flexible ones. *Flexible expenses* vary from time to time. They are often expenses for items and services that you want rather than need. You might decide to buy a concert ticket or spend money on a hobby. In your financial record, write down these costs by category. You will probably find that your categories change each week.

As you study your weekly records, compare the totals of your income and your expenses. Do you spend all the money that you get, or do you have some left over? Look closely at your expenses. Are you spending too much in a particular category? Are you wasting money on things you don't really need? Are you satisfied with your spending habits?

Planning for Better Money Management

After identifying how you are managing money now, you can plan to manage your money better. You can change spending habits that don't please you by making different choices about how you will use your money. For example,

Ben decided to spend less on snacks after school — something he didn't need — and save money for more important things in the future. If you want to save money for future use, you can choose to cut back your spending now.

A good way to accomplish managing your money is to create a **budget**. A budget is a plan for using the money you have available. When you make a budget for yourself, you are setting up financial guidelines. By following these guidelines, you will be able to reach your personal money management goals and live within your income. Here are some tips for creating a budget:

- First, record the income that you plan to have during the period of your budget. Base your income figure on what you learned from keeping weekly records.
- Next, write down what you plan to spend on fixed and flexible expenses. This information should reflect the choices you have made. Be sure to categorize your expenses. On what will you spend your money? How much will you spend? Be as realistic as you can. This will help you make a budget that you can live within.
- Review your budget periodically to see how it is working. If you have allowed too much or too little for some items, adjust your plan accordingly. If you have forgotten one or more expenses, include these as you update your budget.

In working with your budget, you learn to manage your money through practice. As time passes, your money management skills will be improving.

AROUND THE WORLD

The price of goods and services is not always the best indicator of the cost of living in a country. A more accurate measure is *purchasing power,* or the amount of goods and services your money can buy. For example, a recent survey by the United Bank of Switzerland shows that Zurich, Switzerland is one of the most expensive cities in the world in which to live, based on expenses such as housing, clothing, and food. However, the study also shows that workers there are among the highest-paid in the world, and that their purchasing power is 75% higher than the worldwide average. Workers in Mexico City are among the world's lowest-paid, and their purchasing power is only 21% of the average. In more concrete terms, the average consumer in Zurich has to work 20 minutes to earn enough to buy a hamburger; in Mexico City, it takes almost four hours of work — half a day — to buy a hamburger.

There are several types of financial institutions including banks, savings and loan associations, and credit unions.

Understanding and Using Financial Services

Financial institutions, such as banks and credit unions, can help you manage your money. These businesses offer services to assist you, both as you spend and as you save. You may use some of these services now. Others will be part of your future. By learning how the main financial services work, you will be better equipped to use them when you need to.

Checking Accounts

You've probably seen your parents writing checks as they make purchases and pay bills. You may also have received checks as payment for work or, perhaps, as gifts. Checks represent money that has been placed in a checking account by the person who writes the checks. A check is a written order to a financial institution to pay a specific amount to the person or business named on the check.

Having a checking account is a convenience. It means that you can use checks instead of always carrying money to pay in cash. You can send checks through the mail instead of paying bills in person. Never send cash through the mail — it can be easily stolen.

When you open a checking account, you will be agreeing to certain terms, or conditions. One term is that you will not write checks for more than the amount of money in your

When writing a check, you need to include the date the check was written, the person or business to be paid, and the amount of money to be paid written in numerals and words. You also need to endorse or sign your check.

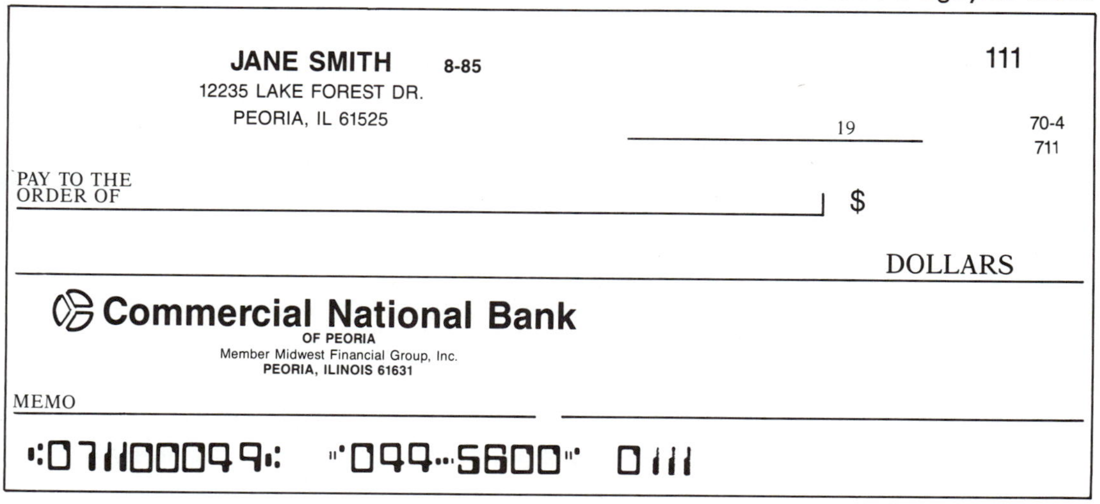
JANE SMITH 8-85
12235 LAKE FOREST DR.
PEORIA, IL 61525

111

19

70-4
711

PAY TO THE ORDER OF $

DOLLARS

Commercial National Bank
OF PEORIA
Member Midwest Financial Group, Inc.
PEORIA, ILINOIS 61631

MEMO

⑆071100049⑆ ⑈044⑉5600⑈ 0111

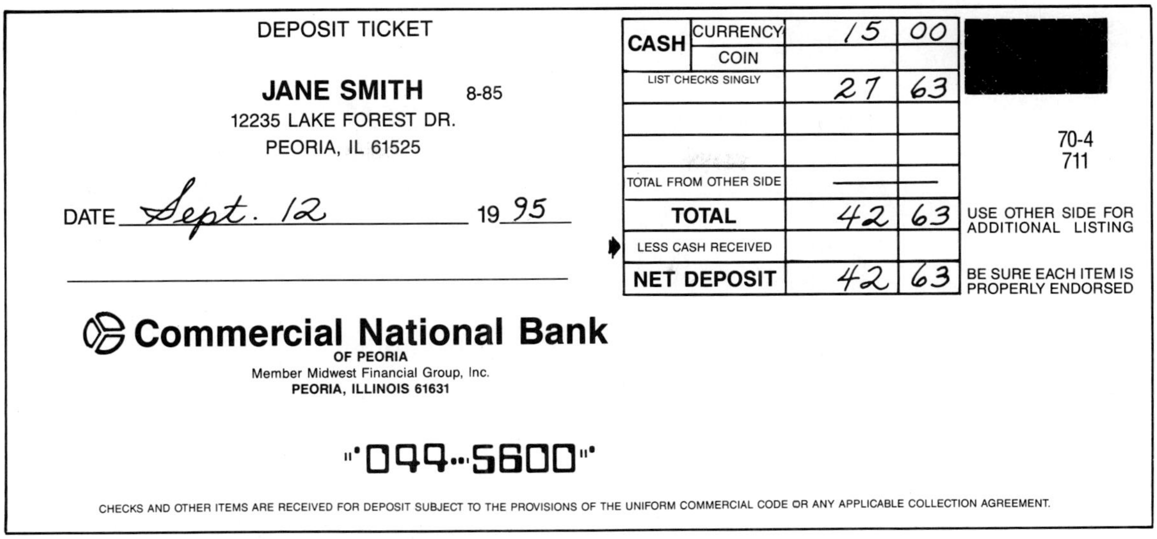

DEPOSIT TICKET

JANE SMITH 8-85
12235 LAKE FOREST DR.
PEORIA, IL 61525

DATE Sept. 12 19 95

CASH	CURRENCY	15	00
	COIN		
LIST CHECKS SINGLY		27	63
TOTAL FROM OTHER SIDE		—	—
TOTAL		42	63
LESS CASH RECEIVED			
NET DEPOSIT		42	63

[redacted]

70-4
711

USE OTHER SIDE FOR ADDITIONAL LISTING

BE SURE EACH ITEM IS PROPERLY ENDORSED

Commercial National Bank
OF PEORIA
Member Midwest Financial Group, Inc.
PEORIA, ILLINOIS 61631

"'099"'5600"'

CHECKS AND OTHER ITEMS ARE RECEIVED FOR DEPOSIT SUBJECT TO THE PROVISIONS OF THE UNIFORM COMMERCIAL CODE OR ANY APPLICABLE COLLECTION AGREEMENT.

You must fill out a deposit slip to deposit money into your checking account.

account. Another common term is that you will pay fees for the handling of your account by the bank. There may be a service charge every month. Some financial institutions may charge a fee for each check you write. Fees on checking accounts vary greatly depending on where you have your account and how much you keep in it. Compare the terms on accounts at different financial institutions. Before you select your account, be sure you understand the terms.

To begin using your checking account, you must first make a deposit, or put money into your account. You will deposit money periodically, as it is needed, to cover checks you will be writing. You may deposit cash or checks written to you by other people or businesses. Before depositing a check, you have to **endorse** it, or sign your name on the back. (This transfers your right to the check over to someone else — in this case, the bank.) Each time you make a deposit, you will need to fill out a **deposit slip**. This slip must have your checking account number on it. If the number is not preprinted, you will have to write the number on the slip. On the deposit slip, you write in the amount of cash being deposited (if any) and also individually list the amount of each check (if any) you want to deposit. You then total the amounts of all checks and the cash. If you want any cash back, you enter the amount desired and subtract it from the total. Your final total will be the amount you will be depositing in your account.

Your checkbook has two important parts. The first is the checks, which you will fill out as needed by writing the date, the name of the person or business you are paying, an amount written first in figures then in words, and your signature.

How to . . .

Reconcile Your Bank Account Statement with Your Checkbook Balance

Follow these simple steps to reconcile your bank account statement with the balance in your check register:

1. Write the last balance shown on your bank account statement.

$____________

2. Total any deposits you have made that do not appear on this statement or any previous statements. **Add** this amount to the one that appears on your statement.

New Total: $____________

3. Write down all the checks that you have written that do not appear on this or any previous statement. Then total all the amounts.

Check Number	Amount of Check
____________	______________
____________	______________
____________	______________
____________	______________
____________	______________
____________	______________

Total of checks still out: $____________

4. After you have added the amounts for the checks that are still out, *subtract* this total from the total in Step 2. This amount should agree with the balance in your check register.

Final Balance: $____________

The second part of your checkbook is for keeping a record of your account as you go along. It is called a **check register**. Each time you make a deposit or write a check, you record this information in your check register. When you make a deposit, you record the amount deposited and the day's date and then add this amount to the amount you already have in your account. When you write a check, you record the check number, the date the check was written, the party paid, and the amount. Then you subtract the amount of the check from the total you have in your account. The new total is called your **balance**, or the total amount of money remaining in your account.

It's as easy as that. Addition and subtraction are the only math skills required for using a checkbook. Careful record keeping is essential, however, if you want to manage your checkbook well.

Your financial institution will also keep records on your account and send them to you. These records, called statements, will tell you which checks have been paid, what deposits have been made, and what fees you have been charged. Go over each statement to be sure that your own records are correct. Subtract any fees you haven't already subtracted. Be certain your balance agrees with that on the statement. You may also receive your cancelled, or paid, checks back when you receive your statements. If you do, keep these as proof of bills you have paid and money you have spent.

Savings Accounts

Unlike checking accounts, savings accounts don't help you manage the money that you spend. Instead, their purpose is to assist you in managing your efforts to save. You might save money toward an expensive purchase. You might also put money away to pay for college. Families often save up for future vacations, new cars, new homes, and unplanned expenses, such as emergencies.

One advantage of savings accounts is that they keep your money safe until later. They also help you increase the amount you put away by paying you something called interest. **Interest** is the money a financial institution pays you at regular intervals for allowing it to use your money. The interest will be a certain percentage of the amount in your savings. Different financial institutions pay different percentages, or interest rates. It pays to compare interest rates before opening your account.

Many people open savings accounts to save for large expenditures such as a college education or an automobile.

You can start your savings account with a deposit of as little as $10. As with checking accounts, you may deposit cash or checks. You may also need to fill out a deposit slip.

When you are ready to use money from your savings, you can take out, or withdraw, part or all of your balance. The procedure for this is to complete a withdrawal slip with your name, account number, signature, and the amount.

You will receive a record of your savings account, showing deposits, withdrawals, and your current balance. This record may be a booklet known as a passbook. For accounts that don't use passbooks, you will be sent printed statements at regular intervals.

▼ Credit ▼

Credit cards are convenient to use. However, you must discipline yourself to purchase only what you can afford.

Right now, you have limited income, and your expenses are relatively low. You probably pay cash for the small number of items and services that you buy. In the future, you will have more income, more expenses, and many more responsibilities. At that time, you may decide to use credit as a tool to help you manage your money. **Credit** is an arrangement by which you purchase things now and are allowed to pay for them later.

One type of credit is loans. With loans, you borrow money from banks, credit unions, or loan companies. You use the money you borrow to pay for your purchases, and you pay back your loan little by little to the lending institution.

Another type of credit is sales credit, which is another name for charge accounts. With this type of credit, you receive your purchase now and pay a store or credit card company later for what you owe.

Both of these types of credit are helpful because, in a sense, they buy time. You don't have to wait until you have all the money you need to make your purchases. Even when you have no shortage of money resources, you may choose to use sales credit. Some people use it all the time because it is convenient not to always have to carry cash. They then pay for their purchases once a month when they receive their statements. Before you decide to use credit, think carefully about the convenience it offers. Also remember that credit is seldom free. It is a service that usually costs.

What Does Credit Cost?

In most instances, using credit costs money. In addition to the money you owe, you must also pay the lender a certain percentage of **interest**. This is the fee you must pay for the privilege of using someone else's money when you use credit, just as a financial institution pays you interest when it uses your money. When you take out a loan, for example, you agree to pay back the amount you borrow — plus interest. Each monthly payment on your loan will include an interest charge. If you use credit cards, you will pay interest unless you pay the total of your bill every month. The interest will be a percentage of the unpaid balance on your credit card account.

Many credit card companies charge 1½ percent a month, which doesn't seem like very much. However, if it takes you a year of 12 monthly payments to pay off your bill, you will be paying 1½ times 12, or 18 percent! This amount adds greatly to the total cost of the items or services you purchase. Since interest rates vary, shop around for credit. You can save money by taking the time to find the lowest rate.

When making purchases with a credit card, be sure to carefully consider the cost of credit.

What Does It Take to Get Credit?

Just as credit users want a good interest rate, businesses that give credit want good customers. Stores, banks, credit unions, and credit card companies prefer to give credit to dependable people.

When you apply for credit, you will be asked to provide information about yourself. Credit businesses will check your information and consider the following:

- ***Your credit rating.*** This is your record of paying debts in the past. Credit businesses look for good credit ratings — ones that reflect prompt, responsible payment.
- ***Your income and your money resources in general.*** Credit businesses want to know if you will have enough money to make payments on your sales credit or loan.
- ***Your property.*** Credit businesses often ask if you own a home, stocks, bonds, or automobiles. The reason for this question is that your property could be sold to get money if you fail to make payments.

Credit businesses do what they can to protect themselves against loss. After all, they are in business, and they want to stay in business.

What Are Your Credit Rights?

Laws have been passed to protect credit users as well as credit businesses. The 1968 Truth-in-Lending Act, for example, guarantees information about what credit really costs.

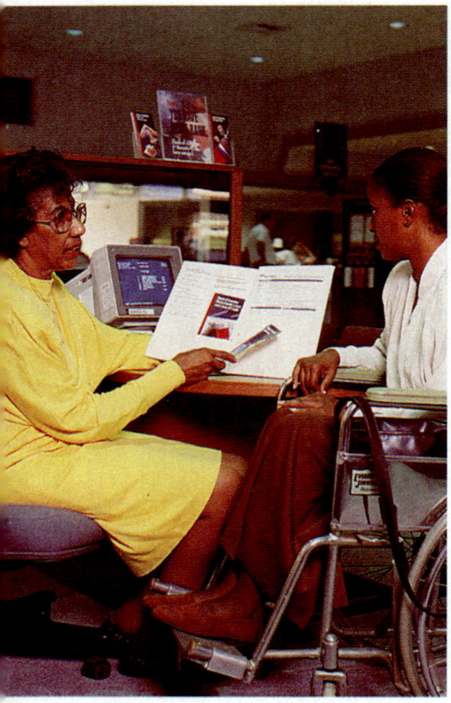

Lenders must tell you the total amount of interest on loans in dollars and cents.

According to this law, lenders must state what the *total* amount of interest on loans will be in dollars and cents. The law also provides that interest for any kind of credit must be stated as yearly costs, or annual percentage rates. With all credit companies stating interest the same way, people can compare credit costs. This allows people to make better decisions about the credit they will use.

The Truth-in-Lending Act also protects people whose credit cards are stolen or lost. According to this law, credit card holders must report the loss of their credit cards promptly. When they do, their responsibility for charges made without their permission is limited.

The advertising of credit is also controlled by law to prevent credit users from being misled. If one credit condition is mentioned in advertising, all other important conditions must also be stated. For example, an advertisement might say that you can purchase a sofa for $10 down. In such a case, the advertisement must also explain that you will pay $10 a week for the next two years.

In 1975, another important law, the Equal Credit Opportunity Act, went into effect. This act makes it illegal to refuse credit to people because of their sex, race, religion, or marital status. The purpose of this law is to prevent discrimination in the awarding of credit privileges.

TAKING ACTION

"I'm a spendaholic," Wendell admits, "and I need your help. By Sunday, any money I've tried to save is long gone. In fact, I'm $15 to $30 short. I was hoping to save for a used car. However, the way I spend money, there's no chance. I asked my mother for a car loan, but she turned me down."

"My weekly allowance is $10, and I earn $60 per week from my part-time job at the car wash. I spend $15 a week or more on fast-food dinners when my mom works late. Going out on weekends costs at least $20, and I spend about $50 a week on everything else. That includes things like basketball tickets, a baseball cap, a cool shirt, or sneakers. It's not like I just throw my money away, but somehow it always disappears."

Using Your Resourcefulness

- Identify some ways that Wendell throws his money away.
- Identify some ways that Wendell could save money on his meals.
- List several activities that would allow Wendell to spend less on weekends and still have fun.
- Prepare a weekly income and expense record that will show Wendell his current financial picture.
- Make a budget for Wendell to help him manage his money better and save $10 a week.

Chapter 19 Review

Summary

In this chapter, you have read about:

- The importance of good money management skills.
- Identifying your spending habits by recording your income and expenses.
- Establishing and following a budget.
- How to use a checking account.
- How savings accounts function.
- The advantages and costs of buying with credit.
- Laws governing how lenders do business.

Facts to Recall

1. Explain the benefits of managing your money well.
2. What can you learn from studying a record of your weekly income and expenses?
3. Explain how to make and follow a budget.
4. Explain how to balance a checking account using a check register.
5. What is the difference between interest paid on savings and interest paid on loans?
6. How does a loan differ from sales credit?
7. Identify two advantages and one disadvantage of using credit.
8. Identify three factors that businesses consider when deciding whether to give credit.
9. According to the Truth-in-Lending Act, how must interest be stated? What is the reason for this?
10. What action is forbidden by the Equal Credit Opportunity Act? What is the purpose of this law?

Ideas to Explore

1. Do you think most teens handle money responsibly? Explain your answer.
2. Do you think it is a good idea to give children a regular, set allowance? Discuss reasons for and against this practice.
3. What responsibilities are involved in having a checking account?
4. Many people spend more than they can afford when using credit. Why do you think this occurs?

Activities to Try

1. Bring to school pamphlets from different financial institutions explaining the services each one offers. As a class, compare them on such points as interest rates on savings accounts, terms of checking accounts, and requirements for receiving credit. What other services do these institutions provide?
2. Do research and then write a short report on different types of financial institutions, such as banks, credit unions, and savings and loans. Explain how they vary in purpose, in services, and in where they get their funds.

LINK TO *Math*

FIGURING SIMPLE INTEREST

Many financial institutions pay *simple interest* — interest paid only on the money you place in your savings account. The interest earned on the account does not earn interest. The following formula is used to figure simple interest: $i = prt$ (interest = principle × rate of interest × time in years). Use this formula to figure the interest earned on the following amounts of money:

- $300 invested at 6% for 6 months
- $275 invested at 4½% for 2 years
- $464 invested at 7% for 1½ years

CHAPTER 20 Consumer Challenges

OBJECTIVES

- Identify factors that influence consumer choices.
- Describe steps wise consumers take when making purchases.

TERMS TO LEARN

- *consumer*
- *impulse buying*
- *comparison shopping*
- *warranty*
- *Better Business Bureau*

Every time you pay for a pizza or a haircut, you are acting as a **consumer**. Consumers are people who purchase and use goods and services. What kind of consumer are you? Do you get the most for your money? Are you satisfied with your purchases, or do you wish you had shopped more wisely? You can learn to improve your consumer skills. This chapter will show you how.

Understanding Influences on Consumers

A good way to start becoming a better consumer is to realize that each purchase involves a choice. You, as the consumer, are the one making the choices. However, many factors influence your choices.

- ***Your income affects your spending.*** You can't spend more than you earn — at least not for long.
- ***The job you have affects what you buy.*** For example, you buy clothing suitable for your job. If you work in outdoor construction, you will need a very different kind of wardrobe than if you worked indoors in a mall or an office.
- ***The environment in which you live makes certain purchases necessary.*** In a cold climate, you might need to buy snow tires. In a hot one, you might want and need air conditioning.

With careful management, you can make your money go farther — to purchase the items you need and the top priorities of things that you want.

- ***Your personal interests tend to direct your buying.*** You choose to spend money on those things that interest you most. It might be books. It might be music. It could be software for your computer.
- ***Advertising is designed to influence and increase your purchasing.*** It makes you want to buy all kinds of things. As a consumer, you must remember that you *do* have a choice over what to buy. You do not have to let advertisers influence your decisions about purchases.
- ***Peer pressure may cause you to buy things in order to feel like part of a group.*** It may be hard to make your own buying decisions at times. However, only you know what you need, want, and can afford.

Taking Charge of Your Purchasing

By keeping in mind the influences on your consumer choices, you can decide to make better choices from now on. One way to do this is to follow a plan for taking charge of your purchasing.

Identify What You Will Buy

This is an essential first step toward effective purchasing. You have to decide what you're going to buy and what you're *not* going to buy. Make your decisions based on your needs and wants, letting your values guide you. What is important to you? Can you afford to buy it and still have money left for other things you want and need?

Another way of taking charge of your buying is to resist **impulse buying**, or making unplanned purchases on the spur of the moment. For example, Blake saw a shirt he liked in a store and bought it. When he got the shirt home, he wasn't very happy with his unplanned purchase — it was the wrong color and didn't fit well. The money Blake spent on the shirt was really needed for new shoes.

Gather Information

Become well informed about the products you decide you want or need to buy. One source of information is people you know who own a product that you are thinking about buying. They can tell you if they like the product and if it has given them problems.

Literature put out by manufacturers is good for technical information. You can use it to compare the features of various brands — an important task before you choose which brand to buy.

Consumer magazines, such as *Consumer Reports*, are also helpful for comparing products. These publications test and rate different brands for quality, safety, and price.

Product advertising can be useful, and it is plentiful. You will find advertisements in newspapers and magazines, as well as on radio and television. Ads have their place in information gathering. For one thing, they can alert you to sales that may help you save money. However, beware. You can't always count on advertising to provide all of the facts about a product. Because ads are designed to appeal to emotions, they sound and look good. However, they may be misleading. They don't give all the facts; they may even misrepresent the facts. Sometimes if you really think about what an ad says, you may find out it really tells you nothing worthwhile about the product — it just offers a tune with a great beat or an attractive picture. Protect yourself by evaluating ads carefully. Never rely on them as your only information source.

When making purchases, it is a real benefit to be informed about the products you are buying. There is much literature available to help you make informed decisions.

▼ Decide When You Will Buy ▼

Knowing when to purchase something can be as important as deciding what to buy. Timing your purchases means planning to make them when it is best for you to do so. It may also save you money. For example, Shelly was able to buy the sweater she wanted at an end-of-season sale for less money than she would have at the beginning of the season. She was able to save credit costs by paying for the sweater with the cash she had set aside for the sweater.

Smart shoppers become aware of typical sale times, and they plan their purchases accordingly. For example, a preseason coat sale often occurs in July or August. One way to

AROUND THE WORLD

Consumers in India have a new decision to make — whether or not to buy an automatic dishwasher and, if so, which brand. About five manufacturers have begun producing the dishwashers that vary in price and features. These companies recently were very successful in introducing other major electric appliances, such as clothes washing machines and food processors, to Indian households. They believe Indian families will be eager to acquire this latest appliance, also. What factors might Indian consumers consider before buying an automatic d shwasher?

Impulse buying can cause you to run out of money before you purchase the items you really need.

find out when sales are going to occur is to refer to local advertising. Then you can get more for your money by buying what you've decided to buy when its price is reduced.

Choose Where You Will Buy

Comparison shopping — or taking the time to shop around and compare products, prices, and services — is a good strategy to use when choosing a place to buy a product. One place may have the product you want at a low price. However, it may not offer the services that you need or want.

As an example, assume you're purchasing a stereo. One need you may have would be the convenience of repair service in case anything goes wrong. One place may offer free repair right in the store. Another store may require you to go elsewhere for service. Still another may charge you for repair by selling you a service contract. By comparison shopping, you can find the place that offers the best balance of price and services that you want and need.

Before you decide where to buy, remember to consider these possibilities.

- ***Department stores.*** These stores sell a variety of goods such as clothing, jewelry, shoes, housewares, appliances, and furniture. Department stores also provide various services for their customers. These might include free delivery and special credit terms.
- ***Discount stores.*** Low prices are the main attraction of these stores. They can offer low prices because they buy in large quantities and limit the number of clerks and customer services.

- ***Neighborhood stores.*** These small businesses usually can't compete with the prices of discount stores. However, they are conveniently located and may carry merchandise not found in larger stores. Neighborhood businesses have clerks available to help their customers. They may also offer certain services, such as free delivery.

- ▶ ***Mail-order firms.*** These businesses have catalogs from which you can order products to be sent to you. Catalogs often include at least some items that are not available in stores near your home. Mail-order shopping can save you time. Sometimes it saves you money. However, often there is a charge for shipping your order. When you are comparing prices, remember to add in this charge.

- ▶ ***Door-to-door sales.*** These involve salespeople who come to your home to sell products. Products sold door-to-door include cosmetics, magazine subscriptions, cooking utensils, and other goods. Some buyers find it convenient to look at merchandise and test it in their own home. Before buying this way, however, it's still a good idea to compare prices and quality.
- ▶ ***Garage sales, yard sales, and flea markets.*** These are a source of merchandise at very low prices. Such sales are not businesses that operate all the time. Instead, they are ways for families and individuals to sell possessions. Garage sales, yard sales, and flea markets offer no customer services. Items are frequently used and must be purchased as they are. Such sales are often a source of unique or unusual items. Remember that you cannot return anything that is defective or otherwise unsatisfactory.

▼ Examine Before You Buy ▼

Learn as much as you can about a product before you actually purchase it. As discussed earlier, information gathering will get you started on this. Once you've narrowed down your choices, investigate some more.

- ▶ ***Inspect a product's quality.*** See how well or how poorly the item was made. For example, check clothing to see if seams are durable and buttons are attached securely. Remember, a high price is not necessarily a reliable sign of good quality.
- ▶ ***Look at the price tag.*** Can you afford this purchase? Is the product worth what it costs? Can you find a better buy?
- ▶ ***Consider the brand.*** Is it one you're familiar with and have had good luck with in the past? Is it a name brand or a store brand? Remember that name brands usually cost more than store brands. Manufacturers of name brands advertise more and this cost is passed on to the customer. Store brands generally are not advertised. You may find that the quality of store brands equals that of name brands while the price is much lower.
- ▶ ***Read product labels.*** Labels and packages give useful facts that may affect your buying decisions. For example,

Compare prices between name brands and store brands to get the best value for your dollar.

TIPS: *Know Your Consumer Rights*

The "Consumer Bill of Rights" was introduced by President John F. Kennedy in 1962. Presidents Nixon and Ford added to the bill. It now includes the following:

- ***The right to safety.*** Consumers are protected against the sale of dangerous products.
- ***The right to be informed.*** Consumers have the right to ask for all the facts needed to make good choices. They are also protected against advertising that is dishonest or misleading.
- ***The right to be heard.*** Consumers have a voice in making laws that affect consumers.
- ***The right to choose.*** Consumers are assured the right to choose from a variety of goods at competitive prices.
- ***The right to redress.*** This is the right to have problems quickly and fairly corrected.
- ***The right to consumer education.*** All consumers and students are entitled to information about consumer issues.

a clothing label gives you information about the fabric from which a garment is made. It also tells you how to care for the garment. Perhaps it needs to be washed by hand or dry-cleaned. In addition, the information on clothing and food labels is regulated by the federal government. Manufacturers decide what facts to include on labels for most other items. Carefully consider all label information before you decide which product is best for you.

- ***Inquire about a warranty.*** A warranty guarantees that a product will work as it should for a certain length of time unless it has been misused or mishandled by the customer. If the product fails to work properly during the specific time period due to any defects in parts, materials, or workmanship, the seller or manufacturer agrees to repair or replace the product or refund your money. Getting a warranty on merchandise is a little bit like getting insurance. In the event that the product has serious defects within the time period of the warranty, you won't have to pay for the repair or replacement. Some warranties cover an entire product for a specific period of time; other warranties are limited and may exclude some parts of a product. Read the warranty carefully to fully understand its conditions.

Your Consumer Responsibilities

Along with understanding your rights as a consumer comes consumer responsibility — the two go hand in hand. For example, if you are guaranteed the right to information about a product and product safety, then your responsibility is to learn as much as you can about the product and use it safely, according to the manufacturer's directions. The same holds true for making wise choices, speaking up when change is needed, and seeking redress when goods and services do not measure up to specified standards.

What other responsibilities do you have as a consumer? First, be as fair and honest with stores and businesses as you expect them to be with you. The biggest responsibility you have as a consumer is to pay for your purchases. If you don't pay, you're stealing. This is not only unfair, but it is also a crime for which you can be put in jail. In the long run, stealing raises prices on goods and services for everyone. Business owners have to cover the cost of their losses. They do this by passing on those costs to customers.

Another responsibility of all consumers is to take care of merchandise they handle or try on. Do your best not to get merchandise dirty or to damage it in any way. You owe it to the store owners and other customers to keep all products in good condition.

When you make a purchase, watch closely while the sales transaction is being completed. Make sure the price is registered correctly and you get any change that is due you. However, if you get too much change, be honest. Give it back.

▼ Learn How to Handle Consumer Complaints ▼

Have you ever purchased a product only to find that it didn't work as it should a short time after purchase? You have the right to complain when a product you purchased was damaged or when a service you paid for wasn't performed correctly. You also have the right to complain when a product was sold to you for more than the advertised price.

The following steps may prove helpful in dealing with consumer problems.

1. Check your warranty. If the problem you have is covered, follow the instructions on the warranty.
2. If you have no warranty, or if your problem isn't covered, go to the store or business where you made the purchase. Politely and firmly explain your problem, and propose a fair solution. Go to a salesperson first. If he or she can't help you, go to the customer service department or the manager. Expect to be treated fairly. Most stores and businesses want to keep their customers.
3. Clearly state to the customer service representative what the problem is and how you would like it to be corrected. Do you want a damaged item fixed or replaced? Do you want a poorly done service performed again?
4. If your trip to a store or business doesn't bring satisfaction, put your complaint in writing. A librarian can help you find out the correct address and to whom to write. Write a letter briefly stating the problem and the solution that you think would be fair. Be sure to include the date; your name, address, and telephone number; the place and date of your purchase; and the model number of the product. In addition, enclose copies of your receipt and your warranty. (Do not send original receipts and warranties.) Keep a copy of your letter for your files, along with the originals of your receipt and warranty.
5. If your letter doesn't bring results, you may choose to take your complaint to the **Better Business Bureau**. This is a private agency that works to improve local business practices and settle consumer complaints.
6. Another option is to take your problem to small claims court to be resolved. In this type of court, you present your complaint before a judge, and the store or business involved must respond. Fees for small claims court are very small. If you win your case, your fees are refunded.

3008 W. Willow Knolls
Peoria, IL 61614
August 15, 1995

YOUR ADDRESS

TODAY'S DATE

NAME AND TITLE OF PERSON YOU'RE WRITING

Mr. Richard Jackson
President
Universal Clocks, Inc.
974 Universal Drive
Anderson, IN 46016

PRODUCT MODEL NUMBER

Dear Mr. Jackson:

Last week I purchased a clock radio, model ST-1062, at XYZ Appliances, 200 Pioneer Parkway, Peoria, Illinois 61615.

NAME AND ADDRESS OF STORE WHERE YOU MADE THE PURCHASE

THE PROBLEM

Unfortunately the clock radio has not performed satisfactorily. Last night the tuner knob came off in my hand. The clock radio has not been mistreated or dropped. To solve the problem, I would appreciate your repairing the knob or replacing the clock radio. Enclosed are copies of my receipt and warranty.

HOW YOU WANT THE PROBLEM SOLVED

COPIES OF RECEIPTS AND WARRANTIES

I am looking forward to your reply and resolution of this problem, and will wait three weeks before seeking third-party assistance. I can be reached at the above address or by phone at 309-555-1234.

Sincerely,

Natalie Ragusa

Natalie Ragusa

TAKING ACTION

"It was love at first sight when I saw these fluorescent-colored baggy pants," exclaimed Brooke. "I absolutely had to have them, but I've only worn them once. This aqua blouse looked wonderful in the store's soft lights, but, once I got it home, it looked awful. I'll have to admit these new red pants don't really fit right. I bought them because of the designer label. I got this skirt because Mindy bought one, and she said we should have skirts alike. Unfortunately, the skirt looks great on Mindy, but it looks terrible on me. See this sweater? I really loved it, and it fit perfectly when I bought it. However, the first time I washed it, it shrank. I didn't see the instruction label ..."

Using Your Resourcefulness

- Identify the mistakes that Brooke made with her clothing purchases. In each case, what could she do in the future to become a better consumer?
- Have you made consumer mistakes similar to Brooke's? Offer an example from your own experience.
- Describe your general pattern as a clothes-buying consumer. Where and how do you shop? Are there ways you could get more clothing value for your money? Explain your answer.

Chapter 20 Review

Summary

In this chapter, you have read about:

- Factors that affect how you spend your money.
- Making decisions about what you will buy, and when and where you will buy it.
- Points to consider when selecting a product.
- Consumers' rights and responsibilities.
- Effective ways of getting consumer problems corrected.

Facts to Recall

1. How do advertising and peer pressure influence your purchasing? How can this create problems?
2. Identify one advantage and one disadvantage to using advertisements as an information source when choosing a product to buy.
3. Explain three ways timing and planning your purchases saves you money.
4. What three points should you consider when comparison shopping?
5. Identify one advantage and one disadvantage of buying from discount stores.
6. Identify two advantages and three disadvantages of buying items at garage and yard sales and flea markets.
7. What three questions should you ask yourself when examining an item's price tag?
8. Explain how brand name and store brands compare in price and quality.
9. Briefly explain the six steps in resolving consumer complaints.
10. Identify three consumer responsibilities.

Ideas to Explore

1. Which of the six influences on spending affect you the most? Explain your answer.
2. Using your most recent purchase as an example, identify which factors affected your decision and explain how they did so.
3. In general, do you believe advertisements are truthful? Defend your answer. Describe ways that they can be misleading.

Activities to Try

1. Choose one item you would like to purchase. Using a consumer magazine such as *Consumer Reports*, see how different brands of the item compare in quality, safety, price, and other categories. Write a short summary of the findings. Identify which of the tested brands you would buy, and why.
2. Practice writing a letter of complaint. Be sure to: explain your problem clearly and briefly; include all the necessary information as discussed in the chapter; and to state how you would like to have the problem corrected.

LINK TO *Communication*

MAKING A COMPLAINT

Toys for children are often found to have some unsafe features. Some may have trim or other small features that fall off and can be easily swallowed by an infant or young child. Bring a toy from home (or a picture of a toy from a catalog) that you think might be dangerous for young children. Respond to the following:

- Explain why you think this toy is dangerous.
- If you had purchased this toy, explain what course of action you could take as a consumer to complain to the manufacturer or place of purchase.
- What might you do if you get no response from the place of purchase or the manufacturer?

CHAPTER 21

Technology as a Resource

OBJECTIVES

- Give examples of technology at home, at school, and in the workplace.
- Describe ways technology might be used in the near future.

TERMS TO LEARN

- ***technology***
- ***modem***
- ***ATMs (automatic teller machines)***
- ***UPC (universal product code)***

We live in a "high tech" age, one in which technology is abundant. **Technology** is the way in which science and inventions are put to practical use in everyday life. Technology includes time-saving and labor-saving devices, such as computers, appliances, and other machines. It also includes new materials for making things safer and stronger and improved methods for doing things faster and more efficiently.

Technology is a resource that people can use for various purposes in different areas of their lives. Today, technology can be found everywhere — at home, at school, and in the many places people work.

Technology at Home

Have you ever thought about how technology touches your life at home? Many people take for granted the day-to-day ways in which technology touches their lives — saving time and energy.

Computers at Home

Much of the technology in people's homes today involves computers. Families that have home computers rely on this resource to help them in a number of ways. Computers are excellent tools for financial planning because they can calculate figures so quickly and accurately. Computers can also aid in time management. They provide a good way to make up, store, and review schedules. If you have letters to write, you can use your computer's word processing capabilities. These allow you to write your letter, change it as you go along, print a neat copy, and file your letter in the computer's memory. Computers also supply many families with a source of home entertainment. These families obtain software for computer games, which are not only fun to play but also challenging.

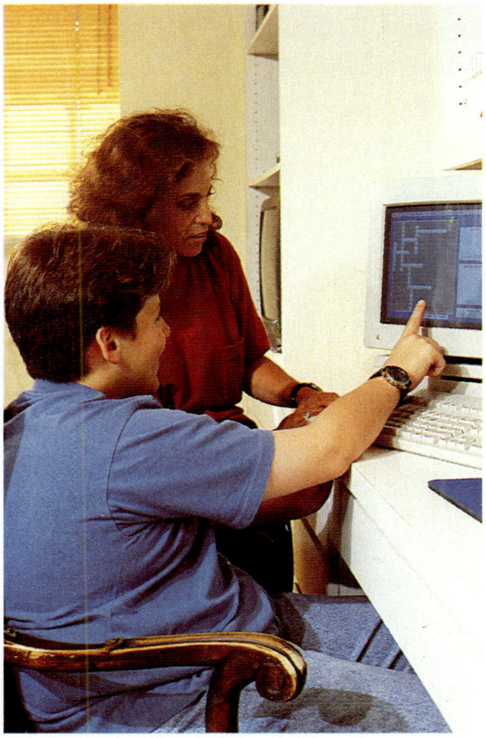

Many families use home computers for money and time management as well as entertainment.

If you have a modem, your home computer can be used for even more functions. A **modem** is a special piece of equipment that connects a computer to a telephone line. This connection allows your computer to communicate directly with other computers. You can both transmit and receive information. By using a modem, you can do your

AROUND THE WORLD

Technology is often accused of weakening ties between people. However, in Costa Rica, it is bringing them together. Since 1988, a group of American scientists and teachers have been showing people in rural Costa Rican communities how to build simple solar-powered ovens. After learning about this design, community members construct their own ovens from locally-produced materials — glass, wood, and cardboard. The teachers believe that this community involvement, which was missing from similar projects in the past, is helping to make this project a success.

banking from home, transferring money between accounts and checking your bank balance. You can also make reservations for airlines, hotels, and rental cars. It is even possible to transmit your taxes this way.

Hidden Computer Technology

Computer technology is often present in homes even when there is no home computer. Many appliances contain hidden computers that help them perform some kind of special function. Electronic home sewing machines contain a microcomputer which allows for the creation and storage of hundreds of new designs and makes sewing faster and easier. There are irons that shut themselves off when they are not in use. A microchip — which acts like a minicomputer — inside these irons is responsible for the shut-off. Microwave ovens include computers that must be programmed in order to cook your food just right. Some coffee makers are equipped with microcomputers that can be programmed at night before you go to bed. This programming turns your coffee maker on in the morning, and your coffee is ready when you wake up.

▼ Technology and Home Appliances ▼

What technology do you have in your home? Do you and your family make use of a VCR? Video technology is popular for homes because it offers such convenience. You can watch movies on your VCR instead of going out and spending money at a theater. You can see what movie you want when you want to, instead of adjusting to the theater's programming and schedule. You can also use your VCR to tape TV shows while you are away or busy. This allows you to do what you need to do and watch your favorite shows later, at the time that suits you best.

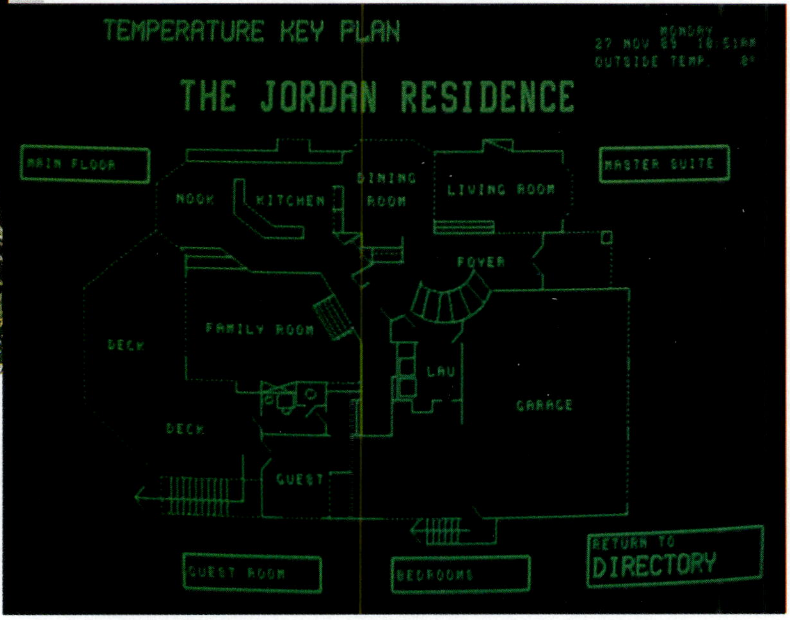

In "smart houses," all gas and electrical systems and appliances are controlled by a central computer. This computer can control outdoor lighting systems, set thermostats, and even start coffee brewing in the morning before the residents of the house are awake.

Much home technology aims at convenience, as in the case of computers and VCRs. Other technology makes your home more comfortable. Central heating and air conditioning are examples. Still other technology is directed at keeping your home safe, such as sensors that sound an alarm when doors or windows are opened. Motion-sensing and solar-powered lights are safety devices that turn on automatically, giving you light where you need it and when you need it most. Automatic garage door openers are technology that provides both safety and convenience. In addition, fully-automated home systems are now available. These control many home functions, such as heating, cooling, and lighting, through one computerized panel.

Technology at School

Computer technology is a vital part of education in many schools today. Teachers depend on computers for creating tests and other materials that students use for class work or homework. Such materials are written on computers, printed out, and stored by computer for possible future use.

Students may also work directly with computers as a learning tool. For example, in home economics, you might use a computer when you are studying food. Computers can be utilized to calculate the calories and healthful ingredients in the foods you eat.

How to . . .

Coordinate Family Needs and Technology

Technology is a positive thing. However, if it isn't managed well, it can cause problems in the family. For each situation below, suggest how family values could be put to work to solve the problem of meeting family needs and effectively using technology:

- The Klopner family rarely talks anymore. Their leisure time is spent watching television and videotaped movies.
- Sixteen-year-old Chad and his older brother argue over using the family's second car.
- The Blonski family has a very full schedule. They eat frozen dinners almost every night, and they're getting tired of them.
- Fourteen-year-old Ellen talks on the telephone every chance she gets. She complains when other family members ask her to let them use the phone.
- Fifteen-year-old Devon spends all his allowance on computer games. Then he asks his sister to lend him money for his other expenses.

Library computers help you find information.

When you are studying home design, you might take advantage of a computer program for trying out furniture arrangements. Moving furniture around by computer is easy. All you have to do is push a few buttons. You can see the results of each arrangement immediately on the computer screen. You can also print out copies of different arrangements to compare and see which you like best.

Your school library probably has a computer that stores a list of its entire collection. This means that you can use the computer to see if the library has a book or other publication you want. You can find out what materials are available on a certain subject or by a particular author. You can also locate your choice on the library's shelves by using information from the computer.

Some school libraries have special software programs for assisting students in choosing a career. (At your school, this material may be in the counselor's office instead of the library.) One purpose of this software is to inventory your interests and supply you with a list of appropriate careers. Another purpose is to research available college programs and other training for certain careers. Some of these software programs are good resources for the most up-to-date information about specific careers. You can use them to learn the duties of a particular job as well as its usual salary range and its future outlook.

School offices make use of computers for various administrative tasks. Computers are often used for alphabetizing class lists and filing away other assorted information. Computers calculate, print, and store students' academic and attendance records. Some schools even depend on computers for making phone calls to parents of students who are absent.

Technology in the Workplace

Wherever you see people working today, you will probably see technology working, too. Technology saves time and human effort at work. It also helps to reduce the number of human errors. Various workplaces use different kinds of technology in different ways and amounts.

Banking

Banks count heavily on technology for help in performing various tasks. When you go to a teller to make a deposit or a withdrawal, the teller uses a computer to complete the transaction. Most banks also provide **ATMs**, or **automatic teller machines**. ATMs are computers that bank customers can use to make their transactions when tellers are busy or when the bank is closed.

Banks also rely on technology when they service your checking account. Computers read the code numbers on your checks and subtract the amount of each check from your balance.

Retail Stores

Technology is employed extensively by retail businesses today. Most large stores use computers for such functions as ordering, stocking, and keeping track of inventory (the amount of merchandise on hand). Many stores also have scanners connected to computers at the checkout stand. These

SAFETY CHECK ✓

Here are some guidelines for safely using your ATM card:

- Never tell anyone your personal identification number (PIN number).
- Only use an ATM in a well-lighted public place.
- Avoid using an ATM late at night.
- Check your bank statements as soon as you receive them to make sure that only the transactions you made are recorded. If there are ATM transactions listed that you did not make, this might indicate an error on the bank's part or that someone has used your pin number to access your account.

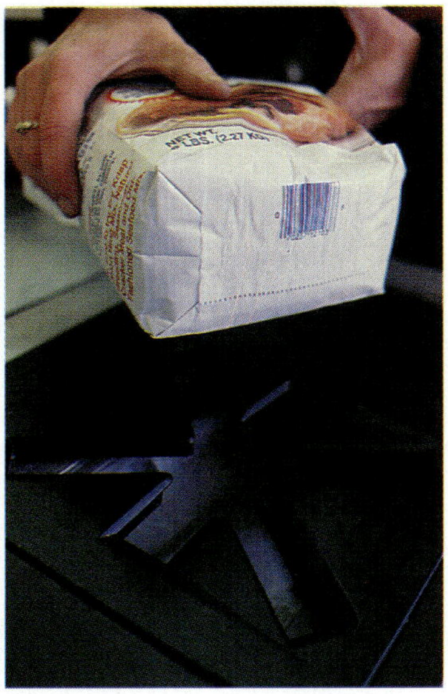

Scanners read the UPC labels on products and send this information to a central computer. The computer sends price information to the cash register which prints your receipt. What are some other ways that bar codes are used?

scanners are designed to read **universal product codes**, or **UPC**, printed on each product or price ticket. A UPC is a bar code — or pattern of stripes that identifies a product. Each product has its own UPC. The checker passes each item across a scanner that "reads" the code and sends it to the computer. The computer sends information about the product's price back to the cash register, which then prints an itemized receipt. The computer also sends the product's code number to an inventory file which helps a store know when supplies of a product are getting low and must be reordered. Using bar coding reduces the time it takes to complete sales transactions. It also reduces the number of errors that occur when prices are recorded by hand.

Credit card purchases also involve computer technology. Computers permit store clerks to check a credit card before the purchase process is completed. The clerk can easily tell if the credit card has been reported as stolen and make sure that the current purchase won't exceed the customer's credit limit.

Another kind of technology often found in stores is video technology. In a department store, you might see a videotape that demonstrates the application of cosmetic products. In a supermarket, tapes may show how to use food products in delicious recipes.

Design

Technology has vastly changed the way that design work is done. Drafters, architects, engineers, and interior designers now use computers. Computer-aided design (CAD) makes it possible to draw houses, bridges, cars, and airplanes quickly and easily. CAD also makes it possible to experiment with a variety of changes in the design of these items in order to determine the best design. In addition, CAD offers the option of working in three dimensions at a computer terminal. This allows architects and interior designers to plan the space in a room quite easily. By using CAD, they can visually "walk" through the space and decide how to use it.

Law enforcement officials use computers to help solve crime.

Transportation

People who work in transportation depend on the latest technology to assist them. For example, both pilots and ships' captains rely on computers to help them navigate, or remain on course. Some new jets have computers that are capable of landing the plane without the pilot's help. Workers on high-speed trains use computers for mapping out routes and for keeping track of railroad traffic.

Law Enforcement

Computer technology serves law enforcement agencies in many ways. One example is that many officers' vehicles are now equipped with computer terminals. Officers count on these computers as an information source. When they need to learn more about a suspect or a stolen car, they turn to their computers for quick answers.

Technicians in crime labs also use computers in the course of their work. National data banks (central computers that store information from all over the nation) help technicians identify fingerprints of suspects. Computers are also used to analyze such things as fibers found on a suspect's clothing. Careful computer analysis helps technicians determine whether a suspect was present at the scene of the crime.

Protective technology also plays an essential role in law enforcement work. This involves the latest developments in things such as bulletproof and flame-resistant clothing. Protective technology is important because it helps keep officers and fire fighters safe.

MEETING SPECIAL NEEDS

Helping the Hearing and Visually Impaired

Special technology has also been designed to help people with disabilities. One example is the TDD, or Telecommunications Device for the Deaf. This technology uses a keyboard connected to a telephone. The hearing-impaired person communicates by sending and receiving printed conversations. Other technology is available for people with visual disabilities. Some computers read aloud from printed books or tell the user what appears on the computer screen.

Health Care

Health care is a field in which scientific knowledge advances very rapidly. Therefore, it is important for physicians and other health care workers to keep up with the latest information. Computer technology is used to gather data about various illnesses and treatments.

Computers are also used today in diagnosing patients' conditions. One way is with the CT scan. With a CT scan, the patient's body is scanned by several X-ray machines. The information that is collected is then used to reconstruct an image on a computer screen so the doctor can "see" graphic images of what is inside the patient's body.

Physicians and hospitals use computers to identify illnesses and treatments.

Future Technology

Right now, technology provides tools that can make life better for individuals and families. Homes, schools, and workplaces are using technology to solve problems and perform tasks quickly and easily. While you are reading this book, new discoveries are being made, and technology is advancing even farther. In the near future, you are likely to see some of these uses of

Technology helps people with special needs.

technology. Some things you may well see in the near future include:

- More people earning a living by doing their job at home from a computer terminal.
- Robots being used in the home for household tasks.
- Closed-circuit TV in the home for monitoring children.
- Home computers that will automatically contact supermarkets to place orders for food and household supplies.
- Computerized devices for medical patients that will allow doctors to monitor health from a distance.
- Tiny implanted computers that will automatically measure the number of calories eaten and used by a person's body.

Managing Technology

Now, and in the future, it will be up to you to make the best possible use of technology in your life. Remember that technology is a resource that you can learn to manage well. Making good use of technology means choosing the equipment, materials, and methods that will work best for you. This will save you time, energy, and money that you can then devote to those things you value most.

TAKING ACTION

Drew has a big idea. He hopes to start a neighborhood shopping service. The purpose of Drew's service will be to help elderly residents and working parents who have a hard time getting out to shop.

Drew already has quite a few names and addresses of neighbors who might be interested. He plans to write a letter explaining his idea and inviting these neighbors to try his service.

Once he gets customers, Drew will collect their shopping lists once a week. To help people make up their lists, Drew will comparison shop and circulate a list of available bargains. Customers will pay an estimated amount for their groceries, plus a reasonable fee for Drew's time and effort. This will allow Drew's service to make a profit. He plans to keep accurate records of all aspects of his business. Drew wonders how he can best use technology in operating his new business.

Using Your Resourcefulness

- In what ways would a computer be helpful for Drew's business? Offer some specific advantages of using a computer.
- How could a computer help *you* manage your own life more efficiently?
- What are some ways that you could learn more about the uses and programs of different computer systems?

Chapter 21 Review

Summary

In this chapter, you have read about:

- How technology can make home life more convenient, efficient, and enjoyable.
- How technology at school can help in learning, creativity, and choosing a career.
- How technology is used in various jobs to increase efficiency and reduce mistakes.
- Possible uses for technology in the future.

Facts to Recall

1. List five tasks performed with home computers that make life more convenient or enjoyable.
2. Give three examples of how microcomputers are used in home appliances.
3. Identify three ways in which technology is used to help keep your home safe.
4. Explain three ways in which specially designed software programs can help you choose a career.
5. What are three advantages to using a UPC to check out items at a store?
6. What is CAD? Who uses it, and how it is helpful?
7. Identify three uses for computers in the field of transportation.
8. Describe two examples of technology that helps people with disabilities.
9. List two ways technology is used in health care.
10. Name two ways in which computers may someday help you prepare meals.

Ideas to Explore

1. How do you think the increasing use of technology will affect the job market in the future?
2. Technology has done much to improve the quality of life. What problems might arise from our growing use of technology?
3. Name three technological advances or inventions that you feel have had the greatest impact on your life, and explain how they have affected you. How would your life be different without them?

Activities to Try

1. On a sheet of paper, write down all the ways you depend on technology every day. What does your list tell you about the importance of technology in your life?
2. With a partner, make two lists: one, of the technological advances made in your lifetime; the other, of advances made in the first 12 to 15 years of your parents' generation. Draw conclusions about in which time period you think technology has advanced more quickly.

LINK TO *Science*

PREDICTING TECHNOLOGICAL CHANGE

Technology is rapidly changing the world in which we live. It is affecting every aspect of our lives, making the unthinkable commonplace in only a short period of time. Locate and read an article describing ways technology is helping scientists in their work.

- What new research efforts are possible as a result of new technology?
- What recent discoveries have been made using new technology?
- Make five predictions of scientific advances that might result from technological development in the future. Your predictions may sound like science fiction today, but tomorrow — who knows?

CHAPTER

22 Natural Resources

OBJECTIVES

- Give examples of renewable and nonrenewable resources.
- Explain the importance of resource management and identify conservation measures.

TERMS TO LEARN

- *natural resources*
- *renewable resources*
- *nonrenewable resources*
- *conservation*
- *recycling*

What do a glass of water, a chunk of coal, a clump of dirt, and a tree have in common? Water, coal, soil, and trees are **natural resources**. These are resources that occur in nature.

Some natural resources keep human beings alive and healthy. The air we breathe and the water we drink are two examples. Other natural resources, including coal and natural gas, are fuels that we use to provide heat and light and to power machines. Some natural resources, such as minerals and trees, are made into products that we use in our everyday lives. Many natural resources add quality to life. What would life be without forests, rivers, lakes, and blue skies to enjoy?

The Supply of Natural Resources

Technology, which you read about in Chapter 21, is a man-made resource. People create technology and control its availability. In contrast, natural resources can't be made by people. Only nature creates these resources and controls the amounts of them available to us.

Some resources renew, or replace, themselves over time. These are called **renewable resources**. Plants renew themselves by producing seeds, which, in turn, produce new plants. Air, water, and soil are also replaced, not by reproduction but through natural cycles. Supplies of air, water, and soil are always being produced unless something interferes with their natural cycles.

Other natural resources do not replace themselves. These are known as **nonrenewable resources**. The supply of these resources is limited. No more is available than what is on the planet right now. Oil is a nonrenewable resource. So are minerals, such as zinc, copper, and iron. Supplies of these resources could last a long time or run out — what happens will depend on how quickly existing supplies are used up.

Planting trees is one way that people can help our environment.

Natural Resources Today

One only needs to look at a newspaper or news broadcast to learn about the condition of natural resources today. Forests have been destroyed. Oil is in short supply. Air, water, and soil have been poisoned by pollution. The whole environment is threatened because resources have been misused

Around the World

The rain forests of South America and Africa are very important to the worldwide environment. They clean the air and are home to many types of plants and animals. However, farmers in that region need the land to plant crops and graze animals. They also need the wood for building and for fuel. Environmental groups like the World Wildlife Fund are trying to teach farmers new techniques to help save the rain forests. However, many problems remain. Where else are there conflicts between protecting the environment and preserving a people's way of life?

and natural cycles have been disturbed. Good resource management is needed to avoid the misuse of resources and ensure the availability of resources now and in the future.

Your Role in Resource Management

The natural resources of planet Earth are shared by everyone on the planet. Therefore, it is the responsibility of everyone to help manage these resources effectively. You have already learned to take charge of your personal resources, such as time, energy, and money. Now you will discover what you can do to participate actively in managing natural resources.

Natural resource management involves **conservation**, which is protecting resources against waste and harm. The following sections describe conservation measures that you and your family can take on a regular basis.

Water

Have you ever wondered what your life would be like without the availability of fresh water? Water shortages exist in some areas today, and water supplies are polluted and unusable in other areas. Water conservation measures involve managing water use so that available water isn't wasted. Here are some ways that you can conserve water:

- Turn faucets all the way off each time you use them, and repair all plumbing leaks. A faucet leaking one drop of water per second can waste 650 gallons of water a year.
- Install aerators on your faucets and your shower heads. These inexpensive devices mix air with water. The result is that the water pressure remains the same, but less water is used.

- Take quick showers instead of baths. You will use as little as one-fifth the amount of water. Wet yourself. Turn off the water while you lather. Then turn the water back on to rinse yourself off.
- Run full loads in your washing machine or dishwasher. Wait until you have a full load to make better use of the water.
- Fill the sink with water instead of leaving the water running wastefully down the drain when washing dishes by hand.
- Use only as much water as you need for brushing your teeth, shaving, or scrubbing fruits and vegetables. Don't let water run needlessly throughout the entire process.
- Sweep driveways and walkways outside your home rather than using water to hose them down.
- Use food scraps as compost for plants or a garden instead of using a garbage disposal, which requires the use of running water.

Heating and Cooling

It is essential to be aware of natural resources when you heat and cool your home. Some heating requires the use of fuels that are nonrenewable resources. Other kinds of heating and air conditioning depend on electricity. However, remember that electricity is often produced by burning a nonrenewable fuel. If we want fuel supplies to last, we must do our best to reduce fuel use now. Here are some ideas for conserving energy when heating or cooling your home:

- Set your heater no higher than 68°F (20°C) during the day to save fuel. At night, turn the temperature down even farther to 55-60° F (13-16°C).
- Keep your heat inside by using weather stripping and caulking to prevent heat from escaping around windows and doors.
- Install storm doors and windows in winter if your climate is cold. This will help you keep the heat in and keep out cold drafts. You will use less fuel.
- Close shades and draperies at night in cold weather to keep in the heat and keep out the cold. If the days are sunny, open shades and draperies in the daytime. This will allow you to heat your home using the sun's energy.
- Set your air conditioner no lower than 78°F (26°C) during the summer months. Have your air conditioner checked yearly to avoid coolant leaks, which can damage the Earth's atmosphere.
- Use a fan instead of an air conditioner. Fans use less electricity and, therefore, less fuel.

- Keep windows covered during the day in hot weather. This will keep heat out, and you will have to cool less.
- Close outside doors promptly when you enter or leave your home. This will keep out heat or cold that will change your home's temperature.
- Avoid heating or cooling rooms that no one is using. Doing so is a waste of fuel.
- Look into using solar energy for heating. The supply of sunlight is unlimited — and free.

Lighting and Appliances

Like heating and cooling, lighting and appliances draw on the Earth's reserves of fuel. Gas ranges and some other appliances use fuels directly, while lighting and electrical appliances make indirect use of fuels. You can help stretch the planet's fuel resources by carefully managing lighting and appliance use in your home.

- Clean lamps and lighting fixtures regularly so that as much light as possible can come through them.
- Replace high-wattage light bulbs with lower-wattage ones or with fluorescent lights, which use less electricity.
- Turn off lights, television sets, radios, and appliances when you leave the room for more than just a few minutes. It doesn't make sense to leave them on when they are not in use, and it takes electricity to run them.

- Choose the appliance that takes the smallest amount of energy for whatever task you do. For example, use an electric skillet to cook food rather than a regular skillet on a burner of an electric range. The electric skillet uses less energy.
- Use your oven to cook several items at once. Don't open the oven door unnecessarily while you are cooking. This allows heat to escape, which means that additional fuel must be used to bring the oven temperature back up to the correct temperature.

- Defrost foods in your refrigerator instead of in your microwave. This takes planning, but it saves energy. As frozen foods defrost, they will help to keep your refrigerator cool.
- Limit the number of times you open your refrigerator and the length of time you leave it open. When cool air escapes and warm air gets inside, your refrigerator has to run longer to stay cool.

- Run the dryer only as long as necessary to dry laundry. Drying laundry too long wastes fuel directly or indirectly, depending on the kind of dryer.
- Consider air-drying clothes instead of using a dryer. Take advantage of solar energy, which uses no nonrenewable fuels.

Transportation

Motor vehicles are powered either by gasoline or by diesel fuel. These products are made from crude oil, or petroleum, which is a nonrenewable resource. There are several ways to cut fuel use and still meet your transportation needs.

- Use transportation possibilities that don't require fuel, such as biking or walking.
- Use public transportation, such as buses and subways, if possible. It uses less fuel because it transports so many people at once.
- Join a carpool. Sharing rides is an efficient use of fuel.
- Maintain your car to insure that it makes the best possible use of gas. Change the oil, maintain the correct air pressure in tires, and have a tune-up regularly as recommended in your owner's manual.
- Plan car trips ahead to make good use of them. Accomplish as many tasks as you can during a single trip.
- Eliminate unnecessary trips in your car. For example, be sure that the store has what you want before you get into your car and drive there.

Using alternate sources of transportation helps save fuel — a nonrenewable resource.

Consumer Goods

The products that you buy are manufactured, using natural resources as raw materials. Paper, for example, is made from wood pulp, a substance that comes from the wood of trees. Manufacturing processes often involve using water, and they always require energy. Fuels are burned to produce energy directly or to produce electricity, which then runs machines. Some manufacturing processes result in pollution, particularly of water and air. Used consumer goods eventually become waste, which is usually buried and may pollute soil and ground water.

Making Wise Consumer Decisions

As a consumer, it is up to you to consider natural resources *before* you buy. By keeping resource conservation in mind when making consumer choices, you will be able to make decisions that are "resource-wise."

- Always ask yourself if you really need your purchase. If not, don't buy something that took a lot of resources to produce.
- When you do buy, avoid disposable items. They quickly become trash and aren't worth the use of resources.
- Choose items that last as long as possible. Examples include rechargeable batteries and long-lasting light bulbs.
- Select items with very little packaging. It takes resources to make wrappers and boxes. Since packaging is usually thrown away once the product is removed, the resources used to make the packaging are wasted.

Keep conservation in mind as you make consumer purchases.

- ▶ Bring reusable bags to the supermarket, and use them to carry groceries home. This saves the resources needed to make paper and plastic bags, which tend to become trash very rapidly.
- ▶ When buying appliances, consider carefully how much electricity or gas they will use. EnergyGuide labels, such as the one on page 519, will help you choose appliances that make good use of fuels.
- ▶ When purchasing a car or other motor vehicle, find out how many miles per gallon various models get. Select a model that gets excellent mileage and, therefore, uses as little fuel as possible.

Cars vary in fuel efficiency. When you or your family are shopping for a car, compare fuel consumption estimates before making your purchase.

Making the Best Use of Consumer Goods

Existing supplies of natural resources will last longer if good use is made of products after they are purchased. Here are some ways that you can stretch a product's usable lifetime:

- ▶ Keep items longer. Don't throw them away because you are tired of them or because styles change.
- ▶ If you don't want a product anymore, give it to someone else who will use it. Charity organizations clean and repair used items so that they can be used further. Adding to product life in this way means that fewer resources are needed to manufacture new products.
- ▶ Contribute to recycling efforts. **Recycling** is using used, discarded products or scrap and waste materials to make new products. Glass, paper, tin, aluminum, iron, steel, and plastics are collected for recycling. In your community, there may be curbside pick-up of materials for recycling. If not, you can take your materials to official recycling centers.

Recycling saves new resources and cuts down on the amount of materials that end up in sanitary landfills.

Recycling old materials saves new resources. It also reduces the number of items that end up in the trash. In addition, producing products with recycled materials may save fuel because it uses less energy.

▼ Fighting Pollution ▼

Pollution makes resources such as air, water, and soil unusable or unhealthy. You and your family can do much to combat the harm that pollution does to our natural environment.

- Become informed about pollution in your community, the nation, and the world. Find out exactly what is happening, where it is happening, and what is being done to solve problems.
- Learn what laws are presently in effect to control pollution. Encourage leaders to get new laws passed as needed to stop pollution.
- Join with others who are interested in improving environmental conditions. For example, you might start a recycling drive at school so that materials won't become waste that pollutes the environment. There might also be a group that picks up roadside litter or one that is helping clean up a polluted waterway. Think about what you can do — and do it! Fighting pollution requires responsible action.

TAKING ACTION

Mrs. Arnold, your home economics teacher, asks your class to enter a national competition. Your goal is to identify an environmental problem or hazard in your community and develop a plan to improve or solve it. The problem might be as simple as a recycling drive or as complex as dealing with pollution or waste.

First you may need to brainstorm to identify the problem. Then you need to research a variety of resources to write a step-by-step plan that is both practical and effective. Mrs. Arnold will submit the best ideas to the competition, which offers college scholarships to winning students.

Using Your Resourcefulness

- Either singly or in groups, identify an environmental problem or hazard in your community.
- What resources will you need to use to learn more about the problem?
- How will you determine if these solutions are practical for your community?

Chapter 22 Review

Summary

In this chapter, you have read about:

- How people depend on natural resources in daily life.
- The supply and condition of natural resources today.
- Things you and your family can do to conserve natural resources.
- Ways to fight pollution.

Facts to Recall

1. Explain four ways in which people use natural resources.
2. Explain the difference between renewable and nonrenewable resources. Give two examples of each.
3. List four things you and your family can do to conserve water.
4. Name five ways in which you and your family can conserve energy when heating and cooling your home.
5. Identify four ways of conserving natural resources through managing lighting and appliance use.
6. List four ways of cutting fuel use in transportation.
7. Identify four ways in which natural resources are involved in the production of consumer goods.
8. Tell four "resource-wise" things you can do when buying products.
9. Name three ways in which recycling helps conserve existing supplies of natural resources.

Ideas to Explore

1. Give examples of laws designed to promote the conservation of natural resources or to fight pollution.
2. Would you and your family be willing to pay a higher price for products that created less pollution or used fewer natural resources to make? Why or why not?
3. Discuss how conserving natural resources affects your family's financial resources.
4. Identify four types of workers whose jobs depend directly on the continued availability of natural resources. What statement can you make about the relationship between wise use of natural resources and a region's or a nation's economy?

Activities to Try

1. In newspapers or magazines, find articles about natural resources. Make a report about their conservation, their destruction, or controversy about their use.
2. Find out about groups or companies that collect materials for recycling in your community. Learn where they are located, what materials they accept, and how much — if anything — they pay for the materials. Report your findings to the class.

LINK TO *Health*

HEALTH AND WATER

Many health problems have been linked to polluted water. Investigate what types of diseases and illnesses can be caused by polluted water. Respond to the following items as you complete your investigation:

- What are the most common water-related illnesses around the world?
- Describe the symptoms and treatments for these illnesses.
- What are some ways that we can take an active part in protecting our water supply?

CAREER *Connections*

Get Ready for Your Future Through Volunteering

"Last year all the schools in our rural community organized a fundraising drive to launch a county-wide recycling program. The organizers asked for student and adult volunteers with computer experience to help record the names of donors, the amount of each donation, and input other important information.

"I'd learned how to use computers at school, so I volunteered to enter this information on the computer. I enjoyed working with computers so much I started to research job possibilities to pursue after high school. After all, I was already doing what many data-entry operators are paid to do — enter and verify data on the computer. I found out word processing operators organize data, list logical steps for the computer to follow, and solve computer program problems. Computer sales personnel use their knowledge of hardware and software capabilities to sell and match systems and programs to their customers.

"I'm still not sure which direction I'll follow, but at least I know that the growing use of computers increases the need for employees with computer knowledge and training. The career opportunities seem limitless."

"Along with Lorenzo I volunteered as a computer operator for our county recycling program. I work full-time as a bank teller. Even though I enjoyed math classes in school, I never thought about working in a bank. I took a business class in which I learned calculator skills on a computer. The class took a tour of the local bank which gave me new insight into career opportunities.

"During the summer, I worked as a cashier at a pharmacy. I quickly learned I liked working with the public. After high school, I took classes for an associate's degree in business at a junior college. I also kept applying for a job at the bank, which I finally got!

"My daily activities involve counting money quickly and accurately, processing withdrawals and deposits on the computer, cashing checks, selling money orders, and taking utility payments. At the end of each day, I make sure that my cash drawer is in balance with the deposits and withdrawals I handled that day. Then assist my supervisor with any additional work that needs to be done. I'm now being considered for promotion and hope to be a bank officer one day. I'm so glad I found and pursued the right career for me."

"As a job placement counselor, I see many people like Naomi. They are young, skilled, and looking for a good job. Though my business and counseling courses in college helped prepare me for this position, hands-on experience has been my best training.

"The first thing I check carefully is a person's application form. I look at grammar and how well this person expresses himself or herself in writing. When I meet the person, I listen carefully to how the person communicates during the initial interview. Appearance, courtesy, and enthusiasm are equally as important as a person's resumé.

"People who come to see me are often inexperienced in the job marketplace. I need to consider their personal resources such as interests, skills, and classes they've taken in high school and college. I believe in giving young people like Naomi a chance to prove themselves, especially when they've worked hard to make the most of themselves."

MAKING THE CONNECTION

- Do you think working with computers might interest you as a career? Why or why not? How might you use a computer in the career field of your choice? Explain your answer.
- Do you think working with money might interest you as a career? Why or why not? Besides banking, what other money-related careers can you name?
- What resource materials might help you choose the right career for you? Would you think about talking with a career counselor or job placement counselor to find work? Why or why not?

4 UNIT Housing

CHAPTERS

HOUSE
FOR SALE
555-5023
PMI
INSTRUCTIONS
1. PULL PIN. HOLD UNIT UPRIGHT.
2. STAND BACK 6 FEET, AIM AT BASE OF FIRE.
3. SQUEEZE LEVER AND SWEEP SIDE TO SIDE.
KIDDE
DRY CHEMICAL

CHAPTER

23 Looking at Housing Choices

OBJECTIVES

- *Name major factors that influence housing choices.*
- *Identify various types of housing and their advantages and disadvantages.*
- *Explain reasons for renting or purchasing housing.*

TERMS TO LEARN

- ***multiple-family dwelling***
- ***duplex***
- ***multiplex***
- ***townhomes***
- ***landlord***
- ***tenants***
- ***lease***
- ***mortgage***
- ***condominium***
- ***cooperative***

Lori and her sister live in an apartment with their mom. Mike and Carlos live in a duplex with their parents. Kim and her family share a house with her grandparents. It's easy to see why housing needs and decisions vary.

In most towns and cities, you don't have to go far to see several kinds of housing. This chapter will help you learn how individuals and families can make good housing choices.

The Meaning of Housing

Housing includes the many different types of shelter in which people live. Suppose you could look at all the housing that ever existed, everywhere in the world. Imagine the variety! Yet each was influenced by the same factors: society, culture, climate, available materials, and technology, to name just a few.

Housing can fulfill important needs of individuals and families. Everyone has certain basic needs in common.

- ***Physical needs.*** Physical needs are those necessary for survival, such as shelter, air, sunlight, sleep, and food. Housing should offer safety for you and your belongings.
- ***Emotional needs.*** Emotional needs can also be met by housing. A home can provide privacy, comfort, and a place for fun and relaxation. You can make your home reflect your personal taste.
- ***Social needs.*** These needs include the need for love and belonging. The home can serve as a gathering place for family and friends.

Housing that offers opportunities to meet emotional and social needs is more than just a structure. It becomes a home.

Influences on Housing Decisions

Although people share basic human needs, they are also individuals. When you and your family are choosing a place to live, think about your specific needs and wants. Then try to find a way to balance those needs and wants with available resources.

MEETING SPECIAL NEEDS

Aiding Independent Living

Everyone wants to live as independently as possible. The elderly and people with disabilities are no exception. If someone in your family has physical limitations, there are many ways you can improve the person's independence at home.

- ***Floors***. Many people have problems walking or must use wheelchairs. Smooth flooring such as vinyl or wood is a good, safe choice. If carpeting is used, choose a level-loop type without padding. Avoid throw rugs. They cause many falls.
- ***Stairs.*** Railings on both sides of stairs and in hallways are helpful. For those in wheelchairs, stairs are a barrier. Outside the home, ramps can replace stairs. Inside, stairs may limit the person to one part of the house. If so, arrange a room for privacy.
- ***Lighting.*** Adequate lighting is especially important for those with poor vision. Check the number, placement, and brightness of lights. In each room, there should be a light that can be turned on near the entrance.

(Continued on next page)

What types of needs and wants might this family have for housing?

Needs and Wants

Needs and wants differ because families differ. What one family considers essential might be unnecessary or even a drawback to another family. Here are some factors to consider.

- ***Family size.*** An-Sook lives with his foster parents and five other children. His family's needs are quite different from Tanya's. Her family includes only herself and her father.
- ***Family life cycle.*** As explained in Chapter 12, every family goes through a life cycle. Changes during the life cycle can affect housing needs and wants. Rona and Jared just had their first baby. Soon they will start looking for a larger place to live with an outdoor play area nearby. Meanwhile, Rona's grandfather Carl is also planning ahead. Now that he lives alone, he would prefer a smaller place that requires little upkeep.
- ***Special needs of family members.*** Consider any special housing needs of family members. For example, someone with limited mobility may require a home that is all on one level. Existing housing can often be adapted to meet special needs. See the feature on pages 252-253 for suggestions.
- ***Location.*** Is it important to be close to a job or public transportation? Would the family prefer a quiet location or a neighborhood with lots of children?

- ***Lifestyle.*** The interests and activities of family members also influence housing decisions. Most people want a home that suits their way of life and sense of style.

These are just some of the factors that affect housing needs and wants.

Considering Your Resources

Resources play an important role in housing decisions. Available housing is one material resource. Only a limited number of housing units are on the market at any given time. If you cannot find what you are looking for, you may have to change some of your ideas about what you want.

The housing you choose must be not only available, but affordable. Most financial experts recommend that no more than about 28 percent of the family income be budgeted for housing. This includes not only monthly payments for the housing unit itself, but other costs such as insurance, repairs, and *utilities* (basic services such as electricity, gas or oil, and water).

Most people must make some compromises in order to find housing that fits their budget. Lori's mother wanted a larger place with a separate bedroom for Lori and her sister.

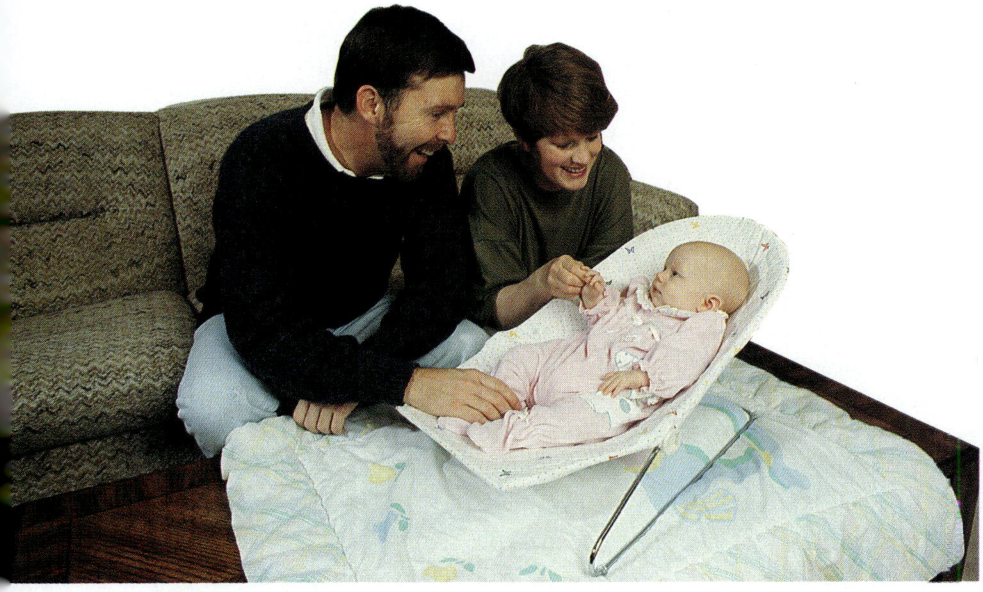

Changes in the family life cycle can affect housing needs. How might this family's needs be different from a family that includes several teens?

Aiding Independent Living (Continued)

- ***Kitchens.*** Kitchens present problems for people with disabilities. Cabinets may require too much bending or reaching. Open shelves are often better. People with wheelchairs need lower countertops. A sink without a cabinet beneath it allows a wheelchair to roll into position. Special faucets with longer spouts and handles are also available. Braille knobs, control panels, and appliance instruction books can be ordered for those who are blind.
- ***Bathrooms***. Grab bars by the bathtub and toilet can increase safety. A seat added to the shower or tub and a hand-held shower make bathing easier for many. Also, add nonslip strips to the shower floor or tub bottom.

Few builders consider the needs of the elderly and those with disabilities. If someone in your family has a physical limitation, you can make a difference. Find out what tasks the person finds difficult. Then think of solutions that would increase independence. Check the library for books and pamphlets.

Affordable housing is sometimes a challenge to find. How can using the telephone be a benefit when looking for affordable housing?

However, high housing costs in their area prevented this. A place that size would have required nearly all of her monthly paycheck. The family finally located a three-room apartment near her mother's job. Location, cost, and available choices played a major role in their selection.

Human resources, such as skills, time, and energy, can stretch housing dollars. For instance, An-Sook's foster parents bought an old house that needed repairs and used their skills to improve it. Without their skills, they would have had to settle for a much smaller house.

Types of Housing

Taking a look at your needs, wants, and resources is one step in making good housing decisions. Another is learning about the various types of housing available. Each type has advantages and disadvantages.

Single-Family Homes

Single-family homes are freestanding. That is, they do not share any walls with another housing unit. They may be small or large, one story or several stories high.

Single-family homes offer more privacy than other types of housing. They are also usually more expensive because they require more land.

One type of single-family home is a manufactured home (sometimes called a "mobile home"). Manufactured homes are houses that are built in a factory then moved to their final location. Most manufactured homes are less expensive than a traditional single-family house. They may come complete with furniture, carpeting, window coverings, and appliances.

AROUND THE WORLD

Housing choices are influenced by available building materials and other uses for land. For the Hopi (HO-pee), Navajo (NAH-vah-ho), and Pueblo (PWEB-lo) Indians of the American Southwest, this resulted in the construction of hogans. These homes were built of logs or stone with domed clay roofs. They were round or hexagonal (six-sided). Hogans were usually spaced far apart, since much of the land was needed to graze sheep. What materials are available for home-building today? How does land use continue to affect housing choices?

What might be the advantages and disadvantages of living in this manufactured home?

▼ Multiple-Family Dwellings ▼

A **multiple-family dwelling** is a structure that contains several housing units under one roof. There are many variations.

- A **duplex** is one building that contains two separate units. The units may be side by side, sharing one wall, or they may be on separate floors.
- A **multiplex** is similar to a duplex, but three or more units share one building.
- **Townhomes** are houses built in rows and attached at the side walls.
- Apartment buildings range from a large older home divided into three or four apartments to a high-rise with hundreds of units. Apartment complexes are made up of a number of separate apartment buildings.

All of these types of multiple-family dwellings use less land than single-family houses. They are especially common in large cities where land is scarce and housing is expensive.

Individual units may be small or large. Residents may share the use of a laundry, swimming pool, or other special features.

As with all types of housing, multiple-family dwellings have their disadvantages. Some people are concerned about noise or lack of privacy. They may want more space for storage and outdoor activities. Children and pets may not be allowed.

However, multiple-family dwellings meet the needs of many people. They are often more affordable and more readily available than single-family houses.

Multiple-family dwellings are often more affordable and meet the needs of many people.

Building Technology

New technology is making it possible to build homes more efficiently. One example is the use of *modular construction*. With this building technique, homes are built in sections at a factory. Then the sections are moved to the building site and assembled. Any type of housing, from apartments to single-family houses, can be built by modular construction.

The cost of modular construction varies widely. It depends on the size, number of rooms, and special features. In general, however, assembling sections inside a factory helps keep costs down and quality high.

Ways to Obtain Housing

Some individuals and families own the housing unit they live in, while others rent it from the owner.

Renting a Home

Renting means paying money to live in a housing unit that is owned by someone else. Owners of rental housing are sometimes called **landlords**. Renters are sometimes called **tenants**. Rental housing is available either furnished or unfurnished and at a range of prices.

All the types of housing units described in this chapter may be rented. In addition, you might rent a room in a house or dormitory. A room just for sleeping, with no private kitchen or bath facilities, is a relatively inexpensive form of housing.

When you rent a housing unit, you may have to fill out an application and sign a **lease** — a written rental agreement. The lease states that you agree to pay rent for a certain number of months. It specifies the monthly fee and any rules you must follow. Always read a lease carefully before you sign it. Many landlords require a security deposit equal to one month's rent or more. The deposit is returned when you move out if the unit has not been damaged.

Many people enjoy the advantages of renting. They include:

- ***Convenience.*** Tasks such as painting and household repairs usually are done by the owner rather than the tenant.
- ***Flexibility.*** Renters don't have to sell their home when it is time to move. Selling a home can be a long and costly process.
- ***Financial advantages.*** Both renting and owning have month-to-month costs. However, tenants do not face unexpected costs for repairs.

What are the pros and cons of renting a home with another person?

Owning a Home

Many people choose to buy a place to live because they value a feeling of permanence. Homeowners also are free to redecorate or remodel their home to meet their personal needs and tastes. Others consider a home as an investment and value the financial security it may give them.

Most people plan for years before buying their housing. Purchasing a place to live is not a decision to be made lightly. Buying a home costs more than any other purchase most families will ever make.

Buying a home is often the largest purchase a family will make. What are some reasons why owning a home may not be for everyone?

Most people take out a long-term loan, called a **mortgage**, to buy a home. The mortgage is typically for 15 to 30 years. Buying a home requires that part of the purchase price be paid in cash. This sum, called a *down payment*, can be quite large.

Other costs must also be considered. A homeowner usually must pay property taxes and insurance, as well as utility and repair costs.

Any type of housing may be owned. Units in a multiple-family dwelling, such as an apartment building, are sometimes owned individually. In that case, they are called **condominiums**. One person does not own the entire building. The owner of each unit pays a fee to help cover the cost of maintaining common areas, such as hallways, lawns, and parking lots.

Another form of ownership is a **cooperative**, or co-op. In a co-op, residents of a multiple-family dwelling form an organization that owns the building. Instead of buying or renting an individual unit, they buy shares in the organization and contribute to its monthly costs. In return, they receive use of one of the living units.

Condominiums and cooperatives combine the advantages of home ownership and apartment living. Many people want to invest in a home but don't want the responsibilities of yard work and outside maintenance.

Sharing a Home

Sharing a home is an option that works well for many people. They can combine their resources with those of other individuals or families to better meet their housing needs.

Almost any type of housing may be shared with others. Friends just out of school may share an apartment to save money. Adult children sometimes return to live with their parents for a time. An older person may move in with a child's family for care and companionship.

Considering the needs of others is a top priority when sharing a home.

Sharing a home only works if people are thoughtful of one another. It is important for people to have some degree of privacy in the home — a place to call their own. They also need a place to visit with friends and a storage area for personal belongings.

Choosing a Place to Live

People often live in several different types of housing during their lifetime, as their needs and resources change. Each time, the decision is an important one. Here are some important points to consider.

- What price range can you afford?
- Is renting or owning right for you at this time?
- What type of housing would best suit your needs?
- What area would you like to live in?
- What specific features are you looking for? Which ones are priorities? On which would you be willing to compromise?

Few people are lucky enough to live in their "dream home." However, the more information you have to make a housing decision, the more satisfied you're likely to be. Finding a place you will call home can be both challenging and rewarding.

Comparing your needs and the many types of housing available is a real benefit when choosing a place to live.

TAKING ACTION

Scott, a friend of your family, has just graduated college and landed a good job as an assistant mechanical engineer. Now he has an important decision to make about housing. He's undecided whether to rent an apartment, or to try to arrange a mortgage for a condominium or small house.

He likes the idea of his own yard. On the other hand, he wonders if he would meet more people in an apartment complex. He knows he wants to settle in the area and hopes to marry someday. Scott comes to you for advice and would like to hear your views.

Using Your Resourcefulness

- Given Scott's needs, wants, and resources, what is your advice?
- Make a list of the advantages and disadvantages of each choice.
- Do you think Scott would be able to arrange a bank loan easily? Why or why not?
- How should Scott go about his housing search? What steps should he take?

Chapter 23 Review

Summary

In this chapter, you have read about:

- How a family's needs, wants, and resources influence its housing decisions.
- Different types of housing available and their advantages and disadvantages.
- How renting and buying housing compare.
- Ways existing housing can be adapted for family members with special needs.

Facts to Recall

1. What three types of basic needs can housing fulfill? Give at least one specific example of each type.
2. Name four factors to be considered when thinking about a family's housing needs and wants.
3. What are utilities?
4. What is the difference between a manufactured home and a traditional single-family house?
5. What is a multiple-family dwelling?
6. How does a multiplex differ from a duplex?
7. What are two advantages and two disadvantages of living in a multiple-family dwelling?
8. What are the advantages of renting a home rather than owning one?
9. What are the advantages of owning your own home?
10. How does a cooperative differ from a condominium?

Ideas to Explore

1. List ten features you would look for in a home. Of these, which three are the most important to you? Why?
2. How might a person who has lived all of his or her life in a single-family home have trouble adapting to living in an apartment?
3. Identify housing concerns common at each stage of the family life cycle.
4. Brainstorm a list of situations when sharing housing might be a good option.

Activities to Try

1. Compare the types of housing being built in your community today with that built 50 to 75 years ago. What changes in families are reflected in the changes in housing? Consider points such as housing choices, size and types of room, and kitchens.
2. Using the ad section of a newspaper, choose 15 apartments that might interest you. Calculate the average monthly rent for these apartments.
3. Imagine that you are in a wheelchair. What difficulties would you encounter trying to get around in your own home?

LINK TO *Communication*

HOUSING ISSUES

You and a friend are thinking about sharing housing together after graduating from high school. Choose one of the following topics and develop a skit showing how you and your friend will identify: needs and wants, determine how much to spend on housing, determine the type of housing needed, or identify household responsibilities. What other topics might enter into your conversation? Why should you work through these issues before moving in with another person? Share your skit with the class.

CHAPTER

24 Understanding the Art of Design

OBJECTIVES

- Explain the elements of design.
- Describe color schemes.
- Identify the principles of design.

TERMS TO LEARN

- *space*
- *line*
- *shape*
- *texture*
- *harmony*
- *proportion*
- *scale*
- *balance*
- *rhythm*
- *emphasis*

Whenever you look at a car, a garden, a pair of running shoes, or a new sweater, you are seeing the results of others' designs. *Your* designs are around for people to see, too. For example, you create a design every time you decide which clothes to wear together, arrange food on a table, or decorate the space where you live. Design is everywhere!

Good design emphasizes the best features of a room or a person's appearance. At the same time, the design makes weaknesses less obvious. This ability to fool the eye is sometimes called *illusion*.

Some people seem to have a natural talent for design. Stephanie, for example, is considered a trend-setter in her choice of clothes. Most people don't realize she has fewer clothes and less expensive clothes than most of her friends.

Even without natural talent, you can learn to create pleasing designs. Understanding the parts — or elements — that make up designs is the first step. Then you will learn how to use these elements by following a set of guidelines called the principles of design.

Elements of Design

The elements of design are five basic building blocks of any design: space, line, shape, texture, and color. As you read about these elements, think about how each is used to make your favorite room comfortable and attractive.

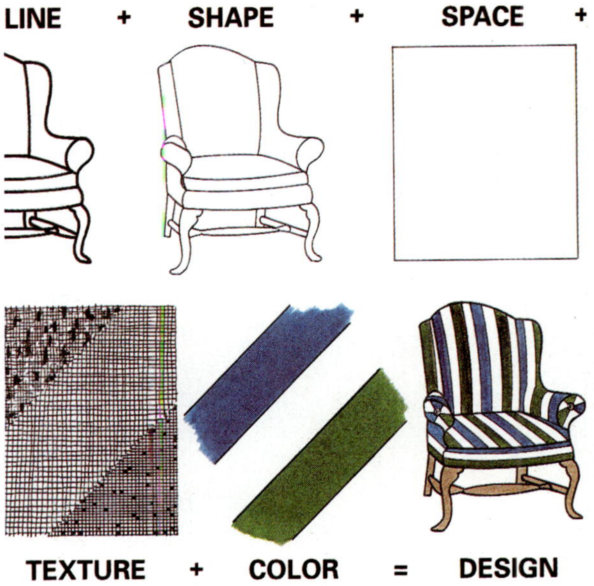

Space

Space refers to the three-dimensional area that is to be designed — a room or a backyard, for example. Space can give different feelings depending on how it is used. For example, a room that contains many pieces of furniture may make some people feel cozy. Others may find the same room uncomfortably crowded. How would you feel in a large room with little furniture?

TIPS: *Creating Feelings with Line*

Lines can be used to create any number of feelings in a room. Think about the purpose of each room. How can line be used to enhance the purpose? Here are some examples:

- Use horizontal lines in a room to create a feeling of restfulness. How might you use horizontal lines in a bedroom?
- Vertical lines suggest action. They might be especially helpful in a family room or play room.
- Using vertical and diagonal lines together suggests a feeling of excitement.

Whenever you arrange furniture, think about how it will be used. People must be able to move easily from one area to another and from one room to another.

Be sure to leave space for the furniture to be used. Can you open the drawers in your bedroom without sitting on the bed? If you pull out the chairs to sit down for a meal, is there still space to walk around the table? Keep the space needs of people and objects in mind for successful decorating.

Line

Line refers to the outline of an object or to obvious lines within it. Lines can cause your eyes to move up and down or across an object. For example, horizontal lines (those that go from side to side) can be used to draw attention to the length of a room. Long, low bookshelves do this. Vertical lines (those that go up and down), can create the illusion of height. Tall bookcases draw the eyes upward. Diagonal and zigzag lines add excitement and interest but should be used only in small amounts. Curved lines are softer and more graceful. The width of lines also makes a difference. Wide lines, especially in bright colors, catch the eye more than narrow lines.

Shape

Shape, or the form of a solid object, is created when lines are combined. Shapes take up some of the space in a room. The shapes of objects can make them seem to be heavy or light. For instance, compare an easy chair in a living room to a chair at a kitchen table. Both would look out of place if their locations were reversed.

Texture

Bumpy, soft, silky, shiny, rough. All these words could be used to describe the **texture** of objects — the way their surfaces look and feel.

A basic rule in combining textures is that they should seem to go together or to relate to each other. For example, dried grasses and berries, being rough in texture, would look appropriate in a piece of old pottery or in a basket. On the other hand, they would look out of place in a shiny plastic dish. Rough texture gives an informal feeling. Smooth, shiny textures seem more formal.

The texture of an item can affect its apparent color. Two fabrics with different textures may not look the same, even though they are of identical color. This is important to keep in mind when trying to match colors.

AROUND THE WORLD

In England, one of the latest home-decorating trends includes the use of handmade fabrics and handmade items such as quilts. Some designers believe this is due to an increased awareness of the environment. How might this trend express concern for the environment?

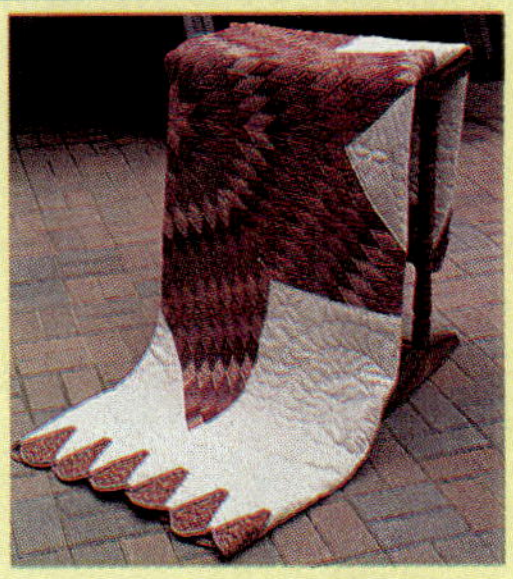

Color

Color is one of the most important design elements. It even has its own language. When you understand the basics of color, you can use it to give the look you want.

In the study of color, *value* refers to the lightness or darkness of a color. For instance, pink is the lightest value of red, and maroon is its darkest value. Light values are sometimes called *tints* and dark values are called *shades*.

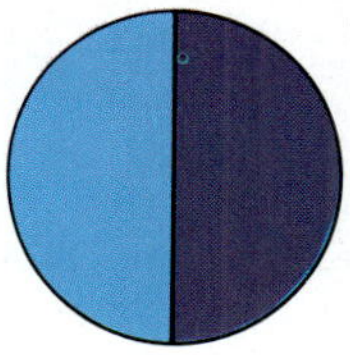

Value affects how large a room or object looks. For example, Inez painted the walls of her small apartment pale blue and light peach to make the rooms appear larger and more open. Dark walls would have made the room seem smaller.

The term *intensity* describes how bright or dull a color appears. A color at full intensity, such as bright red, is very striking. It tends to stand out. Colors with lower intensity, such as dusty rose, are less obvious. In general, low-intensity or dull colors are better for large areas, such as walls and floors. Bright colors often are used for smaller accents, such as pillows and pictures.

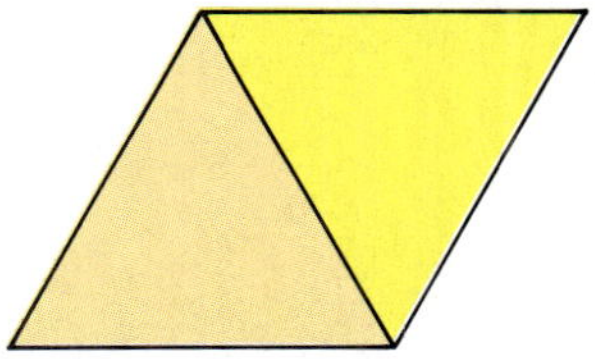

When choosing colors, think about the way they make you feel. Yellow, yellow-orange, orange, red-orange, and red are associated with warmth. Warm colors also make objects appear larger and closer to you.

Green, blue, blue-green, blue-violet, and violet are called cool colors. They may remind you of water, trees, and sky. Cool colors tend to make objects look smaller and farther away. Using cool colors in a small, sunny room would give feelings of coolness and space.

The Color Wheel

The color wheel is a helpful tool for understanding and using color. It starts with a circle divided into twelve pie-shaped sections.

Red, yellow, and blue are called the *primary colors*. All the other colors on the color wheel can be made from them. The primary colors are placed an equal distance apart on the color wheel (every fourth section).

When two primary colors are mixed in equal amounts, a *secondary color* is formed. The three secondary colors are violet, green, and orange. Violet is made by mixing red and blue. Green is a mixture of yellow and blue, and orange is made from red and yellow. The secondary colors go on the color wheel halfway between the primary colors from which they are made.

When you mix a primary and a secondary color, a *tertiary color* (TUR-shee-air-ee) is formed. There are six tertiary colors: yellow-green, blue-green, blue-violet, red-violet, yellow-orange, and red-orange. These tertiary colors fill in the remaining spaces on the color wheel. (Note that the primary color comes first in the name of each tertiary color.)

Black, gray, and white are neutral colors. Sometimes ivory, beige, and tan are also considered neutrals. They are not found on the color wheel.

THE COLOR WHEEL

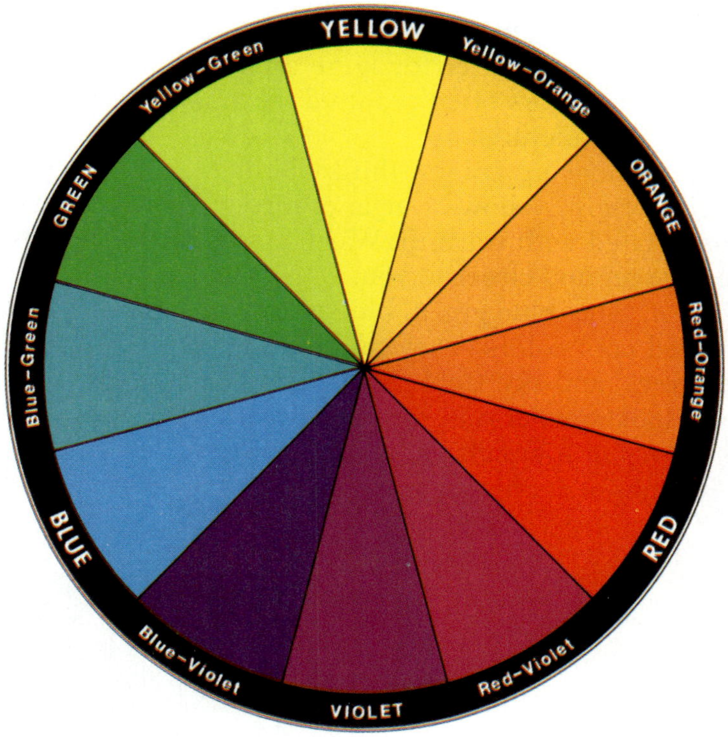

Pocket Lab

Mixing Secondary Colors

MATERIALS:
Red, yellow, and blue tempera paint; white paper

EQUIPMENT:
Small paint brush; paper plate for mixing paint

Directions: Mix equal parts (3 drops each) of the following primary colors to make the secondary colors:

- red + yellow = orange
- yellow + blue = green
- blue + red = violet

After mixing the secondary colors, compare them to the secondary colors on the color wheel on page 266 of the text. Are the colors the same as or different from those found in the text? Why or why not? What happens when primary colors are mixed in unequal proportions?

Color Schemes

There are a number of color schemes, or combinations, that are pleasing to the eye. Each one is based on the color wheel.

- ***Monochromatic.*** This color scheme uses tints and shades of only one color. For example, grass and trees form a monochromatic color scheme made of various values and intensities of green.
- ***Analogous*** (uh-NAL-uh-gus). This color scheme is made up of two or more colors next to each other on the color wheel. Blue-green, green, and blue, for example, form an analogous color scheme.
- ***Complementary.*** This color scheme is made up of two colors that are directly opposite each other on the color wheel. Examples are blue and orange, red and green, and yellow and violet.
- ***Split-complementary.*** This scheme results when a color is combined with colors on either side of its complement. Blue, red-orange, and yellow-orange form a split-complementary scheme.
- ***Triadic.*** This color scheme uses three colors the same distance from one another on the color wheel. For example, the primary colors — red, blue, and yellow — form a triadic scheme.

Triadic

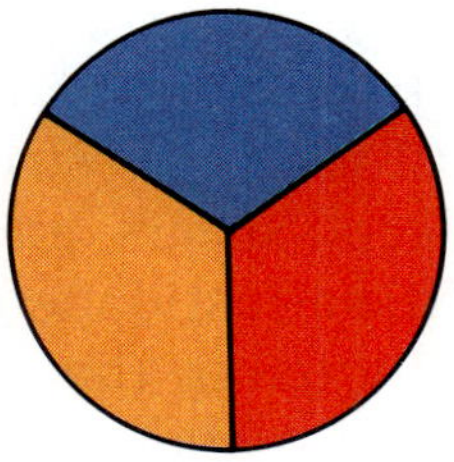
Split-complementary

Complementary

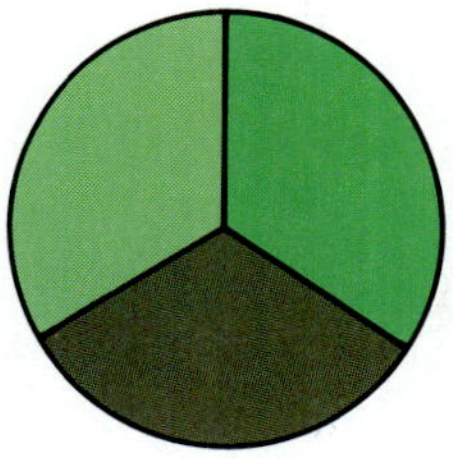
Monochromatic

Analogous

How to . . .

Bring Design into Everyday Life

Have you ever walked into a room and felt that something didn't look quite right? Perhaps a chair wasn't in the right place, or the carpeting seemed to be fighting with the wallpaper. You may have that same feeling as you put together an outfit or prepare a meal. As you will see, the elements and principles of design that are used to decorate a room also apply to clothing and food.

In drawing A, the teen girl is wearing a denim skirt and jacket with a tucked-in chambray shirt. Her accessories include black shoes, a simple black belt with a gold buckle, a gold pendant, and hoop earrings. Notice how line and color are used to create vertical movement. The point of emphasis draws your eye to the neckline.

In drawing B, the same girl changes the look of her outfit by wearing the shirt over the skirt and adding some bold jewelry. Horizontal lines are created at the waist and neckline. In both cases, all parts of the design are attractive and seem to go together.

Look at the food examples in drawings C and D. In drawing C, the plate contains a nutritious meal. However, baked white fish with mashed potatoes, cauliflower, and cottage cheese salad isn't very appealing to the eye. All of the foods are light in color and have a soft texture.

In drawing D, the same white fish is garnished with colorful vegetable strips and served with boiled new potatoes, broccoli spears, and a crisp tossed salad. Notice how paying a little attention to design brings real appeal to this meal.

By using the principles and elements of design when choosing what to wear, preparing food for you and your family, or decorating your room, you can bring beauty into every part of your life.

Drawing A

Drawing B

Drawing C

Drawing D

Using the principles of design effectively can increase your enjoyment of a room. In what ways can you identify the use of harmony, proportion, scale, balance, rhythm, and emphasis in this room?

Principles of Design

The recipe for your favorite cookies is based on principles of baking developed over the years. The same is true of design. The principles of design have been tested for centuries. They can help you combine the ingredients, or the elements, of design to fit *your* personality.

Harmony

Harmony is the feeling that all parts of a design belong together. That doesn't mean that everything has to match. Variety is interesting if the objects grouped together have something in common, such as style, shape, color, or size.

Proportion

Choosing a centerpiece for a table or placing furniture in a room involves **proportion**. It is the way one part of a design relates in size or shape to another or to the whole.

The ancient Greeks discovered that certain uneven proportions create the most pleasing effects. For example, a table that is 2 feet wide by 3 feet long is more pleasing to the eye than one 2 feet square. Proportions are usually expressed as ratios. The first table would have a ratio of 2:3 (2 to 3). Other pleasing proportions include 3:5 and 5:8.

Scale

Scale refers to the overall size of an object or its size compared to other objects. For example, a very small lamp seems even smaller when placed on a large table. Both are considered out of scale with each other.

▼ Balance ▼

A design that has **balance** gives a feeling of equal weight among all parts of a design. Balance can be formal or informal. In formal balance, the objects on each side of an imaginary center line are the same — or at least the same in several elements. One side seems like a reflection of the other. In informal balance, the objects on each side of the center are different in size, form, texture, and/or color.

▼ Rhythm ▼

Rhythm, or a feeling of movement, leads the eye from one point to another. This is done by repeating one or more elements of design. For instance, there is rhythm in the folds of a skirt or the increase in size of kitchen canisters.

▼ Emphasis ▼

In a design, your eyes are attracted to the point of greatest interest, or **emphasis**. A room's point of emphasis might be a poster. An outfit's might be a bright scarf.

Using Design Effectively

Whether you're designing an outfit, a table setting for a meal, or the space where you live, you can make it reflect your tastes and interests. By putting the elements and principles of design to work, you can increase your enjoyment and your family's, too.

TAKING ACTION

Mr. Raible, your friend Jenine's father, plans to open a cafe. His idea is to offer inexpensive but nutritious foods such as salads, soups, and sandwiches. He hopes to attract teens, as well as adults.

Mr. Raible has asked you and Jenine what you would do if you were the interior designers on the project. The dining area is a narrow room with a low ceiling and one large window.

Using Your Resourcefulness

- Decide on an overall design theme that will appeal to both teens and adults.
- Choose a color scheme.
- Sketch your design suggestions. Keep the elements and principles of design in mind.
- Find out where you can learn about fire and safety regulations that may affect the design.

Chapter 24 Review

Summary

In this chapter, you have read about:

- The ways design is used in many aspects of everyday life.
- How every design is made up of five elements.
- How understanding color can help you use it effectively.
- The ways color schemes are formed.
- How the principles of design can be used to create an attractive living space.

Facts to Recall

1. What are the five basic elements of design?
2. What are two practical things to remember when using space?
3. How do vertical lines affect an object or a room? Horizontal lines?
4. What is one basic rule of combining textures?
5. Define value as it relates to color.
6. Define warm and cool as they relate to color. Give two examples of each.
7. What are the three primary colors? Why are they called primary?
8. What is the difference between a secondary and a tertiary color?
9. What are the six principles of design?
10. What is the difference between formal and informal balance?

Ideas to Explore

1. Why might someone paint a room a dark color?
2. What textures might be appropriate for a two-year-old's playroom? How might they differ from those in a formal dining room?
3. Explain how rhythm is created by hanging three pictures on a wall, with the picture in the center higher than the ones on the side.

Activities to Try

1. Analyze your appearance today in terms of design elements and principles. For example, what type of color scheme do your clothes form? What is your point of emphasis?
2. Make a poster showing at least one example of each of the five types of color schemes. You may use rooms, clothes, or foods as examples.

LINK TO *Art*

VALUES OF COLOR

Value refers to the lightness or darkness of a color. Use the following guidelines to create a light value (a tint) and a dark value (a shade) of your favorite primary color:

1. On a sheet of white construction paper, use a ruler and a pencil to draw three, 2-inch (5-cm) squares. Number the squares 1, 2, and 3.
2. Using tempera paint in your favorite primary color, paint square number 1.
3. Mix equal parts (3 drops each) of primary color tempera paint with white tempera paint to create a *tint*. Paint square number 2.
4. Mix equal parts (2 to 3 drops each) of primary color tempera paint with black tempera paint to create a *shade*. Paint square number 3.

Which square of paint appears to look larger? Smaller? Why?

CHAPTER

25 Making Design Work for You

OBJECTIVES

- Identify the backgrounds in a room.
- Select and arrange furniture and accessories.
- Describe ways to make sharing space easier.

TERMS TO LEARN

- *functional furniture*
- *furniture joints*
- *upholstery*
- *traffic lanes*

Whether your home has a single room or many, you can use your knowledge of design to make it more comfortable. Remember that good design doesn't mean starting with an empty room and buying everything new. Even small changes can make a big difference. A few bright pillows, a can of paint, or simply rearranging furniture can add new appeal to a room.

Of course, a home is meant for people to live in. A good design must be both pleasing to the eye and comfortable and convenient for those who use it.

Designing Living Space

Whether you are a professional interior designer or simply someone trying to make a bedroom more appealing, the task is similar. Here's a step-by-step plan you can follow for improving any room.

- ***Step 1: Identify needs and wants.*** Planning a good design starts with identifying needs and wants of those who will use a room. Is there a major goal to be achieved? What activities will take place in the room? What type of storage is needed? The Sanchez family wants to make space in their kitchen for a table and chairs. Stephanie and Tim Rogy have a small apartment. Their decorating plan includes painting their living room to make it brighter and adding storage space. Carlos and Mike want more privacy in their shared bedroom.
- ***Step 2: Evaluate the current room using the elements and principles of design.*** What aspects work well and which need improvement? This analysis will help you make your design plan.

What elements and principles of design are used in this room? How might the way the elements are used be improved?

TIPS: *Decorating Walls*

Here are some tips for arranging wall decorations:

- Hang decorations at eye level.
- Place single wall decorations over a piece of furniture that is in proportion to the decoration.
- Choose frames that complement the artwork or needle work.
- Use an uneven number of items if you are creating a wall arrangement. Uneven numbers are more pleasing to the eye.
- When arranging a wall grouping, try tracing each item on paper and cutting them out. Practice arranging your paper "wall decorations" (using masking tape on the back) before fastening the hangers or nails to the wall.
- Avoid hanging items where they could be damaged by heating vents or dirt.

- ***Step 3: Consider your resources.*** Changing your room's look doesn't mean you have to start from scratch. Adding a few new touches to what you already have can make a big difference. So can reducing clutter by giving away things you no longer want or need. Remember that *resources* mean more than money. You also can put your skills to work. Perhaps a friend or relative can help you learn a new skill as you work.

Careful planning will help you meet your design goals. Backgrounds, furniture, accessories, and storage areas must all work together in a successful design.

Backgrounds

Walls, windows, and floors serve as backgrounds for furnishings and accessories. They help show off furniture and decorative objects to their best advantage.

Walls

Walls form the shape of a room and divide a large area, such as an apartment, into smaller areas. Walls also help give people privacy and cut down on noise.

The number of ways to make walls attractive is limited only by your imagination. The two most popular ways use paint or wallpaper. With paint, you can have your choice of colors or even paint a design. Wallpaper can add interesting patterns and textures to walls and ceilings.

You can combine wall treatments, or finishes, in a room. For example, you might wallpaper one wall and paint the other three. Another option is to paint the lower half of each wall and wallpaper the upper part.

In what ways do the walls, windows, and floors show off the best features of the furnishings in the photo? How do these backgrounds help create interest?

Windows

Window treatments (sometimes called window coverings) provide both privacy and decoration. There are many choices including curtains, drapes, shutters, blinds, or shades.

You can use one or more window treatments. For instance, you might use curtains or drapes along with fabric shades or mini-blinds. With basic sewing skills you might make simple curtains yourself. Window coverings can really change the look of a room. Think about the options and check their costs before making your choice.

Floors

Floor coverings can add both comfort and beauty to a room. Many people like flooring materials such as wood, vinyl, and ceramic tile. They are durable and easy to clean. Carpets and rugs can provide extra comfort and color. Wall-to-wall carpet covers the entire floor in a room. Rugs usually cover only part of the floor. Rugs come in many shapes and sizes.

Furniture

Furniture has many roles. It provides a place for all kinds of activities: visiting with your family and friends, watching television, relaxing, eating, and sleeping. Most furniture is **functional furniture**. That means it meets specific needs. Chests, for example, provide storage space. Tables give space for eating and, perhaps, doing your homework. Of course, functional furniture is usually decorative as well.

Around the World

The use of wood lattice was brought to Mexico by Spanish explorers and is still popular there today. Lattice (LAT-iss) is a design created by criss-crossing strips of material, leaving space between them, or by cutting patterns in the material to achieve the same effect. These patterns can be intriguing and appealing. Lattice is also practical since it partially hides whatever is behind it. It is used in chest doors, bookcases, and over windows. How could you use lattice to improve your living space?

How to ...
Paint a Room

Painting is one way to give a room a quick facelift. Whether you paint one wall in an accent color or the entire room, you will quickly see the results of your work.

Painting isn't a difficult skill to learn. You do need a steady hand and a willingness to work carefully. Here are the steps to follow.

- ***Step 1: Choose the paint.*** Use what you have learned about color to choose paint that will highlight the room's features. Interior paint comes in latex and oil varieties. Walls and ceilings are usually painted with flat (not shiny) paint. Choose gloss or semi-gloss for the trim, such as window frames.

- ***Step 2: Get the room ready.*** Move everything possible from the room, including curtains and rugs. Cover the floor and any remaining items with plastic or canvas drop cloths. Next, clean the areas to be painted. Use spackle — a plasterlike material that comes in a can — to fill any cracks or holes. Scrape or sand away any loose paint.

- ***Step 3: Assemble your equipment.*** Walls and ceilings can be painted with a roller or brush. For window and door frames and other trim, use an angled trim brush. Use masking tape or special painting tape to protect areas (such as windowpanes) that will not be painted. Keep at least one rag handy to wipe up any paint spills or splatters.

- ***Step 4: Plan your job.*** The best order for painting a room is ceiling first, walls second, and trim last.

▶ ***Step 5: Begin painting.*** Stir the paint thoroughly with a clean mixing paddle. If you are using a roller, pour paint into the roller tray. First use a trim brush to paint a strip on the ceiling where it meets the wall. Use the roller to paint the remainder. Repeat the procedure with the walls. Some rooms may need a second coat of paint to cover the existing color.

▶ ***Step 6: Paint trim.*** Carefully, paint any trim with the trim brush. This includes windows and doors and baseboards. Use pieces of cardboard to shield the nearby walls as you paint the trim.

▶ ***Step 7: Clean up.*** When you are finished, clean your brushes, roller, and tray thoroughly. With latex paint, use water for cleanup. With oil paint, use turpentine or paint thinner. Keep any leftover paint tightly sealed in the can. Make a record of how much paint you used, what brand, and what color. That information will help if you need to touch up problem areas or decide to paint the room again.

TRADITIONAL

EARLY AMERICAN

CONTEMPORARY

What might be the advantages and disadvantages of each type of furniture for a family with young children, an elderly couple, and a single person?

Looking at Furniture Styles

Because people's tastes differ, manufacturers make many styles of furniture. These styles can be divided into two basic types: traditional and contemporary.

Traditional styles are based on designs that have been used for hundreds of years. Wealthy people who lived in cities had fine furniture made of beautiful woods and elegant fabrics. This furniture often had carving or other decorations. Those who lived in the countryside made similar furniture but with simpler lines and less decoration. Thus traditional furniture can be formal or informal and fancy or plain. English and French furniture influenced much of the traditional furniture you see today.

Early American furniture is another traditional style. It was developed in the American colonies. It often is made of maple, pine, or oak and has a simple, informal design. Many people like the warm, relaxed feeling it gives.

Oriental furniture generally has very simple lines. The furniture is made of dark or black wood with a shiny finish. Oriental design also influenced traditional European furniture.

Contemporary furniture is simple and reflects today's lifestyles. It has straight or smoothly curved lines with little or no decoration. Although some pieces of contemporary furniture are made of plastic, glass, and metal, wood and fabric are often used, too.

Should you use only one furniture style in a room? Sometimes it is more interesting to combine furniture from several periods. For example, you might try using an Early American rocking chair in a contemporary bedroom. It's best to choose styles that have a similar feeling, such as simple country styles from different time periods. This can help give a room a special look.

Choosing Furniture

Before selecting furniture, determine what you have and what you need. Maybe your bed and chest of drawers are in good condition, but you would like a desk and chair. If money is limited, put your creativity to work. Garage sales, flea markets, and consignment or secondhand shops often have used furniture bargains just waiting for you. With a coat of paint or a new cushion these pieces may be just what you have in mind.

When selecting furniture, new or used, evaluate it carefully. See the "Furniture Buying Checklist" on page 279 for points to consider.

When buying furnishings, whether new or used, evaluate them carefully. What characteristics should you look for before making a purchase?

Furniture Buying Checklist

Will the proportion and scale fit the room and other furnishings?

- ✔ Can the piece serve more than one purpose?
- ✔ Does the piece feel sturdy?
- ✔ Do drawers slide smoothly in and out?
- ✔ Are the **furniture joints**, (the points at which any two furniture parts connect) firm and tight?
- ✔ Do knobs and handles all match and are they firmly attached?
- ✔ Does upholstery have straight seams and well-fitted corners? (**Upholstery** refers to materials such as fabric, padding, and springs, that are used on covered sections on furniture.)
- ✔ What kind of upkeep does the furniture need?

Arranging Furniture

The smart way to arrange furniture is to use paper before muscles. All you need is graph paper and a measuring tape. Measure the size of the room. Use your measurements to draw the outline of the room on graph paper. Make each square represent 6 inches (15 cm) or 1 foot (30.5 cm). Be sure to mark the size and placement of windows, doors, and other features. On another piece of graph paper draw the sizes and shape of each piece of furniture. Cut them out. Then try different arrangements just by moving the paper "furniture."

You can also buy kits that contain precut furniture shapes. The shapes are made of plastic that clings to an outline of your room. The "furniture" is easy to move around.

There are also computer software programs that can help you try out various furniture arrangements. Some are simple, inexpensive programs that function much like the graph paper approach. Others (often called CAD programs for computer-aided design) can give lifelike views of how a finished room will look. Professional designers find these very useful.

Take time to think about your arrangement plan. Ask others for their ideas. Check to see if the **traffic lanes** — paths from one area or room to another — are uncluttered and fairly direct. Don't block them with furniture.

Planning effective traffic lanes makes a room more functional.

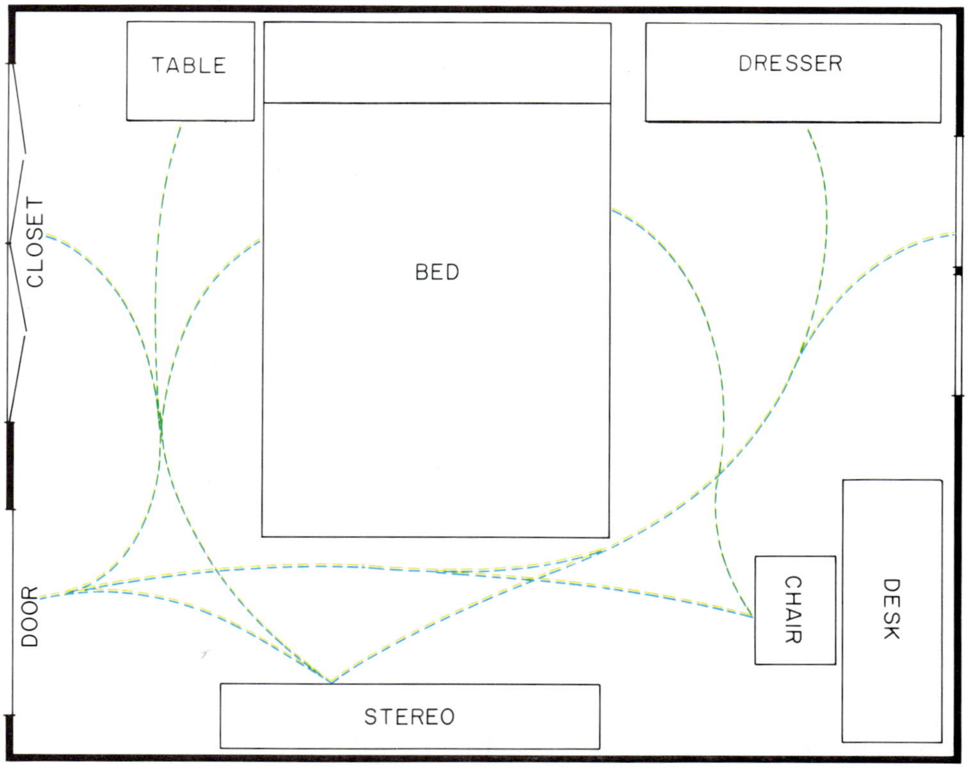

How are accessories used to enhance the appearance of this room?

Accessories

Accessories can make the difference between an uninteresting room and an exciting one. Lamps, plants, posters, books, baskets, and pictures are just a few possibilities. What other low-cost ideas can you add?

When selecting accessories, keep in mind the elements and principles of design. A large lamp, for example, would overwhelm a small delicate table. Remember that a few carefully selected accessories can be far more effective than many less attractive ones.

Storage Areas

No matter how much storage space a family has, there never seems to be enough. A first step is to organize existing storage space to improve its usefulness. If more storage is needed there are many options.

Boxes, plastic crates and containers, pegboards, and baskets are just a few inexpensive storage stretchers.

Not all storage needs to be hidden. Think of ways to make stored items part of your room design. You might, for example, display your baseball cap collection or scarves on a pegboard on the wall. The next chapter gives additional storage tips.

Effective storage allows you to make the best use of space.

Sharing Space

Everyone must share space. It may be at home, at work, in a shopping mall, or even on the beach. In a family, everyone shares areas such as the kitchen and living room. Bathrooms usually are shared, too.

Agreeing on a few ground rules helps make sharing living space a positive experience. What types of rules do you think would be most helpful?

Many teens share a bedroom with one or more siblings. If you share a room, you've probably discovered that differences in age, interests, types of friends, and study habits can create problems.

Whenever people share the same space, it helps to agree on a few ground rules. You will enjoy each other more and have fewer conflicts. This also will help keep conflicts at a minimum. Respect and consideration for the other person are the keys. You might, for example, agree not to use each other's books or clothes without permission. Stick to the rules you make.

If you have different needs and schedules, let your furniture arrangement help solve the problem. For example, try separating the sleeping and activity areas of the room. In a shared bedroom divide the room so you each have a private area.

Think of sharing space as a plus, not a minus. Learning how to share space can teach you a lot about yourself and others. The cooperation and communication skills you learn will help you both now and in the future.

TAKING ACTION

In a few months, Guy will have to begin sharing his bedroom with his ten-year-old brother Kirk. The new baby the family is expecting will go in Kirk's room. Guy isn't happy about the idea but knows there's no other choice. Mrs. Thompson has agreed to redecorate the room in order to make both sons as comfortable as possible.

Guy asks you for your ideas. The bedroom is 12 feet (3.7 m) square with one large closet. There are two twin beds, chests of drawers, and desks. Guy also wants to keep a big arm chair and a bookcase. He's concerned about overcrowding the room, and he knows his mother's budget is limited.

Using Your Resourcefulness

- Design a furniture plan that takes into account comfort, privacy, and traffic lanes.
- How can you involve Kirk in this process?
- What are inexpensive ways Guy and Kirk might accessorize the room?
- Where could you turn for more information or help in planning?

Chapter 25 Review

Summary

In this chapter, you have read about:

- A three-step plan for designing or improving your living space.
- How a room's background elements can be used for the most pleasing effect.
- Furniture styles from different time periods and parts of the world.
- How to select and arrange furniture.
- How accessories can personalize a room.
- Creative use of space for storage.
- Tips on sharing space with others.

Facts to Recall

1. What two basic characteristics must a good design have?
2. List the three steps in planning improvements to living space.
3. What parts of a room are considered as the backgrounds for furniture?
4. What are the two most popular types of wall treatments?
5. Identify four types of window treatments.
6. Describe two ways in which traditional furniture differs from contemporary furniture.
7. List five signs of quality in furniture.
8. Explain how to test different furniture arrangements using paper.
9. What are traffic lanes and why are they important?
10. What are the keys to successfully sharing living space with another person?

Ideas to Explore

1. What pieces of furniture can you think of that serve more than one purpose?
2. Identify the accessories in your classroom. Are they functional, decorative, or both? How might you use accessories to make the room more appealing without making it distracting?
3. Develop a list of the ten rules you think would be most important if you shared a bedroom with a brother or sister.

Activities to Try

1. Decide what background materials and colors you would choose to make a cold room seem warmer. What would you choose to make a warm room seem cooler? (Refer to Chapter 24 for ideas.)
2. Examine two pieces of classroom furniture. Discuss both their good and poor construction features.
3. Draw sketches or write descriptions of at least three ways to use items as decorative accessories instead of storing them out of sight.

LINK TO *Social Studies*

FURNITURE STYLES AND HISTORY

At the library, research three traditional furniture styles. Furniture styles that you might choose to research include Colonial, William and Mary, Queen Anne, Chippendale, Federal, Shaker, or Victorian. Use the following questions to guide your research:

- Describe the unique design features of each style of furniture.
- What historical factors influenced each furniture style? Include the needs of people, era of time, tools available, etc.
- How did other cultures influence traditional furniture styles in America?

CHAPTER

26 Keeping Your Home Clean and Safe

OBJECTIVES

- *Develop a maintenance plan for your home.*
- *Identify important home sanitation, safety, and security practices.*
- *Identify repairs best left to professionals.*

TERMS TO LEARN

- ***maintenance***
- ***sanitation***
- ***hazard***

It's not just people, pets, and plants that need regular care. Your home also needs care to keep it running smoothly. You and your family will find life much easier if you work together to keep your living space clean, safe, and organized.

Keeping belongings put away, disposing of garbage, and cleaning your home regularly are necessary for your family's comfort, health, and safety. Also important are caring for equipment and repairing or replacing broken or worn-out items.

Getting Organized

The first step in organizing for home maintenance is to develop a plan of work. Home **maintenance** includes cleaning, making repairs, and checking appliances and equipment regularly. A good maintenance plan can catch small problems before they become large expensive ones.

To develop a maintenance plan, list the jobs for each room or area of your home. Decide how often each should be done — daily, weekly, or occasionally. Then consider how much time each job will take and the order in which it needs to be done. The last step is deciding who will be responsible for each job. Even small children can be given simple tasks. Many families rotate job assignments.

When family members work together to keep a home clean and safe, the results are rewarding. How can families benefit by working together?

THE VALDEZ FAMILY'S MAINTENANCE PLAN

		MOM	DAD	HOLLY (15)	CALVIN (13)	BECKY (10)	ANDY (4)
DAILY	Make your bed. Put away clean clothes and place dirty clothes in the laundry.	■	■	■	■	■	■
	Wash and rinse dishes. Take out the garbage.				■		
	Dry and put away dishes. Sweep kitchen floor.			■			
	Clean table, countertops, and appliances.					■	
WEEKLY	Dust your room. Straighten closets and drawers.	■	■	■	■	■	■
	Vacuum carpeting.		■				
	Mop hard floors. Clean oven. Change linens.	■					
	Clean all bathtubs, showers, sinks, toilets, and mirrors.			■		■	
	Dust all the furniture in living, dining, and family rooms.				■		■
MONTHLY	Clean refrigerator. Dust upholstery and the draperies.	■					
	Clean medicine cabinets and lampshades. Check for burned out light bulbs and replace them.					■	
	Conduct fire drill.				■		
	Polish furniture in living, dining, and family rooms.				■		■
	Clean all throw rugs. Dust walls and ceilings for cobwebs.			■			
	Check smoke detectors and fire extinguishers. Change filters in heating/cooling system. Turn all bed mattresses.		■				
SEASONALLY	Clean basement, garage, and/or attic.	■	■	■	■	■	■
	Clean all woodwork (i.e. baseboards, doors, windowsills).				■		■
	Wash windows and screens.			■		■	
	Shampoo carpeting.		■				
	Air blankets and pillows. Clean out kitchen cabinets and hall closets.	■					

Some maintenance tasks, such as cleaning the refrigerator, need only be done occasionally. What other tasks can you think of that need to be done seasonally or occasionally?

▼ Daily, Regular, and Occasional Tasks ▼

Look around, and you can see that people have different standards of cleanliness. For example, Kim's family likes to keep their home spotless, with everything in its place at all times. On the other hand, Eric's parents don't mind a certain amount of clutter. Although there is no right or wrong, you and your family need to agree on an acceptable standard of tidiness. This may take some compromise on everyone's part.

Many families consider these to be daily tasks:

- Washing dishes.
- Disposing of garbage.
- Wiping up food spills as they occur.
- Putting away clothes and other belongings.

When everyone is willing to help, these chores can be finished more quickly.

Each family decides how often other cleaning tasks must be done. Many schedule a general cleaning of their living space once a week. Others may do these tasks more or less often. The kitchen and bathroom need frequent and careful cleaning to keep germs under control.

Your list of maintenance tasks will also include some to be performed occasionally or seasonally. Occasional tasks include cleaning the refrigerator, washing walls and windows, and cleaning out closets. Check the instruction books that come with furnishings and equipment for proper maintenance. Add those tasks to your list. Many families also need to list outdoor tasks such as raking leaves or cutting grass.

Storage

Clothes, toys, towels, dishes, cleaning supplies, and tools are found in every home. Where do they belong? Each room needs space for storing items that normally are used there. Having organized storage space available encourages family members to put things away after each use.

Two basic rules to follow when organizing storage space are:

- Store items near the area they are used.
- Store frequently used items where they can be reached easily.

Storage that is easy to use is especially important in kitchens, bathrooms, and children's rooms. One of the best ways to save time cleaning is to keep items picked up as you go along.

How can well-organized storage space make home maintenance easier and safer?

How does clutter affect family safety?

Cleaning Products and Equipment

Part of getting organized for cleaning your living space involves selecting appropriate products and equipment. Household cleaning products come in such a wide variety that you may find it hard to choose among them. Many products serve the same function, so read labels carefully before selecting the one you need. Whenever possible avoid dangerous products. Warning labels on the container mean a product requires special caution. Always follow product directions exactly.

Many basic cleaning products are both inexpensive and kind to the environment. Baking soda, for example, makes a good, gentle cleansing powder for sinks, refrigerators, and microwave ovens. It can also be used to remove odors. Products that clean more than one type of surface often are a good buy. However, remember that no matter what advertisements say, cleaning products cannot work without your help. You'll have to do some wiping or scrubbing to loosen dirt and grime. Fortunately, a thin layer of dust and dirt is easy to remove. Only when the dirt piles up do you need to spend extra time and energy on cleaning.

Using the proper equipment also makes cleaning easier. Brooms, mops, buckets, brushes, sponges, dusting cloths, and vacuum cleaners are the major pieces of cleaning equipment needed for home maintenance.

Using the proper equipment makes cleaning easier. What equipment do you find most useful in cleaning your home?

Keeping Your Home Clean and Healthy

Keeping your home neat and organized makes it a pleasant place to live. Proper care makes furnishings and equipment last longer. Actual cleaning is even more important. By removing dust and dirt, disposing of garbage, and controlling pests, you keep your home a healthy place to live. These tasks are sometimes called **sanitation**. Dirt and bacteria can lead to illness.

- ***Dust and dirt.*** To remove dust and dirt, you need to sweep, dust, vacuum, wash, and mop. Sweeping with a broom removes dirt from hard floors. Brooms also can be used for seasonal jobs such as cleaning window screens and dusting cobwebs from walls and ceilings.

  Use a clean cloth or a duster to wipe window sills and baseboards. Then dust all furnishings except upholstered pieces. Don't forget areas such as chair legs and lamp shades. Wood furniture needs occasional polishing to keep it in good condition.

  For cleaning jobs, it helps to know that certain tasks will just naturally come first. For example, as you are dusting work from the top to the bottom. That way dust doesn't fall on areas you have already dusted. It also helps to clean your way around the outside edges of a room. Then clean the center and finish with the floors. This way you won't forget any areas.

Regular vacuum cleaning removes dust and dirt from carpets, hard floors, upholstered furniture, and draperies. How often should vacuuming be performed?

SAFETY CHECK✓

Though you may not have thought about it, cleaning itself can be dangerous. Here are some guidelines to keep you safe and your home clean:

- Follow the directions on cleaning products exactly. Never mix products. The results could be poisonous, explosive, or fatal.
- Keep cleaning products in their original container. That way you will always know what they are and how they should be used.
- Never store cleaning products near food.
- Store cleaning products in a locked cabinet, out of the reach of small children.
- Some cleaners give off powerful fumes. Use a fan and open windows to bring in fresh air.
- Use a sturdy stepladder, not a chair, to reach items stored in high places.
- Be sure the braces on the ladder are fully extended. Never climb all the way to the top step. Follow the ladder manufacturer's directions carefully.

A vacuum cleaner can remove dust and dirt from carpeting, hard floors, upholstered furniture, and draperies. Through suction, it draws soil into the machine where it is trapped inside a bag or container. Vacuum bags and containers must be removed or cleaned frequently for the machine to operate properly.

Washable hard floors need regular washing to remove stubborn dirt. Use a mop, water, and a cleaner safe for the type of floor you have. Mopping generally is done weekly.

- ***Garbage.*** To be sanitary, you should dispose of garbage daily. It's a good habit to empty all the wastebaskets into a central container at the end of each day. Garbage not only looks bad, but also can endanger your family's health. Garbage contains thousands of germs and gives off an unpleasant odor.

  Leftover food on dishes in the kitchen sink is a form of garbage. Make sure food scraps are disposed of properly. Dishes should be washed after meals in hot, sudsy water to remove germs.
- ***Pests.*** Roaches, ants, mice, flies, and termites are all types of household pests. They carry germs that can make you and your family sick. Pests love dust, dirt, and garbage. By keeping your housing clean, you can usually keep pests under control. If you use pest control products, read and follow the directions carefully. If a pest problem becomes severe, call a professional pest control service.

Keeping Your Home Safe

A clean and well-maintained home usually is safe and secure. In fact, maintenance plays a big role in the safety and security of your home. On the other hand, when maintenance jobs are neglected, accidents and even illnesses can occur. For example, toys on the floor can cause someone to fall. Electrical equipment that isn't used properly can become an electrical **hazard** (HAS-urd), or source of danger. Open garbage can lead to fires or illness. An open, improperly stored cleaning product could be poisonous if swallowed.

How might this fall have been avoided?

▼ Falls ▼

Good home maintenance cannot guarantee your family's safety. However, it can prevent unnecessary risks. For instance, many falls can be avoided by:

- Wiping up spills promptly.
- Securing throw rugs to the floor.
- Using a ladder or stepstool to reach items in high places.
- Storing items properly.
- Using adequate lighting.

▼ Electrical Hazards ▼

It's easy to forget the dangers of electricity. Electricity is powerful and should be treated with respect. To avoid electrical hazards:

- Never plug too many cords into an outlet.
- Never use electrical appliances near water.
- Never run electrical cords underneath rugs or carpeting.
- Never leave outlets that small children can reach uncovered.

Electrical hazards can also be avoided by keeping appliances in good working order. Items that are broken or don't work properly can be a safety hazard, and should be unplugged immediately, then repaired or replaced. Check appliances regularly.

Never use electrical appliances near water. The risk of electrical shock greatly increases.

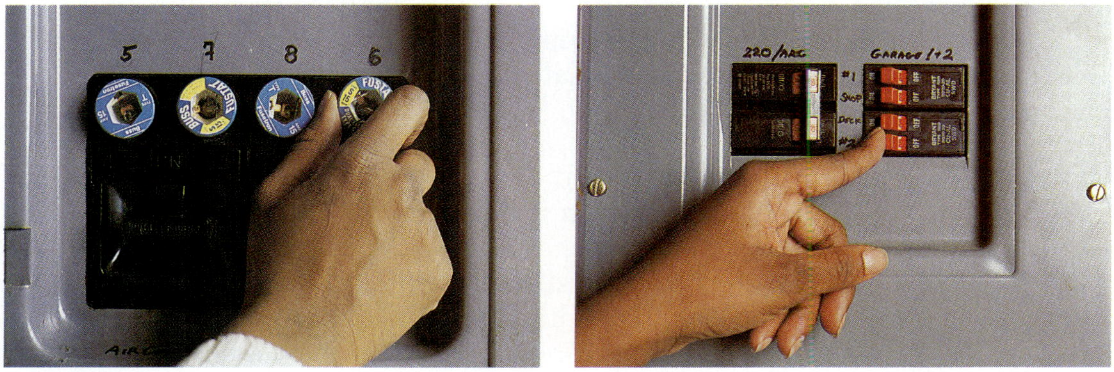

When circuits are overloaded, fuses melt and circuit breakers turn off to prevent damage to the electrical wiring in your home. Be sure to replace fuses with the correct sizes for your system. If you have a circuit breaker box, simply unplug appliances on the overloaded circuit and turn the breaker back on.

AROUND THE WORLD

For many Chinese and Chinese-American people, a home is not hazard-free unless it possesses feng shui (feng-shway). This ancient Asian belief stresses the importance of harmony between people and their surroundings, both natural and manmade. For example, a house with feng shui will not have the front and back door in a straight line with each other. It is believed that this could result in poor health or financial trouble. Some home builders in areas with large Chinese-American populations consider feng shui when building houses.

How does testing all smoke detectors once per month help keep your family safe?

Fires

Matches, cigarettes, candles, grease, and electrical appliances are the most common causes of fires. Garbage cans, mattresses, and upholstered furniture are ideal places for a fire to start. Keep matches out of children's reach. Store flammable products away from all heat sources.

Every home should have fire extinguishers. Keep a chemical extinguisher near the kitchen range for grease and electrical fires. Be sure you know how to use it.

Smoke detectors can provide early warning in case of fire and smoke. Make sure your home has smoke detectors near bedroom areas and on each floor. Check all detectors once a month to see that they are functioning properly.

Saving your home isn't as important as saving your life. It is a good idea to include a monthly fire drill, along with a smoke detector test, in your home maintenance plan. You and your family need to know how to escape from every room. If you live in a building with an elevator, always use stairs instead if there is a fire. Plan for the family to meet in a specific place outside if there's a fire. That way, you will know everyone is safe.

Poisons

Poisons exist in nearly every room of your home. Soaps, bleach, shampoos, aspirin, paint, prescription drugs, most cleaning products, and even some house plants can be deadly. Small children are usually the victims of accidental poisoning. Therefore, poisonous products need to be stored out of children's reach in a locked cabinet. Never tell children that medicine is candy. Also, remove poisonous house plants if there are young children or pets in the home.

If someone swallows something poisonous, act quickly. Call your community's Poison Control Center or a hospital emergency room. Be ready to say what was swallowed and how much. You will also need to know the approximate age and weight of the victim. Carefully listen to the professionals' instructions, and follow them immediately. Quick action can save a life.

Common household products can be very poisonous. Where do you store poisonous products for safety?

Keeping Your Home Secure

Everyone wants to feel safe and secure at home. That means keeping both your family and your belongings safe from harm.

In a home, strong doors with good locks are the most basic need. Deadbolt locks are the best choice. When you turn the key (from inside or outside the door), a strong metal bar slides into the door frame. Some other types of locks can easily be opened by someone trying to break in. Windows and sliding glass doors also need locks. Check with a lock shop for advice on the best types to use.

Make sure the area around outside doors is well lighted. This will help you get in and out of your home safely. One type turns the light on automatically whenever motion is detected. This provides safety yet saves energy. Experts also advise eliminating large bushes near entrances where intruders may hide.

Many other security devices are available. Some, like home alarm systems, are expensive. Others, such as forming a neighborhood watch system, are free. People in the neighborhood simply make it a point to look out for each other and report any suspicious activity. You must also watch out for your own personal safety. As you come and go from your home, especially at night, stay alert. Make it a point to avoid dangerous places.

Simple household repairs, such as repairing bathroom caulking, can help save a family money. What types of simple repairs might you learn to help with?

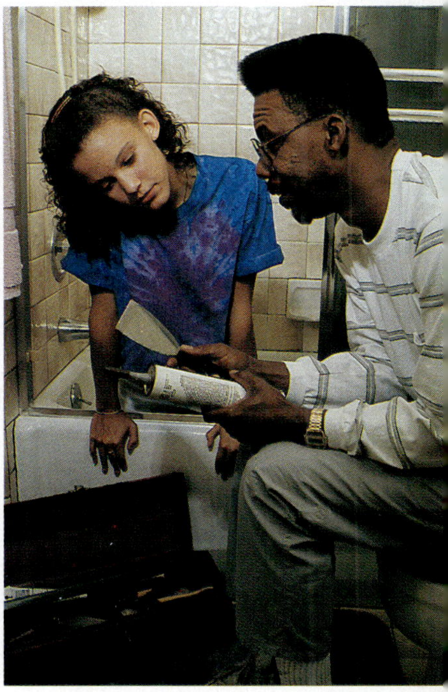

Making Repairs

You and your family can do some repairs yourselves. For example, you should know what to do if the toilet overflows, the kitchen sink becomes clogged, or a fuse blows. You should know how to handle a hammer, screwdriver, wrench, caulking gun, and paintbrush. However, leave difficult repairs

A well-maintained home is good for the environment. How is this family helping to take care of the environment?

to the experts. Hire a licensed electrician to do wiring, a qualified heating technician to repair the furnace, and a licensed plumber to do major plumbing repairs.

In many communities, low-cost classes are available to teach repair skills. Learning these skills can save your family money.

Keeping a Positive Attitude

Attitude plays a major role in the level of maintenance within your home. If all members do their share, the family's maintenance plan will save a lot of time, money, and energy. Instead of having to replace items that are neglected, the family can spend its resources on items and activities that everyone will enjoy.

A well-maintained home is also better for the environment. The more regular cleaning and repairing you do, the less often you will need harsh chemical cleaners or poisonous substances that could pollute the air or water. When you take good care of your *own* environment, you are actually helping everyone else's.

TAKING ACTION

Your friend Kelly offered you a part-time job twice a week helping her clean Mrs. Ellinger's house. You need extra money and agree to give her a hand. Mrs. Ellinger is Kelly's 75-year-old neighbor who often bakes cookies for the two of you. While she's very kind, she is not very neat. Mrs. Ellinger is the first to admit her small house — with one bedroom, bathroom, living and dining area, and kitchen — often looks like it was "struck by a tornado."

To complicate things, Kelly isn't the most organized person you know. She has asked you to think of a fair way to split the cleaning and chores.

Using Your Resourcefulness

- Devise a general maintenance plan for Mrs. Ellinger's house, broken down into daily, weekly, and monthly chores.
- How will you and Kelly divide the chores? Will you repeat the same chores or rotate them?
- What are four ways to insure the house is sanitary and healthy?

Chapter 26 Review

Summary

In this chapter, you have read about:

- Organizing your family's home maintenance plan, according to when tasks are done and who does them.
- Basic cleaning products and equipment and their use.
- Cleaning tasks and maintenance habits that help keep your home safe and attractive.
- Important safety practices to follow.

Facts to Recall

1. List four steps in organizing a home maintenance plan.
2. What are two basic rules to follow when organizing storage space?
3. Which five major pieces of cleaning equipment would you consider most important? Explain your choices.
4. When cleaning a room or area, in what order should the jobs be done?
5. How can garbage and pests endanger your family's health?
6. What is a hazard? Give three examples.
7. Name three ways falls can be avoided.
8. What two types of equipment should every home have to prevent the spread of fire?
9. Name three ways to prevent the accidental poisoning of children.
10. Name three household repairs that you and your family can do yourselves. Name three types of repairs that should be handled by qualified professionals.

Ideas to Explore

1. Which five qualities do you think are most important for a clean and safe environment?
2. At what age should children become involved in home maintenance and cleaning? What tasks might be appropriate for a three-year-old? For an eight-year-old?

Activities to Try

1. You are having a problem keeping your room neat. You know that one reason is lack of closet and drawer space. Devise at least three ways to improve storage using free or inexpensive materials.
2. Identify three cleaning or maintenance tasks you dislike doing. Come up with a plan for making each easier or more enjoyable.

LINK TO *Health and Safety*

PLANNING AN ESCAPE ROUTE

Having a plan of escape from your home in case of fire can be the key to saving your life and the lives of your family members. Use the following guidelines to develop a fire escape plan for you and your family:

- Draw a floor plan of your home. Be sure to indicate the location of all windows and doors.
- On the floor plan, mark the location of smoke detectors.
- Draw two escape routes from your home. Include one escape route from the bedrooms and another from some other area of the home such as a basement or family room. If there is more than one floor in your home, plan a way to escape from additional floors, too.

After you have finished your plan, discuss it with your family. Some authorities suggest having a monthly fire drill to make sure all family members understand how to get out of the home safely.

CAREER *Connections*

Get Ready for Your Future Through Volunteering

"I'd like to become an architect one day, though I've heard jobs may be hard to get in the future. I know I have to get a head start. I looked around for a part-time job or volunteer work in a related area. I asked everybody I knew, and finally Ruth Kendricks — a friend of my uncle's — suggested I help her out in her interior design firm.

"Although I had no actual knowledge, I had formed ideas about interior design and didn't know if the work would prove valuable for architecture. I started out answering phones and learning how to write purchase orders for furnishings that Mrs. Kendricks bought for clients. I also watched her deal with architects. After a time, I realized that architecture and interior design work to complement each other in a successful housing or commercial design project.

"Mrs. Kendricks is very tuned in to how clients will use their living or working space. She chooses furniture, fabrics, and wall treatments that are as practical as they are pleasing to the eye. As I watched her work, I learned that architects need to be extremely sensitive to their clients' needs. They need to understand the intended use of each room they design. I can't predict my career future, but I know this experience has been far more valuable than I ever imagined."

"Designing buildings was my dream. However, I knew it wouldn't be an easy dream to make come true. I worked hard to build a solid educational foundation by taking art, design, drafting, and math courses in high school and college.

"After four years of study in college and two years of working on a master's degree in architecture, I started looking for a job. There were some very discouraging moments. After many weeks of searching, I was hired by an architectural firm as a draftsperson.

"When I look back on school, I think of all the time I used to spend in the computer and drafting labs —

sometimes 30 or 40 hours a week. It turns out that the self-discipline and the skills I developed were incredibly helpful when I took the state licensing exam.

"Now that I'm a licensed architect, I have a wide range of responsibilities. The part I like most about my job is working on my firm's design projects for apartment complexes in a local retirement community."

"I always loved the idea of designing buildings, but I also love computers. In college, I took both architectural and computer-software design courses. It's no accident that in my chosen career I help design computer-aided design software (CAD) for architects. The team I work with develops computer programs that help architects consider design variations at the touch of a few buttons. Other programs can quickly prepare materials lists and cost estimates. It's amazing how computers have streamlined work that would have taken hours or perhaps days to complete in years past."

MAKING THE CONNECTION

- What other related volunteer work would give Brad valuable experience to reach his goals?
- Amy freely admits that searching for a job was frustrating at times. What steps can someone looking for a job take to make the search go as smoothly as possible?
- If Barry were unable to find a job designing computer software for architects, what other jobs might he consider that would employ his professional skills?

UNIT 5 Clothing

CHAPTERS

POLY COTTON

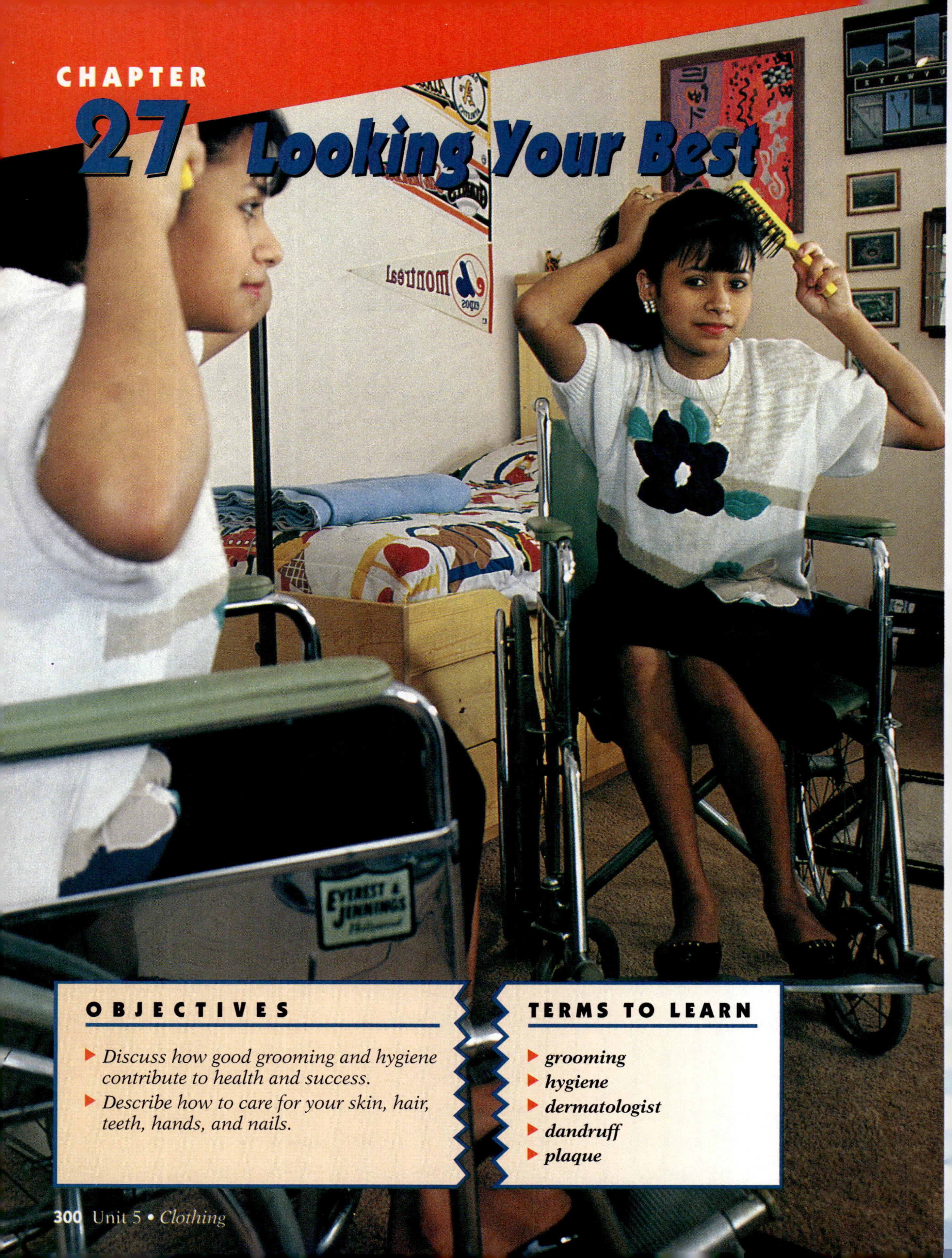

CHAPTER 27 Looking Your Best

OBJECTIVES

- Discuss how good grooming and hygiene contribute to health and success.
- Describe how to care for your skin, hair, teeth, hands, and nails.

TERMS TO LEARN

- ***grooming***
- ***hygiene***
- ***dermatologist***
- ***dandruff***
- ***plaque***

"Hey, you look great today!" That kind of a compliment would brighten anyone's morning.

People make an impression on others within the first few minutes after meeting. You often base decisions about whether you want to get to know someone better on your first impression of them. At the same time, they are using their impression of you to decide whether they want to learn more about you. The way people look, as well as the way they act, affects first impressions.

What does it take to look great? If you put "the right clothes" on the top of the list, think again. Being beautiful or handsome isn't a requirement either. The first key to looking your best is actually good grooming. Even the latest clothes can't make up for dirty hair, grimy fingernails, or lack of a shower. This chapter includes helpful suggestions for looking your best.

Good Grooming

Good **grooming** means developing a personal care routine to keep yourself clean, neat, and attractive. Not everyone is born with perfect looks, but everyone can be good looking by paying attention to the details of his or her grooming.

Cleanliness is essential for both good health and attractiveness. Following some simple guidelines of proper **hygiene**, or cleanliness, can give you a head start on making yourself a more attractive person. How does your routine measure up? Do you take a bath or shower each day? Do you take care of your complexion? Do you keep your hair clean and neatly styled? Do you brush and floss your teeth regularly? Are your nails clean and neatly trimmed? Neglecting any of these areas can keep you from looking and feeling your best.

Taking the time to be well-groomed reflects a positive self-concept. In what ways do your grooming habits show how you feel about yourself?

AROUND THE WORLD

The desire for social unity is a traditional Japanese value that influences modern dress. Many Japanese people strictly follow the latest fashion trends, choosing neutral colors and simple accessories to avoid drawing attention to themselves. Some people are critical of this, saying it puts too much pressure on individuals to conform. Is this true in the United States? How do you personalize your appearance? How do others?

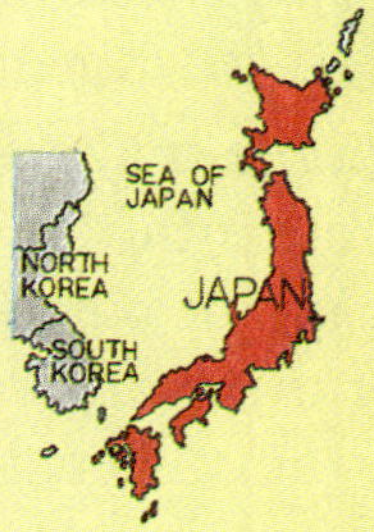

▼ Your Skin ▼

Your skin is like a fabric that covers and protects your body. Skin has important functions. It protects your body. It can feel heat, cold, and pain. Skin helps rid your body of wastes. It gives off oils to keep itself soft and moisture to help regulate your body temperature.

You look your best when your skin is in good condition. Healthy skin starts with eating right. Chapter 39 gives more information on healthy eating habits. Keeping clean is the most important habit for both good looks and good health. Soap and water wash away dirt. They also remove dried skin, extra oil, and surface bacteria that can cause odors and infections.

Start with a daily bath or shower. Remember, just dipping in and out of water doesn't get you clean. You need to use soap. Start washing at the hairline and work down. If you are taking a shower, step from under the spray while you lather so the soap has a chance to work. If you can't take a bath or shower every day, wash well from head to toe.

Eating a variety of healthy foods and drinking plenty of water helps keep skin in good condition. How healthful are your eating habits?

A small brush can help you clean your hands, elbows, ankles, heels. For your back, use a long-handled brush. Rinse well with clean water so that no soap is left on the skin.

If you have dry skin, use lotion after your shower or bath. Many people have dry skin in some areas and oily skin in others. Tanya, for example, has dry skin on her legs and arms but an oily face. She treats each part differently.

Hygiene doesn't end with a shower or bath. Your face needs washing at least twice a day. Your hands need frequent washing. Throughout the day, they pick up dirt and germs. These can easily make you and others ill. Always wash your hands well before meals and snacks. Hands also need to be washed after you use the toilet, touch a pet, or complete cleaning chores. Put germs down the drain. Don't share them with your family and friends.

Antiperspirants and Deodorants

As part of your daily cleanliness schedule, remember to use an antiperspirant or deodorant. You can't count on a daily bath to prevent perspiration odor. Only regular use of a good deodorant or antiperspirant will do this. Many people who offend others with perspiration odor never suspect it. Their own sense of smell does not warn them.

A deodorant controls odor. It does not affect the flow of perspiration. An antiperspirant controls odor and also checks perspiration in the area to which it is applied. Both products come in several forms, such as solid, liquid, spray, or cream. Apply them to clean, dry skin.

Acne

About 80 percent of all teenagers develop acne. Many adults also have this problem.

No one knows exactly what causes acne. A number of factors can play a role. If one of your parents had acne, you are more likely to have it, too. Stress and strong emotions, such as anxiety and fear, can trigger acne. Some medicines can cause skin problems. There is no medical evidence that foods such as chocolate, cola drinks, or potato chips can cause acne or make it worse.

Acne develops when glands below the pores (tiny openings) in the skin become blocked. The oils that normally move through the pores to soften the skin are trapped beneath it. As more oil becomes trapped, blackheads and whiteheads develop. Often, these areas become irritated or infected and develop into pimples.

Acne is most common in teens. The body begins to produce more oily substances. Problems are most common on the face, upper chest, and the back.

How to . . .

Enjoy the Sun and Protect Your Skin

A suntan may help to make a person look healthy. However, you pay a high price for bronzed skin. Too much exposure to the sun's rays damages the skin and causes sagging and wrinkling. The major threat of too much sun is skin cancer (or melanoma).

Ultraviolet light doesn't feel hot, so it's easy to think you don't need extra protection from the sun's ultraviolet rays on cooler days. Clouds or even thin clothing offer little protection. Ultraviolet rays also pass through wet T-shirts and penetrate through several feet of water. The rays also reflect off beach sand and water, increasing your exposure.

What can you do to protect your skin from overexposure to the sun's ultraviolet rays? Doctors recommend using sunscreens for protection. Sunscreens work by absorbing or scattering the harmful rays of ultraviolet light.

Sunscreens are sold with an SPF (sun protection factor) number. The SPF number indicates the amount of protection you receive against the harmful rays of the sun and sunburn. An SPF of 10, for example, allows a person who would normally burn after 30 minutes exposure to the sun to safely be in the sun for five hours or 10 times longer than usual.

How do you select and use sunscreens?

- If you burn easily with minimum exposure, you would want to pick a sunscreen with a 15 SPF or higher, especially in a hot climate.
- As a rule of thumb, you'll get the best SPF protection by applying the sunscreen liberally over your entire body.
- It's best to apply a sunscreen approximately 30 minutes before exposure to sunlight. This allows it to be absorbed so it will be less likely to be washed off by perspiration.
- If you perspire heavily or go into the water often, reapply the sunscreen.

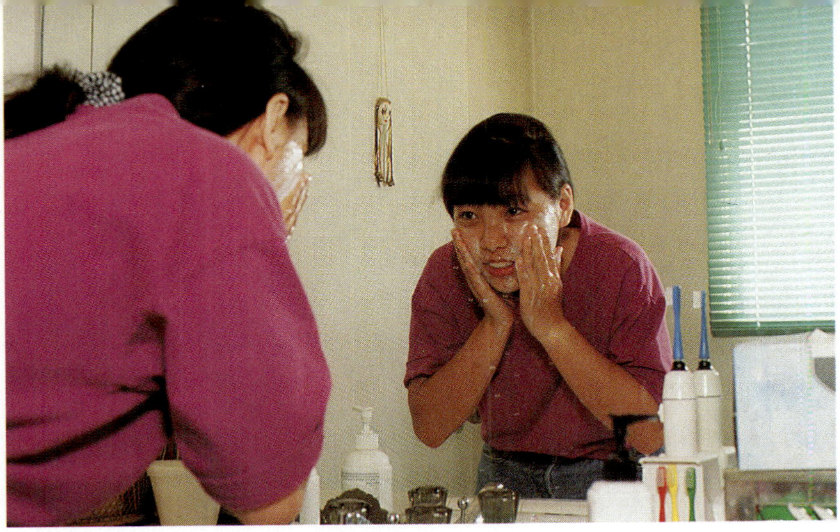

Cleansing your face several times per day can help you treat acne. Choose soaps and other cleansing products that are suited to your type of skin.

What can you do if you develop acne? Mild or slight cases of acne are best treated by washing your face twice daily. You can blot your face with a tissue between washings to remove the oil. Acne medicine that you can buy without a doctor's prescription may help. Avoid using oily makeup or other skin products on the problem areas. Avoid picking or squeezing the acne. This can injure the skin. It can also spread bacteria.

A serious case of acne needs treatment by a doctor. **Dermatologists** are doctors specializing in skin problems. They can usually help minimize acne.

Your Hair

Hairstyles change just as clothing styles change. Experiment to find a look that flatters your face. People often find that an easy-to-care-for style works best. A professional hairstylist can help you choose a good style for the shape of your face and type of hair.

Did you know that hair reflects your general health? Beautiful hair begins inside. A poor diet, emotional upsets, or a bad cold can change the appearance of your hair.

There are many products on the market to clean your hair and to keep it healthy. How can you choose the ones that are best for you? Consider the type and condition of your hair. Dry hair is harsh to the touch and has a strawlike texture. Hair is oily if it becomes stringy and sticky within a day or two after shampooing. Your hair is normal if you have none of the above problems. Choose products that match your hair type. High prices don't necessarily mean a shampoo or conditioner will work better for you. (Conditioners add shine and make hair more manageable.) Look for small sample-size bottles at first, so you can try out new varieties for a small price.

A flattering, easy-to-care-for hairstyle works best for most people.

Carefully read the labels on hair care products to choose the product best for your hair.

TIPS: *Buying Shampoo*

Are you confused by the many different types and brands of shampoo on store shelves? These facts may help you choose:

- Shampoos do one thing only — clean hair — regardless of advertised promises.
- Shampoos containing protein can make your hair look and feel fuller and less limp temporarily. However, getting enough protein in your diet is the only way to get it in your hair.
- Dandruff can sometimes be controlled by washing hair 3 or 4 times a week. You may not need a special anti-dandruff shampoo.

Shampooing

How often you shampoo depends on your hair. Many teens have so much natural oil in their hair that they need to shampoo every day. Wash your hair often enough to keep it looking good.

While regular shampooing won't harm your hair, you do have to be careful about how you shampoo. Hair is weaker when it is wet. To prevent damage, avoid vigorous rubbing during washing or drying.

Washing your hair is so routine, you probably never think about how you do it. Do you skip any of these steps?

1. Gently brush your hair from the scalp to the ends.
2. Wet hair with warm water.
3. Work the shampoo into a lather with your fingertips. Massage both the hair and scalp.
4. Rinse thoroughly. Hair is clean when it squeaks between your fingers.
5. If you are using a separate conditioner, apply it according to the package directions.
6. After rinsing, squeeze extra water from your hair. Blot dry with a towel, but don't rub.
7. Comb your hair gently with a clean comb. If the hair is tangled, work the snarl out carefully with a wide-toothed comb. Take care not to yank or pull.

Dandruff

Dandruff, or scales and flakes on the scalp, is a problem for many people. There are many causes.

To help control dandruff, keep your hair clean. Special dandruff shampoos are often helpful. Keep combs, brushes, and other hair care equipment clean. Change pillow cases often. Avoid scratching the scalp with sharp combs or fingernails. If dandruff is severe and does not improve, consult a dermatologist.

Your Teeth

If your teeth are to last a lifetime, they need regular care. What are the greatest enemies of healthy teeth? Until your mid-twenties, decay is the biggest cause of problems. After this age, gum disease becomes the biggest dental problem — causing more tooth loss in adults than any other dental disease.

The chief cause of tooth decay is **plaque** (plak). This is a sticky film of harmful bacteria that is constantly forming inside your mouth. Foods, especially those with a lot of sugar, cling to the teeth. The sugar and plaque form an acid that eats away at your tooth enamel and gums.

You can help prevent decay by:

- Eating nutritious food.
- Limiting between-meal snacks.
- Brushing properly and flossing after meals and snacks.
- Seeing a dentist regularly.

If possible, brush your teeth right after eating. Brushing will take away plaque and food particles from easy-to-reach tooth surfaces. However, a toothbrush can't reach between teeth and the gumline. This is where most dental disease starts. Use dental floss, a string-like material, to reach these areas. Floss your teeth every day.

What if you're not always able to brush after eating? Rinse with water after you eat. Swish the water around to help remove small bits of food.

Every few months, replace your toothbrush. When the bristles begin to show signs of wear, the brush can't do a good job of cleaning.

At least once a year, have your teeth checked by a dentist. A cleaning will help your gums. Cavities can also be discovered and treated while they're still small.

Flossing your teeth daily helps remove plaque and food particles that you can't reach with your toothbrush.

Your Nails

Nail care should be part of your good grooming routine. Dirty, broken, or bitten nails hurt your appearance. Here are some tips:

- Clean your hands and nails at least once a day. Use a small brush to remove stubborn dirt.
- Cut toenails straight across.
- Fingernails look best in a slightly oval shape. Be careful, however, not to cut or file too close to the corners.
- Use an emery board or file to smooth nail edges.
- Wear gloves for cleaning, gardening, and other activities that are hard on the hands.
- Use lotion to keep dry hands smooth.
- Nail biting is a habit that can be broken. Gradually decrease the number of nails you bite until you eliminate the problem.

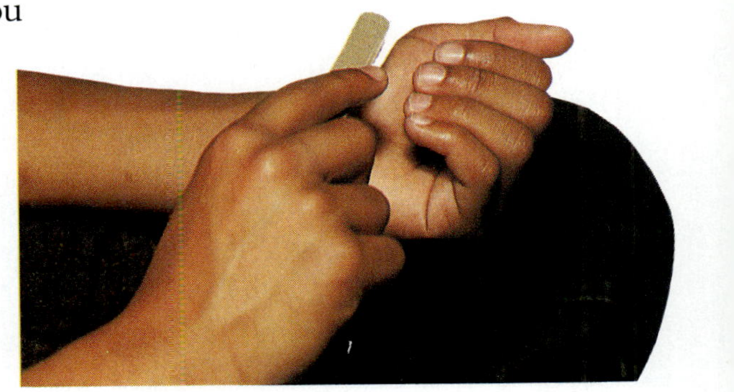

How does proper nail care lead to attractive hands?

The Confident Look

Confidence in your appearance grows as you begin taking responsibility for your own cleanliness and personal grooming. The grooming habits you develop now will tend to stay with you for a lifetime. As you develop positive grooming habits, you will look and feel better all the time. This sends a positive message to others around you that you really care about looking your best.

Good grooming habits help build confidence and last a lifetime. In what ways is this teen showing he feels confident about himself?

TAKING ACTION

Breanne's first thought is, "What can I wear?" Mr. Shanks, the principal, wants her to represent Irving High School at the city council meeting next month. A citation for the school's community service project will be presented, and he has asked Breanne to accept the award.

Having never done anything like this before, Breanne turns to you, her good friend, for advice. You know that new clothes will not be possible for her. Breanne's family does not have much money for extras. Breanne wants to feel good about herself when she stands before the council. She wants you to help her figure out how to put her best foot forward.

Using Your Resourcefulness

- What kinds of clothes would be appropriate? What would be inappropriate?
- What might Breanne do to present a good appearance by spending little or no money? What resources can she draw on other than money?
- Do you think appearance is related to self-esteem? Explain your answer.
- In what ways might healthy self-esteem be a resource?

Chapter 27 Review

Summary

In this chapter, you have read about:

- How to care for your skin by washing regularly and using lotion if needed.
- What causes acne and how you can treat it.
- Selecting and using the shampoo and other hair care products that are right for you.
- How to prevent tooth decay.
- How to keep your nails clean and attractive.

Facts to Recall

1. Name three functions of your skin.
2. Besides dirt, what three things do soap and water wash away?
3. What is the difference between a deodorant and an antiperspirant?
4. How can washing your face daily help prevent acne?
5. How can you tell if hair is clean when you are washing it?
6. Name three things you can do to prevent dandruff.
7. How does plaque contribute to tooth decay?
8. What are four things you can do to help prevent tooth decay?
9. List five tips for keeping your nails clean and attractive.
10. Name two ways that you can protect your skin from the ultraviolet rays of the sun.

Ideas to Explore

1. In what ways can being well-groomed reflect a good self-image? How can good grooming reflect your attitude toward life? What message does poor grooming send to others?
2. Suppose your best friend believes that the way to look healthy is to have a deep suntan. What would you say to your friend? How would you encourage your friend to protect his or her skin?

Activities to Try

1. With a partner, brainstorm a list of characteristics you notice about a person the first time you see them. How do these characteristics influence the way you respond to a person?
2. Write a public service announcement about protecting skin from the sun's ultraviolet rays. The announcement should be geared towards teens. What message would you send to teens that would effectively convince teens to take better care of their skin?

LINK TO *Math*

THE COST OF GROOMING PRODUCTS

Identify three types of grooming products that you use regularly. Comparison shop for five different brands of each product. Write down the product name, manufacturer's name, a brief description of the container, weight, and cost. Use the following guidelines for a cost comparison:

1. Compute the unit price for each product by dividing the weight of the product into the cost.
2. Compute the average cost for each type of product by adding the costs of all five products together and dividing by five.
3. Suggest some factors that contribute to cost differences.

CHAPTER

28 Selecting Clothing

OBJECTIVES

- *Develop a wardrobe plan.*
- *Select attractive clothes using the elements and principles of design.*
- *Give guidelines for shopping for clothes.*

TERMS TO LEARN

- ***clothing inventory***
- ***multipurpose clothes***
- ***fashions***
- ***classics***
- ***fads***
- ***separates***
- ***silhouette***

Look around the classroom. Are most people wearing similar clothes, or is there great variety? Some similarities might be explained by the weather or a school dress code.

If all your classmates were strangers, what clues might each one's choice of clothes give you about that person? Your clothes also send a message to others about how you want to be seen.

Being well-dressed does not necessarily require closets full of clothes. It's more important to have clothes you enjoy wearing and that mix and match well together. This chapter will help you choose flattering clothes that are both comfortable and well-made.

Planning Your Wardrobe

A wardrobe that works well for you doesn't just happen. It takes some thought. If you want to avoid having to say, "I don't have anything to wear," take some time to plan your wardrobe. You may discover ways to combine clothes you already have to make new outfits. An inventory can also help you decide which new clothes would make the biggest impact on your wardrobe.

Taking an Inventory

The best way to start planning your wardrobe is to take a look at what you already have. Making an organized list of your clothes is called taking a **clothing inventory**. An inventory can help you decide what you need and set priorities for shopping.

To take a clothing inventory, first sort your clothes into three groups:

- Clothes you like and wear regularly.
- Clothes you no longer wear and don't want.
- Clothes that you aren't certain about.

This "maybe" or "if" group is for items you might like to wear *if* they were repaired ... or *if* you had something to wear with them ... or *if* they were more in style.

Next, make a separate list for each different type of activity in which you participate. These might include school, sports, special occasions, relaxing, and possibly a job. List the items you put in your first pile — the clothes you wear and like — under the appropriate activities. Some items may

Classic designs in clothing stand the test of time. What are some ways the clothing worn by this teen will stand the test of time?

AROUND THE WORLD

For the Amish people of Lancaster County, Pennsylvania, clothing expresses important religious beliefs. These "plain people" dress conservatively. Attire for men and boys includes black broadfall (zipperless) pants without hip pockets, black vests and coats fastened with hooks and eyes, and broad-brimmed hats. Women and girls are often seen in simply designed, solid-color dresses, black aprons, and black or white bonnets. The Amish believe that plain dress emphasizes the virtues of simplicity, modesty, and humility by which they try to live.

be listed under several activities. Your favorite sweater, for example, might look good with both casual and dressier clothes. **Multipurpose clothes** — those suitable for a variety of situations — stretch your wardrobe.

Now look again at the clothing items in your "if" pile. Would repairing or updating some of the items make them more appealing? If so, add these garments to your inventory. Plan what you will do to make the items usable. In Chapter 36, you'll find directions for making minor repairs and ideas for updating garments.

What about the pile of clothes you don't want? Give them to someone else who can use them. You might offer them to a younger brother or sister or donate them to a charitable organization.

Also take time to check the basics in your wardrobe. To be well-dressed you need shoes, nightwear, undergarments, and other basic items.

Planning New Purchases

After you complete your clothing inventory, look over your lists. Do you see any gaps? You should have the most clothing for the activities you participate in most often. For activities that come up less often, one or two outfits may be enough.

By planning for additions to your wardrobe, you can make choices that will make a real difference. Some points to consider are:

- ***Needs and wants.*** Which items do you really need? Which do you want but could get along without? Needs are usually more important than what you want. You may also have to consider how your needs fit in with the needs of others in your family.

- ***Budget.*** How much money do you have to spend on clothes? If a family's clothing budget is limited, decisions must be made about whose needs are most important.
- ***Fashion.*** Be aware that advertising, fashion, and fads influence what you may want. **Fashions** are styles that are currently popular. Some fashions are considered **classics**. These styles never seem to disappear completely, although they may be changed a little from time to time. Fashions that last for only a short time are called **fads**. It's usually not wise to spend a lot of money on fads, because you can't wear them too long.
- ***Versatility.*** Choose multipurpose clothing items that can be used for several activities.
- ***Mix-and-match possibilities.*** You'll be more pleased with the new clothes you buy if they fit in with what you already own. Shop for **separates**, garments that can be combined with one another to make several different outfits. Shirts, pants, jeans, skirts, sweaters, and jackets are all separates. Choose colors that will go with the clothes you already own. If the colors of your clothes go together, you will have many more possible outfits to wear.
- ***Accessories.*** Using accessories — small items of clothing that complete an outfit — is an inexpensive way to update clothes in your wardrobe. Belts, ties, scarves, and jewelry can give new life to the clothes you already own.

Pocket Lab

Mix and Match Math

MATERIALS:
current fashion catalogs; advertisements

EQUIPMENT:
pen; paper, 4" × 6" index cards; glue; scissors

Directions: Select pictures of twelve separate items of clothing. Choose 2 jackets, 2 sweaters, 4 skirts/pants, and 4 shirts. Choose solids/ prints in two colors that go well together such as black and white. Choose a third color, like red, for accent if you wish. Select shapes, patterns, and textures that go well together. Glue each picture on a separate card. Number the cards 1 to 12. Now see how many different outfits you can create by mixing and matching the separates. Record the numbers of the combinations you used.

- How many different outfits did you create? Did all of the different items go well together?
- What are the advantages of buying compatible separates?
- How could you mix and match six separates for a weekend trip?

Individualizing Your Clothes

The way you dress communicates messages you want to send to others. Why not select clothing that will highlight your best features and downplay problem areas? If you know something about design, you can use it to say, "Look at my best features. This is the person I want you to see."

Many of the illustrations in this chapter show you how to apply basic design elements and principles to the way you dress. Chapter 24 discusses the design elements and principles in more detail.

Elements of Design

In clothing, three of the most important elements of design are line, color, and texture. Understanding how they work will help you choose attractive styles.

Line

Lines in garments can be formed by fabric design, such as a striped pattern. They can also be formed by seams, pleats, and trims. The **silhouette** (sill-uh-WET), or outline of a garment, creates an important line. Think of the difference between narrow, straight pants and loose, baggy ones.

Lines guide eye movement up and down or across an area. Clever placement of lines can actually change what people see. Vertical lines can make you seem taller. Horizontal lines lead the eyes across the body making it seem broader.

Color

What are the best colors for you? They may not be your favorites or the latest fads. Your best colors are the ones that flatter the colors of your hair, skin, and eyes.

One good clue is to decide which of your clothes bring you the most compliments. Those colors are probably good choices.

You can also experiment by holding up different colors to your face and looking in a mirror. Which colors are most flattering? Do you look better in bright or soft colors? Do certain colors seem to make your eyes and hair shine? Your best colors should make your face look healthy and glowing. This is a good way to discover which colors make you look and feel your best. You can also learn which you should avoid.

MEETING SPECIAL NEEDS

With Clothing

It's frustrating! Clothing is designed for the "average" person. It's often not suitable or comfortable for people with physical disabilities.

Jennifer Dalton uses a wheelchair to get around. Like most teens, she likes to look her best. She is active in the student council and the debate team. As she explains, clothing is a real problem for her.

"Most people don't realize what it's like for me to shop for clothes. When you are in a sitting position, most clothes pull in the back and bunch up in the front. It's very uncomfortable. Since my legs are paralyzed, it's hard for me to get in and out of clothes. My grandmother helps by sewing some of my clothes and altering others.

I wish more clothing manufacturers would realize that there's a real need for stylish clothes for people with physical limitations. I know they can't meet everyone's individual needs. But there are lots of people — even without disabilities — who would choose clothes that are easy to put on and take off. Maybe that's what I'll do after college — design my own clothing line!"

Choosing a warm or cool color can reflect your clothing image. For example, warm colors tend to draw attention and can give the illusion of increased size. Cool colors, on the other hand, seem to pull back and give the illusion of reduced size. Whatever colors you choose, be sure that they flatter your hair, skin, and eyes.

Texture

Texture is the surface characteristic that you can see or feel in a fabric. The texture of your clothing can also affect your appearance. A bulky sweater can seem to add pounds, while one with a flat, smooth knit has the opposite effect. Shiny fabrics also tend to increase apparent size.

▼ Principles of Design ▼

The principles of design discussed in Chapter 24 apply to clothing, as well as homes. Two of the most important are proportion and emphasis. They help you combine the elements of design you have just read about to compliment your personality.

- ***Proportion.*** Proportion involves the relationship of one part to another. If you make one section of your body look long, wide, or large, then another section will appear shorter, narrower, or smaller.
- ***Emphasis.*** Emphasis, or the point of interest, is what one's eyes see first. Use emphasis to draw attention to your best features. A splash of color in a tie or scarf highlights the face. A bright belt could emphasize a slim waist.

LINE

COLOR

EMPHASIS

TEXTURE

PROPORTION

Labels on each garment list the care guidelines for that garment. How might reading the care guidelines affect your clothing purchases?

Shopping for Clothes

Have you ever shopped at dozens of stores to find the right shirt? Have you ever looked for a winter coat in January, only to find racks of bathing suits? Shopping is not always easy.

You can better meet the shopping challenge if you are an organized and well-informed consumer. You are not born with shopping savvy, or know-how. However, you can learn the "how-tos" of being a smart consumer. Chapter 20 has basic information that applies to all types of shopping. This chapter will help you sort through some of the decisions you have to make when buying clothes.

Getting Ready to Shop

Before you leave home to go shopping, have a good idea of what you need to buy. If you completed a clothing inventory, you should know what you need to fill the gaps in your wardrobe. You may also want to talk with family members about the needs of others in the family. Do others have some high-priority needs? Where do your needs fit in to the family budget? You may need to prioritize your "needs" list and buy the highest priority items first.

Allow enough time to shop and make comparisons. Avoid waiting until a week before a big event to find something new to wear. Remember to dress in comfortable clothing.

TIPS: *Dressing to Save Energy*

You can actually dress with energy conservation in mind. Just remember these guidelines:

- Dark colors can help you stay warm by absorbing heat from the sun. Light colors help you feel cooler in sunlight.
- Close-fitting clothes trap body heat to keep you warmer. To feel cooler, wear clothes with large neck, arm, and leg openings, open-type shoes, and fewer accessories.
- Clean clothes keep you warmer in the winter. Dirt clogs open spaces and decreases a fabric's insulation quality. In the summer, clean clothes are more comfortable to wear.

SAFETY CHECK✓

Tips for buying safe children's clothing include:

- Buy children's sleepwear labeled "flame-retardant."
- Avoid garments with long strings and ties for infants. If they get wrapped around an infant's neck, they could cause strangulation.
- Avoid garments with buttons that could easily be pulled off and swallowed.
- Buy pants that are hemmed, not cuffed. They are less likely to catch and cause falls.
- Choose outdoor wear with separate hats or hoods. One-piece outfits may keep children from seeing well.

How does checking garment quality before you buy help save you money? What benefits does this have in the long run?

Shopping Strategies

Try to stick with your shopping plan. At the same time, you have to be flexible. You may not be able to locate the exact item you want. If not, decide what would be the best substitute. You might use sewing skills to make the garment you want.

You may breathe a sigh of relief when you do find the right style, color, and size garment for which you are searching. Should you buy it? Not yet. You will want to look more closely at a few key areas first.

- ***Check the care label.*** Make sure you have the time, energy, and money needed to give the garment proper care.
- ***Check the price tag.*** Will the price of the garment fit in your budget? Don't buy something just because it is on sale. If an item is not the right color or style for you, it's not the bargain you may think it is.
- ***Check the fit.*** Try the garment on to be sure the garment doesn't pull or wrinkle when you walk, sit, bend, or move your arms. Waistbands should be comfortable, not too loose or too snug. Uncomfortable clothes are never a good buy.
- ***Check the quality of workmanship.*** If you plan to wear a garment often, buy the best quality you can afford. Remember, the garment will have to stand up to the strain of being worn and laundered frequently.

Carefully examine children's clothing for durability and safety.

How to . . .
Select Quality Clothing

Shoppers who know quality when they see it look for these points:

- Machine stitching is straight, even in length, and appears strong. Thread color should be close to the color of the fabric.
- Seams are smooth and straight, and stitches are even. They don't show any signs of puckering or pulling. Seam edges are finished to prevent raveling.
- The hem of the garment is even and parallel to the floor.
- Plaids, stripes, and large designs are matched at the seams.
- Points of strain are strengthened with double stitching or seam tape.
- Buttonholes are closely stitched and reinforced with extra stitching at the ends. Buttonhole openings fit the buttons and lie flat when closed.
- Zippers zip easily. When they are closed, zippers lie flat and are covered by the fabric.

Responsible Shopping

As you begin your shopping trip, think about the way you care for the clothing you look at and try on. You are responsible for keeping it clean and undamaged. Here are some tips for responsible shopping:

- Look at clothes carefully. Make sure your hands are clean.
- Avoid wearing jewelry that could snag or catch on clothing.
- Carefully remove clothes from hangers when you try them on. Unbutton buttons and unzip zippers.
- If you wear make-up, be careful not to get it on the clothing you try on.
- Alert a sales clerk if you find a damaged garment.

- When you are through trying on a garment, return it to the rack or a sales clerk if you do not buy it.
- Shoplifting is illegal. Most stores turn shoplifters over to the police.

Deciding to Buy

WAREHOUSE POLICY

• NO CASH REFUNDS

• NO CHARGE CARD CREDITS

EXCHANGE WITHIN 7 DAYS WHEN ACCOMPANIED BY REGISTER RECEIPT AND PRICE TICKET

• LAY-A-WAYS 1/3 DEPOSIT — 14 DAYS TO PICK UP

THANK YOU!

Exchange policies vary from store to store.

After checking the care instructions, price, fit, and quality, you should have a good idea of whether this garment is right for you. Don't buy anything if you have serious doubts about it.

Check stores' exchange or return policies before you buy. Discount stores and factory outlets have stricter rules than most department stores. If the policy is "exchanges only, no returns," you know that you won't get your money back. Instead, you're able to exchange an item for one of equal value.

Keep the sales slip until you are absolutely certain you won't return the item. Many stores make exchanges only with the original sales slip. Some stores have a time period during which items may be returned. Usually this period is between 7 and 14 days.

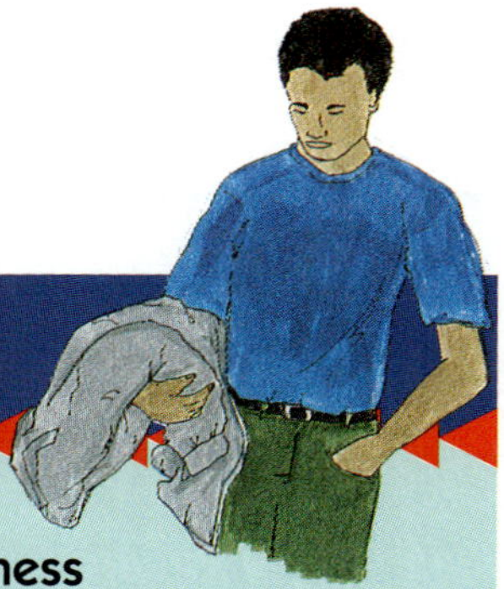

TAKING ACTION

Lionel takes one look at the classic leather jacket in the store window and says to you, "I've got to have it." The two of you walk into the store and Lionel tries on the jacket in his size. It not only looks great on him, but it is on sale for half-price. The salesman assures him, "You won't find a deal like this again."

Lionel is in a dilemma. He intended to go shopping for some badly-needed fall clothes. Most of his pants are too short for him, and several shirts need repairs. The amount he planned to spend on new clothes equals the sale price of the leather jacket. If he buys the jacket, he'll have to wait at least three months before he can afford to buy anything else. Lionel wants your advice.

Using Your Resourcefulness

- What would you suggest Lionel do? Offer three reasons to support your answer.
- If Lionel decides to shop for pants and shirts, what choices does he have in terms of where to shop? What are the advantages and disadvantages of these choices?
- If Lionel decides to buy the jacket, what can he do about shirts and pants until he can save some more money?
- What options does Lionel have if he decides he would like to have the jacket and the shirts and pants?
- How is Lionel effectively using his resources? Explain your answer.

Chapter 28 Review

Summary

In this chapter, you have read about:

- How careful planning can help you build a wardrobe that will meet your needs.
- How to take a clothing inventory as the first step in wardrobe planning.
- How the elements and principles of design can help you choose flattering clothing.
- Strategies that can help you make wise decisions when you shop for clothing.
- How to evaluate the quality of a garment.

Facts to Recall

1. Describe how to take a clothing inventory.
2. Define multipurpose clothing and give an example.
3. Name four points to consider when planning what to add to your wardrobe.
4. Give an example of using design elements to highlight one's best features.
5. Describe how proportion and emphasis enter into clothing design.
6. Name four key areas to check before deciding whether to buy a garment.
7. List five signs of quality workmanship in a garment.
8. Name at least four guidelines to follow when buying clothing for people with special needs.

Ideas to Explore

1. What do you think is the most common mistake people make when shopping for clothing? Why is it a problem? How could the problem be prevented?
2. Why do fashions change?
3. Give three examples of classic fashions and three examples of fads. In general, how do classic fashions differ from fads?
4. Suppose you have enough money to buy a good-quality pair of slacks. Then you find another pair that is half the price of the first, but of poor quality. Which would you buy and why? What is the importance of quality when buying clothing?

Activities to Try

1. Using magazines and newspapers, find pictures of clothes that are examples of fads and classics. Cut out the pictures and label them. Write an explanation for your selections.
2. Create a clothing design that would minimize one of the following: wide shoulders; long, thin legs; short arms; large hips; small chest.

LINK TO *Communication*

MAKING CLOTHING CHOICES

Develop a skit showing the positive and negative aspects of peer pressure concerning clothing choices. Include some ways that you and your friends affect each other's clothing choices. In addition, act out situations in which teens and their parents may have conflicts over clothing choices (you may want to incorporate ways in which peer pressure affects the teen/parent conflict). Be sure that your skits *fairly* represent different points of view as well as express ways to resolve conflict over clothing choices.

CHAPTER 29

Fibers to Fabrics

OBJECTIVES

- Describe how natural and manufactured fibers differ.
- Identify the characteristics of common fibers.
- Explain three methods of making fabric.
- Describe how finishes change fabrics.

TERMS TO LEARN

- *fibers*
- *natural fibers*
- *manufactured fibers*
- *luster*
- *generic name*
- *trade name*
- *fabric blends*

Alicia's new shirt was made from a soft rayon fabric. She had several washable rayon shirts that were easy to care for. After wearing the shirt once, Alicia washed and dried it the same way she washed and dried her other rayon shirts. Alicia wondered what she had done wrong when the shirt came out of the dryer covered with little matted balls and sleeves that were several inches shorter than when it went into the dryer.

When you buy clothing, do you stop to think about the fabric from which it is made? Taking time to learn about fabrics will help you to:

- Become a smarter consumer.
- Take care of clothing correctly so it looks better and wears longer.
- Be happier with your clothing and fabric purchases.

Fibers

Fibers are hairlike substances that are twisted together to make yarns and fabric. There are two groups of fibers: natural and manufactured.

Natural fibers come from plants or animals. They include cotton, linen, wool, silk, and ramie, among others.

Fabrics are used in many things besides clothing that affect your life daily. How many products can you name in which fabrics are used?

Liquid nylon is forced through the spinnerette and hardens into fibers. How might nylon fibers be used?

Manufactured fibers, also called synthetic (sin-THET-ik) fibers, are made all or in part from chemicals. Some manufactured fibers are made from products such as coal and oil. To make the fibers, a syrupy substance is forced through a spinnerette — a metal plate full of very tiny holes that looks similar to a shower head. The liquid coming through the spinnerette is hardened to form stringlike fibers. The fibers are about the thickness of sewing thread. Some new fibers, called *microfibers*, are forced through a spinnerette with micro-sized holes. The microfiber yarns are twice as fine as the best silk yarn.

Cotton is the most widely used natural fiber.

Linen is made from the stems of the flax plant. It is used in clothing and home decorating products.

Natural Fibers

Natural fibers have been used for thousands of years. Cotton is the most widely used natural fiber. Both cotton and linen come from plants. These fibers absorb moisture well. This makes them comfortable to wear in warm weather. Cotton and linen also wrinkle, shrink, and mildew easily.

Wool comes from the fleece of sheep. It absorbs moisture and still feels dry. It resists wrinkling and is valued for its warmth. Wool fibers trap air and prevent the loss of body heat. Wool shrinks when washed in hot water. It also burns when exposed to very high heat.

Silk is the strongest of the natural fibers. It is spun by silkworms. It is comfortable to wear because it absorbs body moisture and resists wrinkles. Silk is a luxury fiber and is very expensive. However, there are many other less costly fibers that have the look and feel of silk.

Ramie comes from the stalks of China grass in Southeast Asia. It is a strong, durable fiber. It is often combined with other fibers, such as cotton, in making fabrics. Ramie absorbs moisture and dries quickly. It has a natural **luster**, or shine, and can be dyed easily.

The fleece of sheep is fine and soft. Fabrics made from wool are good to wear in cold weather.

Luxurious silk fibers are being spun into yarn at this textile factory in Thailand.

AROUND THE WORLD

Americans are most familiar with the satiny smoothness of finished silk, but it is used raw in other countries, such as India. When first spun, silk is a stiff yarn that is woven into a coarse, crisp fabric called tussah (TUSS-ah). The silkworm's natural gum makes these fabrics dye-resistant; if the gum is removed, however, the yarns can be dyed and woven into bright, colorful patterns.

▼ Manufactured Fibers ▼

Manufactured fibers are generally strong. They have a natural ability to spring back to their original shape. Many manufactured fibers are sensitive to heat. They can be damaged by a hot iron.

Manufactured fibers are made to look, feel, and act like natural fibers. However, several qualities make manufactured fibers unique. Almost all of these fibers tend to shed

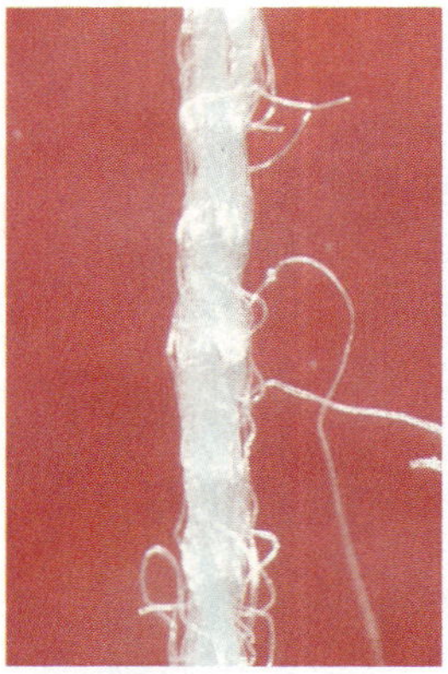

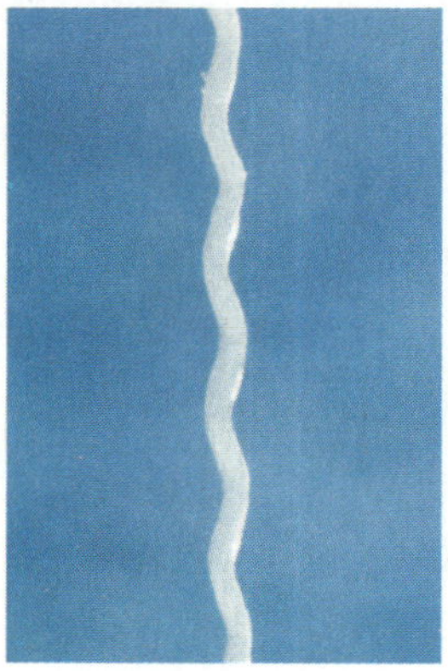

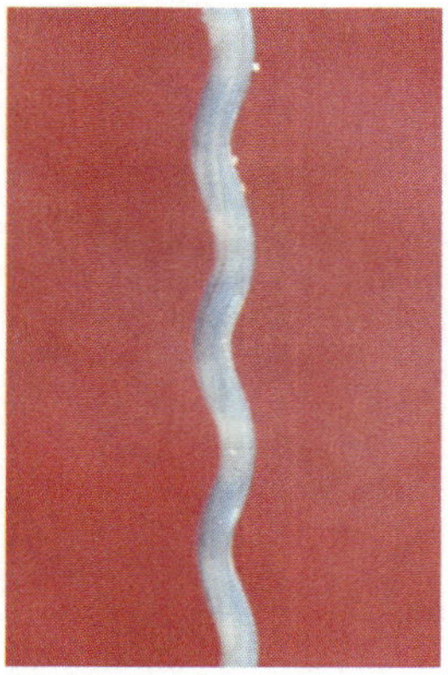

Above are three common manufactured fibers. The top photo is an example of nylon; the middle photo is an example of Dacron© polyester; the lower photo is an example of Orlon© acrylic. Many labels often provide the trade names and the generic names of fibers.

water rather than absorb it. As a result, they dry quickly and shrink very little. They also tend to be warm to wear. Some manufactured fibers have been improved to absorb moisture better. For example, fabrics can be made to have more volume or bulk. The added bulk allows more air to move through the fabric in order to absorb perspiration. This makes clothing made from manufactured fibers more comfortable to wear in warm weather.

Manufactured fibers, such as nylon, rayon, spandex, and polyester, add to your choices of fabrics. Each manufactured fiber has two names. It has a **generic name** — or the common name for a group of similar fibers, and a **trade name** — or the manufacturer's name for a specific fiber or fabric. Every manufactured fiber is put into a group depending on the materials from which it is made. For example, Dacron®, Fortrel®, and Kodel® are all trade names for polyester fibers. All members of the polyester family have similar characteristics and need the same type of care. Labels on garments and fabrics usually carry both names.

Blends

Every fiber has good qualities. However, no fiber is perfect. As a result, manufacturers have developed **fabric blends** — fabrics containing two or more fibers. Blends combine the best qualities of each fiber. As an example, mixing cotton and polyester offers the moisture absorbency of cotton and the quick drying and wrinkle resistance of polyester.

The percentage of each fiber needed in order to build in certain qualities varies. For example, a blend of 50 percent polyester and 50 percent cotton with a durable-press finish resists wrinkling. Without a durable-press finish, a blend of 65 percent polyester and 35 percent cotton is needed to resist wrinkling.

Fabric Construction

Fibers are twisted together to make yarns. These yarns are usually about the thickness of sewing thread. Yarns are then put together to form fabric. The final yarn arrangement affects the wear you can expect from the fabric. It also affects the care a fabric needs. Three common methods of making fabric from yarn are weaving, knitting, and bonding.

Natural and Manufactured Fibers

Natural Fibers	Characteristics	Uses
Cotton	Dyes and prints easily. Absorbent and comfortable. Wrinkles. Easily laundered.	Jeans, shirts, sportswear, socks, undergarments and household textiles such as towels and sheets.
Linen	Very durable. Very absorbent. Wrinkles. Easily laundered.	Suits, jackets, dresses, tablecloths.
Ramie	Strong. Dyes well. Wrinkles easily.	Knit tops, scarves, sweaters, upholstery.
Silk	Strong. Lightweight. Weakened by perspiration. Damaged by chlorine bleach. Sometimes washable, usually dry-cleaned.	Shirts, dresses, ties, scarves.
Wool	Warm. Resists wrinkling. Absorbent. Attracts moths. Usually dry-cleaned, sometimes washable.	Coats, suits, slacks, sweaters, hats, gloves.
Manufactured Fibers	**Characteristics**	**Uses**
Acetate	Drapes well. Poor abrasion resistance. Usually dry-cleaned. Heat sensitive.	Sportswear, shirts, dresses, ties, scarves.
Acrylic	Resists wrinkling. Lightweight and soft. May pill or form small matted balls. Dry-cleaned or laundered.	Knitted garments, sportswear, blankets, upholstery.
Modacrylic	Soft. Resists wrinkling. Not absorbent. May pill. Dry-cleaned or laundered.	Sportswear, knitted garments, fake furs, blankets.
Nylon	Strong. Resists wrinkling. Poor absorption. Washable. Dries quickly.	Swimwear, hosiery, undergarments, sportswear.
Polyester	Resists wrinkling. Retains pleats and creases. Low absorption. Holds oil stains and soil. Washable. Dries quickly.	Shirts, dresses, slacks, sportswear, pillow stuffing.
Rayon	Highly absorbent. Easy to dye. Drapes well. Wrinkles. Usually dry-cleaned. Sometimes washable.	Dresses, shirts, ties, scarves, window coverings, undergarments.
Spandex	High degree of stretch. Lightweight. Weakened by chlorine bleach. Washable.	Swimwear, undergarments, skiwear, support hosiery.

FABRIC WEAVES

PLAIN

TWILL

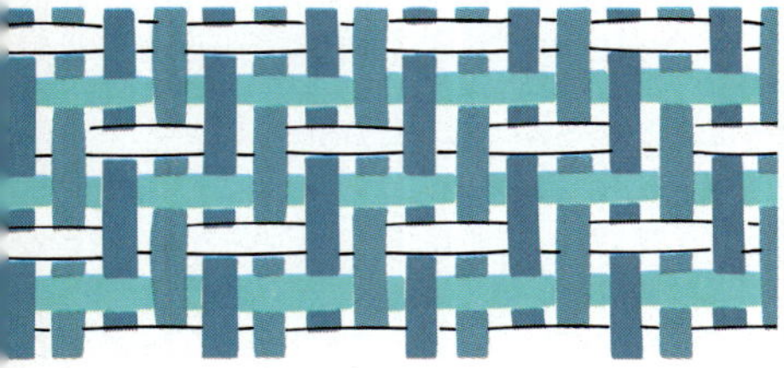

SATIN

OXFORD CLOTH

DENIM

SATIN

▼ Weaving ▼

In weaving, lengthwise and crosswise yarns are laced together at right angles. The tightness of the weave determines the firmness of the fabric and affects how it will wear. Generally, tightly woven fabrics wear better than those that are loosely woven.

Different types of weaves are used to make fabric. Plain, twill, satin, and pile weaves are the most common.

- ***Plain weave.*** In this simple weave, each crosswise yarn passes over and under each lengthwise yarn. Broadcloth and gingham are examples of plain weave fabric.
- ***Twill weave.*** The lengthwise yarns pass over two and then under two crosswise yarns. In twill weave fabrics, the diagonal ridges made by yarns can be seen on the surface of the fabric. The twill weave produces a stronger fabric than other weaves. Jeans are usually made of denim fabric, a hard-wearing twill weave.
- ***Satin weave.*** A satin weave produces a shiny fabric. The lengthwise yarns pass over four or more crosswise yarns and generally under one crosswise yarn. The satin weave is not as strong as the twill or plain weave.
- ***Pile weave.*** Three sets of yarn are used to make the pile weave. Pile fabrics such as velvet and corduroy are first woven in a plain, twill, or satin weave. Then an extra set of yarns is woven in to form a pile, or cut surface.

▼ Knitting ▼

Another way of making fabrics is by knitting. Knitted fabrics are stretchy and comfortable. They are made by interlocking loops of yarn together row after row. Yarns of various fibers, weights, and textures are knit by machine or hand. Knits are more easily snagged and pulled than woven fabrics.

Clothing made from knitted fabrics allows free movement. It generally holds its shape well. As with woven fabrics, knitted fabrics may be made by several different methods.

- ***Single knits.*** These are often used for T-shirts and simple dresses. Single knits have a flat, smooth appearance on the front side and horizontal loops on the back side. Single knit is sometimes called jersey.
- ***Double knits.*** These knits are made with two interlocking layers on the front and back that cannot be separated. Double knits are durable and wrinkle resistant. They stretch well and are comfortable to wear.

- ***Tricot knits (TREE-coh).*** Narrow vertical ribs on the front and crosswise ribs on the back, characterize tricot knits. They have plenty of stretchability and are runproof, snag-resistant, and nonraveling. These qualities make tricot knits useful for undergarments, dresses, shirts, blouses, and swimwear.

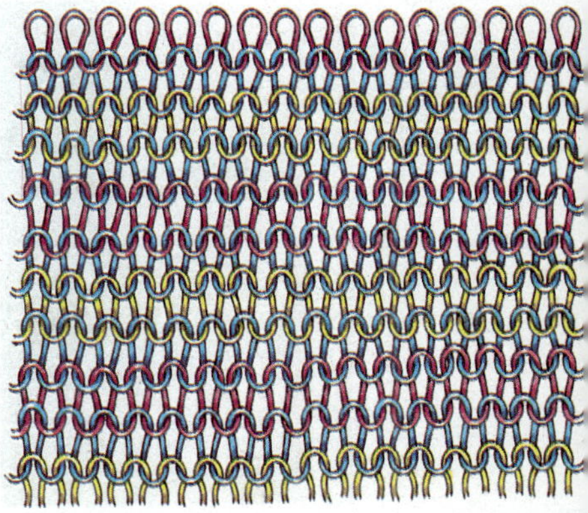

Knitted fabric.

Bonding

Bonding is a method used for making nonwoven fabrics. Fibers are mechanically or chemically joined together. Steam or heat, used with an adhesive, bonds nonwoven fabrics together. Bonding gives shape to nonwoven fabrics, helps make them flexible, and helps prevent wrinkling.

Long-lasting nonwoven fabrics may be used for blankets, carpet backing, and interfacing — a fabric used inside garments that gives hidden support and stability. Some nonwoven fabrics are disposable and may be used for items such as disposable diapers.

Fabric Finishes

Finishes are one of the final touches put on yarns or fabrics. Finishes change some of the natural characteristics of fabrics to make them more appealing and useful. Many different finishes can be added. These range from dyeing and printing, to waterproofing.

Dyeing and Printing

Fabrics are dyed in machines such as these.

Adding color to fabric is an age-old art. It also is as new as the most complex computer. Some dyes come from nature and some are developed in the lab. The way dye is applied varies. Sometimes yarn is dyed before it is woven into fabric. The most common method of dyeing is called piece dyeing. The dye is applied after the yarn is made into fabric.

Color can also be applied by using a printing process. Patterns, such as flowers, ducks, or polka dots, can be rolled onto fabric by using rollers or cylinders. Sometimes patterns are applied by screen printing, in which dyes are forced through a screen onto the fabric. This process is similar to stenciling.

Weaving patterns out of selected colors of pre-dyed yarn is another way to create a design in fabric. Patterns such as plaids can be formed this way.

This machine is used for screen printing fabric.

▼ Other Finishes ▼

A number of fabric characteristics can be changed by finishing processes. Some finishes are permanent, and some are not. It's best to check the label. Here are some finishes you will see when you read the labels on textile products.

- ***Flame-retardant.*** Helps fabric resist burning.
- ***Permanent or durable press.*** Requires little or no ironing of fabric after washing.
- ***Sanforized.*** Prevents fabric from shrinking more than 1 percent.
- ***Stain- and spot-resistant.*** Helps fabric resist stains and spots.
- ***Waterproof.*** Helps fabric shed water.
- ***Water-repellent.*** Helps fabric resist water but does not waterproof it.

Many fabric finishes can be destroyed if fabrics are not cared for properly. Check the care labels and follow the manufacturer's directions carefully. You will learn more about caring for clothing in Chapter 30 of the text.

TAKING ACTION

The "Pop Choir" at your school has been asked to perform at the opening ceremonies for the *Fourth of July* celebration in your community. The choir members would like to have new performance outfits for the occasion.

You are a choir member and part of the teacher-student committee that has been asked to choose the new outfits. The choir director has several concerns about the outfits and has shared them with the committee. They include: the outfits need to be easily and inexpensively cared for; the outfits need to be comfortable and allow for movement; the outfits must be durable enough to last several years; and the outfits need to be suitable for the celebration.

Using Your Resourcefulness

- What fibers and fabrics may meet the outfit needs of the "Pop Choir"? Discuss the advantages and disadvantages of each.
- What fabric finishes might be most suitable for the performance outfits?
- How can the committee best make use of community resources in locating outfits to meet the needs of the "Pop Choir"?

Chapter 29 Review

Summary

In this chapter, you have read about:

- The characteristics and uses of natural and synthetic fibers.
- How fabrics are formed by weaving, knitting, and bonding yarns.
- How colors and patterns are added to fabrics.
- Other fabric finishes and how they affect the fabric's characteristics.

Facts to Remember

1. List three benefits of learning about fabrics.
2. Name three natural fibers and their sources.
3. What advantage is there in the tendency of manufactured fibers to shed water rather than absorb it? Disadvantage?
4. Why have manufacturers developed fabric blends?
5. How does a plain weave differ from a twill weave?
6. How are knitted fabrics made?
7. Name three qualities of knit fabrics. Give three examples showing how knits are used.
8. Describe two ways that patterns can be applied to fabric.
9. Name four fabric finishes and a benefit of each.

Ideas to Explore

1. Why might articles made from natural fibers be more expensive than those made from manufactured fibers?
2. How can an increase in the use of manufactured fibers affect a region's or a nation's economy and way of life?
3. Using the chart "Natural and Manufactured Fibers" on page 327, identify the different fibers you would wear in the following situations: a safari in Kenya; a ski trip in Colorado; a formal dinner at the White House.

Activities to Try

1. Debate the use of natural and manufactured fibers. Defend your position stating the advantages and disadvantages of each.
2. Collect small samples of different natural and manufactured fabrics. Mount each sample on its own index card or in a pocket-size spiral notebook. On the back of each card or page, write the fabric characteristics and care suggestions. Use your fabric notebook as a shopping guide when you are buying clothing or fabric.
3. Using ½ inch (1.3 cm) by 12 inch (30.5 cm) strips of construction paper, make the following weaves: plain, twill, and satin. Use different colors for lengthwise and crosswise yarns. You will need about 20 strips for each weave. Mount your weaves on construction paper and label them.

LINK TO *Art*

DESIGNING A T-SHIRT

Draw the silhouette of a basic T-shirt on a piece of paper. Assume you are producing a decorative fabric design that will be stenciled or painted on the T-shirt. (Refer to Chapter 28, pages 314-316 on individualizing your clothes.)

Use markers or paint to develop the design on paper. Explain how you used the elements and/or principles of design in developing the decorative fabric design to be applied to the T-shirt.

CHAPTER

30 Caring for Clothing

OBJECTIVES

- Describe routine clothing care and storage.
- Describe how to launder and press clothes.
- Explain how to make simple clothing repairs.

TERMS TO LEARN

- ***routine***
- ***pretreatment***
- ***pressing***
- ***ironing***
- ***dry clean***
- ***shank***

It's Wednesday morning. With eyes half open, you reach in the closet for a shirt. There isn't one. How could you have forgotten to do the laundry last night? Yesterday's shirt has been in the hamper with the other dirty clothes all night. That's not an option. Finally, at the back of the closet, you discover a clean one. It's your least favorite, but at least it's clean. Relief! Oh, no ... not one, but two buttons are missing. What a choice! A pullover sweater may be the answer. As you frantically search for something to wear, you realize the importance of taking good, daily care of your clothes.

When you change clothes, what do you do with the clothes you have taken off? Do they end up on the chair or the floor rather than in the drawer or closet? By looking after your clothes, putting them away, and making repairs when needed, you come out ahead. It takes a few extra minutes, but your clothes will be ready to go when you are.

Routine Care

The purpose of **routine**, or regular, care of your clothes is to avoid such disasters. You will have clean clothes ready to wear when you need them. If you want to save time caring for your clothes, look for easy-care fabrics. Check hangtags and labels on garments before you buy. Find out what type of care clothes will require. Do they have any special finishes?

You can prevent many problems by taking a little extra time in the routine. Then, when you get ready to put on your favorite shirt, you won't have to use a safety pin in place of a button or apply tape to keep up a hem. You can be sure you are looking your best.

When you dress or undress, open all the fasteners, such as buttons, zippers, and snaps. This helps to keep rips and tears to a minimum. Allow deodorant to dry before dressing, so you don't stain your clothes. Put cologne and perfumes on your body, not on your clothes. They can stain and weaken fabric. If possible, put clothes on and take them off over your head, rather than getting in and out of them feet first. This prevents picking up dirt and lint from the floor. For pants or shorts, taking your shoes off before getting in and out of these garments will help them stay cleaner.

Check for spots, ripped seams, and loose buttons right after taking off your clothes. Remove spots as soon as you

Which one of these roommates displays a good example of clothing care?

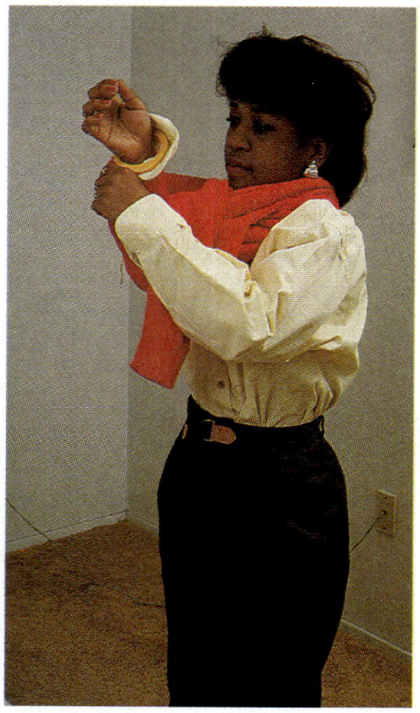

Carefully remove clothing when dressing and undressing.

can. The longer stains remain in clothing, the harder they are to remove. Repair clothes as soon as possible.

Wet clothes need special attention. Hang clothes in a cool, well-ventilated area away from direct heat. Heat may cause some garments to shrink. Stuff the toes of wet shoes with paper and also dry them away from heat.

Put clothes that need to be washed in a dirty clothes bag or basket. If you store dirty and clean clothes together, the clean clothes will take on the odor of the dirty ones.

Storage

It's easy for a closet to become disorganized, especially when you are in a hurry. Here are a few ideas to get you started on shaping up your closet:

- Organize space by hanging similar clothes together, such as shirts, pants, or skirts. Some people group outfits frequently worn together.

- Use hangers that are wide and strong enough to support your clothes. Wooden or plastic ones are a good choice.
- Help pants to keep their shape by hanging them by the bottom of the legs or over hangers, as shown in the photo. Hang skirts by the waist. Press-type or clothespin-type hangers are useful for pants and skirts.
- Use shelf space, the floor, and walls of the closet to store accessories. You can buy special closet organizers or create your own. You might use different-sized boxes to store accessories like scarves and hats. Hooks or nails can be used to hang other accessories like belts and purses.

An organized closet saves you time and frustration.

If drawer space is limited, organization can again come to the rescue. Use drawer dividers or small boxes to keep items in place. Group similar items together. This makes them easier to find.

Avoid putting too many clothes into a drawer. Garments are less likely to be damaged or wrinkled when you allow enough storage space.

If you live in an area where the seasons change, you will probably store some clothes while you're using others. Before putting clothes away for a season, check to be sure they are repaired and clean. Dirty clothes invite textile-eating insects to have a banquet at your expense.

Before storing clothes, remove all belts and close all fastenings so that garments will keep their shape. Hang clothes carefully or fold and put them in boxes or drawers. Sweaters or loosely knitted garments should be stored flat. Tissue paper or thin plastic bags placed between folds helps to prevent creases from forming. Be sure to store clothes in a place that's cool, dry, and out of direct sunlight. Garment bags are good to use for storage.

Putting too much into a drawer can wrinkle your clothing. How might these drawers be better organized?

AROUND THE WORLD

Classics are garments that always seem to be in style. The people living in some parts of Mexico wear clothes that have been in fashion there for almost five hundred years. Researchers studying Indian groups in the mountains of Mexico have found strong similarities between their garments and those of the Aztecs, people who lived in Mexico in the 1500s. A man's fringed vest, for example, looks much like ones seen in Aztec statues. A shawl worn by present-day women villagers is also very similar to those seen in Aztec drawings. Why do you think these styles have remained popular for so long?

Washing Clothes

Because of busy schedules, many families share responsibility for doing the laundry. Laundry isn't a difficult job. However, it isn't quite as fast or effortless as commercials make it seem.

Jeff's first laundry experience wasn't the snap he expected. He tossed all the clothes into the washer. They didn't quite fit until he packed them down a bit. All the boxes and bottles of laundry products had him thoroughly confused. Finally, he added some of each, turned the washer on "soak," and left for a ballgame.

How many of Jeff's errors did you catch? What ending would you write for this story?

Laundry isn't difficult — if you know what you're doing. Here are some tips.

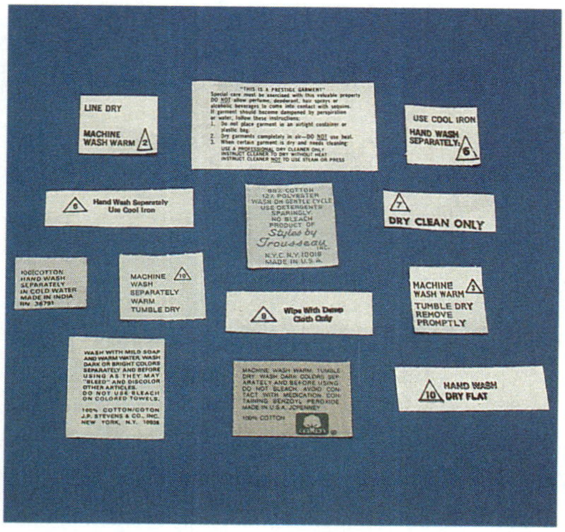

Care labels provide important information about how to clean garments.

Check Care Labels

When it comes to clothing care, your best source of information is the care label sewn into the garment. If the garment is washable, the label will tell what steps to follow in washing and drying. Care labels also tell you what *not* to do, such as "Do not bleach."

Sort Clothes

Sorting is important in order to get clothes clean, to prevent colors from running together, and to keep garments in good condition. Not all clothes need the same water temperature, washing action, and washing time.

Using the care labels, sort the clothes to be machine washed into separate piles as follows:

- Delicate fabrics that require warm water and a gentle cycle.
- Sturdy white and light-colored clothing.
- Permanent press and knit fabrics.
- Dark-colored clothes.
- Heavily soiled garments that should be washed separately.

As you sort the clothes empty all pockets. Also close all zippers, snaps, hooks, and buttons.

Sorting clothes before you do laundry can keep you from damaging your clothes.

Use laundry products according to the manufacturer's directions to get clothes clean.

Pretreat Clothes

Pretreatment refers to any special attention you give a garment before laundering. Pretreatment helps remove heavy soil and stains. Necklines and the cuffs of long-sleeve shirts, for example, often need special attention. Washing alone may not be enough to get such areas clean. Rub undiluted liquid detergent on the soiled or stained area or use a special pretreatment product. Follow label directions.

Also check carefully for stains. Stains that are not removed in the wash cycle may become permanent when the garment is machine dried. The longer any stain remains, the more difficult it is to remove. Different types of stains require different treatments. Stain removal charts are helpful in deciding the best method to use. For many stains, try sponging them with cool water.

Choose Laundry Products

Many different kinds of products are available for doing laundry. Detergents, bleaches, and fabric softeners each have special jobs to do.

- ***Detergents.*** The primary job of detergent is to remove the dirt from clothes. Detergents also aid in removing grease by breaking it into fine particles. These particles are held in the water until it is drained. Regardless of what brand of detergent you use, be sure to put in the recommended amount. If too little is used, clothes will not get clean. If too much is used in an automatic washer, it is difficult to rinse out all the suds.
- ***Bleach.*** Bleach helps to remove grayness, stains, and, in some cases, germs from clothes. Liquid chlorine bleach is so strong, it must be diluted before use. Be sure to read all the instructions carefully before you use a bleach product.

If you don't follow directions, garments may be ruined. Putting chlorine bleach directly on fabrics can even make a hole in the fabric.

- ***Fabric softeners.*** These help to soften fabric, control static electricity, and reduce wrinkling. Some fabric softeners are added to the rinse cycle of the washer, some are contained in the detergent, and others are added to the dryer in sheet form. Follow the manufacturer's instructions for use.

Pocket Lab

Effects of Chlorine Bleach on Stains and Fabrics

MATERIALS:
6 stained fabric samples obtained from your teacher; chlorine bleach; water

EQUIPMENT:
pan; tongs

Directions: Observe the stains on the fabric samples. Try to identify the cause of each stain. Carefully, make a solution of 1 quart water and 2 tablespoons bleach. Place fabric samples in the pan for 5 to 10 minutes and observe the results.

- Which stains did the bleach remove?
- Which fabrics were damaged by the bleach?

Select Cleaning Action

Different types of clothing require different water temperatures, water levels, and wash cycles. Be sure to choose the right settings for each load of laundry. For example, use a cold temperature and a low water setting for a small load of brightly colored clothing.

Garments need to circulate freely while being washed and rinsed. The movement of water through clothes helps to force dirt out of the fabric. Avoid overloading the washer. A washer is fully loaded when garments placed loosely in the empty washer tub almost reach the top.

Use a cold water rinse for every load to save energy. Rinse water temperature has no effect on the cleaning process.

Hand Washing

Some clothes require the gentle handling of hand washing. Of course any machine washable item can also be washed by hand. Here are a few tips:

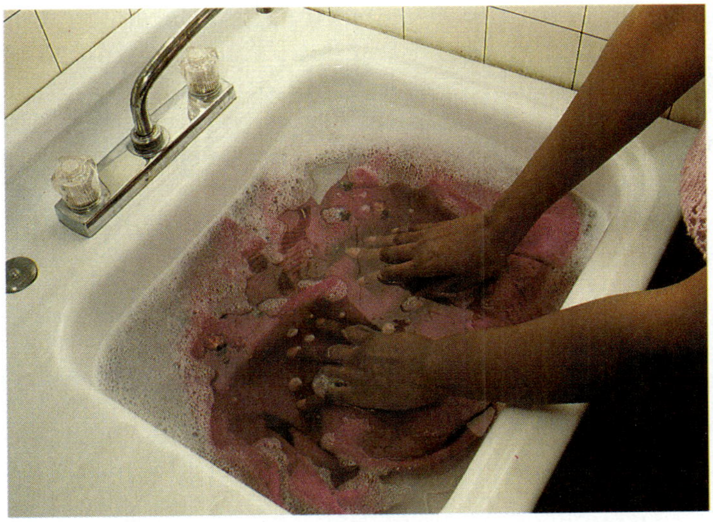

Gently squeeze sudsy water through delicate hand washables for the best results.

- Use a sink or container large enough for the clothes to move freely. You may be able to wash only one or two items at a time.
- Choose a soap or detergent to match the clothes.
- Put water into the sink, add the detergent, mix, and then put in the clothes.
- Soak the clothes for 5 to 30 minutes, depending on the amount of soil and detergent directions. The detergent will do most of the work for you.
- Drain the sink and add fresh water. Gently squeeze sudsy water through the garments. You don't have to do a lot of hard rubbing. Be sure to have at least two clean rinses to remove both suds and soil.

Drying Clothes

Most clothes can be either air-dried or dried in a dryer. Generally, articles that can be washed together can be dried together. However, some need to be dried in a particular way. Check the information on the care label.

Machine Drying

Always shake out laundered clothes before tossing them into the dryer. This will help them dry faster. Avoid overloading the dryer. Overloading increases drying time and can cause uneven drying and wrinkles.

TIPS: *Getting Out Stains*

To get out some of the most common stains, follow these guidelines:

- **Blood.** First soak stain in cold water for 30 minutes, then in a presoak product. Wash in cool or warm water. (Hot water will set a protein stain, such as blood.)
- **Oil and grease.** Use a prewash stain remover, according to label directions. Wash in hottest water recommended on garment care label.
- **Soft drinks, tea, and coffee.** Sponge with cool water. Use prewash stain remover. Wash in hottest water recommended on garment care label.

Avoid overloading the dryer. Clothes won't dry efficiently and are more likely to wrinkle.

SAFETY CHECK✓

To press and iron safely:

- Don't touch a hot iron.
- Keep your hands and face away from the steam.
- Position the cord so the iron doesn't get pulled off the ironing board.
- Keep the iron upright when not in use.
- Turn off and unplug the iron after each use. Steam irons should also be drained of water.
- Let the iron cool completely before storing it.

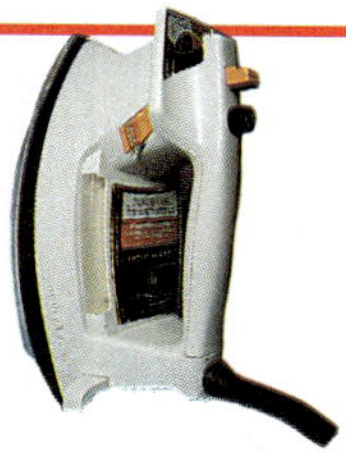

Select the dryer setting designed for the load you're drying. (The instruction book is your best source of information.) Most dryers, for example, have a permanent press cycle that cools down clothes after drying to minimize wrinkles. Avoid overdrying clothes. This can cause shrinkage. For best results, remove clothes from the dryer as soon as it stops. Remember to clean the lint filter each time after using the dryer.

Air Drying

Air drying is an energy-saving alternative to machine drying. After washing, clothes are placed on a clothesline, rack, or on plastic hangers to dry. Loosely woven or knit garments should be laid on a flat surface to dry.

Pressing and Ironing

After washing and drying, some clothes need additional treatment to remove wrinkles. This is done with moisture, heat, and pressure. Pressing and ironing are the two techniques used. **Pressing** is the process of lifting and lowering the iron onto an area of fabric. **Ironing** involves moving the iron back and forth over the fabric to remove wrinkles.

The correct iron temperature depends on the garment's fiber content. Check the care label before pressing or ironing. If the fabric is a blend, set the iron for the fiber that requires the lowest setting. If you do not know the fiber content, test a hidden seam or hem.

Knits and wool should be pressed, not ironed, to avoid stretching. Most woven fabrics can be ironed.

Always press or iron articles that need the lowest setting first. Move to higher settings later. Begin with small areas, such as collars, sleeves, and cuffs. Then move on to the body of the garment. Remember to press dark and wool fabrics inside out. These fabrics will become shiny when heat and pressure are applied to their right side. Pile fabrics like velvet and corduroy need special care. They should be steamed to avoid flattening the pile.

Dry Cleaning

Some care labels tell you to dry-clean garments. To **dry-clean** means to clean with chemicals rather than with detergent and water. The cleaned garment is steamed to remove wrinkles. Not all fabrics can be successfully dry cleaned. Check the care label.

There are two types of dry-cleaning services available. Professional dry cleaners are more expensive, yet they can remove most spots and stains from your garments. Coin-operated machines cost less, but do not provide special treatment for spot or stain removal.

Clothing Repair

Clothes kept in good repair look better and last longer. Making simple repairs is easy. Here are some of the most common problems you will find.

Rips and Tears

Ripped seams are easily repaired. Use a color of thread that matches the fabric. By hand or with a sewing machine, make a new line of stitching. Begin and end the stitching just beyond the ripped section. (See Chapter 35 for more on machine stitching.)

Tears on your clothing can be straight, diagonal, or three-cornered. Iron-on mending tape can help you repair them. Choose a color that matches the garment. The tape is ironed on the inside of the garment, following package directions.

Tears can also be repaired with patches on the right side of the garment. Choose a fabric similar to the garment fabric. Use hand or machine stitching to attach the patch to the garment.

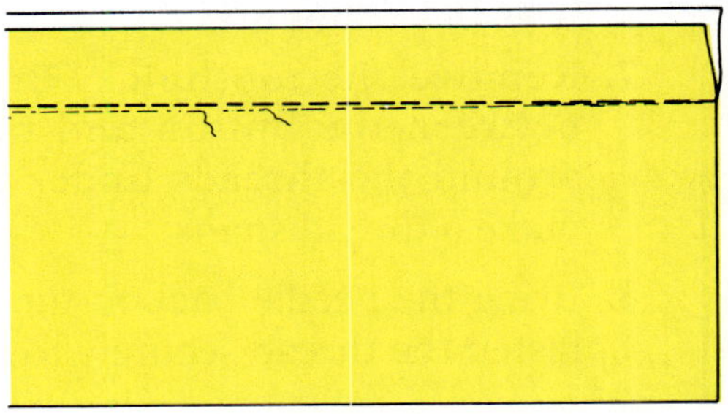

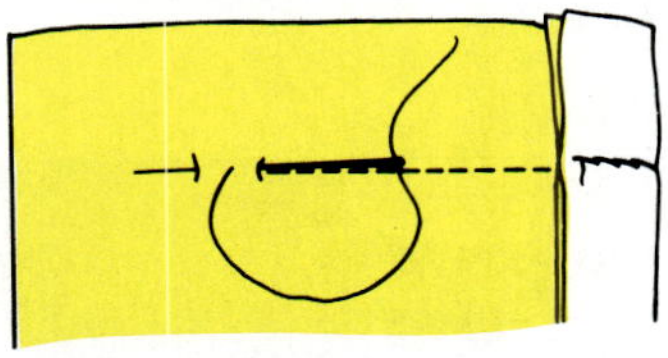

Learning how to make simple clothing repairs is a step you can take toward being well-groomed, and it can save you money, too. Ripped seams are easily repaired on the sewing machine or by hand sewing.

Buttons

Buttons should be securely attached to the garment. Continued buttoning and unbuttoning causes threads to weaken and break. Therefore, it's important to know how to replace buttons.

There are two types of buttons — sew-through and shank. With sew-through buttons, the thread comes up through the button and shows on the top side. Shank buttons have a **shank**, or stem, on the bottom to hold the thread. The shank gives you room to work the button through the buttonhole. Because sew-through buttons don't have shanks, you must make a thread shank for them. See page 342 to learn how to make a thread shank.

How to ...
Replace Buttons

1. Place a pin where the missing button is to be located. Select a matching thread color.
2. Double the thread in the needle and knot both ends together. Bring the needle up from the wrong side to the right side of the garment.
3. Take a small stitch to secure the thread knot.
4. Remove the pin you used to locate the button.
5. Bring the needle through the button. Place a toothpick across the top of the button to allow for a thread shank.
6. Make several stitches through the fabric, the button, and over the toothpick.
7. Remove the toothpick. Bring the needle and thread between the button and the fabric. Wrap the thread around the threads under the button several times to make a thread shank.
8. Bring the needle back to the wrong side of the fabric and fasten the thread securely to the fabric. Clip the thread.
9. Your finished button.

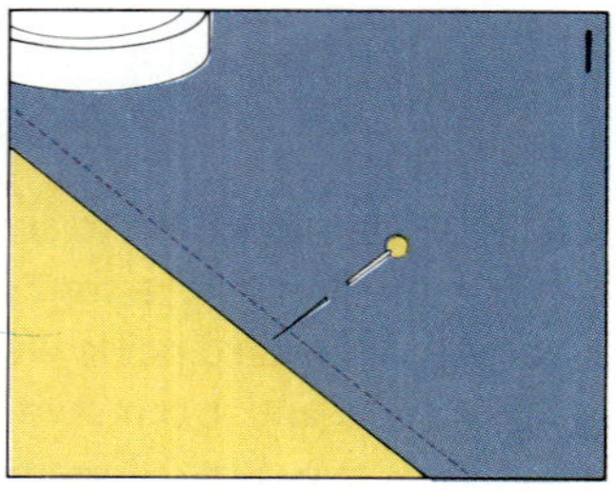

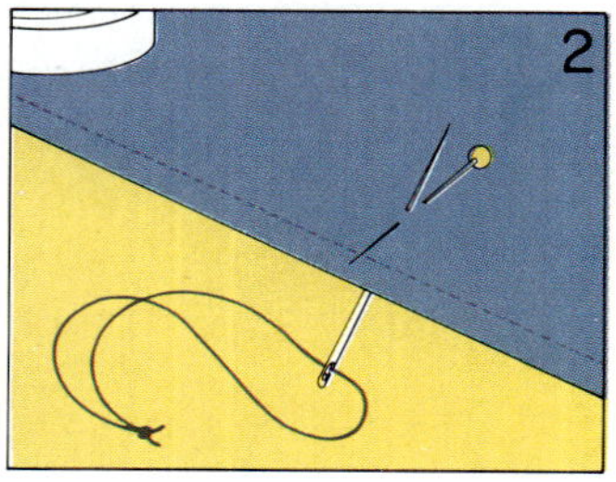

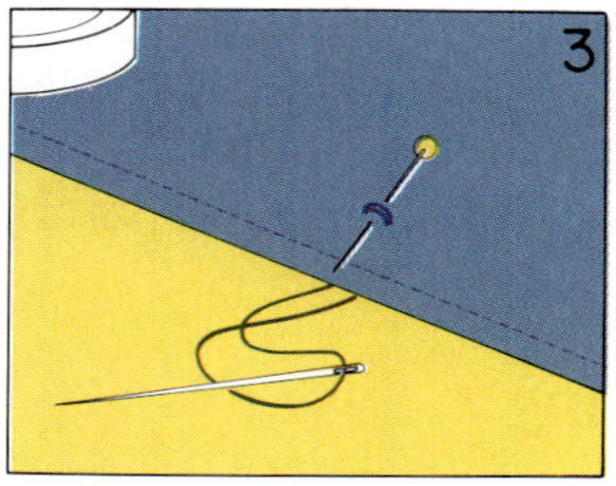

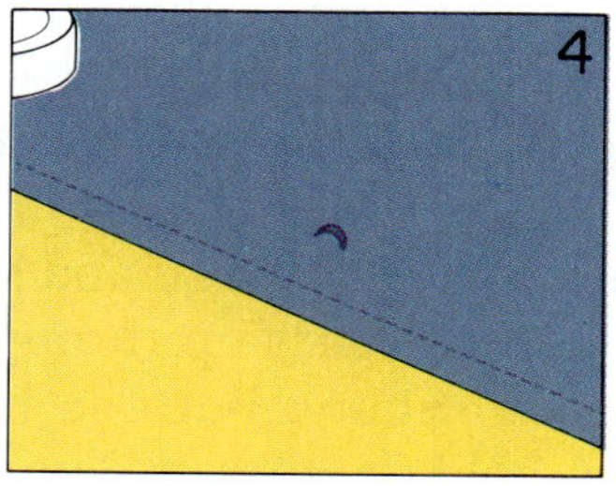

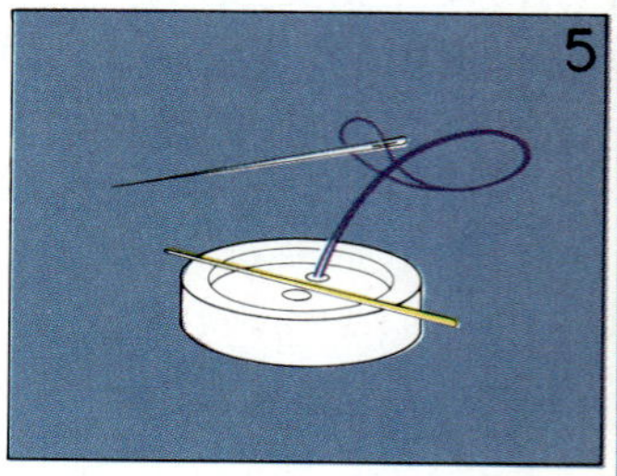

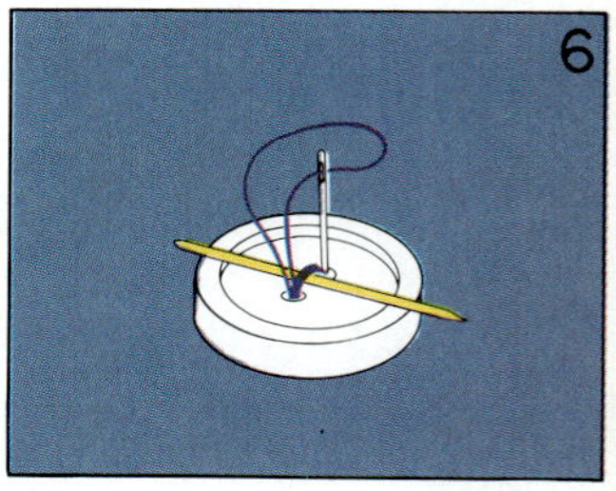

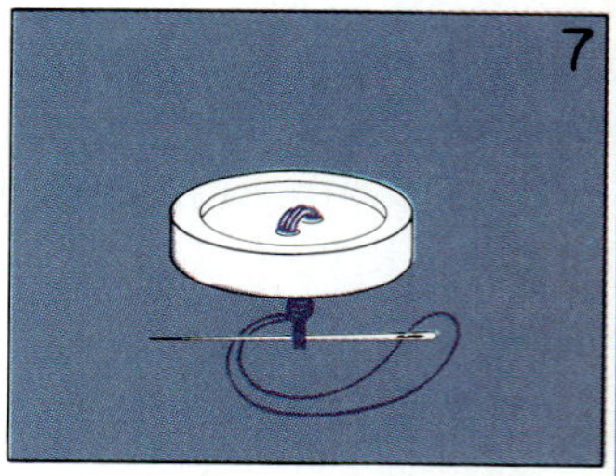

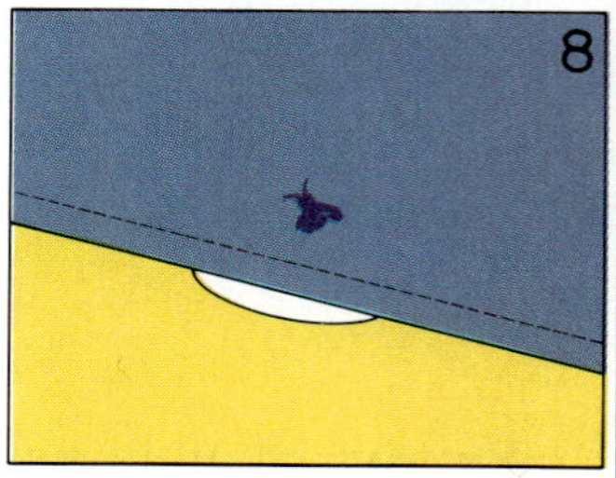

▼ Hooks and Eyes ▼

Hooks and eyes are often used to fasten openings on which there is a strain. They are often found on the ends of collars, neck edges, and waistbands. Use black hooks and eyes for dark fabrics and silver ones for light-colored fabrics. On edges that overlap, as on a waistband, use a straight eye. On edges that meet, as on a neck edge, use a round eye. To sew on hooks and eyes:

- Place the hook on the underside of the overlap at least 1/8 inch (3 mm) from the edge. Using small stitches and a single thread in the needle, stitch around each loop or ring. Sew through one layer of fabric so that the stitches will not show on the right side. Bring the needle between the two thicknesses of fabric to the end of the hook. Take three to four stitches around the end of the hook so it is held down firmly. See pages 406-407 for more information on hand sewing stitches.
- Overlap the edge and mark the position of the straight eye on the left-hand side with a pin. Stitch the eye in place around both loops using small stitches. Fasten the thread securely and clip.
- For edges that meet, sew the hook 1/8 inch (3 mm) from the edge. Stitch around each loop. Match the garment edges. Position the eye so that the loop extends 1/8 inch (3 mm) beyond the edge. Stitch in place. When the hook and eye are attached the edges should meet exactly. Secure the thread, and clip close to the fabric.

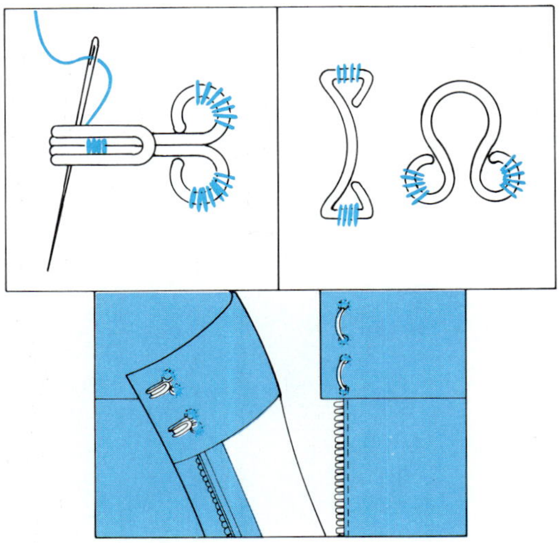

The hooks and eyes shown here are attached to the waistband of a garment with a whipstitch. See Chapter 35 for directions on how to sew a whipstitch.

▼ Snaps ▼

An opening that doesn't have much strain, such as the top of a buttoned neckline, is often fastened with a snap. Use black snaps for dark fabrics and silver ones for light-colored fabrics.

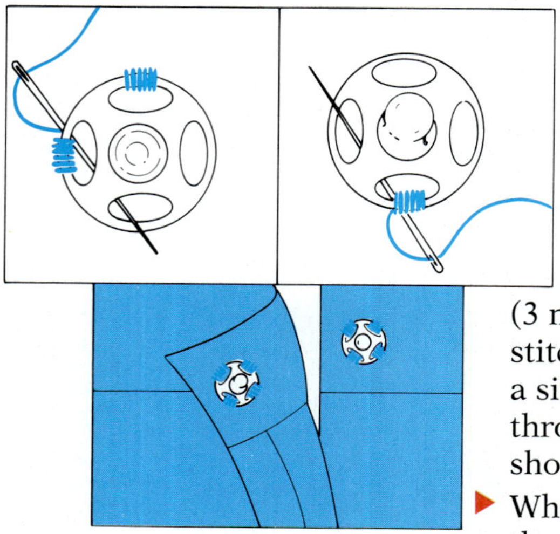

Snaps are used for openings that do not have much strain, such as the top of buttoned necklines. Snaps are sewn onto a garment with a whipstitch.

- The ball section of the snap is usually sewn to the underside of the overlap. Then, pin the closing together and mark the location of the socket, or flat part of the snap. Mark the position of the socket by placing a pin through the center hole of the ball section after it is sewn in place.
- Place the ball section of the snap about ⅛ inch (3 mm) from the edge of the overlap. Make several stitches close together in each hole of the snap using a single thread in the needle. Use small stitches. Sew through only one layer of fabric so that stitches don't show on the right side.
- When going from hole to hole, slide the needle through one hole and under the snap to the next hole. Fasten the thread when finished.

TAKING ACTION

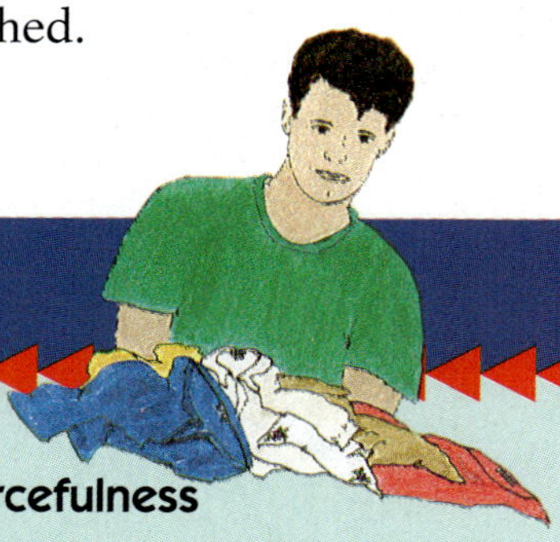

When his uncle asked him, Warren agreed to help out at the family business, "Garcia Cleaners." The business offers services such as dry cleaning, machine or hand washing and drying, and ironing. Warren has had no training because the place is usually so busy that none of the experienced employees have time to help him.

On his first day, the manager said to him, "Sort this bundle of clothes into three baskets. Put the clothes that need dry cleaning in the first basket, those that need machine washing in the second, and those that need hand washing in the third." Warren is left with the following items to sort: soiled denim pants, cotton slacks, stained rayon pants, a silk blouse, a linen sports jacket, a polyester bathrobe, a wool coat, lace handkerchiefs, and a satin dress.

Using Your Resourcefulness

- What resources might Warren draw upon to find out more about clothing care and fabrics?
- At the present time, how should Warren sort the clothes? Where might he find information that would help him right away?
- Should any articles be pretreated? How?
- Clothing care is one skill Warren needs on the job. What other skills will help him succeed at work?

Chapter 30 Review

Summary

In this chapter, you have read about:

- How routine care and proper storage of clothing can help make them last longer.
- How to sort and treat soiled garments for washing.
- Laundry products and how to use them.
- How to press and iron clothes when needed.
- Sewing on hooks and eyes and snaps.

Facts to Recall

1. Name four things to remember when dressing and undressing to help keep your clothes clean and in good repair.
2. Identify three ways to organize your closet.
3. What are five tips for machine washing clothing?
4. Identify five groups that clothes can be sorted into for machine washing.
5. When should clothes be pretreated?
6. List four things to remember when machine drying clothes.
7. In what three ways can rips and tears be mended?
8. Briefly explain how to make a thread shank for a sew-through button.
9. Briefly describe how to fasten overlapping fabric edges using a hook and eye.

Ideas to Explore

1. Discuss the benefits of properly taking care of clothes. Is wearing stained or torn clothing a fashion statement or a statement of neglect?
2. How can having garments professionally dry-cleaned when indicated save money over time?
3. What is your biggest clothing storage problem? What are some possible solutions to this problem?

Activities to Try

1. Using magazines, catalogs, or newspapers, cut out pictures of clothing you might typically find weekly in the laundry basket. Sort the pictures of clothes into appropriate loads using the guidelines found in this chapter. Mount each load onto a piece of paper and write a brief explanation about your sorting decisions.
2. Develop a care chart for your clothes. Use the care labels in your clothes as a guide. Make a column for each different type of care and label the top of each column on your chart. List each of your clothing items under the appropriate label.

LINK TO *Science*

How Detergents Work

Try the following experiment to see how detergent works.

- Fill a glass with water and then pour 2 tablespoons (30 mL) of vegetable oil on top.
- Stir the oil and water mixture with a spoon. Observe the results.
- Add 2 tablespoons (30 mL) of laundry detergent to the oil and water mixture. Stir briskly. Observe the results.

What happened after you stirred the oil and water mixture together? What happened when you added the detergent to the mixture and stirred it together? How could the results that you observed explain the cleaning action of a detergent?

CHAPTER

31 Selecting a Pattern

OBJECTIVES

- *Take measurements to determine pattern size.*
- *Select a pattern that matches your skill level.*
- *Interpret pattern envelope information.*

TERMS TO LEARN

- ***ease***
- ***yardage***
- ***view***
- ***notions***

Have you ever struggled to find clothes that fit just right? Are shirt sleeves always too short? Are pant legs always too long?

If you have struggled with problems like these and others, then learning to sew can be a real benefit and a lot of fun, too. Practice and a little patience are all you need to sew clothing that fits well and does the most for you.

The Right Pattern Size

The success of any sewing project depends on choosing the right pattern. Making a pillow or tote bag does not require taking personal measurements. However, if you are making a garment for yourself or someone else, knowing how to take measurements will help you to select the best pattern size. Read on to learn how to determine pattern size for both females and males.

Ready-to-wear sizes are not always the same as pattern sizes. However, pattern sizes are similar among the major pattern companies. Pattern sizes will vary slightly, depending on the amount of **ease**, or room needed for comfort and movement, allowed for in the pattern.

You will need to take several body measurements. Accurate measurements can be taken over any garments that fit well. Bulky sweaters, jackets, and belts should be taken off before taking measurements.

In order to take accurate measurements, work with a partner and measure each other. Take each measurement twice. Check to be sure both measurements are within ½ inch (1.3 cm) of each other. If they are not, check again.

When taking measurements, hold the tape measure so it fits comfortably. It should not be too tight or too loose. If you are unsure about the correct size even after following these directions, check with your teacher.

As you and your partner take each other's measurements, write the measurements down. You will need them to select the correct pattern size. Measurements are also used to make any pattern adjustments that may be needed.

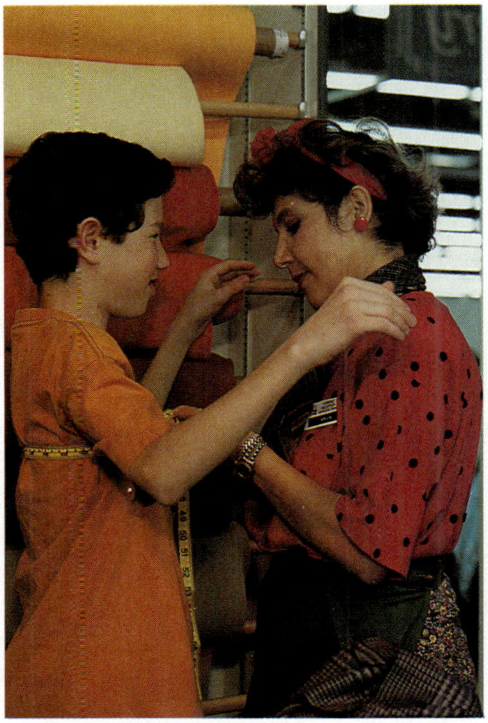

Taking accurate measurements will help you select the correct pattern size.

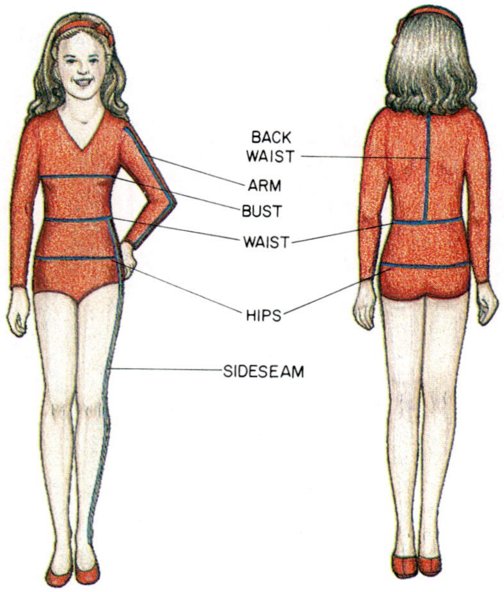

Female Measurement Record

	Your Measurement	Total	Pattern Measurement	Difference
Bust				
Waist				
Hips				
Back Waist Length				
Arm				
Height				

Measurements for Females

Before selecting a pattern size, you need to determine your measurements and figure type. Take the following measurements:

- ***Bust.*** Measure over the fullest part of the bust and straight across the back.
- ***Waist.*** Tie a string around your waist to identify the narrowest point. Measure around the natural waistline with a tape measure.
- ***Hips.*** Measure around the largest part of the hips, anywhere from 6-9 inches (15-23 cm) below the waist.
- ***Side seam.*** Measure from the waist along the side seam to the top of the foot or desired pant length.
- ***Back waist length.*** Measure from the bone at the base of the neck to the natural waistline.
- ***Arm length.*** Measure from the top of the shoulder and over the bent elbow down to the wrist.
- ***Height.*** Measure when standing tall, without shoes, against a wall.

Figure Types

Figure types are based on body proportion and two measurements — height and back waist length. Today, pattern companies divide female figure types into two main groups — girls' and misses'. Compare your body proportion, height, and back waist length with those on the chart on page 349 to determine your figure type.

After identifying your figure type, compare your body measurements with those on the chart. Your measurements may not exactly match those given. The following guidelines can help you in selecting the pattern size that most closely matches your measurements:

- Use the bust measurement for garments requiring fit in the top, such as blouses, dresses, suits, and coats.
- Use the hip measurement for garments that fit snugly over the hips and are not affected by bust measurement. This includes fitted skirts, pants, and shorts. The hip measurement is more important than the waist measurement because the waist is easier to alter.
- Use the waist measurement for skirts with pleats or fullness beginning at the waistline.
- If you fall between two sizes, pick the smaller size if you are small-boned. Select the larger size if you are large-boned. Pattern companies also have adjustable patterns that make it easier to cut the pattern to the right size. For example, many patterns may be adjusted for petites by shortening the pattern pieces in certain areas.

GIRLS'
Girls' patterns are designed for the girl who has not yet begun to mature. See chart below for approximate heights without shoes.

Size	7	8	10	12	14
Breast	26	27	28½	30	32
Waist	23	23½	24½	25½	26½
Hip	27	28	30	32	34
Back Waist Length	11½	12	12¾	13½	14¼
Approx. Heights	50"	52"	56"	58½"	61"

MISSES'
Misses' patterns are designed for a well-proportioned and developed figure: about 5'5" to 5'6" without shoes.

Size	6	8	10	12	14	16	18	20	22	24
Bust	30½	31½	32½	34	36	38	40	42	44	46
Waist	23	24	25	26½	28	30	32	34	37	39
Hip	32½	33½	34½	36	38	40	42	44	46	48
Back Waist Length	15½	15¾	16	16¼	16½	16¾	17	17¼	17⅜	17½

Measurements for Males

Take the following body measurements to help you select your best pattern size:

- ***Chest.*** Measure around the fullest part of the chest.
- ***Waist.*** Measure over the shirt at the natural waistline.
- ***Hips.*** Measure around the fullest part of the hips anywhere from 6-8 inches (15-20 cm) below the waist.
- ***Neck.*** Measure around the base of the neck and add ½ inch (1.3 cm) for shirt neck size.
- ***Arm length.*** With the arm bent up at the elbow, measure from the bone at the base of the neck, around the elbow, and up to the wrist bone.
- ***Inseam.*** A simple way to take this measurement is to use a favorite pair of pants that are the correct length. Place the pants on a flat surface. Measure from the crotch seam to the bottom of the pant leg.
- ***Side seam.*** Measure from the waist down to the point where the pant leg breaks slightly on the shoe.
- ***Height.*** Measure when standing tall, without shoes, against a wall.

Body Type

To determine your body type, compare your body proportion, height, and back waist length with those on the chart on page 350.

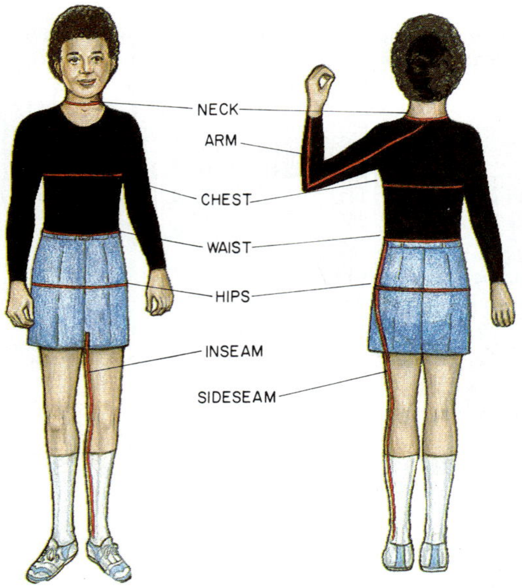

Male Measurement Record

	Your Measurement	Total	Pattern Measurement	Difference
Chest				
Waist				
Hips				
Neck				
Arm				
In-Seam				
Side Seam				
Height				

After determining your body type, compare your body measurements with those on the chart. Your measurements may not exactly match those given. Use the following guidelines to pick the correct pattern size:

- Use the chest measurement to select the pattern for a coat or jacket.
- Use the neck and chest measurements to select shirt patterns. If measurements vary, use the chest size and alter the neck.
- Use the waist measurement as a guide to select a pants pattern. If the hips are very large or small in comparison to the waist, buy the pattern by the hip measurement and alter the waist.
- Body measurements may fall between two sizes. Choose the larger size if you are husky or like a looser fit. Use the smaller size if you are slim or like a snug fit.

	BOYS'				TEEN BOYS'			
Size	**7**	**8**	**10**	**12**	**14**	**16**	**18**	**20**
Chest	26	27	28	30	32	33½	35	36½
Waist	23	24	25	26	27	28	29	30
Hip (Seat)	27	28	29½	31	32½	34	35½	37
Neckband	11¾	12	12½	13	13½	14	14½	15
Height	48	50	54	58	61	64	66	68
Shirt Sleeve	22⅜	23¼	25	26¾	29	30	31	32
	MEN'S (height approximately 5'10")							
Size	**34**	**36**	**38**	**40**	**42**	**44**	**46**	**48**
Chest	34	36	38	40	42	44	46	48
Waist	28	30	32	34	36	39	42	44
Hip (Seat)	35	37	39	41	43	45	47	49
Neckband	14	14½	15	15½	16	16½	17	17½
Shirt Sleeve	32	32	33	33	34	34	35	35

Measurement charts can be found in the back of pattern catalogs. They also provide you with pattern illustrations and skill-level sections to help you develop sewing skills with success.

Using a Pattern Catalog

After you have determined your figure or body type and pattern size, you will be ready to look through a pattern catalog.

All pattern catalogs are divided into sections. Sections cover such topics as different figure/body types, size ranges, and garment and craft categories. Take a minute or two to look over the titles of the various sections. You will find the titles helpful in selecting sections that fit your skill level.

As you look through the catalog, you will see sketches and pictures of different garments or crafts. For each picture, there will be a description and the **yardage** — the amount of fabric needed for each project. Although the pictures and sketches don't tell it all, they can give you a clue as to how easy or difficult each pattern will be.

Body measurement charts, like those used to determine your pattern size, are at the back of the catalog. There is also a numerical listing of all the pattern numbers and the page numbers on which they can be found. This makes it easy to look for a special pattern number.

The three main parts of a pattern are the envelope, the instruction sheet, and the pattern pieces.

Choosing the Right Pattern

Selecting a pattern that is right for your skill level generally leads to a more positive sewing experience. If you tackle a pattern that is too difficult at first, it is easy to become discouraged and unhappy with the finished product.

If you are a true beginner, look for the "easy-to-sew" section of the pattern catalog. Patterns in this section have several things in common:

- They have a small number of pattern pieces.
- They don't require a great deal of fitting.
- The designs are simple and have very few sewing details, such as darts, pleats, sleeves, collars, trim, and pockets.

After mastering some of the basic sewing skills, you'll be ready to take on the challenge of more complicated patterns. If you like sewing, try a new construction technique or fabric type when selecting each new pattern.

The front of the pattern envelope shows different views and details of each pattern.

Reading the Pattern Envelope

The three main parts of a pattern include the envelope, the guidesheet, and the pattern pieces. The pattern envelope contains the instruction sheet and pattern pieces. Both the front and back of the envelope contain important information.

The Envelope Front

The front of the envelope shows several colorful **views**, or garment styles that can be made from a pattern. Slightly different details, such as long or short sleeves, types of collars, and trims, make each view unique. Views are also shown in various fabrics, so you'll get an idea of how different one pattern can look. It also identifies the pattern number, size, figure/body type, and any special information such as "Suitable for Serger Sewing." (A serger stitches, trims, and finishes a seam all at the same time.)

AROUND THE WORLD

When a garment has religious meaning, it can cause conflict. In France, for example, school officials have been debating whether to allow female students of the Islamic faith to wear head scarves. The students' religious teaching requires them to wear the scarves in public, but French public schools, like those in the United States, may not show support or favoritism for any one religion. School officials find themselves caught between their duty to remain neutral and the students' right to practice their faith through dress. How would you resolve this conflict?

PICK-A-KNIT® RULE | **FOR THIS PATTERN—4"(10cm) OF KNIT FABRIC MUST STRETCH CROSSWISE FROM HERE →** | **TO HERE →**

REGLE "CHOISISSEZ-UN-TRICOT" | **POUR CE PATRON—4"(10cm) DE TRICOT DOIVENT S'ETIRER EN TRAVERS D'ICI →** | **JUSQU'ICI**

000

10 PIECES

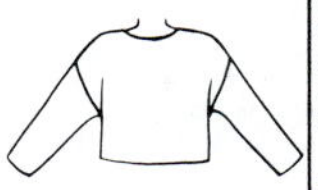

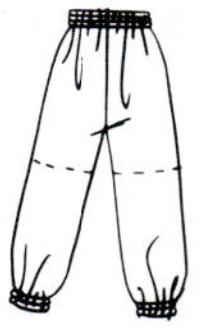

MISSES', MEN'S OR TEEN BOYS' PANTS OR SHORTS AND KNIT TOPS. . . TANK TOP SIZED FOR STRETCH KNITS ONLY: Tank top has racer back. Cropped loose-fitting top has extended shoulders and three-quarter length sleeves. Pull-on pants or shorts with side seam pockets have triple elastic waistline casing with optional purchased drawstring. Pants have double elastic ankle casings. Shorts can be made in border printed or plain fabrics.

Fabrics—Cotton interlock, cotton-lycra blends, jerseys. Top, pants and shorts also in sweatshirt knits. Pants and shorts also in broadcloth, challis, lightweight faille, supplex. Shorts also in border printed fabric. See Pick-A-Knit® Rule for tank top. Not suitable for obvious diagonals. Extra fabric needed to match plaids, stripes or one-way design fabrics. For pile, shaded or one-way design fabrics, use with nap yardages/layouts.

Notions: Thread. Look for Simplicity notions.

Multi-Sized Pattern

BODY MEASUREMENTS						
Chest/Bust	30-32	34-36	38-40	42-44	46-48	Ins.
Hip	31-32½	35-37	39-41	43-45	47-49	"
Sizes U.S.A. ONLY	(X-Small	Small	Medium	Large	X-Large)	
Sizes	(X-Small	Small	Medium	Large	X-Large)	
Tank-Top—Sized for stretch knits only						
60"**	1	1	1	1	1	Yd.
Top						
60"**	1¼	1¼	1¼	1¼	1⅜	Yds.
Interfacing—¼ yd. of 22" to 25" fusible						
Pants						
45"**	2¼	2⅝	2¾	2¾	2¾	Yds.
60"**	1¾	2	2¼	2¼	2¾	"
Elastic—5⅝ yds. of ½" wide						
Shorts—Plain Fabric—Cut lengthwise						
45"**	1½	1½	1½	1⅝	1¾	Yds.
60"**	1⅛	1⅛	1⅛	1⅝	1⅝	"
Shorts—Border Printed Fabric—Cut crosswise						
45"*	1¾	1⅞	2	2⅛	2¼	Yds.
Shorts Elastic—3¾ yds. of ½" wide						
Pants or Shorts Drawstring (opt.)—1¾ yds. of ¼" cord or one novelty shoe lace approx. 63" long						
Pants side length	40	40½	41	41½	42	Ins.
Shorts side length	19	19½	20	20½	21	"

*without nap **with nap ***with or without nap

PANTALON OU SHORT ET T-SHIRTS POUR JEUNE FEMME, HOMME OU ADOLESCENT . . . DEBARDEUR EN JERSEY EXTENSIBLE SEULEMENT: Débardeur avec dos cycliste. T-shirt court et ample avec emmanchures tombantes et manches trois-quarts. Pantalon ou short avec poches dans les coutures de côté, triple élastique coulissé à la taille et cordon acheté facultatif. Pantalon avec élastique double coulissé aux chevilles. Le short peut être réalisé dans du tissu imprimé à bordure ou en tissu uni.

Tissus–Coton interlock, coton Lycra mélangé, jersey. T-shirt, pantalon et short en jersey molletonné pour sweatshirt. Pantalon et short en popeline, étamine, faille légère, supplex. Short en tissu imprimé à bordure aussi. Voyez la Règle "Choisissez-Un-Jersey" pour le debardeur. Les tissus à diagonales apparentes ne conviennent pas à ce patron. Prévoyez davantage de tissu pour raccorder les écossais, rayures ou motifs unidirectionnels. Pour les tissus à long poil, de différents tons ou à motifs unidirectionnels, utilisez métrages et plans de coupe "avec sens".

Mercerie: Fil. Demandez la mercerie Simplicity.

Patron à tailles multiples

MESURES NORMALISEES						
Poitrine	76-81	87-92	97-102	107-112	117-122	cm
Hanches	79-83	89-94	99-104	109-114	119-124	"
Tailles/Sizes	(X-Petite	Petite	Moyenne	Grande	X-Grande)	
Tailles-Europe	(X-Petite	Petite	Moyenne	Grande	X-Grande)	
Débardeur-En jersey extensible seulement						
150cm**	0.90	0.90	0.90	0.90	0.90	m
T-shirt						
150cm**	1.10	1.10	1.10	1.10	1.30	m
Entoilage–thermocollant–0.30m de 55cm à 64cm						
Pantalon						
115cm**	2.10	2.40	2.50	2.50	2.60	m
150cm**	1.60	1.80	2.00	2.10	2.50	"
Elastique–5.10m de 1.3cm de large						
Short–Tissu uni–coupé dans la longueur						
115cm**	1.30	1.40	1.40	1.50	1.60	m
150cm**	1.00	1.10	1.10	1.40	1.50	"
Short—Tissu imprimé à bordure–coupé dans la largeur						
115cm*	1.60	1.70	1.80	1.90	2.10	m
Short Elastique—3.50m de 1.3cm de large						
Pantalon ou Short–cordon (facult.)–1.70m de 6mm ou un lacet de soulier fantaisie de 160cm de long						
Longueur côté du pantalon	102	103	104	106	107	cm
Longueur côté du short	48.5	49.5	51	52	53.5	"

*sans sens **avec sens ***avec ou sans sens

▼ The Envelope Back ▼

There is more detailed information on the back of the envelope. Look for the following information:

- ***Views.*** The envelope back often includes sketches of a garment's back and front views. These show design lines and details that are not easily seen in sketches or photographs on the envelope front.
- ***Garment description.*** A detailed description of the garment will give you lots of information about how each view is constructed.
- ***Suggested fabrics.*** The pattern company lists the types of fabrics that will work well for every pattern. A wide choice is usually given for each view.
- ***Notions.* Notions** are the smaller items needed to make a garment. Thread, buttons, zippers, snaps, hooks and eyes, and any trims you will need are listed.
- ***Advice on special fabrics.*** For example, the advice for one pattern might read, "Extra fabric needed to match plaids, stripes, one-way designs. Not suitable for obvious diagonal fabrics."

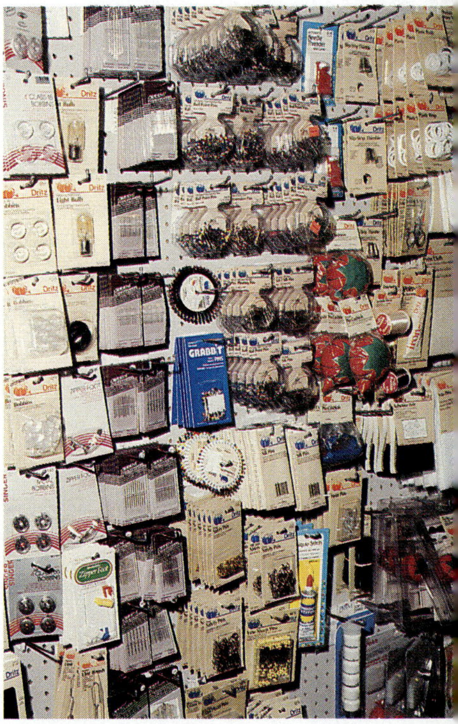

Each type of notion has a different function. Check your pattern for what you need.

Selecting the right pattern results in a well-fitting garment.

- ***Body measurements.*** To select the correct size, compare your measurements with those listed. The measurements and sizes are listed on the back of the pattern envelope as an easy reference.
- ***Yardage chart.*** Usually the largest amount of space on the back of the envelope is devoted to a chart that helps you determine the amount of fabric to buy. The pattern sizes, different views, and fabric widths are listed. Typically, you will see 36-inch, 45-inch, and 60-inch (90-, 115-, and 150-cm) fabric widths. The size and the view you are making will determine the amount of fabric you need to buy. Identify and circle the size, view, and fabric width you will be using on the chart. This will help you avoid making mistakes. Next, draw a line down the size column and another across from the fabric width until the lines intersect, or cross each other. At the point the lines cross, you will find the exact yardage needed to sew the garment.
- ***Garment measurements.*** These measurements may vary depending on what you are making. They may include finished back length or width of the lower edge.

Using the information on the pattern envelope can help you to successfully begin your sewing project.

TAKING ACTION

Brenda wants to give special presents to her brother and sister, who are twins, for their tenth birthday. She can't afford to buy ready-to-wear clothes at this time. However, she owns a sewing machine and decides to make her presents for David and Cleo.

Brenda is a beginner and intends to choose an "easy-to-sew" pattern for tank-tops and shorts. In the summer, the twins are outside all day long — biking, swimming, or playing in a nearby park.

Brenda needs David's and Cleo's measurements in order to buy a pattern. David's measurements are: Chest 29", Waist 25", Hips 30", Height 55". Cleo's measurements are: Chest: 28", Waist 25", Hips 31", Back waist length 13", Height 56". Brenda wants the outfits to be fun, colorful, and comfortable. She turns to you for help.

Using Your Resourcefulness

- What pattern sizes should she choose for David and Cleo? Since Brenda has little money to spend, what options does she have concerning the size needs of David and Cleo and the pattern(s) she buys?
- Describe a pattern style that Brenda could use for David's and Cleo's outfits. Give examples of colors and fabrics that could be used for this pattern. Give a reason for each of your choices.
- In what ways is Brenda being resourceful?
- Would you consider making something special for a relative's birthday? Why or why not?

Chapter 31 Review

Summary

In this chapter, you have read about:

- Taking body measurements for females and males.
- Determining the most important measurement for sewing different garments.
- Locating information on pattern envelopes.
- Using a yardage chart.

Facts to Recall

1. Name four things you should do to take accurate body measurements.
2. Where should the hips be measured on a female?
3. What is the most important measurement to consider when selecting a pattern for a fitted skirt, pants, or shorts?
4. How is the shirt neck size determined for males?
5. Name three characteristics of patterns found in the "easy-to-sew" section of a pattern catalog.
6. Identify three types of information found on the pattern envelope front.
7. List five types of information found on the pattern envelope back.

Ideas to Explore

1. What are some advantages to knowing how to sew your own clothing?
2. Suppose your waist and hip measurements fall between two sizes listed for a pants pattern in the catalog. Your waist is 1 inch (2.5 cm) smaller and your hips are 2 inches (5 cm) larger. Which measurement would you use to buy the pattern? Why?
3. How can simple sewing skills help improve or personalize ready-made garments?

Activities

1. Obtain two patterns, each from different companies. How are the patterns similar and different? Locate information such as body measurements, fabric suggestions, notions needed, and yardage needed for several sizes. Is the information easily found? Which pattern brand did you prefer? Why?
2. Using one or more pattern catalogs, select three patterns you think would be good for someone who is learning to sew. Why do you think these patterns would be good for beginners? What are the similarities and differences in the patterns?

LINK TO *Math*

TAKING MEASUREMENTS

With a partner, take your body measurements as described in this chapter. Measure your body in the following locations: bust or chest, waist, and hips. Use these measurements and a pattern chart (from the back of a pattern book or pages 349-350 in the text) to determine the pattern size that you need. Answer the following questions:

- How should you choose a pattern size if your measurements do not match the measurements on the pattern charts?
- If you wear a different size shirt than you do pants, how should you choose your pattern size? What alternatives do you have?

CHAPTER

32 Fabric and Notions

OBJECTIVES

- *Select fabric appropriate for your pattern, appearance, and skills.*
- *Choose interfacing and notions.*
- *Compute the total cost of a sewing project.*

TERMS TO LEARN

- ***grain***
- ***interfacing***
- ***fusible interfacing***
- ***applique***
- ***casing***

Have you ever been shopping for that perfect garment — something unique that expresses who you really are? Is it sometimes discouraging to see the same type of clothing in store after store?

By using your imagination and creativity when selecting fabric and notions, you can create clothing that is as original and unique as you are. Personal touches such as trims, interesting fabric combinations, or unusual buttons, will help you create fashionable clothing.

Browsing through a fabric store will give you a good idea about the types of fabrics, patterns, and notions that are available. How will you know which fabrics and notions are right for your pattern? As you read this chapter, you will discover some helpful guidelines for making wise fabric and notion choices.

Selecting Fabric

Before you buy a piece of fabric, think about how appropriate the fabric is for your pattern, your appearance, and your sewing skills. What kind of care will the fabric need?

Buy fabric you like and will enjoy working with. After all, you are investing your time, money, and creativity. You will want to enjoy using the finished product.

Selecting fabric that is appropriate for your pattern, appearance, and sewing skills will result in a sewing project you can be proud of.

▼ Consider Your Pattern ▼

When you shop for fabric, bring your pattern and the money needed to buy the fabric and notions. Both your pattern and the money you have to spend will influence your decisions about fabric and notions.

Where do you begin? Your pattern envelope is a good place to start. As you learned in Chapter 31, both the front and back of the envelope provide important tips on selecting fabric. Give special attention to the advice about suitable fabrics.

Using your own good judgment is a key to wise fabric choices. If you are making an active sportswear garment, look at fabrics that are durable and hard-wearing. The fabric will also have to stand up to frequent washings. If you are making something for a dressier occasion, a more delicate fabric might be just what you want.

▼ Consider Your Appearance ▼

When making a garment, think about how the fabric will look on you. Do the design elements of the fabric accent your best features? Use design to your advantage just as you would when buying clothes. Consider each of the following items:

- ***Color.*** In Chapter 28, you learned that everyone looks better in some colors than in others. When you find a fabric you like, locate a mirror and hold the fabric close to your face. Try a few different colors against your skin. Which ones bring out the best in your natural coloring? Also consider whether the color you choose will go with the main colors in your wardrobe. Coordinating colors is a good way to expand your wardrobe with fewer articles of clothing.
- ***Line.*** If you want to look taller, pick fabric with vertical (up-and-down) lines or design. Continuous vertical lines also have a slimming effect. If you want to look shorter, pick horizontal (side-to-side) lines or patterns. To emphasize curves or to appear more full-bodied, try a pattern with diagonal lines.
- ***Proportion.*** Keep fabric designs in proportion with your body. If you are short and have a small bone structure, choose smaller designs. If you are tall or have a large bone structure, a larger design may be the choice for you.

Fabric colors affect your appearance in many ways. What colors enhance your best features?

- ***Texture.*** Fabrics with a great deal of texture — bulky, heavy, rough, and coarse-looking — will make a body appear larger. In contrast, smooth-looking fabrics will minimize body size.

Consider Your Sewing Skills

Confidence in your ability is a real benefit for a successful sewing experience. If you are just learning to sew, choose a fabric with qualities that are easy for a beginner to handle. After learning the basics of sewing, you can move on to more challenging fabrics.

Here are some fabric qualities to consider:

- ***Construction.*** How is the fabric made? Is it woven, or is it knit? Firmly woven fabrics, in a plain weave, are easier to work with than loosely woven or knitted fabrics. They are less likely to stretch or unravel.
- ***Weight.*** Medium-weight fabrics are easier to work with than sheer, heavy textured, or bulky fabrics.
- ***Grain.*** **Grain** refers to the direction in which yarn run in fabric. A fabric is *on-grain* when lengthwise and crosswise threads are at right angles to each other. It is *off-grain* when lengthwise and crosswise threads do not meet at right angles and are curved or slanted. Check fabric carefully before you buy it. Do not buy fabric that is badly off-grain, no matter how little it costs. Straightening fabric takes time, and sometimes it cannot be done at all. If fabric is printed, make sure the print matches the fabric grain. It's difficult to work with off-grain prints. You will learn more about grain in fabric in Chapter 34.
- ***Design.*** Solid-colored fabrics or those with a small design are easiest to work with.
- ***Challenging fabrics.*** If you are a beginner, avoid plaid or striped fabrics and those with one-way designs. These fabrics, along with corduroy and velvet-type fabrics, all require special handling and extra fabric. Lines in plaids and stripes need to be matched in order to have a quality look.
- ***Wrinkle resistance.*** Check for wrinkle resistance by squeezing a small amount of fabric in your hand. Hold it for 30 seconds and release it. If most of the wrinkles disappear quickly, the fabric's wrinkle resistance is good.
- ***Imperfections.*** Look at the large piece of fabric you want to buy. Check for snags, spots, defects, and faded colors.

Consider Fabric Care

The care needed by a fabric will depend on the fiber content and any special finishes applied to the fabric. If you don't want to spend time hand washing or pressing, choose washable fabrics with a permanent press finish. If you don't want to spend money on cleaning bills, avoid fabrics that require dry-cleaning.

Ready-to-wear garments must have care instructions sewn into a seam. Fabric sold by the yard must also come with a care label that you can sew into the seam. Ask the salesperson for the care label. The label on the end of the bolt of fabric will list the fiber content and any special finishes that are used.

Interfacing must match the characteristics of your fabric.

Buying Interfacing

Interfacing is a special fabric that gives support and body to a garment. Although the interfacing isn't visible in finished garments, it makes them look better and last longer. Interfacing is often used at necklines, openings, and collars.

A variety of types of interfacings are available. You will find woven, nonwoven, and fusible interfacing. **Fusible interfacing** has an adhesive coating that bonds it to the fabric when pressed with a hot iron.

Here are some helpful tips for choosing interfacing:

- Choose an interfacing that has weight, body, and care requirements similar to those of your fabric.
- Drape your fabric over the interfacing before you buy it. The interfacing should not show through the fabric.
- Check to see that the interfacing has give, or stretch, that matches your fabric. Some interfacings have stretchability that is ideal for knit fabrics where some stability is needed.

Most interfacings come in white, black, or tan. Use white or tan with light-colored fabrics and black with dark fabrics.

Notions provide the finishing touches to your garment.

Buying Notions

Notions are small items, such as thread, zippers, buttons, trim, seam binding, snaps, and hooks and eyes that are needed to complete a garment. The back of the pattern envelope lists the notions needed to complete a sewing project.

Be sure the care requirements for notions are the same as those for the fabric. For example, if the fabric is washable, all notions should be washable.

▼ Thread ▼

Thread holds your seams together. Buy the best quality thread you can find. It will be stronger and easier to use in sewing. For solid-color fabrics, select thread that is slightly darker than the fabric. For prints, look for thread that matches the main color in the print.

For most projects, either cotton-covered polyester or 100 percent polyester thread would be a good choice.

Always select a good quality thread that matches the main color in printed fabrics. For plain colored fabrics, thread should be the same color or slightly darker than the fabric.

▼ Zippers ▼

Zippers come in a variety of colors, lengths, and styles. Some open at the bottom, and some are closed. Check the pattern envelope for the zipper length and type suggested. Match the color of the zipper to the fabric as closely as possible. If the fabric has several colors, match the zipper with the background color.

AROUND THE WORLD

The little nut of the tagua (TAG-wah) tree is making a big difference for the environment. The tagua tree grows in the Ecuadoran rain forest. The nut, which looks like ivory, is gathered and sold by villagers to be made into buttons and jewelry. This has several benefits. First, it provides the villagers with an income. Secondly, it encourages the preservation of the rain forests, which are important to the global environment. Finally, it discourages the illegal hunting of elephants for their tusks. The tagua tree nut is one example of how helping the environment helps us all.

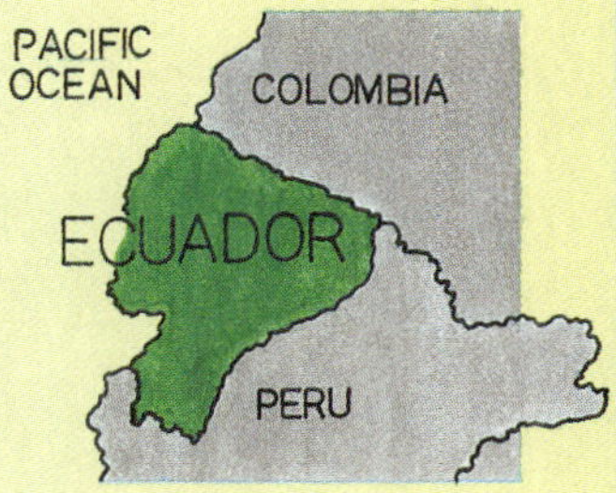

▼ Trims ▼

Trims are available in a wide variety of shapes, sizes, and colors. Ribbon, piping, lace, eyelet, and braid are all types of decorative trims. An **appliqué** (ap-pluh-KAY), a cut-out fabric decoration that is sewn onto a larger background, can also be used as a trim. Most trims can be purchased ready-made and are easily attached by hand or machine stitching.

Sewing skills can be used for more than just garments. You can make items for your room, for gifts, or for your personal use. What are some other items you could make by using your sewing skills?

Trims give you an opportunity to personalize your project. They can add color or give an item a totally different look. Be sure to coordinate trims with your fabric and project design. The trims that you select should be able to be cleaned the same way as your fabric. Preshrink trims by placing them in hottest water the fiber content will allow for 30 minutes. Allow trims to air-dry.

Other Notions

Depending on the sewing project, you may need seam binding, bias tape, elastic, buttons, hooks and eyes, or snaps.

- ***Seam binding.*** A flat tape that is used for finishing hem edges. It is either a woven or a lace-type tape. Since the lace tape stretches, it is often used on knitted fabrics. When purchasing tape, try to match the fabric color as closely as possible.
- ***Bias tapes.*** Folded strips of fabric tape. The word "bias" tells you that the tape has give or stretch. It is used on curved hems and as a **casing** — a closed tunnel of fabric that holds a piece of elastic or a drawstring inside.
- ***Elastic.*** A stretchable fabric tape available in several different types and widths. The type of elastic you choose will depend on whether it will be used in a casing or stitched directly to a garment. Read the label when purchasing elastic to be sure it will serve the correct purpose.

- ***Buttons.*** Help to keep a garment closed. They are also decorative and can be the center of interest. You may want to match the color of your buttons with the fabric color or create interest by choosing a button that contrasts with your fabric.
- ***Snaps and hooks and eyes.*** Used for holding small openings, such as waistbands and neck openings, together. They come in black and silver. Black is good for dark-colored fabrics. Silver is better with light-colored fabrics. Plastic snaps are also available.

Considering Costs

The total cost of a sewing project will include the price of the pattern, fabric, and any notions or interfacing that are required to complete the project.

Remember, the amount of fabric needed is listed on the back of the pattern envelope. It is based on your size, the garment view you are using, and the fabric width.

To figure the cost of the fabric and interfacing, multiply the yardage you need by the cost per yard. For example: Lakisha needs 3 yards of fabric at a cost of $4.95 per yard. She will pay $14.85 for the fabric. In addition, she needs 1 yard of interfacing at $1.89 per yard for a total cost of $1.89. To these amounts, Lakisha must add the cost of the notions (one spool of thread at $1.25 and a zipper at $1.10), the pattern (which costs $4.95), and five percent sales tax. After she totals the costs of all these items, Lakisha will have a good idea about how much her project will cost by the time she reaches the cashier.

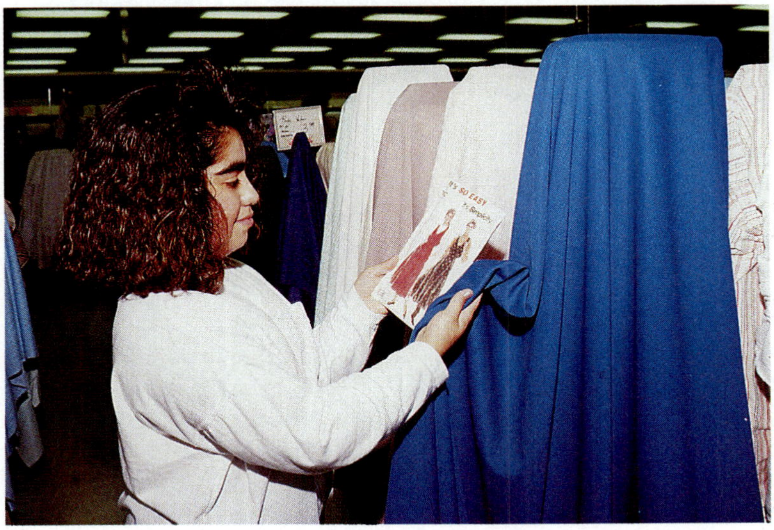

The amount and type of fabric your pattern requires often affect your choice of fabric.

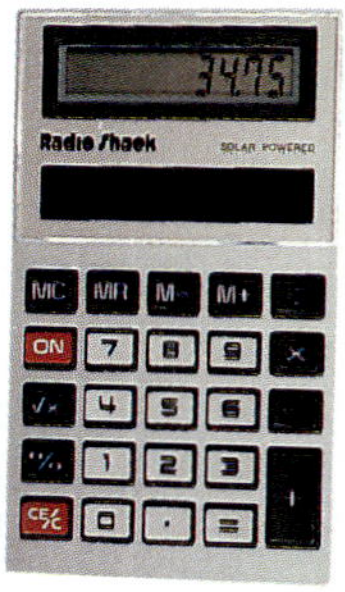

Figure the Cost of a Sewing Project

Here is the way Lakisha figured the cost of her sewing project:

Fabric ($4.95 per yard × 3 yards)	$14.85
Interfacing ($1.89 per yard × 1 yard)	$ 1.89
Notions (Thread at $1.25 + zipper at $1.10)	$ 2.35
Pattern	$ 4.95
Subtotal	$24.04
+ **Tax (5 percent)**	$ 1.20
= **Total Cost**	$25.24

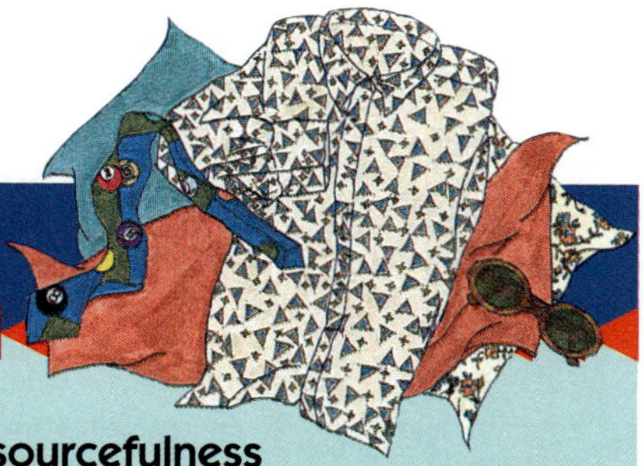

TAKING ACTION

Your school is celebrating its 50th anniversary this year. As part of the school celebration, the senior class historian has asked the FHA chapter to do some research about the types of clothing that students wore when the school first opened. The idea has been suggested that the FHA chapter sponsor a "Now and Then" style show sometime during the celebration.

As part of the FHA chapter, you have been assigned to find out about the fabrics and notions used in garments 50 years ago.

Using Your Resourcefulness

- Brainstorm a list of resources that you might use to find out about fabrics and notions used in garments 50 years ago.
- What are the similarities and differences between the fabrics and notions used 50 years ago and those used today? What has influenced some of the similarities and differences?
- How are the needs of people reflected in the types of fabrics and notions used in garments?
- What suggestions do you have for putting together a "Now and Then" fashion show? Where might you find the garments needed?

Chapter 32 Review

Summary

In this chapter, you have read about:

- Factors to consider when selecting a fabric for a sewing project.
- How to select interfacing and notions that are right for your project.
- How to determine your project's total cost.

Facts to Recall

1. What four things should you consider before buying a piece of fabric?
2. What effect do heavy, bulky fabrics have on body appearance?
3. How can the weave of a fabric affect your ability to work with it?
4. Name two kinds of fabrics someone just learning to sew should avoid.
5. List four guidelines to selecting appropriate interfacing.
6. How do you match a zipper to a multicolored fabric?
7. What is seam binding?
8. What should be included in figuring the total cost of a sewing project?

Ideas to Explore

1. Determine what colors, lines, proportions, and/or textures would be appropriate in each of the following situations: a small woman with a light complexion who wants to look taller and slimmer; a tall, thin man who wants to add bulk to his frame; a woman with a dark complexion who wants to emphasize her face.
2. Suggest ways in which notions might be used to make a plain black shirt look brighter or more interesting.
3. Do you think there is a stigma, or negative feeling, attached to wearing homemade clothing? If so, how can this attitude be changed?
4. Sewing has traditionally been thought of as something only women should be interested in. How might young men get more involved in the activity?

Activities to Try

1. Collect five small pieces of different types of fabrics. Mount each fabric type on a separate sheet of paper. On each paper under the fabric, explain whether or not the fabric would be a good choice for someone who is just learning to sew.
2. Choose a pattern out of a pattern catalog that you would like to sew. Make a checklist of all the items you will need to sew this garment. Include types of fabrics and notions on your checklist. Take your checklist with you to the fabric store.

LINK TO *Math*

SEWING COSTS

Compute the cost of your sewing project. Identify the pattern view and size to determine the yardage needed and the notions such as thread, trim, elastic, or buttons. Use the actual cost of your fabric and notions to determine the total cost of your project. Remember to include the state sales tax. Answer the following questions:

- How would the cost of your project change if you received a 10 percent discount?
- How would the cost of your project change if you received a 25 percent discount?

(**Note:** To determine the discount, multiply the pre-taxed total by the percentage of discount and then figure the amount of tax.)

CHAPTER

33 Sewing Equipment

OBJECTIVES

- *Identify and explain the use of small sewing equipment.*
- *Demonstrate operation of a sewing machine.*
- *Explain the usefulness of sergers in sewing.*

TERMS TO LEARN

- ***trim***
- ***backstitching***
- ***tension***
- ***serger***

The equipment section of a fabric store can seem a bit overwhelming for someone learning to sew. There are dozens of tools. Fortunately, you will need only a few basic items for most sewing projects. As you expand your sewing skills, you might find other equipment helpful for special techniques.

This chapter will introduce small equipment that is used for cutting, marking, measuring, and pressing. Your teacher will tell you which equipment is available in the clothing lab and which items you will need to buy.

In addition to small equipment, this chapter also explains the types and features of sewing machines and how to care for them. Learning to use a sewing machine takes some practice, but it is a skill you will have for life.

Small Sewing Equipment

Having the right tools can make sewing faster, easier, and more fun. The small articles of equipment you will be reading about are organized in groups according to their use.

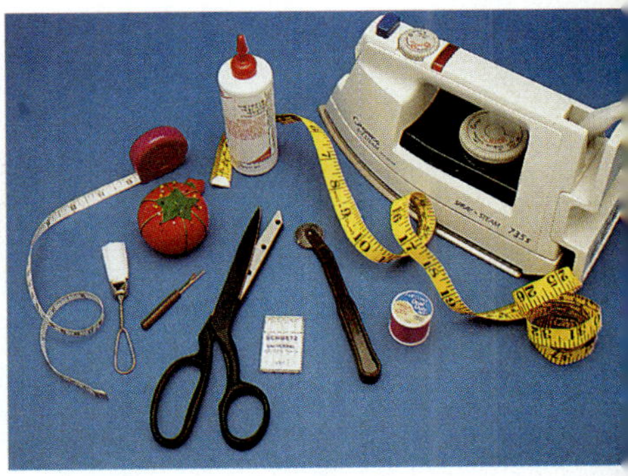

Every piece of sewing equipment has a purpose. You can save time and personal energy by using the right equipment for the job.

Cutting Equipment

All the pieces of cutting equipment belong to the scissor family. Keep cutting equipment sharp by using it only for sewing. Never cut paper with a sewing scissors. Basic cutting equipment includes:

- ***Small scissors.*** Use small scissors to clip threads and **trim**, or cut off, extra fabric from seams.
- ***Shears.*** Shears are used for cutting the fabric. They have long blades with either bent or straight handles. The finger holes on shears are a different shape than those on scissors. Bent-handled shears improve accuracy since the fabric is hardly lifted from the table when it is being cut. Both right- and left-handed shears are available.
- ***Pinking shears.*** Use pinking shears to finish the edge of a firmly woven fabric or a knit fabric. They help to prevent raveling by cutting a zigzag edge.
- ***Seam ripper.*** The seam ripper has a hooklike point. It is handy for cutting and removing stitches.

Pinking shears, shears, small scissors, and a seam ripper help make sewing easier. Keep safety in mind when working with sharp objects.

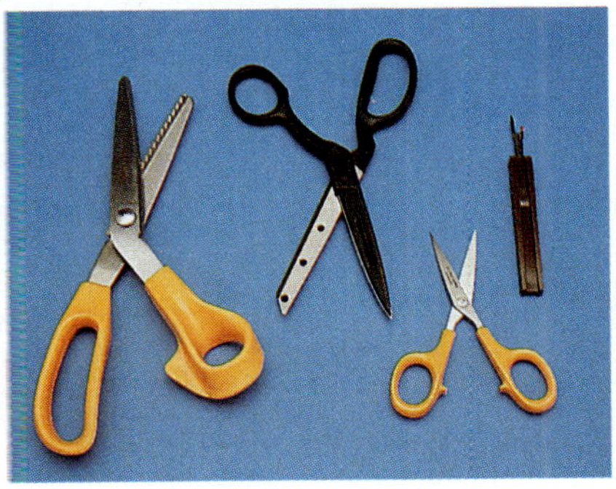

Measuring Equipment

To accurately measure the pattern, fabric, and garment pieces as you sew, the following measuring equipment will be helpful:

SAFETY CHECK ✓

To use equipment safely:

- Keep shears, scissors, and seam rippers closed when not in use.
- Pass sharp objects handle first.
- Keep pins in a pin cushion — not in your mouth or clothing.

- ***Tape measure.*** A narrow strip of durable plastic or firm fabric. Many are marked with both inches and centimeters.
- ***Measuring stick.*** A measuring stick, or yardstick, is useful for measuring both the pattern and fabric on a flat surface. Choose one with smooth edges to prevent snagging the fabric.
- ***Seam gauge.*** This small ruler has a slide marker that can be set to measure specific lengths. It can be used for measuring small areas, such as hems, buttonholes, and seams.

Marking Equipment

Marking equipment will help you transfer important construction markings from your pattern pieces to your fabric. It can be used to mark the correct position of features such as pockets, buttonholes, hems, and collars. Here is some of the most common marking equipment:

- ***Tracing wheel and paper.*** A tracing wheel is used with special fabric tracing paper to transfer pattern markings to the wrong side of fabric.
- ***Tailor's chalk.*** This is a pencil or small square made of chalk or wax used to mark fabric. Wax is used for wool fabrics. Chalk can be used on all other fabrics.
- ***Fabric marker.*** This is a special pen that puts markings on fabrics temporarily. Some fabric pen marks can be removed with water. Others fade in a short period of time. It's best to test fabric markers on a scrap of fabric before using them. Never use markers meant for writing on fabric. The marks may be permanent.

Using measuring and marking equipment accurately leads to a better-fitting, professional-looking garment.

▼ Pressing Equipment ▼

In Chapter 30, you learned how pressing and ironing can give your clothing a crisp, neat appearance. In addition, pressing your project as you sew will give it a finished and professional look. Basic pressing equipment includes:

- ▶ ***Iron and ironing board.*** A steam iron and a well-padded ironing board are necessary for pressing as you sew.
- ▶ ***Press cloth.*** Using a press cloth between the fabric and iron when pressing helps to keep dark fabrics from developing a shine. You can buy ready-made press cloths, or you can make your own from lightweight muslin or cheesecloth.

A *tailor's ham* is a very firm cushion that is used to press curved seams and darts.

A *sleeve board* is a small ironing board. It is helpful when you need to press sleeve seams or small pieces.

Good pressing is done carefully and safely. Pressing equipment gets very hot and can easily cause injuries if not handled properly. Review the "Safety Check" box on page 340 for tips about safe pressing.

▼ Other Small Equipment ▼

You will use some additional equipment to complete sewing projects.

- ▶ ***Hand Sewing Needles.*** Needles are numbered from 1 (very thick) to 12 (very fine). A sharp point and medium length makes "sharps" best for general hand sewing. Try a size 7 or 8. Ballpoint needles are helpful for knit fabrics. They have rounded points, which separate the knit as you sew.
- ▶ ***Machine Needles.*** Machine needles come in both United States sizes and European sizes. The sizes range from very fine — U.S. size 10 (European size 70) for lightweight fabrics, to U.S. size 14 (European size 90) for mediumweight fabrics, to very coarse — U.S. size 18 (European size 110) for heavyweight fabrics. Select the size best suited to your fabric. Choose ballpoint needles for knit fabric.
- ▶ ***Straight pins.*** Straight pins are used to hold the pattern to the fabric and to hold pieces of fabric together for sewing. Most pins are made from stainless steel. There are sharp pins for woven fabrics and ball-point pins for knit fabric.
- ▶ ***Pin cushion.*** Use the cushion to keep needles and pins handy while you work. An emery bag, a strawberry-shaped bag, is attached to many pin cushions. You can clean rusty or sticky needles and pins by pushing them into this bag a few times.
- ▶ ***Thimble.*** A thimble can be used to push a needle through the fabric while hand sewing. A thimble should fit snugly on the third finger of the hand that holds the needle.

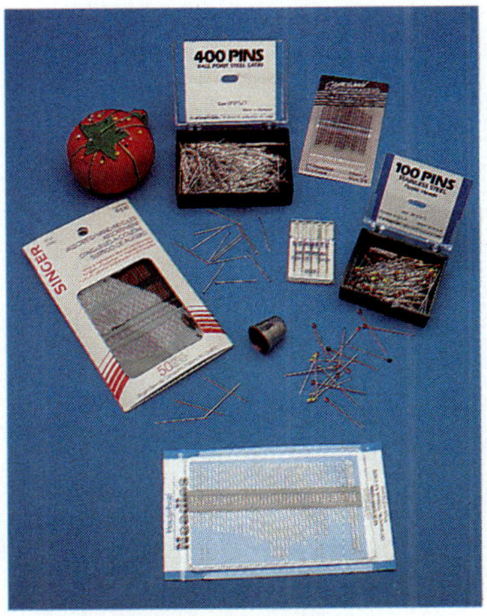

A variety of pins, needles, and other sewing equipment are very useful for sewing projects.

Most highly automated sewing machines provide an assortment of decorative and functional stitches. Basic models stitch straight, zigzag, and often have a built-in buttonhole feature. What sewing machine features would be most useful to you?

Sewing Machines

A sewing machine is one of the most important and most expensive pieces of sewing equipment you will need. Machines available today range from basic models to computerized machines that do a variety of jobs (like decorative stitches) at the touch of a button. Basic models can handle most general sewing. Look for one that can do both straight and zigzag stitching. Attachments, such as a buttonholer, can also increase a basic machine's usefulness.

For successful sewing, take time to learn about the sewing machine you will use. Read the instruction booklet or have someone show you how to operate and care for the machine before you start to sew.

AROUND THE WORLD

The machines that make socks and hosiery must work very quickly and precisely. At a recent garment industry fair, some new machines from Italy were introduced. The wheels of some of these models are capable of 450 rpm (revolutions per minute), and some have over 200 needles. The action of these needles more closely resembles that of knitting needles or a crochet hook than of a regular sewing machine.

▼ Parts of the Machine ▼

All sewing machines function in a similar manner. Knowing the major parts will help you operate the machine easily and accurately. The parts that follow are found on most machines. Check the instruction booklet to see where they are located on your machine.

1. ***Hand wheel.*** This is the large wheel on the right side of the machine. It controls the up-and-down movement of the needle and thread take-up lever.
2. ***Thread take-up lever.*** This lever feeds thread from the spool to the needle.
3. ***Throat plate.*** This is the metal plate under the machine needle. On most machines, the throat plate also contains seam allowance markings for accurate sewing.
4. ***Bobbin.*** A small, flat spool that holds the bottom thread.
5. ***Bobbin case.*** This holds the bobbin and is found beneath the throat plate. Some bobbin cases are removable.
6. ***Bobbin winder spindle.*** This spindle holds the bobbin while thread is wound from the thread spool to the bobbin. The location of this spindle varies with each machine.

TIPS: ***Buying a Sewing Machine***

Look for these basic features when buying a sewing machine:

- The machine starts and stops smoothly.
- The bobbin is easily wound and inserted into the bobbin case.
- The foot pedal is comfortable to operate.
- The needle area is well-lighted.
- You can understand the instruction manual.

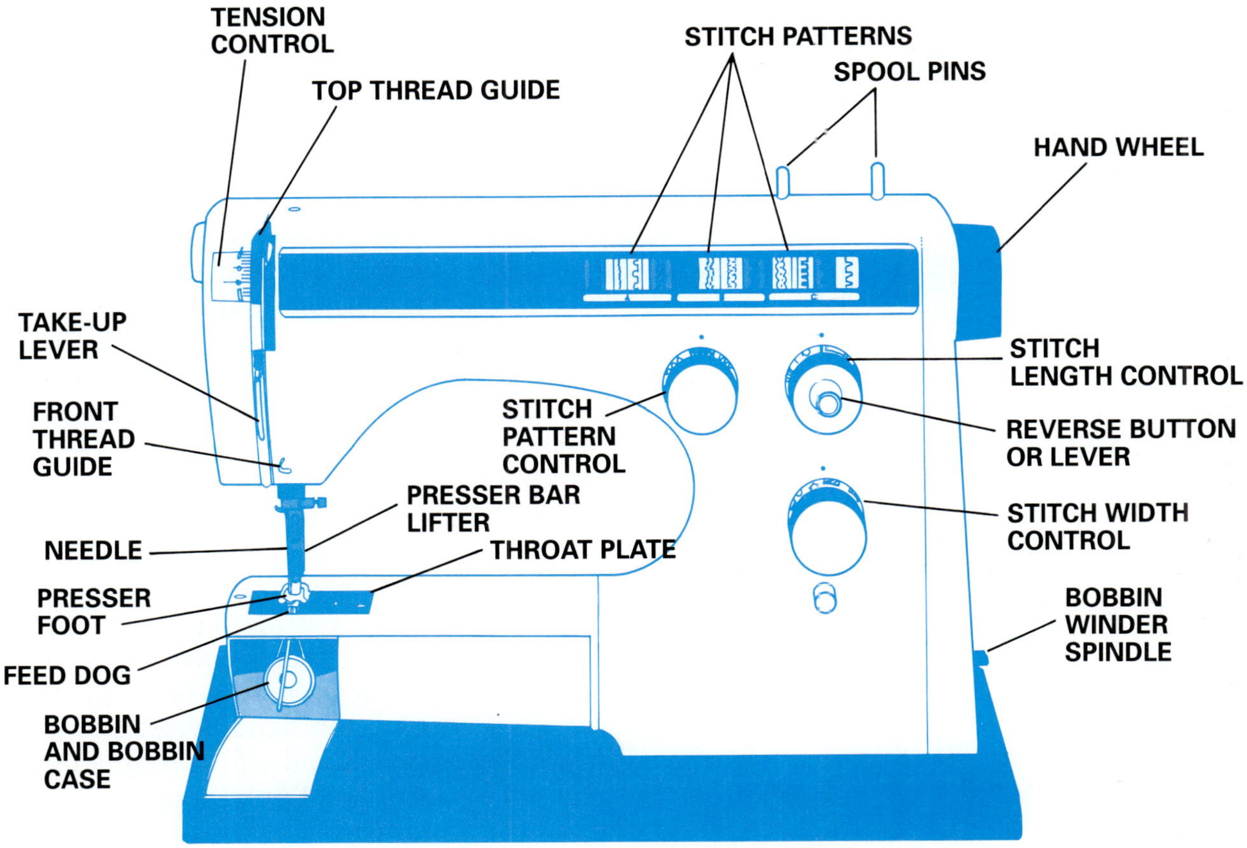

7. ***Feed dog.*** The feed dog has a toothlike surface that moves the fabric during stitching.
8. ***Presser foot.*** The presser foot holds the fabric firmly in place against the feed dog for sewing.
9. ***Presser-bar lifter.*** This raises and lowers the presser foot.
10. ***Tension control.*** The tension control adjusts the tightness or looseness of the upper thread.
11. ***Stitch length control.*** This is used to adjust the length of stitches from short to long.
12. ***Stitch width control.*** This control is used to adjust the width of a stitch when using zigzag or decorative stitches.
13. ***Stitch pattern control.*** The stitch pattern control can be adjusted to make different decorative stitching patterns.
14. ***Reverse button or lever.*** Depending on the machine, this will be a button or a lever that allows you to stitch backward to secure the end of the seam.
15. ***Spool pin.*** This holds the spool of thread.
16. ***Thread guides.*** Thread guides hold the upper thread in place as it moves through the machine.
17. ***Knee or foot control.*** The position of this depends on the machine. It regulates the starting, running, and stopping of the machine by the amount of pressure applied to the control.

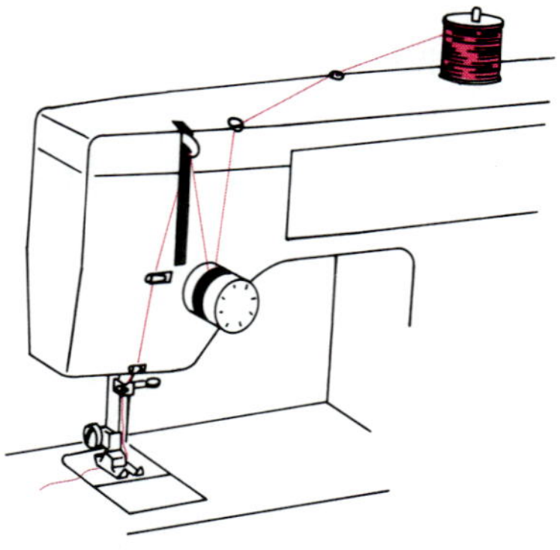

Correctly thread your sewing machine to prevent stitching problems.

Winding a bobbin.

Threading the Machine

Raise the needle and take-up lever to the highest position before threading the machine. The general order for threading all machines follows a similar pattern. The thread passes from the spool pin, through the tension control and thread take-up lever, and then through the hole in the needle. The thread guides help hold the thread in place and keep it from getting tangled. To make threading the needle easier, try cutting the thread on a slant.

The bottom or bobbin thread must also be wound onto a bobbin. The method will vary depending on the machine. Check your machine instruction booklet for specific directions for winding the bobbin thread of your machine.

After threading the machine and putting the bobbin into the bobbin case, bring the bobbin thread up through the hole in the throat plate before you begin to sew. Hold the end of the needle thread while turning the hand wheel one full turn toward your body. The upper thread will pull up a loop of bobbin thread. Pull up on the loop of bobbin thread until the thread end is above the throat plate.

▼ Machine Stitching ▼

All machines straight stitch the same way. If you haven't sewn before or will be using a different machine, take time to practice stitching. Here are the general directions:

- Use a sharp needle for woven fabrics and a ball-point needle for knits. See page 369 about correct needle sizes to use.
- For general-purpose sewing, use the zigzag foot and zigzag throat plate on the machine. Other accessories, such as a zipper foot, can be put on the machine for specific sewing techniques.
- Raise the take-up lever and needle to the highest point by turning the hand wheel toward your body before starting to stitch. Do the same when stitching is finished. This keeps the thread from pulling out of the needle.
- Before starting to sew, pull both the upper thread and bobbin thread to the right side of the presser foot. The threads should also be underneath the presser foot. This keeps the threads from becoming tangled in the bobbin case.
- Place the fabric under the presser foot. The beginning of the stitching line should be just under the point of the needle. First, lower the needle into the fabric and then lower the presser foot. The bulk of the fabric should be to the left of the machine.
- Start the machine slowly. A smooth, steady speed is better than speed-ups and slow-downs.
- Use the throat plate markings to guide your fabric through the machine. This will help you keep an even seam width.
- Slow the machine speed down for the last few stitches. This will help prevent you from stitching beyond the edge of the fabric.
- Secure stitching at both ends of a seam. There are several ways to do this. **Backstitching**, or retracing your stitches about ½ inch (1.3 cm), is done by using the reverse button or lever on your sewing machine. Another way to secure stitching is to tie the thread ends after the fabric is removed from the machine. Cut the thread ends long enough for tying. Bring both threads to the wrong side, tie a knot, and clip off the ends.

▼ Adjusting Stitch Length and Tension ▼

Some fabrics require different stitch lengths and tension adjustments. **Tension** refers to the tightness or looseness of the thread. Check the machine stitching on a two-layer scrap

SAFETY CHECK ✔

To use a sewing machine safely:

- Stitch slowly when learning how to use the machine.
- Keep your fingers away from the needle.
- Don't lean too closely over the machine, in case the needle breaks. Safety glasses can help prevent eye injuries.
- Position the cord so that people won't trip over it.
- Disconnect the cord from the outlet before disconnecting it from the machine.

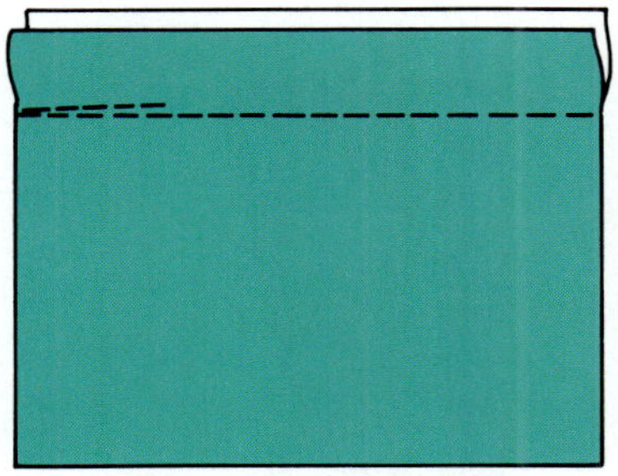

REVERSE STITCHING OR BACKSTITCHING

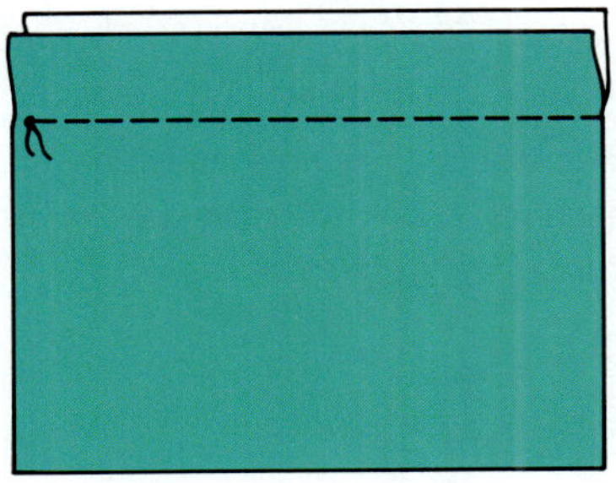

TIED THREADS

of your fabric before beginning to sew. The correct stitch length and tension make a seam that is both attractive and strong. You can make changes in the stitch length by adjusting the stitch control.

The tension is balanced when the stitching looks the same on both sides. It is not in balance when the stitches are too tight on one side and too loose on the other. Here are some guidelines for correcting tension problems:

- Check the machine and bobbin threading first. Often times, tension problems are due to incorrect machine threading.
- If the upper tension is too tight, the upper thread lies straight on the top of the seam, and loops of the lower thread can be seen on the lower side of the seam. You can correct this problem by loosening the upper tension. Turn the tension control a little at a time while testing the stitch on a scrap of fabric. Look in the instruction booklet for the direction to turn the tension control.
- If the upper tension is too loose, the lower thread lies straight on the bottom of the seam, loops of the upper thread can be seen. Correct this by tightening the upper tension a little at a time.

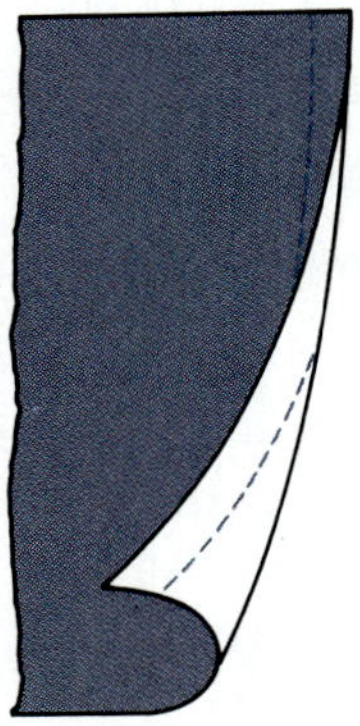
BALANCED TENSION

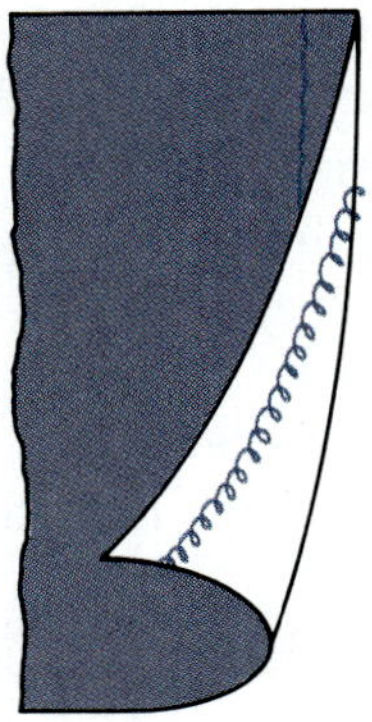
UPPER TOO TIGHT

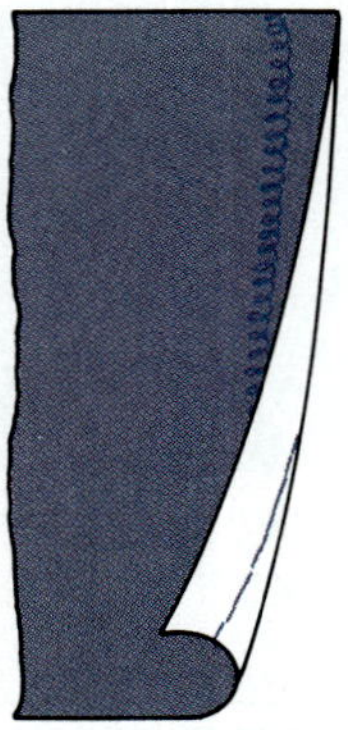
LOWER TOO TIGHT

Before changing your tension settings, check the machine threading first.

Choosing Stitch Length

U.S. Machine Settings	Other Machine Settings	Uses and Fabrics
6	4	▶ Basting ▶ Sewing bulky, heavy fabrics
8	3	▶ Topstitching
10-12	2-2.5	▶ Staystitching ▶ Sewing mediumweight to lightweight fabrics
14-16	1-1.5	▶ Reinforcement stitching at points of strain

- Turn your stitch length control to set the desired stitch length.
- Zigzag stitches vary in width. Narrow width zigzag stitches are used to make stretchable seams for knitted fabrics. Wider zigzag stitches are used for mending, decoration, or finishing seams.

Common Causes of Sewing Machine Problems

In most cases, poor sewing results are due to an improperly threaded machine or a blunt or damaged needle. Always check the machine threading and the needle before taking any other action.

Problem	Possible Causes
Needle breaks	▶ The needle is dull, the wrong size, or put in wrong. ▶ Pulling on fabric while sewing. (This bends the needle. It breaks when it hits the throat plate.)
Upper thread breaks	▶ Needle is blunt, bent, or put in wrong. ▶ Upper machine thread is not threaded correctly. ▶ Tension on the upper thread is too tight. ▶ The thread has knots.
Lower thread breaks	▶ Bobbin case is put in wrong. ▶ Bobbin thread is not threaded correctly. ▶ Lower thread tension is too tight. ▶ Bobbin is wound too full.
Unattractive stitches Unattractive seam	▶ Needle is blunt, bent, or put in wrong. ▶ Thread tension is not correct. ▶ Machine is not threaded correctly. ▶ The needle, thread, and fabric are not well matched. ▶ Bobbin thread unevenly wound. ▶ Bobbin is not correctly inserted in the bobbin case.
Skipped stitches	▶ Heavy finish on fabric keeps stitches from forming. (Wash fabric before sewing.) ▶ The needle is dull, bent, or put in wrong. ▶ Machine is not threaded correctly.

- If you still have stitching problems after checking for possible causes, ask your teacher for help.
- Before adjusting the tension control on your classroom sewing machine, ask your teacher for help.

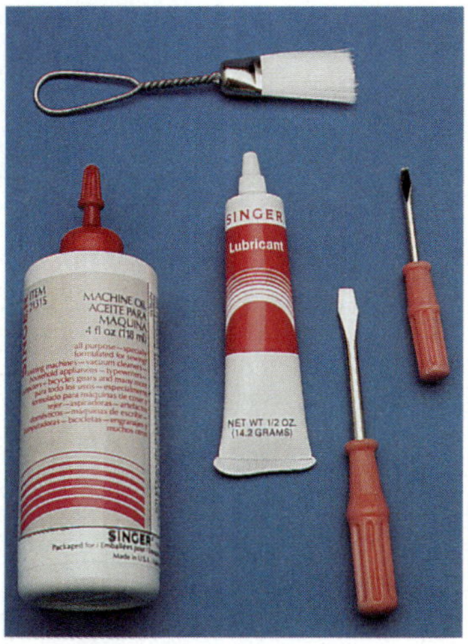

Use the proper equipment and materials to properly clean and lubricate your sewing machine.

Machine Care

To sew properly, the sewing machine needs to be cleaned regularly. Remove the throat plate and clean the teeth of the feed dog with a small brush. Also brush the bobbin case clean. Most machines will need occasional oiling in order to keep all working parts lubricated. Check the instruction booklet for details.

If the machine jams because thread has become tangled in the bobbin or under the throat plate, the thread must be removed carefully. Turn off the machine. Remove your foot from the foot control (or from the knee control) and check the sewing machine instruction booklet for further directions.

Serger Sewing

Have you ever wondered why the seams in ready-to-wear clothing look so smooth and neat? Thanks to some new technology, people can now make garments that have the appearance of the finest ready-to-wear clothing at home.

A **serger** — or overlock sewing machine — is a machine that stitches, trims, and finishes a seam in one step. It sews the special stitches you have seen along the seam edges on the inside of most ready-to-wear clothing.

Some garments, such as sweatshirts, can be sewn entirely on the serger. However, many people combine the use of a conventional sewing machine and a serger.

Sergers are different from conventional sewing machines in the following ways:

- Sergers sew much faster than conventional sewing machines.
- Sergers have "knives" that trim the seam before it is stitched.
- Sergers use more thread. Most serger thread is on a cone that holds 1000 or more yards. Depending on the model, the serger uses two, three, four, or five cones of thread for stitching.
- Sergers may use one or two needles depending on the model.
- Sergers have no bobbins. Two loopers in the lower part of the serger take the place of bobbins.
- Lifting the presser foot is not necessary when starting to sew unless fabric is thick. The serger grabs onto the fabric as you begin to sew.

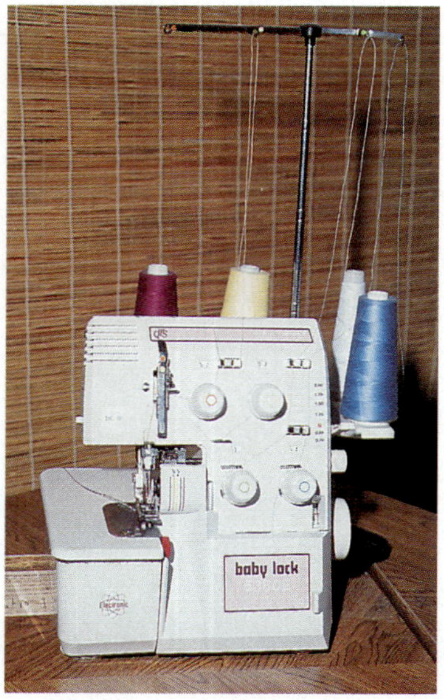

A serger conveniently decreases the amount of time that you spend sewing a garment. It completes many steps all at the same time.

▶ All pins must be removed when sewing with a serger to prevent the knives from becoming dull. This could lead to poor stitching.

All brands of sergers basically sew the same way. As you feed the fabric into the machine, the feed dogs grab onto the fabric and pull it toward the knives. The knives trim the edges of the fabric before the fabric reaches the loopers and needles for stitching. After stitching, the fabric moves off the serger behind the needles. Instead of backstitching, you simply run the fabric off the serger and tie the loose ends. See page 416 for more information about securing serger seams.

Sewing with a serger has inspired many people to begin making their own clothing. Clothing items, such as sweatshirts, swimsuits, pants, shirts, and dresses, can be made quickly and easily with a professional look.

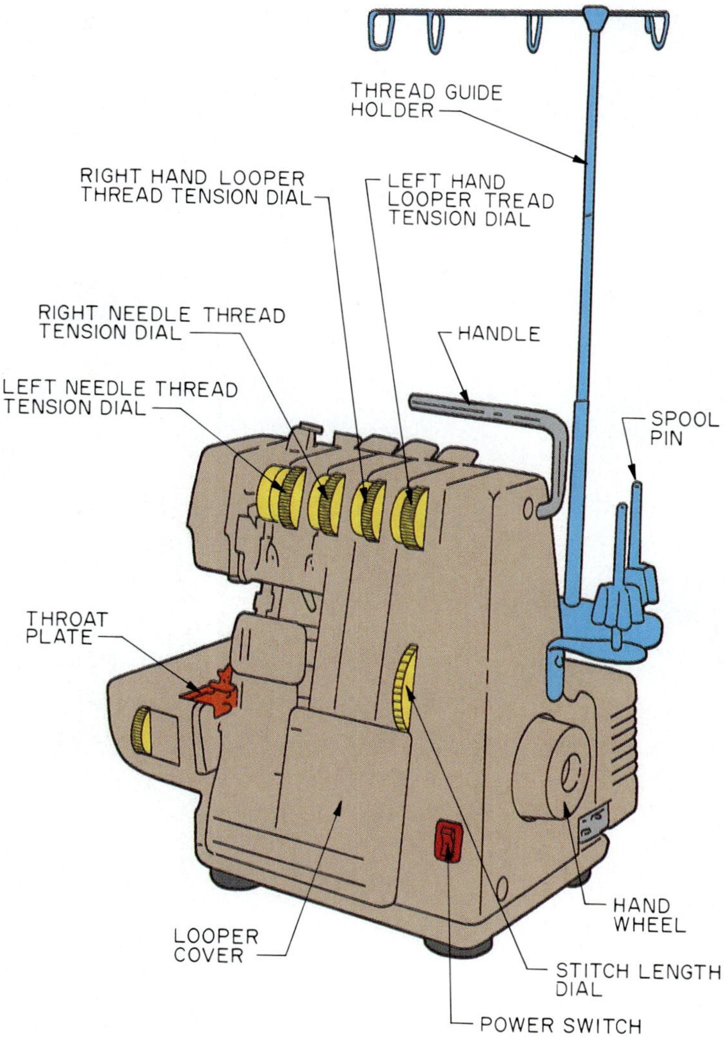

The serger loopers and knives shown in the diagram below are found under the looper cover. When the looper cover is open on most sergers, the machine will not sew — a real safety benefit.

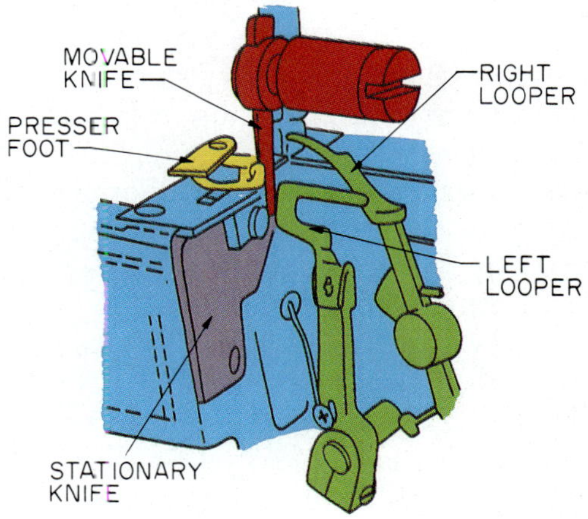

Pocket Lab

Shortcut to Serger Threading

MATERIALS:
extra cones of serger thread

EQUIPMENT:
threaded serger; scissors

Directions: Observe a demonstration on how to thread an unthreaded serger, then try this shortcut method. Cut the threads on the serger just above the thread cones. Remove the thread cones and replace them with the extra cones of serger thread. Tie the thread ends of the new cones to the clipped threads about two inches from the thread ends. Gently pull the thread ends coming from the needle(s) and loopers to pull the new thread color through the machine. Release the tension, if necessary, to allow the knots to pass through the tension disks. For the needle threads, continue pulling until the knot reaches the needle. Clip the thread, removing the knot, and rethread the needle. The knots in the looper threads should easily pass through the eye of the looper.

- Which method was faster?
- Why should you learn how to thread an unthreaded serger?
- Why would you want to use the shortcut method whenever possible?

TAKING ACTION

Aleatha was ready to start a sewing project at home when she discovered that she did not have some sewing equipment that might be necessary for her project. Some of the items Aleatha was missing included a sewing gauge, measuring stick, chalk, pincushion, and a press cloth.

The stores were about to close and there was no time for Aleatha to go buy the items she needed. Aleatha remembered a discussion that was held in a Social Studies class about reusing and recycling common household items for other purposes. She decided to think about that discussion as she started her project.

Using Your Resourcefulness

- Brainstorm a list of items Aleatha could use in place of (or use to make substitutes for) the sewing equipment she did not have.
- If Aleatha is unable to think of some alternatives on her own, where might she go for help?
- In what ways is Aleatha making wise use of all of her resources?

Chapter 33 Review

Summary

In the chapter, you have read about:

- The different pieces of equipment used for cutting, measuring, marking, and pressing fabric.
- The parts of a sewing machine and the function of each part.
- Safety tips for hand and machine sewing.
- Sergers and how they can be helpful in sewing.

Facts to Recall

1. Identify four different pieces of cutting equipment. Explain the use of each.
2. Briefly explain the purpose of using marking equipment. Give four examples of different types of marking equipment.
3. When machine sewing, how can you keep the thread from coming out of the needle?
4. Describe two ways of securing stitches at the end of the seam.
5. List four safety tips for using a sewing machine.
6. What are three ways to keep a sewing machine clean and running smoothly?
7. Why should you remove the pins from the fabric when using a serger?
8. Briefly explain how a serger sews a seam.

Ideas to Explore

1. What personal traits do you think would help make a person good at sewing?
2. What might be some hazards of not knowing how to use a sewing machine properly?
3. Respond to the statement: "Sewing is its own reward. It is a skill that can be used throughout life." Do you agree or disagree with the statement? In what ways can sewing be a useful skill in life?

Activities to Try

1. Using your pattern or a pattern you have selected from a pattern catalog, predict how you might use the sewing equipment described in this chapter to sew the garment from this pattern.
2. Examine the seams and the hems on the clothing you are wearing. Which seams and hems do you think were sewn on a serger? Which do you think were sewn on a conventional sewing machine? Discuss your responses in class.
3. Using your machine instruction booklet, a spool of thread, and a bobbin, practice winding the bobbin and threading your machine. Be sure to check with your teacher if you have a problem.

LINK TO *Communication*

USING SMALL SEWING EQUIPMENT

Select an article of small sewing equipment from one of the following groups: cutting, measuring, marking, or pressing equipment. Organize a brief oral presentation to be given to your classmates concerning this article of equipment. Use the following guidelines in preparing your presentation:

- Describe the article of equipment and tell about how it can be used.
- Include information about buying a quality article of equipment. What should you look for? Are there important safety features?
- Demonstrate how to use this article of equipment correctly and safely.

CHAPTER

34 Preparing to Sew

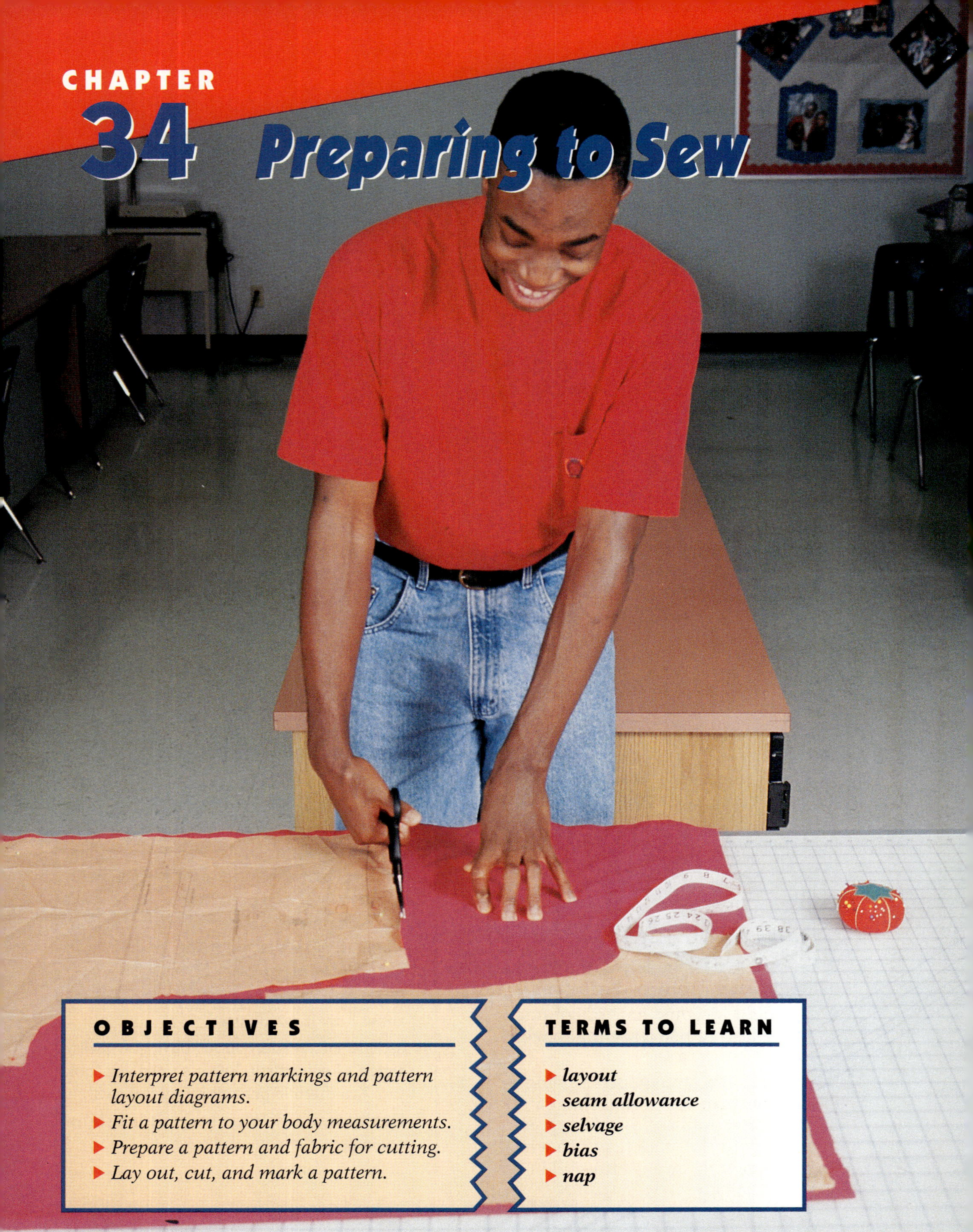

OBJECTIVES

- *Interpret pattern markings and pattern layout diagrams.*
- *Fit a pattern to your body measurements.*
- *Prepare a pattern and fabric for cutting.*
- *Lay out, cut, and mark a pattern.*

TERMS TO LEARN

- ***layout***
- ***seam allowance***
- ***selvage***
- ***bias***
- ***nap***

As Kendra looked at the fabric, pattern, notions, and equipment spread on the table in front of her, she wondered, "How will all of this turn into the shirt on the pattern envelope?" At this point, you may be feeling as confused as Kendra. However, beginning to sew is not as complicated as it may seem. Before starting to sew, you will need to lay out the pattern on the fabric, cut the pattern out of the fabric, and mark the construction points on the fabric. This chapter will help you complete those steps with ease and accuracy.

Using the Pattern

Inside the pattern envelope, you will find the guide sheet and pattern pieces. The guide sheet and the information printed on each pattern piece are your guides to successful sewing. The guide sheet contains:

- Sketches of different styles or views that can be made from the pattern.
- A list and diagram of pattern pieces.
- Cutting **layouts**, or diagrams, that show how to lay pattern pieces on the fabric for different sizes, fabric widths, and types of fabric.
- Step-by-step instructions for sewing the garment or project.

Carefully following these seven basic steps before you start sewing leads to a successful sewing experience.

Each individual pattern piece has a number of pattern symbols or markings. Use the pattern symbols to guide layout of the pattern and to mark your sewing project. The most common symbols include:

1. ***Cutting line.*** The heavy line on the outside of the pattern should be followed when cutting out the fabric.
2. ***Grainline.*** This straight line with arrows on each end must be placed in the direction of the lengthwise grain, crosswise grain, or bias. Check the pattern layout on the instruction sheet.
3. ***Place on fold.*** This is a bracketed grainline that indicates that the pattern edge is to be placed exactly on the fold of the fabric.
4. ***Darts.*** The broken lines show the stitching line. The solid center line indicates where to fold the dart before stitching.
5. ***Solid line.*** A solid line is often used to show where pockets, trims, and other features will be located.

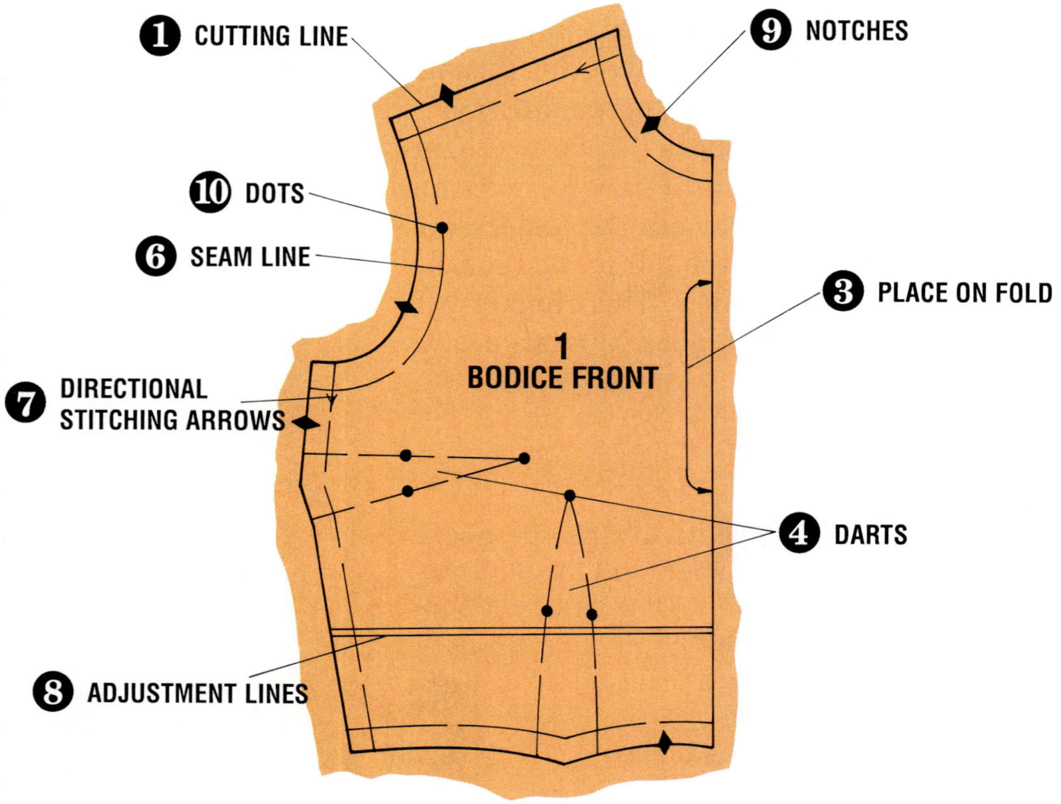

1 CUTTING LINE
9 NOTCHES
10 DOTS
6 SEAM LINE
3 PLACE ON FOLD
1
BODICE FRONT
7 DIRECTIONAL
STITCHING ARROWS
4 DARTS
8 ADJUSTMENT LINES

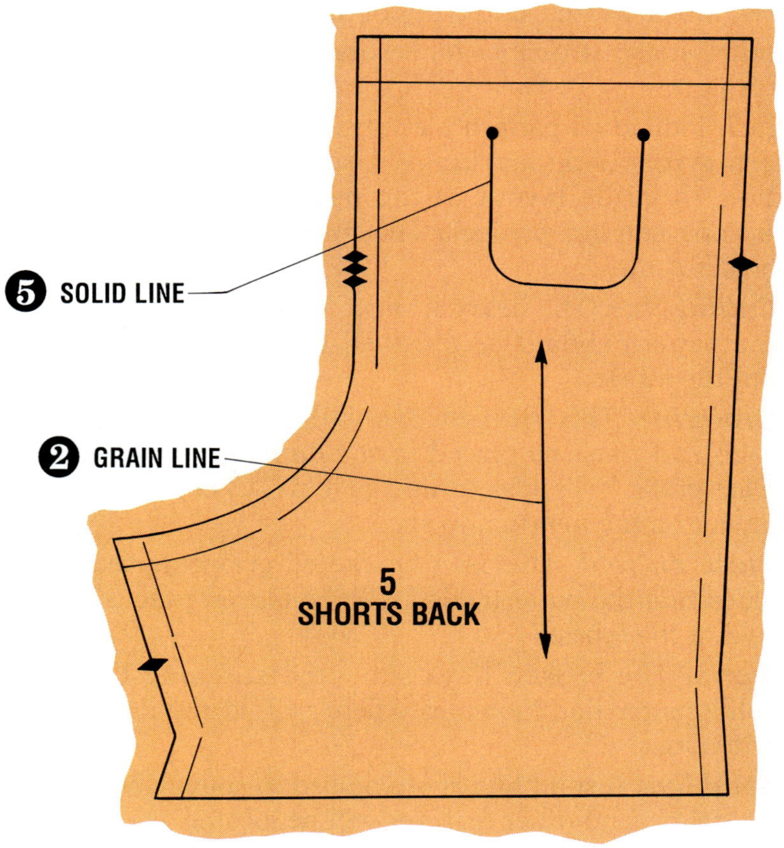

5 SOLID LINE
2 GRAIN LINE
5
SHORTS BACK

6. ***Seam line.*** This is a broken line, usually $\frac{5}{8}$ inch (1.5 cm) inside of the cutting line. You stitch along the seam line.
7. ***Directional stitching arrows.*** These arrows indicate which way to sew seams.
8. ***Adjustment lines.*** Two parallel lines indicate where a pattern is cut or folded for lengthening or shortening.
9. ***Notches.*** These diamond-shaped symbols along the cutting line show where the pattern pieces are joined together.
10. ***Dots.*** Small dots are used for matching seams and construction details such as pocket placement.

Pocket Lab

Using Marking Equipment

MATERIALS:
tracing paper; tailor's chalk; fabric markers; fabric samples

EQUIPMENT:
tracing wheel

Directions: Experiment using different methods of marking each fabric sample.

- On what types of fabric did the tracing wheel and tracing paper work well?
- What factors influence the color of tracing paper that you choose?
- When would you choose tailor's chalk for marking? When did the pencil work best? When did the square of chalk work best?
- When did you prefer the fabric marker? Was the marker easy to remove from all fabric samples?

Fitting the Pattern

When checking how well a pattern will fit you, match your own measurements with those on the pattern envelope. By matching your measurements closely to the measurements on the pattern envelope, you can select a pattern with enough wearing ease for comfort. *Wearing ease* — the extra the room needed in a garment for movement and comfort — allows you to sit, bend, and stretch without tearing your clothes. Wearing ease is built into patterns by the pattern companies.

Some garments also have built-in *design ease* which allows garment designers to create different styles. Design ease is additional ease built into a pattern beyond the wearing ease. It allows for details such as wider pant legs, fuller skirts, or over-sized shirts.

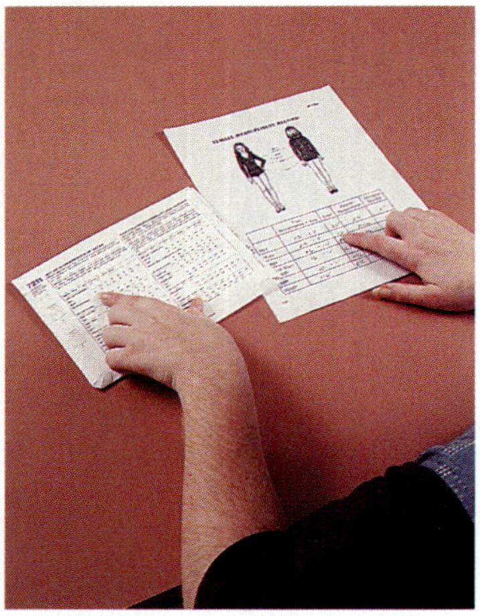

Compare your measurements with the measurements on the back of the pattern envelope to determine the best size to use.

Pattern pieces can be measured to help determine how a pattern will fit. When comparing your measurements, follow these simple guidelines:

- Press the pattern with a warm, dry iron, or smooth it out with your hands.
- Check measurements on the pattern at the same places where the body measurements were taken and write them down.
- Do not include **seam allowances** — the fabric between the cutting line and the stitching line — or darts when measuring the pattern pieces.

In most cases, you can expect your pattern pieces to be larger than your exact body measurements. Don't panic! Your pattern should be larger to account for wearing and design ease. How can you tell if there is enough room for wearing and design ease? Start by looking at the picture on the front of your pattern envelope. Also read the description of the garment on the back of the pattern envelope. Should the garment fit closely to your body or is it supposed to be loosely fitted? If the garment is loosely fitted and the pattern measurements are larger than your body measurements, any fitting problems can generally be taken care of in the sewing stage. However, if the garment is closely fitted and the pattern measurements are significantly larger (or smaller) than your body measurements, some adjustment in the pattern will be needed. It is easier to make changes before, rather than after, a pattern is cut.

Preparing Fabric

Both woven and knitted fabrics need to be preshrunk and straightened before you lay out the pattern and cut your fabric.

Fabric that is off-grain will not hang correctly when made into a garment. Straightening the grain makes sure the garment will hang properly on your body.

Preshrinking Fabric

Preshrinking makes sure that your fabric will not shrink once the fabric is made into a garment. Washable fabrics should be preshrunk according to the manufacturer's directions. Some fabrics, such as wool, need to be professionally dry-cleaned for preshrinking.

It is best to preshrink all fabrics. In addition to preventing further shrinkage, preshrinking removes fabric finishes that can leave a sticky substance on sewing machine needles that may cause skipped stitches. All woven interfacings, zippers, and trims should also be preshrunk.

To preshrink washable fabrics, follow the fabric care instructions for washing and drying listed on the bolt or care label. For fabrics that ravel easily, you may want to zigzag stitch the cut edges before washing the fabric.

Washable knits should always be washed and dried before cutting. Knits are made up of loops that stretch as much as 10 to 35 percent during the knitting process. Knits will usually shrink more than woven fabrics.

Around the World

Someday you may be wearing a dress or a shirt made from pineapple leaves. Scientists at a university in Colombia have discovered that material made from the leaf fibers is much like raw cotton and some synthetic materials. Each pineapple leaf produces about one pound of usable fiber. What effect might this discovery have on pineapple-growing regions? On producers of other textiles?

Fabric Grains

In Chapter 32, you learned that on-grain fabric is made of two sets of yarns that are at right angles to each other. The lengthwise grain is formed by the yarns that run the length of the fabric. Lengthwise grain has little or no stretch. The **selvage** is the finished lengthwise edge of the fabric. It will not ravel. The crosswise yarns run horizontally from selvage to selvage. This is called the crosswise grain. The crosswise grain has more stretch than lengthwise grain.

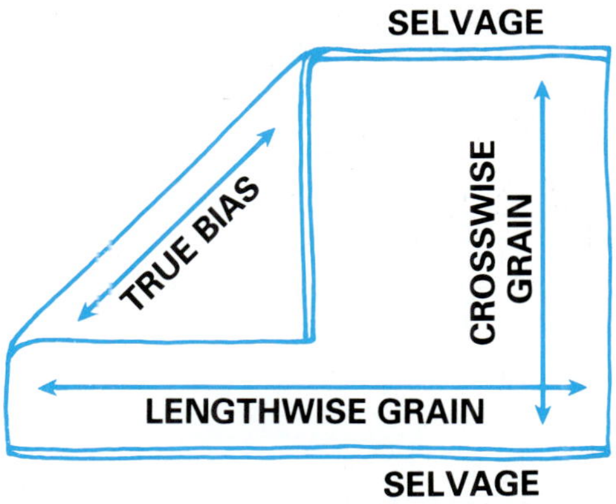

Knowing the characteristics of fabric grains will help you lay your pattern on the fabric correctly.

The true bias has the most stretch. True **bias** is the diagonal edge formed when the fabric is folded so that the crosswise grain is parallel to the selvage, or lengthwise grain.

Knits do not have a grain. However, knitted fabrics have a lengthwise chain of loops that correspond to the lengthwise grain. The crosswise row of loops corresponds to the crosswise grain. In most knits, the crosswise loops have more stretch.

How to ...
Alter Your Pattern

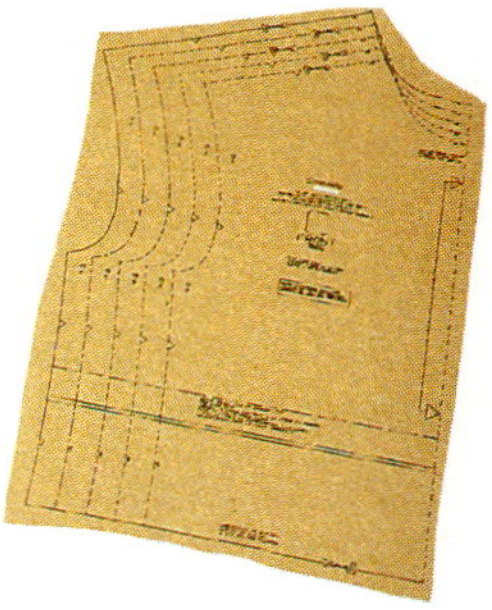

Successful pattern alterations result from using the following guidelines: make adjustments for length and width on both front and back pattern pieces; use a measuring stick to extend the grainline; make sure the grainline is straight; and redraw any design details or darts changed by the pattern alteration.

The following illustrations and directions tell about some common pattern adjustments.

Adjusting Width

An adjustment of 2 inches (5 cm) or less can be made along the side seams of a garment. Divide the adjustment needed by the number of seam allowances. If a garment has two side seams and four seam allowances, the amount to be adjusted on each pattern piece is one-fourth the total amount. For example, to increase the waistline by 1 inch (2.5 cm), you will add ¼ inch (6 mm) to the side seam of the front pattern piece and ¼ inch (6 mm) to the side seam of the back pattern piece. Both side seams will be increased by ½ inch (1.3 cm) and the total garment will be increased 1 inch (2.5 cm).

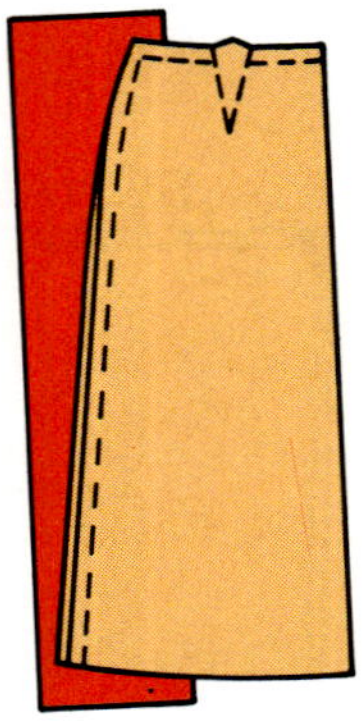

Increasing Pattern Width

Tape tissue paper along the pattern piece edge. Divide the total adjustment needed by the number of seam allowances. Measure out the amount needed from the cutting line. Carefully redraw the cutting lines and seam lines to blend in with areas of the pattern that did not need adjustment.

Decreasing Pattern Width

To decrease the width of a pattern, divide the total amount of adjustment needed by the number of seam allowances. Measure in the amount needed and redraw cutting lines and seam lines to blend in with the areas that did not need to be decreased.

Lengthening a Pattern

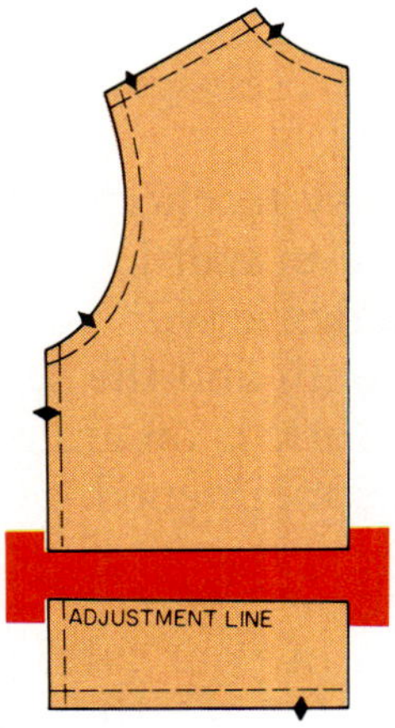

Cut the pattern apart on the adjustment lines. Tape one pattern piece to the tissue paper. Using a measuring stick, draw the grainline as one continuous straight line through the tissue paper. Measure down the amount needed for length and tape the second piece of the pattern to the tissue paper at that point. Make sure the grainlines match up. Connect the cutting lines. Use the same method to adjust the back pattern piece.

Shortening a Pattern

Measure the amount to be shortened upwards from the adjustment line on the front pattern piece. At that point, draw a second line that is parallel to the adjustment line. Fold the adjustment line and bring it up to the second line. Match the grainline markings. Tape the fold in place. Use the same method to adjust the back pattern piece.

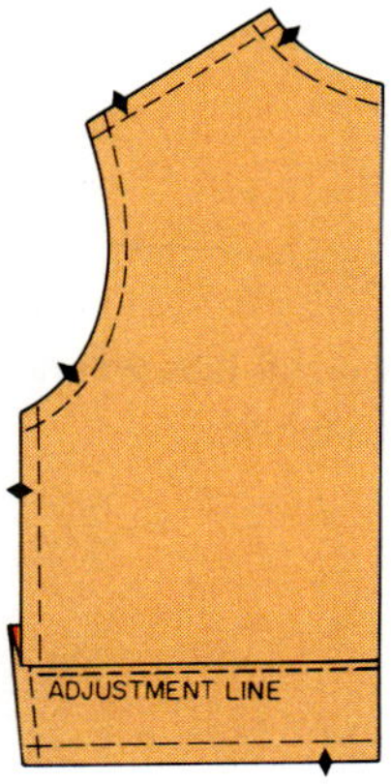

Checking the Grain

Fabric that is off-grain or is cut off-grain does not hang correctly when made into a garment. It is difficult to check the grain of the fabric if the cut edges are uneven.

If you can clearly see the individual crosswise yarns, cut along one yarn from selvage to selvage. If not, clip the selvage and pull one thread (yarn) across the fabric. Pull it gently with one hand while pushing the fabric back with the other hand. When the entire thread is pulled out, the empty space shows as a line. Cut along this line. If the thread breaks before it is completely pulled out, cut along the line where the thread was removed. Pick up the end of the broken thread and continue pulling it across the fabric. Cut off the remaining fabric along the line. Your fabric edge will be straight on the crosswise grain. Repeat on the other cut edge.

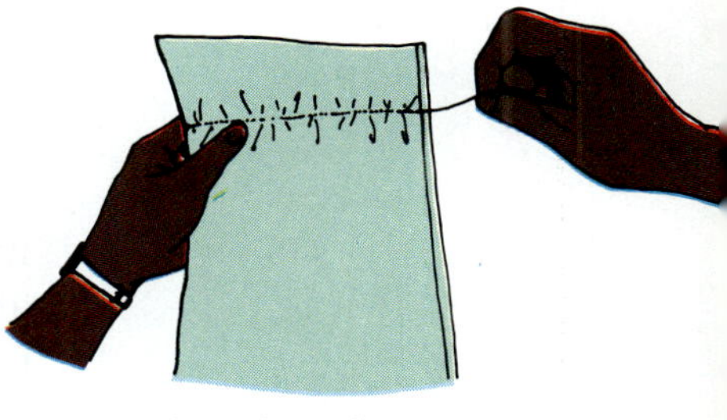

Pulling a thread on the crosswise grain determines whether or not a woven fabric is on-grain.

To straighten the edge of knitted fabrics, simply cut across a crosswise row of loops from selvage to selvage. Knit fabrics do not have a thread that can be pulled.

After making the cut edges even, it is easy to check the grain. Work on a flat surface. Fold the fabric in half lengthwise with the selvages together. Smooth the fabric with your hands, but do not pull it. If the fabric is smooth and the selvages and raw edges are perfectly even, the fabric is on-grain. If the edges are not even, the fabric must be straightened.

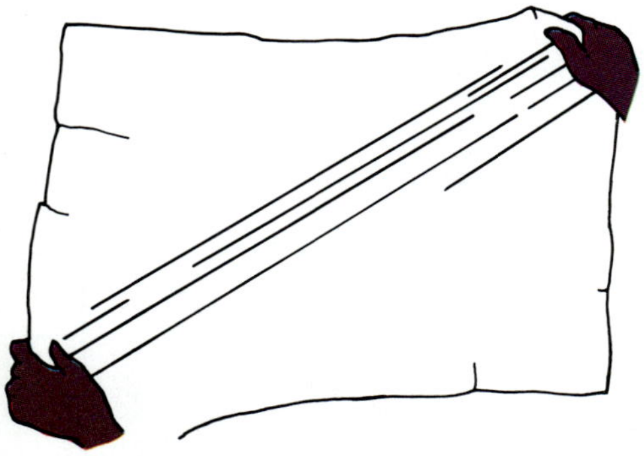
Pulling fabric on the bias will help straighten the grain of the fabric.

Straightening the Grain

In order to straighten the grain of your fabric, the fabric must be pulled on the true bias. Unfold the fabric and pull it in the opposite direction from the way the ends slant. Ask someone to help you pull the fabric — it is easier than straightening the fabric alone. After pulling the true bias, refold the fabric. If the selvages and cut edges match up perfectly at right angles, you have pulled enough. Press the fabric with steam to set the yarns in the on-grain position.

Pattern Layout

After you have prepared your fabric, the next step is to place the pattern pieces on the fabric. The pattern guide sheet lists the pattern pieces needed for each view. To prepare your pattern, follow these steps:

- Cut apart the pattern pieces you need. To avoid accidentally trimming away the cutting lines, leave some extra paper outside of the cutting lines on all pieces.
- Check off the pattern pieces needed as you find them. Place the extra ones back into the envelope.
- Press pattern pieces with a warm, dry iron.
- Write your name on the pattern pieces. When you are working in a clothing lab with other people, pattern pieces can easily get mixed up.

Positioning the Pattern Pieces

Placing the pattern pieces on the fabric correctly is an important step. Once the fabric has been cut, you may not be able to correct layout mistakes. To position the pattern pieces, follow these steps:

1. Find and circle the correct layout on your pattern guide sheet. This shows how to place the pattern pieces for the view, fabric width, and the pattern size you are making.

2. Check the layout instructions carefully. Note the following markings: the right and wrong sides of the fabric; the right and wrong sides of the pattern; and the pattern pieces to be cut a second time. Are any pieces to be cut from a single layer of fabric?
3. Fold the fabric as shown in the layout diagram. Generally, fabric is folded in half on the lengthwise grain with the right side on the inside. Because layouts can vary, however, check how the fabric should be folded. If your fabric is longer than your work table, keep extra fabric folded at the end of the table until it is needed.
4. Carefully place the pattern pieces on the fabric as shown. By following the layout diagram, all the pattern pieces you need should fit on the fabric you have. Remember that each pattern piece has the grainline indicated by an arrow or a "place on the fold" symbol. Use your eyes to line up those markings with the grain of the fabric. Use one or two pins to secure each piece. After you have pinned on a pattern piece, check it off on the guide sheet.
5. Pin each pattern piece securely to the fabric, checking grainlines. Start with large pattern pieces placed on the fold. Pin securely, inserting the pins perpendicular to the cutting line and smoothing out the pattern as you go.
6. Pin the remaining pattern pieces so the grainline symbol is straight on the fabric grain. Pin one end of the grainline symbol to the fabric. Measure the distance from both ends of the arrow to the selvage. If the measurements are not the same, move the pattern at the unpinned end until they are. Smooth the pattern and pin.

Be sure to read the layout instructions carefully and choose the correct layout for your view, size, and type of fabric.

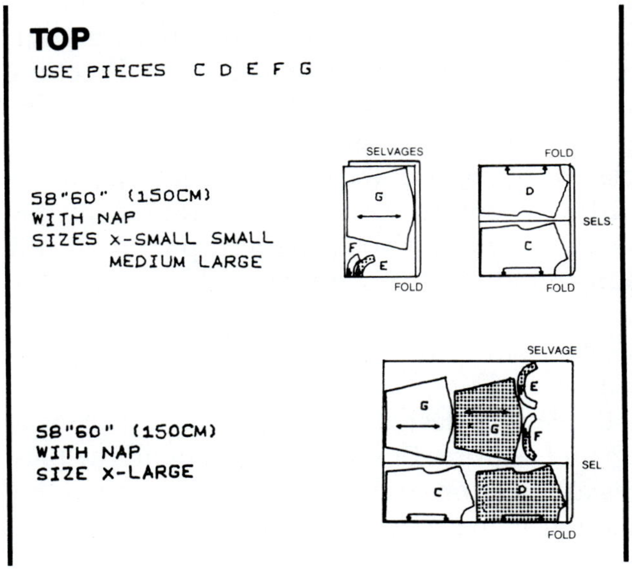

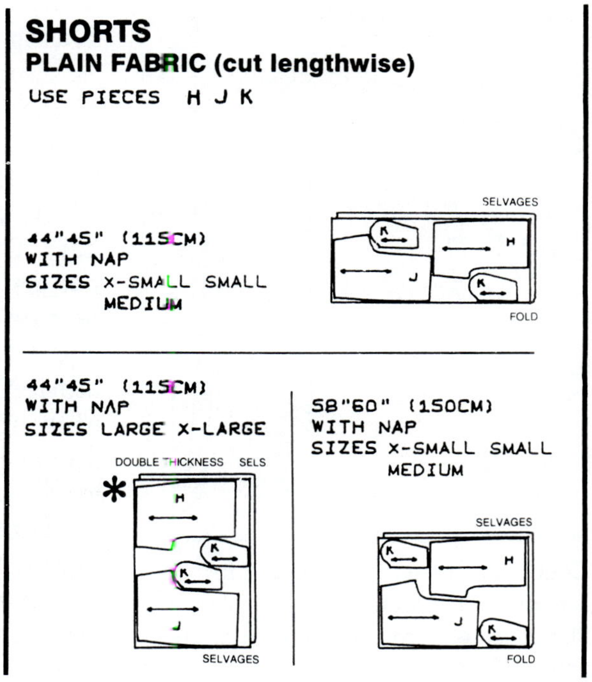

Right Side or Wrong Side

How can you tell which side of the fabric should be used for the outside of your garment? For many fabrics, it is easy to determine which side is the right side. However, some fabrics make it more difficult for you to decide. One clue is to fold back an edge and compare the two sides. The right side is often brighter and has a clearer print or a more obvious surface weave. However, some plain-weave fabrics are the same on both sides. Knitted fabrics can be stretched on a cut edge to determine the right side. The edge will usually roll toward the right side of a knitted fabric.

If you can't decide which side is the right side, then pick one. Mark the wrong side of the fabric with chalk so you'll use the same side as the right side throughout your project. Forgetting to mark the wrong side may leave you with a project of varying colors or degrees of shine.

Special Layouts

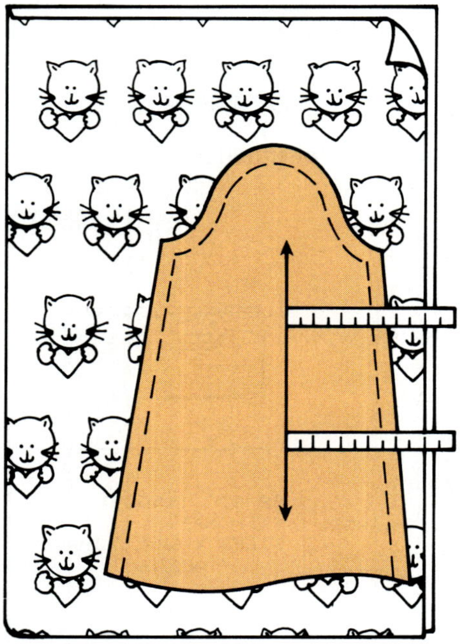

Check your pattern instructions for special fabric layouts to avoid problems. Place each pattern piece straight on the grain of fabric.

Checks, plaids, and stripes need special layouts. Each of these fabrics can present a problem unless pattern pieces are carefully placed. The lines of these designs should match along the seams. Check a sewing book for directions.

Some fabrics have a **nap**, or brushed surface. These include corduroy, suede cloth, and velveteen. To find the direction of the nap, stroke it with your hand. If it feels smooth, you are going in the direction of the nap. If it is rough, you are going against the nap. The nap must lie in the same direction on all pattern pieces. Otherwise, the garment may appear to be two different colors. You need to decide on the effect you want before placing pattern pieces on the fabric. Many napped fabrics are cut with the pile running up, so the color will be darker. However, corduroy is often cut with the pile running down for longer wear.

Look at one-way designs to determine if there is a logical top and bottom. Be sure the tops of all the pattern pieces and the top of the fabric design face in the same direction. Otherwise, the design will be upside down on the garment.

Cutting Out the Pattern

Use a sharp shears with a long cutting blade to cut out your fabric. Follow the outside edges of the cutting lines carefully. Do not cut on the fold line. Hold the pattern and fabric flat with one hand as you cut with the other to prevent the pattern from moving under the fabric. Move around the table as you work instead of moving the fabric.

Cut the notches outward, not inward. Cutting inward can weaken the seam. You could also accidentally cut into the garment. If there are two or three notches together, cut them across the top as one long notch.

Keep pattern pieces pinned to the fabric for marking and identification. If you are using interfacing, cut out the interfacing when you finish cutting the fabric.

Marking Fabric

The lines and symbols on your pattern pieces serve as a guide for sewing accurately. These markings need to be transferred to the wrong side of your fabric before the pattern is unpinned. They must be visible as you sew, but should not show on the outside of the finished project.

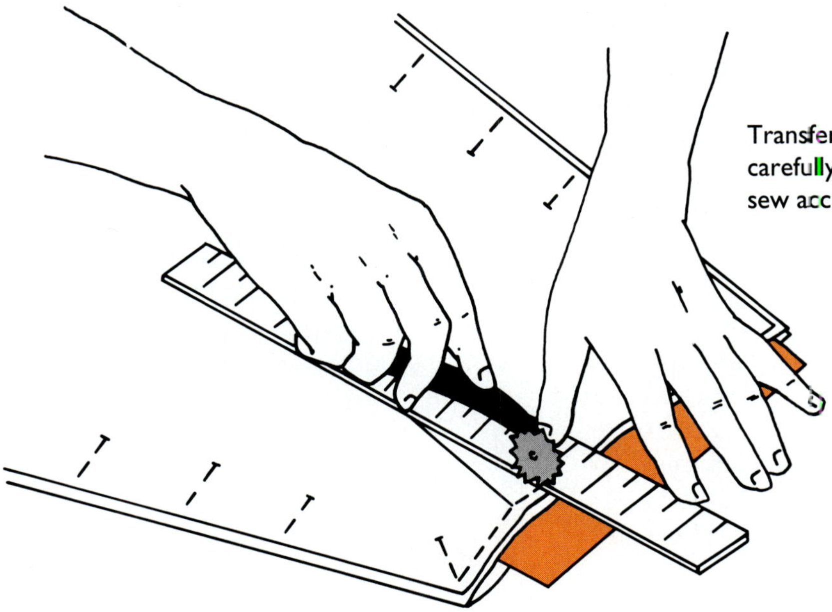

Transferring the pattern markings carefully to your fabric helps you sew accurately.

Markings can be transferred to fabric with a tracing wheel and tracing paper, tailor's chalk and pins, or fabric markers. Here are some guidelines for marking your fabric:

- ***Tracing paper and tracing wheel.*** Choose a color of tracing paper that can be easily seen, but is close to the color of your fabric. Slide the tracing paper under the pattern so that the colored side is against the wrong side of the fabric. If you need to mark two layers of fabric, use two sheets of tracing paper. Roll the tracing wheel along the necessary markings. Using a ruler will help keep the lines straight. Mark the dots with an "X."
- ***Chalk and pins.*** Put a pin through the pattern and fabric at the place to be marked. Make a chalk mark on the wrong side of both fabric layers at the pin marking.
- ***Fabric markers.*** Special liquid fabric markers can be used to make temporary markings on fabric. Some can be removed with water, and others will fade after several hours. Test markers on a scrap of fabric to be sure the markings will come out.

After carefully marking the fabric, you will be ready to start sewing your project together. You will learn about special sewing methods in the following chapters.

TAKING ACTION

Luther is having a problem and needs your help fast. His sewing project is due next week for Mrs. Burkett, the home economics teacher, but Luther is having trouble getting past the pattern stage.

Luther decided to save money by borrowing a pants pattern from a friend. Luther's friend is shorter than Luther and wears one size smaller. Luther thinks he needs to add 1 inch (2.5 cm) to the width and 1 inch (2.5 cm) to the length.

Luther was in a hurry when he took his own measurements and thinks that he may not have been very accurate. He's also having a hard time figuring out where to make the needed adjustments. Luther hopes to finish his project on time.

Using Your Resourcefulness

- What were the advantages and disadvantages of borrowing a pattern?
- What are some ways that Luther can make the most of the time he has available to finish his project? Suggest a plan of action.
- Describe to Luther the benefits of having someone help him take his measurements.
- In what ways are accurate measurements a valuable resource for Luther?
- Where can Luther find help in learning how to adjust his pattern?

Chapter 34 Review

Summary

In this chapter, you have read about:

- Pattern symbols that help you lay out, mark, and cut your sewing project.
- How to check your pattern for fit.
- How to alter pattern width and length.
- Preparing your fabric for sewing by preshrinking it and/or straightening its grain.
- Pattern layout, including pinning and cutting out your pattern, and marking your fabric.

Facts to Recall

1. Explain the meaning of each of the following pattern symbols: grainline, darts, notches. How can you recognize these symbols on a pattern piece?
2. What is wearing ease? How is it different from design ease?
3. Briefly explain how to check for fit by measuring pattern pieces.
4. When adjusting pattern width, how do you determine the amount to be adjusted on each pattern piece?
5. Give two reasons for preshrinking fabric before cutting and sewing it.
6. Explain how to straighten the crosswise ends of a piece of fabric when the crosswise yarns are not easily seen.
7. How can you straighten the grain of an off-grain fabric?
8. List the four steps to prepare your pattern for placement on the fabric.
9. What should you do if you can't decide which side of your fabric is the right side?
10. Briefly explain how to pin a large pattern piece to the fabric.
11. Name three methods you can use for transferring pattern markings to your fabric.

Ideas to Explore

1. What safety tips may be helpful when working with your pattern and fabric?
2. What might you do if you find that a garment is too small for you after you have started sewing it?
3. Predict what might happen if you don't preshrink your fabric.

Activities to Try

1. Lay out and pin a pattern on fabric following a pattern guide sheet. Do at least two things wrong. Have a partner see how quickly he or she can tell you what is wrong and how to correct the error.
2. With a partner, demonstrate how to straighten fabric that is off-grain.

LINK TO *Communication*

CREATING SEWING ENTHUSIASM

Write a one-page motivational article that is designed to encourage people just learning to sew. The article should be well organized and the main points should be clearly written. Address the following points as you write your article:

- Emphasize carefully following the major steps in preparing the pattern; layout and cutting the pattern out of the fabric; and transferring the pattern markings to the fabric.
- Create enthusiasm concerning the advantages of sewing your own clothing.

CHAPTER

35 Basic Sewing Essentials

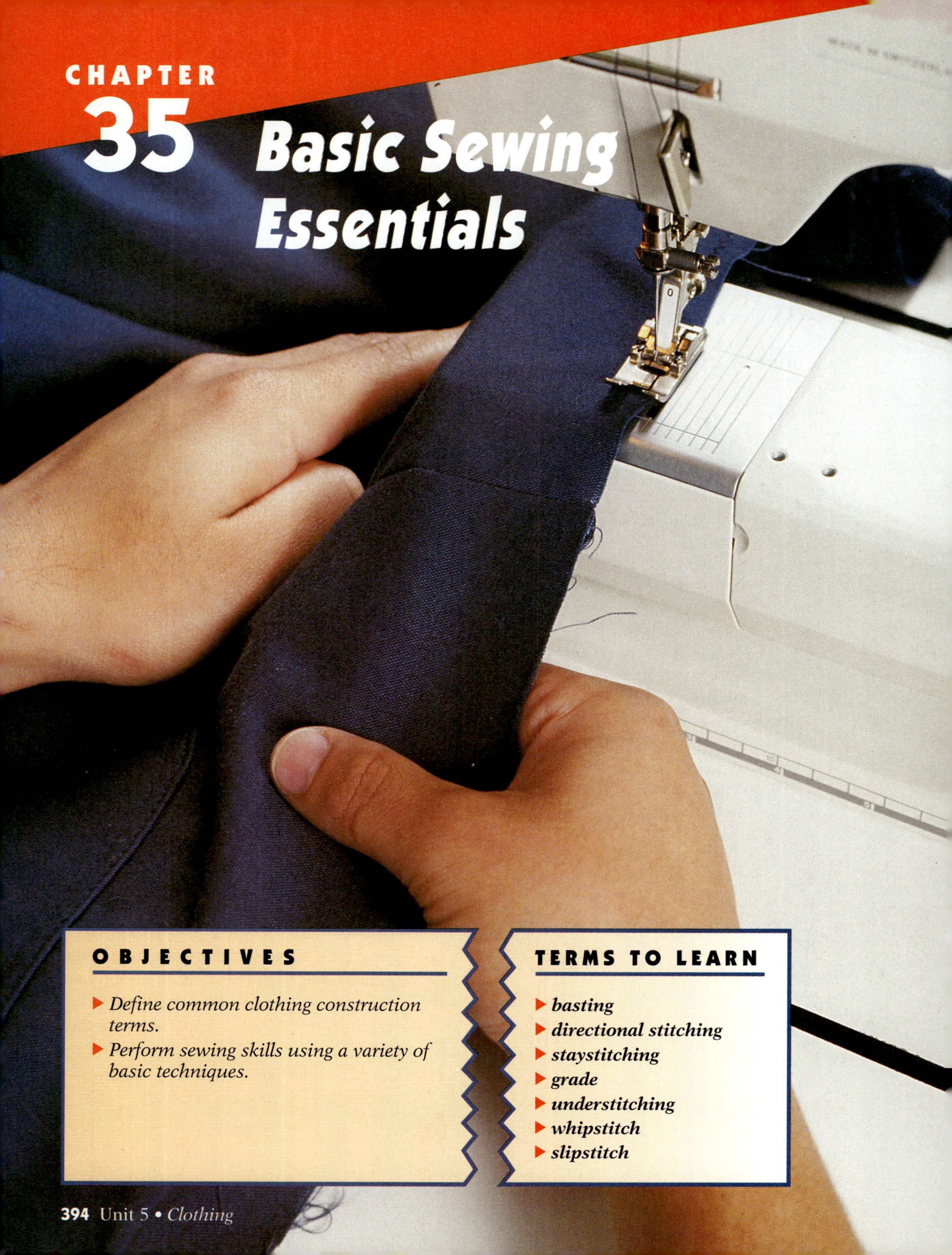

OBJECTIVES

- *Define common clothing construction terms.*
- *Perform sewing skills using a variety of basic techniques.*

TERMS TO LEARN

- ***basting***
- ***directional stitching***
- ***staystitching***
- ***grade***
- ***understitching***
- ***whipstitch***
- ***slipstitch***

Spencer was ready to start sewing his project. As he started to read his pattern guide sheet, he discovered that there were a few things left that he had to learn. "How should a seam be sewn? What is understitching, grading, and clipping? How should I sew the pocket on my shirt?"

As you begin to sew your project, you may discover that you have as many questions as Spencer did. The directions and the pictures in this chapter will help you learn many new sewing skills.

Fitting a Garment

If you altered your pattern correctly before cutting it out, you will probably have few adjustments to make as you sew. However, it is best to check the fit of a garment while you are making it instead of waiting until it is finished. Changes can be made quickly and easily when they are done early.

- Fit the garment right side out.
- Fit at major construction seams, such as side seams, waistline seam, underarm seams, and major darts. It is easier to alter a garment at major construction seams.
- Make adjustments on both sides of a garment rather than on just one side.
- Check to be sure there is enough ease for movement and comfort. See if you can walk, sit, bend, and raise your arms without straining and pulling the garment.
- Be on the lookout for seams that do not hang straight. Watch out for wrinkles and sags. These are all signs of a poor fit.

To be certain about fit, you may need to baste parts of your garment together. **Basting** means holding fabric in place temporarily with pins or long stitches. There are several types of basting. Hand and machine basting use long stitches of thread. In pin basting, the pins substitute for actual thread stitches.

When basting, make sure the stitches or pins are next to, but not directly on, the seam line. This makes the basting easy to remove after the permanent seam is sewn.

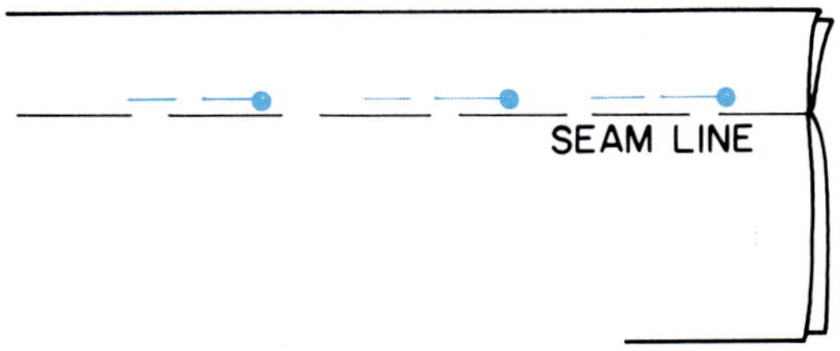

The figure on the left is an example of pin basting. The figure on the right demonstrates hand basting.

AROUND THE WORLD

Making and exporting clothing is a growing industry in Caribbean nations such as Jamaica, Haiti, Costa Rica, and the Dominican Republic. Wages are lower in these countries, so garments are less expensive to make. In addition, these countries are close to the United States, so shipping costs are lower. Since 1988, this industry has created over 100,000 new jobs for people in the Caribbean region. What impact do you think this has on the economy in the Caribbean and the United States?

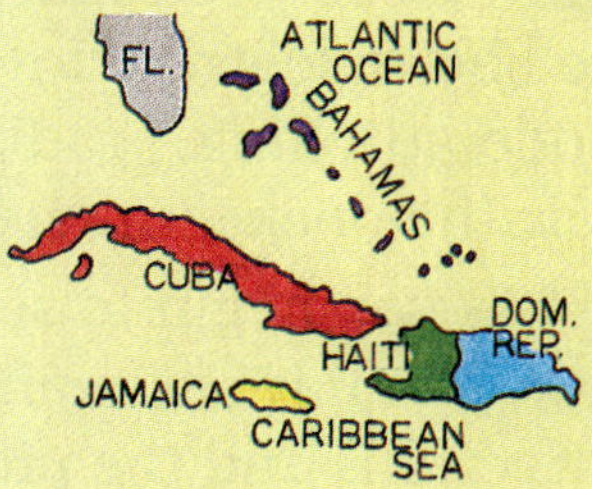

Machine Stitching

Machine stitching is used for the major seams of the garment. It can be used for many different sewing techniques. Review the chart on page 374 in Chapter 33 to determine the stitch length to use for your fabric.

Pattern instructions generally use specific terms to describe each method of stitching. Two of the most common methods are directional stitching and staystitching.

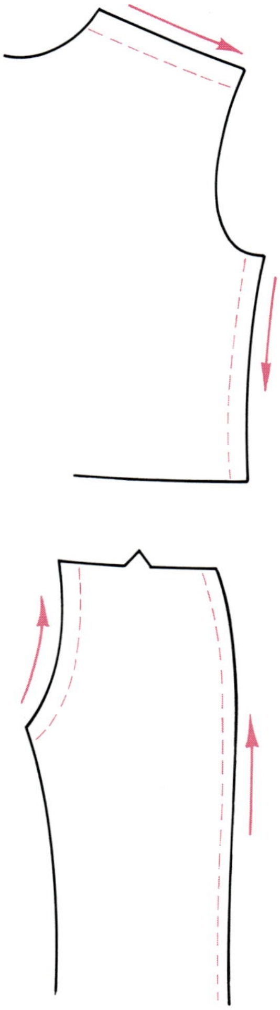

Directional stitching requires that you stitch in the direction of the arrows shown on the pattern. It helps keep the fabric from stretching as you sew.

Directional Stitching

All the stitching on a garment should be sewn with the grain of the fabric. Stitching in the direction of the grain is called **directional stitching**. If you sew with the grain, you are less likely to stretch the fabric.

There are several ways to determine the direction for stitching:

- Move your finger along the raw edge of the fabric. The direction that smooths the yarns against the fabric is with the grain. This is the direction you are going to stitch.
- Pattern tissues have arrows pointing to grain direction.
- As a general rule, stitch from the wide to the narrow part of the garment. For example, sew from the neckline to the shoulder line.

Staystitching

Before you begin to put a garment together, it should be staystitched. **Staystitching** is a row of stitching on one layer of fabric that prevents fabric edges from stretching as you sew. To be effective:

- Staystitch in the direction of the grain.
- Use the same thread, tension, and stitch length you will use for the garment seams.
- Staystitch ½ inch (1.3 cm) from the raw edge. This is ⅛ inch (3 mm) from the seam line. Staystitching should not show on the outside.
- Staystitch edges that are curved, on the bias, or cut off-grain (such as shoulder seams, necklines, armholes, waist-lines, and the hiplines of garments). These areas are most likely to stretch.
- Staystitch armhole and neckline facings only along the curved edges to be attached to the garment.
- Do not staystitch vertical or straight seams.

SAFETY CHECK ✓

As You Sew:

- Remove pins as you sew and put them into the pin cushion.
- Never put pins in your mouth.
- Keep your fingers away from the machine needle while sewing with the machine.
- When using a seam rip-per to remove stitches, hold the point away from your body.

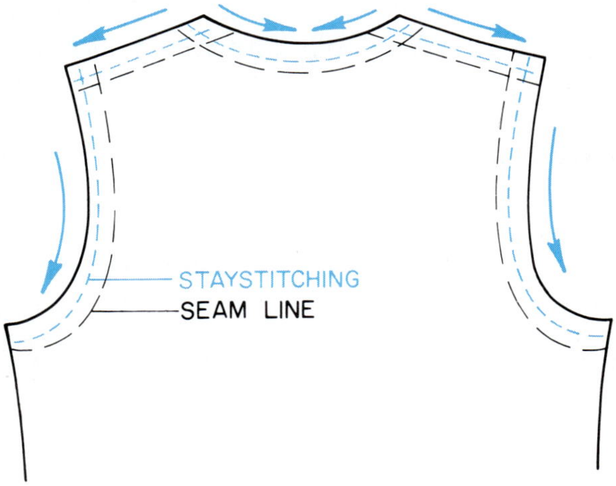

Staystitching is done on curved areas to keep the fabric from stretching.

Sewing Techniques

The sewing techniques described in this chapter are basic techniques you will use in many projects. Learning them is the next step on your sewing adventure.

Darts

Darts help a garment to fit more smoothly over curved areas of the body. They are most often used at the waistline and the front underarm seam.

A single-pointed dart has a point at only one end and is stitched before the seams are sewn. Follow these guidelines in making a dart:

1. Fold the fabric (right sides together) on the center line of the dart. Pin baste on the stitching line, carefully matching the lines accurately. Place the heads of the pins toward the point of the dart for easy removal as you stitch.

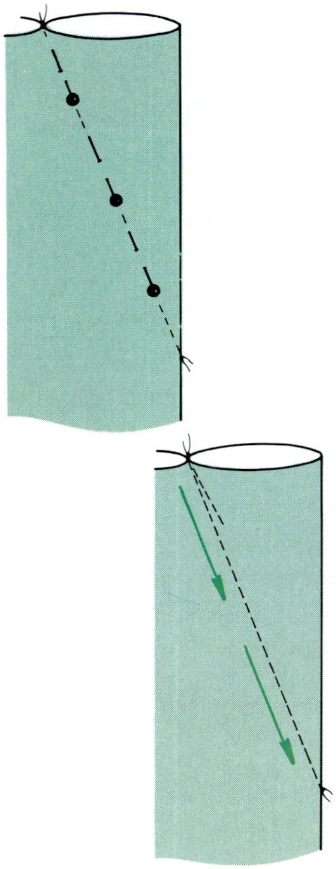

Pin baste and then stitch a single-pointed dart from the wide end to the point.

2. Stitch from the wide end to the point. Backstitch to secure the stitching at the wide end of the dart. Follow the stitching line, removing the pins as you sew. The last few stitches should be on the fold to give a smooth point. Secure the threads at the point of the dart by tying them together. Clip the thread ends to ¼ inch (6 mm) from the fabric.
3. Press the dart flat. Then press the dart to one side. Press underarm darts toward the waistline. Press all other darts toward the center of the garment.

▼ Seams ▼

Seams hold a garment together. They are formed by sewing two pieces of fabric together. A well-made seam affects the way a garment looks and wears. When stitched too tightly, the seam may pucker. If a seam is stitched too loosely, it may pull apart.

A plain seam is most commonly used in garments. In general, seams are ⅝ inch (1.5 cm) wide unless another width is given in the pattern directions. As you learned in Chapter 34, the fabric between the seam line and the cut edge is called the *seam allowance*.

Before you begin your project, sew a sample seam on a scrap of your fabric. Check the tension, stitch length, and general appearance. To make a plain seam follow these steps:

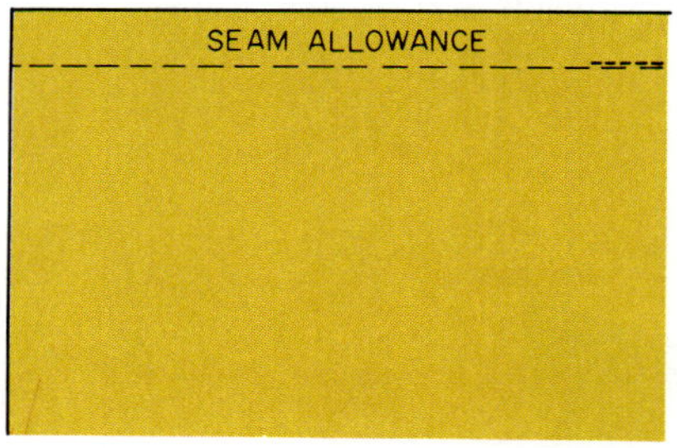

Secure the ends of a plain seam by backstitching on both ends.

1. Put right sides of the fabric together. Match notches, cut edges, and both ends of the fabric. Place pins at right angles to the seam line at the ends and notches. Pin the rest of the seam, placing pins 2 to 3 inches (5 to 7.5 cm) apart.
2. Put the fabric under the presser foot with the cut edges of the seam allowance lined up with the proper seam guide on the throat plate. Turn the handwheel and insert the needle ½ inch (1.3 cm) from the top of the fabric. Lower the presser foot.
3. Backstitch to secure the top end of the seam.
4. Using a medium speed and an even pace, stitch to the other end of the seam.
5. Backstitch to secure the bottom end of the seam.
6. Press the seam open flat unless directed otherwise.

SUCCESSFUL SERGING

Serging a Seam

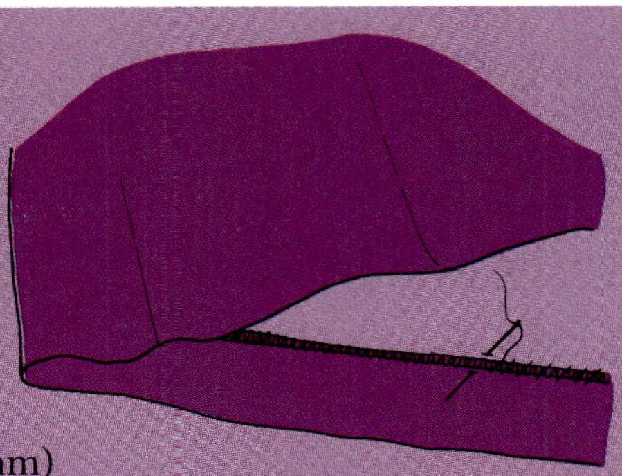

Serged seams work well on many garments. They are especially good on knits since the seams must stretch with the garment. You can also use serged seams with woven fabrics for loose fitting garments and with lightweight fabrics that pucker easily.

Planning ahead is important when using a serger. Sew a test seam first. Remember, the seam line is where the needle enters the fabric — not where the knives cut. If you begin with a ⅝ inch (1.6 cm) seam allowance, and your knives cut off ⅜ inch (1 cm), a ¼ inch (6 mm) seam allowance remains.

If your serger does not have a guide mark for sewing a ⅝ inch (1.6 cm) seam, simply measure ⅝ inch (1.6 cm) from the needle and mark the spot with a permanent marker or piece of tape.

Generally, pins are not needed for serger sewing. The serger feeds fabric evenly through the machine. If you do use pins, remove them before they hit the knives. If a pin hits the knives, the blades can be seriously damaged. In addition, pins that break and fly away from the machine, could cause injury.

Press serged seams to one side, front or back, depending on the garment you are making.

Seam Finishes

In many fabrics, the cut edge ravels as a garment is worn and laundered. Seam finishes are often used to prevent raveling on seams and facings.

The seam finish selected depends on the type of fabric and the amount of raveling. If you are unsure which to use, try different finishes on scraps of fabric. Use the one that appears to be the best for the fabric.

Here are the guidelines for several types of seam finishes:

- ***Stitched and pinked finish.*** Fabrics that ravel slightly can be stitched and cut with a pinking shears. Stitch ¼ inch (6 mm) from the cut edge. Pink the edge after stitching, being careful not to cut the stitching.

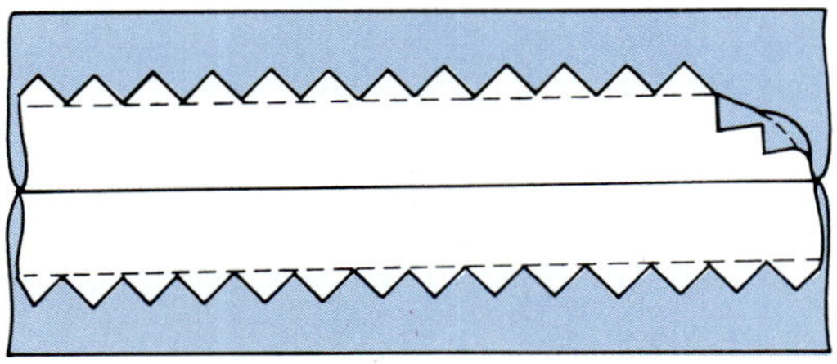

Stitched and pinked finish.

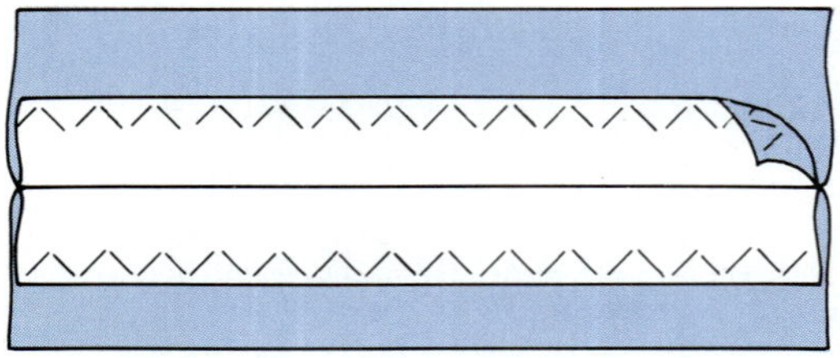

Zigzagged finish.

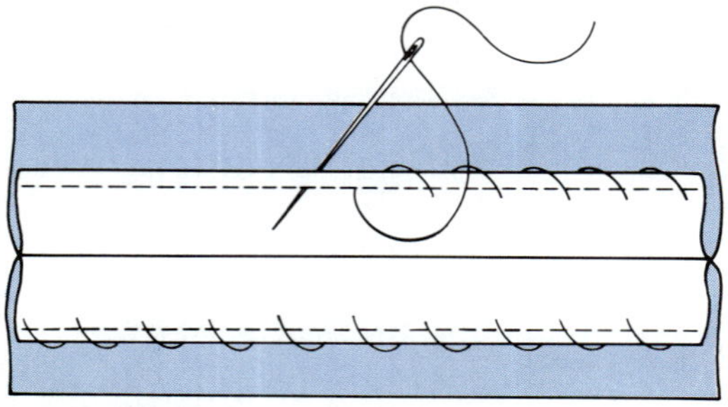

Overcast finish.

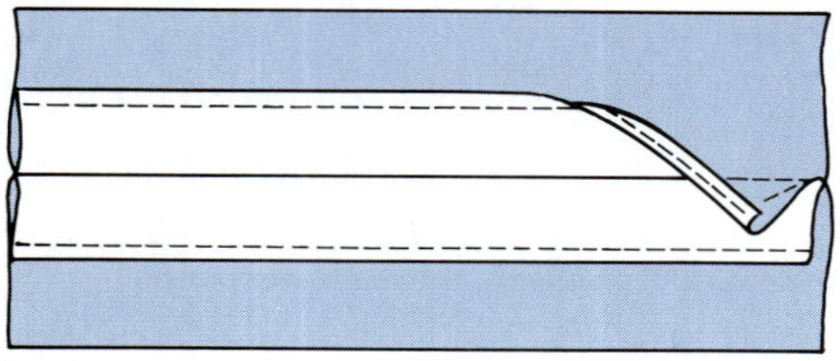

Clean finish.

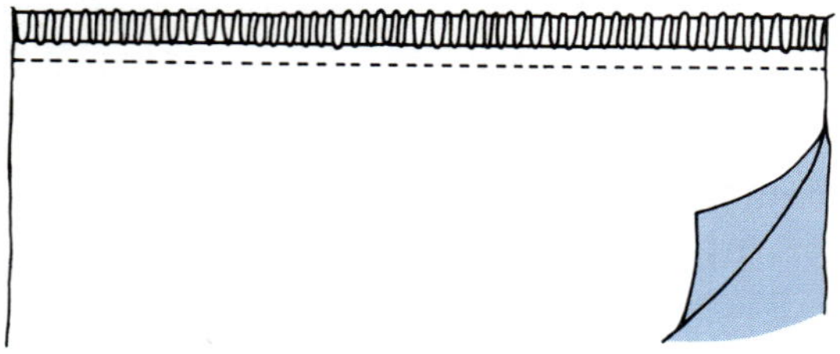

Serged finish.

- ***Zigzagged finish.*** For fabrics that ravel, zigzagging is a good seam finish. Use a medium-width machine zigzag stitch and sew along the edge of each seam allowance.
- ***Overcast finish.*** If your machine does not zigzag, you can overcast the edge of a fabric by hand. Stitch at a slant with large, even, closely-spaced stitches that go over and around the edge of the fabric.
- ***Clean finish.*** A clean finish is a turned and stitched finish used on lightweight and mediumweight fabrics. Machine stitch ¼ inch (6 mm) from the cut edge. Turn the cut edge toward the inside along the stitching line. Press. Machine stitch close to the folded edge. Facings, seams, and hems can be clean-finished.
- ***Serged finish.*** This may be used on any fabric. Serge along the cut edge of the seam, trimming ⅛ inch (3 mm) or less as you sew. A serged finish is especially helpful on heavy or bulky fabric and fabric that ravels easily.

Interfacing

Interfacing gives body and support to places where it is needed, such as necklines, buttonhole openings, and cuffs. Interfacing is applied before the facing is attached to the garment. Depending on the type used, it is either sewn or pressed onto the garment.

Applying Sew-on Interfacing

Here are some guidelines for applying sew-on interfacing:

1. Cut the pointed corners off the interfacing about ⅛ inch (3 mm) past the seam line to reduce bulk. This means ⅛ inch (3 mm) of the fabric corners will be without interfacing. Pin the interfacing to the wrong side of the fabric piece.
2. Machine baste the interfacing to the fabric ½ inch (1.3 cm) from the outer edges. Stitch with the direction of the grain.
3. Trim the interfacing as close to the stitching line as possible.
4. Handle the interfacing and the fabric as one piece when sewing the seams.

Applying Fusible Interfacing

Follow these guidelines for applying fusible interfacing:

1. Trim fusible interfacing before it is pressed onto the fabric. Mark and trim ½ inch (1.3 cm) along the seam lines. Also, cut any pointed corners off the interfacing about ⅛ inch (3 mm) past the seam line to reduce bulk.
2. Place the coated side of the interfacing on the wrong side of the fabric. Be sure the cut edges are ½ inch (1.3 cm) from the fabric edges.
3. Follow the pressing instructions that come with the interfacing.

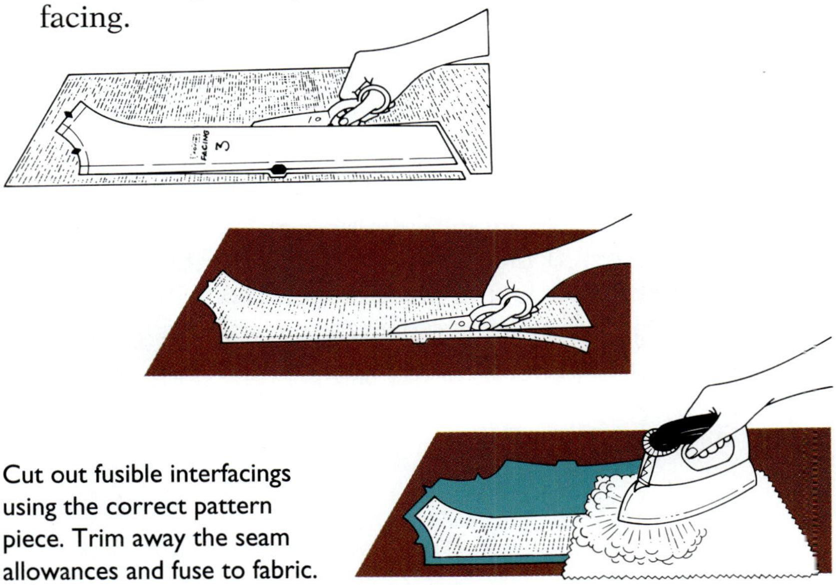

Cut out fusible interfacings using the correct pattern piece. Trim away the seam allowances and fuse to fabric.

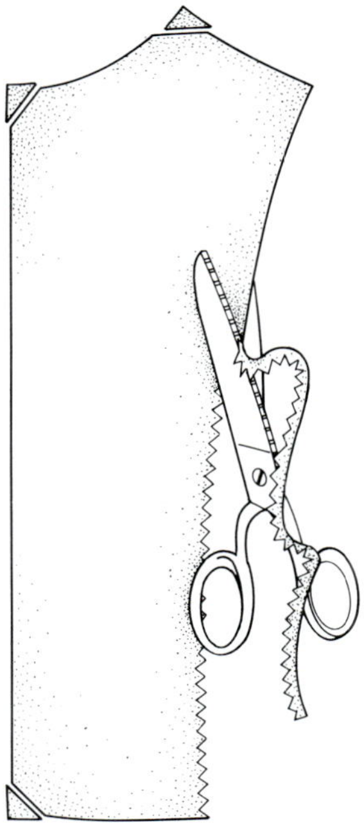

Trim sew-on interfacing before basting to fabric.

▼ Facings ▼

Facings are often used to finish the neckline, front opening, armholes, and collars of garments. There are several different types of facings. However, a shaped facing is used most frequently. It is cut the same shape as the edge onto which it is sewn.

Before learning to sew a facing to a garment, there are several techniques you will need to understand.

- ***Grading a seam allowance.*** After facings are joined to a garment, the seams are **graded**, or cut in layers to reduce bulk. To grade a seam: trim the interfacing as close as possible to the seam line; trim the facing seam to ¼ inch (6 mm); then trim the garment seam to ⅜ inch (1 cm). The wider seam on the outside cushions the narrower one and keeps it from showing when the seam is pressed. **Note:** Trim the seams together diagonally across sharp corners, such as collar points and neck facing edges, before continuing to grade the seam.

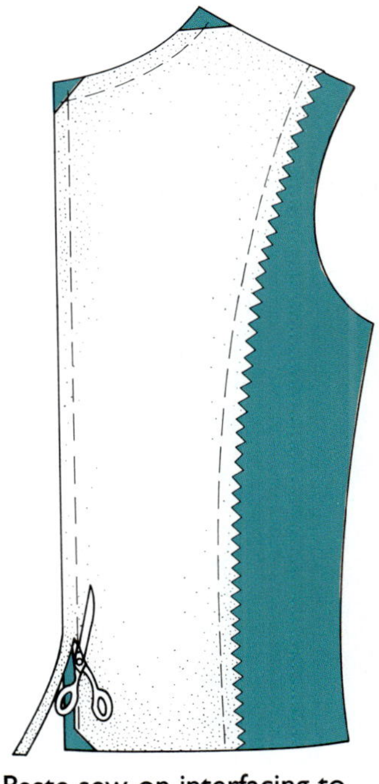

Baste sew-on interfacing to garment. Then trim the interfacing close to the basting.

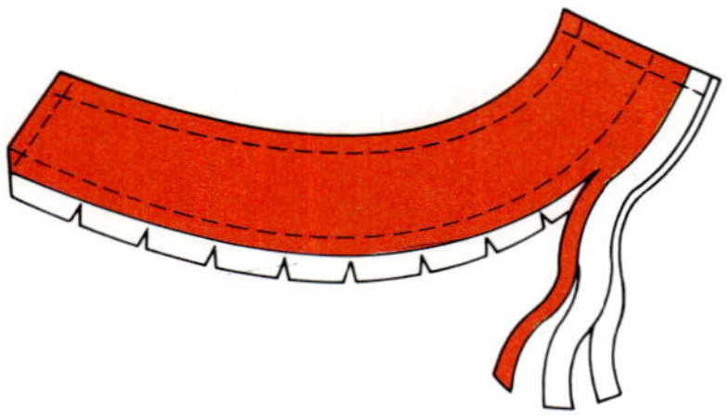

Grading and notching on an outward curved seam.

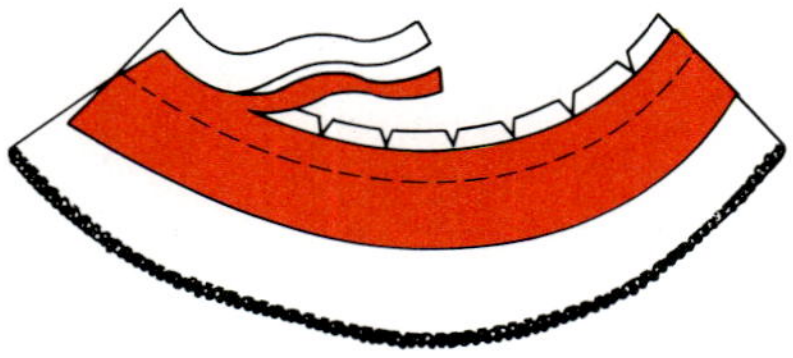

Grading and clipping on an inward curved seam.

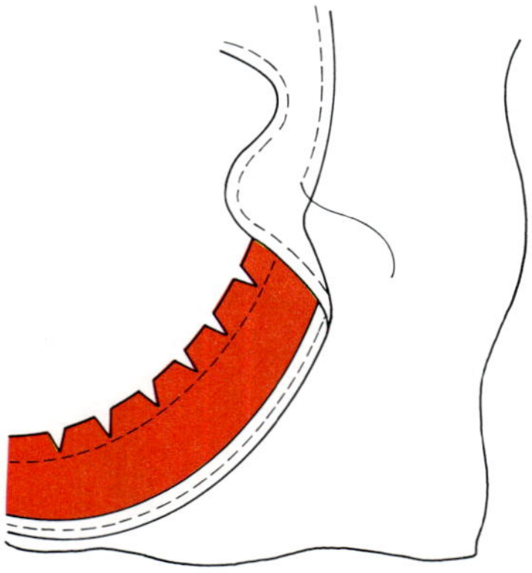

Understitch through all layers of the seam allowance and facing to keep the facing from rolling to the right side of the garment.

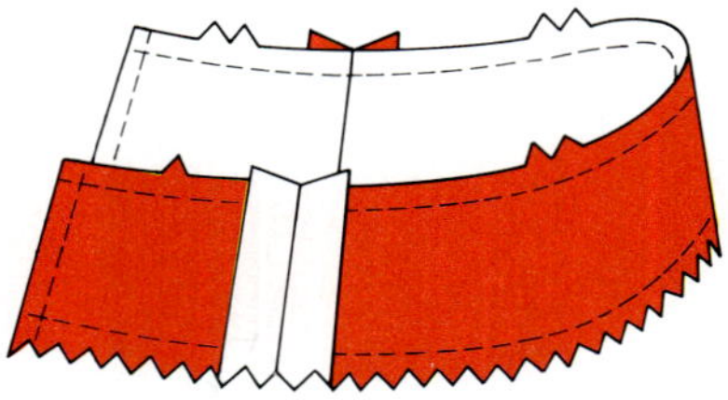

Join facing pieces together and finish the outer edges.

- ***Notching and clipping a seam allowance after grading.*** Outward-curved edges on collars and inward-curved edges on necklines need special treatment to lie flat. Cut V-shaped notches from the seam allowance on outer curves. Make small clips in the seam on an inner curve. Space the clips and notches around the edges so the curve will lie flat. Be careful not to clip through the stitching.
- ***Understitching.*** Understitching gives a smooth, flat edge to facings. It keeps the seams and facings from rolling to the right side of the garment. Before understitching, press seam allowances on both garment and facing toward the facing. Grade and clip the seams as needed. Work with the right side of the garment facing up. Sew, using a regular machine stitch, through the facing and the two seam allowances about ⅛ inch (3 mm) from the seam line. Press.

Now you are ready to learn how to sew on a facing. Follow these steps to attach a facing:

1. Staystitch curved facing edges that are to be attached to the garment. Sew facing pieces together as directed in the pattern. Trim the seams to ¼ inch (6 mm) and press open.
2. Finish the unnotched outer edges of the facing to prevent raveling. Use one of the finishing methods discussed earlier in this chapter. Press.

Press as You Go

"Press as you go" is a good rule to keep in mind. If you press each piece after it is sewn, your work will go faster and will be more accurate. Pressing as you sew gives your garment a professional look.

Here are some guidelines for pressing as you sew:

- Use pressing equipment correctly.
- Check the correct temperature setting on the iron by using a scrap of fabric.
- Press with the grain of the fabric.
- Press each seam and dart before joining that section to another one.
- Use the point of the iron to press seams open.
- Press flat garment areas on a flat surface. Use a tailor's ham — an oblong stuffed cushion that is shaped like a ham — for curved areas.
- Avoid pressing over pins. They can scratch the bottom of the iron and mark the fabric.

3. Place the right side of the facing against the right side of the garment. Match notches, seams, and pin together.
4. Stitch the facing to the garment at ⅝ inch (1.3 cm), sewing as evenly as possible.
5. Grade and clip the seams to reduce bulk.
6. Press the facing and seam allowance away from the garment.
7. Understitch the seam allowance. Press.
8. Fasten the facing to the inside of the garment by hand sewing it to the seam allowances or darts. Take a few tiny stitches over and over at the same place. Avoid sewing the entire facing edge to the inside of the garment. This will cause the garment to pull along the stitching line and look unattractive on the outside.

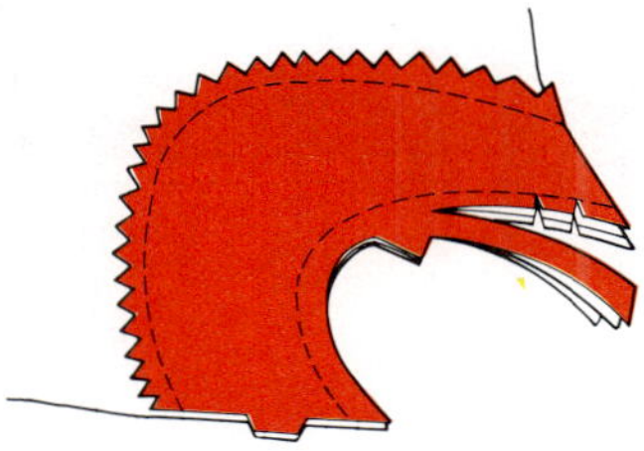

Sew facing to garment. Then grade and clip or notch the seam allowance.

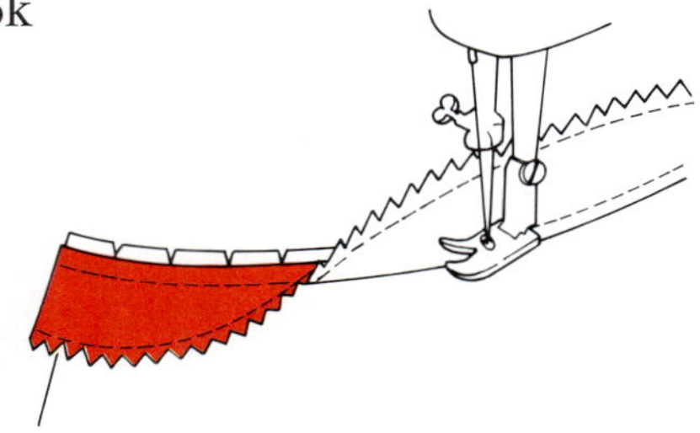

Understitch the facing.

Gathering

Fullness on shirts, dresses, and skirts is often created by gathers. To make gathers, sew two evenly spaced rows of machine basting on the right side of the fabric, using a long machine stitch. Leave a 2 inch (5 cm) length of thread at the beginning and the end of each row. Stitch the first row on the seam line. Stitch the second row about ¼ inch (6 mm) from the seam line inside the seam allowance.

If a large amount of fabric is to be gathered, divide the amount to be gathered into four equal parts. Stitch and gather each part separately.

Pin the edge to be gathered to the corresponding straight edge (such as a sleeve to a cuff, a gathered skirt to a waistband, or a ruffle to a curtain edge) with the right sides together. Match all markings, notches and seams.

Adjust gathers to fit the straight edge. First, secure one end of the basting stitches by wrapping the thread ends around a pin in a figure eight. Working from the other end, gently pull the loose ends of the bobbin threads. Slide the fabric along with your fingers. After gathering the amount you think is needed, secure threads by wrapping them around a pin. Measure the exact width needed, and adjust the gathers. Pin about every ½ inch (1.3 cm).

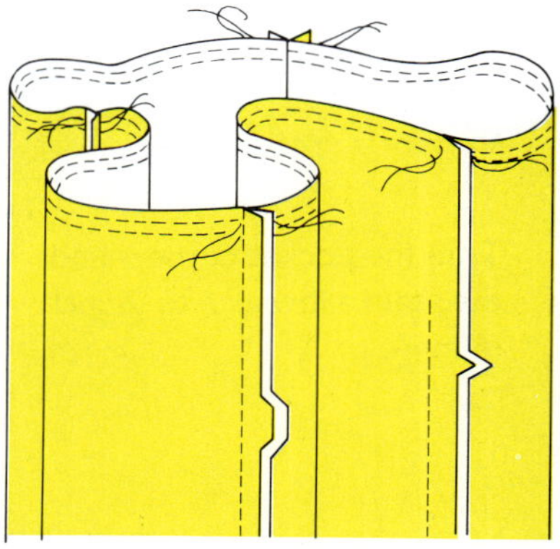

Gather each section using basting stitches.

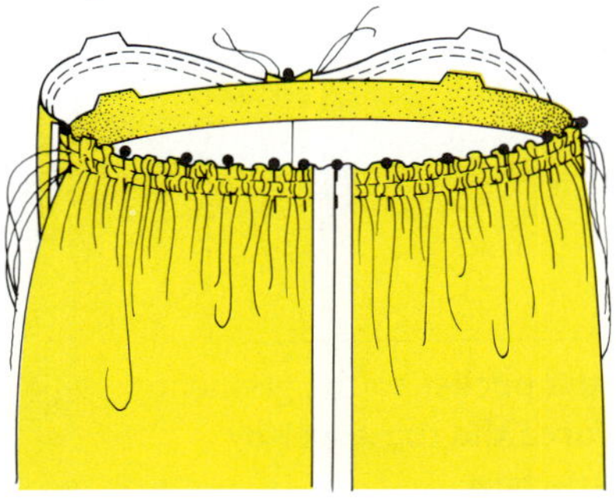

Pin the gathered edge evenly to the corresponding straight edge.

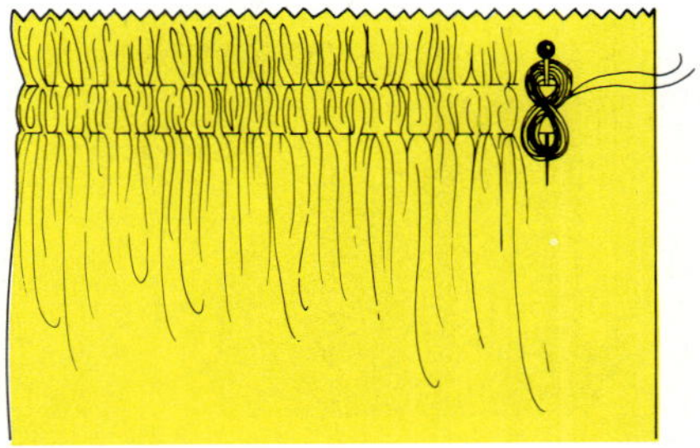

Secure the gathers around a pin, as shown.

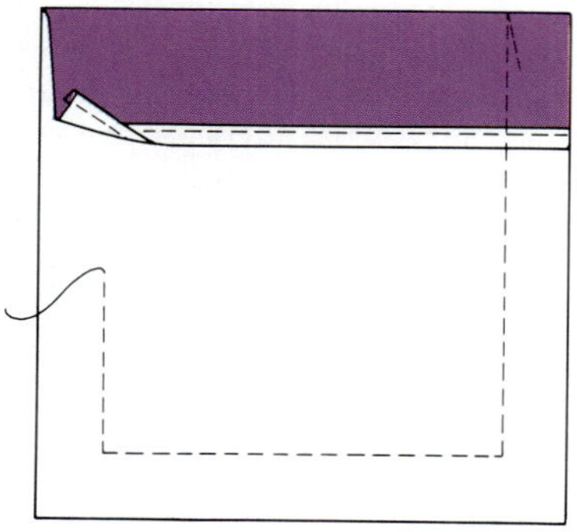

Finish and face the pocket edge. Stitch along the seam line.

When stitching a gathered seam, sew with the gathered edge on top. In this way, stitching is more accurate and the gathers will not be caught in the stitching. For safe sewing, remove the pins as you sew.

Patch Pockets

A patch pocket is made from a separate piece of fabric and is attached to the outside of the garment. Follow these directions for a square patch pocket:

1. Turn the top edge of the pocket under ¼ inch (6 mm) to the wrong side of fabric. Press. Stitch close to the edge.
2. Turn the top pocket edge to the outside (right sides of fabric together) along the fold line to form the pocket facing. Pin.
3. Stitch along the seam line from the top of the pocket on one side to the top on the other side. Backstitch at both ends.
4. Trim the corners and seam allowance on the pocket facing to about ¼ inch (6 mm). Turn pocket facing right side out and press.
5. Fold the seam allowances under along the stitching line. Press. This will give you a guideline to work with to form a square corner.
6. To form a square corner, open the seam allowances. Fold the corners under diagonally to the stitching line and press. Trim the diagonal seam allowance to ¼ inch (6 mm). Refold the seam allowances on both sides of the corner to form a square edge. Press again.
7. Place the pocket on the outside of the garment, with the wrong side down. Follow placement markings. Pin and baste.
8. Machine stitch close to the outer folded edge. Use the inside edge of the presser foot as a seam guide. Reinforce the top edges of the pocket by backstitching.

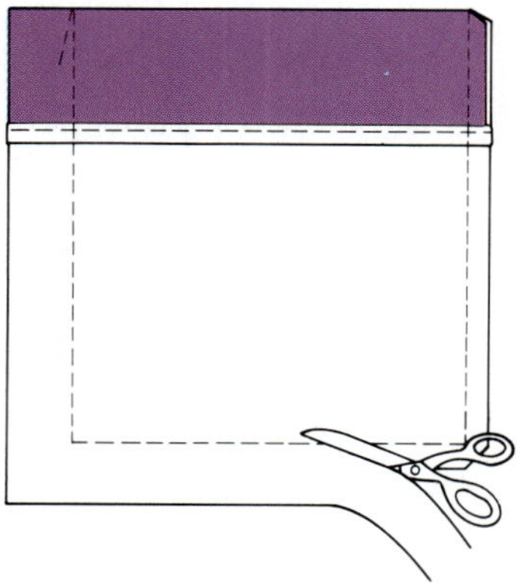

Trim the pocket corners and the seam allowance to ¼ inch (6 mm).

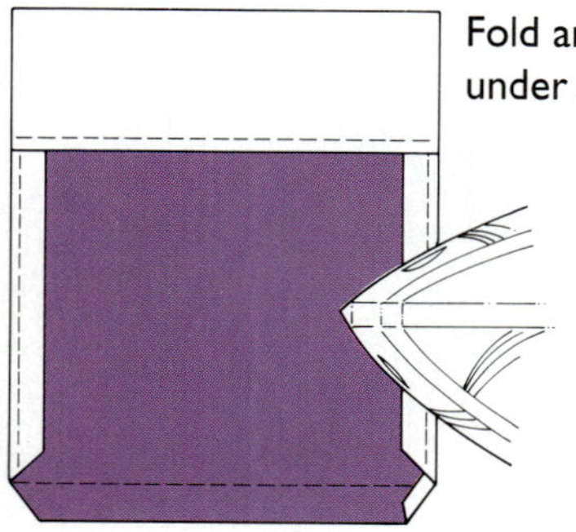

Fold and press seam allowances under along the stitching line.

Sew the pocket to the garment. Reinforce the top edges by backstitching.

▼ Hems ▼

All hems are not the same. The type of hem you put in depends on the type of fabric and the amount of fullness to be handled. Some casual garments have a narrow, machine-stitched hem. However, most garments have hems that are finished by hand. This way the hem is almost invisible.

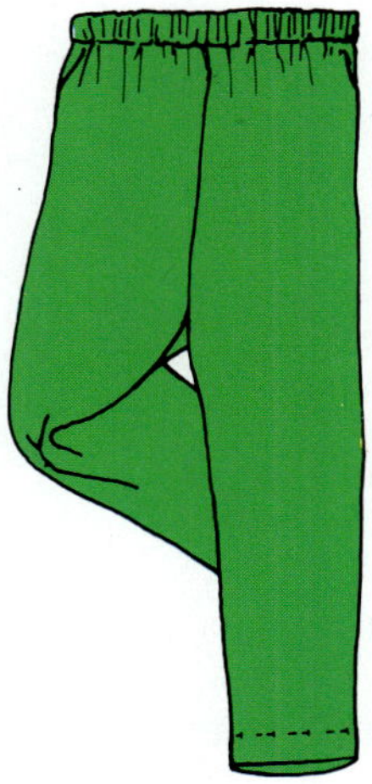

Mark the hemline accurately.

Marking the Hem

To mark the length of the hemline, put on shoes of the heel height you expect to wear with the finished garment. Decide on the most attractive length for the garment. Have another person measure the correct length up from the floor using a measuring stick. Place pins or chalk marks at the same distance all the way around the garment. Stand straight and still while the hem is being marked. Check to be sure the markings form an even line. Make any changes needed.

Using the marked line as a guide, turn the hem to the wrong side of the garment. Pin along the fold line. Place pins at a right angle to the folded edge.

Hem width varies depending on the fullness of the garment. Garments with less fullness can have deeper hems. Pants usually have a hem of 1½ to 2 inches (3.8 to 5 cm). Skirt hems vary from 1 to 3 inches (2.5 to 7.5 cm). For example, the hem in a straight or gathered skirt may be 2 to 3 inches (5 to 7.5 cm) deep. However, the hem of a circular skirt should be no more than 1 inch (2.5 cm) deep.

Measure the hem width needed plus ¼ inch (6 mm) for finishing. Use a sewing gauge, cardboard notched at the correct hem width, or a ruler to mark the correct width. Cut off extra fabric from the edge of the hem.

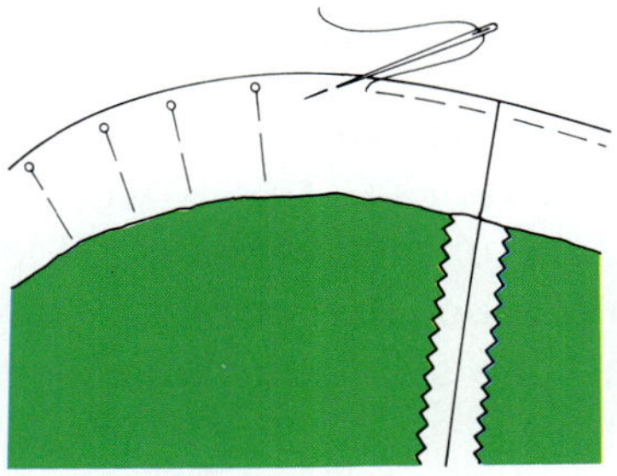

Pin and baste the hem along the fold.

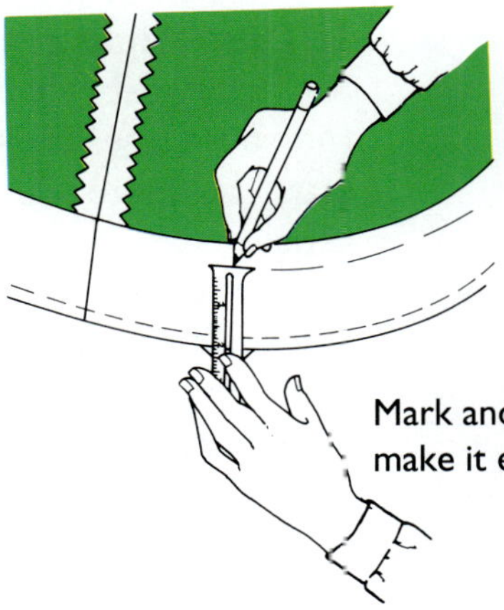

Mark and trim the hem depth to make it even.

Machine stitch ½ inch (1.3 cm) from the cut edge. Stitch only through the hem, not the outside of the garment.

If necessary, ease in extra fullness at the hemline so the hem will not be bulky and lumpy. Some fabrics shrink with steam. In this case, shrink the fullness along the hem by steam pressing in the direction of the grain. For fabrics that do not shrink, ease out the fullness by pulling up on the bobbin thread at different points along the stitching to take out fullness. Press with steam to flatten the eased material.

Shrink hem fullness in with steam on fabrics that shrink.

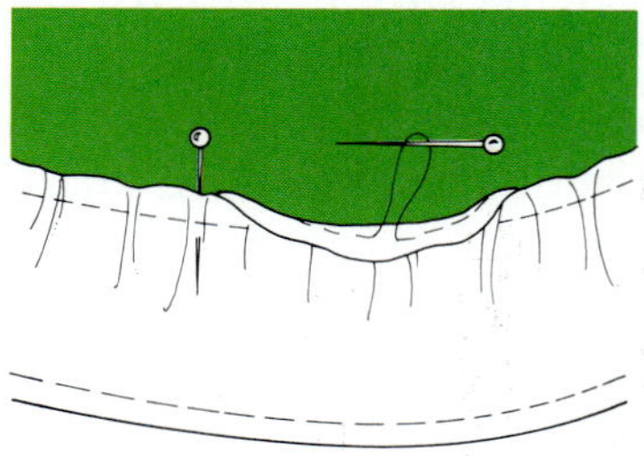

For fabrics that do not shrink with steam, machine baste close to cut edge. Pull up bobbin thread to ease in fullness.

SUCCESSFUL SERGING

Serge and Hem

Use the serger to give a smooth, finished edge to your hem. Simply mark and measure the hem as directed. Serge the hem allowance only to the desired width. Turn the hem under and press. Attach the hem to the garment with hand or machine stitching.

Some hems require only serger stitching. For example, serge off the bottom of a T-shirt or tuck-in shirt for a quick hem.

Check your serger directions for several decorative serger hem ideas.

Completing the Hem

Woven or lace seam tape can be used to finish raw edges of lightweight and mediumweight fabrics. Use woven tape for heavy fabrics that ravel. Pin tape or lace to the outside of the raw edge. Be sure ¼ inch (6 mm) of the seam tape overlaps the edge of the fabric. Machine stitch the tape to the fabric.

Attach the hem to the garment by using a **whipstitch**, a small diagonal handstitch. Using a single strand of thread in the needle, attach the thread to the hem at a seam. Take small, even stitches by catching both the garment and the edge of the tape or lace in each stitch. Pick up only one or two threads of fabric as you sew. The finished hem should have evenly-spaced diagonal stitches over the edge.

Sometimes the raw edge of a hem is simply turned under and machine stitched before hemming. A **slipstitch** is used to attach the hem to the garment. Using a single thread in the needle, attach the thread to a seam at the hem. Slip the needle through the folded clean-finished edge. With the same stitch, catch one or two threads in the outer layer of fabric. Continue the stitches, always slipping the needle through the fold and then into the outer layer of fabric. Slipstitches should be spaced evenly along the hem about ½ inch (1.3 cm) apart. Be careful not to make the stitches too loose or too tight. The slipstitch is an almost invisible stitch when sewn correctly.

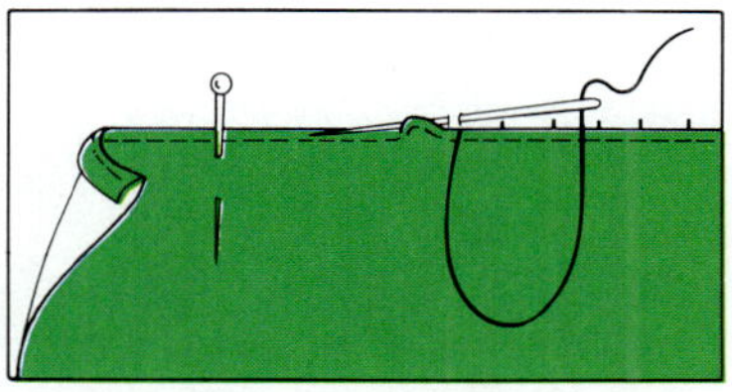

Whipstitch or slipstitch the hem edge to the garment.

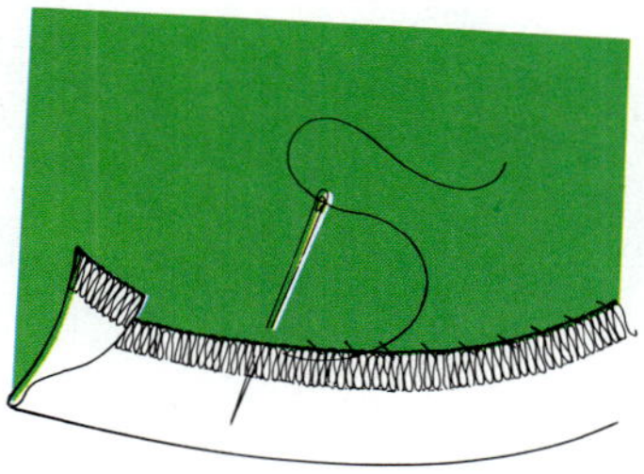

Hem edge finished by serging the fabric edge.

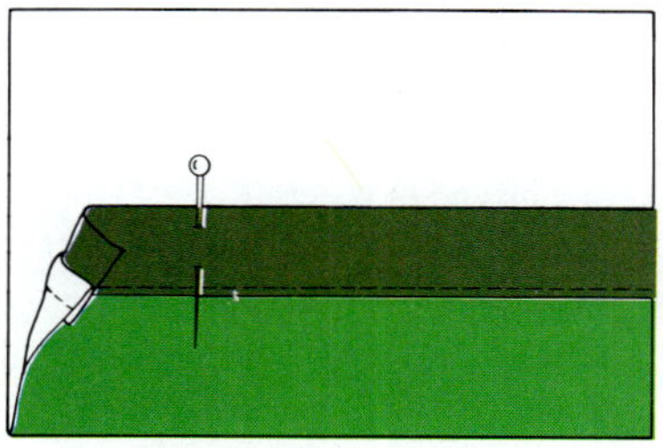

Hem edge finished with woven tape stitched to fabric edge.

Pocket Lab

Choosing Seam Finishes

MATERIALS:
Three 6-inch (15-cm) square scraps of heavyweight, mediumweight, and lightweight fabric

EQUIPMENT:
sewing machine, serger, pinking shears

Directions: On each side of each fabric sample, use a different type of seam finish: clean finish, stitched and pinked finish, machine zigzagged finish, serged finish.

- Which finish would you avoid using on a heavyweight fabric? Why?
- Why would just pinking a seam edge be a poor seam finish? For what types of fabrics would you choose a stitched and pinked finish?
- When would you choose a machine zigzagged finish? Why?
- When would you use a serged finish? Why?

Knowing how to hem garments is a good skill to have.

TAKING ACTION

A new family, the Chans, recently moved into your apartment building. For the past six weeks you have been babysitting for their three-year-old son, Michael, every Thursday evening and Saturday morning. Although Michael knows most of his letters and colors, you have noticed that he has a hard time turning the pages of books and coloring pictures. He also gets very frustrated when it is time to get dressed in the morning or change into his pajamas at night. He can never seem to get his clothes on the right way.

Michael's birthday is next month. You have decided to make him a fabric book that will give him practice with various types of fasteners used on clothing.

Using Your Resourcefulness

- Make a list of the most common types of clothing fasteners you might include in the book. Which are commonly found on clothing for children?
- Which fasteners do you know how to sew? How could you learn others?
- Sketch out your plan for the book page by page. How can you use a story to make playing with the book fun?

Chapter 35 Review

Summary

In this chapter, you have read about:

- Fitting a garment as you work on it.
- Making darts.
- Stitching and finishing seams.
- Applying facings and interfacings.
- Sewing gathers, patch pockets, and hems.

Facts to Recall

1. List four tips for fitting a garment.
2. Why should all stitching on a garment be directional?
3. What is the purpose of darts? Where are darts most often used?
4. Briefly explain how to sew a dart.
5. How should the top and bottom ends of a seam be secured?
6. On what fabrics can serged seams be used?
7. Name three seam finishes. Give an example showing when each seam finish could be used.
8. How do you make the outward-curved edges of a collar lie flat?
9. Why is pressing as you go a benefit when sewing your project?
10. Briefly explain how to slipstitch a clean-finished hem to a garment.

Ideas to Explore

1. What are the advantages of having someone help you to measure and pin a hem?
2. How might you trim a patch pocket to make it more attractive?
3. What factors may influence your choice of interfacing? How would you choose interfacing for your fabric?

Activities to Try

1. Choose three seam finishes you think would work with the fabric for your project. Prepare a sample of each finish. Press. Compare the samples. Which appeared to work best? Why?
2. Assume you are a video script writer. You have just been assigned to write a script for a new video series called "Sewing Basics for Beginners." The producer indicated that you may choose one of the following topics for the script: applying interfacing (sew-on and fusible); seam finishes; or sewing darts and seams. The producer wants you to be as creative as possible. Share your script with the class.

LINK TO *Art*

ILLUSTRATING SEWING TECHNIQUES

Draw a colorful illustration for one or more of the following basic sewing techniques: stay stitching, dart, plain seam, or serged seam. After your drawing is complete, make a fabric sample of the technique showing the correct way to do the technique. Use contrasting fabric and thread so the technique can be easily seen. Display the sample and illustration attractively on poster board.

CHAPTER

36

Challenging Sewing Essentials

OBJECTIVES

- *Practice challenging sewing techniques.*
- *Recycle and make basic garment alterations.*

TERMS TO LEARN

- ***lapped zipper***
- ***adjustable zipper foot***
- ***tapestry needle***

Now that you have started your sewing adventure, you may be beginning to realize that sewing can be very rewarding (and sometimes challenging). It is a creative way to personalize your clothes. Learning to sew also gives you a skill that you will be able to use throughout your lifetime.

Challenging Techniques

The techniques explained in this chapter will help you to further develop your sewing skills. You will learn how to make a collar, put in a zipper, sew a sleeve, and sew a waistband or elastic casing. Although these skills are still considered basic, you may find them more challenging than those in Chapter 35.

Collars

Collars come in many different shapes and sizes. Most collars have two parts — the *uppercollar* and the *undercollar*. The basic steps for making all collars are similar. Here are the guidelines for making a collar:

1. In general, pin the interfacing to the wrong side of the undercollar. (Check your directions to be sure which side of the collar you are to interface. There are some exceptions to the general rule.) Machine baste the interfacing to the undercollar ½ inch (1.3 cm) from the outer edge. If the collar is pointed, trim the corners off the interfacing before attaching it to the undercollar. If you are using fusible interfacing, trim off the interfacing ½ inch (1.3 cm) on all edges. Follow the manufacturer's directions for fusing.
2. With right sides together, pin the uppercollar and undercollar together.
3. Stitch the collar together on the seam line except at the neck edge. Use a short stitch length. Take one stitch diagonally across each corner of a pointed collar. This makes a neater point when the collar is turned.

Collar — Step 1

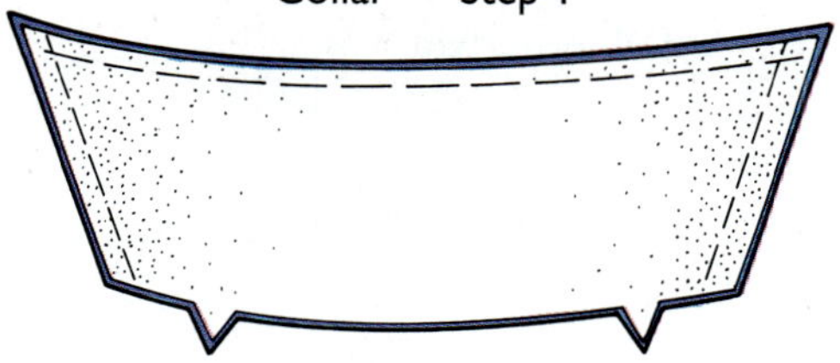

Collar — Step 3

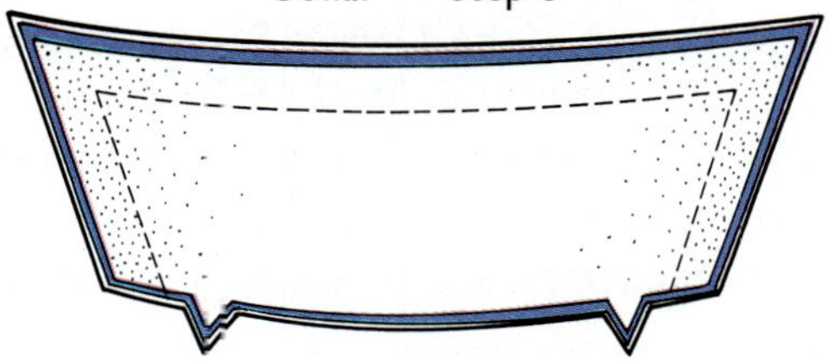

4. Grade the seams. Trim the interfacing close to the stitching; trim the undercollar seam allowance to ¼ inch (6 mm); and trim the uppercollar seam allowance to ⅜ inch (1 cm). Trim both seam allowances diagonally across the collar points about ⅛ inch (3 mm) from the stitching line. Clip the seam as needed.
5. On a pointed collar, understitch to within 1 inch (2.5 cm) from each point. On a round collar, understitch all around the seam. Refer to page 402 for information about understitching.
6. Turn the collar right side out and gently push the points out. (Never use a scissors to do this. Use a point turn — a small piece of equipment you can buy at a fabric store.) Press the collar flat, being sure to roll the seam to the undercollar side so it will not show on the finished collar.
7. Baste the notched, raw neck edges together. Attach the collar to the garment as directed.

Collar — Step 4

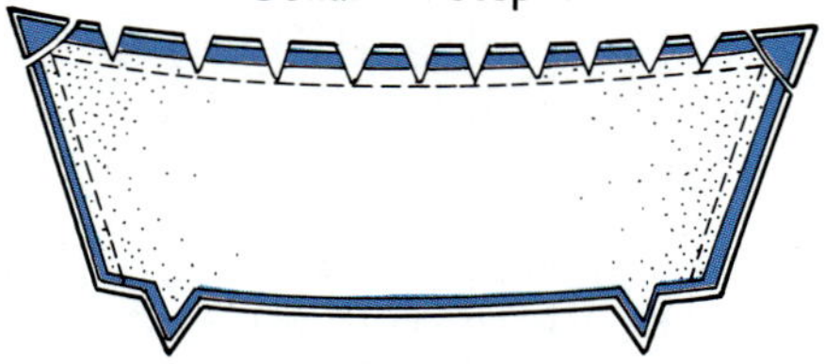

Collar — Step 5

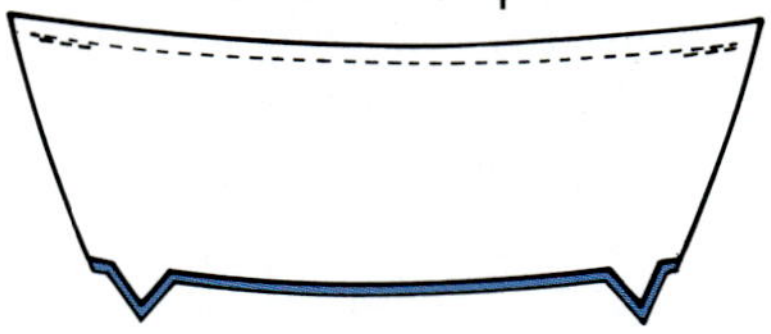

For many years, European fashion designers set the trend in women's clothing in the United States. Often, the garments they created were beautiful but difficult to care for and not durable. Now American fashions, noted for comfort and practicality, are becoming very popular in Europe. Many designers believe this is because the lifestyles of the European women who buy these clothes are becoming more like those of American women. Busy with families, careers, and social activities, they need versatile clothes that are easy to care for.

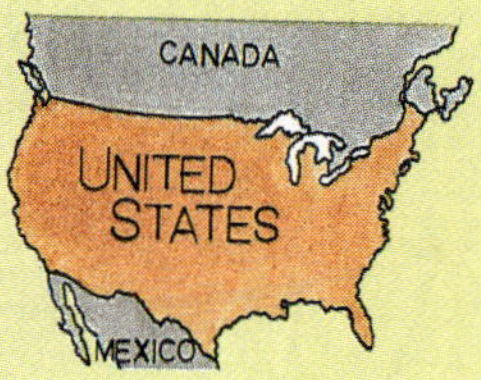

▼ Lapped Zippers ▼

With a **lapped zipper**, a single flap of fabric and one row of stitching can be seen on the outside of the garment. This method of putting in a zipper can be used for lightweight or mediumweight fabrics. It totally hides the zipper and looks attractive on back, front, or side openings.

You will be using an **adjustable zipper foot**, a presser foot that can be positioned to the left or the right of the needle. This allows stitching to take place on either side of the zipper.

Follow these steps to insert a lapped zipper:

1. With the right sides together, pin the seam that will include the zipper. Make sure the top edges are even. With the wrong side up, place the zipper along the seam allowance. Position the top of the zipper teeth 1 inch (2.5 cm) from the top edge. Measure the length of the zipper opening. Use chalk to mark the bottom location of the zipper teeth on the seam allowance.
2. Using a standard presser foot and regular stitch length, sew the seam from the bottom of the garment up to the mark for the bottom of the zipper opening. Backstitch. Without removing the fabric from the machine, change the stitch length to basting. Continue sewing the seam to the top edge of the garment.
3. Press the seam open.
4. Attach the adjustable zipper foot to the machine. Position the foot to the right of the needle.
5. Open the zipper. With the top edge of the garment facing you, place the zipper — right side down — on the right-hand side of the seam allowance. The zipper teeth should be on the seam line. Match the bottom of the zipper teeth with the chalk mark made in Step 1. Pin the zipper in place.
6. Machine baste from the bottom to the top of the zipper, ⅛ inch (3 mm) from the zipper teeth. Stitch only through the zipper tape and seam allowance. Remove the pins as you reach them.
7. Close the zipper and turn it face up. Keep the garment to the left of the needle. Fold the seam allowance back from the zipper and pin in place. Move the zipper foot to the left side of the needle. Stitch through the folded edge of the seam allowance and the zipper tape from the bottom to the top of the zipper. This row of stitching should be close to the zipper teeth.

Zipper — Step 5

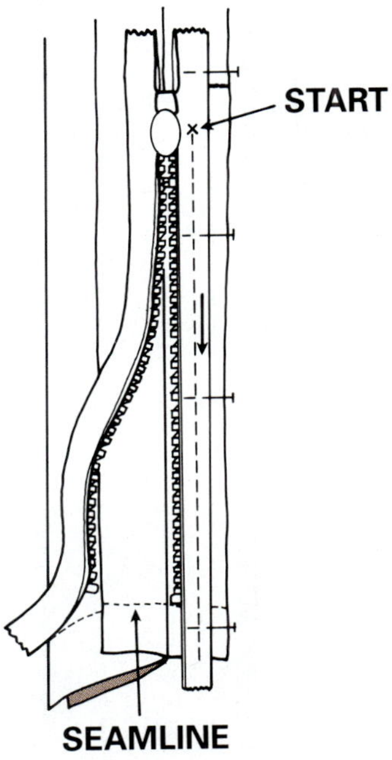

Zipper — Step 7

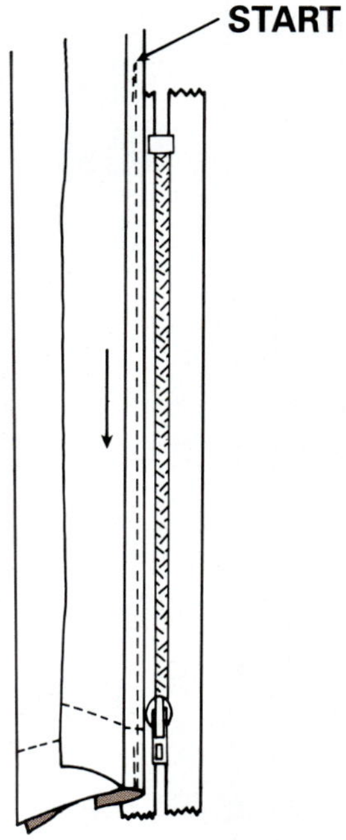

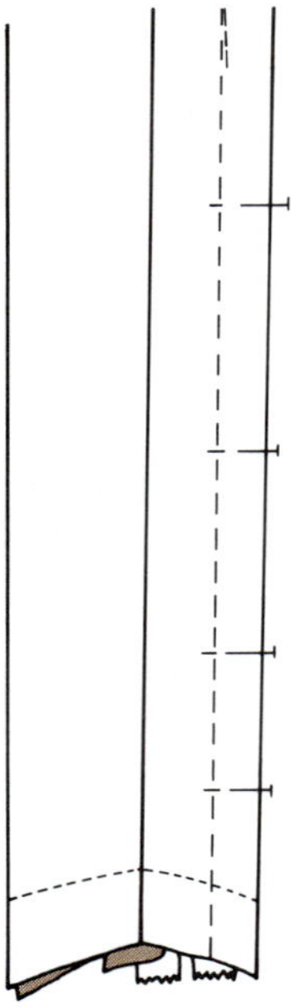

Zipper — Step 9

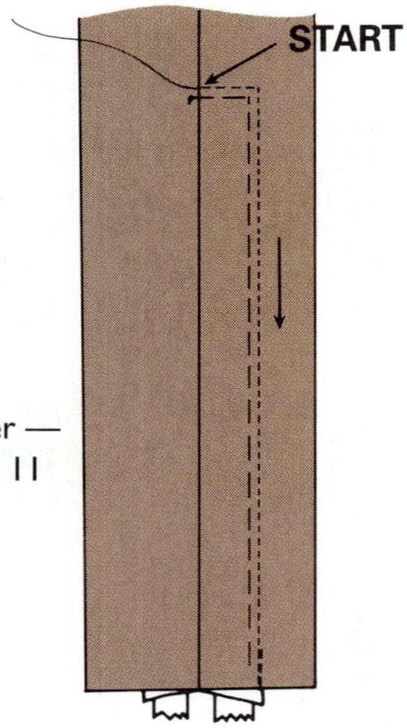

Zipper — Step 11

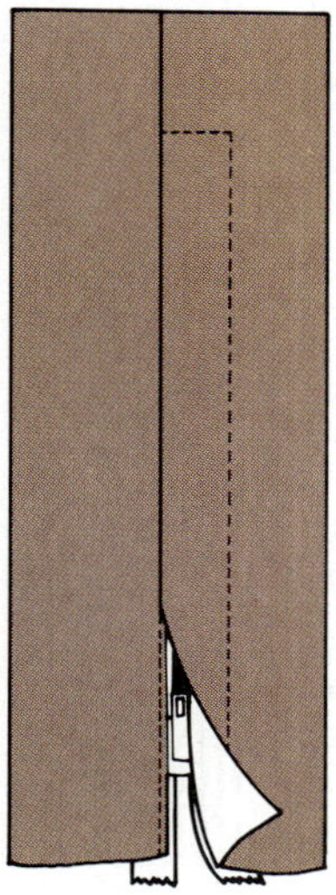

Zipper — Step 12

8. Fold the zipper over so the right side is flat against the other seam allowance. Turn the garment to the right. A tuck should form at the bottom of the zipper. Pin the zipper tape to the seam allowance only.
9. Machine baste the zipper to the seam allowance from the bottom to the top of the zipper. Stitch ⅛ inch (3 mm) from the zipper teeth.
10. Remove the garment from the machine and turn it right side out. Press lightly over the zipper area. Hand baste across the bottom of the zipper and up the side of the zipper, ⅜ inch (1 cm) from the seam.
11. Move the zipper foot to the right side of the needle, and begin stitching at the bottom of the zipper. Sew along the basting across the bottom of the zipper, stitching out from the seam ½ inch (1.3 cm). To pivot the corner: stop with the needle in the fabric; lift the presser foot and turn the fabric so the top edge of the garment is facing you; lower the presser foot. Continue stitching along the basting, ½ inch (1.3 cm) from the seam, to the top of the garment. Backstitch ¼ inch (6 mm) at the top of the zipper to secure the stitching.
12. Pull the upper thread at the bottom of the zipper to the wrong side of the garment by using a hand sewing needle. Tie the upper and bobbin threads together and clip the threads close to the garment. Remove all basting stitches. Press.

▼ Set-In Sleeves ▼

Set-in sleeves are sewn into the armholes of the garment after the side seams have been sewn. The top of the sleeve is larger than the armhole to allow room for movement. Although it may seem difficult to ease in the extra fullness, it helps to make the garment comfortable to wear. Here are the guidelines for sewing a set-in sleeve:

1. With the right side facing up, machine baste around the top of the sleeve on the seam line between the notches. Do not clip off the thread ends. Sew a second row of basting stitches ¼ inch (6 mm) from the first, inside the seam allowance.
2. To avoid making two sleeves to fit the same armhole, put both sleeves on a table with the right sides facing up. With right sides together, pin the underarm seam on each sleeve. Stitch the underarm seams. Finish the seam edges. Press the underarm seams open.

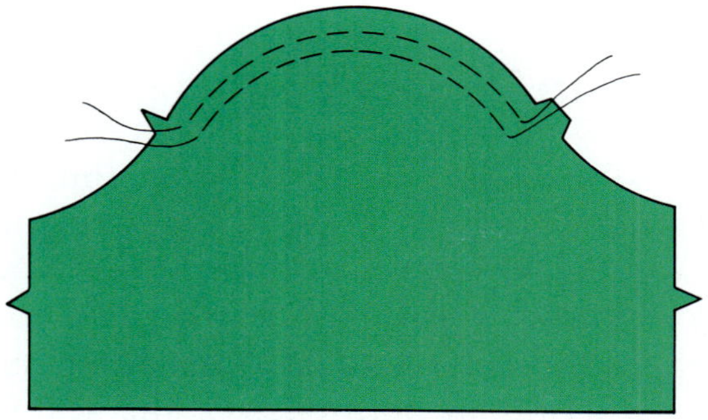

Sleeve — Step 1

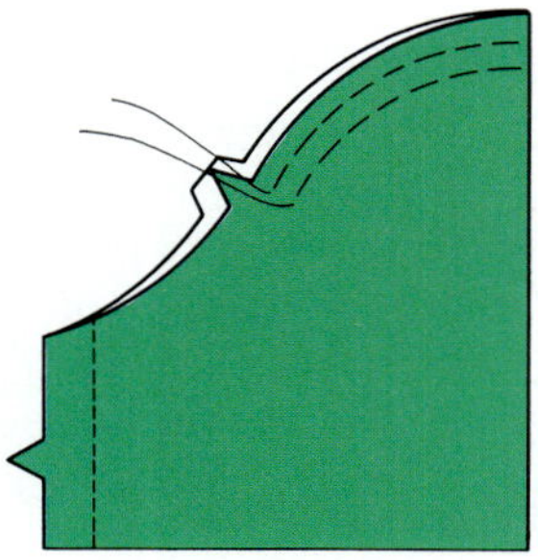

Sleeve — Step 2

Sleeve — Step 4

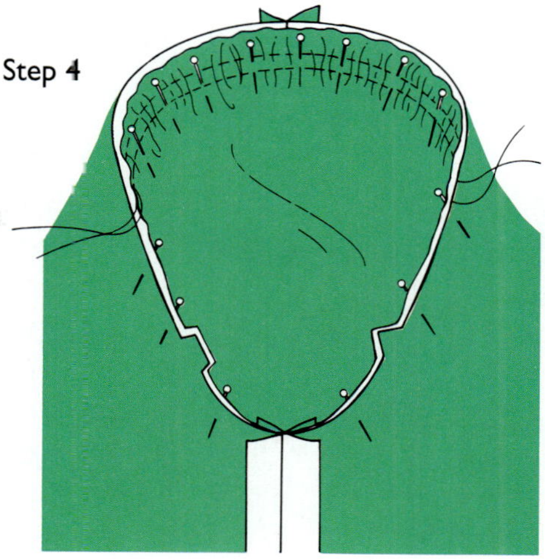

Sleeve — Step 5

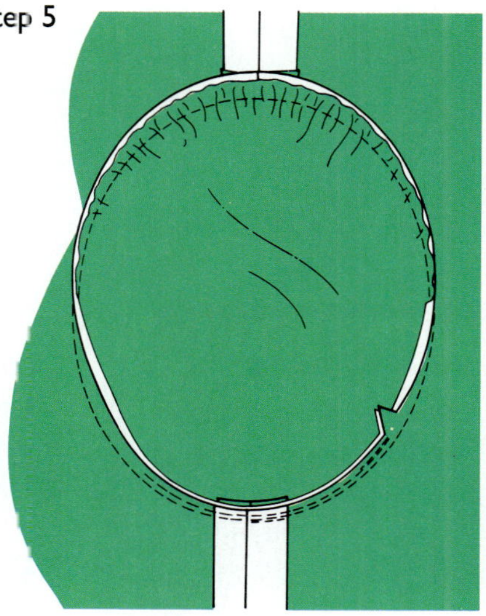

3. Match each sleeve to the garment with the right sides together. Pin each sleeve on the garment at the underarm seams, shoulder seams, notches, and markings. Insert pins on the seam line to hold the seam securely. Use the following directions to finish pinning and sewing each sleeve.
4. Pull the bobbin thread ends, starting at each notch and ease the fabric toward the top until the sleeve fits the armhole. Secure threads around a pin in a figure eight. Distribute fullness evenly. Place pins ½ inch (1.3 cm) apart along the seam line. Keep the raw edges even. The sleeve should fit smoothly without puckers.
5. Machine stitch on the inside with the sleeve side facing up to be sure no puckers are caught in the seam. Begin and end the stitching at the underarm seam, backstitching to secure the seam. Then make a second row of stitching between the notches along the underarm area. Sew ⅛ inch (3 mm) from the first row of stitching, inside the seam allowance. This stitching gives extra strength to the area of strain.
6. Trim the seam between the notches at the underarm to ¼ inch (6 mm). Zigzag the seam allowances together to finish the seam. Press the armhole seam toward the sleeve.

SUCCESSFUL SERGING

Finishing the Armhole

After sewing the armhole seam on your conventional sewing machine, serge the seams together ⅛ inch (3 mm) away from the seam line. This provides a neat finish and saves time too!

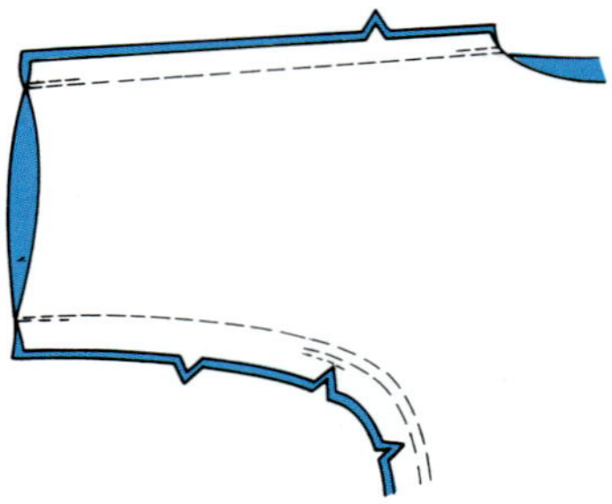

Kimono Sleeve — Step 3

▼ Kimono Sleeves ▼

Kimono sleeves are the easiest sleeve for a beginning sewer to make. They are cut as part of the of the garment front and back with a shoulder seam and underarm seam. Here are the guidelines for sewing a kimono sleeve:

1. With right sides together, pin the shoulder seam. Stitch on the seam line, backstitching at both ends of the seam. Press the seam open.
2. With right sides together, pin the underarm seam. Stitch the underarm seam on the seam line. Stitch again at the underarm curve, ¼ inch (6 mm) from the seam line.
3. Clip the underarm curve of the seam and press the seam open except at the underarm curve.

▼ Attached Waistbands ▼

Attached waistbands are usually interfaced to prevent stretching. Cut the interfacing the same length as the waistband and half of its width. Follow these steps for attaching a waistband:

1. With wrong sides of the fabric together, fold the waistband in half lengthwise matching the raw edges evenly. Press along the fold. This will mark the lengthwise fold.
2. Pin the interfacing to the wrong side of the waistband along the notched edge. The inside edge of the interfacing will be on the lengthwise fold.
3. Machine baste the interfacing to the waistband ½ inch (1.3 cm) from the notched edge. Stitch through the interfacing and one layer of fabric. Begin and end stitching ½ inch (1.3 cm) from each end of the band. Machine baste the interfacing to the remaining edges of the band ½ inch (1.3 cm) from the cut edge. Trim the interfacing to the stitching line. Refer to page 401 for instructions on using fusible interfacing.
4. Press the seam allowance on the unnotched edge to the wrong side along the seam line.
5. Pin the waistband to the garment, with the right sides together. Match the notches and ease the garment to the waistband between the markings. One end of the waistband will be longer than the other to give an underlap when the waistband is fastened. Check your pattern guide sheet to make sure the extension is on the correct side of the opening.

SUCCESSFUL SERGING

Sewing Kimono Sleeves

The seams for kimono sleeves can be sewn on the serger. This saves time in two ways. It eliminates the need for trimming and finishing the seams. The serger does this all in one step.

Because a serger does not backstitch, you will need a way to secure the seam ends. Using a **tapestry** (TAP-uh-stree) needle — a needle with a large eye and a blunt point — thread the chain of serger stitches through the needle eye and pull it under the looper threads of the seam about 1 inch (2.5 cm). Trim off any excess chain.

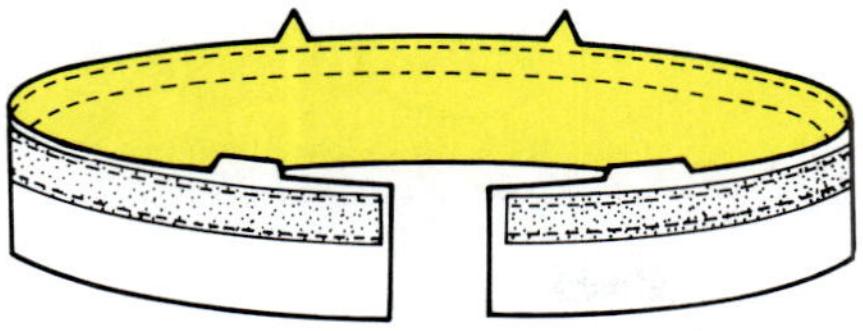

Waistband — Step 3

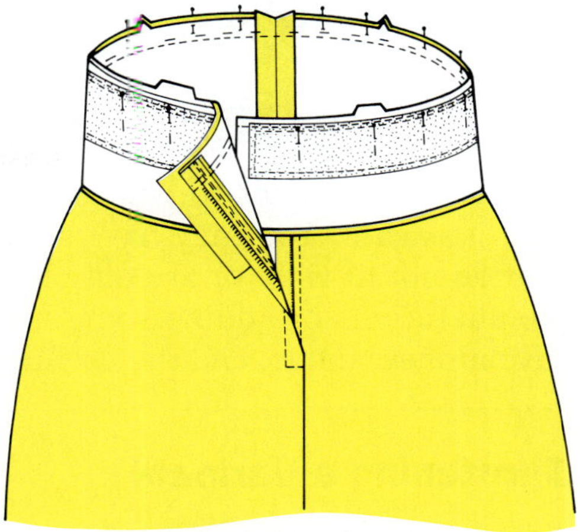

Waistband — Step 5

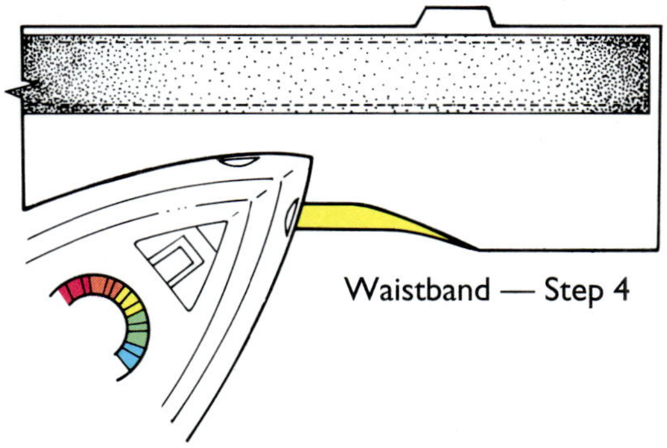

Waistband — Step 4

6. Stitch on the seam line from one end of the waistband to the other. Backstitch on both ends. Grade the seam. Trim the waistband seam allowance to ¼ inch (6 mm) and the garment seam allowance to ⅜ inch (1 cm). Press the seam flat and then up toward the waistband.
7. Fold the waistband in half lengthwise with right sides together. Pin and stitch the seam at each end of the waistband. The stitching will be even with the folded edge of the zipper on the overlap. The underlap will be longer. Trim the seams to ¼ inch (6 mm). Trim the corners diagonally being careful not to cut the stitching.
8. Turn the waistband right side out. Check to be sure the corners are square. Press along the fold line.
9. Pin the unnotched side of the waistband to the seam allowance on the inside of the garment. Slipstitch the turned edge to the waistline seam.

SUCCESSFUL SERGING

Finishing a Waistband

Instead of pressing under the unnotched side of a waistband to finish it, try a serged finish. Simply serge off the seam allowance on the unnotched edge. This provides a smooth finish and takes more bulk out of the waistband seam.

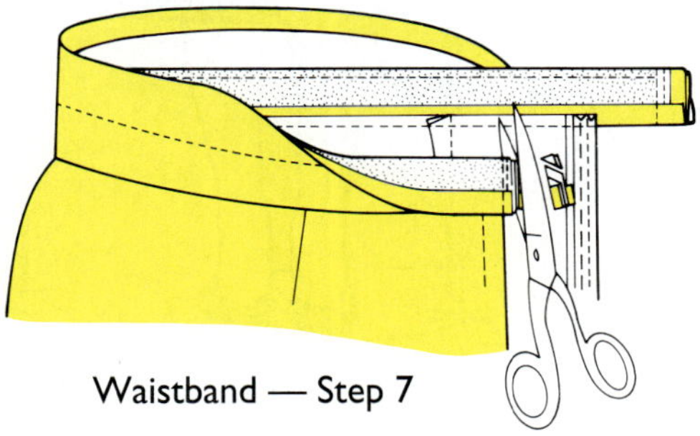

Waistband — Step 7

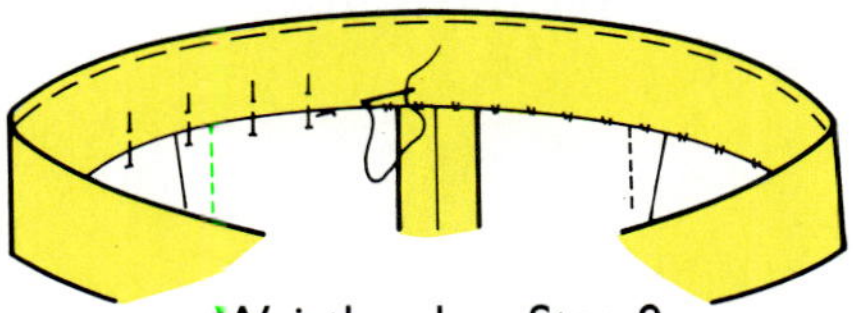

Waistband — Step 9

How to ...

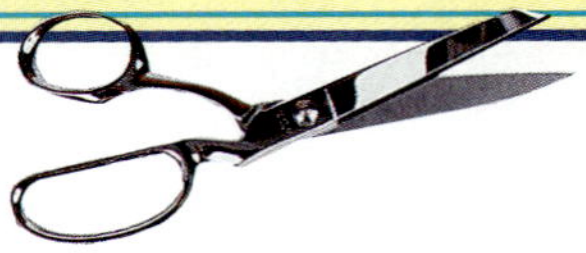

Alter and Recycle Clothing

Recycling means to change something into an item you can use again. You may have some garments in your closet that do not fit right or are out of style. By making some simple alterations or adding some trim, you can prevent waste, save money, and extend the usefulness of a garment.

Shortening a Garment

1. Remove the old hem stitching, and press out the crease.
2. Put on the garment and have someone mark the bottom of the hem.
3. Turn the hem to the inside along the new hemline. Pin the hem in place, matching the seams.
4. Baste the hem close to the folded edge. Try the garment on once more to make sure the hem length is correct.
5. Measure and mark the desired hem depth. Trim off the extra fabric.
6. Finish the raw edge of the hem.
7. Pin the top of the hem to the garment.
8. Machine or hand stitch the hem to the garment. Remove the basting. Press.

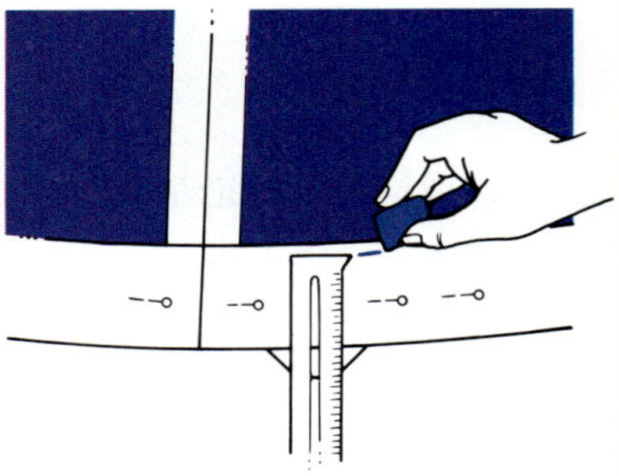

Lengthening a Garment

Follow the same steps for lengthening as you did for shortening hems. Creases from old hemlines may not always press out. A decorative trim or band of contrasting fabric may help cover the old hemline.

If the new hem allowance is too narrow, sew wide hem facing tape to the hem edge to create a new hem allowance.

Turn the hem facing tape to the inside and press. Hand or machine stitch the hem facing tape to the garment.

Adjusting Width

Small width adjustments can be made at the side seams of a garment. Here are some guidelines for adjusting width.

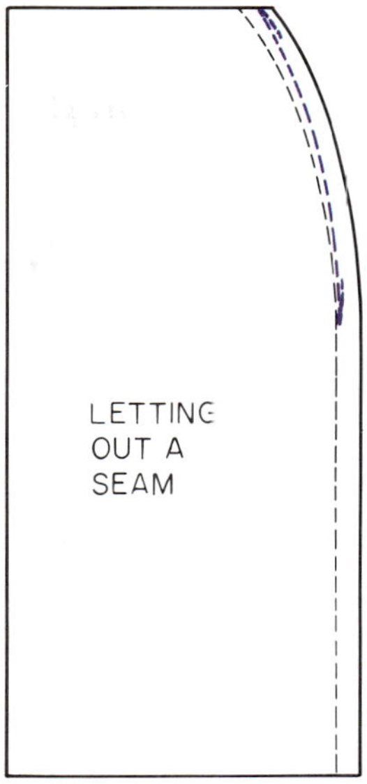

- **Making a garment larger.** Check the seam allowances to be sure there is enough fabric for new seams. Remove the old stitching in the seam section to which the width will be added. Try the garment on inside out and have someone pin the new seams. Machine baste the seams. Try the garment on to check fit. Stitch the new seams with a regular stitch length, carefully tapering the stitching into the old seam line. Backstitch at each end of the seam. Remove the basting. Press the seam open.
- **Making a garment smaller.** Put the garment on inside out and have someone pin the new seams on each side of the garment. Machine baste along the pin line, removing the pins as you stitch. Try the garment on to check fit. Stitch the new seams using a regular machine stitch, carefully tapering the new stitching into the old seam. Remove the basting stitches and old seam line. Press the seams open.

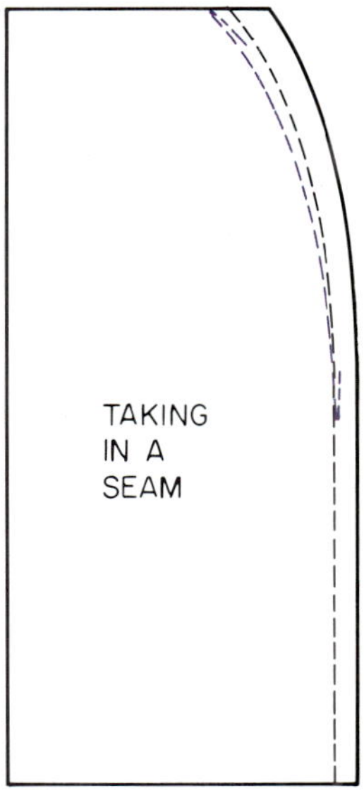

More Tips for Recycling Clothing

- Pass a garment on to another family member.
- Have a clothing swap with your friends.
- Sell used clothing at a garage sale, bazaar, flea market, or secondhand store.
- Recycle fabric from clothing that can no longer be worn. Make accessories, clothing for children, or craft projects. What accessories could you make from an old pair of jeans?

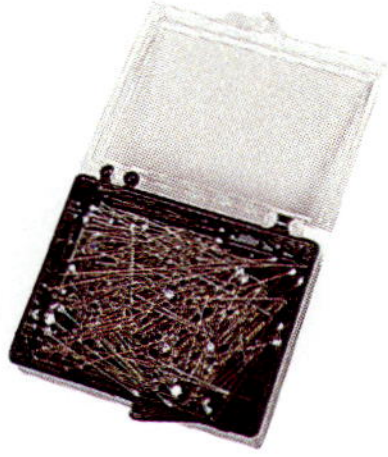

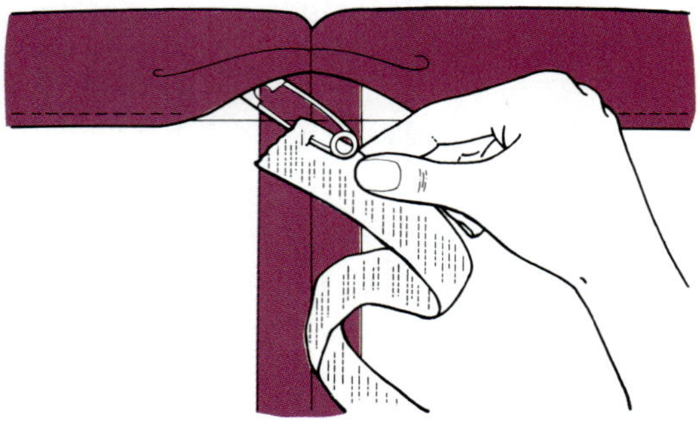

Elastic Waistband — Step 5

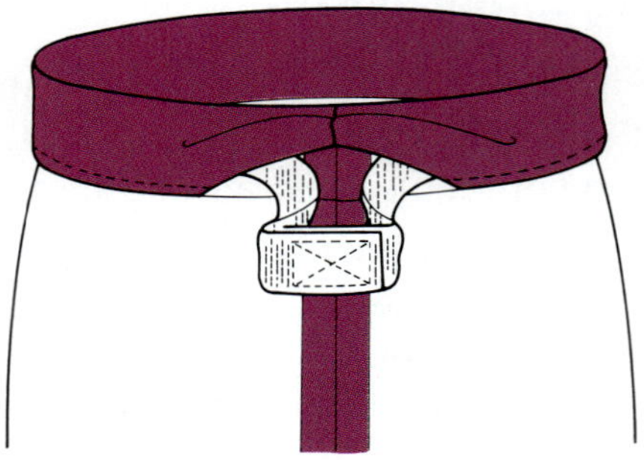

Elastic Waistband — Step 6

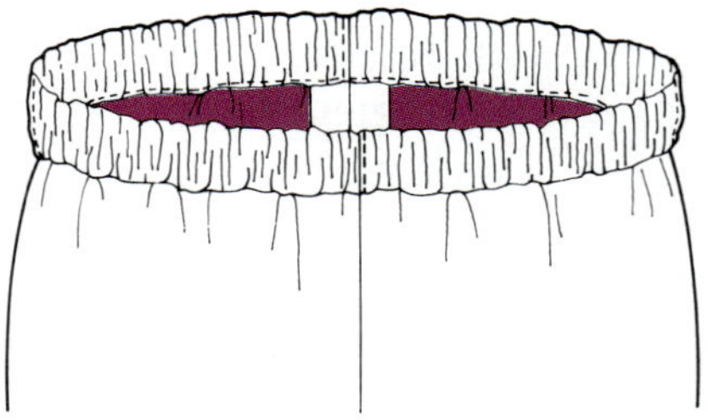

Elastic Waistband — Step 8

▼ Elastic Waistbands ▼

The elastic waistband is popular in both pants and skirts because it allows movement and is comfortable. The directions given here are for making a casing that is 1 inch (2.5 cm) wide, which will enclose ¾ inch (2 cm) wide elastic.

1. Use a zigzag stitch (or serge) around the top edge of the garment if the raw edges need to be finished.
2. Fold the waistline edge of the garment over 1¼ inches (3.2 cm), matching the wrong sides together to form a casing. Press the folded edge.
3. Stitch a seam 1 inch (2.5 cm) from the folded edge of the casing. Begin stitching at the center back or side seam. Leave a 1½ inch (3.8 cm) opening to insert elastic. Backstitch at each end of the seam.
4. Cut a piece of elastic to fit snugly around your waist. Remember, it must be able to slide over your hips. Add 2 inches (5 cm) to overlap and stitch the elastic together.
5. Put a safety pin in one end of the elastic. Insert the pin and elastic into the opening in the casing. Pull the pin and elastic through the casing, using the pin to guide the elastic. Hold onto the loose end of the elastic.
6. Overlap the elastic ends 1 inch (2.5 cm). Machine stitch the overlap securely in a square pattern.
7. Stitch the opening of the casing closed. Backstitch at each end of the opening.

8. Adjust the fabric evenly around the elastic waistband. Stitch through the casing and elastic at all seam lines, backstitching to secure all stitching. This will prevent the elastic from twisting in the casing.

Casings can be used at sleeve edges, necklines, and hemlines, as well as waistlines. The elastic makes the garment adjustable. It also helps to control fullness. Casings are much easier to make than attached waistbands or cuffs. You will find casings used in many beginner and easy-to-sew patterns.

▼ Drawstring Waistbands ▼

Drawstring closures are popular on many types of sport clothes. Drawstring openings that are in the seam are made as you sew the seam. Here are the guidelines for a drawstring casing:

1. At the seam where the drawstring is to be pulled through to the outside, stitch 1¼ inches (3.2 cm) of the seam starting at the top of the garment. Backstitch at both ends.
2. Leave a ¾ inch (2 cm) opening in the seam below the 1¼ inch (3.2 cm) stitched seam. Complete the seam below the ¾ (2 cm) opening. Backstitch at both ends of the seam.
3. Fold ¼ inch (6 mm) of the top edge of the garment to the inside. Press.
4. Fold the top edge of the garment over 1 inch (2.5 cm) to the inside, forming a casing. Press along the fold line. Stitch close to the lower edge of the casing. Backstitch at the beginning and end of the stitching.
5. Put a safety pin in one end of the drawstring. On the outside, insert the pinned drawstring through the casing opening and pull the drawstring through the opening. (Be sure to hold on to the loose end of the drawstring so it will not be pulled through). Tie a knot in each end of the drawstring. Distribute the fullness evenly.

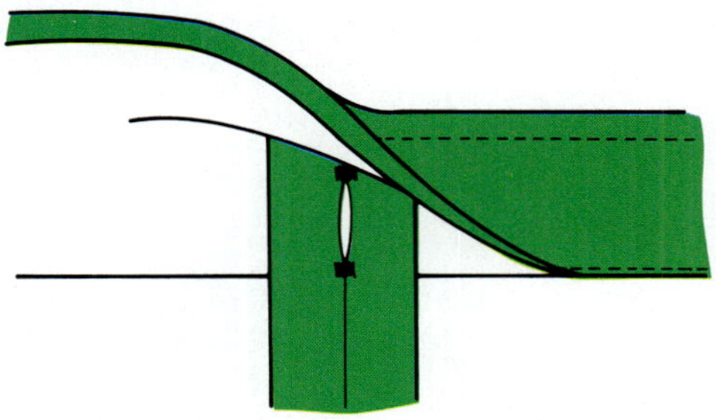

Drawstring Waistband — Step 2

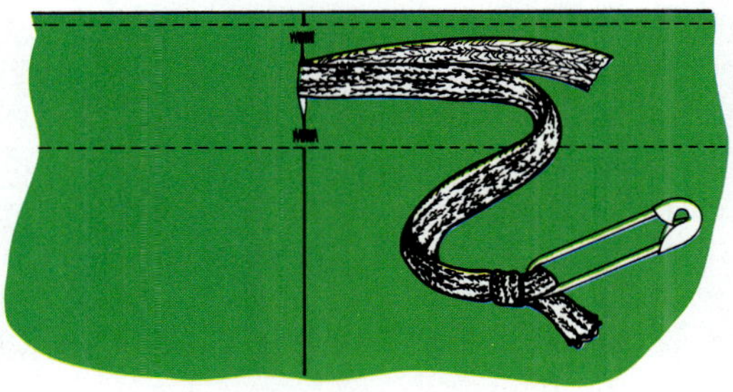

Drawstring Waistband — Step 5

Successfully finishing a sewing project builds your self-esteem and gives you a sense of accomplishment.

TAKING ACTION

Mrs. Carlisle asks you to help her teach beginners in an adult education sewing class. The class includes people of all ages who are learning to sew for the first time.

Mrs. Carlisle has asked you to come up with an idea for a simple yet appealing project. What sewing project (other than an item of clothing) would appeal to people of various ages? The project should include one or more basic sewing techniques. You will be assisting with a small group of the students after Mrs. Carlisle gives some basic instructions. Remember to keep your own skill level in mind in choosing a project.

Using Your Resourcefulness

- Brainstorm a list of possible nonclothing sewing projects suitable for beginners. What skills will be needed to complete these projects?
- What interests and needs should you consider in selecting a project?
- What resources could you use to find out more about the interests and needs of people of different ages?
- What other qualities or skills in addition to sewing skills would make your efforts in Mrs. Carlisle's class a success?

Chapter 36 Review

Summary

In this chapter, you have read about:

- Using an adjustable zipper foot to attach lapped zippers to garments.
- Sewing set-in sleeves and kimono sleeves.
- Making attached, elastic, and drawstring waistbands.
- Recycling and updating your clothes.

Facts to Recall

1. Describe how interfacing is attached to a collar.
2. How do you keep the seam from showing on a finished collar?
3. When first sewing a seam that will include a lapped zipper, at what point do you change from a regular to a basting stitch and why?
4. Explain how set-in sleeves are attached and fitted to a garment before they are stitched in place.
5. How do you insert the elastic into the casing when making an elastic waistband?
6. Name three benefits of recycling clothing.
7. If you are lengthening a garment and find that the new hem allowance is too narrow, what can you do to make it wider?

Ideas to Explore

1. On what types of garments might kimono sleeves be more suitable than set-in sleeves?
2. What garments do you own that could be updated or recycled for another use? How would you do this?
3. How will accurately performing the sewing techniques discussed in this chapter increase your self-esteem?
4. Give three examples of ways the sewing techniques discussed in this chapter could be used in making clothing for people with special needs (such as someone in a wheelchair, someone with a broken arm, a teen with juvenile arthritis, etc.).

Activities to Try

1. If your project does not include a casing with elastic, make a sample casing to fit your wrist out of some scrap fabric. Practice putting in the elastic and securing it to fit your wrist.
2. Draw a cartoon to illustrate a variety of ways to recycle clothing or the fabric used in clothing.
3. Locate drawings or photographs of different collar shapes using a pattern catalog or sewing book. Trace and cut out at least six collars. Using an illustration of a person wearing a shirt, try the different collars around the neck. Which collars look best? What reasons can you give for some collars looking better than others? Write a brief summary of your findings.

LINK TO *Art*

SEWING TECHNIQUES AND CLOTHING DESIGN

Fashion designers use the principles of design to create unique and attractive clothing. Look in fashion magazines, catalogues, and newspapers to find examples of the following advanced construction techniques that creatively use the principles of design: collars, zipper closings, set-in sleeves, kimono sleeves, elastic waistbands, and drawstring waistbands.

Arrange an attractive display (such as on a bulletin board) that illustrates how these techniques create interest in clothing design. Create an appealing caption.

CAREER *Connections*

Get Ready for Your Future Through Volunteering

Meredith

"When I think about it, I've been working with clothing in some way since I was in fifth grade. My mom couldn't afford to buy the clothes that I wanted, but she gladly bought patterns and fabric and taught me how to sew. Now I use these skills in my volunteer work at the *Community Clothes Closet*.

"I started working at the *Community Clothes Closet* for my FHA volunteer project. We take in donated clothing and sell it at a minimal charge to people who can't afford new clothing prices. Several days each month are *free* days, when people can come and take the clothing they need at no charge.

"Some of my responsibilities are sorting through incoming clothing, looking for anything that needs minor repairs, and making the repairs before the clothing is offered for sale. This is a practical way to put my skills to use.

"I know that I'd like to have a clothing-related career in the future. The choices in this field are many, but I am seriously considering learning how to restore antique clothing and design clothing for people with disabilities. Whatever type of job I decide on, I feel confident that I will succeed, because I will be doing something that I love."

Nicholas

"My wife and I used to tease each other about working together one day, but I didn't take the idea seriously until Maureen came up with a brainstorm. She'd worked for a children's wear designer for several years and wanted to branch out on her own. She did some informal market research, which seemed to show that children's athletic clothing was a fast-growing market. I'd had some marketing and manufacturing experience. Maureen's idea seemed solid.

"We started small, working out of our home. Maureen had a few friends help out part-time making samples. I made contacts for supplies, sales, and kept our books. Maureen uses a computer program (CAD, for computer-aided design) to help develop her ideas and get them quickly on paper.

"Now after several years, we sell to stores around the country. We lease part of a small factory and have 25 full-time employees. The business has grown, and we've grown personally in these last few years."

"My official title is sales associate; however, some people call me a salesperson. This job involves so much more than showing customers to the size they need or ringing up a sale. Customers sometimes need help selecting an outfit for a special occasion, or they want to know the latest trend in colors. It's very rewarding to know you have helped someone find an outfit that enhances their best features and makes them feel good about their appearance.

"My experience here will also be valuable if I want to explore other careers in the fashion industry. For example, the information I'm learning about trend cycles and people's likes and dislikes in clothing will help me if I decide to become a merchandise buyer. Developing my ability to communicate with customers could lead to a job in public relations. My current job offers a lot of training, not only for my career but also for life."

MAKING THE CONNECTION

- In what ways does Meredith seem to have high self-esteem? How does Meredith's volunteer work contribute to her self-esteem? How will it help her succeed at work?
- In what other ways did Meredith benefit from her volunteer work?
- How can working as a volunteer be a benefit to a future entrepreneur?
- In what ways can you use the clothing skills that you have as a volunteer?

UNIT 6 Foods

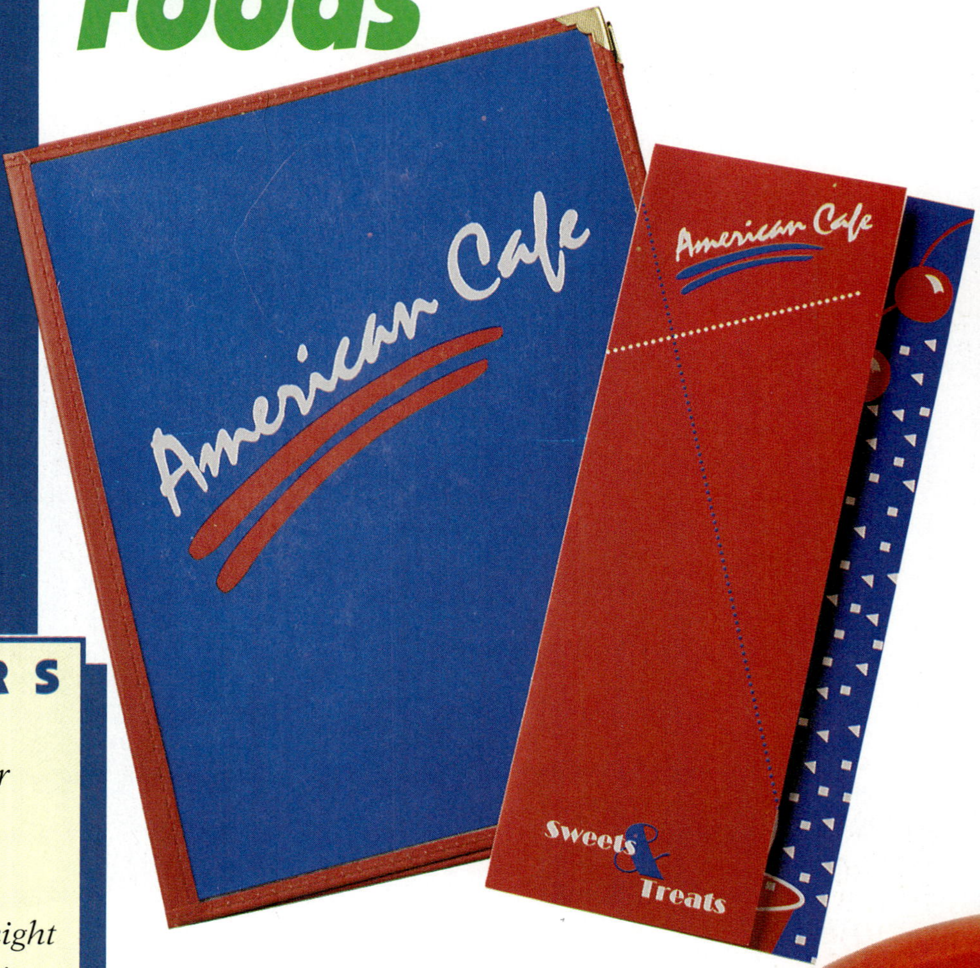

CHAPTERS

CHAPTER

37 Staying Healthy

OBJECTIVES

- *Describe ways to promote physical, mental, emotional, and social health.*
- *Explain the dangers of tobacco, alcohol, and other drugs and how to avoid them.*
- *Identify safety and family health care concerns.*

TERMS TO LEARN

- ***health***
- ***wellness***
- ***aerobic exercise***
- ***immunizations***

How would you define good health? Some people might answer "Not being sick" or "Being in good physical shape." There is more to it than that, however.

Health refers to the total state of your well-being. It includes:

- Physical health — the condition of your body.
- Mental and emotional health — as reflected in your thoughts, attitudes, and feelings.
- Social health — as reflected in your relationships with others.

Physical, mental, emotional, and social health are interrelated. All are affected by your day-to-day actions and decisions. For instance, one night Gary didn't get very much sleep. The next day he felt grouchy and irritable. He didn't do as well on the math test or run as fast at track practice as he could have. He even snapped at his best friend Roger, who avoided him the rest of the afternoon. How would you rate Gary's overall health that day?

Sharing time with and getting support from friends is essential for wellness. In what ways do you get support from others?

Some Signs of Good Health

Physical

- Having enough energy for all your daily activities
- Looking and feeling your best

Mental and Emotional

- Feeling good about yourself
- Expressing your emotions in a mature way
- Being able to handle problems and manage stress

Social

- Getting along with others
- Giving and getting support when needed

Wellness

Fortunately, you can do something about your health. **Wellness** is a way of living based on healthful attitudes and actions. It means taking an active role in improving and maintaining your health.

Choosing healthful foods helps you maintain your physical health.

Practicing wellness can have a positive effect on your life right now. It can help you look, feel, and perform your best. In addition, the choices you make today will influence the quality of your life in the future. Taking care of your health can help you reach your future goals.

Good Habits for Physical Health

Your body is the only one you will ever have. How well do you take care of it? Everyday habits such as eating, exercising, and sleep influence your physical health.

Eating Right

The food choices you make have a direct effect on your health. Every section of your body — skin, hair, teeth, nails, and blood — was once food! Your body uses food for energy, for growth, and to keep all its systems working properly.

Experts advise eating a variety of foods including lots of grains, fruits, and vegetables. In later chapters, you will learn more about making wise food choices.

Exercise

A regular exercise program helps to keep you physically fit. Exercise helps your body work more efficiently and adds firmness and tone to your muscles. It can also help you get rid of tension, sleep better, and feel more alert and energetic.

You need a variety of activities to benefit your body in different ways. A total exercise program works on all four of these elements:

- ***Heart and lungs.*** Your heart, lungs, and blood vessels deliver oxygen to your body tissues. You can train them to work more efficiently with regular aerobic exercise. **Aerobic exercise** (uh-ROE-bik) is any vigorous activity that causes your heart to beat faster for a sustained amount of time. Jumping rope, running, cycling, swimming, and walking are good aerobic exercises.
- ***Muscular endurance.*** This is the ability of your muscles to work for a long time without stopping. Most aerobic activities also improve muscular endurance.

- ▶ ***Muscular strength.*** Strength is what enables your muscles to push or pull with force. Having strong muscles can also improve posture and help prevent injury. Strengthening exercises work specific muscles of the body. For example, sit-ups strengthen the stomach muscles.
- ▶ ***Flexibility.*** This means the ability to move easily. You should be able to move muscles and joints through their normal range of motion without pain or stiffness. Slow, gentle stretching exercises help improve flexibility.

Getting regular exercise helps keep you physically fit. What activities do you participate in that benefit your heart and lungs, muscular endurance, muscular strength, and your flexibility?

An Exercise Program for You

In order to get the most benefit from exercise, you should make it a regular habit. Remember to include all four elements of fitness in your program. However, you don't have to work on all four every day. Here are some guidelines for planning your exercise program.

- ▶ Include aerobic exercise three to five times a week. Each session should consist of at least 20 minutes of brisk, nonstop activity.
- ▶ Include a strength-building session two times a week. Be sure to work all the major muscle groups: chest, stomach, back, legs, and arms. Allowing at least 48 hours between strength workouts lets the muscles rest and build new tissue.
- ▶ Perform stretching exercises several times a week. You might do them before and after your workouts or before going to bed.

SAFETY CHECK ✓

To keep your workouts safe:

- Find out how to perform each exercise or activity correctly. Ask an instructor to show you, or read a reliable exercise guide.
- Drink plenty of water before, during, and after vigorous exercise.
- Begin each exercise session with a warm-up period. A warm-up prepares your body for the activity to come and helps prevent injury. You might march in place for a few minutes to warm your muscles, then do some stretching exercises. Finally, begin a "light and easy" version of the activity you are preparing for. After about ten minutes, you should be ready to exercise at your normal pace.
- End each exercise session with a cool-down period. Otherwise, you may feel lightheaded and muscles may cramp or tighten up. Gradually reduce the level of your activity to let your body slow down. Then stretch again to help prevent soreness.
- Don't overdo. If you feel any dizziness, nausea, or sharp pain while exercising, stop. If you feel exhausted after a workout, have trouble sleeping, or are not making progress in your exercise program, you may be trying to do too much.

It's easier to stick with an exercise program if you select activities that you enjoy. To keep from getting bored, vary your activities from time to time.

Lack of time or money should not keep you from exercising. Running, walking, and jumping rope are inexpensive and can be done almost anytime.

Think of ways to change your lifestyle to include exercise. You might walk or ride a bike to school instead of taking a car or bus. Plan social activities that include exercise, such as basketball, roller skating, or bowling. Exercise with a friend or participate in an organized team sport. Make exercise a lifelong habit and you will reap the rewards for many years.

Sleep and Rest

Sleep is important for good health. While you sleep, your body repairs itself, removes waste products from cells, and builds a supply of energy for the next day's activities.

You may think that you can do more if you sleep less. Actually, when you don't get enough sleep, it becomes harder to concentrate. It takes you longer to get things done.

Most people need seven to nine hours of sleep a night. Teens often need more because of rapid growth. If you have trouble getting up in the morning or feel tired during the day, try going to bed earlier. It may make a big difference in the way you feel.

Adequate sleep and rest play an important role in wellness. Is the amount of sleep you get each night adequate?

Other Health Habits

There are many other ways to promote your physical health. Most of these are a matter of "preventive maintenance" — taking simple steps now to avoid big problems later on. Here are some examples.

- Use adequate lighting for reading and other activities. Rest your eyes periodically by looking away from close work.
- Use a sunscreen to protect your skin.
- Protect your hearing by avoiding loud sounds. Turn down the volume when listening to the radio, stereo, or television.
- Make hygiene a habit. Follow the suggestions for good grooming in Chapter 27.
- Practice good posture. It will improve your appearance and allow you to stand, sit, or move without getting tired. Your organs, bones, and muscles will develop and function better.

Good posture improves your appearance and helps your body function better.

Mental, Emotional, and Social Health

Many of the skills discussed in other units of this book can help you improve your mental, emotional, and social well-being. For example, having a positive attitude can help you face challenges. Communicating and resolving conflicts can help you build strong relationships.

Learning how to manage stress is essential for a balanced, healthful life. As you learned in Chapter 4, you cannot avoid stress. You can, however, learn to deal with stress before it causes physical and emotional problems. Following the healthful habits already mentioned — such as eating right, exercising, and getting enough sleep — will help. Keep in mind these other ways to manage stress:

- Set aside time for the activities you enjoy and the people you enjoy being with.
- Spend a few minutes each day just relaxing.
- Try not to get upset over little things.
- Look on the bright side. Don't lose your sense of humor.
- When you have a problem, find someone to talk to. You might try going to a close friend, a family member, a member of the clergy, or a community counseling center.

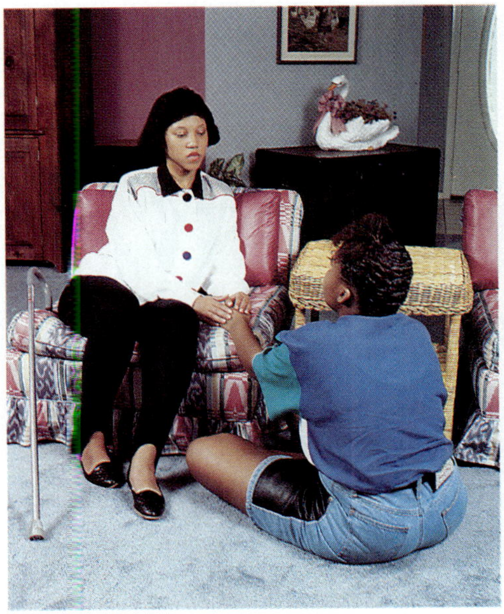

Talking about a problem with someone you trust is a healthful way to cope.

Avoiding Harmful Substances

Tobacco, alcohol, and other drugs are health abusers. They can cause serious problems for individuals, families, and society.

Tobacco

The use of tobacco products can shorten your life. Smokers have an increased risk of cancer, heart disease, and lung diseases. People who use chewing tobacco are increasing their risk of cancer of the mouth.

It is best never to begin smoking or chewing tobacco. However, once the habit is developed, it can be stopped with determination and effort.

Alcohol

It is illegal to sell alcohol to minors. Why? Alcohol has a number of negative effects that even many adults find hard to handle.

Alcohol is a depressant drug, a chemical that slows down the body's processes. The more people drink, the more they lose their sense of judgment. They cannot think clearly. Normal actions, such as hand movements, walking, and talking, become very clumsy.

Alcohol has a reputation as a killer. Medical science has proven there is a strong link between heavy drinking and heart disease, cancer, liver disease, and birth defects.

Drinking large amounts of alcohol can cut off the supply of oxygen to the brain, killing brain cells. Once brain cells are destroyed, they can't be replaced.

Drinking and driving is often a deadly combination. Alcohol is the nation's primary cause of traffic accidents, resulting in nearly half of all traffic deaths. Heavy drinking is also the cause of more than half of all home accidents.

For many people, it's easy to drink too much. Even though they aren't old enough to drink legally, some teens are alcoholics. They often deny they have a problem. Not only do they try to deceive others, but they often deceive themselves as well. Many drop out of school and, as a result, limit their future chances.

If you know someone who has an alcohol problem, encourage him or her to get help. See Chapter 14 for suggestions of where to find help for alcohol problems.

Avoiding harmful substances is a positive approach to maintaining wellness.

How to ...

Say "Yes" to Life and "No" to Drugs

You may face pressure to use harmful substances. What can you do?

- Learn the facts about tobacco, alcohol, and other drugs. The more you know about the harm these substances can do to you, the easier it will be to say "no" to them.
- Be alert to the signs of drug and alcohol use by friends. Try to persuade them to get help.
- Combat boredom. Take up a hobby, get a job, do volunteer work, or become active in school clubs.
- Learn how to have a good time with friends without using alcohol or other drugs.
- Decide ahead of time how you will handle the pressure to use harmful substances. Practice what you will say. NO is a powerful word. People won't like you more if you drink or take drugs. They will, however, respect you for not doing so.

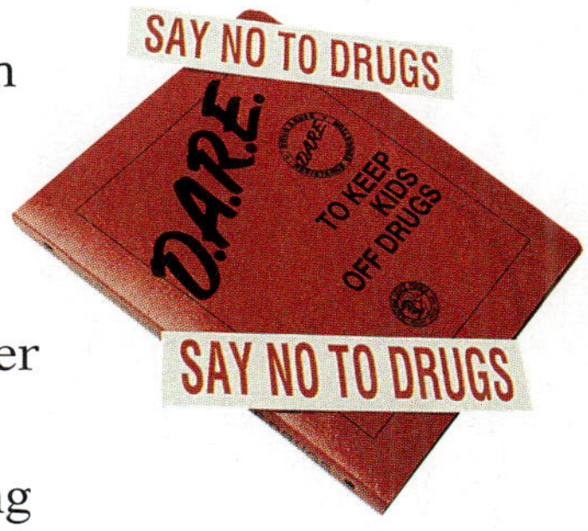

Other Drugs

Alcohol is not the only drug that can cause problems. Drug abuse occurs whenever a person:

- Uses an illegal drug, such as marijuana or cocaine.
- Misuses medicines by taking more than directed or a drug prescribed for someone else.
- Uses substances not intended to be taken into the body. Inhaling the spray from an aerosol can is an example.

People who abuse drugs are hoping for a pleasant effect. However, the effects of drugs can be most unexpected and unpleasant. The person may become confused or violent. Physically, drug abuse can damage the body and lead to death.

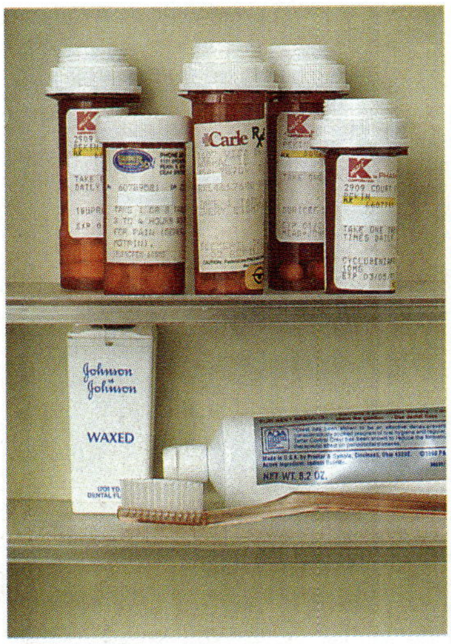

Use medicines safely as directed by your physician.

Many drugs are habit-forming. Over time, the body develops a physical and emotional need for the drug. Without it the person becomes ill. As the body becomes used to the drug, it may require more and more to produce the same effect.

Some people think that using drugs will help them escape their problems. In fact, drug use only causes new problems. At the same time, it reduces the person's ability to cope with life.

People who misuse or abuse drugs are not just hurting themselves. They are hurting the family members and friends who care about them. They hurt their employers because they cannot perform their jobs effectively. If the drug problem leads to an accident or crime, innocent people may be hurt or even killed. The cost of drug abuse to society is measured both in money and in human lives.

Overcoming a drug problem is not easy, but it can be done. See Chapter 14 for information on sources of help.

What steps are you taking to keep yourself safe?

Safety

It's easy to think, "Nothing could ever happen to me." However, accidents can and do occur. It's also true that most accidents can be prevented.

You have to take the lead in watching out for your safety. Safety is important 24 hours a day, in every situation. For example:

- ***At home.*** You are more likely to have an accident at home than anywhere else. Chapters 26 and 47 include important information on safety in the home. Many of these guidelines apply to other situations, too.
- ***At school or work.*** Schools and workplaces have rules for everyone's protection. Following the rules will help you avoid hurting yourself or others.
- ***In recreational activities.*** When you're having fun, it's easy to forget about safety. It can also be easy for accidents or injuries to occur. Always wear the proper protective gear, such as a helmet for bicycling or a life jacket for boating. Learn and follow the rules of your activity.
- ***On the road.*** Always wear a seat belt when driving or riding in a car. Obey traffic laws, whether you are driving, bicycling, or walking.

Safety also means protecting yourself against crime. When you are out, be aware of your surroundings. Notice where you are, who is around you, and what they are doing. Avoid unsafe areas, such as a poorly lit street, if at all possible.

TIPS: *Stocking a First Aid Kit*

Every first aid kit should include these basic items:

- Adhesive strip bandages, in a variety of shapes and sizes.
- Sterile gauze pads.
- Gauze rolls.
- Adhesive tape.
- Medicated soap.
- Antibiotic ointment.
- First aid manual.
- List of emergency telephone numbers.

Preparing for Emergencies

Having a list of emergency numbers next to the telephone is essential in crisis situations.

Prepare for an emergency before it occurs. Keep a list of emergency telephone numbers at your phone. In many areas, you can call 9-1-1 for fire, police, or medical emergencies. The telephone book has a listing of other hotline and crisis numbers.

If you call for help, the person answering your call will ask you important questions. Try to stay calm and state the facts.

You should also learn simple first aid for minor injuries. You can contact the local chapter of the American Red Cross. They can help you with basic information.

Family Health Care

Health care is an important consideration for families. An accident or illness may strike at any time. Children need **immunizations**, shots to protect against disease. Even if family members stay well, they should have regular medical and dental checkups and eye examinations. Planning and decision-making can help families meet their health care needs.

Depending on where you live, a number of different health care resources may be available. These might include hospitals, clinics, government and private agencies, and physicians. In addition, there may be ambulance and paramedic services that respond to emergencies. Families should be aware of the resources in their community, the services provided by each, and the relative costs.

Many people choose a family doctor to handle most of their health care needs. That way, one physician or group of physicians has information about each family member's medical history and special needs. If additional treatment is necessary, the family doctor refers the patient to another health care provider.

What health care resources might you and your family need?

Families should also keep their own health care records. These might include information about doctor visits, immunizations, allergies, and major illnesses.

Health care can be costly. Families can ease the financial burden by:

- Setting aside savings for unexpected medical costs.
- Learning about health care resources in their area.
- Obtaining health insurance. Although the insurance itself may be costly, it can be far less expensive than paying hospital bills. Many employers offer health insurance at low or no cost as a benefit to their workers.

Around the World

For over 100 years, people in Egypt have had an unusual source of health care — their barbers. A symbol of this practice was the white pole with a spiraling red stripe — a symbol still used by many barbers today. Since the 1880s, barbers have been licensed to practice basic medical care. They were given training to treat simple ailments such as coughs, stomach aches, and abscesses. Today, because of the rapid advancements in medicine, doctors must be more specialized. The one-stop service of the barber-surgeon of long ago has become a lost profession.

Long-Term Health Care Needs

Some family members may have long-term health care needs. For example, Ray's father takes medication for high blood pressure. Sonya has cerebral palsy and walks with crutches. Ladonna's grandmother has arthritis.

The impact of a long-term health problem on the family may be small or large. A family that works together to talk about their needs, examine their resources, and make the necessary adjustments is likely to meet the challenge successfully.

TAKING ACTION

Lately Gary seems different. You've known him since fifth grade. His family life has had its share of problems, but in the past he seemed able to handle it. Now he often seems depressed and moody.

The other day before school, you asked Gary how his weekend was. He told about going to a party and getting drunk. You've heard similar stories about Gary from others. This is happening more and more often.

It's obvious to you that Gary has a problem. As a friend, you want to help — but how? You're not sure how Gary will react if you try to talk with him. He usually listens to you and respects your advice, but he's not comfortable talking openly about his feelings. You don't want to put him off. Still, you feel you need to do something.

Using Your Resourcefulness

- What might happen if you talk to Gary about his problem? If you do nothing?
- What other possible courses of action can you think of?
- To whom might you go for help and advice?
- Your community may have resources that can help teens who abuse alcohol or have other problems. How could you find out about those resources?
- List the resources in your community that might be able to help in this situation. Include how a person could get in touch with them.
- After thinking about possible courses of action, what is the first step you would take in this situation?

Chapter 37 Review

Summary

In this chapter, you have read about:

- The meaning of health and wellness.
- Habits that help you maintain your physical health.
- Ways to promote mental, emotional, and social health.
- The dangers of tobacco, alcohol, and other drugs.
- How to prevent accidents and handle emergencies.
- Ways for families to meet their health care needs.

Facts to Recall

1. What is health? What is wellness?
2. Name three everyday habits that affect physical health.
3. How does aerobic exercise improve fitness?
4. Suggest three ways to incorporate exercise into daily routines.
5. How is sleep important to good health?
6. Name three ways of managing stress.
7. Name four negative effects of alcohol use or abuse.
8. Identify four ways alcohol and drug abuse is harmful to the user and to others.
9. Give an example of a guideline for personal safety.
10. Name two ways you and your family can prepare for emergencies.
11. Identify three health care resources available to families.

Ideas to Explore

1. In what ways do you think mental, emotional, and social health can affect physical health? Explain.
2. What motivates a person to choose a wellness lifestyle? Why do you think some people neglect their health?
3. Discuss this statement from the text: "Taking care of your health can help you reach your future goals."

Activities to Try

1. Design a cartoon or poster promoting wellness. It may encourage people to practice health habits, such as exercising and eating right, or discourage them from developing poor habits, like smoking and alcohol abuse.
2. In small groups, brainstorm a list of activities or events that add stress to your lives. Then make another list of healthful ways to relieve stress.
3. Write an exercise plan that fits the recommendations made in this chapter.

LINK TO *Math*

FIGURING YOUR TARGET PULSE RATE

The best way to figure out if you are exercising hard enough to benefit your heart and lungs is to check your pulse rate. Immediately after exercising, your pulse should fall within a range called your *target pulse rate*. This tells you your exercise is giving you a good aerobic workout. Here's how to figure your target pulse rate:

1. Subtract your age from 220.
2. Multiply the result of Step 1 by 70 percent (.70). This gives you the *lower* number for your target pulse rate.
3. Multiply the answer from Step 1 by 85 percent (.85) to find the *upper* number for your target pulse rate.

For the most benefit from exercise, try to keep your pulse rate within this range.

CHAPTER

38 Nutrients and Their Functions

OBJECTIVES

- *Identify six types of nutrients and their roles.*
- *Explain nutrient deficiencies.*
- *Describe digestion.*
- *Explain how to meet energy needs nutritiously.*

TERMS TO LEARN

- ***nutrients***
- ***carbohydrate***
- ***fiber***
- ***protein***
- ***legumes***
- ***cholesterol***
- ***deficiency***
- ***calorie***
- ***nutrient density***

"Wait a minute," Luis said as he stopped in front of the snack shop in the mall. His friends, Alex and Carolyn, waited patiently while Luis bought a pretzel with cheese sauce and a large soft drink. "That's the third time you've stopped for food," Carolyn said as Luis rejoined them. "Have you got a bottomless pit for a stomach?"

"I just didn't have time for breakfast or lunch today," Luis said. "But I figured I'd find plenty of food in this mall to fill me up — and I was right!"

Snacks can be fine, but Luis is forgetting something. Food is more than something that tastes good and fills you up when you're empty. It is your body's source of nutrients. **Nutrients** are substances that are found in foods and that the body needs in order to work properly. That's why choosing the right foods is so important.

The Nutrient Team

Your body needs nutrients for a number of jobs — energy, growth, repair, and basic processes. The six basic types of nutrients work together as a team. They are carbohydrates, proteins, fats, vitamins, minerals, and water. Each type of nutrient has a special role in keeping your body healthy.

Carbohydrates

Carbohydrates are the body's main source of energy. They consist of the starches and sugars in foods.

Sugars are also called *simple carbohydrates*. You don't need much sugar in your diet. Fruits, vegetables, and milk naturally contain a small amount of sugar plus other nutrients. Sugar is also added to some foods. Candy, soft drinks, and other sweets are high in added sugar and often lack more important nutrients.

Starches are also called *complex carbohydrates*. They should make up a large part of your diet. Good sources include breads, cereals, rice, pasta, dry beans and peas, and starchy vegetables such as potatoes and corn.

Many foods high in complex carbohydrates also contain fiber. **Fiber** consists of plant materials that do not break down completely when food is digested. Fiber is an important part of a healthy diet. It helps the body get rid of waste products and may have other health benefits as well. Whole-grain products, beans, fruits, and vegetables are good sources of fiber.

Carbohydrate foods are the main source of energy. They also contain fiber — an essential component in the digestive process.

Pocket Lab

Sugar Sleuth

MATERIALS:
food labels

EQUIPMENT:
none

Directions: Find the food(s) listing the largest number of sugars and sweeteners such as corn syrup and dextrose. Write down the food's name and ingredient list. Circle each form of sugar listed. Ingredients are listed on the label in order by weight — from greatest to least. Note which foods list sugars as one of the first three ingredients or include several sugars.

- What kinds of sugars and sweeteners did you find?
- What did this activity tell you about sugars in food?
- Which products appear to be high in sugar?

Every part of your body contains protein — your hair, your skin, and your internal organs such as your heart and lungs. Eating a variety of protein foods is essential to good health.

Proteins

Protein is a nutrient used to build and repair body tissues. It is important for other reasons, too. It helps regulate a number of body functions. Protein can also provide energy if your diet doesn't include enough carbohydrates.

Protein is made up of chemicals called *amino acids*. Different kinds of protein are made up of different combinations of amino acids.

There are about 22 known amino acids. The body manufactures all but nine of them. Those nine are called *essential amino acids*. It is essential you get them from the food you eat because your body can't make them.

Foods from animal sources — meat, fish, poultry, milk and milk products, and eggs — contain all of the essential amino acids. That is why these foods are called *complete proteins*.

Plant foods, such as grains, dry beans and peas, nuts, seeds, and some vegetables, also contain proteins. However, these proteins are lacking one or more of the essential amino acids. Therefore, they are called *incomplete proteins*.

To understand incomplete proteins, think of a safe with a combination lock. If you know only one or two of the numbers in the combination, you're locked out. If you have all three numbers, you can use them together to open the safe.

In the same way, your body cannot use one incomplete protein by itself. You need the right combination. To get complete protein from plant foods, you can:

- Combine two or more incomplete proteins which make up for each other's shortcomings. These food combinations are called *complementary proteins*.

- Combine an incomplete protein with a small amount of a complete protein food.

To find out more about combining proteins, read "How to Mix and Match Proteins" on pages 444-445.

Fats

Fats are the most concentrated form of food energy. They also carry the fat-soluble vitamins (A, D, E, and K) in the body. In addition, fats provide substances that your body needs for normal growth, reproduction, and healthy skin.

Foods such as butter, margarine, salad dressing, and sour cream add fats to the diet. Fats are also hidden in foods such as meat, fish, poultry, egg yolks, whole milk, cheese, pastry, and nuts. For most people, getting enough fat in the diet is easy. The challenge is to avoid getting too much.

There are two main types of fats:

- ***Saturated fats*** are solid at room temperature. They are found in animal foods such as meat, poultry, fish, egg yolks, and dairy products. Saturated fats are also found in tropical oils — coconut, palm, and palm kernel.
- ***Unsaturated fats*** are usually liquid at room temperature. They are found mainly in vegetable oils, with the exception of tropical oils.

While dietary fat is essential to a healthy diet, we need only one tablespoon (30 grams) per day. Yet many of the foods we eat are high in fat. How might you alter your food choices to include foods that are lower in fat?

Cholesterol and Saturated Fats

Cholesterol is a fat-like substance which the body uses to make necessary chemicals and to help in digestion. Your body manufactures all the cholesterol it needs.

Physicians can measure the amount of cholesterol in the bloodstream. When the level of certain types of cholesterol is high, there is a greater risk for heart disease. Therefore, health professionals advise people to reduce their cholesterol levels.

One way to reduce cholesterol in the bloodstream is to eat less cholesterol in foods. Cholesterol is found in foods from animal sources. Foods from plant sources are naturally cholesterol-free.

Another way to reduce cholesterol in the bloodstream is to cut down on fats, especially saturated fats. Researchers have discovered that saturated fats seem to raise the level of cholesterol in the blood.

Vitamins

In the early part of this century, researchers found that unknown substances seemed to be needed by the human body in very small amounts. These substances are now called vitamins.

How to ...
Mix and Match Proteins

You can mix and match proteins from different sources to round out those that are incomplete by themselves. The proteins can be eaten together or at another meal the same day. Here's how it works.

Plant Protein Plus Plant Protein

One of the easiest ways to get complete protein from plant foods is to combine grains with legumes. **Legumes** are a class of vegetable that is high in protein. Examples include dry beans, such as kidney beans; dry peas, such as split peas; and peanuts. The amino acids supplied by grains and legumes work together to give the body complete protein.

The chart below will help you mix and match plant proteins. Pick one food from each column and put them together for complete protein. Some ideas are given to help you get started.

Complementary Plant Proteins

Legumes:	Grains:
Peanuts	Whole-grain bread
Peanut butter	Enriched bread
Soybeans	Pita bread
Tofu	Bagels
Lentils	Tortillas
Black-eyed peas	Cornbread
Split peas	Other breads
Kidney beans	Pasta
Navy beans	Noodles
Pinto beans	Rice
Other dry beans and peas	Cereals

Possible Combinations:

Baked beans and cornbread
Peanut butter sandwich
Red beans and rice
Split-pea soup and bagel
Bean burrito

Plant Protein Plus Animal Protein

You can also make better use of plant proteins by combining them with a small amount of complete protein, such as meat, poultry, fish, eggs, milk, or cheese. For example, whole-wheat cereal contains incomplete protein. Milk contains complete protein. When you eat both cereal and milk, the complete protein in the milk helps your body make better use of the incomplete protein in the cereal.

Combining plant proteins with a small amount of complete protein is economical. It also adds variety to meals. Here are some examples:

- Macaroni and cheese
- Chicken noodle soup
- Spanish rice with diced ham
- Bean tostada and a glass of milk

How many other combinations can you think of?

Vitamins are chemicals that regulate body processes. Unlike carbohydrates, proteins, and fats, vitamins do not provide energy or become part of the body. However, a lack of vitamins can result in poor health. Generally, you get all the vitamins you need if you eat a variety of foods.

Vitamins can be grouped into two categories:

- ***Fat-soluble.*** Vitamins A, D, E, and K are taken into the body with foods containing fat. The body can store fat-soluble vitamins, so it does not have to depend on a day-to-day supply. If you get too much of vitamins A and D, the excess builds up in the body and can be harmful. This can happen if a person takes large doses of vitamin pills.
- ***Water-soluble.*** Vitamin C and the B-complex vitamins are water-soluble. Water-soluble vitamins are not stored in the body as fat-soluble vitamins are. Therefore, try to eat foods containing them every day. If you get too much of a water-soluble vitamin, the extra generally is passed out of the body in urine. Even so, very large doses may be harmful.

The charts on page 446 give more details about vitamins.

Choose a variety of foods daily to meet your need for vitamins.

AROUND THE WORLD

When you are eating a nutritious diet, it is easy to forget its importance. In some parts of India, however, many children die of malnutrition. Their families simply cannot afford to feed them properly. When these children were given a daily supplement of vitamin A, though, their death rate dropped by over 50% after just one year. To them, this one nutrient was literally the difference between life and death.

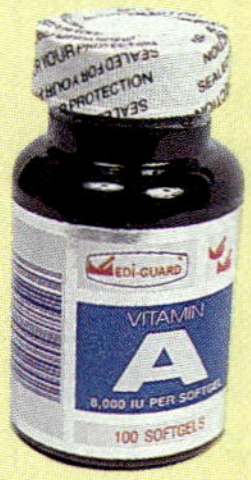

Fat-Soluble Vitamins

Vitamin	Sources	Functions
Vitamin A	▶ Dark green, leafy vegetables, such as spinach ▶ Deep yellow and orange fruits and vegetables, such as carrots, sweet potatoes, and apricots ▶ Liver ▶ Milk, cheese ▶ Eggs	▶ Helps keep skin and hair healthy ▶ Aids night vision ▶ Helps build strong bones and teeth
Vitamin D	▶ Milk with vitamin D added	▶ Helps build strong bones and teeth
Vitamin E	▶ Vegetable oils, margarine ▶ Whole-grain breads and cereals ▶ Dark green, leafy vegetables ▶ Dry beans and peas ▶ Nuts and seeds ▶ Liver	▶ Helps form red blood cells, muscles, and other tissues
Vitamin K	▶ Dark green, leafy vegetables ▶ Cabbage	▶ Helps blood to clot

Water-Soluble Vitamins

Vitamin	Sources	Functions
B-complex vitamins (including riboflavin, niacin, thiamine, B_6, and B_{12})	▶ Whole-grain and enriched breads and cereals ▶ Dry beans and peas, peanut butter, nuts ▶ Meat, poultry, fish ▶ Eggs ▶ Milk	▶ Help body use carbohydrates, fats, and proteins ▶ Help produce energy in cells ▶ Help maintain healthy nervous system, muscles, and tissues
Vitamin C	▶ Citrus fruits ▶ Many other fruits and vegetables, such as strawberries, broccoli, tomatoes, potatoes	▶ Helps maintain bones, teeth, blood vessels ▶ Helps heal wounds

▼ Minerals ▼

Your body needs a large number of minerals, but only in small amounts. If you look at the chart, "Some Important Minerals," you can see that minerals have two important jobs. They make up part of the hard and soft body tissue, and they assist in body functions.

If you eat a variety of foods every day, you will generally meet your mineral needs. Getting enough calcium is especially important to you at this point in your development. Calcium is an important part of the structure of your bones and teeth. Developing a good bone structure now is essential to having strong bones when you are older. If you do not drink milk or or eat milk products every day, it can be difficult to get enough calcium.

Some Important Minerals

Mineral	Sources	Functions
Calcium	▶ Milk and milk products ▶ Sardines, salmon (eaten with bones) ▶ Dark green, leafy vegetables ▶ Dry beans and peas	▶ Helps build and maintain strong bones and teeth ▶ Helps heart, muscles, and nerves work properly ▶ Helps blood to clot
Phosphorus	▶ Meat, poultry, fish ▶ Eggs ▶ Dry beans and peas, nuts ▶ Milk and milk products	▶ Helps build and maintain strong bones and teeth ▶ Helps body use carbohydrates, fats, and proteins
Iron	▶ Liver ▶ Red meats ▶ Egg yolks ▶ Dark green, leafy vegetables ▶ Dry beans and peas, nuts ▶ Whole-grain and enriched breads and cereals ▶ Dried fruits, such as raisins	▶ Helps enable red blood cells to carry oxygen to all parts of the body
Potassium	▶ Oranges and orange juice ▶ Bananas ▶ Dried fruits ▶ Dry beans and peas, peanut butter ▶ Meats	▶ Helps heart and muscles work properly ▶ Works with sodium, another mineral, to keep fluid balance in cells ▶ Helps regulate blood pressure

Drinking six to eight glasses of water a day is essential to good health. What beverages do you choose when you are thirsty? Why might water be a better choice?

Water

You can live longer without food than without water. Water is needed for digestion and to carry nutrients throughout the body. It also helps remove body waste and controls body temperature.

Foods with a high water content, such as soups, provide some of the water you need. The rest must come from the liquids you drink, such as milk, juice, and water. Do you drink the recommended six to eight glasses of liquid daily?

Deficiencies

When nutrients are not eaten in large enough amounts, a **deficiency**, or shortage, results. The symptoms, or effects, depend on the seriousness of the deficiency.

At first, the symptoms may not seem very serious. They may include tiredness or difficulty sleeping or concentrating. Colds or other illnesses may be more frequent. Nutrient deficiencies can also cause weight gain or weight loss.

If a deficiency becomes more serious, specific parts of the body can be affected, such as the skin, eyes, tongue, or bones. It depends on which nutrient is lacking.

The key to avoiding nutrient deficiencies is to eat a variety of foods daily. Each food has a different mix of the nutrients you need for good health.

Frequent illness may be a sign of a nutrient deficiency. Are you eating a variety of foods necessary for good health?

Digestion

In order to use the nutrients in food, your body must first digest the food. The digestive process begins when the thought, sight, aroma, and taste of food stimulates the flow of saliva. The chemicals in saliva, along with chewing, begin to break the food down.

Food moves from the mouth through the esophagus to the stomach. There digestive juices break the food down further. Food remains in the stomach an average of three to five hours, but that depends on the type of food. Carbohydrates are digested more quickly than proteins and fats.

From the stomach, the food moves to the small intestine. From there, the nutrients are absorbed into the bloodstream. Some nutrients are used as building materials, some for energy, and some are stored. Unneeded nutrients and any undigested food are eliminated as body waste.

Energy and Calories

Food supplies the body with energy. Some energy is needed for normal processes, such as breathing and pumping blood. You also need energy for all your activities.

Calories are units for measuring energy, just as inches measure length. Calories are used to measure both the energy you take in from food and the energy you use up.

How many calories you need daily depends on factors such as your age and activity level. Taking in more calories than needed causes weight gain, while taking in fewer calories than needed causes weight loss. Chapter 40 discusses weight management in more detail.

The number of calories you need depends on your age and activity level.

Meeting Your Energy Needs

The source of the calories you take in is also important. The energy in foods comes from fats, carbohydrates, and proteins. Vitamins, minerals, water, and fiber do not provide energy. Fat is the most concentrated source of energy with 9 calories per gram. Carbohydrates and proteins have 4 calories per gram. (A gram is a metric unit of weight.)

For good health, experts recommend that:

- At least 55 percent of the calories you take in should come from carbohydrates (mainly complex carbohydrates).
- About 15 percent of your calories should come from protein.
- No more than 30 percent of your calories should come from fat (mainly unsaturated fat).

Foods such as chips and soft drinks have low nutrient density. How might you change your food choices to increase the number of nutrient-dense foods?

▼ Nutrient Density ▼

When you choose foods, consider nutrient density. **Nutrient density** is a comparison of the nutrients in a food to the number of calories.

Foods such as candy, potato chips, and sugary soft drinks have low nutrient density. They add to your calorie intake, but contribute few important nutrients. Most of the nutrients they do supply are ones you probably don't need more of: fat and sugar.

Foods such as fruits, vegetables, whole grains, lean meats, and low-fat milk have high nutrient density. They do more than just help meet your energy needs. They also supply important nutrients such as proteins, vitamins, minerals, and fiber.

The way a food is prepared or served can make a difference in nutrient density. A plain baked potato, for instance, has higher nutrient density than french fries. Because they are cooked in oil, the french fries have more fat and calories.

Most of the foods you eat should be high in nutrient density. If you fill up on foods with low nutrient density, you may get too many calories and not enough of some nutrients. The next chapter will help you learn more about making wise food choices.

TAKING ACTION

The school cafeteria menu has been pretty much the same for as long as you can remember — sloppy joes, pizza, french fries, chocolate cake, and other traditional, popular items. Now the school board has decided some changes may be needed. In particular, the board members are concerned about foods that are high in fat and sugar. However, they also know that these foods are among the most popular. They want to be sure the revised menu will appeal to students.

The school board has asked the FHA/HERO (Future Homemakers of America/Home Economics Related Occupations) club to help with this project. You have been chosen to lead the committee that will work with Mrs. Ragusa, head of the school food service. Where do you begin?

Using Your Resourcefulness

- How can you identify the nutritional pros and cons of each menu item?
- Where can you find suggestions on how to prepare food with less fat and sugar?
- How can you find out students' feelings about specific foods?
- List the different resources, both material and human, that can help you get the information you need to offer useful suggestions.

Chapter 38 Review

Summary

In this chapter, you have read about:

- Sources and functions of important nutrients.
- How incomplete proteins can be combined to help meet your protein needs.
- What can happen if your diet lacks nutrients.
- How your body digests food to obtain nutrients.
- Recommendations for meeting your body's energy needs.

Facts to Recall

1. Name the six basic types of nutrients.
2. What are simple carbohydrates? Complex carbohydrates? Which is the most important part of a healthful diet?
3. What foods contain fiber? Why is fiber important to good health?
4. What foods are sources of complete proteins? Incomplete proteins?
5. What are the dangers of getting too much saturated fat?
6. What are vitamins? How do they differ from other nutrients such as proteins?
7. What mineral is especially important to teens for growth and development? Why?
8. Identify three early symptoms of a nutritional deficiency.
9. How does saliva help in digestion?
10. What do calories measure?
11. What percentage of calorie intake should come from carbohydrates? From proteins? From fats?
12. Explain the importance of nutrient density.

Ideas to Explore

1. What are some advantages of mixing and matching incomplete proteins to meet your protein needs?
2. Health experts recommend getting vitamins and minerals from foods rather than from pills. Why do you think this is so?

Activities to Try

1. In the chapter, find examples of how nutrients work together to perform related functions. Use your examples to write a paragraph on nutrient teamwork.
2. Carmen's food choices one day had a total of 85 grams of fat. How many calories does that equal? (Remember, one gram of fat has 9 calories.) If Carmen's total calorie intake that day was 2250 calories, what percentage of those calories came from fat? How does this compare with recommended guidelines?

LINK TO *Science*

Identifying Fat in Foods

Here's a simple experiment to check for the fat content in foods. Choose several different types of food (such as meat, french fries, potato chips, carrots, apple juice) to test. Cut as many 3-inch (7.5 cm) squares from a paper bag as you have foods. Rub each food on a paper square labelled with the food's name. Let the squares dry. Then hold each square up to a high-intensity lamp and observe the results.

- What effect did the different foods have on the paper?
- Can you determine the amount of fat in the different foods using this test? Explain.
- How may this information affect your food choices?

CHAPTER 39

Guidelines for Healthful Eating

OBJECTIVES

- *Identify and explain the Dietary Guidelines for Americans.*
- *Name the food groups in the Food Guide Pyramid and give recommended servings for each.*

TERMS TO LEARN

- ***Dietary Guidelines for Americans***
- ***obesity***
- ***Food Guide Pyramid***

You may not have control over all of the factors that influence your health. However, you do make choices about the foods you eat.

What can you use as guidelines in making healthful food choices? Not all of the guidelines you read or hear about are reliable. Two simple sets of guidelines, based on scientific evidence, come from the U.S. government. They are known as the Dietary Guidelines for Americans and the Food Guide Pyramid.

Dietary Guidelines for Americans

Health experts are continually studying the relationship between eating habits and health. They have found that poor eating habits contribute to many serious health problems, such as heart disease, high blood pressure, stroke, diabetes, and some forms of cancer. Fortunately, good eating habits can reduce the risk of these diseases.

The **Dietary Guidelines for Americans** were developed to help you make healthful food choices. They include these six simple suggestions:

- Eat a variety of foods.
- Maintain healthy weight.
- Choose a diet low in fat, saturated fat, and cholesterol.
- Choose a diet with plenty of vegetables, fruits, and grain products.
- Use sugars only in moderation.
- Use salt and sodium only in moderation.

These guidelines are suggested for healthy people ages two years and over. They are not for younger children and infants, since their food needs are different.

Eat a Variety of Foods

You need more than forty different nutrients for good health. (Some of the most important nutrients were discussed in Chapter 38.) No one food can supply all the nutrients in the amounts you need. For example, milk supplies calcium but no fiber. Whole-grain breads supply fiber but little calcium.

Eating a variety of foods is the best way to insure that you get all the nutrients you need. Later in this chapter, you will learn how to use the Food Guide Pyramid to plan varied food choices.

Which is the better snack choice, the apple or slice of apple pie? Why?

AROUND THE WORLD

In Canada, people are ordering fewer hamburgers when dining out. A recent survey has shown that in 1990, 13.5% of all meals ordered in restaurants included a hamburger, compared to 17.1% in 1985. In that same period, the percentage of meals including chicken rose from 11.2% to 16.1%. How might this be related to a growing concern about eating more healthfully?

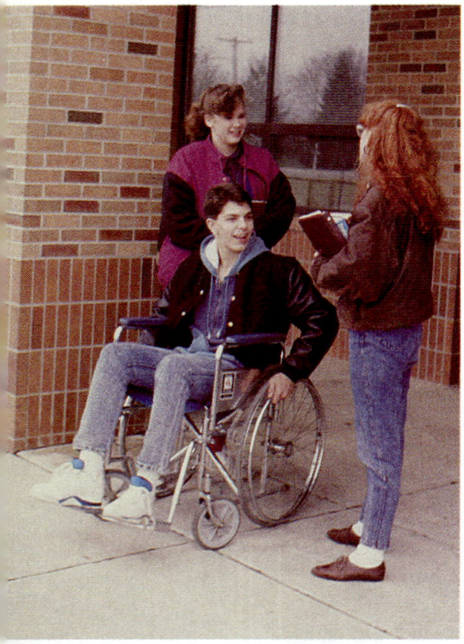

Maintaining a healthy weight may reduce potential health problems.

▼ Maintain Healthy Weight ▼

If you are too heavy or too thin, your chances of developing health problems increase. Somewhere between those two extremes there is a healthy weight for you.

Researchers are still trying to define "healthy weight" more exactly. They do know there is no magic number that is right for everyone. Whether your weight is a healthy one for you depends on factors such as:

- Your age, height, and gender (male or female).
- How much of your weight comes from body fat compared to muscle, bone, and other lean tissue. Having too much body fat is called **obesity**. It is linked to a number of health problems.
- Whether you or others in your family have high blood pressure or other weight-related medical problems.

Many people who think they have a weight problem actually do not. However, someone who is truly overweight, obese, or underweight is taking serious chances with his or her health. If you feel concerned about your weight, check with your doctor. Chapter 40 gives more information and suggestions for managing your weight.

Choose low-fat foods for health.

▼ Choose a Diet Low in Fat, Saturated Fat, and Cholesterol ▼

Although fat is an essential nutrient, most Americans eat more than they need. Too much saturated fat and cholesterol in the diet increases the risk for heart disease. High-fat diets also contribute to obesity. Therefore, the Dietary Guidelines recommend cutting down on fat — especially saturated fat — and cholesterol.

Fortunately, eating the low-fat way can be not only healthful, but easy and good-tasting. For suggestions, read "How to Lower the Fat" on page 455.

How to . . .

Lower the Fat

Health experts recommend that you get no more than 30% of your calories from fat. This guideline applies to your eating habits as a whole, not individual foods or meals. Eating less fat doesn't mean you have to give up favorite foods. Here are some suggestions you may want to try.

- Choose skim or low-fat milk instead of whole milk.
- Eat meat in moderation. One serving is just 2 to 3 ounces (55 to 85 grams) of cooked meat. Vary your protein sources, making sure to include dry beans and peas, poultry, and fish as well as meat.
- When buying meat, choose lean cuts. Some examples are beef round steak or ground round, pork tenderloin, and veal. Also look for "Select" or "Lean" on the meat label. Cut down on luncheon meats, bacon, and sausage.
- Trim the fat off meat before cooking or eating.
- Take the skin off chicken or turkey before eating. White meat has less fat than dark meat.
- Eat light-colored fish. Darker fish usually has a higher fat content.
- Buy tuna packed in water. If you buy oil-packed tuna, rinse off the oil.
- Try broiled, baked, or steamed foods. Avoid those that are fried.
- Add less butter, margarine, mayonnaise, and gravy to foods.
- Use plain yogurt instead of sour cream in dips and on potatoes.
- Look for low-fat products when buying foods such as salad dressings.
- Go easy on foods such as hard cheese, nuts, and peanut butter. They are nutritious, but high in fat.

▼ Choose a Diet with Plenty of Vegetables, Fruits, and Grain Products ▼

Do you know why this guideline was included? Vegetables, fruits, and grain products have so many benefits that it would be hard to eat too many of these foods.

- They are high in complex carbohydrates and usually low in fats. By eating vegetables, fruits, and grain products more often, you can increase carbohydrates and decrease fats in your diet.
- They are good sources of fiber, which you need for good health. Scientists are continuing to research the benefits of fiber.
- They are high in vitamins and minerals.

In addition to great taste, fruits, vegetables, and grain products supply your body with many important nutrients.

▼ Use Sugars Only in Moderation ▼

Sugar is added to many foods, such as ice cream, candy, cakes, pastries, and sweetened cereals. Although sugar is a nutrient, it is not needed in large amounts. It's more important to get plenty of complex carbohydrates and enough vitamins, minerals, and protein. Eating foods with a high amount of sugar added may limit the number of other, more nutritious foods you eat. It might also cause you to gain too much weight.

Eating too many sweet foods can also contribute to tooth decay. The longer sugary or starchy foods stay in the mouth before teeth are brushed, the greater the chance that cavities will develop.

Most regular soft drinks contain one teaspoon of sugar per ounce. What other beverages would be better choices on a regular basis?

TIPS: *Flavoring Foods for Lower Sodium*

If you automatically reach for the salt shaker to season foods, consider these low-sodium or no-sodium alternatives:

- Buy or make your own salt-free seasoning blends, for example, a combination of lemon pepper, garlic powder, basil, and thyme.
- Flavor vegetables with lemon or lime juice, or with flavored vinegars.
- Baste meats with fruit purées or preserves to enhance flavor. Try cranberry sauce on pork or poultry.
- Use bottled teriyaki sauce instead of soy sauce for a savings of 260 milligrams of sodium per tablespoon.

Use Salt and Sodium Only in Moderation

Most Americans eat more salt and sodium than they need. In addition to table salt sprinkled on food, sodium is added during the processing and manufacturing of food.

Eating too much sodium seems to increase the risk of high blood pressure in some people. You can cut down on sodium by:

- Flavoring foods with herbs or spices instead of salt.
- Eating salty foods less often and in smaller amounts.
- Reading labels and choosing foods lower in sodium.

Pocket Lab: Shaking the Habit

MATERIALS:
plate covered with waxed paper; salt shaker; ingredient and nutrition labels

EQUIPMENT:
none

Directions: About one-third of the average person's daily intake of sodium comes from salt added to food in cooking or at the table. Try this test: Salt the covered plate as you would if it contained food. Collect the salt and measure it. If you used about 1/8 teaspoon, that amounts to 250 milligrams of sodium. Much of the sodium we consume is found in processed foods. Sodium is also naturally present in many foods such as oatmeal. Check the ingredient and nutrition labels for a variety of foods and specifically look for the words salt and sodium.

- Did you use more salt than you expected?
- Which foods have added salt?
- Which foods are high in sodium?
- How could you cut back on sodium in your diet?

Food Guide Pyramid
A Guide to Daily Food Choices

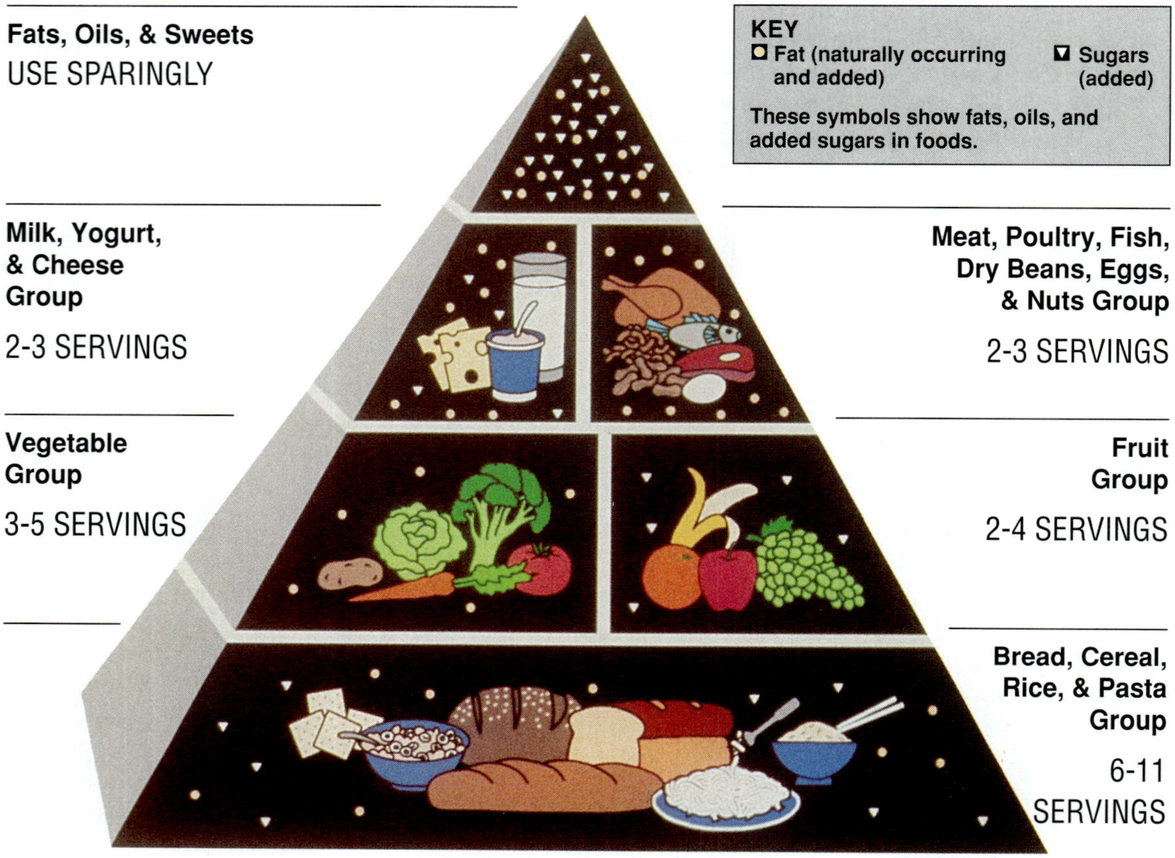

Food Examples for One Serving

Milk, Yogurt, and Cheese Group
- 1 cup milk or yogurt
- 1½ ounces ripened cheese
- 2 ounces processed cheese

Meats, Poultry, Fish, Dry Beans, Eggs, and Nuts Group
- 2 to 3 ounces of cooked lean meat, poultry or fish
- 1 cup cooked dry beans
- 2 Tbsp. peanut butter — ½ serving

Vegetable Group
- 1 cup leafy raw vegetables (lettuce, spinach)
- ½ cup other vegetables, cooked or raw
- ¾ cup vegetable juice

Fruit Group
- 1 orange, apple, banana, pear
- ½ cup chopped, cooked, or canned fruit
- ¾ cup fruit juice

Bread, Cereal, Rice, and Pasta Group
- 1 slice bread
- ½ cup cooked cereal, rice, or pasta
- 1 ounce ready to eat cereal

The Food Guide Pyramid

The **Food Guide Pyramid** is a simple method of diet planning based on food groups. Foods are organized into five major groups based on the nutrients they contain. If you eat the recommended number of servings from each of these five groups every day, you will probably get all the nutrients you need.

The Food Guide Pyramid can help you and your family put the Dietary Guidelines for Americans into practice. The guide is shown on page 458.

How Many Servings?

Notice that the Food Guide Pyramid gives the recommended number of servings from each food group as a range. Most people should have at least the lowest number of servings in the range. Some people may need more, depending on their age, body size, and activity level. For example, most teens need more because of rapid growth. A male teen who is very active would probably need the highest number of servings.

Some people wonder how they could possibly eat as many servings as the Food Guide Pyramid recommends. However, note that the serving sizes are not large. If you have cereal and toast at breakfast, a sandwich at lunch, and spaghetti and a roll at dinner, you've had six servings from the breads, cereals, rice, and pasta group.

Some foods, such as pizza or a salad, are mixtures of foods from more than one group. When you are figuring up your total number of servings, think of the individual items in each food mixture. A pizza, for instance, includes crust (a grain product), cheese, vegetables, and perhaps meat.

Limit your choices of sugary products to an occasional treat. What other food choices offer a sweet flavor, but are packed with nutrients?

Choosing Foods from the Food Groups

Be sure to choose a variety of foods from each food group. Although foods within a group are similar, they do not contain exactly the same nutrients. If you limit yourself to only a few choices, you may come up short.

The Food Guide Pyramid includes a reminder to use fats, oils, and sweets sparingly. It's fine to have small amounts once in a while, as long as your overall food choices are healthful ones. However, foods high in fat and sugar should not be a major or frequent part of your eating plan.

Keep the Dietary Guidelines in mind when you use the Food Guide Pyramid. Choose foods from each group that are low in fat, cholesterol, sugar, and sodium. By following the Dietary Guidelines and the Food Guide Pyramid, you will help yourself stay healthy, fit, and active for years to come.

TAKING ACTION

Your school is preparing for National Wellness Week. Each class has been asked to create a campaign promoting some aspect of wellness. Your class has been given the task of informing the community about the Dietary Guidelines for Americans. For this project, you and your classmates will rely not only on your knowledge of the Guidelines, but also on your understanding of people's active lifestyles and attitudes toward health. Your job is to convince them that practicing healthful habits can fit into their busy schedules. How will you find the information you need to get your message across?

Using Your Resourcefulness

- How will you encourage people to eat a wide variety of foods? Where will you find specific examples of the basic food groups and the nutritional benefits of each?
- How will you find out about the price and availability of different food items, to convince people that the products are inexpensive and easy to find?
- Where will you find more information on maintaining a healthy weight, including facts on body fat, weight-related medical disorders, and factors affecting healthy weight levels?
- Where will you find suggestions on ways to cut down on sodium, sugar, and fats?
- Where will you find different ways of preparing vegetables, fruits, and grain products, to encourage people to include more of these in their diets?
- Where will you learn more about Americans' present health habits, to know which guidelines need special emphasis?
- List all the resources that you think would help you to put your knowledge of nutrition to use in everyday life.

Chapter 39 Review

Summary

In this chapter, you have read about:

- The Dietary Guidelines for Americans and the reasons for following each.
- How to lower the fat in your diet without giving up your favorite foods.
- How to use the Food Guide Pyramid to plan a healthful diet.

Facts to Recall

1. Why is eating a variety of foods important to maintaining good health?
2. Identify three factors that help determine whether your weight is a healthy one for you.
3. Name three ways to reduce fat when buying and preparing meat and poultry.
4. Name three reasons for eating plenty of vegetables, fruits, and grain products.
5. Why should sugars be used in moderation?
6. What are three ways of cutting down on sodium in your diet?
7. According to health experts, what percentage of your calories should come from fat?
8. Name the five major food groups and give the recommended number of servings for each.
9. What four types of nutrients can be found in vegetables?

Ideas to Explore

1. Many food labels or advertisements include phrases such as "no cholesterol," "light," "less fat," "low in sodium," or "good source of fiber." What examples have you seen or heard? How might these statements be helpful to consumers? How might they be misleading?
2. Why do government agencies play a role in developing nutrition guidelines and bringing them to the public? What might happen if this source of information was not available?

Activities to Try

1. Using the Food Guide Pyramid, create a three-day menu that includes at least the minimum number of servings from all five major food groups.
2. Imagine you are a writer or artist working for an advertising agency. Your client is a vegetable growers' association that wants your help in promoting its product. Use your creativity to design an advertisement or ad campaign to improve the image of a specific vegetable, such as broccoli, cauliflower, or brussels sprouts.

LINK TO *Math*

FIGURING PERCENTAGE OF CALORIES FROM FAT

For good health, no more than 30% of your daily calories should come from fat. Have you ever wondered how some of your favorite foods measure up? Using food labels from two foods and the formula below, determine the percentage of calories from fat for these foods:

1. Multiply the number of grams of fat by 9 (the number of calories in 1 gram of fat). This gives you the total calories from fat.
2. Divide the total calories from fat by the number of calories per serving.
3. Multiply the answer from Step 2 by 100%.

Example: 1 serving corned beef hash has 490 calories and 34 grams of fat.

1. $34\text{ g} \times 9 = 306$ calories from fat.
2. $306 \div 490$ calories per serving $= 0.63$
3. $0.63 \times 100\% = 63\%$ of the calories in corned beef hash come from fat.

CHAPTER

40 Managing Your Weight

OBJECTIVES

- *Discuss how to safely reach and maintain a healthy weight.*
- *Identify characteristics and hazards of fad diets.*

TERMS TO LEARN

- ***body image***
- ***basal metabolism***

Question: What is the perfect weight or the perfect body build?

Answer: When it comes to people's sizes and shapes, there's no such thing as "perfect." After all, everyone is an individual.

However, there is a weight range and fitness level that is right for you — one that helps you stay healthy and feel your best. Finding and reaching that level is what weight management is all about.

What Weight Is Right for You?

Weight management is a matter of good health, not just appearance. If you have read Chapter 39, you know that one of the Dietary Guidelines is "Maintain a healthy weight." Weight management can help you avoid the health risks of being overweight or underweight.

If you are a teen who is still growing, it is natural for you to be gaining weight. How can you find out whether your weight is within a healthful range? The best way is to consult a physician or other health professional.

Keep in mind that weight is only part of the story. How much of your weight comes from body fat may actually be a better clue to health. Extra pounds are not a problem if they come from muscle or bone. On the other hand, even a person who is underweight may have too much body fat.

If you need to gain or lose weight, or get rid of extra fat, this chapter can help you learn how to do it successfully and safely. If your current weight is about right, learning about weight management can help you keep it that way.

What Affects Your Weight?

Your weight depends on a number of factors. Some of these cannot be changed. You inherited your basic body type: short or tall, large-boned or small-boned. You may have inherited a tendency to gain weight more or less easily than others.

However, you *can* change your activity level and eating habits. Together, these factors have a great effect on your weight and percentage of body fat. Recall the discussion of energy and calories from Chapter 38. Whether you gain, lose, or maintain weight is largely a matter of balancing energy.

Your activity level is one factor that affects your weight.

Body Image and Self-Esteem

Your **body image** is a mental picture of how you think your body looks. This mental picture may or may not be accurate.

It's difficult to see yourself objectively, or as you really are. Often people dwell on what they consider their flaws. They compare themselves to models or athletes with "ideal" body builds. When they look in the mirror, all they may see is their weight, the shape of their thighs, or the size of their arm muscles.

However, being critical of yourself will not help you make positive changes. It will only make you feel worse. Instead, learn to feel good about the person you are. Remember that you are more than just a number on a scale or a clothing size. You are a whole person with many good qualities, inside and out.

When you have high self-esteem — when you feel good about yourself — it's easier to see yourself objectively. You may still decide that you want to make changes in the outer you. However, it will be because you care about yourself, not because you are trying to fit some image of perfection.

- If the energy you take in from food *equals* the energy you use, your weight stays the same.
- If the energy you take in from food is *more* than the energy you use, you gain weight. Why? Your body converts the extra energy to body fat and stores it.
- If the energy you take in from food is *less* than the energy you use, you lose weight. Why? To get the extra energy it needs, your body converts body fat back to energy.

A Weight Management Plan for You

Good choices in eating and exercising can help you reach and maintain a healthy weight. Start by setting a goal and planning how to reach it. A good plan would include evaluating your exercise and eating habits and finding specific changes to focus on. Then carry out your plan. Evaluate your progress regularly to see how well your plan is working.

Pocket Lab

How Much Is a Serving?

MATERIALS:
mashed potatoes; grape jelly

EQUIPMENT:
plate; serving spoons; measuring cups and spoons

Directions: On your plate, serve the amount of mashed potatoes you would normally eat at a meal and the amount of jelly you would use on one piece of toast. Using measuring cups and spoons, measure the amounts of potatoes and jelly you took as a serving and record the amounts. Using a Nutritive Values of Foods table and the serving size listed on the jelly jar, compare your serving size with a standard serving size.

- Were your servings larger or smaller than the standard serving sizes?
- Why is it important to compare serving sizes when checking the number of calories you consume?
- Why is serving size an important consideration in maintaining your weight?

Losing Weight

Health experts recommend that if you want to lose weight, try to lose about a pound a week. Losing weight at a slow, steady rate is safer than trying to lose more rapidly. It's also more likely to be successful in the long run.

People often think of losing weight as "going on a diet." Instead, think of combining exercise with healthful, lifelong eating habits. Research has shown that when it comes to losing weight, the combination of exercise and healthful eating habits is more effective than any diet.

Why do so many weight-loss diets fail? People who try to follow a too-strict diet will often feel hungry and deprived. Eventually they go back to their old eating habits. In fact, they often eat more than ever and end up weighing more than when they started. This pattern of weight loss and gain is very dangerous. So is any strict diet that does not provide your body with enough energy and nutrients. See the box on page 466 for more information about dangerous diets.

If you need to lose or gain a large amount of weight, talk with a physician to get sound advice. Extreme changes can affect your health.

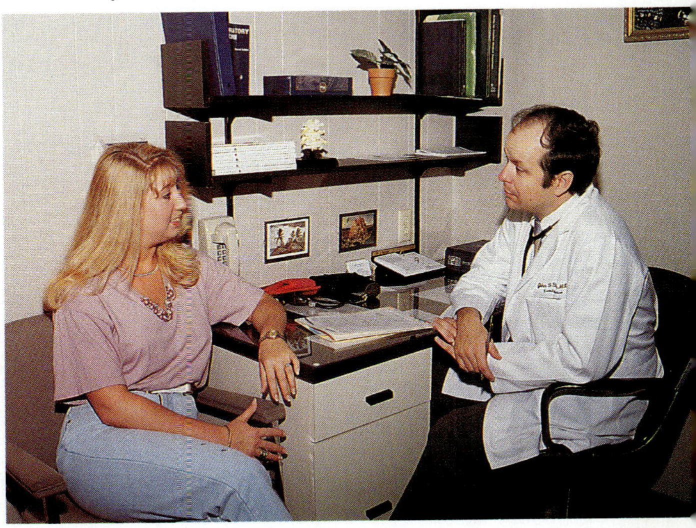

Beware of Fad Diets

Weight-loss diets and products are everywhere these days. They are discussed in books and magazines, advertised in print and on radio and television, and passed around among friends. Many of these diets are costly. Many don't work. Some are even health hazards. How can you tell? Here are some warning signs.

- ***Very few calories.*** No one should take in fewer than 1200 calories a day unless he or she is under a physician's care. Most people need more than that, even to lose weight.
- ***Unrealistic promises.*** Some advertisements promise that fat will "melt away" without exercise. They may tell stories of people who lost dozens of pounds in just a few weeks. However, there is no fast, easy way to lose weight.
- ***Limited food choices.*** Some diets require you to eat one food or just a few foods day after day. This type of diet does not take into account the nutritional needs of your body. Variety is the only way to be sure you are getting all the nutrients you need.
- ***Special products.*** Some diets are based on using special milkshake mixes, candy bars, or other products. You can't be sure of getting complete nutrition, but you can be sure that you have spent a lot of money. These weight-loss plans don't help you learn healthful eating habits.
- ***Diet pills.*** So-called "diet pills" are drugs that are supposed to cut down your appetite. They can have dangerous side effects. People taking these pills have been reported to have very high blood pressure, kidney failure, and strokes. Pills can also lead to drug abuse.

A safe weight-loss plan:

- Is based on real foods, not powders, pills, or special diet liquids.
- Has enough calories per day to maintain energy.
- Includes a variety of foods from all five major food groups in the Food Guide Pyramid.
- Emphasizes whole grains, fruits, vegetables, and other low-fat foods.
- Does not promise weight loss without exercise.
- Does not promise weight loss of more than one to two pounds per week.

Exercise

Being more active can help you lose weight. One reason is the extra calories you burn while exercising. However, exercise has other weight-loss benefits as well.

Up to 12 hours after vigorous exercise, your body burns calories at a higher rate than it would have otherwise. If you exercise in the morning and later in the day, you will burn bonus calories all day long. The extra exercise will even be working for you while you sleep.

If you become more physically active, you will probably look trimmer even if you don't lose weight. The reason is that you are likely to lose body fat and replace it with lean muscle tissue. A pound of muscle tissue takes up less space than a pound of body fat.

Muscle also requires more energy to maintain itself than body fat. Adding muscle can increase your **basal metabolism** — the number of calories needed for normal body processes. Raising your basal metabolism means you'll lose weight a little more easily, or can eat a little more without gaining weight.

Many people find that when they exercise regularly, they are more motivated to eat healthfully. And of course, exercise has many other health benefits, as you learned in Chapter 37.

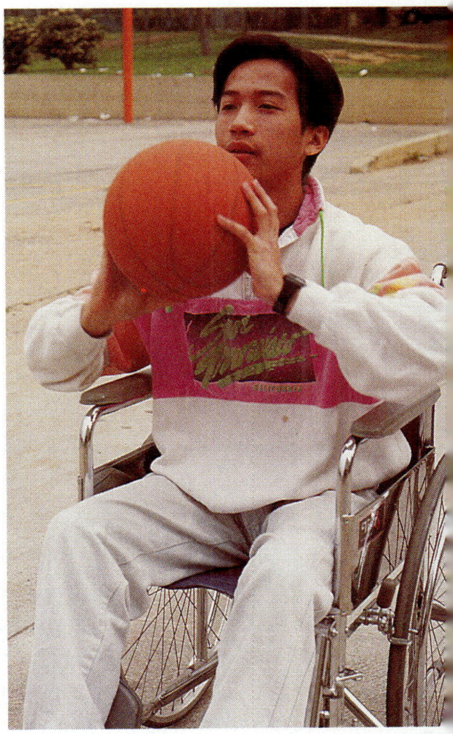

Regular exercise helps you burn calories.

Eating Habits

The first step in improving your eating habits is to understand what your current habits are. Try keeping a food diary for one week. Each time you eat something, write down what it was and the amount. Also describe the situation — the time of day, where you were and with whom, and how you felt.

At the end of the week, look for patterns. Try to see when you're most likely to overeat or make poor choices. Is it when you're bored? When you're away from home? While you watch TV? Then think of a way to solve the problem. The next time you're bored, for example, try calling a friend or going for a bike ride.

Remember, healthful eating habits are based on the Dietary Guidelines and the Food Guide Pyramid. Many people find that they lose weight just by following these basic guidelines.

In particular, choose foods low in fat. Low-fat, nutrient-dense foods make it easier to meet your nutrient needs without exceeding your calorie needs. For a low-fat eating plan, follow the suggestions in Chapter 39. Be sure to eat plenty of whole grains and fresh fruits and vegetables.

When are you most likely to make poor food choices?

Notice the serving sizes given in the Food Guide Pyramid (see page 458). In the beginning it may be helpful to measure the servings out so you'll know exactly what the portions look like.

If you want to keep track of calories, use food labels and a good calorie chart. Remember, calories are not bad for you. They are a measurement of the energy your body needs. Your physician can give you advice on the number of calories you need each day.

AROUND THE WORLD

A new product called Oatrim, developed at a U.S. Department of Agriculture research lab in Peoria, Illinois, could be good news for weight-conscious people and oat farmers alike. Oatrim is an oat bran-based fat substitute. In taste tests, ice milk and a frozen dessert made with Oatrim compared well against ice cream in taste and texture, while containing far fewer calories and much less fat and cholesterol. If Oatrim becomes popular, it could also open up a new market for oat farmers, who often have trouble getting good prices for their crop.

Making sensible food choices and varying your exercise routine are essential for successful weight loss.

Tips for Losing Weight

The formula for losing weight is fairly simple: get plenty of exercise and make sensible, nutritious food choices. The challenging part is sticking to your plan. Here are some tips from people who have been successful.

- Vary your exercise routine to keep from getting bored.
- Exercise with a friend. You'll be less likely to skip a session.
- Don't skip meals. People who do usually end up eating more food, and less nutritious food, than if they had eaten the meal.
- Sit down at a table and eat slowly. It's more relaxing and you will enjoy the food more. You'll also be less likely to overeat.
- Plan for snacks in advance. Choose nutritious snacks such as fresh fruit, whole-grain crackers, or raw vegetables.
- When eating away from home, look for healthful choices. Many restaurants offer grilled chicken, baked potatoes, salads, and low-fat milk. Ask for food to be served without high-fat condiments such as mayonnaise, sour cream, and regular salad dressing.

- Avoid thinking of certain foods as "bad." Your overall food choices are what counts. If you love ice cream or potato chips, eat a small amount once in a while to satisfy your craving. Just don't make a habit of eating these foods frequently or in large amounts.
- Avoid weighing yourself every day. Normal ups and downs can be discouraging. Instead, check every week or two weeks. You'll see more of a change.
- If you still don't see progress when you weigh yourself, try keeping track of your measurements instead. You may be losing inches, not pounds, as you replace fat with muscle.
- Remember that one slip doesn't mean you've failed. If you eat too much or miss an exercise session, don't punish yourself or give up. Just go back to your plan the next day.
- Have patience. The extra weight wasn't gained all in one day, so you can't expect to lose it overnight.

Gaining Weight

If you want to gain weight, you should still follow the Dietary Guidelines and Food Guide Pyramid. Just add extra servings or make servings slightly larger. Here are some suggestions:

- Split up the usual three meals a day into six small ones. This reduces the chances of feeling full before you have eaten enough food.
- Eat nutritious snacks between meals.
- Pass up water in favor of milk and juice. Milk and juice are more nutritious and add calories.
- Include nutritious but calorie-dense foods, such as nuts, cheese, peanut butter, or dried fruits, in meals and snacks. Avoid filling up on low-calorie foods, such as lettuce.

If you are trying to gain weight, look for nutrient dense food choices that are higher in calories.

Exercise is just as important for gaining weight as for losing it. If you eat more but don't exercise, you will gain fat. Too much body fat is not healthful no matter what you weigh. Exercise is essential for building muscles. Moderate exercise can also help stimulate your appetite for healthful foods.

A look at your day-to-day habits may help you see a reason for being underweight. For example, Yolanda often felt she was too busy to eat. Her active, growing body needed more calories than she was giving it. Once she slowed down and ate regular meals, her weight reached a healthy level and stayed there.

Stress and tension can cause you to lose your appetite. Before sitting down to a meal, you might relax for a few minutes or take a short walk. Learning how to manage the stress in your life can help you maintain a healthy weight.

Some people are underweight because of an eating disorder. (See page 481 in Chapter 41.) Because they see themselves as fat, they work hard at losing weight. In reality, they may be dangerously thin. A person with an eating disorder needs professional help to overcome it.

Making wise food choices leads to a healthful way of life.

Maintaining Your Weight

After losing or gaining weight, keep the good habits you've developed. Just remember to adjust your calorie intake and activity level to stay at your target weight.

If your weight is fine now, try to keep it that way by eating right and staying active. This will be especially important as you grow older and your lifestyle and energy needs change.

When you are at a weight that's a good one for you, and you are sensible about the way you keep your weight, you'll have gone a long way toward healthful living.

TAKING ACTION

Robin is quite a bit overweight. She doesn't exercise often and is the first to admit her favorite food is french fries. Though she has a sense of humor and laughs at herself, you know weight management is a real and difficult issue for her.

One day Robin is unusually frank with you. "I suppose I'll never be slim. Maybe I'm just meant to be this way." There is an awkward silence. You think Robin might want your help, but you're not sure.

Using Your Resourcefulness

- Do you think you should offer to help Robin with her weight problem? Why or why not? If so, how would you bring up the subject? If not, what would you do instead?
- Suppose Robin asks for your help. What, specifically, could you offer to do?
- What personal or material resources do you have that might be helpful to Robin?
- What questions could you ask Robin to help her take stock of her own resources?
- What types of community resources might be helpful in this situation? How could you find out about them?
- Suppose Robin comes to you one day, very excited and happy. "I just read about these amazing diet pills! I can't wait to try them." What would you do?
- How can you encourage Robin and help her feel successful on the way to her goal?

Chapter 40 Review

Summary

In this chapter, you have read about:

- The best way to determine whether your weight is within a healthful range.
- Factors that affect your weight.
- The relationship between self-esteem and body image.
- How to lose weight through exercise and healthful eating habits.
- How to recognize dangerous fad diets.
- How to gain weight safely and sensibly.
- The importance of maintaining a healthy weight.

Facts to Recall

1. Why is weight management important?
2. What is a person's body image? How is it affected by self-esteem?
3. Name two factors affecting your weight that you can control.
4. A weight loss of how many pounds per week is considered safe?
5. Why is it unwise to try to lose weight by "going on a diet"? What is a better alternative?
6. Explain three ways in which exercise is of benefit in a weight-loss program.
7. List six tips for sticking with a weight-loss plan.
8. List four characteristics of a dangerous fad diet.
9. Why is exercise important for someone who wants to gain weight? Give two reasons.

Ideas to Explore

1. What do you think most people base their ideas of the "right" weight on? Why? What can happen as a result?
2. Recent studies have shown that many young people are overweight and in poor physical condition. What are some possible reasons?
3. Why should special care be taken when designing a weight loss program for young people?
4. What fad diets do you know of? What are the health hazards of each?

Activities to Try

1. Keep a food diary for two days. Identify at least one good habit and one poor habit based on your food diary. Make a plan for improving your food choices.
2. Evaluate a diet or diet aid using the guidelines listed in "Beware of Fad Diets" on page 466. Write a newspaper article explaining why you do or do not recommend this diet or product.

LINK TO *Math*

Figuring Calorie Intake

Balancing the calories that you eat with the calories you burn up is essential in maintaining a healthy weight. Use the following guidelines to figure the average number of calories you eat in a day:

1. Keep a food diary for three days. Write down everything that you eat and the amount that you eat.
2. Use a calorie chart to identify the calories per serving for each serving of food that you ate.
3. Add up the total number of calories that you ate for the three days.
4. Divide the total from Step 3 by 3 to figure the average number of calories you ate per day.

(**Note:** If you are maintaining your weight, the calories you burn in daily activities are balancing with the calories you eat.)

CHAPTER

41 Facts for Food Choices

OBJECTIVES

- *Identify influences on food choices.*
- *Recognize accurate information about food.*
- *Explain how individual needs affect nutrition.*
- *Describe common eating disorders.*

TERMS TO LEARN

- ***myth***
- ***megadoses***
- ***organically grown***
- ***additive***
- ***vegetarian***

When Hannah was a girl, a typical family dinner included foods like fried chicken, dumplings, and corn fritters. For dessert, there was often chocolate cake or ice cream.

Today, Hannah's fourteen-year-old son helps prepare the family meals. Brandon is an athlete who wants to be sure he gives his body the right fuel. They fix meals like broiled chicken, pasta with fresh tomatoes and green peppers, and broccoli with lemon juice. Sometimes they have a vegetarian meal. For dessert, they enjoy fresh fruit served over angel food cake. Their meals are planned with nutrition as well as taste in mind.

Hannah likes this new attitude toward food. Still, she sometimes misses the favorite dishes she grew up on.

Influences on Food Choices

Have you ever thought about why you choose the foods you do? When it comes to food, your likes, dislikes, and habits are influenced by:

- ***Family and culture.*** Most people tend to like the dishes and food customs they grew up with. Dislikes, too, may be learned from family members.
- ***Religious beliefs.*** Many of the world's religions include beliefs and practices relating to food.
- ***Friends.*** Eating is often a social event. You might have lunch at a fast-food restaurant just because your friends are going there.
- ***Emotions.*** People often associate certain foods with feelings of comfort or love.
- ***Trends.*** When certain foods are popular and readily available, you are more likely to choose them. How many pizza restaurants do you think there are today?
- ***Geographical area.*** Different regions or countries often have their own food traditions.
- ***Advertising.*** Food companies and restaurants spend millions of dollars each year to convince you to buy their products.
- ***Lifestyle and values.*** How much time do you have for meals? How important is your good health? Your answers to questions like these can make a difference in the foods you choose.

Many of your food preferences have been influenced by your family.

Culture and tradition influence our food choices. In the United States, for example many people enjoy eating turkey on Thanksgiving Day. In China, many people enjoy dishes such as stir-fried snake, deep-fried scorpion, and peppered rat. While some may find these foods unusual, in the Chinese culture they are thought to be quite special and delicious.

Getting the Facts

Information about food and nutrition comes to you from many sources. For example:

- Your best friend tells you, "My brother heard someone say that bee pollen makes you stronger." Should you believe it?
- You see a television commercial for a breakfast cereal. The ad says, "Look at all the vitamins and minerals you get in one bowl." Should you buy the cereal?
- You see a newspaper headline: "Study shows chicken livers prevent cancer." Should you eat chicken livers every day from now on?

The information on food and nutrition in this book is based on scientific evidence. However, not all sources of information are reliable. The advice about bee pollen is a **myth**, an untrue statement that some people believe. The box on page 475 gives other examples of myths and compares them with the facts.

In the second example, the television commercial is trying to sell a product. The cereal may indeed be nutritious, but so are many other cereals. You can get all the vitamins and minerals you need by eating a variety of foods throughout the day. There's no need to get them all in one bowl of cereal. You'd be wise to compare the price of this cereal with others before you buy.

Even information based on scientific research may be misleading. The newspaper report mentioned above is just a made-up example, but it is typical of reports you might see.

Food Myths

There's a lot of gossip circulating about certain foods, nutrients, and diets. Stories get passed along and changed. Sometimes, there is no factual basis for what you hear. Here are some examples of food myths and the real facts.

Myth:	Fact:
"Honey is more wholesome than sugar."	Honey is a mixture of several different sugars. Your body uses all sugars the same way, whether they come in liquid or granular form.
"Eating carrots will help you see better."	Carrots do help supply your body with vitamin A, and vitamin A is needed for healthy eye tissues. However, no vitamin can correct conditions like nearsightedness and farsightedness.
"An apple a day keeps the doctor away."	Apples are a low-calorie, high-fiber snack food. Eating one every day isn't a bad idea, but it won't prevent illness.
"Starchy foods are fattening."	Naturally starchy foods, such as potatoes, are usually low in fat. The real culprits are high-fat spreads and sauces. For instance, a small baked potato, a slice of bread, and a third of a cup of noodles all have fewer than 100 calories. However, a single tablespoon of butter adds *over* 100 calories.
"Margarine has fewer calories than butter."	Margarine and butter have exactly the same number of calories. They differ in the type of fat they contain. Butter is a highly saturated fat, while most margarines are made from unsaturated vegetable oils.

These reports are often based on the early results of just one study. Many other studies would have to confirm the results before scientists accept them as fact. Even then, you shouldn't jump to conclusions based on that information alone.

How can you be sure you are getting the facts? Here are two strategies to use.

- ***Think critically.*** Question what you read or hear. Is the person telling or writing about the information an authority? What is his or her training or education in nutrition? Is this person being paid to make certain claims or statements?
- ***Get reliable information.*** Some people who know the facts about nutrition are registered dietitians, home economics teachers, family doctors, and school nurses. The library has magazines and books about health and nutrition. Be cautious about publications put out by organizations trying to sell their products.

Following is some information about topics that many people are concerned with today. These include nutritional supplements, "natural" and "health" foods, organically grown foods, and food additives. Knowing the facts about these topics can help you make better decisions.

Nutritional Supplements

Pills, liquids, and powders that are supposed to supplement, or give a boost, to your diet are expensive. Do you need them? The answer is "probably not." If you eat foods from the five food groups, you will have a balanced diet. The only exception is if a physician recommends taking a supplement.

Some products claim to provide complete nutrition. However, there is no way to guarantee that a product provides all the nutrients you need. Foods may contain vital nutrients that science has not discovered yet.

Some people think that taking **megadoses**, or very large amounts, of a vitamin or mineral will cure disease. This is not only untrue, it is dangerous. Taking too much of any nutrient can be harmful.

Eating a balanced diet eliminates the need for nutritional supplements.

"Natural" and "Health" Foods

Companies that make and sell food products know that many people today are concerned about their health. That is why you often see terms like "natural" and "health" on food labels. These terms may mean different things to different people.

For example, Jana wanted to buy some fruit juice. She chose a bottle labeled "100% natural." When she looked more closely at the label, she was surprised to find that the beverage was mostly added sugar and water. Jana thought "natural" meant pure fruit juice. To the food manufacturer, however, "natural" simply meant that sugar and water come from nature.

You will notice that claims for many health food products do not explain exactly what the product will do. If this was done, government agencies could investigate and take legal action about the false statements. Instead, indirect claims are made. For example, an ad may have quotes from people who say the product helped them.

Many so-called "health" foods are neither more nor less nutritious than regular food products. There is one difference, however. Health foods almost always cost more. On the whole, these foods can cost from two to three times as much as regular food.

Before you buy a "natural" or "health" food, read the label carefully. Compare it with regular products. Then decide whether the product is worth the extra cost.

The nutritional value of organically grown foods and those grown with chemical fertilizer is the same.

Organic Foods

"Organic" is another popular word today. The term **organically grown** describes food produced without manufactured chemicals.

There is no nutritional difference between a food grown with organic fertilizers and the same food grown with chemical fertilizers. However, some people prefer to buy organic fruits and vegetables. They are concerned about the long-term effects of chemicals on people's health and the environment.

One problem is that people who sell organically grown food can't be certain it was organically grown. Foods fertilized with chemicals could be passed off as being organically grown. It is difficult to be sure about growing conditions unless you actually see how the plants are cultivated or you buy from a person you know.

Pocket Lab

Analyzing the Effects of Additives

MATERIALS:
one slice store-bought bread; one slice homemade bread

EQUIPMENT:
plate; labels; plastic wrap

Directions: Place one slice of store-bought bread and one slice of homemade bread each on a plate. Label and date each plate. Cover each plate with plastic wrap and leave them out at room temperature. Observe the bread slices daily. Record the date that mold appears on each slice of bread. After the mold appears, answer the following questions:

- How many days did it take for mold to appear on each slice of bread?
- What additives are listed on the store-bought bread label?
- Draw some conclusions about the importance of food additives.
- What might happen to our food supply if all additives were banned?

Food Additives

An **additive** is a substance added to food for a particular purpose. Additives may be used to:

- ***Prevent spoilage.*** BHT is a chemical often added to foods to keep them from spoiling. Vitamin C may be added to foods to keep them from turning brown.
- ***Add nutrients.*** For example, vitamin D is added to milk to help prevent deficiencies. Often, some nutrients are lost in the process of turning raw food into the food products you buy. Nutrients are then added to replace those lost.
- ***Add flavor.*** Vanilla, salt, sugar, and various seasonings are added to many foods for flavor.
- ***Add color.*** Food coloring is added to many foods to make them more attractive.

Many food additives help preserve the quality of food. Without their use, the food supply would be more limited in quantity and quality.

Before any new food additive can be used, it must be tested for safety and approved by the federal government. Some additives, originally thought to be safe, have been banned or withdrawn if there was any evidence they could be harmful.

Nutrition for Individual Needs

Did you know that good food choices for you may not be the best choices for someone else? Basic nutrition guidelines, such as the Dietary Guidelines, apply to almost everyone. However, people also have individual differences that can affect their nutritional needs.

Extra calories and nutrients are needed during pregnancy.

Nutrition Through the Life Cycle

Everyone goes through different stages of life. At each stage, the need for calories and nutrients is slightly different.

- ***Pregnancy*** is the start of the life cycle. The food choices made by an expectant mother affect not only her own health, but that of the unborn baby. Women who are pregnant or breastfeeding need extra calories and nutrients. They should be especially sure to get enough calcium.
- ***Infants*** first get their nutrients from breast milk or formula. As babies grow, they can be introduced to other foods, such as cereal, fruits, vegetables, and meats. Foods for infants are specially prepared so that they are safe and easy to digest.

Older adults have the same nutrient needs as younger people, but may need fewer calories.

- ***Children*** need good nutrition for growth and health. Toddlers and young children should have a variety of foods from the five major food groups. Because their bodies are small, they need smaller servings. By the time children are in school, the normal serving sizes can be used.
- ***Teens*** need a lot of energy for rapid growth. During this time, you need the best nutrition you can get. In particular, be sure to get enough calcium for strong, healthy bones now and in later life.
- ***Young, middle, and older adults*** should continue to follow the Dietary Guidelines and the Food Guide Pyramid. Adults are no longer growing, and some may not be as physically active as they were when they were younger. Therefore, they usually need fewer calories.

Illness and Medical Conditions

Nutrition is a particular concern when someone is ill. Good nutrition, along with rest and proper care, can help the body get back to normal and regain strength. However, a person who is ill may not want to or be able to eat normally. It is best to follow a physician's advice about what the patient should eat.

Chronic, or long-term, medical conditions can also affect food needs. Some examples of chronic conditions are diabetes (dy-uh-BEE-tis), food allergies, or high blood pressure. A physician may prescribe a special diet to help control the condition.

Good nutrition and rest are needed during an illness. When you or someone you know is ill, it is best to follow a physician's advice about what to eat.

Eating Disorders

Another concern related to nutrition is the topic of eating disorders. The causes of eating disorders are not well understood. However, the effects are all too clear.

One such disorder is *anorexia nervosa* (an-uh-REX-ee-uh ner-VOH-suh). It basically means self-starvation. People with this disorder have a strong fear of being overweight. They eat very little and can become extremely thin, yet still think they weigh enough or too much. They become obsessed with thoughts of food, their weight, and dieting.

Another eating disorder is *bulimia* (buh-LIM-ee-uh). It is similar to anorexia in that the person is overly concerned with weight. People with bulimia will eat large quantities of food in a short period of time. This is sometimes referred to as binge eating. After eating, the individual will try to rid the body of the food to avoid weight gain. They may induce vomiting, abuse laxatives, go on a very strict diet, or over-exercise.

Anyone can have an eating disorder. Usually, however, the affected person is a teen or young adult. Females are affected more often than males.

Both anorexia and bulimia can cause serious medical problems. If left untreated, either one can become severe enough to cause death.

People with anorexia or bulimia need qualified professional help. If you recognize the signs of an eating disorder in yourself or someone you know, check with your school nurse or family doctor.

Nutrition for Vegetarians

A **vegetarian** is a person who does not eat meat, fish, or poultry. Some vegetarians also avoid other foods derived from animals, such as eggs or milk.

People who become vegetarians do so for a variety of reasons. It may be for religious reasons or because they are opposed to the use of animals for food. Some are concerned with conserving natural resources. (It takes more resources to produce animals for food than to raise crops.) Others see a vegetarian diet as a way to eat less fat and cholesterol and more fiber. It is also economical.

Vegetarians need to carefully balance the types of foods they eat to get all the necessary nutrients. Many people who are not vegetarians enjoy adding vegetarian dishes to their meals for variety.

Evidence shows that a well-selected vegetarian diet is a healthy one. In fact, vegetarians are less likely to develop some of the common health problems related to diet, such as heart disease, high blood pressure, cancer, and obesity. This does not mean vegetarians will never have these health problems. It does mean that their diets are less likely to contribute to these conditions.

Since vegetarians limit their selection of foods, they must be careful to balance their diets nutritionally. The need for protein can be met by eating complementary plant proteins, such as legumes and grains. (You may want to review the discussion of complete and incomplete proteins in Chapter 38.)

If there is any nutrient lacking in a vegetarian diet, it is likely to be vitamin B_{12}. This B vitamin is found only in foods of animal origin. Vegetarians who do not eat dairy or egg products may need to take vitamin B_{12} tablets.

If milk is not included in the diet, it can be difficult to get enough calcium. Vegetables high in calcium include broccoli, kale, collard greens, and mustard greens. Tofu, a soybean product, is also a good source of calcium.

There are many good vegetarian cookbooks with lots of recipes and ideas. Looking through them can help you see that a vegetarian diet can have a lot of variety. Many people who are not vegetarians often use vegetarian dishes to add variety to the foods they eat.

▼ Nutrition for Athletes ▼

Everyone wants to be a winner or play on a winning team. It's a reward for the training and effort put into getting ready for an event. However, wanting to win can also present problems for athletes and their coaches. They become perfect targets for misinformation about nutrition.

If you want to get your body in top form physically, you must practice good nutrition. Even if you are an occasional athlete who bicycles, hikes, jogs, or plays tennis, nutrition is important. The fuel you feed your body affects your performance, your enjoyment, and the physical benefits you obtain from the activity.

What Athletes *Don't* Need

A great deal of incorrect information is passed along to athletes. Here is a sample of poor advice that you would be better off without.

- ***Salt tablets.*** Some people advise taking salt tablets to replace the salt lost when sweating. This can be dangerous. When you take extra salt, water is pulled out of muscles to dilute the amount of salt in your system. As a result, your muscles cannot work efficiently and your performance is lowered. You can replace the salt lost during heavy exercise by eating regular foods with normal seasonings.
- ***Extra protein.*** Will eating a huge steak or taking protein powder make you stronger? No. Only exercise can strengthen and build muscles. A normal diet supplies all the protein your body needs. Extra amounts are usually converted to fat and stored. Breaking down the protein puts a heavy workload on the liver and kidneys and can create a water shortage in body tissues.
- ***Vitamin and mineral supplements.*** You do not need supplements to stay in top form or to give you energy. The extra fat-soluble vitamins are stored in your body fat. When the vitamins stored reach high levels, they can be toxic, or poisonous. If you are eating a variety of foods, why spend money for pills you don't need?
- ***"Quick energy" drinks that are high in sugar.*** Fluids with too much sugar draw water into the stomach so that the sugar will be diluted. The tissues and cells in the rest of your body won't have enough water. Sometimes this can cause an upset stomach or diarrhea. It's better to drink plain water or beverages low in sugar.
- ***Rapid weight loss.*** Athletes in some sports are often encouraged to "make weight" just before a competition. They may try crash diets, diet pills, or "sweating off" pounds. Such rapid weight loss programs are dangerous. They hurt your performance and can permanently damage your health. To make safe, long-term changes in your weight, follow the guidelines in Chapter 40.

A balanced diet is a key to better athletic performance.

What Athletes Need

Good training and a balanced diet are the keys to peak performance. Because of the heavy energy demands on their bodies, most athletes need extra calories. A male teen athlete, for instance, would probably need the highest number of servings suggested in the Food Guide Pyramid.

Carbohydrates are the most efficient fuel your body can get. Athletes, like everyone else, should eat plenty of nutritious complex carbohydrates, such as breads, pasta, potatoes, rice, and fruit. Candy bars and sweet drinks are too sweet and don't carry the nutrients your body needs. If you eat a high-protein, high-fat, and low-carbohydrate diet, you'll be tired and perform poorly.

Timing is important, too. Smart trainers have their athletes eat three to four hours before an athletic event. This time lapse allows the athletes to digest their food before heavy exercise. A pre-event meal should be high in carbohydrates and low in fats and proteins.

If you are involved in athletics, follow this sound advice. You'll feel better and see a difference in your performance.

TAKING ACTION

Your mother has just returned from a medical checkup. Her doctor is concerned about her high blood pressure and cholesterol levels. In addition to prescribing medication, she has told your mother to follow a low-sodium, low-fat, low-cholesterol diet and to avoid stress.

You want to help your mother by preparing meals that are both good for her and enjoyable to eat. You also want to do what you can to reduce the stress in her life.

Using Your Resourcefulness

- Where can you find information about the food sodium, fat, and cholesterol content in foods?
- Where can you look for recipes that would fit your mother's special nutritional needs?
- You and your mother would like to learn more about high blood pressure and how to manage it. Where do you start?
- How will you find time to prepare meals while still keeping up with your studies?
- Suppose other members of the family still want to eat their traditional favorite foods that your mother should not eat. What problems might this cause? What are some possible solutions?
- What could you do to help reduce the stress in your mother's life?

Chapter 41 Review

Summary

In this chapter, you have read about:

- Factors that influence eating habits.
- How to distinguish food facts from myths and misleading statements.
- Facts about nutritional supplements, "natural" and "health" foods, organic foods, and food additives.
- How nutritional needs vary throughout the life cycle.
- How nutritional needs can be affected by illness and medical conditions.
- How a vegetarian diet can meet nutritional needs.
- Good and poor nutritional practices for athletes.
- Symptoms of anorexia nervosa and bulimia.

Facts to Recall

1. List four influences on food choices.
2. A friend tells you that eating chocolate causes acne. The school dietitian says it does not. Whom do you believe and why?
3. Are nutritional supplements necessary to a balanced diet? Explain.
4. How can terms like "all natural" and "health food" be misleading? Give an example.
5. Identify four purposes for food additives.
6. Why are food choices especially important to pregnant women? To teens? To people who are ill?
7. Identify two possible nutritional deficiencies in a vegetarian diet and explain how they can be avoided.
8. List three nutrition guidelines for athletes.

Ideas to Explore

1. Which of the influences on food choices do you think has the strongest effect on most people? Why?
2. According to the chapter, news reports about nutrition research can sometimes be misleading. Would it be better not to publish the results of scientific studies until they are confirmed? Explain.

Activities to Try

1. Find a news report about scientific studies on food, drugs, or nutrition. Be prepared to explain what claim is being made, who is making it, and the facts or research behind it.
2. Plan a day's meals for one of the following: Sondra, a 25-year-old pregnant woman; Harold, a 60-year-old executive; Luisa, a 10-year-old who is allergic to milk; Darlene, a 16-year-old soccer player; Jim, a 34-year-old vegetarian. Explain how your plan suits the person's individual needs.

LINK TO *Geography*

GEOGRAPHIC INFLUENCES ON FOOD CHOICES

The availability of food choices around the world are often linked to geographic conditions. Select an area other than where you live (such as North Africa, the Middle East, Asia, Southeast Asia, South America, Europe, etc.). Locate information about this area. Use the following questions to guide your research:

- How do the climate and soil conditions affect the available food choices?
- What kinds of crops (foods) are generally grown in this area?
- How do the available foods fulfill nutritional needs? Is there a need to import some foods to fulfill nutritional requirements?
- How do economic conditions affect the availability of food in this area?

CHAPTER

42 Planning Meals and Snacks

OBJECTIVES

- *Explain how meal patterns and resources affect meal planning.*
- *Give suggestions for simple and nutritious meals.*
- *List the elements of meal appeal.*

TERMS TO LEARN

- ***meal pattern***
- ***convenience foods***

"I know I should eat better," Melanie sighed. "Take today, for instance. A doughnut was all I had for breakfast. The only vegetables I've had were the ones on that slice of pizza. But I don't have time to think about nutrition! I just have to grab whatever's handy."

By now, you have learned a lot about nutrition and how it affects your health. Will you be like Melanie, who has trouble following through? Or will you apply what you've learned in your day-to-day life? This chapter will help you use your resources to plan meals and snacks that are nutritious and appealing.

Putting Nutrition to Work for You

Over a period of time, you develop a set of eating habits. Some of your habits may be good, and some may be less desirable. What are your habits? Do you nibble when studying or watching TV? Do you eat plenty of fresh fruits and vegetables? Do you snack on foods high in fat and salt? Think of ways to replace poor habits with better ones.

Keep the Dietary Guidelines and the Food Guide Pyramid in mind. As you learned in Chapter 39, they are valuable tools for planning nutritious meals and snacks.

The best way to be sure you get good nutrition is to plan for the whole day. That doesn't mean you need to carry around a list of everything you plan to eat. It simply means that all the food you eat — whether it comes from meals or snacks, early or late in the day — is part of your total nutrition picture. Good planning helps you make sure that all those individual food choices add up to good nutrition.

Using Meal Patterns

A **meal pattern** is the way your daily food choices are grouped into meals and snacks. Over a period of time, people establish meal patterns that work for them. Some people eat three meals a day and one or two snacks. Others prefer to have four, five, or even six smaller meals.

Having a meal pattern in mind can make it easier to plan how you will get your daily servings from the five major food groups. For instance, you need six or more servings of breads and cereals a day. You might plan to have two servings at each meal and get the rest from snacks.

Breakfast is an important part of any meal pattern.

AROUND THE WORLD

Do you think of sandwiches only as peanut butter or ham salad? In Denmark, a sandwich is a smorrebrod (smer-er-BREWTH). It is made with a wide variety of fillings and served open-faced. The ingredients include traditional Scandanavian staples: dark breads, fish, and milk products. Try making your own smorrebrod. Start with a nutritious multi-grain bread like rye or pumpernickel, fill it with tuna, lettuce, cheese, or onion, top it with a dollop of mayonnaise and a sprinkle of parsley. What other interesting combinations can you think of?

A typical meal includes a main dish, several side dishes, a beverage, and sometimes dessert. The main dish often supplies protein. Grain products, vegetables, and fruits can be included as side dishes or in other parts of the meal. You might use milk as the beverage or include another milk product, such as yogurt or cheese. Look at the sample food choices on page 489. You will find a good representation of foods from the five major food groups.

Meal planning becomes easier once you get in the habit. Eventually you may want to plan meals and snacks for several days or even a week at a time.

Resources for Meal Planning

Meal planning involves many decisions. What to eat is only one of them. You must also choose how to make the best use of your resources.

Available Choices

Choose convenience foods carefully for good nutrition.

Years ago, pioneer families ate food that they had raised or hunted themselves and prepared at home. Today you have many more choices. Your next meal might come from a restaurant or be delivered to your door. At the supermarket, you can find fruits and vegetables from all around the world and complete dinners that microwave in minutes.

Convenience Foods

Convenience foods, those purchased partially or completely prepared, are a big help to beginning cooks and busy people. Convenience foods range from ready-to-serve canned soups to entire frozen meals. They can be a good choice when time and skills are limited.

SAMPLE FOOD CHOICES FOR A DAY

	B	V	F	ME	MI
Breakfast:					
Cereal with milk	x				x
Toast	x				
Orange juice			x		
Snack:					
Apple			x		
Lunch:					
Turkey sandwich	xx			x	
Carrot sticks		x			
Milk					x
Snack:					
Whole-wheat crackers	x				
Peanut butter				x	
Milk					x
Dinner:					
Beans and rice	x			x	
Broccoli		x			
Corn		x			
Wheat roll	x				
Fruit cocktail			x		

B = Bread, Cereal, Rice and Pasta Group
V = Vegetable Group
F = Fruit Group
ME = Meat, Poultry, Fish, Dry Beans, Eggs, and Nuts Group
MI = Milk, Yogurt, and Cheese Group

However, convenience foods also have some disadvantages. Most are high in sodium. Many have significant amounts of fat and sugar. Look for nutrition information on the label and compare products before you buy.

Convenience foods can also be more expensive than ingredients you put together yourself. However, some convenience foods actually cost less than those you prepare. Check it out.

Money

Food costs can take up a large part of the family budget. Fortunately, nutritious food is not necessarily expensive. By making wise choices, you can have tasty, nutritious meals without spending a lot of money.

Another way to save money on food is to plan for the use of leftovers. Sometimes people call them "planned-overs." You can make more than needed for a meal and plan to use the remainder at another time. For example, leftover meat loaf can be used for sandwiches at lunch. Extra rice can be made into fried rice. Planned-overs can save time and cut down on food waste.

When family members help to get a meal on the table, it can be ready in just a few minutes.

Other Resources

Time, energy, skills, and equipment are also resources for meal planning. Remember, if some resources are in short supply, you may be able to make a tradeoff. For instance, if family members get home from work and school late in the day, there may not be very much time or energy to prepare the evening meal. What are some possible solutions? The family might decide to spend more money on convenience foods to save time. They might use a microwave oven to speed meal preparation. They might cook on the weekend when there is more time and freeze the meals for use during the week.

Personal skills are a valuable resource to consider. The rest of the chapters in this unit will help you learn how to use recipes and prepare many kinds of foods. People who know the basics of food preparation have more options. They can use their skills to prepare a meal that is more nutritious and less expensive than eating out. Can you think of other advantages of preparing food at home?

Planning Your Own Meals

If you are like most teens, you are on your own for at least some of your meals and snacks each week. Whether you prepare food at home, eat out, or "grab-and-go," your food choices deserve thought. The following suggestions will help you plan quick and easy meals and snacks.

▼ Breakfast ▼

Breakfast is often called the most important meal of the day, and with good reason. If you skip breakfast, your body goes for up to 18 hours without a new energy supply. It can't function well. Even a small nutritious breakfast can help you feel better and work better each day.

Some people dislike breakfast foods or say they don't have time to eat breakfast. Breakfast doesn't have to be boring or time-consuming. Any food is fine for breakfast as long as it's nutritious. You might try:

- A sandwich of peanut butter and sunflower seeds on whole-wheat bread.
- A container of yogurt with chopped nuts and raisins.
- A bean tostada.
- Leftover pizza.
- Milk, fresh or canned fruit, and wheat germ whirled in a blender.

There are many other fast and tasty possibilities. Use your creativity to think of interesting combinations.

▼ Packing a Lunch ▼

Many people take a packed lunch to school or to work. Use the Food Guide Pyramid to help you plan a nutritious packed lunch.

Dairy products, cooked meats, and some other foods can spoil if not kept cool. An easy way to keep your lunch safe is to include something cold in your lunch container. You might use a frozen gel pack or freeze some water or juice in a sealed container. Using an insulated lunch bag will also help keep foods safe.

What can you pack in your lunch? Sandwiches are popular because they are easy to pack and eat. Try different combinations of breads and fillings for variety. A tossed green salad is also a good choice. So are fresh fruits and crunchy vegetables, such as carrot or celery sticks, cauliflower chunks, cherry tomatoes, red bell pepper rings, or zucchini sticks. If you have a wide-mouth vacuum bottle, you can pack soup or other hot foods, such as spaghetti. You might round out the meal with milk, yogurt, or cottage cheese.

To save time, you can prepare part or all of the lunch ahead of time. Refrigerate or freeze the foods in their containers. In the morning, just pop them in your lunch bag and you're on your way. See page 492 for more tips on packing a lunch.

What food choices do you enjoy in a packed lunch?

How to . . .
Pack a Lunch

Here are some suggestions to help you keep packed lunch foods safe and fresh.

- ***Sandwiches.*** Wrap the sandwich well or use an airtight container to keep it fresh. You might want to try making sandwiches ahead of time and freezing them. (Avoid freezing sandwiches with raw vegetables, mayonnaise, or hard-cooked eggs.) Pack the still-frozen sandwich in your lunch to help keep the other foods cold. By lunchtime it will be thawed and ready to eat.
- ***Sandwich additions.*** You can add flavor and texture to sandwiches with tomato slices, sprouts, green pepper rings, or other additions. Pack them separately and add them to the sandwich just before eating. Otherwise they might get soggy.
- ***Salads and vegetables.*** Pack in an airtight container. Pack dressings or dips separately.
- ***Hot foods.*** Preheat a vacuum bottle by filling it with hot water. When the food is steaming hot, pour the water out of the vacuum bottle and fill it with the food. Seal the bottle tightly.
- ***Milk.*** If you can't buy milk at lunchtime, bring your own in a vacuum bottle. Make sure the vacuum bottle and the milk are both cold when you pack your lunch.
- ***Other dairy foods.*** Pack chilled cottage cheese or yogurt in tightly sealed containers. Use an insulated lunch bag or include a frozen item to help keep them cold.
- ***Utensils.*** Don't forget to pack a napkin and a spoon or fork, if needed.

Snacks

Nutritious snacks can help active, growing teens to meet their nutrient needs.

Would it surprise you to learn that snacking isn't bad for you? In fact, most growing, active teens need snacks. They would have a hard time getting the nutrients they need from meals alone.

The real problem is poor snack choices. Many popular snack foods, such as potato chips, candy bars, and cookies, have low nutrient density. They are high in fat and sugar and supply few of the nutrients you need. Filling up on these foods can lead to real problems.

Instead, snack on low-fat foods from the five major food groups. You might choose fresh fruit, raw vegetables, fruit juice, plain popcorn, or crackers with a little peanut butter.

Some foods that you might normally think of as part of a meal also make good snacks. Try a small sandwich, a cup of soup, or a glass of skim milk.

Quick and Easy Dinners

Sometimes you may want to prepare a quick evening meal for one. Many simple and nutritious dinners can be made using a combination of fresh and convenience foods. Following are some ideas for main dishes. To complete the meal, add simple side dishes such as a cooked frozen vegetable, a green salad, fresh fruit, or bread.

- Cook leftover chicken with frozen stir-fry vegetables. Serve over instant rice.
- Bake a potato. (It takes just five minutes in the microwave.) Top with scrambled egg or cottage cheese.
- Top bagel or English muffin halves with bottled pizza sauce and the toppings of your choice. Heat in a microwave or toaster oven.
- Combine canned kidney or pinto beans (mashed) with seasonings and chopped vegetables. Roll up in a tortilla.

A baked potato can be part of a quick, nutritious meal when topped with a protein food.

Choosing from a Fast-Food Menu

When you eat at a fast-food restaurant, keep the Dietary Guidelines in mind. Many fast-food menu items are high in fat, sodium, or sugar. For instance, a large cheeseburger, an order of fries, and a shake can easily provide about half the calories a typical teenager needs each day, along with about 60 grams of fat. (That's probably about two-thirds of a typical teenager's daily "fat budget.")

Fortunately, fast-food menus are changing in response to the needs and wants of customers. Many restaurants now

You can choose nutritious, low-fat foods at many fast food restaurants.

offer items lower in fat, calories, and sodium. Look for signs or brochures that give information about the nutrition of menu items. Here are some examples of good choices:

- Sandwiches: lean roast beef or turkey, small hamburger, grilled chicken.
- Side dishes: plain baked potato, mashed potatoes, salad with low-fat dressing, fresh fruit from salad bar.
- Beverages: low-fat milk, water.
- Breakfast items: pancakes, cereal with low-fat milk.

Ask for food to be served without high-fat, high-sodium toppings, such as cheese, bacon, mayonnaise, and tartar sauce or special sauce. Go easy on salt, butter, and other toppings you add yourself.

Try to choose a good balance of foods from the five major food groups. If the meal is short on fruits, vegetables, grains, or dairy products, be sure you get enough of these foods at other meals that day. By following these guidelines, you can enjoy fast foods and still have a healthful diet.

Planning Family Meals

How is meal planning handled in your home? Is it the responsibility of one person or do several people share ideas? No matter how it's handled, planning family meals takes management skills.

If you are planning a meal for the whole family, what do you need to think about? Nutrition is an important consideration, just as it is when you are planning your own food choices. In addition, you need to think about questions such as:

- When will the meal be served? Will everyone eat at the same time or is everyone's schedule different? The box on page 495 gives some suggestions for busy families.
- Who will prepare the meal? If resources such as time, equipment, or cooking skills are limited, try to keep the menu simple.
- What foods do family members like and dislike? Even the best meal plan won't work if people don't eat the foods. Fortunately, each of the five major food groups has enough choices to satisfy even the pickiest eaters.
- Do any family members have special needs? Someone may be on a special diet or be allergic to certain foods, for instance. You may need to adapt the menu for that person.
- How can I make the meal appetizing? A successful menu is more than just nutritious and practical. It has something extra called "meal appeal."

Planning family meals can be a real challenge. How do you and your family handle meal planning?

Eating in Shifts

Meals, especially dinner, are a good time for the family to get together. Unfortunately, in real life it doesn't always work out that way. Families often have to plan meals around work hours, school activities, meetings, and other events. The whole family may not sit down at one time to eat.

Busy schedules don't have to mean another night of takeout pizza or frozen dinners. Here are a few ideas you and your family might want to try.

- Keep individual servings of leftovers or "planned-overs" in the refrigerator or freezer.
- Prepare a food that will keep for several hours. For instance, you might put a main-dish salad in the refrigerator. Family members can serve themselves whenever they are ready.
- Use a slow cooker to prepare a stew, soup, or other dish. The food can cook all day until it is done, then safely continue cooking a few more hours until everyone has had a chance to eat.
- Plan a casserole that can be reheated without losing flavor. Some food mixtures actually taste better after flavors have had time to mingle.
- Set aside a shelf in the refrigerator for do-it-yourself meals. For instance, prepare containers of lettuce, tomatoes, shredded cheese, meat sauce, beans, and other fixings for tacos or salads.

Making meals look appealing is part of good planning and an enjoyable dining experience.

▼ Meal Appeal ▼

Close your eyes and think about your favorite meal. Does it look as good as it tastes? You can perk up appetites by paying attention to:

- ***Color.*** The colors of food come right from an artist's palette — green, yellow, red, purple, orange, and creamy white. Use this wide variety to avoid monotonous one-color meals.
- ***Shape.*** Different shapes make a meal more attractive. For instance, meatballs, peas, and boiled, small potatoes are all round. For variety, try hamburger, slivered beans, and a baked potato.
- ***Texture.*** Contrasting textures also add variety. If you are having mashed potatoes, you might plan on a crisp green salad rather than applesauce. Crispy stir-fried vegetables are a good contrast to rice.
- ***Flavor.*** Vary flavors to add interest to a meal. Plan flavors that go well together. If have too many spicy or strongly flavored foods in one meal, they will fight with each other for your attention.
- ***Temperature.*** You might want a contrast of temperatures, such as a cold salad with steaming soup. Cold foods are appealing on hot days and hot foods on cold days.

TAKING ACTION

Keith is working as a supervisor in a summer day-care program for nine- and ten-year-olds. The service does not include meals or snacks, so the children are required to bring their own. Keith has noticed many children bringing foods that seem like poor choices — cookies and potato chips, for example. He would like to encourage better nutrition among the youngsters, but knows they may not want to part with their sweets. He also realizes he must sell their parents on good nutrition if his plan is to have a lasting effect. He asks for your help in getting the children to eat more nutritiously.

Using Your Resourcefulness

- Where can Keith learn about any special nutritional needs of children in this age group?
- Where can he find out what foods are high in these nutrients?
- Where can he find suggestions on making nutritious snacks appealing to children?
- Where can he get information on what kinds of foods can be safely packed in lunches?
- How can he make price comparisons, to convince parents that simple, healthful foods are also cheaper?
- What suggestions can you offer Keith for talking with the parents about good nutrition?

Chapter 42 Review

Summary

In this chapter, you have read about:

- Applying the Dietary Guidelines and the Food Guide Pyramid to your meal pattern.
- Resources to consider when planning meals.
- How convenience foods fit into meal planning.
- Ideas for easy, nutritious meals and snacks.
- How to pack a lunch.
- Making healthful choices from a fast-food menu.
- Hints for fitting nutritious meals into a busy family schedule.
- Ways to make meals appealing.

Facts to Recall

1. How can planning meals and snacks help ensure nutritious eating?
2. Why does knowing your meal pattern in advance help you eat healthfully?
3. Identify four resources to consider when planning meals.
4. Name two advantages and two disadvantages of convenience foods.
5. Explain how "planned-overs" can save a family money, time, and energy and cut down on food waste.
6. What are two ways of keeping foods from spoiling in a packed lunch?
7. Name two examples of a healthful sandwich choice and side dish at a fast-food restaurant.
8. List four questions to think about when planning a meal for the whole family.
9. Give three ideas for planning meals for a family that does not eat at one time.
10. Name five factors affecting meal appeal.

Ideas to Explore

1. Describe a meal pattern you might follow on a typical weekday. How has this pattern developed to suit your lifestyle? Does it present any problems in getting all your required daily nutrients? How might you change it to help you eat more healthfully?
2. How are current trends and technology influencing the way families plan, prepare, and eat meals? What are some positive results? What are some negative results and how can families respond?

Activities to Try

1. Bring a menu from a fast-food restaurant (or make a list of menu items) to class. Identify those items you would and would not choose as part of a nutritious meal. Explain your selections.
2. Brainstorm a list of snacks that are easy to prepare and eat, yet also nutritious.

LINK TO *Communication*

TEACHING CHILDREN ABOUT BREAKFAST

Learning to make healthful food choices starts in childhood. Plan a five- to ten-minute puppet show designed to teach young children about eating a nutritious breakfast. Emphasize the food groups from the Food Guide Pyramid. (Note: You can make interesting puppets out of socks, paper lunch bags, or other recyclable materials.) Present your puppet show to younger children.

As a follow-up activity, make some nutrition "flash cards" that show different foods from the food groups that can be eaten for breakfast. Involve the children by asking them to identify which food groups the foods come from.

CHAPTER

43 Buying and Storing Food

OBJECTIVES

- Name factors affecting food prices.
- Discuss how to prepare and shop for food.
- Explain how to store food.

TERMS TO LEARN

- *processing*
- *cents-off coupons*
- *unit price*
- *open dating*
- *perishable foods*

Have you ever shopped for food for your family? Everyone at some time has probably had to shop for a container of milk, a head of lettuce, or a loaf of bread. If you shop for a few items, your task is fairly easy.

Shopping for food becomes a more challenging task when the weekly shopping list is involved. Will you be able to get the best value for your dollar? Will you be able to resist many of the tempting treats along the supermarket aisles and buy only what you need?

In this chapter, you will learn more about the food you buy and techniques for buying it. Developing shopping savvy will help you get the most value for your food dollar.

Food Costs and Your Budget

As you learned in Chapter 42, money spent on food can use up a large part of the family budget. Before you start out for the supermarket, you need to figure out how much money you have to spend on food. Talking with family members about the food budget will help you carefully plan food choices.

Planning your food choices helps you stay within your food budget.

The price of food reflects the many steps food goes through before it reaches the marketplace:

- ***Production.*** The food on your plate began with farming or fishing. Factors such as weather and the time of year affect the supply of food, and therefore the cost. If supplies are limited — for instance, after a drought or freeze — prices go up. Foods are generally least expensive and taste best during the peak of their growing season. For example, tomatoes are usually tastier and less expensive in summer.
- ***Processing.*** Part of the cost of food is due to **processing**, or the steps that are taken to prepare and package food for sale. Foods may be processed to increase their safety and storage life, to add convenience, or to make them into specific products (such as flour made from wheat).
- ***Distribution.*** Transportation costs are also figured into the price of food. In most stores, foods have been shipped in from all over the United States and even some foreign countries.

- ***Marketing.*** Food companies spend money to advertise their goods, design attractive packaging, and research new products. These costs are passed on to consumers.

Getting Ready to Shop

Shopping for food involves more than just a trip to the store. It involves using your planning and management skills before you leave home. Taking time to plan ahead can save time and money when you shop.

Deciding Where to Shop

If you live in a populated area, you will probably have a greater variety of stores to choose from than if you live in a small town or rural area.

- **Supermarkets** are large stores that sell a full line of food products and nonfood items. Many supermarkets include a bakery, a cheese shop, a deli, a fish market, a salad bar, or other specialty departments.

When shopping for food, choose a store that sells a variety of good quality foods.

- **Warehouse stores** take a "no-frills" approach to selling food. They carry a limited line of basic items, which are often displayed in cartons. Prices are lower than in a supermarket, but fewer services are offered. For example, you may have to bring your own bags and fill them yourself.
- **Convenience stores** carry a limited line of food and nonfood items. They are designed to attract shoppers who want to make a quick stop for a few items. Prices are usually higher than at a supermarket.
- **Specialty stores** concentrate on one type of food item, such as meat, fish, or baked goods. Often the prices are higher than at other stores. Specialty stores offer personal service and may prepare special items for you.
- **Farmers' markets** are places where local growers bring their harvest to sell. During the growing season, you can find low-cost fresh fruits and vegetables here.
- **Food co-ops** are owned and operated by members of the co-op (cooperative). The co-op buys food in quantity and distributes it among the members. Since members do the work, costs are kept down.

Wherever you shop, choose a store that has a good selection of quality foods. In addition, a store should be clean and neat.

Avoid shopping when you are hungry. You may find yourself buying more food because everything looks good to eat.

Planning Your Shopping Trip

Your schedule will help determine when and how often you shop for food. In most cases, you can make the best use of your time by going on one major shopping trip instead of several small ones.

If you shop when stores are less crowded, you'll spend less time waiting in line. Try not to shop on an empty stomach. Hungry shoppers often spend more than expected because everything looks "good enough to eat."

Make it a practice to check newspaper ads before you shop. By looking at different store ads, you can compare prices and find out what is on sale. Take advantage of sale items and seasonal foods as you plan menus.

Look through magazines, newspapers, and advertising fliers for cents-off coupons. **Cents-off coupons** are certificates that allow customers to buy products at reduced prices. Manufacturers print these coupons to encourage you to use their products. Some stores offer double or triple discounts on coupons.

When available, use coupons for items on your shopping list.

Have you ever returned from the store with bags full of items you didn't intend to buy — and none of the items you really needed? A shopping list can help you avoid this problem. Keep a list posted in the kitchen. When you are planning menus, write down the ingredients you'll need for recipes. Before shopping, check the cabinets, refrigerator, and freezer for items that are running low.

To make your list easier to use, group similar foods together — all the dairy products, all the canned goods, and so on. You can also save time by arranging your shopping list to match the way foods are organized in the store. Remember to take your list and your coupons to the store with you.

Shopping for Food

When you get to the store, keep your shopping list handy. As you select items, cross them off the list. A small calculator can help you keep track of how much you are spending.

Food stores use a number of techniques to encourage impulse buying — making purchases on the spur of the moment.

- Bright, colorful packaging and displays are designed to catch your eye.
- Special displays are often placed in the middle of the traffic lane or at the end of an aisle. You have to slow down to go around them. The items on display are sometimes sale priced, but not always.

Be aware of tactics that encourage impulse buying. The sight, aroma, and taste of food may tempt you to spend more than your budget allows.

- Popular items are often placed at eye level so you will be more likely to see and buy them.
- Slow, relaxing music encourages shoppers to take their time and buy more.
- Some stores offer food samples to encourage consumers to try new products. The sight, aroma, and taste of food can be very tempting.

By following your shopping list and being aware of these tactics, you'll be less likely to make impulse purchases.

Comparison Shopping

As you walk through the store, you will find many choices. Your shopping list may say "green beans," but do you want fresh, frozen, or canned? What brand and size should you choose?

Instead of grabbing a package at random, take the time to comparison shop. By comparing different items, you can be sure you are getting good nutrition and quality at a good price. Comparison shopping is easier if you have an understanding of labels, brands, prices, forms and sizes of food, and signs of quality.

Reading Labels

Are you a label reader? Reading labels is an important part of comparison shopping. The label tells you what is inside the package. A typical label includes:

- The name of the product.
- A description of the product, such as whole, halves, or diced.
- The net weight of the contents. (Net weight does not include the weight of the package.)
- The name and address of the manufacturer, packer, or distributor.
- A list of ingredients. They are listed in order of weight, beginning with the largest amount. For example, if a soup lists noodles before chicken, it has more noodles than chicken in the can.

In addition, you will often see brand names, pictures of the contents, and suggestions for preparation.

Nutrition information is often given on the label or on a sign posted near the item. This information can help you to select more nutritious foods.

Nutrition Facts

Serving Size 1/2 cup (114 g)
Servings Per Container 4

Amount Per Serving	
Calories 90	Calories from Fat 30
	% Daily Value*
Total Fat 3 g	**5%**
Saturated Fat 0 g	**0%**
Cholesterol 0 mg	**0%**
Sodium 300 mg	**13%**
Total Carbohydrate 13 g	**4%**
Dietary Fiber 3 g	**12%**
Sugars 3 g	
Protein 3 g	

Vitamin A	80%	Vitamin C	60%
Calcium	4%	Iron	4%

* Percent Daily Values are based on a 2,000 calorie diet. Your daily values may be higher or lower depending on your calorie needs:

	Calories	2,000	2,500
Total Fat	Less than	65 g	80 g
Sat Fat	Less than	20 g	25g
Cholesterol	Less than	300 mg	300 mg
Sodium	Less than	2,400 mg	2,400 mg
Total Carbohydrate		300 g	375 g
Fiber		25 g	30 g

Calories per gram:
Fat 9 • Carbohydrates 4 • Protein 4

By reading labels, you can choose foods that provide the best nutritional value for your money.

By law, foods that have had nutrients added and products that are advertised as being nutritious must have nutrition labels. These labels include:

- Serving size and number of servings.
- Calories per serving and calories from fat.
- Grams of fat, cholesterol, sodium, carbohydrates, and protein per serving and their percentage of daily value.
- Key vitamins and minerals and their percentage of daily value.

Comparing Brands

When you shop, compare national brands, private labels, and generic products.

- **National brands** are produced by major food companies. They are sold across the country and advertised nationally.
- **Private label**, or store brand, products are packaged for a particular chain of stores. Prices are usually lower than for nationally advertised brands. There may be or may not be differences in the quality. The nutritional value is the same as for the national brands.
- **Generic products** can be identified by their plain, simple packaging. They are less expensive than other brands. The nutritional value is the same as for other products, but the quality and appearance may not be as good.

The unit price allows you to compare the cost of different-sized packages of foods.

Using Unit Prices

Many stores offer a unit pricing system to help consumers comparison shop. The **unit price** is the price per ounce, pound, or other convenient unit of measure. Unit pricing makes it easy to compare the cost of products in different-size packages.

Unit prices are often posted on the shelf near the item. The total price for the package is also given. For example, a 15-ounce can of tomatoes may have a unit price of 3 cents per ounce. The total price for the can is 45 cents (3×15).

If unit prices are not given, you can calculate them yourself. Divide the total cost of the package by the number of units (such as ounces or pounds) to get the cost per unit. Repeat this process for other sizes and brands to determine the best buy.

Comparing Forms and Sizes

Compare the price of foods in different forms whenever you can. Foods may be purchased fresh, frozen, canned, or dried. They may be whole, sliced, diced, or chopped. How you plan to use the food will help you to decide what to buy. There's no point in paying the higher price for whole or extra fancy items if they are going to be used in a casserole.

Buying in quantity or buying larger sizes often costs less. However, compare the unit prices to be sure. Also, if the extra food will be wasted, buying the larger size is not a bargain.

Some stores offer bulk foods that you can select and package yourself. Products are in large containers, and you scoop out the amount you want. Because food is not packaged, prices may be lower than individually wrapped products. Compare unit prices to make sure you are getting the best buy.

Judging Quality

Low-priced food is not a bargain if the quality is poor. It takes careful shopping to select food that is fresh and nutritious.

Open dating is a system used on food labels to help you determine the freshness of a product. Several different methods of dating are used. A "sell by" or "pull" date is often found on bakery goods, dairy products, meats, and other items that lose freshness quickly. This date tells the last day the product can be sold in the store. The product is still safe for home use after this date if stored properly and used quickly.

A "use by" date can be found on refrigerated doughs and packaged cold cuts. This shows the date after which the food will no longer be at its peak of freshness.

Other tools for judging quality include the grade labels, such as "grade A," that are found on some foods. You will learn more about specific grades and signs of quality in Chapters 47 to 51.

TIPS: *Recognizing Signs of Food Spoilage*

How can you tell when food is unsafe to eat? Learn these "danger signs":

- The food has an unusual odor or color.
- The food has an unusual softness or mushy spots.
- The food looks or feels "slimy."
- Raw meat changes to a dull, gray-brown color.
- Cans of food have bulges.

Open dating helps you determine the freshness of products that you buy.

Shopping for Convenience Foods

Many foods are available in a wide variety of convenience forms. You can buy main dishes, side dishes, snacks, and entire meals already prepared. Some are frozen, while others can be stored at room temperature. Many can be heated in the microwave oven for quick meals.

Convenience foods can be part of a healthful diet. However, read labels carefully. Many convenience foods are high in fat, sugar, and sodium. They should be used in moderation and in combination with fresh foods. For instance, you might round out a frozen dinner by adding skim milk, whole-wheat bread, and an apple. Come to think of it, many fresh foods are convenient, too!

How to . . .
Be a Courteous Shopper

As you shop, practice courtesy toward other customers. Here are some tips for courteous shopping:

- Handle foods carefully to avoid damaging them. When careless shoppers damage products, store owners have to increase prices to cover the losses.
- Avoid blocking traffic in the store aisles.
- Have your coupons ready to hand to the checkout clerk.
- If you are paying with a check, write it out (except for the amount) while waiting in the checkout line.

Many supermarkets use a scanner to speed up checkout and maintain an accurate inventory.

▼ Filling Your Cart and Checking Out ▼

As you load your cart, put heavier items at the bottom. Put easily damaged items, such as tomatoes, bread, and eggs, where they will not be crushed.

Select refrigerated or frozen foods last so they don't thaw before you get them home. Many stores are arranged so that the frozen food aisle is your last stop.

In many supermarket checkout lanes, an electronic scanner reads prices automatically. The clerk passes each grocery item over the scanner. The scanner uses a laser to read a bar code — called a universal product code, or UPC — that is found on the package. The bar code identifies the product, size, and manufacturer. When the UPC is read by the scanner, the price of the item is automatically rung up on the cash register. The UPC not only speeds up checkout, it also helps the store keep an up-to-date inventory.

As you place your items on the checkout counter, make sure the prices or UPC symbols are visible. You can also help the checkout clerk by grouping together items that are all the same price, such as several cans of tomato soup.

Familiarize yourself with the grocery prices and check them as they are rung up on the register.

After you pay the bill, make sure you receive the correct change. Make sure all items you paid for are put into bags.

Storing Food

After you have finished shopping, take the food home immediately and store it. Put frozen foods away first to prevent them from thawing. Next, put away foods that belong in the refrigerator. (Any food that was kept cold at the store should be refrigerated or frozen at home.) Put your other items away last.

As you store your purchases, place them behind similar foods that are already in storage. That way, food that has been stored the longest is at the front of the storage area so that it will be used first. This is especially important for fresh and frozen products.

Putting food away after shopping is a quick and easy task when family members work together.

By storing food wisely, you will be able to enjoy fresh and nutritious food. Here are some guidelines for the three basic types of storage areas: refrigerator, freezer, and dry storage.

AROUND THE WORLD

In desert regions such as Morocco and Ethiopia, dairy products do not keep long without refrigeration. The people of these countries have solved part of the problem, however, by using *clarified* butter. Clarified butter is made by melting the butter and skimming off the milk solids as they rise to the top. The oily portion that remains keeps well at room temperature for about a month. It also burns less easily when used in cooking.

Refrigerator Storage

The refrigerator provides safe storage for **perishable foods**. These are foods that spoil easily, such as milk and other dairy products, eggs, meat, fish, poultry, and many fruits and vegetables. Storing perishable foods in the refrigerator helps prevent the growth of bacteria and keeps foods fresh and flavorful.

Inside the refrigerator, the temperature should be between 32°F and 40°F (0°C and 5°C). Cold air needs to be able to circulate in the refrigerator to keep food at proper temperatures.

Make use of the compartments and racks in your refrigerator. The meat keeper is extra cold to keep meat fresher. Vegetable bins help fruits and vegetables retain moisture. The door shelves can hold large bottles and cartons, but are not as cold as those inside the refrigerator.

Keep foods covered in the refrigerator to keep them from drying out and absorbing flavors and odors from other foods.

Put frozen foods away immediately after you arrive home from the supermarket.

▼ Freezer Storage ▼

Using the freezer allows you to store foods for longer periods of time. Freezer storage slows down the growth of harmful bacteria. The inside temperature of the freezer should be 0°F (−18°C) or below.

Foods to be frozen should be sealed in airtight, moisture-proof packaging. Plastic containers, freezer paper, heavy foil, and special freezer bags are good to use. Foods that you buy frozen can be stored in the original packaging.

▼ Dry Storage ▼

Canned and boxed foods that do not require freezing or refrigeration should be stored in a cool, dry place. Once they are opened, cover them tightly to keep out insects.

TAKING ACTION

Zach is on vacation with his best friend's family, the Wilders. One morning he volunteers to walk to the nearest market and buy food for breakfast. "Pick up some good healthy cereal," Mrs. Wilder tells Zach.

Now Zach is perplexed as he faces the cereal shelf. With so many brands to choose from, he doesn't know which to buy. Zach reads the following labels, listing nutritional information for a 1-ounce serving:

- *Knott's Natural Bran* has 4 grams of sugar, 2 grams of fat, and 4 grams of fiber.
- *Short's Shredded Wheat* has 0 grams of sugar, 0 grams of fat, and 6 grams of fiber.
- *Green's All-Natural Granola* has 6 grams of sugar, 4 grams of fat, and no listing for fiber.

Using Your Resourcefulness

- Which cereal appears to be the most nutritious from the label? Why?
- Both *Knott's* and *Green's* say "Cholesterol free" and "Low-fat" on the box. Are the claims misleading? Why or why not?
- Do you read food labels when you shop? Why or why not?
- How could reading food labels benefit you now in your life? In the future?

Chapter 43 Review

Summary

In this chapter, you have read about:

- How production, processing, distribution, and marketing affect food prices.
- Different types of food stores and the items and services found in each.
- How to save time and money when shopping by being prepared and organized.
- The techniques used by stores to encourage you to buy.
- How to get the most for your money by comparison shopping.
- Guidelines to help you be an efficient, courteous shopper.
- How to preserve the quality of food by proper storage.

Facts to Recall

1. Explain how weather can affect the price of food.
2. Name three reasons why food is processed. How does processing affect food prices?
3. What is the difference between a supermarket and a warehouse store?
4. Explain how a food co-op operates.
5. Identify three ways that looking at newspaper ads and magazines before going shopping can save you money.
6. Give two hints for organizing your shopping list for more efficient shopping.
7. List four types of information that you can find on packaged food labels.
8. How do generic products compare with national brands in price, nutritional value, and quality?
9. How is unit price calculated?
10. When is buying in quantity not a bargain?
11. What is the difference between a "sell by" date and a "use by" date?
12. What is the proper temperature range for inside the refrigerator? The freezer?

Ideas to Explore

1. What types of food stores are found in your community? What are the advantages and disadvantages of each?
2. In your experience, what is the biggest mistake people make when grocery shopping, in terms of spending time and money? Why?

Activities to Try

1. Write a sample grocery shopping list of items your family uses regularly. Use the tips found in the chapter to organize your list efficiently.
2. Write a radio public service announcement describing consumer tips for saving money when shopping for food.

LINK TO *Math*

FIGURING UNIT PRICE

Locate canned, boxed, and bottled food items (such as a canned vegetable, boxed cereal, and bottled juice) at the supermarket. For each food item, list a national brand, private label or store brand, and a generic brand. Write the price and the amount the package contains next to each food item. Compute the unit price for each food item using the formula found on page 504 of the text.

- Which brands appeared to be the best buy for each food item?
- Why is buying the lower-priced food items a benefit for the shopper?
- When might the lower-priced items not be the best buy? Why?

CHAPTER

44 Kitchen Equipment

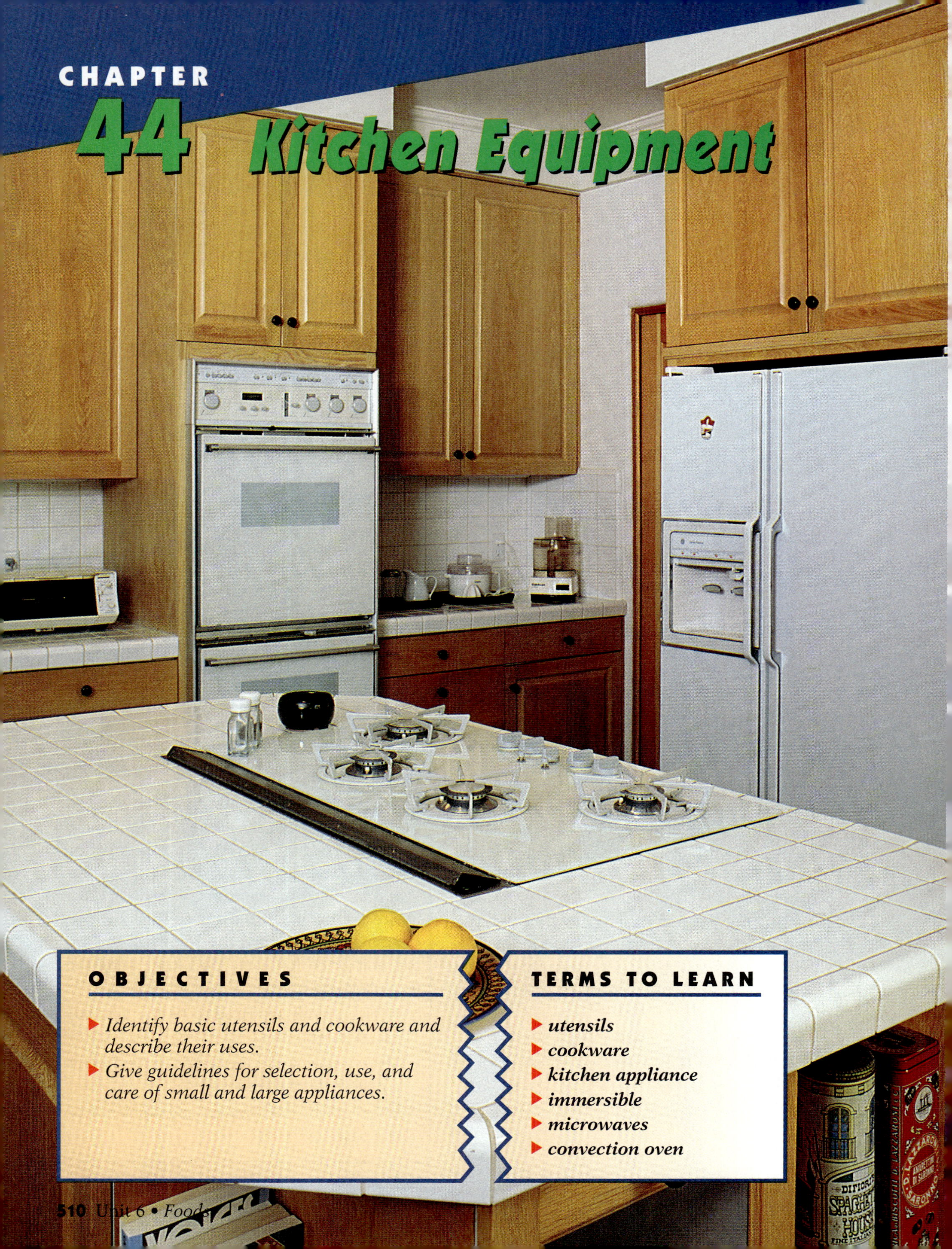

OBJECTIVES

- *Identify basic utensils and cookware and describe their uses.*
- *Give guidelines for selection, use, and care of small and large appliances.*

TERMS TO LEARN

- ***utensils***
- ***cookware***
- ***kitchen appliance***
- ***immersible***
- ***microwaves***
- ***convection oven***

Can you play basketball without a ball or baseball without a bat? You can't. You can ask the same type of question about the kitchen. Can you heat soup without a pan or make stew without a knife? The answer is "no."

However, it's not necessary to own every piece of kitchen equipment sold. If you did, you would run out of storage room! A better approach is to choose wisely and get the most out of each piece of kitchen equipment you have. You'll find some items are more useful than others.

You can often substitute one piece of kitchen equipment for another if you have limited space or the cost is too high. Mixing bowls can be used as serving dishes. A wire whisk could be used instead of an electric mixer.

Safety is an important consideration when using kitchen equipment. You can read about kitchen safety in Chapter 47.

Utensils

Small kitchen tools are called **utensils**. If you have already done some cooking, you know how helpful utensils can be. They save you time and enable you to prepare products you would not otherwise be able to make.

Sturdy, well-made utensils will last a long time. Careful use and storage also extend their life. If you have a dishwasher or microwave oven, buy utensils that are dishwasher-safe or can be used in the microwave.

Measuring Utensils

Measuring utensils help you to accurately measure ingredients for recipes. Some popular measuring utensils are shown here.

Dry measuring cups, used to measure dry ingredients such as flour and sugar, are usually in sets. The most common sizes in the U.S. are ¼ cup, ⅓ cup, ½ cup, and 1 cup. If you use recipes that give amounts in the metric system, you will need metric measuring utensils. Sizes found in a set of metric dry measures include 50 mL (milliliters), 125 mL, and 250 mL.

Dry measuring cups

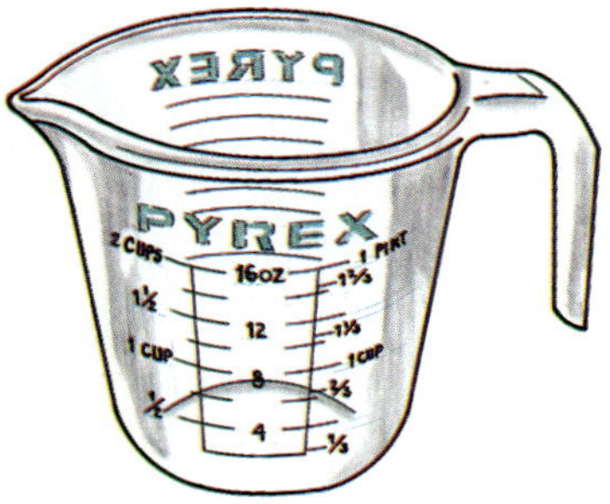

Liquid measuring cup

Liquid measuring cups have a spout for pouring. They have measurements marked on the side in cups, ounces, and milliliters. Common sizes are 4 cups, 2 cups, and 1 cup (1000, 500 and 250 mL).

Measuring spoons are used for measuring smaller amounts of liquid and dry ingredients. The most common sizes are ¼ teaspoon, ½ teaspoon, 1 teaspoon, and 1 tablespoon. A set of small metric measures includes 1 mL, 2 mL, 5 mL, 15 mL, and 25 mL sizes.

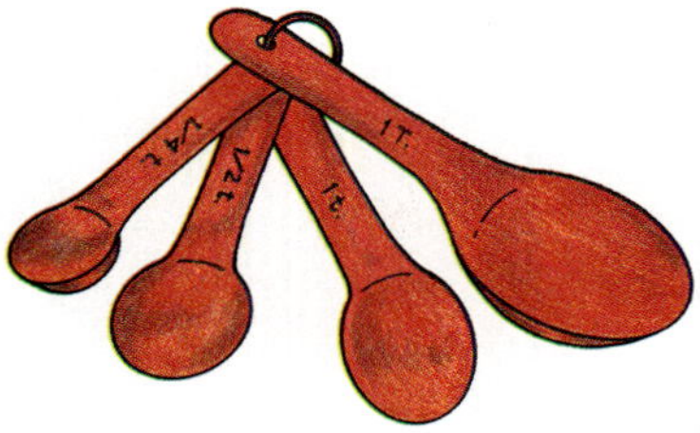

Measuring spoons

Mixing Utensils

Mixing utensils help to blend ingredients together. Some mixing utensils can be used for a variety of tasks. Others are used only for one specific task.

Mixing bowls come in graduated sizes. They are used to hold the ingredients you are mixing.

Mixing spoons have long handles and are used for combining ingredients. You see them in wood, metal, and plastic.

Rubber or plastic scrapers are used to scrape bowls and fold ingredients together. They have a wide, flexible blade.

Sifters sift and mix dry ingredients together as they pass through a mesh screen. They come in various sizes.

A *pastry blender* cuts shortening into flour for piecrusts and biscuits. Sometimes people use two knives or a fork in place of a pastry blender.

Wire whisks are used for beating and blending. Whisks are especially good to use in beating egg white mixtures and stirring sauces.

A *rotary beater* is also known as a hand beater or eggbeater. It is used to beat eggs and mix thin batters, such as pancake batter.

Sifter

Mixing spoon

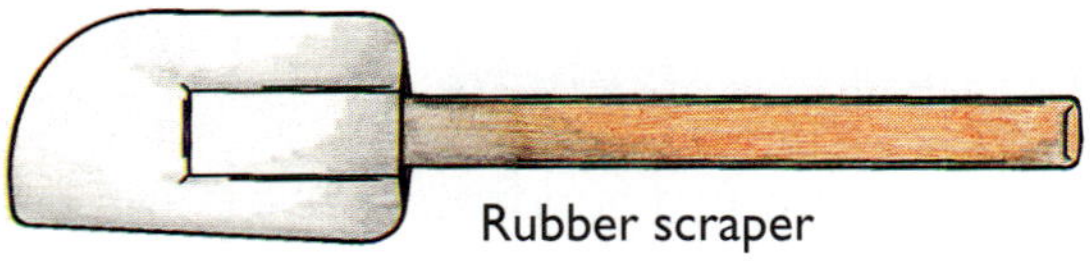

Rubber scraper

Pastry blender

Wire whisk

Mixing bowls

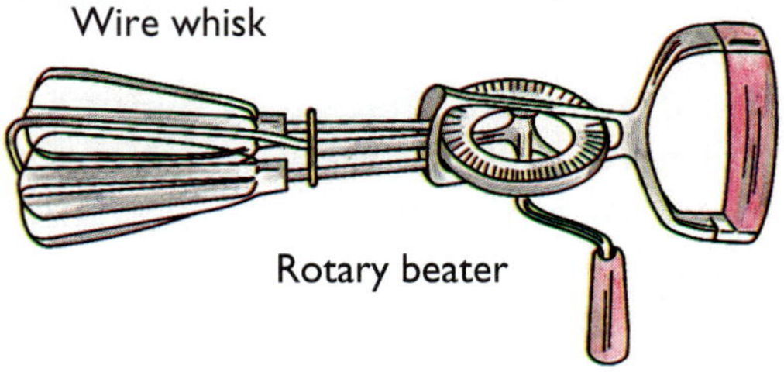

Rotary beater

AROUND THE WORLD

The mortar and pestle are standard equipment in the Vietnamese kitchen. Ingredients to be ground or crushed are placed in a small wooden or ceramic bowl, the mortar, and broken up with a pestle, which looks much like a very small baseball bat. Many cooks have two sets: a smaller one for nuts and spices, and a larger one for seafood and meat. For preparing small amounts of foods, the mortar and pestle are more convenient than an electric food processor.

Paring knife

Utility knife

Chef's knife

Bread knife

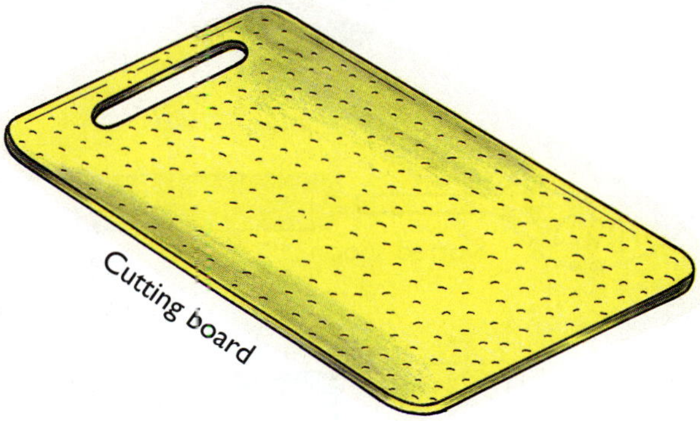

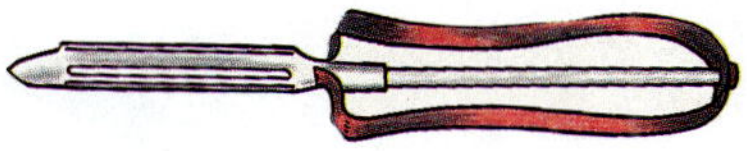
Peeler

▼ Cutting and Chopping Utensils ▼

Cutting and chopping tools cut food into smaller pieces. Keep safety in mind as you use cutting tools.

Knives come in a variety of sizes. *Paring knives* are good for peeling fruits and vegetables. *Utility knives* are all-purpose knives for cutting and slicing many foods. *Chef's knives* are used for cutting, mincing, and dicing. *Bread knives* come in handy for slicing bread or baked goods.

Cutting boards are used as a base for your cutting work. They help to keep knife blades sharp and counters in good shape. When you cut raw meat, poultry, or fish, use a cutting board made of plastic. Plastic boards are easier to keep clean than wooden ones, so there is less chance of spreading harmful bacteria.

Peelers are used to peel vegetables and fruits. The blade swivels.

Kitchen shears are sturdy scissors. They are used to cut vegetables, pastry, poultry, and meat.

Graters are used to shred and grate vegetables and cheeses. Some graters shred both finely and coarsely.

Grater
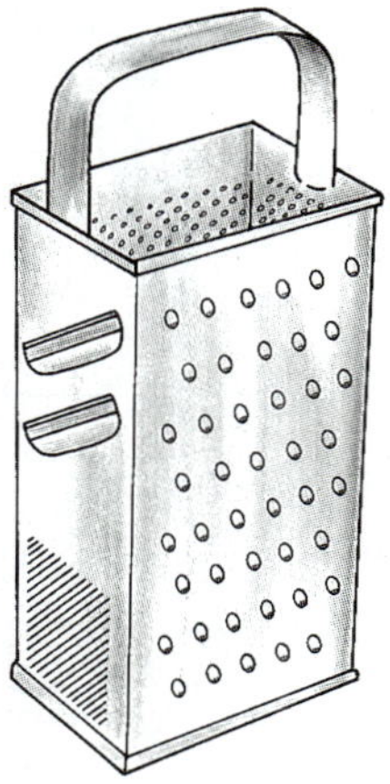

Colander

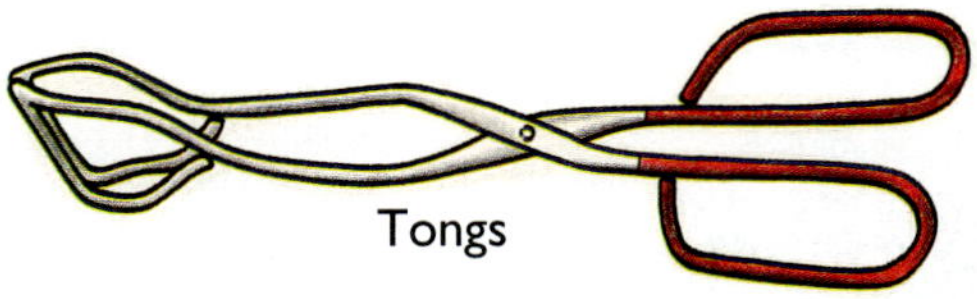
Tongs

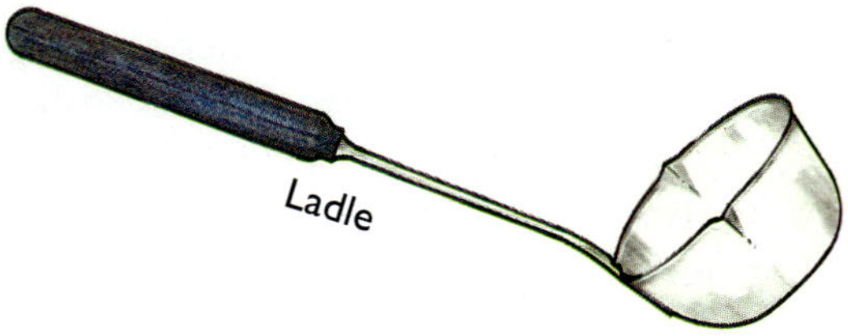
Ladle

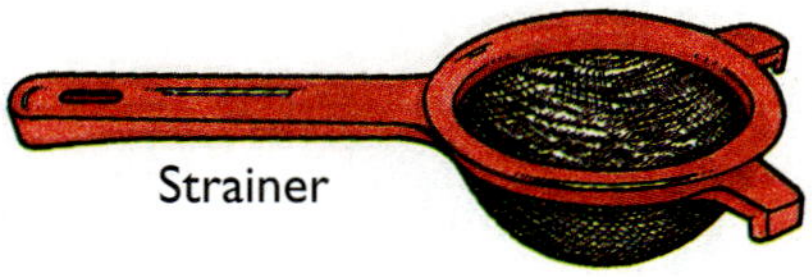
Strainer

Slotted spoon

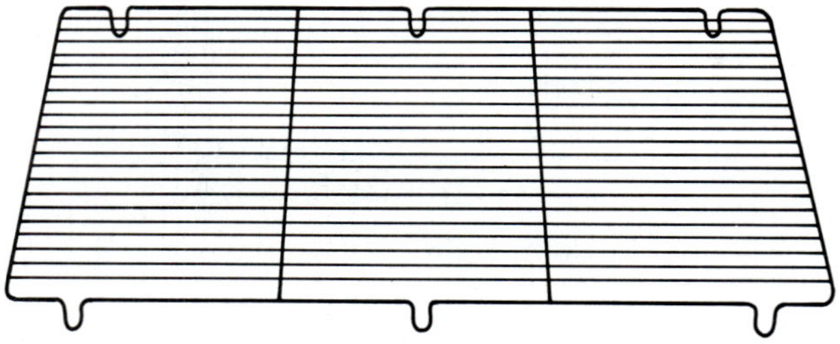
Cooling rack

Spatula

Turner

Cooking fork

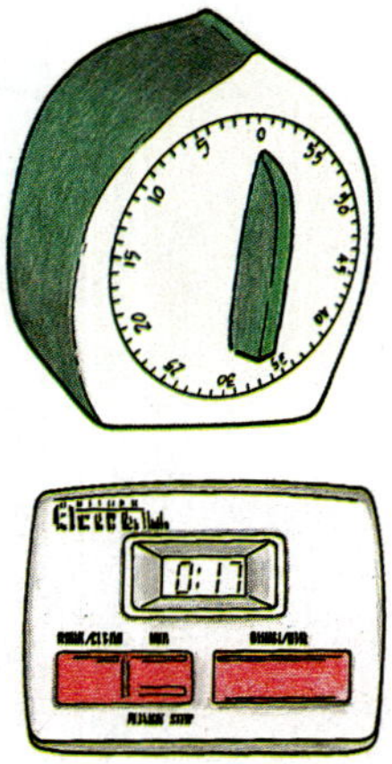
Timers

Other Kitchen Utensils

A variety of other tools help to make kitchen work easier. Several examples are shown here.

Colanders are bowls with large holes that stand on a base or little legs. They are good for draining foods such as cooked pasta.

Strainers are wire mesh baskets with handles. They strain the liquid from smaller amounts of food.

A *slotted spoon* is helpful for lifting small pieces of solid food from liquid.

Narrow metal *spatulas* have wide, dull blades. They are useful in leveling dry ingredients in measuring cups, picking up small cookies from baking sheets, and loosening baked products from the sides of baking pans.

Wide spatulas, or *turners*, are useful. They can lift and turn foods such as pancakes or hamburgers.

Tongs are grasping instruments. They help you lift large pieces of food, such as a chicken drumstick or a corncob.

Cooking forks are also used for lifting and turning foods.

Ladles are helpful when serving foods such as hot soup and stews.

Timers can remind you about cooking times. They usually can be set for periods of time up to 60 minutes.

Cooling racks are also known as cake racks. They are made of wire and allow air to circulate around hot baked products.

Cookware

Cookware includes pots, pans, and other containers for use on top of the range, in the oven, or in the microwave. They are made of various materials. Some of the differences in these materials affect the way you use and care for them. The chart on page 516 explains the different types of materials.

Frying pans, or *skillets*, are shallow and have a long handle. They come in assorted sizes and sometimes have covers.

Saucepans and *pots* are deeper than frying pans. They come in a variety of sizes, usually measured in quarts or liters. Some have covers. Saucepans have one handle, while pots have two — one on each side.

Casseroles, or baking dishes, come in a variety of shapes and sizes. They are deep enough to hold a main-dish mixture and often have covers.

Cake pans are round, square, or rectangular. They can be used for baking many things in addition to cakes.

Baking sheets are rectangular, low-sided pans. They are most often used for baking cookies.

Pie pans are round with sloping sides. They come in different sizes.

Muffin pans have from six to twelve individual cups to hold muffins and cupcakes.

Loaf pans are used for breads and meat loaves. They come in different sizes.

Custard cups are made out of heatproof glass. You might use them to bake custard or microwave eggs.

Frying pan or skillet

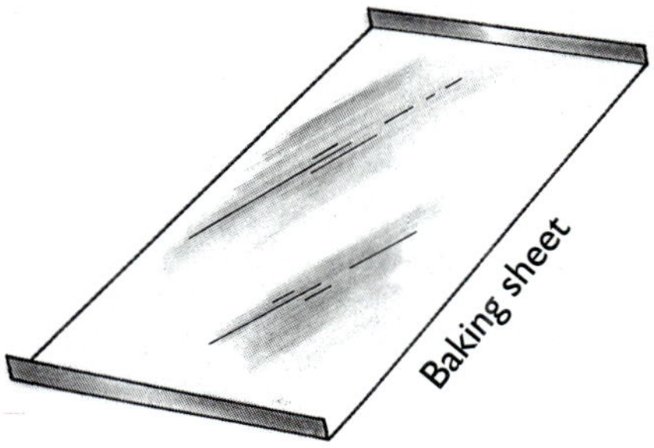

Pie pan

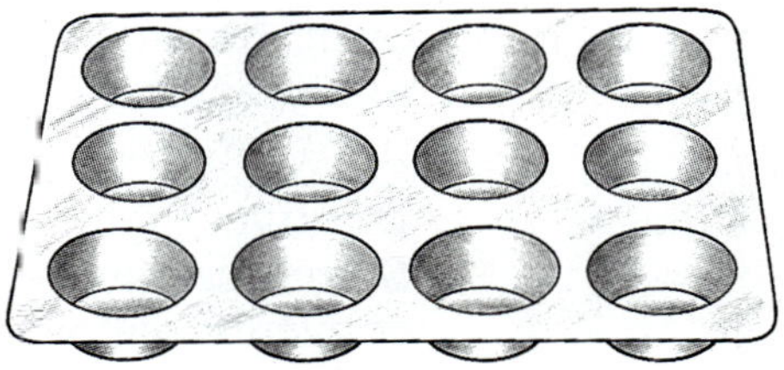
Muffin pan

Custard cups

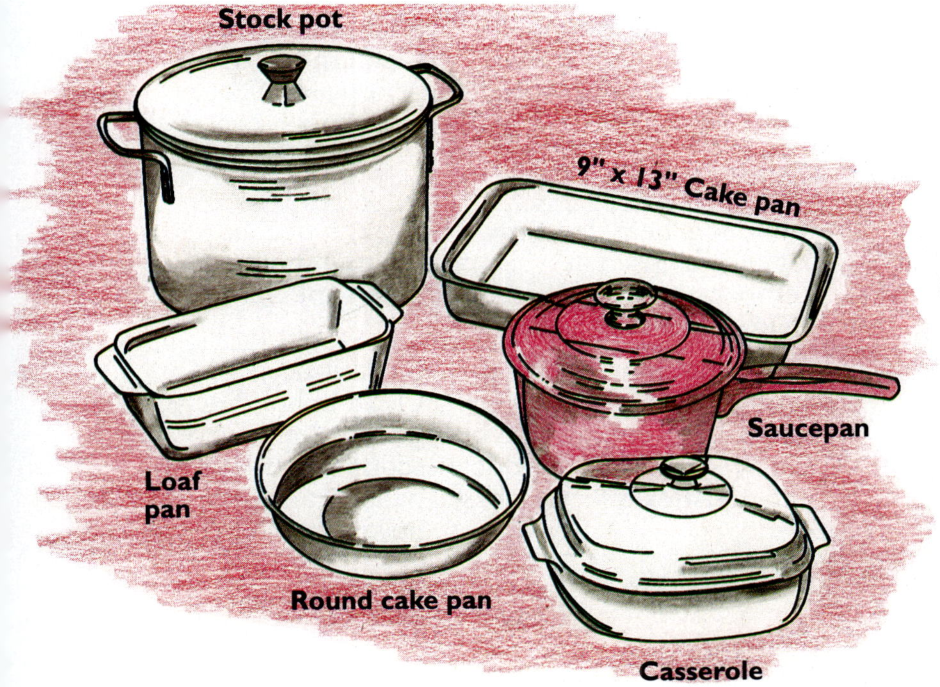

Cookware Materials

Material	Advantages	Disadvantages	Care
Aluminum	Lightweight, durable, good conductor of heat.	Minerals in food and water cause darkening. Dishwasher detergent stains and darkens. (Acid foods remove darkening.)	Soak, if needed. Clean in hot detergent water. Do not put in dishwasher.
Cast iron	Good conductor of heat.	Rusts unless dried thoroughly. Heavy.	Soak, if needed. Clean in hot detergent water. Dry well. Do not scour.
Porcelain enamel (glass on metal)	Spreads heat well.	Chips and stains easily.	Soak, if needed. Clean in hot detergent water. Remove stains with household bleach.
Stainless steel	Strong. Resists stains and rust. Keeps brightness under normal care. Durable.	Does not spread heat evenly. (Aluminum and copper, good conductors of heat, are often used on the bottom or as a core.) Will darken if overheated.	Soak, if needed. Clean in hot detergent water. Scour.
Glass	Transparent — you can see food in container.	Chips and breaks easily. Conducts heat unevenly. Most require wire trivet for use on electric range. Cannot hold up under extreme temperature changes.	Soak, if needed. Clean in hot detergent water. Do not scour.
Glass ceramic	Withstands sharp temperature changes — can go from freezer to oven. Resists scratching and cracking. Some are transparent.	Breaks when dropped. May develop hot spots that cause food to stick.	Soak, if needed. Clean in hot detergent water. Scour.
Plastic	Durable. Lightweight. Some can be used in conventional ovens as well as microwave.	Conducts heat unevenly. Cannot be used at temperatures higher than 350°-400°F (170°-200°C).	Soak, if needed. Clean in hot detergent water.
Nonstick finishes	Allow fat-free cooking and easy cleaning. Durable if used properly.	Will scratch unless used with nylon or plastic utensils. Overheating will cause staining and reduce the nonstick effectiveness.	Soak, if needed. Clean in hot detergent water. Do not scour with metal pads or abrasive powders.

Appliances

Kitchen appliances are pieces of equipment for the kitchen powered by either gas or electricity. Using both small appliances and large appliances makes your cooking time more productive.

Small Kitchen Appliances

Small electric appliances can sit on a table or counter and be moved from place to place easily. There are hundreds of small kitchen appliances available today.

If you use an appliance frequently, it is a good investment. However, people often buy appliances, store them in a cabinet, and forget about them. If you keep appliances handy, you are more likely to use them.

Before buying a small appliance, ask yourself how often you will use it. Is it worth the cost? Consider the size of the appliance. Do you have enough space to store and use it?

Comparison shop to gather information about various appliance brands you're considering. What safety features are included? What is covered by the warranty? Sometimes a warranty covers parts, labor, and shipping costs. Other times, only certain parts are covered and nothing else. Refer to Chapter 20 for additional information on comparison shopping.

Look for the Underwriters Laboratories (UL) seal on the appliance. This seal certifies that an electrical appliance is safe to use.

Some appliances will have the term **immersible** (ih-MUHR-suh-buhl) on them. This means that the entire appliance can safely be put into the water to be washed. On such appliances, the electric unit has been sealed so no water can enter. If you do not see the term "immersible," never put the appliance in water. You could receive a bad shock.

Here are some common small appliances:

- ***Toaster.*** Holds at least two slices of bread for toasting — sometimes more. Some can adjust for thicker breads such as muffins.
- ***Toaster oven/broiler.*** Good for toasting breads, warming foods, and doing small cooking chores, such as broiling hamburgers.
- ***Hand-held mixer.*** Can be used for whipping cream, making cake batter, mixing pudding, and mashing potatoes. It's lightweight and fairly compact, so it's easy to manage and convenient to store.

TIPS: *Buying a Toaster*

Look for these features when buying a toaster:

- Bread wells that are large enough for thicker foods, such as English muffins or frozen toaster foods.
- A snap-down crumb tray for easier cleaning.
- Heat-resistant handles, temperature control, and a well-insulated base.
- Energy-saving features.

Toaster

Toaster oven/broiler

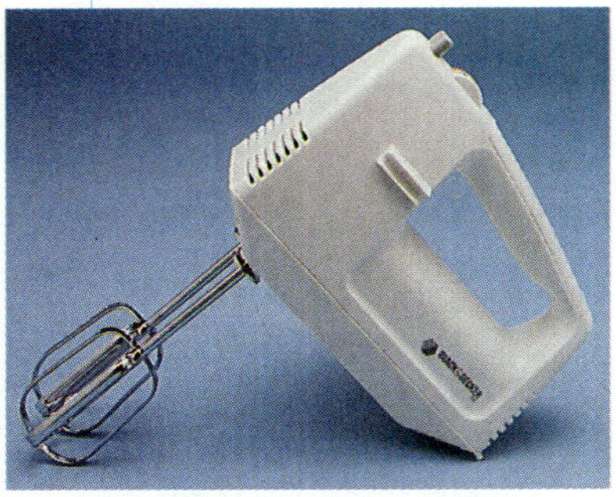

Hand-held mixer

- ***Stand mixer.*** Has a bowl that rotates on a turntable in the base of the stand. Depending on the power of the motor, the mixer is either light-duty or heavy-duty. Heavy-duty mixers are better able to handle heavy cookie doughs and bread batters.
- ***Blender.*** Has push-button speed controls for a variety of mixing and chopping tasks. Good for beverages, such as fruit drinks and milk shakes.
- ***Food processor.*** Different blades and disks allow it to perform a variety of cutting and mixing tasks. Good for slicing or shredding vegetables, for example.
- ***Electric frying pan.*** A control on the handle regulates the cooking temperature. Use to fry, roast, simmer, or bake. Can also serve as a buffet server or hot tray.

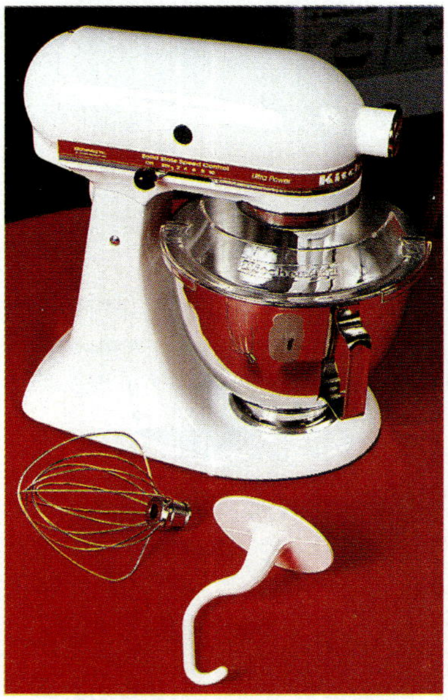

Stand mixer

Food processor

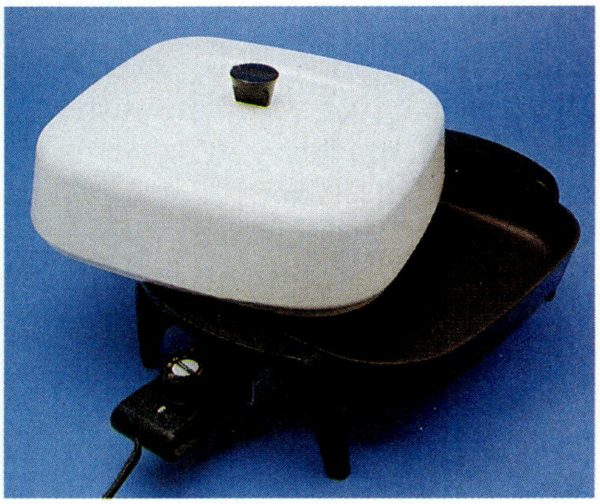

Electric frying pan

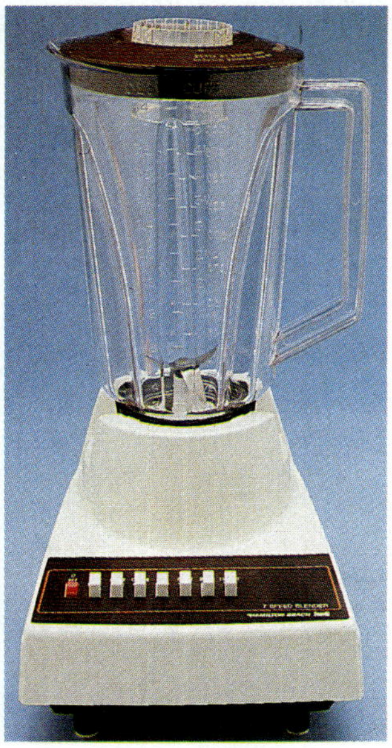

Blender

Large Kitchen Appliances

A large appliance, such as a range or refrigerator, is a major purchase. The cost depends on the style, size, and special features and on whether you buy a new or used appliance.

If you have a new appliance, read and save the owner's manual. It has a lot of valuable information about using and caring for the appliance.

If your family is shopping for a large kitchen appliance, follow the shopping principles outlined in Chapter 20. During your comparison shopping, be sure to compare the Energy-Guide labels for an estimate of the energy use of the appliance.

Another way to judge the quality of appliances is to look for safety and performance seals. You have already read about the Underwriters Laboratories (UL) seal placed on electrical appliances that have been tested for safety. The American Gas Association (AGA) certified seal is placed on tested gas appliances.

UL seal

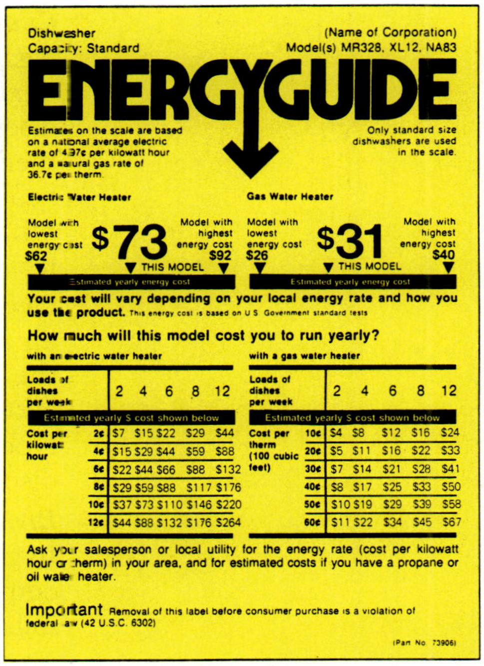

Dishwasher
Capacity: Standard

(Name of Corporation)
Model(s) MR328, XL12, NA83

ENERGYGUIDE

Estimates on the scale are based on a national average electric rate of 4.37¢ per kilowatt hour and a natural gas rate of 36.7¢ per therm.

Only standard size dishwashers are used in the scale.

Electric Water Heater

Model with lowest energy cost $62 — **$73** THIS MODEL — Model with highest energy cost $92

Estimated yearly energy cost

Gas Water Heater

Model with lowest energy cost $26 — **$31** THIS MODEL — Model with highest energy cost $40

Estimated yearly energy cost

Your cost will vary depending on your local energy rate and how you use the product. This energy cost is based on U.S. Government standard tests

How much will this model cost you to run yearly?

with an electric water heater

Loads of dishes per week		2	4	6	8	12
Estimated yearly $ cost shown below						
Cost per kilowatt hour	2¢	$7	$15	$22	$29	$44
	4¢	$15	$29	$44	$59	$88
	6¢	$22	$44	$66	$88	$132
	8¢	$29	$59	$88	$117	$176
	10¢	$37	$73	$110	$146	$220
	12¢	$44	$88	$132	$176	$264

with a gas water heater

Loads of dishes per week		2	4	6	8	12
Estimated yearly $ cost shown below						
Cost per therm (100 cubic feet)	10¢	$4	$8	$12	$16	$24
	20¢	$5	$11	$16	$22	$33
	30¢	$7	$14	$21	$28	$41
	40¢	$8	$17	$25	$33	$50
	50¢	$10	$19	$29	$39	$58
	60¢	$11	$22	$34	$45	$67

Ask your salesperson or local utility for the energy rate (cost per kilowatt hour or therm) in your area, and for estimated costs if you have a propane or oil water heater.

Important Removal of this label before consumer purchase is a violation of federal law (42 U.S.C. 6302)

(Part No. 73906)

An EnergyGuide label estimates the cost of operating an appliance for one year.

Refrigerators

The design of the refrigerator affects how long frozen food can be stored. Some refrigerators have only one outside door with a small freezer compartment inside. This type of freezer compartment does not stay cold enough for long-term storage of frozen foods. Generally, frozen foods should be stored for less than a week in this type of freezing compartment.

Combination refrigerator-freezers have two separate outside doors. One part is for storing fresh foods. The other one is for freezing fresh food and for long-term storage of frozen food. The freezer section may be located above, below, or alongside the refrigerator section. If the temperature in the freezer is at or below 0°F (−18°C), frozen foods can be stored for a long time.

Combination refrigerator-freezers have an outside door for each compartment.

Clean the outside and inside of the refrigerator often. You can use water mixed with a little baking soda. Wipe up spills right away to prevent odors and germs.

Check the owner's manual for other care instructions. You may need to defrost the freezer, clean coils at the bottom or back of the refrigerator, or empty a drip tray, for example.

Ranges

Ranges are used for baking, cooking, and broiling. You can choose from gas or electric models. The features available on ranges vary with the manufacturer and model.

A basic range includes a cooktop, one or more ovens, and a broiler.

- ***Cooktop.*** A range usually has four cooking surfaces. If it is a gas range, they are called burners. When you turn a gas burner on, you have an instant source of heat. With an electric range, the cooking surfaces are called heating elements. Usually these are coils that take a few minutes to heat up or cool off. When you turn the heating element off, the food will continue to cook unless you remove it from the heating element.
- ***Oven.*** Conventional ovens use gas or electricity to heat air in a closed compartment. The hot air flows around the food and cooks it. When putting items in the oven, allow enough space for the air to circulate. (Two other types of ovens — microwave and convection — will be discussed shortly.)
- ***Broiler.*** A broiler is used to cook foods under direct heat. In gas ranges, the oven and the broiler are often separate compartments. The broiler door is kept closed while broiling. In an electric range, the broiler is usually found in the oven compartment. The oven door should be left slightly open when you broil.

The different parts of a range can also be purchased as separate appliances. A cooktop can be built into a kitchen cabinet with storage space underneath. An oven and broiler can be built into a wall. Smaller countertop ovens are also available.

The inside and outside finishes on most ranges are made of stainless steel or porcelain enamel, which is glass on metal. When you clean them, avoid using harsh, gritty cleansers. While the surface is slightly warm, wipe up spills and spattered grease with a warm, sudsy cloth or sponge. Then wipe with a damp cloth rinsed in clear water. If food boils over, wipe off the burner or heating element, drip pan, and drip tray as soon as the unit is cool enough to touch. Hot water and detergent do a good cleaning job.

The broiler compartment in a gas range is underneath the oven.

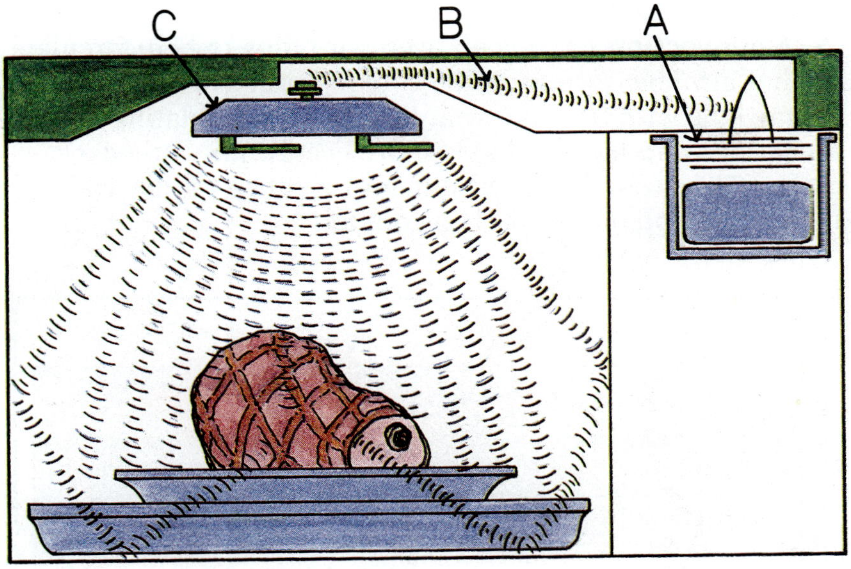

The magnetron tube creates microwave energy. The microwaves are distributed by a slowly rotating fan which causes the microwaves to bounce off the walls, ceiling, and bottom of the oven. Microwave energy causes food molecules to vibrate, producing friction. The friction produces heat and cooks the food.

Microwave Ovens

Some microwave ovens are part of a range or built into a wall. Most, however, are countertop models.

The most important part of a microwave oven is the magnetron tube. It changes electrical energy into tiny waves of energy called **microwaves**. Some of the microwaves hit the food directly. Others bounce around the oven and off the metal walls until they hit the food.

Microwave ovens don't get hot. Instead, the energy passes through the cookware into the food. It causes the water molecules in the food to vibrate, or rub against each other. This friction then produces heat that cooks or warms the food.

There are many advantages to cooking in a microwave oven. Microwave cooking can save time and energy. Baking one potato in a microwave oven takes 5 minutes as opposed to 55 minutes in a conventional oven. There is less cleanup with a microwave oven because spills do not bake on the surface. You can cook or heat foods in individual serving dishes, such as plates or bowls, as long as the dishes are made of microwave-safe materials. One disadvantage is that foods don't brown.

Metal reflects microwaves. This is why manufacturers tell you not to use metal cookware in the microwave oven. It could damage the magnetron tube, an expensive item to replace.

You can learn more about microwave cooking, as well as other cooking methods, by reading Chapter 46.

Convection Ovens

A **convection oven** is an oven with fans to help circulate the hot air. This speeds up the cooking process, although not as much as with the microwave oven. The circulating hot air also cooks and browns foods more evenly. Like other ovens, convection ovens may be built into a range or the wall, or they may stand on the kitchen counter.

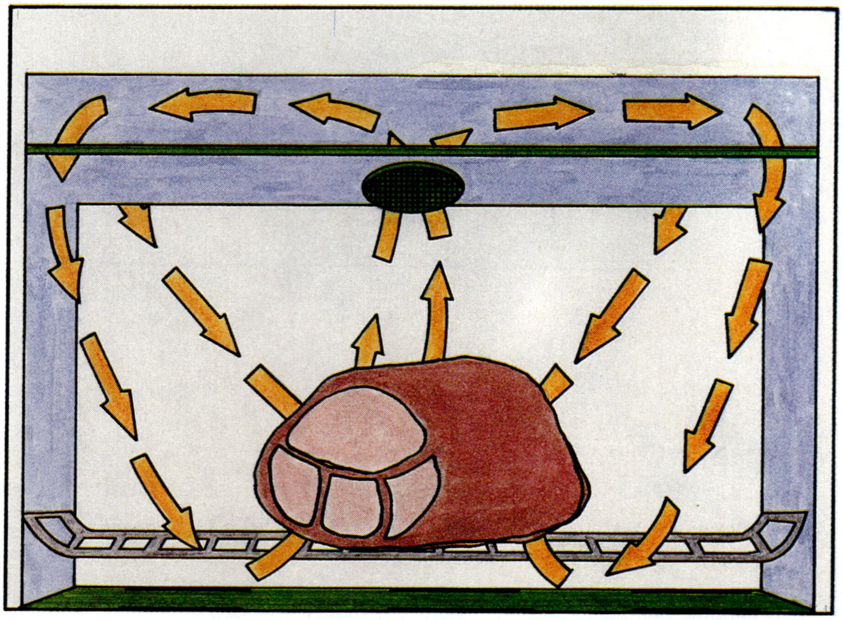

In a convection oven, a fan circulates heated air continuously throughout the oven. Temperatures are usually more even than in a conventional oven. This helps foods cook more evenly.

TAKING ACTION

Your friend Clay has a problem. His older brother Andrew just moved into his first apartment, and Clay wants to get him a housewarming gift. Knowing Andrew has few kitchen utensils or appliances, he has decided to buy him some. "He needs almost everything, but he doesn't have much space," Clay explains. "I'd like to get him some things he can really use. However, I don't have too much to spend, so I want to be sure I'm getting the best buy for my money. What do you think I should do?"

Using Your Resourcefulness

- What resource can Clay use to find out about different kitchen appliances and utensils and their uses?
- What advice can you give Clay about selecting some essential kitchen equipment that might be useful to his brother?
- How might Clay compare the quality and reliability of different brands of the same item?
- How can he determine whether he is getting the most for his money?

Chapter 44 Review

Summary

In this chapter, you have read about:

- Kitchen utensils and their uses.
- Different types of cookware and cookware materials.
- Factors to consider when buying small and large kitchen appliances.
- Types of small appliances often found in the kitchen.
- How to care for refrigerators and ranges.
- How microwave and convection ovens cook food.

Facts to Recall

1. Name four mixing utensils. List the uses of each.
2. Why should plastic cutting boards be used instead of wooden ones for cutting raw meat, poultry, or fish?
3. What two types of utensils might be used for turning slices of bacon in a frying pan?
4. Name two similarities between frying pans and saucepans. Name one difference.
5. List four different types of baking pans.
6. Name four factors to consider when buying a small kitchen appliance.
7. What does "immersible" mean? Why is it important to know whether a small appliance is immersible?
8. List two tips for keeping a refrigerator clean.
9. How do microwave ovens cook food? Convection ovens?
10. What are three advantages of cooking with a microwave oven?

Ideas to Explore

1. Name some instances in which you could substitute one piece of kitchen equipment for another.
2. In what ways are microwave ovens easy for children to use? What are some risks involved in allowing young children (ten years and under) to use a microwave?

Activities to Try

1. Use your imagination to design a new type of utensil or appliance. If you prefer, design an improved version of an already existing article of kitchen equipment. Use words, pictures, or both to describe your invention, its use, and how it works.
2. Find studies or surveys in consumer magazines comparing different brands and models of one type of kitchen appliance. Decide which model you would buy, based on the magazine's findings.

LINK TO *Communication*

Promoting Kitchen Equipment and Appliances

Many people rely on the knowledge of a salesperson when buying kitchen equipment or small appliances. Choose an item of kitchen equipment or a small appliance you find particularly useful (such as a food processor or type of bakeware). Locate as much information as possible about the item (such as how it works, usage, care, etc.). Assume the role of a salesperson who is convincing a customer to purchase this item. In your "sales pitch," talk about the safety features, use and care, the versatility, and advantages of owning this item. Keep your sales pitch to three minutes or less.

CHAPTER

45 Recipes and Measuring

OBJECTIVES

- *Explain how to select and interpret a recipe.*
- *Demonstrate how to measure ingredients.*
- *Alter a recipe's yield and substitute ingredients.*

TERMS TO LEARN

- ***recipe***
- ***abbreviation***
- ***equivalents***
- ***yield***

How do you combine tomatoes, onions, garlic, basil, oregano, parsley, olive oil, salt, and pepper into a great pasta sauce? You can use your imagination and blend the ingredients until the mixture tastes just right. You could also look for a recipe that tells you how to make pasta sauce.

In this chapter, you will learn about choosing recipes and measuring ingredients. The next chapter will help you learn how to follow recipe directions for successful results.

Choosing a Recipe

A **recipe** is a set of directions used in cooking. Recipes list the amounts of ingredients needed and then tell you what to do with those ingredients. Look at the sample recipe on page 526.

Recipes can be found in cookbooks, magazines, and newspapers. Friends and family members often share favorite recipes with one another.

Before you choose, look over several recipes for the type of food you want to prepare. Compare them by asking yourself these questions:

- Is this recipe appealing? If you will be sharing the food with others, consider their preferences and special needs as well as your own.
- How long will the recipe take to prepare? Do I have enough time?
- Do I understand all the steps? Do I have the skills needed?
- Do I have all the necessary equipment? Will I be able to find all the ingredients?

If you haven't had very much cooking experience, look for recipes with fewer ingredients and steps. They are usually easy to prepare.

Measuring

Much of your success in preparing food depends on the way you measure ingredients. Knowing abbreviations, equivalents, and measuring techniques will get you off to a good start.

Homemade Granola

3 cups	rolled oats
1 cup	mixed seeds or grains (such as sunflower seeds, sesame seeds, wheat germ, or shredded wheat)
1 cup	coarsely chopped walnuts
½ cup	vegetable oil
½ cup	honey
1 cup	raisins
1 cup	diced dried fruits

Mix all ingredients except raisins and dried fruit in a large bowl. Spread in a single layer on a jelly roll pan. Bake at 300°F, stirring often, for 30 minutes or until golden brown. Remove from oven. Stir in raisins and dried fruit. Cool. Makes 8 cups granola.

Recipes may be written in different ways, but they all should include the information shown here.

Abbreviations and Equivalents

The chart below shows units of measure commonly used in recipes. Some recipes are written using customary measurements, such as cups and tablespoons. Others use metric measurements, such as milliliters. It's best to use the correct measuring equipment, metric or customary, for the recipe you're using.

Units of Measure

Type of Measurement	Customary Units and Abbreviations	Metric Units and Symbols
Volume	teaspoon (tsp.) tablespoon (Tbsp.) fluid ounce (oz.) cup (c.) pint (pt.) quart (qt.) gallon (gal.)	milliliter (mL) liter (L)
Weight	ounce (oz.) pound (lb.)	gram (g) kilogram (kg)
Temperature	degrees Fahrenheit (°F)	degrees Celsius (°C)

An **abbreviation** is a shortened form of a word. Recipes often use abbreviations or symbols to save space. Be sure to look at the abbreviations and symbols shown on the chart and become familiar with them.

You'll also find it helpful to know some basic equivalents. **Equivalents** are amounts that are equal, such as twelve inches and one foot. Equivalents come in handy when you don't have the right measuring equipment or want to change a recipe. The chart below will help you learn basic equivalents.

Equivalents

Customary Unit	Customary Equivalent	Approximate Metric Equivalent
Dash	Less than ⅛ tsp.	Less than 0.5 mL
¼ tsp.		1 mL
½ tsp.		2 or 3 mL
1 tsp.		5 mL
1 Tbsp.	3 tsp.	15 mL
1 fluid oz.	2 Tbsp.	30 mL
¼ cup	4 Tbsp. OR 2 fluid oz.	50 mL
⅓ cup	5 Tbsp. + 1 tsp.	75 mL
½ cup	8 Tbsp. OR 4 fluid oz.	125 mL
⅔ cup	10 Tbsp. + 2 tsp. OR ⅓ cup + ⅓ cup	150 mL
¾ cup	12 Tbsp. OR ½ cup + ¼ cup OR 6 fluid oz.	175 mL
1 cup	8 fluid oz. OR 16 Tbsp.	250 mL
1 pt.	2 cups OR 16 fluid oz.	500 mL
1 qt.	2 pt. OR 4 cups OR 32 fluid oz.	1 L (1000 mL)
1 gal.	4 qt.	4 L
1 oz. (weight)		30 g
1 lb.	16 oz. (weight)	500 g
2 lb.	32 oz. (weight)	1 kg (1000 g)

Read your recipe thoroughly to become familiar with symbols and abbreviations.

Level off dry ingredients with the straight edge of a spatula.

▼ Measuring Dry Ingredients ▼

Dry ingredients include sugar, flour, salt, and baking powder. To measure ¼ cup (50 mL) or more, use a dry measuring cup. Hold the cup over waxed paper or the ingredient's container. Spoon the ingredient into the cup, heaping it a little over the top. Then level off the ingredient with the straight edge of a spatula. For smaller amounts, use a measuring spoon in the same way.

Some dry ingredients call for special techniques:

- Flour has tiny granules that pack together. If the recipe calls for sifted flour, sift it first, then measure in the usual way. Otherwise, stir the flour before spooning it into the measuring cup. Don't tap the cup to level the flour. Tapping packs down the flour and gives you too much. Whatever you were making would turn out too thick or dry.
- To measure brown sugar, pack it firmly into a measuring cup and level off. It should keep the shape of the cup when turned out of the cup. (Other types of sugar are not packed, but measured in the usual way.)

Read liquid measurements at eye level.

▼ Measuring Liquid Ingredients ▼

Liquid ingredients, such as milk, water, or oil, are measured in liquid measuring cups. These measuring cups are clear so you can see the liquid as it fills the cup. They have extra space at the top to prevent spilling and a spout for pouring. For an accurate measurement, place the cup on a flat surface and read the measurement at eye level.

Small amounts of liquids are measured in measuring spoons. Just fill the spoon to the brim. You don't need to level off liquids.

Measuring Fats

Solid fats, such as shortening, can be measured in a dry measuring cup. Pack the fat into the cup and level off. Use a rubber or plastic scraper to remove the fat from the cup.

Sticks of margarine or butter have measurements marked on the wrapper. One stick equals ½ cup (125 mL). If you need just part of a stick, cut through the wrapper on the appropriate marking.

Solid fats can also be measured in a liquid measuring cup using the water displacement method. Here's an example. To measure ¼ cup of solid fat, use a 1 cup liquid measuring cup. Fill it with cold water to the ¾ cup mark (because 1 cup minus ¼ cup equals ¾ cup). Now add the fat, a little at a time, making sure it is covered by the water. When the water reaches the 1 cup mark, you have measured ¼ cup of fat. Pour off the water and scrape the fat out of the cup.

AROUND THE WORLD

For most cooks, especially beginners, carefully measuring ingredients is a good idea. For the Cajuns (KAY-jenz) of southwest Louisiana, however, experimenting and substituting are valued in preparing meals. This has historical roots. When the first Cajuns settled in Louisiana in the mid 1700s, they lived off the land — and wasted nothing. Leftovers did not keep well in the humid climate, so they were often added to whatever dish was on the menu that day. Also, bartering, the trading of goods and services, brought different foods and spices to Cajun cooking. This spirit of adventure, born of necessity, makes Cajun cooking popular in all parts of America.

Altering Recipes

Very few recipes have to be followed exactly as written. The most common reason for altering a recipe is to change the number of servings. Other times you may need to substitute an ingredient for one that is missing. Some people like to experiment with recipes by adding their own touches. The following guidelines will help you alter recipes successfully.

Use your knowledge of equivalent measurements to alter the yield of a recipe.

▼ Changing the Yield of a Recipe ▼

The amount of food or number of servings a recipe makes is called the **yield**. If you want more or fewer servings, you will have to alter the recipe. Your math skills and knowledge of equivalent measurements will come in handy as you make the changes.

Suppose you are going to prepare a favorite casserole recipe. You want to make four servings, but the recipe yields eight. First, divide the number of servings you want by the original yield. The answer is the number you will use to calculate the new amount for each ingredient. In this example, $4 \div 8 = \frac{1}{2}$. You will multiply the amount of each ingredient by $\frac{1}{2}$.

Here's how it works. If the recipe calls for 2 pounds of ground beef, you would use 1 pound ($2 \times \frac{1}{2} = 1$). Instead of $\frac{1}{2}$ cup milk, you would use $\frac{1}{4}$ cup ($\frac{1}{2} \times \frac{1}{2} = \frac{1}{4}$).

As you multiply, you may need to convert from one unit of measurement to another. Suppose the recipe calls for $\frac{1}{4}$ cup grated cheese. The new amount would be $\frac{1}{8}$ cup ($\frac{1}{4} \times \frac{1}{2} = \frac{1}{8}$). Since you don't have a utensil that will measure $\frac{1}{8}$ cup, use the chart on page 527 to help you figure out an equivalent measure. Can you see that if $\frac{1}{4}$ cup is equivalent to 4 tablespoons, $\frac{1}{8}$ cup must equal 2 tablespoons?

Calculate the new amount for each ingredient in the recipe. Write the new amounts down on a piece of paper. It's easy to forget to change the amounts unless you write them down.

You need to think about some other points as well. Container sizes may have to be changed. For example, if you double a recipe, you will need to use either a pan that is twice as large or two pans of the original size.

The baking or cooking time may also have to be adjusted. If you put the mixture in a larger pan than the recipe called for, the heat will have to pass through a larger amount of food. The mixture will need to bake a little longer.

Be sure to change the size of the cooking container when you alter the yield of a recipe.

▼ Making Emergency Substitutions ▼

It's no fun to be in the middle of preparing a recipe and suddenly discover you are missing one of the ingredients. Before you begin, read through the ingredients list and make sure you have all the items on hand.

If you do find yourself without an ingredient, you may be able to make a substitution. Experience has shown that some ingredients can be used in place of others with fairly good results. Some of these substitutions are listed below. You may find others listed in cookbooks. Substitutions are more successful in some products than others.

Another possible solution is to change your plans slightly. If there's no canned tuna, perhaps you can make an egg salad instead. If you don't have all the ingredients for icing a cake, you can sprinkle confectioner's sugar on top.

Substitutions That Work

- 2 Tbsp. (30 mL) flour = 1 Tbsp. (15 mL) cornstarch (for thickening)
- 1 cup (250 mL) sifted cake flour = 1 cup minus 2 Tbsp. (220 mL) sifted all-purpose flour
- 1 cup (250 mL) whole milk = ½ cup (125 mL) evaporated milk plus ½ cup (125 mL) water
- 1 cup (250 mL) sour milk or buttermilk = 1 cup (250 mL) fresh milk plus 1 Tbsp. (15 mL) vinegar or lemon juice
- 1 square (1 oz. or 28 g) unsweetened chocolate = 3 Tbsp. (45 mL) unsweetened cocoa powder plus 1 Tbsp. (15 mL) butter or margarine
- 1 cup (250 mL) granulated sugar = 1 cup (250 mL) packed brown sugar OR 2 cups (500 mL) sifted powdered sugar

For best results, carefully choose ingredient substitutions.

▼ Making Creative Changes ▼

A recipe is your guide to success. At first, it's a good idea to do exactly what the recipe tells you to do. However, after you have used a recipe several times, you may want to try some variations.

Seasonings can often be changed to suit your tastes. For example, some people like their chili to be extra spicy. They might add more chili powder or hot peppers. If someone in your family doesn't like nuts, you might substitute raisins in a cookie recipe. Trial and error will lead you to the perfect combinations for your tastes.

Some recipes are more difficult to alter successfully than others. Most baked goods, such as breads or cakes, require an exact balance of ingredients. Recipes for foods such as casseroles and stews are more flexible.

Adding your own touches to recipes can bring you special satisfaction. You may even develop recipes of your own someday.

TAKING ACTION

Every year you and your friends in the Washington Junior High French Club have an informal dinner for members and their guests. Each member is asked to bring an authentic French dish to share. This year you have found a recipe for croissants — French crescent rolls — in an authentic French cookbook. You have translated the directions correctly, but realize the ingredient amounts are given only in metric. Your customary measuring utensils are not marked with metric equivalents. You want to use this recipe, but you will need to convert the metric measurements into customary ones. In addition, as a health-conscious person, you are concerned that this traditional recipe calls for butter and whole milk. You are afraid this will make the croissants too high in fat and cholesterol. As you are working on the conversions, you wonder what substitutions could be made to reduce the fat and cholesterol without changing the taste or texture of the croissants.

Using Your Resourcefulness

- Where can you find the customary equivalents for metric measurements?
- Where can you get information about the fats and cholesterol found in butter and whole milk?
- Where can you learn about ingredient substitutions?
- In what way can you determine how these substitutions will affect taste and texture?
- List all the resources that can help you find the facts you need to solve this problem.

Chapter 45 Review

Summary

In this chapter, you have read about:

- What to consider when choosing a recipe.
- Customary and metric abbreviations commonly used in recipes.
- Techniques for measuring dry ingredients, liquid ingredients, and fats.
- How to alter a recipe to increase or decrease its yield.
- Substitutions to try in case you are missing an ingredient.
- Ideas for adding your own touches to recipes.

Facts to Recall

1. List three questions to ask yourself when selecting or comparing recipes.
2. Write the terms the following abbreviations or symbols stand for: oz., tsp., g, Tbsp., pt., mL, °C, lb.
3. How many fluid ounces are in one cup? How many tablespoons are in one cup? How may teaspoons are in a tablespoon? How many milliliters are in one cup?
4. Briefly explain how to measure ½ cup of sifted flour.
5. Explain how the technique for measuring brown sugar differs from that for measuring granulated white sugar.
6. What two things should you do to measure liquid ingredients accurately?
7. Explain how you would measure ½ cup of solid fat in a 1-cup liquid measuring cup.
8. Name two types of ingredients that might be easiest to vary in a recipe.

Ideas to Explore

1. What do you think is the most common mistake made by beginning cooks when choosing a new recipe to try?
2. Why might it be easier to substitute ingredients in a vegetable stew than in a chocolate layer cake?
3. How might a cookie recipe that calls for butter, sugar, eggs, and a frosting be altered to make it lower in fat, sugar, and calories?

Activities to Try

1. Find examples of confusing or poorly written recipe directions. Explain how you would rewrite them to make them clearer.
2. Choose a recipe from this textbook or another source. For each ingredient listed, tell exactly what measuring equipment you would use to measure the required amount.

LINK TO *Math*

ALTERING A RECIPE

Learning to alter recipes can be a real benefit in making recipes meet the needs of you and your family. Find a new recipe or use an old family favorite that includes at least eight ingredients. Alter the recipe to make three times as many servings as the original yield. Use the method described on page 530. Then answer the following questions:

- Which ingredients need to be converted to another unit of measurement for ease in measuring? For example: if an altered recipe called for ⅝ cup flour, the equivalent measure you would need is ½ cup (⁴⁄₈ cup) plus 2 tablespoons (⅛ cup).
- How does altering the recipes affect the size cooking container needed?
- If cooking time is required, how will it be affected by altering the recipes?

CHAPTER

46 Preparation Terms and Techniques

OBJECTIVES

- *Interpret recipe terms.*
- *Describe basic cooking methods.*
- *Give safety guidelines for microwave cooking.*
- *Conserve nutrients during preparation.*

TERMS TO LEARN

- ***broiling***
- ***baking or roasting***
- ***boiling***
- ***simmering***
- ***frying***

Today everyone needs to learn how to prepare food. Many families share kitchen responsibilities. It may mean getting a fast meal together or helping to prepare a meal for a special occasion. Even if you prepare only convenience foods, you still need to know the meaning of basic terms so that you can follow directions correctly.

This chapter explains basic techniques and cooking methods. Once you master them, food preparation won't be a mystery to you.

Stir

Blend, mix, combine

Beat

Whip

Recipe Terms

Some words have special meanings when used in food preparation. At each step in a recipe, pay attention to the exact term used. It is your clue to the tool you need and the technique to follow.

Mixing Terms

A number of recipe techniques are used to combine ingredients or bring about a change in texture.

- ***Stir.*** Use a spoon and a circular or figure-eight motion.
- ***Blend, mix, combine.*** Stir two or more ingredients together thoroughly.
- ***Beat.*** Use this technique to make mixtures smooth or to beat egg whites. Use a quick, over-and-over motion with a spoon or wire whisk. You can also use a rotary beater or electric mixer.
- ***Whip.*** Beat the ingredient (such as cream) very rapidly to bring in air and increase volume. Use a wire whisk, rotary beater, or electric mixer.
- ***Cream.*** Using a spoon, beater, or mixer, combine ingredients until soft and creamy. This technique is often used to combine fat and sugar.
- ***Cut in.*** This is a way to mix a solid fat with dry ingredients. Use a pastry blender, fork, or two knives and a cutting motion.
- ***Fold.*** Use this technique to gently combine a delicate mixture, such as beaten egg whites, with other ingredients. Use a rubber or plastic scraper. See "How to Fold in Egg Whites" on page 536.

How to ...

Fold in Egg Whites

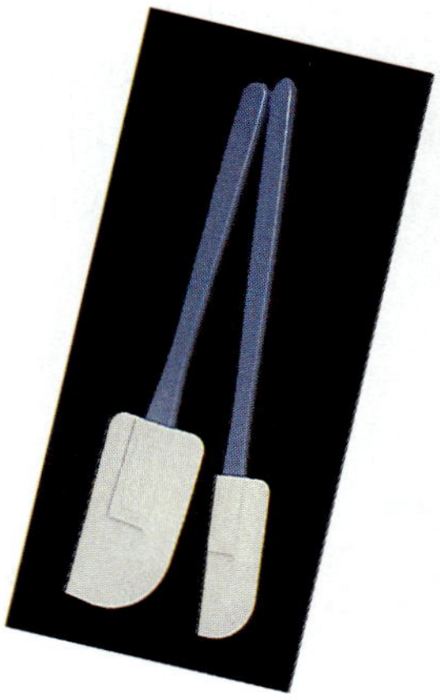

1. Add some of the egg whites to the bowl with the other ingredients.
2. Cut the scraper down through the center of the mixture.
3. Turn the scraper at the bottom of the bowl and gently bring it up along the side. You are bringing some of the mixture from the bottom of the bowl to the top.
4. Give the bowl a quarter turn. Fold again. Repeat several times.
5. Add the rest of the egg whites. Fold until the mixture is uniform.

Cream

Cut in

Fold

Chop

Dice

Pare

Mince

Shred

Cube

Grate

▼ Cutting Terms ▼

Do you know the difference between mincing and chopping, or between cubing and dicing? Becoming familiar with these terms will add to your success in the kitchen.

- ***Chop.*** Cut food into small, irregular pieces.
- ***Mince.*** Chop food into pieces that are as small as possible.
- ***Cube.*** Cut into evenly shaped pieces about ½ inch (13 mm) on each side.
- ***Dice.*** Cut into evenly shaped pieces about ¼ inch (6 mm) on each side.
- ***Pare.*** Cut off the outside covering of a fruit or vegetable. Use a peeler or a paring knife.
- ***Shred.*** Cut or tear food into long, thin pieces. When using a grater, rub the food over the large holes. Depending on the food, you might use a knife, two forks, or a food processor instead.
- ***Grate.*** Rub food over a grater (the side with small holes) to get fine particles.

SAFETY CHECK ✓

To safely use knives:

- Use sharp knives. They are less likely to slip and cause an accident.
- Always use a cutting board. Never hold the food in your hand while cutting or cut toward yourself.
- When using one hand to hold the food steady, tuck your fingers under. That way your knuckles, not your fingertips, are closest to the knife.

▼ Other Terms ▼

Here are some additional terms you might find in a recipe.

- ***Baste.*** Moisten foods, such as meat, while cooking. Basting adds flavor and helps keep the food from drying out. You might baste with meat drippings, a sauce or marinade, or melted butter. Use a brush or a baster.
- ***Brush.*** Use a brush to lightly cover the surface of a food with another food, such as egg white.
- ***Coat.*** Cover the surface of a food with a dry ingredient, such as flour, cornmeal, dry bread crumbs, or sugar.
- ***Garnish.*** Decorate a finished dish with a small food item, such as a sprig of parsley, a carrot curl, or a sprinkling of paprika.
- ***Grease.*** Rub lightly with a fat, such as butter, margarine, oil, or shortening.
- ***Season.*** Add seasonings, such as salt, pepper, herbs, or spices, to improve the flavor of a food.
- ***Strain.*** Remove solid particles from a liquid by pouring the liquid through a sieve or strainer.
- ***Drain.*** Remove excess liquid by placing food in a strainer or colander.

Baste

Brush

Coat

Grease

Strain

Garnish

Season

Drain

Broiling is a quick, nutritious way of cooking food.

Basic Cooking Methods

If you leaf through cookbooks and recipes in magazines, you can get lots of ideas about different ways to cook foods. Most recipes that involve cooking are based on a few basic methods. These include broiling, baking or roasting, boiling, simmering, frying, and microwave cooking.

▼ Broiling ▼

Broiling is cooking directly under or over the source of heat. If you broil in a range, countertop broiler, or toaster oven, the heat is above the food. If you broil on an outside grill, the food is on top and the heat comes from below. To control how fast the food broils, you adjust the distance the food is placed from the source of heat.

Foods that can be broiled include tender cuts of meat and poultry, fish, and some vegetables and fruits. Perhaps you have had broiled tomatoes or broiled eggplant.

Broiling has several advantages. Cooking is quick because the food is tender and usually in small pieces. If the food contains fat, the fat drains away from the food.

▼ Baking or Roasting ▼

Baking and **roasting** both mean cooking in an oven or oven-type appliance with dry heat. You control the heat by setting the temperature control.

Foods commonly baked or roasted include tender cuts of meat and poultry, fish, some fruits and vegetables, breads, pies, cakes, and cookies. Cooking time depends on the size of the food to be cooked. Larger pieces of food take longer than smaller size foods.

Baked foods are cooked uncovered by dry heat in an oven.

Except for occasional basting of poultry and fish, roasting or baking allows you to do other things while the food is in the oven. Check food for doneness at the shortest suggested cooking time.

Boiling

A liquid is **boiling** when bubbles rise and break on the surface. Boiling is usually done on the rangetop. For example, noodles and pasta are cooked in boiling water. The rolling boil helps to keep the noodles from sticking together. However, few other foods are boiled.

Steaming is a method of cooking food over boiling water rather than in it. The food is held out of the water by a metal basket or other utensil. Holes in the basket allow the hot steam to rise up and cook the food. The pan is tightly covered to keep the steam inside. This cooking method is most often used for vegetables.

Boiling water is used for cooking foods such as pasta and corn-on-the-cob.

Simmering

Simmering means keeping the temperature of a liquid or mixture just under the boiling point. Bubbles form slowly and break below the surface. Like boiling, simmering is often done on the rangetop. However, food can also be cooked at a simmer in the oven or using other appliances, such as a slow cooker.

Simmering is usually preferable to boiling. Foods keep their shape better and fewer nutrients are lost. Cooking is sometimes begun by bringing the water or other cooking liquid to the boiling point. Then the heat is turned down and cooking continues at a simmer.

Foods that can be simmered include fresh or frozen vegetables, some fresh or dried fruits, meat, poultry, and fish. Simmering is a good way to tenderize less tender cuts of meat and poultry. Mixtures of food can be simmered together to make a soup or stew.

Braising involves browning food in a small amount of fat, then simmering in very little added liquid. Less tender cuts of meat are sometimes braised.

Simmering cooks foods just below the boiling point. Simmering helps foods such as vegetables retain their shapes and nutrients.

AROUND THE WORLD

The Viking range allows cooks to prepare a number of foods in a variety of ways at the same time. With two gas ovens, six grates, and a grill, it can be used to roast, broil, grill, sauté, and simmer all at once. It also has special insulation to reduce the risk of kitchen fires from an overheated range. The Viking is an all-American creation, designed by a Mississippi contractor and his wife in 1980.

SAFETY CHECK ✓

To safely fry foods:

- Be sure food is dry before putting it in the fat or oil. Moisture can cause hot fat to spatter and burn you.
- Put food into the fat slowly and carefully so it won't splash. Use a spoon or tongs, not your fingers.
- If a grease fire starts, smother the flame with the cover of the pan or with salt. DO NOT put water on the fire.

▼ Frying ▼

Frying means cooking foods in fat. Frying can be done on the rangetop or with small appliances, such as an electric skillet or electric fryer.

If the food is immersed (completely covered) in fat, the method is called *deep-fat frying*. Chicken, sliced potatoes, and some other vegetables can be deep-fat fried. Deep-fat frying browns the food and makes it crisp. However, because this cooking method adds a considerable amount of fat to foods, it should not be used frequently.

Pan frying is done in a skillet with a smaller amount of fat. Pan frying is used for tender cuts of meat, fish, eggs, and some vegetables. When thinly sliced vegetables are cooked in a very small amount of fat, it is called *sautéing* (saw-TAY-ing).

Stir-frying is another variation. Foods such as vegetables, meat, poultry, or fish are cut into small pieces, then quickly cooked and stirred in a small amount of hot oil. Stir-frying is considered a fairly healthy way to prepare foods because little fat is used.

Pan frying

Stir-frying

▼ Microwave Cooking ▼

Why is microwave cooking so popular today? The main reason is that it saves time. Many convenience foods can be prepared even more quickly in the microwave oven. You can also reheat leftover foods, defrost frozen foods, and cook many fresh foods faster than with a conventional range. (Check page 521 for a discussion of the way microwave ovens work.)

Microwave cooking requires different materials and techniques than you would use in a conventional oven. Be sure to read the instruction book that came with the microwave oven you use.

Carefully choose cookware that is safe to use in the microwave oven.

SAFETY CHECK ✓

To safely use a microwave oven:

- Read the owner's manual and follow its instructions for use and care of the oven.
- Do not let young children use the microwave without supervision.
- In case of sparks or fire, leave the oven door closed. Turn off or unplug the oven.

Microwaves pass through some cookware materials and are reflected by others. During cooking, microwave energy is not evenly distributed. Food in some spots gets hotter than the rest. Trapped steam can cause food to "pop" or explode. For these reasons, it is important to follow the recipe or package directions and the guidelines that follow. They will help you cook food evenly and safely.

Materials to Use

Materials that are safe to use in the microwave oven include:

- Heatproof glass containers.
- Plastic containers labeled "microwave-safe."
- Paper plates labeled "microwave-safe."
- Paper towels that do not contain plastic fibers or recycled paper.
- Microwave-safe plastic wrap.
- Waxed paper.
- Metal cookware specifically designed for use in microwave ovens and labeled "microwave-safe."

Other materials are not safe to use in the microwave oven. Brown paper bags or paper towels made of recycled paper may burn when heated. Plastics that are not microwave-safe can melt from the heat of the food or cause chemicals to get into the food. Metal pans made for conventional ovens and large pieces of aluminum foil reflect microwaves. They can cause uneven cooking and damage the oven.

SAFETY CHECK ✓

When microwaving foods:

- Pierce foods with skins, like potatoes, in several places with a fork before placing them in the microwave. Otherwise they may explode in the oven.
- Do not microwave in tightly sealed containers. When using plastic wrap, fold back one corner or pierce the wrap in several places with a fork.
- Do not microwave eggs in the shell. They may explode during or after cooking.

Use a ring or spoke pattern to insure that foods cook evenly in the microwave.

Preparing Food for Microwaving

The recipe or instruction book should tell you what type of container to use. Be sure the container fits into the microwave comfortably without touching the walls, door, or top of the oven. Round or ring-shaped containers are often recommended because they help food cook more evenly.

When heating liquids such as soups or sauces, use a container two to three times larger than the amount of food you are putting into it. Otherwise the liquid may spill over as it cooks or as you stir it.

Keep food pieces as uniform as possible. If they are different sizes and shapes, some will cook faster than others.

Arranging foods as specified in the recipe will also help ensure even cooking. Individual items are often arranged in a ring or a spoke pattern. The parts of the food that will take longest to cook should be placed toward the outside of the container, where they will receive the most microwave energy. These are usually the parts that are thicker, denser, or tougher, such as the thick part of a chicken leg or the tough stems of broccoli spears.

Covering food helps prevent drying out and spattering. If the dish does not have its own cover, use microwave-safe plastic wrap, waxed paper, or paper toweling.

TIPS: *Buying a Microwave Oven*

These are some of the most popular microwave oven features. Consider your family's needs when deciding which features are most important:

- Temperature probes help prevent overcooking by taking the temperature of cooking food and shutting off the oven when it reaches a predetermined temperature.
- Automatic programs determine the right cooking time and power level based on the food, its weight, and how it is to be prepared.
- Multistage cooking allows the oven to automatically change power levels according to preset controls.

Pierce plastic wraps to release steam during microwave cooking. This helps eliminate steam burns.

Many convenience foods are packaged in microwavable containers. You may need to remove part of the package or follow other special instructions. Check the package directions for what to do.

Follow recipe directions for accurate microwave cooking.

Setting the Controls

Set the power level and cooking time as instructed in the recipe or package directions. Be accurate. A few extra seconds or minutes of cooking can make the food too tough to eat.

Cooking time depends partly on the particular microwave oven you use. The cooking power of a microwave oven is measured in watts. Most microwave recipes are written for 600- to 700-watt ovens. If your oven has a lower wattage, the cooking time will be a little longer. If your oven has a higher wattage, food will cook faster. Check the owner's manual to find the wattage of the oven you are using.

Some recipes give a range of time, such as 6 to 8 minutes. It's a good idea to use the shortest time suggested or to set the timer for a few seconds or minutes before you think the food will be done. You can always add more cooking time if needed.

During Cooking

For more even cooking, the directions may tell you to do one or more of the following partway through cooking.

- ***Rotate.*** Turn the dish around. If the directions say "¼ turn," the part of the dish that was facing front should now face the side of the oven. If the directions say "½ turn," the front of the dish should now face the back of the oven.
- ***Stir.*** Stir food from the outsides of the dish toward the center.
- ***Rearrange.*** Move the food around in the dish. Move pieces from the outside to the center and from the bottom to the top.
- ***Invert.*** Turn the food over in the dish.

Standing Time

After the cooking time is up, the directions may tell you to let the food stand. During the standing time, the food continues to cook even though the oven is shut off. Leave the food covered and in the oven for the amount of time specified. Then check the food for doneness. Add more cooking time if needed.

SAFETY CHECK ✓

After microwaving:

- Use potholders when removing dishes from the oven. Hot food heats up the container.
- Be careful when removing covers or opening bags of popcorn. To avoid steam burns, keep the cover or bag tilted so the steam flows away from you.
- Watch out for hot spots that could burn your mouth. Stir to distribute the heat evenly, or let the food cool before eating.

Conserving Nutrients

During preparation, foods can lose some of their nutrients. By taking care when you handle and prepare foods, you can help keep as many nutrients as possible. Here are some guidelines.

- Leave the skins on fruits and vegetables if possible. The skin contains vitamins, minerals, and fiber.
- Consider nutrition when choosing cooking methods. Boiling and frying tend to rob food of the most nutrients. Baking or roasting, broiling, microwaving, and simmering in a small amount of water generally conserve more nutrients.
- Avoid overcooking food. Carefully follow the directions for cooking temperature and time.
- Save the liquid in which food is cooked. It contains valuable nutrients. If the liquid will not be eaten with the food, you might use it for making soup.

Learning to prepare food is like any other skill you acquire. A good beginning is to start with the basics and then practice. Some attempts will be more successful than others, but you will always learn.

Now that you know the meaning of many cooking terms and techniques, you are off to a good start. You may find, like many people have, that preparing food is enjoyable and rewarding.

TAKING ACTION

Jason has an ambitious plan. To celebrate his mother's promotion at work, he is going to cook her a special dinner this weekend with some of her favorite foods — roasted cornish hen, mixed vegetables, and chocolate cake. "I know it's a lot of work," he admits, "but with all our kitchen gadgets, a good cookbook, and the help of a good friend like you, I know I can pull it off."

You know Jason has more enthusiasm than experience. If he is to create a masterpiece — and not a mess — he will need a crash course in cooking terms and techniques. And, if you are to help him, so will you.

Using Your Resourcefulness

- Where can you and Jason find recipes for the dishes he wants to make?
- Where can you find explanations for the cooking terms you don't understand?
- How can you decide which utensil to use for each technique?
- Where can you learn suggestions for preparing the different recipes, for example, ideas on seasoning the hens and vegetables or garnishing the cake?
- Who might you contact if you have questions as you cook, or if a recipe doesn't turn out as you think it should?

Chapter 46 Review

Summary

In this chapter, you have read about:

- Recipe terms for mixing, cutting, and other ways of preparing foods.
- Different cooking methods and their uses, advantages, and disadvantages.
- Tips on using a microwave oven for safe, even cooking.
- How to save nutrients in the foods you prepare.

Facts to Recall

1. When reading a recipe, why should you pay attention to the exact term used?
2. What is the difference between cutting in and folding ingredients? Explain in terms of ingredients, tools, and motion used.
3. What is the difference between shredding and grating food?
4. Why is food basted? Name three types of food products used for basting.
5. Give two guidelines for using a knife safely.
6. What is the difference between boiling and simmering food? Which technique is preferred and why?
7. List three variations of frying.
8. Identify four materials that are safe to use in a microwave oven.
9. When cooking with a microwave oven, what parts of the food should you place toward the outside of the container? Why?
10. When preparing food in a microwave oven, why is it a good idea to use the shortest suggested cooking time?
11. Give three guidelines for conserving nutrients when preparing food.

Ideas to Explore

1. Discuss examples of how using the wrong cooking techniques or tools could affect the way a recipe turns out.
2. Discuss some advantages and some disadvantages of microwave cooking.
3. Think about a problem you have had in using a kitchen tool. What do you think caused the problem? How could this problem have been prevented or solved?

Activities to Try

1. Find a recipe in a cookbook or other source. Identify and explain the different terms used.
2. Find recipes that give directions for both microwave and conventional preparation. What are the differences in tools, ingredients, amounts of ingredients used, and techniques? What do you think are the reasons for these changes?

LINK TO *Science*

CONTAINER SHAPES AND MICROWAVE COOKING

The shape of the cooking container often effects how evenly food cooks in the microwave. Using a canned convenience pasta product, compare how evenly the products cooks in a rectangular, round, and doughnut-shaped container. Microwave each container for 3 minutes at 100 % power. Answer the following:

- Describe how evenly the pasta product cooked in each container. Include the similarities and differences.
- How did the appearance of the pasta product compare in each container? Explain.
- Did any of the pasta products have an overcooked or burnt flavor due to uneven cooking? Explain.

CHAPTER

47 Working in the Kitchen

OBJECTIVES

- *Demonstrate safety and sanitation procedures for working with food.*
- *Work cooperatively in the foods laboratory.*
- *Organize workspace, plan time schedules, and conserve resources in the kitchen.*

TERMS TO LEARN

- ***food-borne illness***
- ***bacteria***
- ***pre-preparation tasks***
- ***kitchen work center***

Working in the kitchen can be an enjoyable experience. To keep it that way, make the kitchen a safe and sanitary place to work and use good management skills.

Kitchen Safety

More accidents take place in the kitchen than any other room in the home. The same accidents can occur in the foods lab, too. To prepare yourself for accidents that do happen, become familiar with basic first aid techniques. Know where first aid supplies are kept.

You can help prevent accidents by thinking ahead and working safely. Following are some guidelines that can help you to make the kitchen or foods lab a safe place to work. Think of other safety rules to add to the list.

How many hazards can you find in this kitchen?

Preventing Cuts and Bruises

It is very easy to cut yourself in the kitchen because of the sharp utensils used. Falls are another common cause of injury. To prevent cuts and bruises:

- Wash knives and other sharp objects separately. Never put a sharp knife in a sink of sudsy water to soak.
- Store sharp knives separately from other utensils.
- Keep knives sharp so they will be less likely to slip while cutting.

To prevent cuts, use a damp paper towel to pick up broken glass.

- Use a cutting board. Keep your fingertips out of the way of the knife.
- Before trying to retrieve an object from a garbage disposal, unplug the unit.
- Close cabinet doors and drawers when not in use. Otherwise, someone could walk into them and be injured.
- Use a safe ladder or step stool for reaching high or hard-to-get items.
- Wipe up spills from the floor right away. Do not walk on a wet floor.

Preventing Burns

You can't be too careful when working around gas and electric appliances. Here are some ways to prevent burns.

- Teach young children not to touch the heating units on a range.
- Use flat-bottomed and well-balanced cooking utensils on the range so they will not tip over easily.
- Turn handles of cooking utensils inward on the range so they will not be knocked off the burner. Be sure handles do not extend over another burner or surface unit that is hot.
- Use thick, dry potholders when handling hot utensils.
- Remove the cover from a pan by lifting the far side of the cover first. That way the steam flows away from you.
- Dry food thoroughly before putting it into hot fat in a pan. Water causes fat to spatter.
- Use kitchen tongs to remove food from hot water and to turn food that is frying. The tongs will help to keep your hand away from the hot fat or water.

Using thick, dry potholders helps prevent injury from burns.

▼ Preventing Fires ▼

Fires can start very easily at the range. If a grease fire starts, do not throw water on the flames — they will spread. Instead, smother the fire with the cover of the pan or with salt. Keep a working fire extinguisher in the kitchen and learn how to use it. Here are some ways to prevent a fire from starting.

- Avoid wearing dangling jewelry or loose-fitting clothes. They can get caught in appliances or catch fire over heating units.
- Keep paper towels, dish towels, and electric cords away from the range.
- Do not use the range as a source of heat to warm the kitchen.
- Avoid using a dish towel to handle hot utensils. Its drooping ends could catch on fire.
- Be sure no more than two appliances are plugged into an electrical outlet at one time. Overloading circuits may result in a fire.

An *electrical octopus* overloads a circuit and may cause a fire.

▼ Preventing Electrical Shock ▼

Electrical equipment should be in good working order and used properly. Remember that water and metal are good conductors of electricity. You could be, too, if you're not careful. To prevent electrical shock:

- Dry hands thoroughly before touching electrical equipment.
- Never connect an electrical appliance while you are standing on a wet surface.
- Do not put the heating unit, motor, or cord of an electrical appliance in water unless it is marked "immersible."
- Always unplug a cord from the wall outlet before removing it from the appliance. Otherwise electricity continues going through the cord, and you can receive a shock.
- Disconnect an appliance by pulling on the plug. If you pull on the cord, it can become damaged and cause a shock.
- Keep forks and knives out of electric toasters. If food gets stuck in a toaster, disconnect the appliance, turn it over, and try to shake the food loose.

▼ Preventing Poisoning ▼

Household chemicals, such as cleaning products, are often kept in the kitchen. Many contain dangerous substances that can be poisonous if swallowed, inhaled, or splashed on the

Store hazardous cleaning agents and chemicals away from food and children.

skin. Keep the number of the nearest poison control center by the telephone and call it in an emergency. To prevent poisoning:

- Keep drain openers, household cleaners, and poisons in their original containers. Read the warnings and directions on the label. Follow directions exactly.
- Keep household chemicals where children cannot reach them. Store them away from food items.
- Avoid mixing household chemicals together. Some mixtures cause dangerous chemical reactions.

Food Safety and Sanitation

Many people get an upset stomach and think they have the flu. Sometimes they do. Other times they may have a **food-borne illness**, often called food poisoning. It is caused by eating spoiled food or food containing harmful bacteria. **Bacteria** are one-celled living things so small they can be seen only with a microscope. Many people call harmful bacteria germs. Food containing harmful bacteria does not always smell or taste spoiled. For that reason, many people aren't aware of the real cause of their illness.

Bacteria require three things to grow: food, moisture, and the right temperature. With just a little carelessness, you can create these ideal growing conditions in your kitchen at home or in the foods lab at school.

You can prevent food-borne illness by practicing sanitation. Sanitation is keeping bacteria down to as small a number as possible through cleanliness and proper food handling. Follow these guidelines to prevent food-borne illness.

Cleanliness

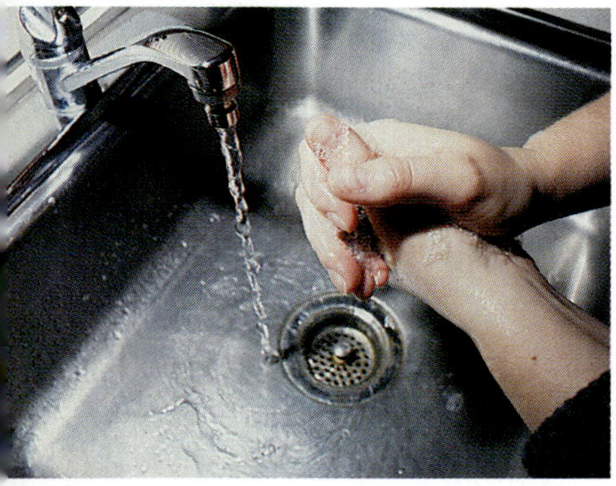

Always wash your hands before handling food.

Bacteria are present everywhere. Practicing cleanliness helps keep harmful bacteria out of food.

- Keep the kitchen clean and free of pests.
- Wear clean clothes when you work with food.
- Wash your hands before you handle food, after you cough or sneeze, after you use the toilet, and after you touch pets. Otherwise bacteria on your hands can be transferred to the food.
- If you have a cut or break in the skin on your hands, wear rubber or plastic gloves.
- If you taste food during cooking, use a clean spoon each time.

Pocket Lab

How Clean Are You?

MATERIALS:
growing medium

EQUIPMENT:
4 petri dishes

Directions: Using the petri dishes with growing medium your teacher has obtained from the science department, contaminate the growing medium with the following samples from your body: scrapings from under fingernails, a hair, and scrapings from your face. As a control, wash your hands thoroughly using soap and warm water, then rub your clean fingers across the growing medium in another petri dish. Be sure to label each of the petri dishes with the contaminant each contains. Allow the bacteria to grow at room temperature. Check the results after 24 hours.

- Which samples did the bacteria grow on?
- Did any bacteria grow on the control dish?
- Draw some conclusions about the importance of cleanliness in the kitchen.

- When handling dishes and other eating utensils, avoid touching surfaces that come in contact with food. For instance, hold forks by the handle, not by the tines.
- Change dishcloths and dish towels often. Have separate towels for wiping hands and wiping dishes.

Handling Meat, Poultry, Fish, and Eggs

Raw meat, poultry, fish, and eggs may contain harmful bacteria. These foods should always be cooked thoroughly so that the bacteria are destroyed. Never eat these foods when raw or only partly cooked. Do not cook the food partway and finish cooking another time — it will not be safe to eat.

When you touch raw meat, poultry, fish, or eggs, the bacteria can get on your hands. They can also get on any utensils or dishes, such as a cutting board, knife, or plate, that came in contact with the raw food. Immediately after handling the raw food, wash your hands and the utensils with hot, soapy water. Otherwise the bacteria could be transferred to other foods, such as a salad or cooked meat, and cause illness.

Use a plastic cutting board for meat, poultry, or fish. Wooden cutting boards are difficult to clean thoroughly.

Store foods at proper temperatures to prevent bacterial growth.

Proper Temperatures

Bacteria multiply quickly between 60°F and 125°F (15°C and 50°C). To make sure food stays out of this danger zone, keep it hot or cold.

- Serve hot foods steaming hot, above 140°F (60°C). If you prepared a large quantity, keep the extra portions hot during the meal rather than bringing all the food to the table.
- Keep cold foods cold until you are ready to use them. Be sure the refrigerator temperature is 40°F (5°C) or below.
- To thaw frozen food, place it in the refrigerator overnight (longer if needed) or use a microwave oven. Never let frozen food sit out at room temperature to thaw.
- After a meal, refrigerate or freeze leftovers right away. Don't let them sit on a counter or table for long. Put hot foods into shallow containers so they will cool more quickly.
- Take special care when packing food for a lunch or picnic. Use ice packs and an insulated container to keep cold foods cold. Use vacuum bottles to keep hot foods hot. (See page 492 for more information.)

Kitchen Management

When you plan and prepare meals, you use resources such as money, food, fuel, water, time, and energy. Good management helps you make the best use of your resources. This is true whether you are working in the foods lab at school or in the kitchen at home.

Working in the School Foods Lab

Most of your work in the school foods lab will be done in groups. Learning how to work with others is as important as any other skill you practice in the lab.

Working with others gives you an opportunity to learn to be a team member and to handle responsibility. Each person in the group is important. You are each responsible for certain jobs. When one member of the team doesn't do a job correctly or on time, it affects everyone else. When all members pitch in and do their share, the group is a winner. They're successful.

In every phase of the lab — planning, working, and evaluating — you'll need to cooperate with others. Cooperation makes the work pleasant for everyone.

Working cooperatively in a group allows all group members to achieve success and have a pleasant experience.

AROUND THE WORLD

In some remote African villages, bread baking is not done in the home. Instead, the bread dough is mixed daily by each family, then taken to a community oven in the village to be baked. In this way, bread baking is as much a social activity as a dietary necessity. As African nations become more developed, however, this practice is growing less common. What do you think might be some consequences of the loss of this custom?

Planning Your Work

To work in the foods lab your group will need a plan, just as a coach has a game plan for a team. Plans are made so that everyone will be successful.

Each part of the plan is important. For example, your teacher may ask you to list the ingredients you need and the amounts. Your supplies will be added to the total grocery list for the lab. If your list isn't accurate, then your group or another group may not have the ingredients needed.

When you are in a foods lab, you'll often be working against the clock. Lab times are usually short, so you'll have to plan to use the time wisely. Work out a schedule by listing the major jobs in the order they need to be done. Estimate how long it will take to do each job.

Be sure your schedule allows time for getting ready to cook. Before you actually begin following the steps in the recipe, you will need to:

- Put on a clean apron, tie back long hair, roll up dangling sleeves, and wash your hands.
- Get out all the ingredients and equipment you'll need. This will save time and steps later and prevent mix-ups.

Following a work plan and time schedule keeps you organized.

MEETING SPECIAL NEEDS

In Kitchen Design

People who are physically disabled are often at a greater risk for home accidents. With careful thought and planning, home design and furnishings can be modified to meet special safety needs. The following modifications in a kitchen will make it easier to maneuver in a wheelchair:

- Providing complete work centers with lower-than-normal counters and sinks with space beneath to accomodate a wheelchair.
- Providing space beneath a built-in cooktop instead of base cabinets to accommodate a wheelchair.
- Including base cabinets with pullout storage trays.
- Placing range controls to the side of the burners to avoid reaching across hot burners.
- Installing a built-in oven at counter level to prevent leg burns from hot oven doors.

For safety, wipe up spills immediately.

- Complete tasks that you need to do before you combine ingredients. For instance, you may need to preheat the oven, grease baking pans, measure ingredients, peel or chop foods, heat water, or melt fat. These are called **pre-preparation tasks**.

After you have listed all the tasks, decide who will do each job. Divide the work fairly so that everyone shares responsibility.

The advantage of teamwork is that several tasks can be dovetailed, or done at the same time. If a casserole calls for several different items to be chopped, more than one person can do the chopping. Someone can wash utensils or set the table while others are finishing the food preparation.

Carrying Out Your Plan

When you go into the lab, be sure you know what your assigned jobs are. Post your time plan where everyone in the group can see it.

Follow the rules about dress, behavior, and lab procedures. The rules are set for your safety and to help you work within the time limits of your class period.

When you complete your work, volunteer to help someone else who is behind. If you see something that needs to be done, pitch in and do it.

Cleaning Up

Cleaning up as you go along will help the final cleanup go faster. If food spills on the counter or floor, wipe it up right away. Have a sink or dishpan of warm, sudsy water ready. When you finish using a utensil, put it in the water to soak (except for sharp knives). Whenever you have a few minutes while waiting for something to cook, wash and rinse the utensils.

When you have finished preparing the recipe, transfer the food to a serving dish or plate. If the cooking utensil is very dirty or greasy, scrape it or wipe with a paper towel. Then put the utensil in warm, sudsy water to soak. If food is stuck to a pan, simmer a detergent-and-water solution in it for about 10 minutes.

After you have enjoyed the food you made, it's time for the final cleanup. Clear the dishes from the table and store any leftovers properly. Scrape food scraps into the garbage container or disposal. If you left pots and pans soaking, empty the sink, rinse the pots and pans, and place them with the other dishes to be washed. Follow the suggestions on page 557 for washing dishes.

Remember to wipe off tables and counters and sweep the floor. Leave the foods lab clean and ready for the next group.

How to . . .
Wash Dishes by Hand

- After scraping, stack dishes carefully at one side of the sink. Fill the sink with hot water and liquid detergent.
- Use a clean dishcloth. For stuck-on food, use a scrubber or scouring pad. (Nylon scrubbers can be used on most dishes and cookware without scratching.)
- Start with the cleanest items and work your way to the dirtiest ones. Usually this means you wash glassware first, then flatware and dishes, and finally pots and pans.
- Handle dishes carefully so they don't break or chip.
- Change the wash water if it becomes cold, greasy, or dirty.
- Rinse dishes with hot water. Place them in a rack or on a towel so water can drain.
- Dry with a clean dish towel or leave the dishes in the rack to air dry.
- Put dishes away carefully as soon as they are dry.

Automatic Dishwasher

- Be sure you have read the instructions in the owner's manual.
- Scrape dishes. Rinse them if the owner's manual recommends it.
- Load the dishwasher as instructed in the owner's manual.
- Add detergent to detergent dispenser. (Rinse agents can be used to prevent spotting.)
- Select correct cycle and start dishwasher. (Note: A cycle will go through several rinses and one or two washes.)
- Use dishwasher dry cycle, or air dry.
- Put dishes away carefully as soon as they are dry.

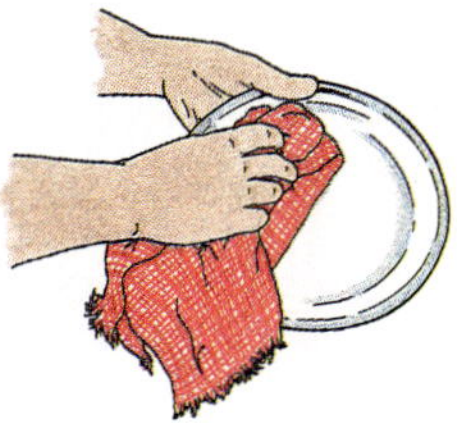

Evaluating the Lab

Evaluation is an important part of the lab experience. When you evaluate your work, you judge the quality of it. Your teacher may have you use a rating sheet to evaluate the way your recipe turned out. You should also evaluate your teamwork by asking yourself some very important questions: Did everything work as planned? What did we do well? How could we have improved? The answers to these and similar questions will be the key to your success in future labs.

Working in the Home Kitchen

In many ways, preparing food in a home kitchen is similar to working in the foods lab. In both situations, time and energy are often limited. Organizing the kitchen and planning your time will help you work efficiently.

Organizing Your Work Space

An efficient kitchen is organized into several work centers. A **kitchen work center** is an area of the kitchen designed to fill a particular purpose. The work center includes all of the appliances and equipment you need for that task. By storing items near the place they will be used, you save time and energy.

Most kitchens include a a mixing center, a cooking center, and a cleanup center. The chart on page 559 shows examples of the items that might be stored in each of these areas. What other work centers might a kitchen include? What items would be found there?

Organizing your work space allows you to prepare delicious meals efficiently.

Examples of Kitchen Work Centers

Work Center	Location	Items to Store Nearby
Mixing center	A counter or other workspace where recipe ingredients can be assembled	▶ Measuring utensils ▶ Mixing bowls and utensils ▶ Ingredients such as flour and spices
Cooking center	Near the range and/or microwave oven	▶ Saucepans, pots, and other cookware ▶ Cooking utensils such as spatulas, tongs, and cooling racks ▶ Potholders and oven mitts
Cleanup center	Near the sink	▶ Dishwashing and cleaning supplies ▶ Everyday dishes, glasses, and flatware ▶ Containers for leftover foods

Managing Your Time

At home as well as at school, it helps to write out a time plan or schedule. Allow a little extra time in your schedule for unexpected delays.

Often two or more family members work as a team. Decide together how you will divide tasks.

When you work alone, you can still be efficient. Look for ways to dovetail tasks. For instance, during the time that it takes for water to start boiling or for noodles to cook, you can be working on another part of the meal.

Planning a schedule is especially important when you are preparing an entire meal. You want all the food to be ready at the same time. Begin your schedule with the foods that take the longest to prepare and cook. For example, it may take 20 minutes to put a casserole together and another 45 minutes for it to bake. If you were also having a canned vegetable and a tossed green salad, you can see that you would need to begin the casserole first.

With more experience, you may not need to write out a schedule every time. Experienced cooks can think through their preparation plans mentally.

▼ Conserving Natural Resources ▼

Conservation and the environment are important issues today. Everyone needs to do his or her part to conserve natural resources. Here are some simple everyday habits you can put to use in the kitchen. Can you think of other ways to conserve?

You can conserve water by:

- Turning off faucets when not in use. For example, don't leave water running constantly while you do dishes.
- Reusing water that would otherwise go down the drain. For instance, when you wash vegetables, catch the water in a container and use it to water your plants.

Recycling as many products as possible saves landfill space. What products do you recycle?

You can conserve electricity and fuel by:

- Cooking an entire meal in the oven at one time.
- Matching the size of the heating element on an electric range to the size of the pot or pan.
- Using hot water only when necessary.

You can conserve food by:

- Buying only as much food as you will use.
- Following recipes carefully.
- Taking a helping that you are sure you will eat. You can always ask for seconds if you want more.
- Using leftovers instead of throwing them away.

You can reduce the amount of trash by:

- Choosing reusable items rather than disposable items.
- Avoiding products with wasteful packaging.
- Buying items that can be recycled or are made from recycled materials.
- Making sure that materials such as glass, newspapers, aluminum cans, and plastic milk jugs are collected for recycling.

See Chapter 22 for more information about conserving and managing natural resources.

TAKING ACTION

"They could have lost everything." Sasha's eyes are wide, her voice somber, as she tells you of her neighbor's calamity. "They were making french fries and forgot to turn off the burner under the oil. It caught on fire and set fire to the curtains — it was a good thing they had a fire extinguisher nearby."

Sasha's friends escaped disaster, but you wonder if your own family would fare as well. You don't have a fire extinguisher — you're not sure you would even know how to use one. You decide right then and there to accident-proof your kitchen. What happened to Sasha's neighbors won't happen to your family. You are not sure, though, where to start.

Using Your Resourcefulness

- Where can you learn how to safely operate your kitchen appliances?
- Who can tell you if your utensils or appliances need repair or replacement to avoid a dangerous accident?
- Where can you find information on using, storing, and disposing of cleaning products safely?
- Where can you learn basic first aid for treating minor cuts and burns?
- How do you decide whom to contact if a serious accident does occur?
- Where can you find tips on teaching young children about kitchen safety?

Chapter 47 Review

Summary

In this chapter, you have read about:

- Preventing accidents and injury when working in the kitchen.
- Preventing food-borne illness through good sanitation.
- Working efficiently in the foods lab and the home kitchen.
- Helping the environment by conserving resources and reducing trash.

Facts to Recall

1. Give five guidelines for preventing cuts and bruises.
2. How should cooking utensils be positioned on the range? Why?
3. List four safety rules for fire prevention.
4. Give two guidelines for safely unplugging an electrical appliance.
5. Where and how should household chemicals be stored to prevent poisoning?
6. Give four guidelines for practicing cleanliness in the kitchen.
7. Explain how to safely thaw meat, poultry, and fish.
8. At what temperature should hot food be served to avoid food-borne illness?
9. List two ways to store leftovers safely.
10. How is dovetailing helpful in planning to prepare food?
11. What is the benefit of organizing a kitchen into several work centers?
12. List four ways to conserve food.

Ideas to Explore

1. Explain how good time management can help reduce the chances of accident or injury in the kitchen.
2. How can you help prevent injury and conserve resources by keeping appliances in good working order?
3. Do you think a kitchen needs to be large to be well-organized? Explain.

Activities to Try

1. Draw a picture of a kitchen with at least three safety hazards. Have the rest of the class identify the hazards.
2. Make posters promoting safe kitchen work habits. Place them in the school foods lab.
3. Find pictures of a kitchen in a magazine. What work centers are included? Which of the basic floor plans is used? Evaluate the storage, work space, and traffic patterns. How might the kitchen be made more efficient?
4. Write a paragraph describing your role as a "team player" in the foods lab. How can working as a team benefit you, your lab group, and the foods class?

LINK TO *Health*

SANITATION SAVVY

Health experts agree that to prevent the spread of bacteria to food, certain sanitation practices should be followed. With a partner, develop a demonstration showing correct procedures for the following:

- **Handwashing.** Show how to thoroughly wash hands and exposed areas of the arms — scrubbing hands and between fingers for 20-30 seconds. Use a brush to clean fingernails.
- **Proper Food Temperatures.** Use a chart or other visual to emphasize the proper temperatures to keep hot and cold foods safe. Include some effective ways to store foods properly in the refrigerator.

CHAPTER

48 Milk and Milk Products

OBJECTIVES

- *Explain the role of milk and milk products in the diet.*
- *Describe how to buy, store, and prepare dairy products.*

TERMS TO LEARN

- ***pasteurized***
- ***homogenized***
- ***reconstitute***

When you were younger, were you often told "Drink your milk"? That's good advice, even now that you are a teenager. Milk is one of the most nutritious and refreshing beverages you can drink. Milk and milk products, such as yogurt and cheese, fit well into meals and snacks. How many of your favorite foods contain dairy products?

Nutrients in Dairy Products

Milk and milk products are good sources of important nutrients. They are high in protein, which you need for growth and repair of the body. The calcium, phosphorus, and vitamin D in dairy products help build strong bones and teeth. Dairy products also supply vitamin A and B vitamins for health and growth. The nutrients dairy products provide are needed throughout life.

Health guidelines recommend two to three servings of milk or milk products each day. They also recommend choosing low-fat versions of dairy products. These have fewer calories and less fat, but the same important nutrients. Milk provides a good example. Compare a 1-cup (250-mL) serving of these three types:

	Calories	Fat (grams)	Calories from fat
Whole milk	150	8	48%
Low-fat (2%) milk	120	5	38%
Skim milk	80	almost none	5%

Milk is a healthy beverage because it contains many nutrients.

Regardless of age, everyone needs the nutrients found in milk and milk products.

AROUND THE WORLD

Blue (sometimes spelled bleu) cheese gets it name from the blue or green veins of mold that run through it. This harmless mold gives the cheese its unusual flavor. Blue cheese is believed to have originated near Roquefort (ROKE-fert), France many years ago. According to legend, a shepherd forgot his lunch in a cave, and returned weeks later to find the cheese, though molded, was still edible and highly flavorful. Roquefort cheese is still made entirely of sheep's milk. Two other types of blue cheese are Stilton, from England, and Gorgonzola (gore-gon-ZOE-la), from Italy.

Almost all dairy products have low-fat versions. You can also buy substitute products, such as nondairy whipped topping to use in place of whipped cream.

Buying Dairy Products

Be a wise consumer when purchasing and storing milk and milk products. Read the labels to be sure you get the product you want. Check the date on the package. This is the last date the product should be sold.

- ***Milk.*** When you shop for fresh milk, you will see the words "pasteurized" and "homogenized." **Pasteurized** (PASS-tyoor-ized) means that the milk has been heated to destroy harmful bacteria. This process increases the length of time you can store milk. **Homogenized** (huh-MAH-juh-nized) means that the fat particles in the milk have been broken up and distributed throughout the milk. If milk is not homogenized, the fat would rise to the top, forming a layer of cream.
- ***Cheese.*** Cheese is another popular milk product. To make cheese, milk is first thickened. The solid part, or *curd*, is then separated from the liquid (called *whey*). The curd is made into cheese. There are dozens of varieties available. Some cheese is aged or ripened. Examples are cheddar and Swiss cheese. Cottage cheese and cream cheese are not aged. Process cheese is made by combining different aged cheeses. Check cheese labels carefully and choose low-fat varieties whenever possible.
- ***Yogurt.*** Yogurt is a milk product with a smooth, thick texture and a tangy flavor. It is available plain or flavored. Frozen yogurt is a popular substitute for ice cream because it is lower in fat. When you buy yogurt, check the labels to compare the fat content and calories in products.

TIPS: *Choosing Cheese*

The type of cheese you use in a dish depends on the flavor you want. Here are some of the most popular varieties and how they are used:

- **Cheddar.** Mild to sharp taste; eaten as is or shredded in cooked foods.
- **Mozzarella.** Very mild flavor; usually used in cooking.
- **Romano.** Very sharp taste, especially if aged; eaten as is or grated to season cooked foods.
- **Swiss.** Mild, slightly sweet and nutty taste; eaten as is or used in cooked foods, salads, and fondues.

Many varieties of cheese are available. When possible, choose varieties that are low in fat.

Other Milk Products

- ***Nonfat dry milk.*** Powdered product made by removing the water from milk. When mixed with water, can be used as fresh milk.
- ***UHT milk.*** Milk processed at very high temperatures to kill all bacteria. It needs no refrigeration until the carton is opened.
- ***Buttermilk.*** A tart, thick product made by adding a safe bacteria culture to milk (usually skim or low-fat).
- ***Evaporated milk.*** Canned milk from which 60% of the water has been removed.
- ***Sweetened condensed milk.*** Canned, concentrated milk with added sugar.
- ***Half-and-half.*** A mixture of milk and light cream. Used in coffee.
- ***Heavy whipping cream.*** Higher in fat than half-and-half or other creams. The high fat content aids whipping.
- ***Sour cream.*** Cream cultured with safe bacteria to give it a tangy flavor.

Milk you buy in UHT packaging is safe and convenient for packed lunches.

Storing Dairy Products

Fresh milk spoils easily. Keep it refrigerated in its original container. Store unopened canned, nonfat dry, or UHT milk in a dry, cool area. Once opened, canned and UHT milk must be refrigerated. When a box of nonfat dry milk is opened, transfer the dry milk to an airtight container. Refrigerate nonfat dry milk when it is mixed with water.

Preparing Dairy Products

Milk, yogurt, and cheese can be eaten as is or combined with other foods. Try blending milk and fresh fruit for a nutritious milkshake. Plain yogurt mixed with seasonings makes a delicious dip to eat with fresh vegetables.

Some recipes, such as puddings and sauces, call for cooking or heating milk products. Since dairy foods are high in protein, they must be cooked over low heat. High heat can cause the protein to scorch or burn easily. It also causes cheese to become rubbery.

Sometimes you will see a recipe that calls for scalded milk. To scald milk, heat it to just below the boiling point.

A film, known as scum, can form on the top of heated milk. The film contains proteins, minerals, and fat. It forms because of the evaporation of liquid from the surface of the heated milk. You can prevent the formation of scum by covering the pan as the milk is being heated. Stirring often during cooking also helps prevent the skin from forming.

Cover or stir heating milk to prevent skin formation.

Pocket Lab: Effect of Acid on Milk

MATERIALS:
1 cup milk; 1 tablespoon vinegar

EQUIPMENT:
glass measuring cup

Directions: Measure 1 cup milk and add 1 tablespoon vinegar. Try different ways of adding acid to milk (such as pouring the milk into the acid, adding 1 tablespoon of milk to the acid and then adding it to the remainder of the milk, etc.) Observe the results.

- Describe what happened to the milk.
- What other products would curdle milk?
- How might you add acid to milk without causing it to curdle?

Hot Cocoa

Customary	Ingredients	Metric
6 Tbsp.	Cocoa	90 mL
6 Tbsp.	Sugar	90 mL
1/8 tsp.	Salt	.5 mL
4 c.	Skim milk	946 mL
1 stick	Cinnamon (optional)	1 stick

Yield: 4 servings

Nutrition Information

Per serving (approximate): 180 calories, 10 g protein, 34 g carbohydrate, 2 g fat, 4 mg cholesterol, 250 mg sodium

Good source of: calcium, riboflavin, and phosphorus

Conventional Directions

Pan: 2-quart saucepan
Temperature: Medium-low

1. **Stir** together cocoa, sugar, and salt in a 2-quart saucepan.
2. **Stir** in about one-fourth of the milk slowly to form a smooth paste.
3. **Stir** in the remaining milk gradually. If desired, add the cinnamon stick.
4. **Heat** milk mixture over medium-low heat, stirring occasionally, until bubbles form around the edge of the pan.
5. **Remove** from heat and stir vigorously with a wire whisk until cocoa is smooth and foamy.
6. **Pour** cocoa mixture into 4 mugs.
7. **Serve.**

Microwave Directions

Pan: 4-cup glass measuring cup
Power Level: 100 percent power

1. **Stir** together cocoa, sugar, and salt in a 4-cup glass measuring cup.
2. **Microwave** the cocoa and sugar mixture at 100 percent power for 30 seconds or until cocoa and sugar dissolve.
3. **Stir** in the milk gradually. If desired, add the cinnamon stick.
4. **Microwave** at 100 percent power for 8 to 10 minutes or until heated thoroughly. Stir after 4 or 5 minutes and again at the end of the cooking time.
5. **Pour** cocoa into 4 mugs.
6. **Serve.**

▼ Microwaving Dairy Products ▼

When heating milk in the microwave oven, keep in mind that microwaves cook rapidly and that milk is sensitive to heat. Be sure to follow directions for the cooking time and temperature. Since milk boils over easily, turn off the power as soon as the milk starts to foam. Stir the milk after heating to distribute the heat evenly.

When microwaving cheese, use care to avoid overcooking. Cheese is less likely to overcook if you grate it or use process cheese. Stop cooking as soon as the cheese starts to melt.

Nonfat dry milk is a nutritious addition to many baked and cooked foods.

▼ Using Nonfat Dry Milk ▼

Nonfat dry milk can be used in both dry and liquid form. When you **reconstitute** (ree-KAHN-stih-toot) dry milk, it means you replace the water which was removed from it originally. Follow the directions given on the package. You can drink the reconstituted milk or use it for cooking. You can also add dry milk granules directly to some recipes to improve foods' nutritional value. Try adding a small amount to baked products, cream soups, mashed potatoes, and meat loaf.

TAKING ACTION

Your friend Carmen has recently become very concerned about calcium. She explains that she has been reading that women, especially teens, need a lot of calcium. She also wants to make sure her four-year-old sister Regina gets enough calcium for her growing bones and teeth. Also, her seventy-five-year-old grandmother will soon be moving in with the family, and Carmen has heard that older people can face special problems with brittle, easily broken bones. Her grandmother has always been very active, and Carmen wants to help her stay strong and healthy.

Carmen has decided that including more milk and milk products in the family's diet will help everyone's nutritional needs, but she is unsure about many things. How much do they need? What products should they buy? How will this affect other aspects of their health? She asks you for advice.

Using Your Resourcefulness

- What resources do you suggest Carmen use to find out about her own, her sister's, and her grandmother's calcium requirements and the role of milk products in a healthful diet?
- Where can she learn about the role milk products play in the physical development of young children and teens, and in the health maintenance of older people?
- Where can she get suggestions for including more milk products in her family's diet? How can she find out which of these products are also best for them in terms of fat, calories, and cholesterol?

Chapter 48 Review

Summary

In this chapter, you have read about:

- Why milk and milk products are an important part of a healthful diet.
- The many different milk products that are available.
- How to store milk products to preserve freshness and nutrients.
- How to prevent common problems when cooking milk products.
- Ways to use nonfat dry milk.

Facts to Recall

1. What important nutrients do milk and milk products contain? How do these nutrients contribute to good health?
2. How does whole milk compare to low-fat and skim milk in fat and calories?
3. What does the date on packages of milk products indicate?
4. Why is milk pasteurized?
5. How is cheese made?
6. What is UHT milk?
7. Explain how nonfat dry milk should be stored, both before and after it has been mixed with water.
8. Describe two ways of preventing scum from forming when heating milk.
9. How can you avoid overcooking cheese in the microwave oven?
10. Why might you add dry milk granules to baked products or meat loaf?

Ideas to Explore

1. Discuss ways in which you could replace one milk product with another one that is lower in fat and calories.
2. In some parts of the world, and for some families, milk products are difficult to obtain and store. Of those milk products that you have read about in this chapter, which might be used to solve this problem? Explain.
3. What might be some ways to incorporate milk and milk products into the diet for someone who doesn't like to drink milk?

Activities to Try

1. Research and write a short report on different sources of milk products around the world. Share your findings with the class.
2. Bring a favorite recipe to class. Be prepared to explain how milk products could be added or substituted for other ingredients to increase the nutritional value of the recipe.
3. Work with a partner to develop a public service announcement (for radio) that encourages people to include milk products as part of a healthful diet.

LINK TO *Art*

FAT IN MILK PRODUCTS

Create a mobile or a collage showing milk products that are higher in fat content and milk products that are lower in fat content. List the percentage of fat in each milk product. Indicate the benefits of choosing low-fat milk products. Use at least one element of design (see Chapter 24, pages 263-268) and one principle of design in the display.

CHAPTER

49 Fruits and Vegetables

OBJECTIVES

- Explain the role of fruits and vegetables in the diet.
- Describe how to buy, store, and prepare fruits and vegetables.

TERMS TO LEARN

- ***produce***

Vegetables and fruits are nutritional bargains. They are rich storehouses of nutrients, yet they are low in calories.

Today, fresh fruits and vegetables from around the world are available in many supermarkets. Try new varieties. You may find some new favorites.

Nutrients in Fruits and Vegetables

Fruits and vegetables have high nutrient density. For the number of calories they supply, most pack large amounts of vitamins and minerals. They make the calories you take in count toward good nutrition.

Calories in Fruits and Vegetables

Most fruits and vegetables are naturally low in fat and calories. However, the way they are prepared and seasoned can make a big difference. Take a look at a popular vegetable, the potato:

1 baked potato, plain	145 calories
20 potato chips	230 calories
1 baked potato with butter and sour cream	240 calories
1 cup (250 mL) potato salad	250 calories
20 french fries	270 calories

Fruits are naturally sweet. When extra sugar is added in processing or preparation, calories add up. For example, take a look at these values for ½ cup (125 mL) of peaches:

Fresh, unsweetened peaches	36 calories
Peaches canned in heavy syrup	95 calories
Frozen, sweetened peaches	118 calories

Although specific fruits and vegetables differ in the amounts and types of nutrients they offer, there are some similarities. Fruits and vegetables are good sources of:

- Carbohydrates (sugars and starches) for energy.
- Vitamin A for good vision, healthy skin, and strong bones and teeth.
- Vitamin C for fighting infections.
- Fiber to aid digestion.
- Minerals such as potassium and calcium.

Choose a variety of fruits to help meet your nutritional needs. What are some of your favorites?

One clue to the nutritional value of fruits and vegetables is color. For example, deep yellow and dark green vegetables and fruits are better sources of vitamin A than those with a pale color. When you buy salad greens, choose varieties that are dark green rather than pale green. Choose dark yams instead of lighter yellow sweet potatoes. Other good sources of vitamin A are apricots, cantaloupes, carrots, collards, kale, broccoli, green peppers, spinach, and turnip greens.

Citrus fruits, such as oranges, grapefruit, and lemons, are outstanding sources of vitamin C. Other good sources are tomatoes, cantaloupes, and strawberries. Vegetables such as broccoli, green cabbage, green peppers, white potatoes, turnip greens, and collards are also good sources of vitamin C.

Green leafy vegetables, such as turnip greens, kale, and collards, provide calcium for your bones and teeth. Spinach, kale, collards, and turnip greens are iron-rich vegetables. Dried fruits, such as raisins and prunes, are also excellent sources of iron, important for your blood.

For good health, you need two to four servings of fruits each day and three to five servings of vegetables. How do your current eating habits measure up?

Nutrient-rich vegetables are available every season of the year either fresh, frozen, canned, or dried. Many provide calcium, vitamins A and C, and iron.

AROUND THE WORLD

On the outside, the breadfruit looks like a big, bumpy, green orange. Inside, though, the fruit's pale color, smooth texture, and starchy flavor do remind you of fresh bread. It is a staple in diets on Caribbean and South Pacific islands, where it is grown. There it is prepared much as potatoes are in the United States. It may be baked or boiled, fried, or roasted. It is often mixed with fish, cheese, or meat.

Buying Fruits and Vegetables

Your family's preferences, the cost, and your need for convenience will determine what fruits and vegetables you buy. You can select from fresh, frozen, canned, or dried fruits and vegetables.

Fresh fruits and vegetables are also called **produce** (PRO-doos). Produce is generally least expensive at the peak of its growing season. For the best value, compare the cost of fresh, canned, frozen, and dried fruits and vegetables.

Buying Fresh Produce

Choose fresh fruits and vegetables carefully. Avoid produce that is wilted, is discolored, or has soft spots. These are signs of age and poor quality. They also mean loss of nutrients.

Most produce loses quality quickly. It's best to shop for produce often and use what you buy within a few days. If packages of produce are too large for your needs, ask a clerk to package a smaller amount for you.

What signs of quality should you look for? Head lettuce and cabbage should feel solid. Citrus fruit, squash, cucumbers, and tomatoes should feel heavy for their size. Celery, asparagus, and snap beans (green beans) are best when crisp. Root and tuber vegetables, such as potatoes and onions, should not have sprouts.

Size is not a sign of flavor or nutritional value. Very large fruits and vegetables can have poor texture and taste.

If produce looks good on the outside, it is probably good on the inside. Examine fresh produce carefully before you buy.

Buying Processed Fruits and Vegetables

Read the labels on frozen, canned, and dried fruits and vegetables. Labels tell whether the item is whole or in halves, slices, or pieces. The label also lists any seasonings, preservatives, or other ingredients that have been added. For example, some frozen vegetables are packaged in sauces that are often high in fat and salt. Would vegetables frozen without sauce provide better nutrition at a lower cost?

Many fruit and vegetable juices are available. Only products labeled "juice" are 100 percent juice. Products with a different name, such as "fruit beverage," may contain added water or sugar.

Be sure cans and packages are in good condition. Avoid buying dented cans. Frozen foods with ice crystals on the packages are a sign that the packages have not been stored under the best conditions.

Carefully examine beverage labels. Only those labeled *juice* contain 100 percent juice.

Storing Fruits and Vegetables

Fresh fruits and vegetables need careful handling after purchase. Store ripe fruits, unwashed, in the refrigerator. Place them in a plastic bag or in the crisper section. Allow unripe fruits to ripen at room temperature before refrigerating them.

Most fresh vegetables need prompt refrigeration. Potatoes and dry onions are the exception. Store them in a cool, dry, dark area.

Keep canned foods in a cool, dry location, if possible at 65°F (20°C). Keep frozen foods at 0°F (−18°C) or below. Long freezer storage is not recommended. Try to use frozen fruits and vegetables within a few months.

Store potatoes in a cool, dry, dark area.

Preparing Fruits and Vegetables

Fruits and vegetables add flavor, texture, appearance, and nutritional value to meals. Preparing them carefully will help maintain the quality in each fruit and vegetable you serve.

Handling Produce

Fresh fruits and vegetables should be washed under cold running water before use. Use a brush to clean hard vegetables, such as potatoes and carrots.

To save nutrients, pare fresh vegetables and fruits as little as possible. In general, most of the nutrients are found just under the skin. If you want to pare, slice, or cut fruits and vegetables, wait until just before you use them. Water-soluble nutrients (the B vitamins and vitamin C) are destroyed by exposure to air. Soaking produce in water also causes water-soluble nutrients to be lost.

Some fresh fruits, such as bananas, apples, peaches, and pears, darken when cut and exposed to the air. If you need to cut them before serving, squeeze lemon, orange, or grapefruit juice on them to prevent browning.

Most fresh fruits and many fresh vegetables can be served raw. For easier eating, cut vegetables into sticks or bite-size pieces.

Pocket Lab

Oxidation of Fruit

MATERIALS:
apple, water, lemon, labels

EQUIPMENT:
peeler, paring knife, cutting board, 3 saucers, 2 small bowls, glass measuring cup

Directions: Set out 3 saucers labeled "lemon juice," "water," and "control." Squeeze the juice from the lemon into a small bowl. Pour $\frac{1}{4}$ cup cold water into another small bowl. Peel and slice the apple. Dip one-third of the apple slices in lemon juice. Spread them on the saucer labeled "lemon juice." Dip one-third of the apple slices in water. Spread them on the saucer labeled "water." Place the rest of the apple slices on the saucer labeled "control." Look at the apple slices on each saucer after 30 minutes and compare what has happened to them.

- Why does fruit turn brown (oxidation) after it is cut?
- What substance prevents oxidation (fruits from turning brown)?
- How do lemons and other citrus fruits keep fruits from oxidizing?
- What other factors might speed up or slow down the oxidation process?

Making Salads

Tossed green salads are popular. Crisp greens are the key. For added appeal, combine several types in the salad. Greens must be cared for properly if the salad is to be crisp and fresh. Before storing, remove discolored leaves, rinse the greens in cold water, and drain them thoroughly.

Some greens, such as spinach, escarole, and curly endive, tend to hold dirt. Put them in a sink or pan of cold water, stir slightly, and lift them out of the water. The dirt settles on the bottom. Greens that are very dirty may need more than one rinsing.

Allow greens to dry before putting them in a salad. This helps the dressing cling to the leaves. If you are making a tossed salad, tear the greens into bite-size pieces. Cutting them with a knife will cause the cut edges to turn brown.

Many other fresh vegetables can be added to a tossed salad. Carrots, onions, broccoli, cauliflower, radishes, tomatoes, cucumbers, and mushrooms are popular choices. Clean the vegetables well and cut them into small pieces for easy eating.

When you add salad dressing, put it on just before serving to keep the greens from wilting. Add just enough to coat the leaves lightly. Many low-fat salad dressings are available.

Cooking Fresh Fruits and Vegetables

When fruits and vegetables are cooked, the starch and fiber in them softens. As a result, fruits and vegetables become less crisp. In addition, some of the nutrients are lost during cooking. Water-soluble vitamins tend to move from the food to the cooking water. The vitamins can also be destroyed by heat. When foods are cooked in a large amount of water for a long time, many nutrients are lost.

To save nutrients, cook fruits and vegetables in a small amount of water until just crispy tender.

Dilled Green Beans with Almonds

Customary	Ingredients	Metric
2 c.	Frozen Green Beans	500 mL
1½ tsp.	Margarine	7.5 mL
1 tsp.	Dill Weed	5 mL
¼ cup	Slivered Almonds	50 mL

Yield: 4 servings

Nutrition Information

Per serving (approximate): 90 calories, 3 g protein, 6 g carbohydrate, 3.5 g fat, 0 mg. cholesterol, 35 mg sodium

Good source of: vitamin A, riboflavin

Conventional Directions

Pan: 2-quart saucepan

Temperature: Medium-low

1. **Simmer** green beans according to package directions until tender-crisp.
2. **Drain** liquid from green beans.
3. **Stir** in margarine and dill weed until well blended.
4. **Add** the slivered almonds and stir.
5. **Serve** hot.

Microwave Directions

Pan: 1-quart microwave-safe covered casserole dish

Power Level: 100 percent

1. **Place** green beans in a 1 quart microwave-safe casserole dish. Add 2 tablespoons (30 mL) of water. Cover.
2. **Microwave** at 100 percent power for 10 minutes or until tender-crisp. Stir after 4 minutes.
3. **Drain** liquid from the green beans.
4. **Stir** in margarine and dill weed until well blended.
5. **Add** the slivered almonds and stir.
6. **Serve** hot.

Proper cooking can help save nutrients. Whenever possible, leave the skins on fruits and vegetables. Cook them whole or in large pieces. When cooking on the range, simmer or steam the fruits or vegetables using a small amount of water. Stop cooking as soon as the food is tender, but still slightly crisp. To get all the nutritional value you can, eat the cooking liquid along with the fruits or vegetables, or save the liquid to use in soup.

Cooking Canned Vegetables

Actually, canned vegetables are already cooked. They need only be heated. Drain the liquid from the can into the saucepan. Gently boil the liquid until it is half the original amount. Add the vegetables to the liquid, cover, and heat to serving temperature.

Cooking Frozen Vegetables

When cooking commercially frozen vegetables, follow the directions on the package. Cook vegetables in a small amount of water and for as short a time as possible to preserve nutrients.

Nutrients and flavor are kept if the food is still frozen when put in boiling water. Separate frozen pieces with a fork after cooking begins so they can cook more evenly.

Cooking fruits and vegetables in the microwave helps save nutrients.

Microwaving Fruits and Vegetables

Microwaving is an excellent way to cook fruits and vegetables. Since little water is needed and the food cooks quickly, nutrients are saved.

To microwave fresh fruits and vegetables, follow the directions in the owner's manual or a microwave cookbook. Usually the food is placed in a dish with a small amount of water and covered. For canned and frozen vegetables, check the label for microwave directions.

TAKING ACTION

A classmate, Christine, greets you Monday morning with exciting news. Several statewide produce growers' organizations are sponsoring a cooking competition for teens. Contestants are to submit menus using fruits and vegetables in as many courses as possible — appetizers, main courses, and desserts. Each group of recipes will be judged on creativity, flavor, ease of preparation, and overall nutritional value. First prize is a two-week summer course at a prestigious food preparation school in France with all expenses paid.

Christine is a talented cook, and would like to become a professional chef. She sees this as an excellent opportunity to advance in her career. She asks you for suggestions on what recipes she should enter.

Using Your Resourcefulness

- Where can Christine find new ideas for using vegetables and fruits?
- Where can she learn about unusual fruits and vegetables?
- How can Christine determine the nutritional advantages and disadvantages of each recipe?
- How can she calculate the time and effort needed to prepare each recipe?
- How might Christine evaluate the recipes for flavor and other meal appeal factors?
- Identify all the resources, human and material, that Christine can use to help her make her decision.

Chapter 49 Review

Summary

In this chapter, you have read about:

- The variety of nutrients found in different fruits and vegetables.
- How to select quality produce.
- What to look for when buying processed fruits and vegetables.
- How to store fruits and vegetables to preserve nutrients and freshness.
- How to prepare fresh, canned, and frozen fruits and vegetables to preserve their nutrients.

Facts to Recall

1. What makes vegetables and fruits "nutritional bargains"?
2. What does color tell you about a vegetable or fruit as a source of vitamin A?
3. Name three fruits and three vegetables that are good sources of vitamin C.
4. How does freshness affect the nutritional value of produce? What are signs of freshness in celery and asparagus? In potatoes and onions?
5. Why should you read the labels on packages of processed fruits and vegetables?
6. Explain how to store unripe fruit.
7. What is the advantage of the leaving skins on fruits and vegetables?
8. Briefly describe the steps in preparing a tossed green salad.
9. How do air, heat, and water affect the nutritional value of fruits and vegetables?

Ideas to Explore

1. Discuss the advantages and disadvantages of buying processed vegetables and fruits instead of fresh produce.
2. One of the appealing features of vegetables and fruits is the many different varieties. What new or unusual types of produce have appeared in supermarkets in the last few years? How might they be used in meals?

Activities to Try

1. Write a short, imaginative essay in which you "invent" a new produce item. The item should combine the best traits of existing fruits and vegetables, such as taste, appearance, availability, and versatility. Explain what characteristics you selected from each fruit or vegetable. Offer preparation and recipe suggestions, and don't forget to name your new creation.
2. Bring to class labels or packages from processed fruits and vegetables. Using the ingredients list and nutrition information, analyze the nutritional value of the product. Use reference books to find the nutrient content of the same food without processing. How does the processed version compare with the fresh version?

LINK TO *Math*

COMPARING COST PER SERVING

Complete a cost comparison study for fruits and vegetables. List three types of fruits and three types of vegetables. Compare the costs per serving for as many forms of these fruits and vegetables as possible (fresh, frozen, canned, and dried). Be sure to compare equal size portions for each form. Answer the following questions about your study:

- Which fruits and vegetables (type and form) have the highest cost per serving?
- Which fruits and vegetables (type and form) have the lowest cost per serving?
- What factors do you think contribute to the differences in cost per serving?

CHAPTER

50 Protein Foods

OBJECTIVES

- *Identify the role of protein foods in the diet.*
- *Describe how to buy, store, and prepare protein foods.*

TERMS TO LEARN

- ***marbling***
- ***tofu***

People often plan meals around a protein food. There are many protein foods to choose from, including meat (beef, pork, veal, and lamb), poultry, fish, eggs, and legumes (dry beans and peas). With so many choices, it's possible to plan an almost endless variety of main dishes. What are some of your favorites?

Nutrients in Protein Foods

What do foods in the Meat, Poultry, Fish, Dry Beans, Eggs, and Nuts Group have in common? All are good sources of protein. Meat, poultry, fish, and eggs have *complete* proteins. As you learned in Chapter 38, that means they have all the essential amino acids your body needs to build and repair its cells. Legumes and nuts contain *incomplete* proteins. When combined with other plant or animal proteins, they too can meet your body's protein needs.

What types of protein foods do you generally eat? Remember to choose protein foods that are low in fat.

Besides protein, each of the foods in this group provides additional nutrients.

- Meat supplies B vitamins and iron.
- Poultry has iron, B vitamins, and phosphorus for strong bones.
- Fish and shellfish are often good sources of iron and vitamins A and D. Most saltwater fish and shellfish supply iodine.
- Eggs have vitamins A and D, as well as riboflavin and iron.
- Legumes are rich in carbohydrates and fiber. They are also good sources of iron, calcium, phosphorus, B vitamins, and vitamin E.

Although all protein sources are nutritious, they differ in fat content. The Dietary Guidelines recommend a diet low in fat, especially saturated fat. Here are some tips to help you follow the Dietary Guidelines when choosing protein foods:

- Eat a variety of protein foods, including lower-fat ones. Skinless, light-meat poultry has less fat than most red meats. Fish is generally low in fat. In addition, the fat found in poultry and fish is less saturated than that in meat. Most legumes have almost no fat at all.
- To reduce the fat in meat, choose lean cuts. You can sometimes tell which cuts have less fat just by looking. Trim away the fat you can see.

- Choose low-fat cooking methods, such as baking or broiling instead of frying.
- Remove skin from poultry before eating. Most of the fat is just underneath the skin.
- Eat moderate portions. Many people eat more protein foods than they really need. Two servings of meat, poultry, or fish — each about the size of a deck of cards (3 oz. or 85 g) — supply all the protein you need for an entire day.
- Limit egg yolks, which contain saturated fat, to three per week. In many recipes, you can replace whole eggs with egg whites or egg substitutes.

AROUND THE WORLD

Many people of India are vegetarians for religious and economic reasons. They get their complete proteins by combining incomplete ones. One common way is by eating a meal of chapatis (chah-PAH-tee) and dal. A chapati is a small flat bread made with whole wheat flour. Dal is a soup or stew named for the Indian legume (similar to split peas) that is its main ingredient. What food groups provide the protein in this meal? What combinations do people in the United States eat that might be similar to chapati and dal?

Buying Protein Foods

Skillful shopping is important with protein foods. Fish, poultry, and meat are expensive. By considering nutrition, quality, and money-saving options, you can make good choices.

Some of the suggestions given for lowering fat can also help you save money. For instance, legumes are a low-cost, as well as low-fat, source of protein. You can also save by combining a small amount of meat with other foods, as in a soup or stew.

Shopping for Meat

Most meat comes from cattle (beef and veal), hogs (pork and ham), and sheep (lamb). Federal laws require that all animals used for food be inspected and found healthy.

Meat is made up of the lean portion (muscle), connective tissue, fat, and bone. The thick white connective tissue holds muscle fibers together.

Smaller pieces of meat, called retail cuts, are what you find in the supermarket. Read the labels carefully to determine the source of the meat and the retail cut.

Cuts and Labeling

Meat is first divided into large pieces called *wholesale cuts*. These wholesale cuts are divided into the smaller pieces called *retail cuts*. Retail cuts are the ones you find in the supermarket. The chart on page 584 shows the wholesale and retail cuts of beef.

Generally, you'll find retail cuts wrapped and labeled. The label identifies the cut with a name such as "Beef Flank Steak." This name tells you the source of the meat (beef), the wholesale cut it comes from (flank), and the specific retail cut (steak).

What to Look For in Meat

You will find many choices in the meat case. How can you decide what to buy? Here are some guidelines to help you find quality meat at a good price.

- ***Grading.*** Beef, veal, and lamb are often graded according to overall quality. *Prime* — the top grade — usually goes to restaurants. *Choice* and *Select* grades are available in many supermarkets. Meat graded "Select" is just as nutritious as meat graded "Choice" but generally has less fat and is less expensive.
- ***Tenderness.*** Meat with less connective tissue is usually more tender. Connective tissue builds up most in body areas which are exercised the most. For example, chuck from the shoulder is less tender than tenderloin from the short loin. Tender cuts usually cost more. Less tender cuts are just as nutritious and can be made tender by long, slow cooking in moist heat.

Cuts labeled "Select" are generally lower in fat.

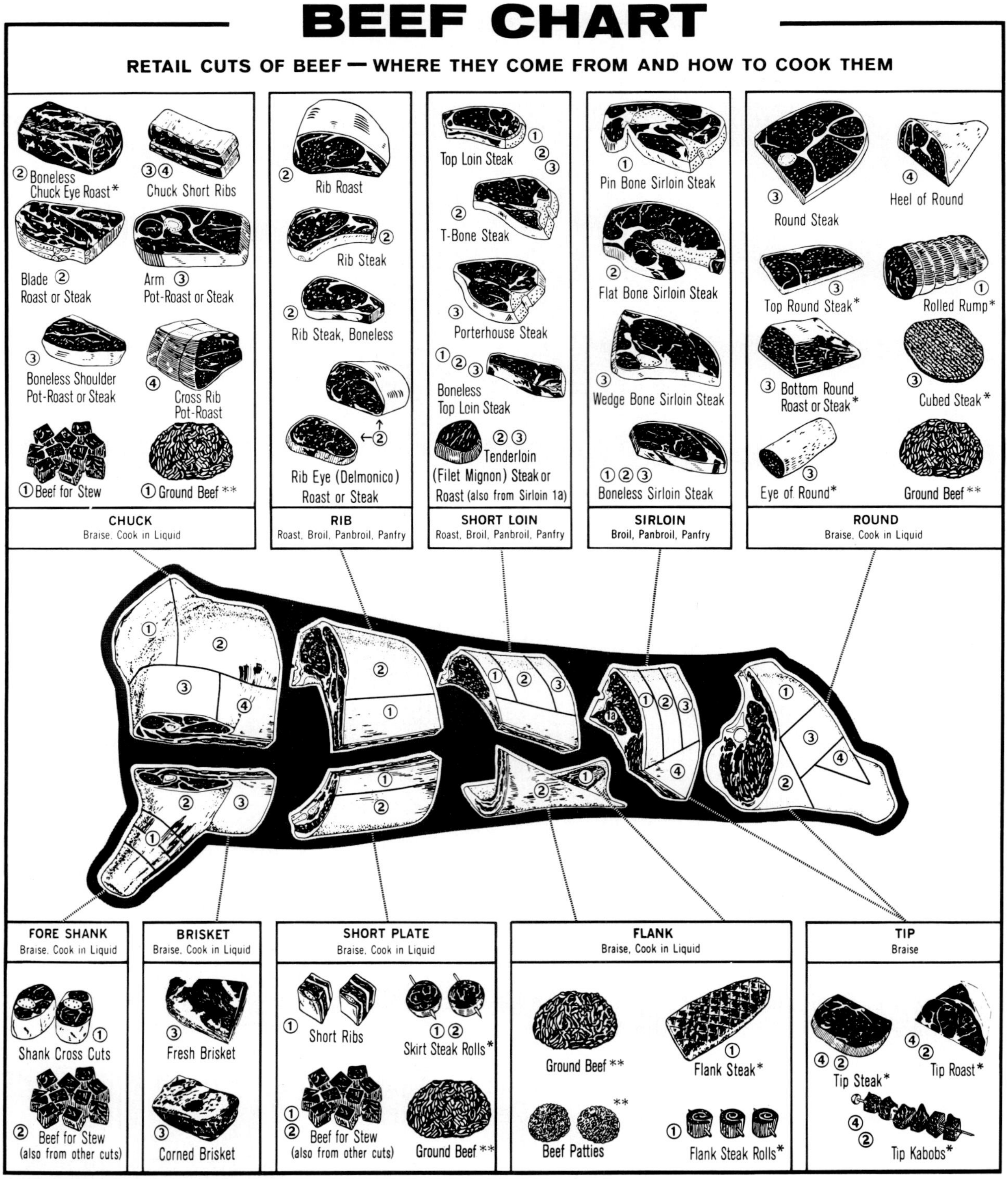

*May be Roasted, Broiled, Panbroiled or Panfried from high quality beef.

**May be Roasted, (Baked), Broiled, Panbroiled or Panfried.

- ***Leanness.*** Fat in meat is found in two forms. The large sections of fat found around the edges of meat can be trimmed away before cooking. **Marbling** refers to small veins of fat scattered throughout the muscle. Marbling adds flavor and juiciness to meat. However, lean meat can also be flavorful and juicy if cooked properly.
- ***Cost per serving.*** Meat labels tell you the cost per pound, the number of pounds, and the price you pay for the package. To find the best buys, you should also consider the cost per serving. With some cuts, you are paying for a large amount of bone or fat that will be wasted. Another cut the same size, but with less bone and fat, will give you more servings. Even if the cost per pound is higher for the second package, the cost per serving may be less.

Shopping for Poultry

The two most common types of poultry are chicken and turkey. Grading for quality is voluntary. You'll usually see Grade A in the store.

When you shop for poultry, compare the prices of different forms. You can buy poultry fresh or frozen. Larger turkeys and chickens usually cost less per pound than smaller ones, and you get more meat per pound. Whole poultry generally costs less per pound than cut-up poultry. You can also buy packages with only specific pieces, such as legs or breast portions, and boneless, skinless pieces. As when buying meat, consider the cost per serving.

You can buy poultry in different forms ranging from whole to cut-up. Whole poultry usually costs the least per pound, but has more waste. Boneless chicken breasts may be the most costly, but have no waste. Check the cost per serving to determine the best buy for you and your family.

Servings per Pound

Meat, poultry, or fish that contains...	Such as...	Will give you...
Little fat and no bone	▶ Ground beef ▶ Boneless chicken breasts ▶ Tuna steaks	3 to 4 servings per pound (500 g)
Moderate amounts of fat and/or bone	▶ Pork chops ▶ Chicken or turkey parts	2 to 3 servings per pound (500 g)
Large amounts of fat, bone, or other waste	▶ Pork spareribs ▶ Whole fish	1 to 2 servings per pound (500 g)

To figure the cost per serving...

Find the cost per pound on the package. Divide it by the number of servings per pound.

Example: Ground beef — $1.99 per pound. Round off to $2. If you get 4 servings per pound, the cost per serving is $2.00 ÷ 4, or 50 cents.

Because they are concerned about saturated fat in the diet, many Americans are enjoying more fish in their diets.

Shopping for Fish

Fish and shellfish are usually bought fresh, frozen, or canned. The cost and supply of fresh fish varies with the season of the year. Frozen and canned fish are available all year.

Fish spoils easily. Fresh or frozen fish should have a fresh fish smell, not an unpleasant odor. You'll know the difference immediately.

As with meat and poultry, consider the cost per serving. The chart on this page shows how many servings you can get from a quantity of meat, poultry, or fish. This will also help you decide how much to buy.

Shopping for Eggs

Eggs provide important nutrients at fairly low cost. An omelet made from eggs might be the main dish for a meal. Eggs are also used as ingredients in other foods ranging from meat loaf to cake.

When buying eggs, you will probably have a choice of size and perhaps of grade. Grade is based on the quality of the egg. Stores most often sell grades AA and A eggs in medium, large, and extra large sizes.

Generally, higher-grade and larger-size eggs are more expensive. However, prices vary depending on the supply of different sizes. Recipes are usually tested using large eggs.

Some stores sell eggs with brown shells. Brown and white eggs have the same nutrients and taste.

Eggs should be refrigerated both before and after purchase. They lose their freshness quickly at room temperature. Open the egg carton before buying to check that the eggs are not cracked or broken.

Eggs provide good nutrition at a lower cost. However, many health experts recommend limiting the number of eggs you eat because they are high in cholesterol.

Shopping for Legumes

Most legumes are packaged in boxes or plastic bags. Some are sold from large sacks or bins by the pound. Beans are also available canned and ready to use.

Allow about ¼ cup (50 mL) of uncooked legumes per serving. Although the amount may seem small, legumes expand greatly when cooked.

Look for firm, clean legumes of uniform size and color. If sizes are uneven, they will not cook evenly.

Tofu (TOE-fu) is a product made from soybeans, a type of legume. Tofu is white in color with a texture somewhat like custard or soft cheese. Its mild flavor is ideal for blending with other foods in soups, casseroles, and stir-fried dishes. It is low in fat and sodium, high in protein and calcium.

Some tofu comes in a special package that can safely be kept at room temperature. Otherwise, it should be found in the refrigerated case. Choose from firm or soft tofu depending on how you want to use it. Make sure the package is tightly sealed, and check the freshness date.

Legumes are an excellent, low-cost source of protein and other nutrients. Combine them with corn muffins and other whole grains for complete protein.

TIPS: *Flavoring Meats*

Meat dishes may be flavored in a variety of ways. Here are some examples.

- **Seasoning.** Sprinkled with salt, pepper, herbs and/or spices while cooking.
- **Marinating.** Soaked in, and sometimes basted with, a seasoned, usually acidic liquid (a marinade). Also tenderizes the meat.
- **Sauce or gravy.** Served with a seasoned mixture of meat juices thickened with flour or cornstarch. The sauce is often passed at table.
- **Coating.** Covered with seasoned bread or cracker crumbs or cornmeal, and baked.

Storing Protein Foods

All protein foods, except legumes, should be refrigerated or frozen. The length of time they will stay fresh in the refrigerator varies:

- Most fresh meat and poultry — 2 to 3 days.
- Ground meat — 1 to 2 days.
- Fresh fish — up to 2 days. Cover tightly to keep odors from transferring to other foods.
- Eggs — 5 weeks. Keep them in the store carton. Do not wash them.

Meat, poultry, and fish can be frozen for longer storage. Use freezer-safe wrap.

Store legumes in a tightly covered container in a cool, dry place. To store tofu, follow package directions.

Preparing Protein Foods

It's best to use low to moderate cooking temperatures for protein foods. Lower temperatures allow the protein to become firm without being tough, dry, or rubbery. The protein cooks evenly and is less likely to shrink.

Cooking Meat, Poultry, and Fish

Cookbooks can give you many ideas for preparing meat, poultry, and fish. You may want to review the basic cooking methods discussed in Chapter 46.

Pocket Lab: Effects of Heat on Protein

MATERIALS:
2 cups of milk

EQUIPMENT:
2 small saucepans

Directions: Place 1 cup of milk in each of two small saucepans. Heat the milk in one saucepan over low heat (below 140°F or 60°C). Heat the milk in the other saucepan over high heat (above 175°F or 80°C). Observe the appearance of the milk in the two saucepans. Carefully taste the milk from each saucepan. Answer the following:

- What results did low heat have on the appearance and flavor of the milk?
- What results did high heat have on the appearance and flavor of the milk?
- How might these results apply to heating other protein foods?

Thawing Safely

Never thaw frozen meat, poultry, or fish at room temperature. It could spoil and cause illness. Instead, place the frozen package in the refrigerator the day before you will need it. (A whole turkey takes 2 to 5 days to thaw.) To save time, you can use a microwave oven to defrost food. Follow the directions in the owner's manual. Food defrosted in the microwave oven must be cooked right away.

Small pieces, such as hamburger patties or fish fillets, can often be cooked while still frozen. Allow extra cooking time.

Most frozen convenience foods are cooked without thawing. Check package directions.

Use a cookbook to determine the time and temperature to cook protein foods.

Choosing a Cooking Method

When deciding how to cook meat, the most important factor is tenderness. Tender cuts of meat usually are cooked by a dry-heat method, such as roasting, broiling, or pan frying. Less tender cuts of meat are cooked with a moist-heat method, such as braising or stewing.

Poultry labeled "broiler-fryer" or "roaster" is young and tender. It can be cooked just as the name states or by other methods, such as microwaving. Mature poultry (a hen or stewing chicken) is the most tender and juicy when braised, steamed, or stewed.

Fish is tender because there is very little connective tissue. Broiling or baking works well with fish.

When Is It Done?

Meat and poultry should be cooked until there is no pink inside and juices run clear. When roasting a large cut of meat or whole poultry, use a meat thermometer. Before cooking, insert the thermometer in the center of the roast or bird. Be sure it does not rest on bone or fat. Cook meat to at least 160°F (75°C) and poultry to 185°F (85°C).

Because fish is tender, the cooking time is usually short. A good time guideline to use is 10 minutes for every inch of thickness. Overcooking dries out fish and causes it to break apart. Fish is finished cooking when the flesh flakes, or separates easily, when tested with a fork.

Perfectly cooked fish separates, or flakes, easily with a fork.

Hot Bean Tortilla Pizza

Customary	Ingredients	Metric
4	Flour Tortillas, 10-inch size	4
4 tsp.	Oil	20 mL
2 16 oz. cans	Red Kidney Beans, drained and mashed	2 453-g cans
5	Green Onions (minced)	5
¼ c.	Salsa	50 mL
1½ c.	Shredded, Low-fat Cheddar Cheese	375 mL

Yield: 4 servings

Nutrition Information

Per serving (approximate):
195 calories, 29 g protein, 69 g carbohydrate, 18 g fat, 0 mg cholesterol, 700 mg sodium

Good source of:
phosphorus, folic acid, iron, calcium, and thiamine

Conventional Directions

Pan: Cookie sheet
Temperature: Broil

1. **Preheat** the broiler.
2. **Sprinkle** each tortilla with 1 teaspoon of oil on one side and place them on the cookie sheet oil-side down.
3. **Combine** mashed red kidney beans, green onions, and salsa in a bowl.
4. **Spread** one-fourth of the bean mixture on each tortilla.
5. **Sprinkle** one-fourth of the shredded, low-fat cheddar cheese on each tortilla.
6. **Place** tortillas under the broiler on the lower rack (about 10 inches from the broiler) to prevent tortillas from burning.
7. **Cook** for 8 to 10 minutes or until the beans are heated through and the cheese has melted.
8. **Serve** hot.

Microwave Directions

Pan: Microwave-safe plate
Power Level: 100 percent power
Note: Omit oil for microwaved tortillas.

1. **Place** each tortilla on a microwave-safe plate.
2. **Follow** steps 3 through 5 of the conventional directions.
3. **Microwave** each tortilla at 100 percent power for 45 seconds to 1 minute or until cheese melts and beans are heated through.
4. **Serve** hot.

▼ Cooking Eggs ▼

Eggs can be cooked in a variety of ways. Whatever method is used, be sure to cook eggs thoroughly — until the yolks are firm or hard. Undercooking may fail to destroy salmonella bacteria found in some eggs. Salmonella can cause food poisoning.

How to ...

Separate Eggs

1. Crack the shell.
2. Pull the shell apart, keeping the yolk in the shell. Some of the white will drop into the bowl.
3. Pour the yolk from one shell half to the other until all the white is in the bowl. Put the yolk in a separate bowl.
4. If a piece of shell falls into the egg white, you can use a shell half to pick it up.

Step 1

Step 2

Step 3

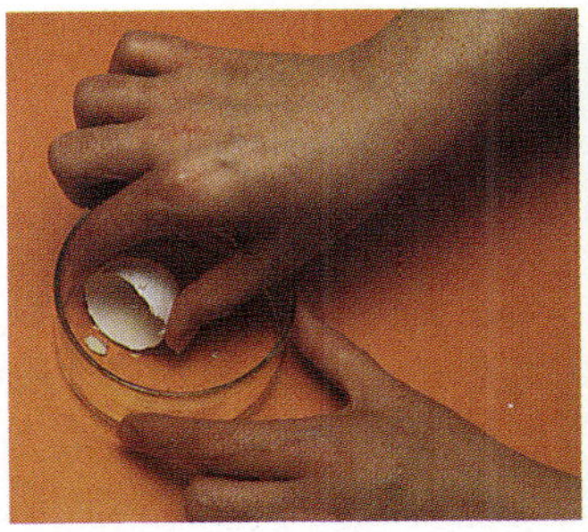

Step 4

- ***Hard-cooked eggs.*** Place the eggs in a saucepan and cover them completely with cold water. Bring the water to a boil. Remove the pan from the heat and cover it. After about 15 to 20 minutes, take the eggs out of the hot water and put them into cold water. If you do this, the shell will be easier to remove. Cold water also prevents overcooking, which could produce a green coating around the yolk.
- ***Separating eggs.*** Some recipes call for egg whites or egg yolks as ingredients. It's not difficult to separate eggs, but it may take a little practice. Follow the steps shown above.

Eggs can be cooked in a variety of ways.

▼ Cooking Legumes ▼

Soak dry beans and peas in water overnight before cooking. This allows them to absorb water. They are softened and the cooking time is shortened.

You can also cover the legumes with water and boil the water for two minutes. Take the pot off the heat and let the legumes stand for one hour. Then follow the recipe directions.

▼ Microwaving Protein Foods ▼

Microwave cookbooks include many recipes for protein foods. Legumes take about as long to simmer in the microwave as they do on the range. However, meat, poultry, and fish can be microwaved quickly.

You can microwave eggs by breaking each one into a custard cup. Pierce the yolk to prevent bursting. Cover and microwave according to the directions in the owner's manual or cookbook. Scrambled eggs are also easy to make in the microwave.

Never microwave eggs in the shell. The egg could explode during or after cooking.

TAKING ACTION

The track team at your school is having its first meet in one month and you have been preparing all winter. You've been jogging in the gym and doing flexibility exercises every morning and night. You feel fit and healthy and ready for your first competition.

In your third hour home economics class, however, you were discussing the need for protein in developing and maintaining a healthy body. You've heard that athletes need extra protein for muscle growth, but you're not sure if that's true — or if it is, how much you need. You want to be in the best possible shape for track season. This sounds like something you should investigate.

Using Your Resourcefulness

- Where can you get correct information about the protein needs of athletes?
- Where can you learn about the different sources of protein?
- What are the advantages and disadvantages of each source of protein?
- Where can you find information about the possible hazards of getting too much protein?
- In what ways can you find tips on preparing protein foods for good nutrition and taste?

Chapter 50 Review

Summary

In this chapter, you have read about:

- How protein foods contribute to a healthful diet.
- Identifying and selecting cuts of meat.
- Buying the best quality poultry, fish, eggs, and legumes.
- Properly refrigerating, freezing, and thawing protein foods.
- Safely and nutritiously preparing protein foods.

Facts to Recall

1. Identify three types of protein foods and the nutrients each supplies.
2. List four ways of limiting fat when choosing and preparing protein foods.
3. Explain why some cuts of meat are more tender than others.
4. Explain how one package of meat, with a higher cost per pound than another, may still be the better buy.
5. What is tofu? Describe its texture, appearance, nutritional value, and uses.
6. Identify one advantage and one disadvantage of convenience foods.
7. Explain the difference in cooking methods used for tender and less tender cuts of meat and types of poultry. Give three examples of each method.
8. Identify a good time guideline for cooking fish, and a sign of doneness.
9. Give two reasons for putting eggs in cold water immediately after they are finished cooking.
10. Describe two methods of softening dry legumes.

Ideas to Explore

1. Discuss ways of choosing and preparing protein foods economically, to get the greatest nutritional value for the least amount of money.
2. Everett is buying chicken for dinner for his family of four people. He is trying to choose between a package of boneless skinless chicken breasts that weighs 1.25 pounds and sells for $2.49 a pound, and a package of chicken parts that weighs 2.25 pounds and sells for 69¢ a pound. According to the chart on page 586, which is the better buy? What factors in addition to price should Everett consider when making a decision?

Activities to Try

1. Bring to school recipes featuring protein foods. Be ready to identify the sources of protein in each recipe, and if possible, to suggest ways of modifying the recipe to make it lower in fat or sodium.
2. Research a short report on protein foods popular in other regions of the world. Present your findings to the class.

LINK TO *Social Studies*

PROTEIN FOODS AROUND THE WORLD

People around the world eat a variety of foods to meet their protein needs. Using cookbooks or other resources, investigate major protein sources used in different countries around the world. Then answer the following questions:

- How does a country's economy (industrial or under developed) influence the types of protein foods available?
- In what ways do the land and climate of a country influence available protein foods?
- How might culture and religion influence the choice of protein foods?

CHAPTER

51 Grain Products

OBJECTIVES

- Explain the role of grain products in the diet.
- Describe how to buy, store, and prepare grain products.

TERMS TO LEARN

- **bran**
- **endosperm**
- **germ**
- **enriched**
- **leavening agent**

Grains are the primary source of food for most of the people in the world. Why? They are inexpensive and can be stored without refrigeration. Grains can be combined with small amounts of other ingredients to be made more nutritious. People from all cultures have found ways to use grains in their diets.

Nutrients in Grain Products

Why are more and more people in the United States finding ways to include grains in their daily diets? Grains, especially whole grains, represent an investment in good health. They are high in complex carbohydrates, especially fiber. They contain iron and B vitamins. When combined with legumes or animal proteins, they also provide high-quality protein. Most importantly, they do not contain saturated fat or cholesterol.

Structure of Grains

Grains are the seeds or fruits of cereal grasses. Though different in size and shape, the structure of grains, such as wheat, corn, and oats, is similar. Each part of the kernel contributes different nutrients. The grain kernels contain the following parts:

- ***Bran.*** The **bran** is the outside covering of the grain kernel. It has six thin layers of protective skin and contains mostly fiber. Bran contains many B vitamins and about 20 percent of the protein in grains.
- ***Endosperm.*** The **endosperm**, the largest part of the grain, is located inside the kernel. The endosperm is made up mostly of carbohydrate, but also contains about 75 percent of the grain's protein.
- ***Germ.*** The **germ** is the sprouting section of the kernel. It contains vegetable oil and is a rich source of vitamins. The germ is removed during processing because its fat content limits how long grains can be stored.

Some grains, such as stone-ground whole wheat, rolled oats, and brown rice, are left practically whole. They contain almost all the nutrients originally found in the grain.

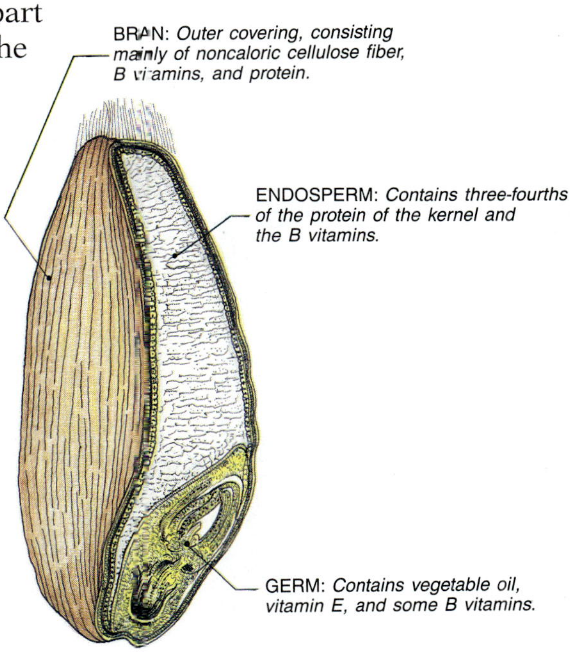

A kernel of grain has three parts — the bran, the endosperm, and the germ. The bran and the germ are the best sources of nutrients. Whole grain products use these parts.

Around the World

Corn is the world traveler of the grain family. Introduced to Europe from Central America in the 1500s, it is now found in many diverse cultures. It appears as a cornmeal mush called *polenta* (poe-LEN-tuh) in Italy; in a spicy stew known as *curry* in India; and as a thickener in coconut-milk ice cream in Thailand.

Some cereals are ready-to-eat and others need cooking.

When grains are processed to turn them into flour or cereals, the bran and the germ are often removed. The nutrients found in the bran and the germ are lost. The carbohydrate and protein in the endosperm remain. Federal law requires that processed grains be enriched. The term **enriched** describes foods that have had nutrients added back after processing.

Buying Grain Products

Since there is such a wide variety of grain products on the market, read the labels carefully to buy the type best suited to your needs. Select products that contain whole grain or bran for a more healthful diet.

When sugar appears near the top of an ingredient list, you receive few nutrients for the calories.

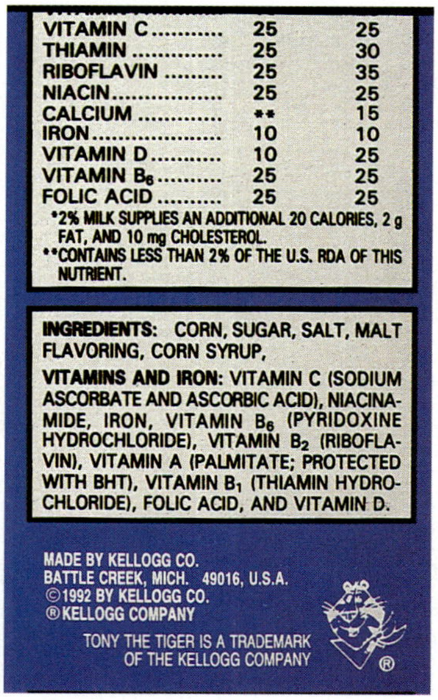

VITAMIN C	25	25
THIAMIN	25	30
RIBOFLAVIN	25	35
NIACIN	25	25
CALCIUM	**	15
IRON	10	10
VITAMIN D	10	25
VITAMIN B_6	25	25
FOLIC ACID	25	25

*2% MILK SUPPLIES AN ADDITIONAL 20 CALORIES, 2 g FAT, AND 10 mg CHOLESTEROL.
**CONTAINS LESS THAN 2% OF THE U.S. RDA OF THIS NUTRIENT.

INGREDIENTS: CORN, SUGAR, SALT, MALT FLAVORING, CORN SYRUP.

VITAMINS AND IRON: VITAMIN C (SODIUM ASCORBATE AND ASCORBIC ACID), NIACINAMIDE, IRON, VITAMIN B_6 (PYRIDOXINE HYDROCHLORIDE), VITAMIN B_2 (RIBOFLAVIN), VITAMIN A (PALMITATE; PROTECTED WITH BHT), VITAMIN B_1 (THIAMIN HYDROCHLORIDE), FOLIC ACID, AND VITAMIN D.

MADE BY KELLOGG CO.
BATTLE CREEK, MICH. 49016, U.S.A.
©1992 BY KELLOGG CO.
®KELLOGG COMPANY

TONY THE TIGER IS A TRADEMARK OF THE KELLOGG COMPANY

Shopping for Cereals

As you shop for cereals, you will find some types that are ready-to-eat and others that need cooking. They may be made from whole or enriched grains or a combination of both.

Ready-to-eat cereals may be flaked, puffed, granulated, or shredded. Simply add milk to the cereal and it is ready to eat. Cereals that need cooking generally come in three forms — instant, quick-cooking, and regular. Follow the package directions to prepare the cereal.

Cereals that are heavily enriched with "a day's supply of vitamins and minerals" and have added dried fruit and nuts are costly. In addition, it is impossible to get all of your nutrients from one bowl of cereal. Eating a variety of foods at regular intervals is the best way to insure a healthy diet. There are no shortcuts to good nutrition.

Sugar-coated cereals may be sweet and tasty. However, they add little to your diet except sugar. If you read the label, you'll find that sugar and sweeteners are the main ingredients.

▼ Shopping for Rice ▼

You will find several types of rice on the market. They include:

- ***Brown rice.*** Whole-grain rice is known as brown rice. It retains its natural nutrients and fiber and has a nut-like flavor.
- ***Enriched rice.*** This type, also called regular white rice, is enriched to replace nutrients lost in processing. It takes less time to cook than brown rice.
- ***Precooked rice.*** Precooked rice is known as instant or quick-cooking rice. It is made from either brown or enriched rice that has been cooked and dehydrated. Your cooking time at home is shorter.
- ***Converted rice.*** Converted rice is partially cooked before the bran is removed. This allows the nutrients in the bran to enter into the endosperm. Converted rice takes longer to cook than regular white rice.

In addition, rice comes in either long-grain or short-grain varieties. Long-grain rice tends to cook up fluffy, while short-grain rice tends to stick together.

▼ Shopping for Pasta ▼

Pasta, or macaroni and noodle products, is an excellent source of carbohydrates. Macaroni is made from a paste of flour and water and contains no fat. Many noodle products have eggs added for tenderness. How may this affect your choice in which product to buy?

Pastas come in a variety of shapes — elbows, shells, long spaghetti strands, spiral pasta or rotini, and flat lasagna noodles. Most pasta is dried and sold in boxes or bags. Fresh pasta is often available in the refrigerated section of the supermarket.

Pasta is an excellent source of complex carbohydrates. It comes in a variety of shapes and sizes.

▼ Shopping for Flour ▼

As you look at the supermarket shelves, you will find an assortment of flours. Here are just some of the types available.

- **All-purpose flour** is also called white flour. It is the most commonly used type. If a recipe simply says "flour," use all-purpose flour.
- **Cake flour** is very fine. It is used in cakes to provide a light, velvety-smooth texture.

- **Self-rising flour** is all-purpose flour that has a leavening agent and salt added. The **leavening agent** (LEV-uh-ning) causes baked products to rise. If you are not sure whether the flour you have is self-rising, taste it. Self-rising flour will have a salty flavor.
- **Whole-wheat flour** is made from the whole grain. It has a coarser texture and stronger flavor than all-purpose flour.

Check your recipe and use the type of flour called for. Substituting a different type of flour without making other adjustments can give poor results in baked products.

Storing Grain Products

Store grain products in a cool, dry place. Tightly seal packages or containers of grain products to keep them fresh and free from insect contamination.

Most bread can be left at room temperature. However, if it is hot and humid, you may want to refrigerate bread to keep it from getting moldy. Freeze bread for long-term storage.

Preparing Grain Products

Ready-to-eat grain products do not require cooking. You can easily combine them with your favorite ingredients. Other grain products require different preparation techniques.

Cooking Pasta, Rice, and Cereals

Pasta expands up to three times its original volume during cooking. Be sure to use a pan size that will accommodate the pasta as it cooks.

Pasta, rice, and other cereal grains are cooked in water. The starch granules absorb water, become soft, and grow in size. For example, pasta generally doubles in size and rice expands up to three times its original volume. Choose a pan large enough to allow room for the expanding grain products as they cook. Rice will absorb all the cooking water. In contrast, cooking water must be drained from pasta.

Follow the package directions for cooking grain products. They list the amount of grain product and water to use per serving and the length of cooking time. The cooking times listed are only approximate. Sample the grain you are cooking close to the end of the cooking time to determine doneness. In general, grain products should be tender but firm, not mushy.

How to ...

Cook Pasta

1. Put 2 qt. (2 L) water into a large saucepan. Add 1 tsp. (5 mL) oil to keep the pasta from sticking together. Bring to a boil.
2. Slowly add the pasta to rapidly boiling water. The water should keep boiling as you add the pasta.
3. Follow the package directions for the length of cooking time. Pasta is done if it is tender but firm in the center.
4. Drain the pasta immediately, but do not rinse — valuable nutrients could be lost. To keep pasta hot, cover the colander with a towel and set it over boiling water.

Step 1

Step 3

Step 2

Step 4

▼ Making Quick Breads ▼

There are two categories of breads:

- **Yeast breads** use yeast as a leavening agent. After the dough is mixed, it requires time to rise before it can be baked. White or whole wheat bread, hamburger buns, and dinner rolls are yeast breads.
- **Quick breads** can be baked shortly after mixing. The leavening agent is usually baking powder or baking soda. Quick breads include muffins, pancakes, biscuits, and waffles.

Ingredients for quick breads usually include flour, sugar, salt, a leavening agent, a liquid, fat, and eggs. These ingredients are mixed using one of two basic methods. The *muffin method* is used not only for muffins, but also for loaf-type quick breads, pancakes, and waffles. In contrast, biscuits are mixed using the *biscuit method*.

Steps 1 and 2

Step 3

Mixing Muffins

To mix muffins, or another quick bread that uses the muffin method, follow these basic steps.

1. Measure the dry ingredients (flour, sugar, baking powder, and salt) into a bowl and mix them together.
2. Make a well with the back of a spoon in the center of the dry ingredients.
3. Measure the liquid ingredients (milk, oil or melted shortening, and eggs) into another bowl and mix them together.
4. Add the liquid ingredients to the dry ingredients.
5. Stir the ingredients together just enough to moisten the dry ingredients. The batter should be lumpy.

Step 4

Step 5

Mixing is the key to success in making muffins. Overmixing generally results in muffins that are somewhat tough. In addition, peaks will form on top, and tunnels or long holes will appear inside the muffins.

After mixing, fill muffin pans according to the recipe and bake in a preheated oven. Remove the muffins from the pan and serve them warm.

Fill muffin pans two-thirds full.

Remove from pan and serve warm.

Cinnamon Oatmeal Muffins

Customary	Ingredients	Metric
¾ cup	Whole-wheat flour	175 mL
¾ cup	White flour	175 mL
1 cup	Uncooked rolled oats	250 mL
1 Tbsp.	Baking powder	15 mL
3 Tbsp.	Sugar	45 mL
½ tsp.	Cinnamon	3 mL
¼ tsp.	Salt	1 mL
1	Egg	1
1 cup	Milk	250 mL
¼ cup	Oil	50 mL

Yield: 12 muffins

Nutrition Information
Per serving (approximate):
150 calories, 4 g protein, 20 g carbohydrate, 6 g fat, 19 mg cholesterol, 135 mg sodium
Good source of:
thiamine, calcium, phosphorus

Conventional Directions
Pan: Muffin pan
Temperature: 400°F (200°C)

1. **Grease** and flour muffin pan.
2. **Combine** flours, rolled oats, baking powder, sugar, cinnamon, and salt. Mix well.
3. **Beat** egg in a separate bowl.
4. **Add** milk and oil to egg. Stir well.
5. **Add** liquid mixture to flour mixture.
6. **Stir** until just blended. Batter should be lumpy.
7. **Fill** muffin cups ⅔ full.
8. **Bake** 15 to 20 minutes or until muffins spring back when touched.

Microwave Directions
Pan: Microwave-safe muffin pan
Power Level: 100 percent power

1. **Line** microwave-safe muffin pan with paper muffin liners.
2. **Follow** steps 2 through 6 of the conventional directions.
3. **Fill** muffin cups half full.
4. **Microwave** at 100 percent power. For 4 to 6 muffins, microwave 2 minutes or until batter is no longer doughy and springs back when touched lightly.

Making Biscuits

Here are the steps for making biscuits. Notice how the mixing method differs from the one used for muffins.

1. Measure the dry ingredients into a bowl and mix them together.
2. Measure the shortening — a solid fat — and add it to the dry ingredients.
3. Cut the shortening into the dry ingredients. Use a pastry blender or a criss-cross motion with two knives. "Cutting in" breaks the solid fat into pea-size pieces and mixes it with the dry ingredients.

Step 3

Step 4

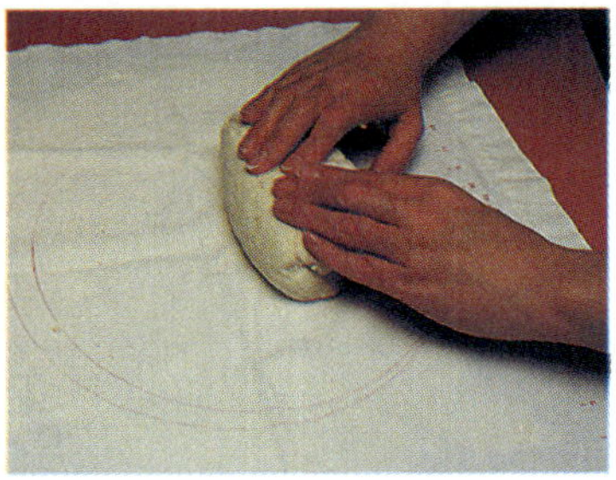

Step 5

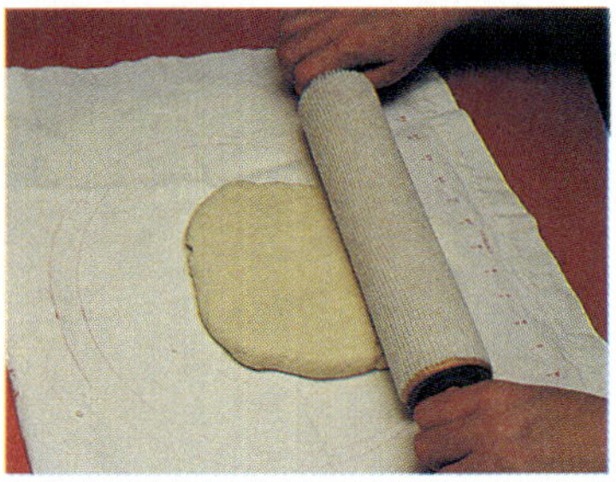

Step 6

Step 7

4. Add the liquid ingredients and mix until a ball of dough forms.
5. Put the dough on a lightly floured board. Knead the dough, using the heels of your hands to press down and away from you. Rotate the dough a quarter turn and fold it toward you. Repeat, kneading about 10 times in all. Kneading the dough makes a flaky biscuit with a fine texture. Overkneading makes a compact and tough product.
6. Use a rolling pin to roll out the biscuit dough until it is about ½ inch (1 cm) thick.
7. Cut out the biscuits using a biscuit cutter or a floured glass.
8. Place the biscuits on a cookie sheet and bake as directed in the recipe.

Rolled biscuits should double in size when baked. They should have lightly browned tops with cream-colored, straight sides.

When done, remove biscuits from pan and serve warm.

Making Cookies

The word "cookie" actually means "little cake." Crisp cookies usually have more fat, sugar, or both than soft cookies or cakes.

There are many types of cookies, including drop, rolled, refrigerator, molded, and bar cookies. They differ in how stiff the dough is and in the way it is handled for shaping.

To bake evenly, all cookies should be the same size and thickness. As a general rule, cookies should be spaced at least 1 inch (2.5 cm) apart on a cookie sheet to allow the cookies to expand during baking.

Arrange the racks in the oven before preheating it. Put the lower rack in the middle of the oven and the upper rack about three inches higher. Place one cookie sheet on the upper shelf and another one on the lower shelf for baking.

Allow cookies to cool on a wire cooling rack before storing.

Occasionally enjoy cookies for desserts or snacks. What are some of your favorites?

Put the cookie sheets in the middle of each rack away from the walls of the oven. This allows the hot air to circulate around the cookies and bake them evenly.

Check the cookies a few minutes before the end of the baking time listed in the recipe. When cookies are done baking, they will be delicately browned. Remove the cookies from the sheet immediately using a spatula. Place them in a single layer on a wire cooling rack. When they are cool, put them in a storage container.

Making Cakes

Have you ever thought about what ingredients go into your favorite cake? Aside from flavoring ingredients such as chocolate and vanilla, most cakes contain flour, sugar, and eggs. Depending on the type of cake, fat may or may not be used. Cakes made with fat, such as butter or pound cakes, are leavened with baking powder or baking soda. Cakes made without fat, such as angel food cakes, use a large number of egg whites. The air beaten into the egg whites is the main leavening agent in these cakes.

Before you mix the batter for a cake, check the recipe to see how to prepare the cake pans. You may need to grease the inside of the pans to prevent the cake from sticking. You can use a paper towel or wax paper to spread a thin layer of solid shortening in the pans. If you prefer, you can use a cooking spray. The recipe may tell you to grease the pans on the sides and bottom or the bottom only. With some recipes, you grease the pans and lightly dust them with flour.

Instead of greasing and flouring cake pans, you can line the bottom of the cake pan with waxed paper. Simply trace the bottom of the cake pan onto the waxed paper, cut along the line you traced, and place the waxed paper into the cake pan.

Some people prefer to cut pieces of wax paper to fit on the bottom of the pan. This makes it easier to remove the cake from the pan without the use of added fat.

There are several methods for mixing cakes with fat. The following method, called the *conventional method,* is used most often.

1. Cream the fat and sugar together until the mixture is light and fluffy.
2. Add the eggs. Beat the mixture again until it is light and fluffy.
3. Measure and combine the dry ingredients in a separate bowl.
4. Measure and combine the liquid ingredients in a separate bowl.
5. Add the dry and liquid ingredients alternately to the creamed mixture. Begin and end with dry ingredients to keep the mixture from separating. After each addition, stir until well blended.

A few minutes before the baking time is up, test the cake for doneness. Lightly touch the center of the cake. If no imprint remains, the cake is done. You can also insert a toothpick or cake tester in the center of the cake. If it comes out clean, the cake has finished baking.

Follow the recipe directions for removing the cake from the pan. Some cakes should be taken out of the pan right away. Others need to cool a short time in the pan. Before removing the cake from the pan, loosen the sides of the cake with a table knife. In most instances, allow a cake to cool completely before applying frosting or other toppings.

TIPS: *Making Cakes*

Whether you use a mix or bake from scratch, follow these tips for a successful cake.

- Preheat the oven.
- Use the size of pan specified in the recipe.
- Prepare pans exactly as directed.
- Follow mixing instructions exactly. For the best volume and texture, stir for the length of time suggested.
- When placing pans in the oven, make sure they do not touch the oven walls or each other. Leave room for air to circulate.

Pocket Lab

Properties of Starch

MATERIALS:
⅓ cup (80 mL) rolled oats, 1 potato, flour, water

EQUIPMENT:
bowl, saucepan, wooden spoon

Directions: Soak ⅓ cup (80 mL) of rolled oats in cold water overnight. Soak thinly sliced potatoes in water overnight. Cook a spoonful of flour in a cup of water. Observe the results.

- How did soaking affect the rolled oats?
- What did you observe in the potato water?
- What effect did heat have on flour?
- What characteristics of starch make it useful as a thickening agent?

Using Thickening Mixtures

Have you ever wondered what gives thickness to a rich gravy or a creamy soup? Gravies, cream sauces, soups, and puddings are often thickened with flour. As the mixture is heated, starch granules in the flour absorb liquid and thicken the mixture. The thickness depends on the amount of flour used.

Thickening liquid mixtures is a basic cooking technique that can be used with many recipes. Follow these steps to thicken liquid:

1. Melt the solid fat, usually butter or margarine, in a saucepan.
2. Add the desired amount of flour to the melted fat. Stir to make a paste.
3. Cook the paste a minute or two over medium heat to avoid a "starchy" or flour-like flavor.
4. Add the liquid all at once. Stir constantly until the mixture is thick.

Why should you stir constantly? Stirring helps keep the starch from forming lumps in the liquid. Starch particles next to the bottom and sides of the pan heat quickly and

Step 1

Step 2

Step 3

Step 4

A smooth sauce results from stirring constantly.

absorb liquid faster than particles in the center. When some starch particles get larger faster than others, you have lumps. Lumps also occur if you add the starch directly to the liquids without first making the fat-starch paste. You can eliminate lumps by mixing with a beater or blending in a blender.

Microwaving Grain Products

In general, it takes almost as long to cook grain products in the microwave oven as it does using conventional cooking methods. Grains such as pasta and rice need time to absorb liquid. Although microwaves speed up cooking time, they cannot speed up the time it takes grains to absorb liquid. Some exceptions to this may be instant or quick-cooking cereals, precooked rice, and precooked pasta.

A variety of baked products, such as muffins and cakes, can be prepared in a microwave oven. However, products baked in the microwave do not brown. They often have a higher volume because there is no crust to stop the product from further rising. The leavening process stops shortly after the microwave oven stops. Recipes developed for microwave cooking usually provide the best results.

To save preparation time, look for convenience grain products that are made for the microwave oven. Some examples are microwave cake mixes and microwave pastas.

TAKING ACTION

Laurel has volunteered to make baked goods for her neighborhood rummage and bake sale. The money raised will be used to buy trees to plant on Laurel's street. She wants to bake breads and cookies that are appealing, but nutritious as well.

She knows that adding or substituting ingredients can make foods more nutritious. Since flour is a major ingredient in all her recipes, she will begin there. She would also like to add other grain products, such as wheat germ and oats, to increase the fiber and vitamins in her baked goods. She asks for your suggestions.

Using Your Resourcefulness

- Suggest ways that Laurel can find out about different types of flour and the nutritional value of each type.
- In what ways can Laurel determine how flour substitutions will affect her recipes?
- Where can Laurel find recipes designed with good nutrition in mind?
- How can she decide whether wheat germ would be an appealing addition to chocolate chip cookies?
- What other resources might be helpful for Laurel?

Chapter 51 Review

Summary

In this chapter, you have read about:

- The different parts of grain kernels and the nutrients found in each part.
- Shopping for grain products to best meet your nutritional needs.
- Preparing grain products, both conventionally and in a microwave oven.
- Baking foods made with grain products, in a conventional oven and in a microwave oven.

Facts to Recall

1. Identify three ways that grains represent an investment in good health.
2. What nutrients are found in the bran? In the endosperm? What percentage of the kernel's protein is found in each part?
3. Give two reasons why it is not an advantage to buy heavily enriched cereals.
4. Identify three differences between brown rice and enriched white rice.
5. How does self-rising flour differ from all-purpose flour?
6. How are rice and pasta similar in cooking? How are they different?
7. Briefly explain the five steps in the muffin method for mixing quick breads.
8. How and why is biscuit dough kneaded?
9. List three ways to prepare cake pans to prevent the cake from sticking.
10. Explain two ways to test a cake for doneness.
11. Why do baked products prepared in a microwave oven often have a higher volume than those baked in a conventional oven?

Ideas to Explore

1. Besides the reasons given in the chapter, why do you think grains are so popular around the world?
2. Discuss some possible hazards of relying on heavily enriched cereals for your daily nutritional needs.

Activities to Try

1. Obtain three kinds of ready-to-eat cereal. Compare the nutrition labels and the prices. Which cereal is the best nutritional value for the money?
2. Assume that you and two friends are on a menu-planning committee for your school. The school board has asked that foods containing more grains be included in school lunches. Your committee must plan lunch menus for two weeks including at least six different grain products each week.

LINK TO *Social Studies*

GRAINS AROUND THE WORLD

Most Americans are familiar with corn, wheat, and rice as nutritious grain foods. However, many other nutritious grain foods are used around the world — and many are gaining popularity in the United States. Select one of the following grains or grain foods to investigate: kasha, couscous, amaranth, millet, or quinoa (KEEN-wa). In your research, find the following information:

- How is this grain food most often prepared?
- What area of the world is this grain food most commonly found in? Why?
- What are the characteristics of this grain food (flavor, texture, etc.)?
- How does the nutritional value of this grain food compare to other grains such as wheat?

CHAPTER

52 Etiquette and Eating Out

OBJECTIVES

- *Set a table correctly.*
- *Describe different methods of serving food.*
- *Give guidelines for appropriate manners and behavior when eating at home or in a restaurant.*

TERMS TO LEARN

- ***etiquette***
- ***tableware***
- ***flatware***
- ***place setting***
- ***course***
- ***appetizer***
- ***entree***
- ***a la carte***

When you eat out or have guests for dinner, you want to know the right things to do so that you and your companions will feel comfortable. Through the years, certain mealtime customs, or ways of doing things, have become common practice. Customs regarded as the "correct" way to do things in social situations are referred to as **etiquette** (ET-ih-ket). By becoming familiar with the customs and etiquette to follow when eating with others and going to restaurants, you will feel much more comfortable. You can be at ease and enjoy the occasion.

Setting the Table

An attractively set table will help make the meal more enjoyable. Customs for setting the table make the table more attractive and the meal more convenient to eat.

The first step in setting a table is to decide what tableware is needed. **Tableware** includes dishes, glasses, and **flatware** (eating utensils). Each person will need at least one plate, glass, fork, knife, and spoon. Depending on what food is being served, other tableware may be needed. For example, a separate, smaller plate and fork are needed for salad, a bowl and soup spoon for soup, and a cup and saucer for a hot beverage. Other essential items include a napkin for each person and a tablecloth or place mats to protect the table.

A **place setting** is the arrangement of tableware for each person who will be eating a meal. To find out how to arrange the items, read "How to Set a Table" on page 610.

Serving Food

Families usually have their own habits and preferences when it comes to serving meals. Your family may serve everyday meals one way and special occasion meals another. The way you serve food often depends on what food you're having, the amount of time and space you have, the number of people eating, and who is helping. The common styles of serving food include:

- ***Family-style service.*** Dinner plates are at each person's place. The foods are in serving dishes on the table and are passed around from person to person to help themselves.

Food is passed from person to person when family-style service is used.

How to ...
Set a Table

1. Arrange a tablecloth or place mats on the table.
2. Place the dinner plate in the center of the place setting one inch from the edge of the table.
3. Arrange the flatware around the dinner plate, following these guidelines:
   - The knife goes to the right of the plate, with the cutting edge facing the plate.
   - Spoons go to the right of the knife, with the bowl of the spoon face up.
   - Forks go to the left of the plate, with the tines or prongs curving upward.
   - If more than one spoon or fork will be used, place the one that will be used first (such as the soup spoon or salad fork) farthest from the plate.
   - The bottom of the handle of each piece of flatware should line up with the lower edge of the plate.
4. If a salad is to be served with the meal, place the salad plate above the forks. If the salad is to be the first course, the salad plate can be placed on the dinner plate and removed after the salad is eaten.
5. Put the water glass just above the tip of the knife. If there is another beverage glass, place it to the right and slightly in front of the water glass.
6. If a hot beverage is to be served, place the cup and saucer to the right of the spoons. Sometimes the cup and saucer are not placed on the table until the hot beverage is served.
7. Place the napkin to the left of the forks. The folded edge should be placed to the outside.

On special occasions, you may use head-of-table service in serving food.

- ***Plate service.*** The food is placed on each person's plate in the kitchen, and then the filled plates are brought to the table.
- ***Head-of-table service.*** This service is often used for special occasion meals. The person at the head of the table puts food on the plates and passes the plates down the table. People wait to eat until everyone has been served.
- ***Buffets.*** This is a good way to serve food when there are too many people to seat around the table. Dishes, flatware, napkins, and serving dishes with food are put on the table or counter. People take what they want and find a place to sit while they eat.

Table Manners

Have you ever felt confused about "what to do when" at mealtime? Here a few guidelines to help you feel more comfortable when eating:

- Place the napkin on your lap.
- Reach for food only if you do not have to lean across the table or reach in front of anyone. Otherwise, ask the person nearest the food to please pass it to you.
- When serving forks and spoons are provided, use them to serve yourself food. Be sure to put them back into the serving dish after you have used them. Try not to use your own flatware when serving yourself.

AROUND THE WORLD

For the Hindus of India, dining etiquette goes far beyond table manners. This belief system teaches respect for all things connected to life, including preparing and eating meals. The cook must bathe before entering the kitchen to prepare a meal. Knives are not used because they are associated with violence and destruction. Food is eaten with the right hand only — the left hand is thought unclean.

- If you're not sure which piece of flatware to use, follow the lead of the person at the head of the table.
- Cut one bite at a time; then eat it. Do not cut all your food into pieces all at once.
- Break, rather than cut, bread and rolls into small pieces.
- Eat as quietly as you can by chewing with your mouth closed. Do not talk with food in your mouth.
- Try to keep your arms and elbows off the top of the table.
- Push foods, such as peas and corn, onto the fork with a piece of bread or a knife.
- It is usually acceptable to eat certain foods with your fingers. Some examples are sandwiches, bread, pickles, carrot sticks, celery, pizza, and corn-on-the-cob.
- When food is too hot to eat, wait until it cools.
- When you are not using a knife or fork, put it across your plate.
- When you have finished eating, put the knife and fork next to each other across the center of the plate. Leave the dishes where they have been during the meal, and put your napkin on the table to the left of your plate.

At many restaurants, food is served to you by a waiter or waitress.

Eating Out

Going out to eat can mean going to a fast-food restaurant, a cafeteria, or a restaurant with table service. You are probably familiar with fast-food restaurants. You select what you want from the menu above the counter, place your order, and then take it out or find your own table. In cafeterias, you take a tray, select your food as you walk through the serving line, and find a table. At a restaurant that offers table service, someone takes your order at the table and brings the food.

Some restaurants require that you telephone ahead and reserve a table. Even if a reservation isn't required, it can help you avoid a long wait if the restaurant is crowded. If you haven't been to the restaurant before, it's also a good idea to find out the price range and what type of dress is appropriate. If you have a reservation, arrive at the restaurant by the appointed time or telephone to cancel the reservation.

At many restaurants, someone will greet you when you come in. This person will probably ask how many are in your party and what type of seating you prefer. If you have a reservation, give the name to the person who greets you. When your table is ready, someone will lead you to it.

If you are eating at a restaurant where no one greets you, seat yourself. Find a table that is agreeable to everyone.

Ordering from the Menu

The menu is often divided into sections for different types of food or different **courses** (parts of the meal). For example, the menu might include appetizers, soups, salads, entrees, desserts, and beverages. An **appetizer** is an optional first course. The **entree** (AHN-tray) is the main course.

The food on a menu may be listed and priced in one of two ways:

- Items may be listed separately, or **a la carte** (ah-la-CART). Each item has an individual price.
- The menu may list a complete meal for a certain price. Be sure to notice what is included in the meal. For instance, the price of a dinner may include your entree, salad, potato, and bread. Other items would cost extra.

Behavior at the Restaurant

When eating out, be considerate of other people. Most people want to eat and talk quietly to their companions. Loud, noisy conversation can bother other diners and interfere with the enjoyment of their meal.

If you need anything during the meal, politely ask the waiter or waitress. Usually he or she will stop by your table several times during the meal. If the problem can't wait until then, get the server's attention by raising your hand and saying "waiter" or "waitress" quietly. If the person waiting on your table is far away, ask a waiter or waitress who is nearby to get the person for you.

Taking ashtrays, glassware, or utensils as souvenirs is theft. The manager could take legal action against you.

TIPS: *Understanding Menu Item Terms*

Avoid confusion — and surprises — when ordering from a menu by learning these frequently used terms:

- **Cacciatore.** Italian for "hunter style." Chicken cooked in a spicy tomato sauce.
- **Alfredo.** Pasta served in a white sauce made with cream, butter, and cheese.
- **Au gratin.** A browned topping of buttered bread crumbs and sometimes cheese. Primarily used for vegetables.
- **Au jus.** French for "in juice." Meat served in its own juices.

Politely get the attention of your waiter or waitress if you need something.

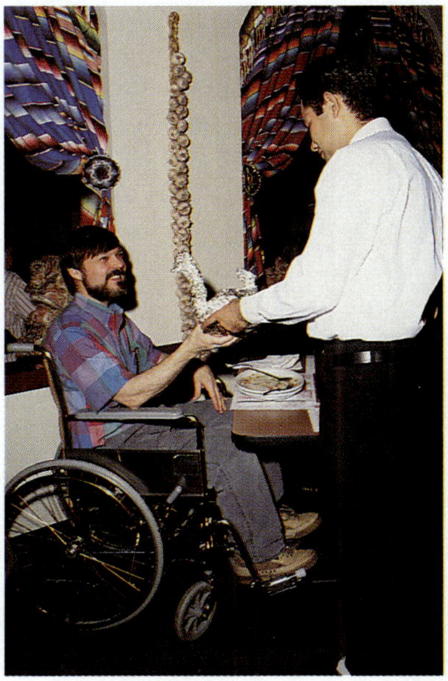

Decide who is going to pay the bill before you get to the restaurant. Be sure to leave a tip for good service.

Paying the Bill and Tipping

At the end of the meal, it's time to pay. If the check is not given to you, say "Check, please."

Who pays? This can often be settled before you get to the restaurant. If you invite someone out, be clear about who is paying. You may say, "It's on me. I'll pay." You may say, "Let's go Dutch," which means each person pays for his or her own meal.

If you are invited out and it's not clear who is paying, bring enough money so you can pay your own bill just in case.

Before paying, check the bill to be sure it is accurate. Remember, many states add a sales tax to restaurant bills.

It's customary to leave a tip for the person who served you. The amount is usually 10 to 15 percent of the bill. A tip is for service, not for food. If the food was bad but the service was good, leave a tip. When no tip is left, the message is clear that the service was poor.

Some checks say at the bottom, "Pay the cashier." In that case, leave a tip at the table and pay on the way out. Sometimes you pay the person serving you, and he or she takes your money and the check to the cashier. You then get the change from the waiter or waitress and leave a tip.

Knowing what to expect in different kinds of restaurants will help you feel more comfortable in a variety of situations.

TAKING ACTION

Kameel is elated and scared. He is thrilled that Jeanette has accepted his invitation to the Garfield Junior High Spring Dance, but he is concerned about the other part of their date — the dinner at a nice restaurant that he has also promised. Kameel doesn't eat out much, certainly not at a restaurant as nice as the one he would like to take Jeanette to. He's worried that he won't be able to afford it, or that he will say or do something terribly inappropriate. He asks for your help in making this an evening that they both will want to remember — and not one they wish they could forget.

Using Your Resourcefulness

- How can Kameel find out which restaurants are within his budget?
- Where can he learn what behavior is appropriate when on a date?
- How can Kameel prepare himself so he will feel comfortable ordering from a menu?
- Where can he find out about different dining utensils and their proper use?
- In what way should Kameel decide how much to tip the waiter or waitress? How should the tip be left?
- List all the sources Kameel might use to help him find the information he needs.

Chapter 52 Review

Summary

In this chapter, you have read about:

- How to arrange the dinnerware, flatware, glasses, and napkins for a meal.
- Different ways of serving food.
- Mealtime etiquette for dining out or at home.
- Proper restaurant behavior, including ordering from a menu, paying the bill, and tipping the waiter or waitress.

Facts to Recall

1. How can knowing mealtime etiquette increase your enjoyment of a meal?
2. Describe the arrangement of flatware around the dinner plate.
3. Identify three factors affecting how food is served.
4. Explain how food is served in *family-style* service.
5. What is a good rule to follow if you're not sure which piece of flatware to use?
6. Give five examples of foods that can be eaten with the fingers.
7. What is meant by "going Dutch"?
8. Is a tip for the food or for the service? Explain your answer.

Ideas to Explore

1. What do you think is the most common mistake people make in mealtime etiquette?
2. What practical benefits can you find in the rules of etiquette discussed in this chapter?
3. How might you tactfully correct a member of your dining party who was showing poor table manners?

Activities to Try

1. With two or three other students, practice proper restaurant behavior in front of the class. Include arriving at the restaurant, being seated, ordering the meal, and paying the bill.
2. Practice and demonstrate eating with different types of utensils, such as chopsticks, fondue forks, or seafood forks.
3. Write a paragraph describing a humorous experience you have had while dining at home or out.

LINK TO Communication

CREATING A TABLE SETTING

Write a menu that you would like to prepare for several friends. Create a demonstration showing how you will properly set the table for this meal. Be sure to include all items of tableware necessary to serve this meal. When setting the table, take into consideration the attractiveness of the table setting. Use the elements and principles of design (see Chapter 24) when deciding about placemats or a tablecloth and centerpiece for the table.

CAREER *Connections*

Get Ready for Your Future Through Volunteering

"After listening to a speaker in my foods class talk about hunger, I started to wonder about people in my own community. I found that there are many hungry people here. There are also groups of people working to help them, like the food pantry not far from my home.

"I started volunteering at the food pantry two evenings a week about six months ago. My job involves stocking and organizing shelves in a small warehouse area. I take careful inventory of the foods on hand and what foods are needed. In this way, those in the community that donate food (and sometimes money) can provide items that are really necessary. Since I've had some computer experience, I was able to create a data base to keep track of our inventory.

"In the future, I'm considering a career in food technology. I would like to find ways to improve the quantity and quality of safe foods."

"My home economics degree and my experience as a volunteer photographer for the college newspaper helped pave the way to my career in advertising. I work in a fast-paced world and create ideas that sell food products. For example, to make a new pasta product a hit, I served a spaghetti dinner to a thousand runners the night before a marathon!

"As an account executive, I supervise magazine ads, work with copywriters, designers, and photographers. I often work with food scientists — mostly home economists — and test new recipes in a test kitchen located in our building. I'm on the scene to supervise when ads are shot for magazines or TV. I love my job and look forward to work every day. What more can you ask?"

"My experience as a hospital volunteer first sparked my interest in dietetics. I saw firsthand how important nutrition is to a healthy way of life.

"You might think a dietitian is someone who is only concerned with other people losing weight. But that's not true. A dietitian promotes better health through better nutrition — whether people are healthy or ill, overweight, or underweight.

"To become a dietitian, I had to earn a college degree plus a one-year master's degree and six months of work experience. Then I took a registration examination so that more career choices would be open to me.

"Generally there are two types of dietitians, clinical and administrative. Clinical dietitians help people learn about food so they can change their eating habits. These dietitians often work in a health care setting such as a hospital.

"As an administrative dietitian, I'm a specialist in food systems. I coordinate buying, budgeting, and serving food for a large company cafeteria. If you like working with people and nutrition, have reasonable math skills and a feel for science, you may want to choose a career as a registered dietician just as I did."

MAKING THE CONNECTION

- Make a list of as many food-related careers as you can think of. Are any appealing to you?
- What skills can you learn through other types of volunteer experiences that you can apply to any career?
- What volunteer experiences in your area could lead to a food-related career? What steps can you take to find out?
- What resources in your school library can help you find out more about food related careers?

Glossary

A

a la carte: having food items listed and priced individually on the menu. (52)

abbreviation: a shortened form of a word. (45)

acquaintances: people whom you know, but who are not your friends. (10)

addicted: physically or psychologically dependent on something. (14)

additive: a substance added to food for a specific purpose. (41)

adjustable zipper foot: a sewing machine attachment that allows stitching to take place on either side of the zipper. (36)

adolescence: the stage of growth between childhood and adulthood. (4)

aerobic exercise: vigorous activity that causes your heart to beat faster for a sustained amount of time. (37)

age span: the number of years between children. (13)

alcoholics: people who are addicted to alcohol. (14)

alcoholism: a disease involving an addiction to alcohol. (14)

alternatives: the different choices you can make to deal with a situation. (3)

apathy: not caring and not trying; the opposite of involvement. (6)

appetizer: an optional first course in a meal. (52)

applique: a cut-out fabric decoration that is sewn onto a larger fabric background. (32)

apprenticeship: on-the-job training with pay. (7)

aptitudes: natural abilities or talents for learning certain skills. (7)

assertive: standing up for yourself in a determined or confident way without bullying others with words or actions. (8)

ATMs (automatic teller machines): computers that customers can use to make their banking transactions when tellers are busy or the bank is closed. (21)

B

backstitching: a reverse stitch used to secure the ends of a seam. (33)

bacteria: one-celled living things so small they can be seen only with a microscope. (47)

baking or **roasting:** cooking in an oven or oven-type appliance with dry heat. (46)

balance: the remaining amount of money you have in your account. (19)

balance: a feeling of equal weight among all parts of a design. (24)

basal metabolism: the number of calories needed for normal body processes. (40)

basting: holding fabric in place temporarily with pins or long stitches. (35)

Better Business Bureau: a private agency that works to improve local business practices. (20)

bias: diagonal line formed when the crosswise grain is parallel to the selvage. (34)

blended families: nuclear families in which one or both adults have been married before and one or both have children from a previous marriage. (12)

body image: a mental picture of how you think your body looks. (40)

body language: nonverbal communication; communication without words. (8)

boiling: cooking at a temperature at which bubbles rise and break on the surface of a liquid. (46)

bran: the outside covering of the grain kernel. (51)

broiling: cooking directly under or over the source of heat. (46)

budget: a plan for how you want and intend to use your money. (19)

C

calorie: unit used to measure energy supplied by food or used by the body. (38)

carbohydrate: a nutrient that is the body's main source of energy. (38)

career: chosen occupation. (7)

casing: a closed tunnel of fabric that holds a piece of elastic or a drawstring inside. (32)

cents-off coupons: certificates that allow customers to buy items at a reduced price. (43)

character: a quality of a person who acts according to a set of high moral principles. (4)

check register: a place in your checkbook where you keep a record of the checks you write and the deposits you make. (19)

cholesterol: a fat-like substance used by the body. (38)

citizen: someone who is a member of a group, such as a city or town, state, or country. (6)

citizenship: the way that you handle your responsibilities as a citizen. (6)

classics: fashions that remain popular year after year. (28)

clique: a group of people who exclude others from their circle. (10)

clothing inventory: an organized list of the clothing you have. (28)

communication: the exchange of information, including facts, opinions, and feelings; sending and receiving messages. (8)

comparison shopping: taking the time to shop around and compare products, prices, and services. (20)

compromise: the result of each person's giving up something to reach a satisfactory solution; give-and-take. (9)

condominium: units in a multiple-family dwelling that are individually owned. (23)

conflict: a disagreement or struggle between two or more people or groups who have opposing points of view. (9)

conservation: protecting natural resources against waste and harm. (22)

conscience: an inner sense of right or wrong. (15)

consumer: a person who purchases and uses goods and services. (20)

convection oven: an oven with fans to help circulate the hot air. (44)

convenience foods: foods that are purchased partially or completed prepared. (42)

cookware: pots, pans, and other containers for use on top of the range or in the oven or microwave. (44)

cooperation: working together for the good of all; teamwork. (9)

cooperative: a form of ownership in which residents of a multiple-family dwelling form an organization that owns the building. (23)

course: part of a meal made up of foods served at one time. (52)

credit: an arrangement by which you purchase things now and are allowed to pay for them later. (19)

credit rating: a record that shows your ability and willingness to pay your debts. (14)

crush: a strong attraction to a member of the opposite gender. (11)

custody: court awarded care of a child or children following separation or divorce. (12)

D

dandruff: scales and flakes on the scalp. (27)

decision making: the act of making a choice or coming to a solution. (3)

deficiency: a shortage of nutrients. (38)

deposit slip: a slip of paper on which you record the amount of money being deposited into your account. (19)

dermatologist: a doctor who treats skin problems. (27)

Dietary Guidelines for Americans: suggestions developed by health experts and the U.S. government to help people make healthful food choices. (39)

directional stitching: stitching in the direction of the grain of the fabric. (35)

discipline: training given by parents and caregivers that helps children become responsible and cooperative. (17)

dry clean: cleaning with chemicals rather than with detergent and water. (30)

duplex: a building that contains two separate housing units. (23)

E

ease: amount of room needed in a garment for comfort and movement. (31)

equivalents: two or more amounts that are equal to each other. (45)

empathy: the ability to understand what someone else is experiencing. (9)

emphasis: the point of interest in a design. (24)

endorse: to sign over your rights to a check by writing your name on the back. (19)

endosperm: the largest part of the grain, located inside the kernel. (51)

enriched: describes foods that have had nutrients added back after processing. (51)

entree: the main course. (52)

entrepreneur: a person who owns and manages a business. (7)

environment: everything around you, including people, places, and events. (1)

ethics: a set of high moral principles. (4)

etiquette: customs regarded as the correct way to do things in social situations. (52)

expenses: the things on which you spend your money. (19)

extended family: a family that includes one or more relatives in addition to the basic family unit. (12)

F

fabric blends: combinations of two or more different fibers. (29)

fads: fashions that last only a short time. (28)

fashions: styles that are currently popular. (28)

fetus: an unborn child. (15)

fiber: plant materials that do not break down completely when food is digested. (38)

fibers: hairlike substances twisted together to make yarns and fabric. (29)

financial: relating to money. (14)

first aid course: instruction on basic emergency care for injuries; provided by the Red Cross and other community agencies. (16)

flatware: eating utensils such as knives, forks, and spoons. (52)

food-borne illness: sickness caused by eating spoiled food; often called food poisoning. (47)

Food Guide Pyramid: a simple method of diet planning based on food groups. (39)

frying: cooking in fat. (46)

functional furniture: furniture that is useful as well as decorative. (25)

furniture joints: points at which any two furniture parts connect, such as a leg to the seat of chair. (25)

fusible interfacing: interfacing with an adhesive coating that bonds to the fabric when pressed with a hot iron. (32)

G

generic name: the common name for a group of similar fibers. (29)

germ: the sprouting section of the grain kernel. (51)

goal: something you plan to be, do, or have, and for which you are willing to work. (2)

grade: to cut seams in layers to reduce bulk. (35)

graffiti: unwanted drawings and writing on walls and other property. (6)

grain: the direction in which yarns run in fabric. (32)

grooming: what you do to make yourself both neat and attractive. (27)

group dating: going places and doing things with a group of both males and females. (11)

growth spurt: a time when your body makes a rapid increase in height. (4)

H

harmony: the feeling that all parts of a design belong together. (24)

hazard: source of danger. (26)

health: the total state of your physical, mental, emotional, and social well-being. (37)

heredity: the qualities and traits passed along from parents to children through the genes. (1)

homogenized: processed to break up the fat particles in milk so they won't separate out. (48)

hormones: chemical substances in your body. (4)

human resources: resources that have to do with people. (1)

hygiene: cleanliness. (27)

I

immersible: capable of being put entirely into water safely. (44)

immunizations: shots to protect against disease. (37)

impulse buying: making unplanned purchases on the spur of the moment. (20)

income: the amount of money that you have coming in. (19)

independence: the ability to take care of yourself. (5)

infancy: the stage of development from birth to one year of age. (15)

interest: on savings — the amount of money the bank pays you for allowing it to use your money; on loans — the money that you pay the lender for the privilege of using credit. (19)

interests: what you like to do. (7)

interfacing: special fabric that gives hidden support and body to a garment. (32)

interpreting: understanding what the speaker actually says and means. (8)

interview: a meeting between a potential employer and a job-seeker. (7)

ironing: the process of moving the iron back and forth over fabric to remove wrinkles. (30)

K

kitchen appliance: a piece of equipment for the kitchen powered by gas or electricity. (44)

kitchen work center: an area of the kitchen designed to fill a particular purpose. (47)

L

landlord: the owner of housing that is rented to someone else. (23)

lapped zipper: zipper style in which a single flap of fabric and one row of stitching show on the outside of the garment after the zipper is sewn into the garment. (36)

layout: a diagram included on the pattern guide sheet that shows how to place the pattern pieces on the fabric. (34)

leader: a person who has influence over a group. (6)

leadership: the ability to lead. (6)

leavening agent: ingredient that causes baked products to rise. (51)

lease: a written rental agreement. (23)

legumes: a class of vegetable that is high in protein, including dry beans, dry peas, and peanuts. (38)

line: the outline of an object or the major lines within it. (24)

luster: shine. (29)

M

maintenance: regular cleaning, repairs and inspections that keep a home in good condition. (26)

management: using your resources to achieve your goals; using what you have to get what you want. (3)

manufactured fibers: fibers made all, or part, by chemicals. (29)

marbling: the small deposits of fat scattered throughout the muscle of meat. (50)

material resources: resources, usually objects, that are not human. (1)

maturity: a process of reaching full development. (5)

meal pattern: the way daily food choices are grouped into meals and snacks. (42)

mediator: someone from outside who helps resolve a conflict. (9)

megadoses: very large amounts, as of a vitamin or mineral supplement. (41)

microwaves: tiny waves of energy produced by a microwave oven to heat or cook food. (44)

modeling: watching and imitating the behavior of others. (5)

modem: a special piece of equipment that connects a computer to a telephone line, linking that computer to other computers. (21)

mortgage: a long-term loan used to buy a home. (23)

multiple-family dwelling: a structure that contains several housing units under one roof. (23)

multiplex: a building similar to a duplex, but with three or more housing units. (23)

multipurpose clothes: clothes suitable for a variety of situations. (28)

myth: an untrue statement that some people believe. (41)

N

nap: brushed surface. (34)

natural fibers: fibers made from plant or animal products. (29)

natural resources: resources which occur in nature. (22)

needs: things that are essential to one's health or well-being. (3)

nonrenewable resources: natural resources that can't replace themselves and, therefore, are limited in supply. (22)

nonverbal communication: communication without words. (8)

notions: the smaller items, such as thread, zippers, and buttons, needed to construct a garment. (31)

nuclear families: families in which two parents share a household with their children. (12)

nurturing: providing love, affection, attention, and encouragement. (17)

nutrient density: a comparison of the nutrients in a food to the number of calories. (38)

nutrients: substances in food that the body must have in order to work properly. (38)

O

obesity: having too much body fat in comparison to the amount of muscle, bone, and other lean tissue. (39)

obligations: things that you must do or have promised to do. (18)

open dating: a date stamped on food packages to help the customer determine the freshness of a product. (43)

organically grown: produced without manufactured chemicals. (41)

P

paraprofessionals: people trained to assist professionals. (7)

parenting: the process of caring for children and helping them grow and develop. (17)

parliamentary procedure: rules used by a leader to keep order while allowing the group to reach a majority decision. (6)

pasteurized: heated to destroy harmful bacteria. (48)

peer pressure: the stress or pressure you feel to do what others your age are doing. (10)

peers: people of similar age. (10)

perishable foods: foods that spoil easily. (43)

personality: a combination of the feelings, character traits, attitudes, and habits that you display to others. (1)

place setting: the arrangement of tableware for each person who will be eating a meal. (52)

plaque: a sticky film of harmful bacteria that forms on the teeth. (27)

poison control centers: a staff of trained people who advise and treat poison victims; often located in a hospital. (16)

potential: the possibility of becoming more than you are right now — all that you can be. (1)

prejudice: an unfair or biased opinion formed without knowing the facts or ignoring the facts. (9)

pre-preparation tasks: tasks that you need to do before you combine ingredients. (47)

preschooler: a child from three to five years of age. (15)

pressing: the process of lifting and lowering the iron onto an area of fabric. (30)

pretreatment: giving special treatment to a garment before laundering it. (30)

prioritize: to rank items according to their importance. (18)

processing: the steps that are taken to prepare and package food for sale. (43)

procrastination: the act of postponing something, or putting it off until later. (18)

produce: fresh fruits and vegetables. (49)

proportion: the way one part of a design relates in size and shape to another part or to the whole. (24)

protein: a nutrient that helps build and repair body tissues. (38)

puberty: the time when boys and girls start to develop the physical characteristics of adult men and women. (4)

R

rapport: harmony or understanding between two people. (8)

recipe: a set of directions used in cooking. (45)

reconstitute: replace water taken out. (48)

recycling: using used, discarded products or scrap or waste materials to make new products. (22)

relationship: a bond between people. (8)

renewable resources: natural resources that can renew, or replace, themselves over time. (22)

resourceful: having the ability to identify and use resources in order to accomplish something or solve a problem. (1)

resource: anything used to help accomplish something. (1)

responding: your reaction, in words and actions, to a communicated message. (8)

rhythm: a feeling of movement caused by repeating one or more elements of design. (24)

role model: someone who, through behavior and attitudes, serves as an example for others. (5)

roles: the parts that people play in life; for example, athlete, student council president, father, or daughter. (5)

routine: taking place regularly. (30)

S

sanitation: the act of keeping your living environment clean and healthy. (26)

scale: the overall size of an object, or its size compared to other objects. (24)

seam allowance: the fabric between the cutting line and the stitching line. (34)

self-concept: the picture you have of yourself and the way you believe others see you. (1)

self-esteem: the way you feel about yourself — the confidence and happiness you have in yourself. (1)

selvage: the finished lengthwise edge of the fabric. (34)

separates: garments that can be combined with one another to make several different outfits. (28)

serger: an overlock sewing machine that stitches, finishes, and trims a seam in one step. (33)

shank: the stem on the bottom of some buttons. (30)

shape: the solid form of an object. (24)

sibling rivalry: competitive feelings between brothers and sisters. (13)

siblings: brothers and sisters. (13)

silhouette: the outline of a garment. (28)

simmering: keeping the temperature of a liquid or mixture just under the boiling point. (46)

single-parent family: a family that has only one parent living in the household. (12)

skills: abilities that come from training and practice. (7)

slipstitch: an almost invisible hand stitch used on a folded edge. (35)

space: the three-dimensional area to be designed. (24)

spouse: a husband or wife. (14)

staystitching: a row of stitching on just one layer of fabric that prevents fabric edges from stretching as you sew. (35)

stereotype: a belief that an entire group of people fit a fixed, common pattern — that they are alike in certain ways. (9)

stress: physical or emotional strain or tension that is caused by changes in your life. (4)

T

tableware: items used to serve and eat a meal, such as dishes, glasses, and flatware. (52)

tapestry needle: a needle with a large eye and a blunt point. (36)

technology: the way in which science and inventions are put to practical use in everyday life. (21)

tenants: people who rent, rather than purchase, their housing. (23)

tension: tightness or looseness of the thread. (33)

texture: the way the surface of an object looks and feels. (24)

time management: planning the use of your time so that you can get the most out of the time you have. (18)

time out: a disciplinary technique in which a misbehaving child is removed from the activity for a short period of time. (17)

toddler: a child from one to three years of age. (15)

tofu: a protein food made from soybeans. (50)

townhomes: houses built in rows and attached at the side walls. (23)

trade name: the manufacturer's name for a specific fiber or fabric. (29)

traffic lanes: the paths people take from one room or area to another. (25)

trim: to cut off extra fabric. (33)

U

understitching: to stitch the seam allowance to the facing to prevent the seam from rolling to the outside. (35)

unit price: the price per ounce, pound, or other unit of measure. (43)

UPC (universal product code): a bar code (or pattern of stripes) that identifies a product and gives the product's price. (21)

upholstery: materials such as fabric, padding, and springs, that are used on covered sections on furniture. (25)

utensils: small kitchen tools. (44)

V

values: the beliefs, ideas, and feelings that are important to you. (2)

vandalism: the destruction of property. (6)

vegetarian: one who does not eat meat, fish, or poultry. (41)

verbal communication: communication with spoken words. (8)

view: a garment style that can be made from a particular pattern. (31)

volunteers: people who offer their services free of charge. (6)

W

wants: things that are not essential but that you desire to make life more enjoyable. (3)

warranty: a guarantee that a product will work as it should for a certain length of time; usually includes the seller's or manufacturer's promise to repair or replace the item or to refund your money if the problem was caused by any defect in parts, materials, or workmanship. (20)

wellness: a way of living based on healthful attitudes and actions. (37)

whipstitch: a small diagonal hand stitch. (35)

work simplification: finding the easiest and quickest way to do each job well. (18)

Y

yardage: the amount of fabric needed to sew a garment. (31)

yield: the amount of food or number of servings a recipe makes. (45)

Credits

Interior Design: Morgan Cain & Associates

Cover Photography: Mark Romine

American Egg Board, 591
American Plywood Association, 260, 288
Arnold & Brown, 61, 78, 452, 474, 560
Jim Ballard, 8
Roger B. Bean, 69, 151, 294
Boatel-Page Division, 260
Uzi Broshi, 437
Burlington Industries, Inc., 330
California Closet Co., 335
Cannon Mills, 329
Todd Carroll, 357
CBI Industries, Inc., 260
Closet Works, 281
H. Wesley Coulter, 163
Howard Davis, 377, 511, 512, 513, 514
Drexel Heritage Furnishings, 262
Laima Druskis, 252, 253, 274, 279, 281, 285, 287, 289, 290, 291, 292, 293
David Falconer, David R. Frazier Photolibrary, 58
David R. Frazier Photolibrary, 103, 130, 183, 237, 312, 325, 336, 580
Ann Garvin, 12, 15, 129, 141, 152, 162, 166, 175, 179, 182, 187, 205, 256, 302, 318, 323, 336, 351, 352, 353, 354, 356, 358, 360, 361, 363, 366, 367, 368, 369, 370, 376, 380, 384, 394, 408, 410, 429, 433, 437, 440, 444, 449, 450, 454, 456, 462, 465, 478, 479, 482, 486, 488, 491, 493, 495, 496, 508, 517, 518, 534, 535, 536, 537, 538, 539, 540, 541, 542, 543, 544, 545, 548, 550, 554, 555, 556, 562, 565, 567, 568, 570, 572, 577, 587, 589, 590, 594, 599, 601, 603, 605, 606, 609, 612, 613, 614
Grand Illusions, 467
Linda K. Henson, 46, 65, 79, 92, 113, 121, 142, 146, 157, 164, 167, 175, 178, 187, 198, 207, 208, 210, 211, 212, 219, 221, 230, 232, 250, 258, 265, 268, 275, 277, 291, 317, 335, 435, 438, 441, 442, 445, 446, 448, 454, 455, 463, 480, 487, 488, 492, 499, 500, 501, 506, 507, 513, 520, 536, 555, 557, 564, 566, 591, 596, 599, 610
Chuck Hofer, 328
Llyn Hunter, 217, 220, 221, 238, 239, 240, 381, 528, 558, 611
Impact Communications, 549
Mike Jenkins, 504
Bob McElwee, 288, 291, 552
Jon McIntosh, 20, 37, 44, 53, 56, 195, 198, 201, 220, 259, 334, 337, 464, 490, 531, 549, 563, 573, 576, 581, 589, 598
Ted Mishima, 100, 101
Monsanto Textiles Co., 324
NASTA Pasta Assn., 597
North Wind Pictures Archives, 254
Pacific Homes Inc., 256
Pennsylvania House, 278
N. A. Peterson, 339
Brent Phelps, 13, 334, 430, 443, 457, 459, 494, 502, 505, 530, 552, 578, 583, 585
Liz Purcell, 197, 280, 328, 329, 341, 342, 343, 344, 348, 350, 371, 373, 395, 396, 397, 398, 399, 400, 401, 402, 403, 404, 405, 406, 407, 411, 412, 415, 416, 417, 418, 419, 484, 496, 595
Mark Romine, 16, 17, 98, 99, 192, 193, 248, 249, 298, 299, 426, 427
Rubbermaid, 574
Simplicity Pattern, 351, 352, 353, 364, 382, 386, 389
Rick Sullivan, 69, 278, 340, 591, 600, 601, 602
Kevin Syms, David R. Frazier Photolibrary, 32

Texas Highways, 324, 325
Thomasville Furnishings, 269
Ken Trevarthan, 254, 524
Unisys, Inc. 233
Unity Systems, 229
USDA, 458, 468, 584
Viking Range Corp., 541
Steve Wertz, 124, 126
Dana C. White, Dana White Productions Inc., 6, 7, 9, 10, 18, 22, 23, 24, 25, 26, 27, 28, 30, 31, 32, 33, 34, 35, 38, 40, 41, 42, 43, 45, 48, 52, 54, 55, 59, 60, 62, 64, 66, 68, 70, 71, 74, 75, 76, 78, 80, 81, 82, 84, 85, 86, 87, 88, 89, 90, 91, 92, 94, 96, 97, 108, 114, 116, 117, 119, 120, 122, 125, 127, 128, 134, 135, 136, 143, 145, 147, 151, 170, 184, 185, 186, 190, 191, 194, 199, 200, 204, 206, 213, 214, 216, 226, 227, 230, 234, 236, 241, 242, 243, 244, 246, 257, 272, 282, 284, 296, 300, 305, 307, 308, 310, 315, 318, 322, 332, 346, 347, 422, 424, 425, 428, 431, 432, 456, 467, 468, 472, 477, 498, 506, 510, 566, 586, 608, 616, 617
Nancy Wood, 102, 103, 104, 105, 106, 109, 110, 111, 137, 138, 164, 165, 166, 172, 173, 177, 454, 470, 484
Duane R. Zehr, 8, 9, 10, 11, 13, 14, 57, 112, 118, 132, 133, 140, 153, 154, 155, 156, 158, 159, 167, 174, 247, 255, 297, 301, 304, 306, 319, 337, 340, 342, 364, 385, 386, 418, 419, 434, 435, 437, 448, 453, 466, 476, 503, 518, 519, 530, 538, 551, 574, 587, 604, 616
Jill Zimmerman, 28, 38, 50, 62, 72, 82, 86, 94, 106, 110, 114, 119, 122, 126, 130, 134, 138, 144, 148, 154, 160, 168, 176, 180, 184, 188, 196, 202, 214, 219, 224, 228, 234, 244, 260, 263, 265, 267, 268, 270, 276, 277, 282, 294, 302, 308, 311, 316, 320, 325, 330, 341, 344, 354, 361, 362, 364, 370, 372, 373, 374, 377, 378, 382, 385, 386, 387, 388, 390, 391, 392, 396, 399, 400, 401, 403, 404, 405, 408, 412, 413, 414, 415, 417, 418, 420, 421, 422, 433, 438, 450, 460, 469, 470, 474, 484, 492, 496, 507, 508, 512, 513, 514, 521, 522, 529, 532, 536, 546, 557, 560, 563, 568, 578, 582, 592, 606, 610, 612, 614

Special thanks to the following individuals, schools, businesses, and organizations for their assistance with photographs in this book. **In Peoria, Illinois:** Adams Furniture; Hotel Père Marquette; Peoria Notre Dame High School; Peoria Police Department, Officers Craig W. Ganda, Mike Doyle, and Robin Turner; Woodruff High School. Limestone Community High School, Bartonville, Illinois. Morton High School, Morton, Illinois. **In Denton, Texas:** Albertson's, Denton County Independent Hamburger Company, El Matador Restaurant, Good Samaritan Village, Piggly Wiggly Market. **In Southern California:** Bank of America, Bobi Leonard Interior Design, Berkley Convalescent Hospital, Elizabeth Casillas, Marie Everett, House of Fabrics, H.U.D.D.L.E., Hughes Markets, John Adams Middle School, Conrad Johnson, Kjersti—Cotton Rainbow, Rosemead Asian Youth Center, The Manuel & Charlotte Myers Family, Mt. Olive Pre-School, Martin Minkardo, Sheriff & Associates Architects, Josea Kramer, Windward School, Sandor Rosenfield, Santa Monica Museum of Art, Santa Monica High School, Santa Monica YMCA, The Wesley and Vicki Tanaka Family, Westside Food Bank.

Models and fictional names have been used to portray characters in stories and examples in this text.

Index

D

N

O

P

U

V

W

Y

Z